Both authors are uniquely qualified, both academically and as practitioners, to write the history of the Institution. Jim Mortimer started his working life as a ship fitter apprentice and subsequently worked in the engineering industry. After working for twenty years as a full-time union official on the executive committee of AUEW–TASS, he became a full-time member of the National Board of Prices and Incomes and subsequently a Board Member of London Transport Executive responsible for personnel and industrial relations. He has been Chairman of the Advisory Conciliation and Arbitration Service (ACAS) since it was established in September 1974.

Dr Valerie Ellis has a long-standing interest in white-collar unionism. After teaching management studies at the University of Manchester Institute of Science and Technology and working with the Commission on Industrial Relations, she became a full-time official of the IPCS in 1970. In 1973 she retained a part-appointment on an Oxford Management Centre research project concerned with change in trade unions. She is presently Assistant Secretary of the IPCS.

D1272587

A PROFESSIONAL UNION:

The Evolution of the Institution of Professional Civil Servants

A Professional Union:
The Evolution of the Institution of Professional Civil Servants

JAMES E. MORTIMER
VALERIE A. ELLIS

London
GEORGE ALLEN & UNWIN
Boston   Sydney

First published in 1980

GEORGE ALLEN & UNWIN LTD *068 474*
40 Museum Street, London WC1A 1LU

© The Institution of Professional Civil Servants, 1980

British Library Cataloguing in Publication Data

Mortimer, James Edward
  A professional union.
  1. Institution of Professional Civil
  Servants – History
  I. Title   II. Ellis, Valerie A
  331.88'11'35441001   HD8013.G73   79–41723

  ISBN 0–04–331076–1

Typeset in 10 on 11 point Plantin
by Northampton Phototypesetters Ltd
and printed in Great Britain
by William Clowes (Beccles) Ltd, Beccles and London

Contents

Preface

The history of the Institution, like that of any other trade union, has been shaped by external political and economic events, and by the actions and attitudes of governments, management and other trade unions. But it has also been shaped by the nature of its membership, by the committed effort of countless honorary officers and committees at every level and by the calibre of those who have been elected and selected to lead it.

Every work of history involves the selection of material. Inevitably in a written account of the development of the Institution the events and controversies are described largely in terms of some of the prominent personalities involved. But there are countless others in the past and present without whom the Institution could not function. There is, above all, the tireless work of a great many members who do the essential work at branch, section and subsection level. Some of these have received long service awards and are mentioned in Appendix 4. To all these members and to all those who follow after we hope this history will provide a fitting tribute.

The history is based primarily on the written sources available, including *State Service*, reports of Institution conferences, and the minutes of the Council and later the National Executive Committee. These sources have, however, been supplemented by the help of several individuals, including both members and non-members of the Institution, who have delved into their memories to provide additional information or who have offered comments on the text. They include from within the Institution: Reg Bartlett, John Beaton, Cyril Cooper, Johnny Fraser, Edward Hewlett, Ardene Hilton, Ted Lawson, Bill McCall, Stanley Mayne, Ruth Miller and Bill Palmer, and from outside, Lord Douglas Houghton, Dr Kay McLeod, Jock Shaw, Eric Wigham, Sir Leslie Williams and Sir John Winnifrith. To all these and to those who typed and reproduced the manuscript, our thanks.

Finally, the authors would like to thank the National Executive Committee of the Institution and the general secretary for commissioning the history and for their encouragement and support throughout its production. It was made clear from the outset that although the Institution was commissioning the history the responsibility for its content rested with the authors. For this trust and degree of discretion the authors are very grateful. Correspondingly for any errors of omission or commission, and for the interpretation of the evidence at their disposal, the authors, and they alone, are responsible.

1 The Birth of the Institution and the Social Background

The initiative for the formation of the Institution came largely from engineers employed within the Admiralty Department. There had been a professional association in the Royal Corps of Naval Constructors since the 1880s, but it was not until 1918, after the Armistice on 11 November, that any real effort was made to extend organisation to other scientific and technical staff. Towards the end of November 1918 a Federation of Professional Officers (Admiralty) was formed representing men in the Royal Corps of Naval Constructors, civil and electrical engineers and cartographers. The Federation was established, according to a letter sent to the Secretary of the Admiralty, 'in order that a central body may be in existence to represent the views of professional officers as and when considered necessary or desirable'.

From the outset the main organisers of the new Federation in the Admiralty recognised that if their efforts were to be effective they would need to join with others for collective representation. This, as they saw it, could take place in one of two main directions: either by combining with other scientific and technical staff employed in the civil service, or, alternatively, with other civil servants employed on administrative, executive and clerical duties. They chose the former course. With this in view, four of the initiators of the Federation of Professional Officers (Admiralty) agreed to have lunch together in the second week of December 1918 to discuss the possibility of forming a wider association to look after the interests and status of engineers in the service of the state. All four were young men and, to that extent, were not strongly inhibited by tradition. It was at their lunch that the idea of forming an organisation for professional staff in the civil service was born.

The first step, they decided, was to call a meeting of professionally qualified civil servants. This was convened for 18 December 1918, in Caxton Hall, Westminster. Notification of the meeting was sent to men in various departments who were known, through informal contact, to be sympathetic to the formation of a representative body of professional staff, and to the secretaries of a number of very small professional organisations within the civil service which had mushroomed into existence during the second half of 1918.

The meeting was well attended and it was agreed that a further but smaller meeting of departmental representatives should be held on 1 January 1919, with a view to forming a permanent organisation. This meeting was attended by sixteen representatives. It was held in an office of the Ministry of Labour, 28 Broadway, Westminster. The departments represented were the Admiralty, the Office of Works, the Post Office, the Air Ministry, the Board of Trade, the Land Registry, the National Physical Laboratory, Greenwich Observatory and the Natural History Museum. A resolution was carried unanimously: 'That an Alliance be now established by this meeting consisting of those Departments which have already formed Associations.' It was not easy to agree on the name of the new organisation. Eventually, after considerable discussion, it was agreed that it should be known as The Professional Alliance, HM Civil Service. A committee was elected consisting of five members, together with one representative from each departmental association. Mr R. C. Bristow of the Federation of Professional Officers (Admiralty) was elected honorary general secretary.

The committee of the newly formed Alliance did not suffer from any false modesty about its aims. One of its first actions was to send a letter to the Prime Minister informing him of the existence of the Alliance, setting forth the accomplishments of its members in the civil service and stating their case for improved conditions.

At the next meeting of the committee, held a week later, Mr Bristow was confirmed as honorary general secretary and undertook to act also as secretary of the Executive Committee. Mr H. E. Seccombe of the Professional and Technical Association of the Office of Works was elected chairman of the Alliance.

No sooner had the Alliance been formally established than the first controversies within its ranks began to emerge. The leading spirits in the Federation of Professional Officers (Admiralty) were sympathetic to trade unionism and wanted the new Alliance to become a closely knit, nationally organised, civil service trade union. They did not like the title 'The Professional Alliance, HM Civil Service' because it suggested a temporary arrangement made between autonomous organisations. The Admiralty men pressed for a change in title. They were successful and the name 'Institution of Professional Civil Servants' was chosen.

The Council of the Institution for 1920 consisted of twenty-five representatives from seventeen separate associations (see Appendix 1). The following professions were represented by one or more associations: civil engineers, mechanical engineers, electrical engineers, naval architects, surveyors, architects, valuers, quantity surveyors, physicians and surgeons, chemists, physicists, auditors. In addition there were a number of professions whose duties were peculiar to the public service, such as Patent Office examiners, HM inspectors of factories and scientific staff of museums.

A TRADE UNION?

The Admiralty men were, however, less successful in their effort to persuade their colleagues that the Institution should openly proclaim itself a trade union and seek registration as a union under the Trade Union Act, 1871. In this controversy the Admiralty engineering representatives were in no doubt that the Institution was, in fact, a union. The real issue, therefore, as they saw it, was not whether it was a union but whether it should acknowledge both to itself and to others that it was a union. They failed to persuade the majority of their colleagues on the committee of the Institution of their point of view. It is recorded in the 1919 report of the Institution that the consensus of opinion was 'unmistakably against trade unionism at present'.

The majority of the committee were opposed to describing the Institution as a trade union because, in their view, many senior members would find themselves in difficulty in the event of a dispute affecting men whom they controlled who were members of manual workers' trade unions. At that time trade unionism was very largely identified with manual workers and there were nowhere near the same number of white-collar trade union members as there are today.

The committee decided that instead of seeking registration as a trade union the

Institution should seek registration as a company. A draft memorandum of association was drawn up by solicitors and put to the Board of Trade. The Board of Trade were not convinced. In what way, they inquired, did the Institution differ from a trade union? The reply of the Institution, framed probably by its solicitors, was that although one of its purposes was to secure higher salaries for its members, it did not consist of workmen. Its members were 'professional civil servants, men of high qualifications and skill, and of good education . . .'. This plea left the Board of Trade unmoved. They had little difficulty in pointing out that the Institution could not qualify as a company but suggested that the Institution might obtain counsel's opinion on what course to take. This advice was followed, but after a further abortive attempt to register as a company the matter was dropped.

The Federation of Professional Officers (Admiralty) continued for a while to fight a rearguard action in favour of identifying the Institution as a trade union. It was the most influential of the constituent associations of the Institution and it had the prestige of having provided the 'founding fathers'. The memorandum of association of the Institution prepared by solicitors for registering the Institution as a company had provoked the Admiralty men even further by the extent to which it eschewed trade unionism and appeared to erect obstacles to prevent the affiliation of the Institution with other organisations. One of the clauses stated:

The Institution shall not support with its funds or endeavour to impose on, or procure to be observed by its members or others, any regulation, restriction or condition which if an object of the Institution, would make it a trade union.

A further clause stated:

The Council shall have power to take common action with other societies in the civil service, or with other professional institutions or other bodies in any manner they think fit, for the object of advancing or protecting the position, status and interests of members of the Institution, but no definite affiliation or official union with any other body shall take place without the consent of a two-thirds majority of a general or special general meeting.

The Admiralty representatives did not conceal their dislike of these clauses. They were faced, however, with two alternatives: either to insist upon the Institution identifying itself as a trade union, at the grave risk of so offending the other constituents that the organisation might disintegrate; or not to press the issue in the belief that it would ultimately be resolved when the other constituents came to recognise, through experience, that the Institution was, in fact, a trade union. The Admiralty engineering representatives chose the latter course. According to the minutes of the Federation of Professional Officers (Admiralty) 26 March 1919:

It was thought best to leave this matter to the discretion of the Executive of the Institution, especially as it was recognised to be important that the Institution should become a working concern at the earliest possible moment and that issues of this nature might tend to delay progress. It was decided that if the Institution's Executive decided to register as a company, there would be nothing to prevent its becoming a trade union at a later date if such a step were deemed desirable by the requisite majority of the Association.

There was also considerable division of opinion over who should be eligible to join the Institution. One clause appeared to go out of its way to differentiate the Institution from organisations of workmen and to model itself on the professional bodies. A distinction was to be made between 'full' membership, which should only be granted to 'permanent officers (established or unestablished), who were in the directing, administrative or higher grades of the service, and were engaged in professional, technical or scientific work', and 'associate' membership. To avoid the separation of interests which were, or should be, the same, however, a second class of 'associates' was formed to include other technical members of the service who assisted the 'professionals', especially those known in most departments as 'draughtsmen'. Those below the grade of draughtsmen and their equivalents, such as laboratory assistants, were excluded altogether until 1939. Thus, an associate had to be one 'Who is engaged on technical or scientific work but not below the grade of draughtsman or its equivalent provided that no person who may be a workman within the meaning of the Trade Union Act shall be eligible . . .'. Full members paid a subscription of 10s 6d per annum, while associates paid 2s 6d, a difference which reflected their subordinate status within the organisation. According to the articles of association, 'associates' were entitled to representation and other benefits at the discretion of the Council. 'No Associate shall, as such, be a Member of the Institution or have any right of voting at its meetings.' The distinction between 'full' and 'associate' members continued until 1946.

SOCIAL BACKGROUND

The events in the closing months of 1918, culminating in the formation of the Institution at the beginning of 1919, cannot be explained solely by reference to the activities of the founding members. Important as their initiative was, it remains to be explained what were the circumstances that motivated them to take it, and what were the conditions that enabled them to evoke a sympathetic response from among many to whom they addressed their appeal.

The founding members had three things in common. First, they were civil servants, secondly they were specialists in their skill, and thirdly they felt the need for some form of collective organisation to protect and advance their occupational interests. Without the substantial growth of the civil service in the late nineteenth century and particularly the growth in the number of specialist civil servants, the preconditions for trade union development would not have existed. Without the establishment of the Whitley machinery, the growth of other civil service unions and the privations of the First World War it is unlikely that the motivation for forming the Institution would have been as strong.

THE GROWTH OF THE CIVIL SERVICE

The existence of a permanent civil service is a comparatively recent development in Britain. Although there were persons employed in the service of the state long before the nineteenth century, it was only towards the middle of that century that a permanent civil service, with some of the features which are now so familiar, began to take shape. The functions of the state greatly expanded in the late eighteenth and early nineteenth centuries with the growth of trade and commerce and with the development of new urban industrial areas. There was an ever-increasing need for public administration affecting, for example, the regulation of trade, sanitation, public health, safety in industry, education and the raising and spending of public money.

With this growth of administrative functions the size of the civil service increased throughout the second half of the nineteenth century and into the opening years of the twentieth century. The non-industrial civil service grew from 39,147 in 1851 to 172,352 in 1911 (Humphreys, 1958, p. 229).

The fundamental features of civil service employment were moulded by the Northcote–Trevelyan Report of 1854. Its principal recommendations were the creation of a uniform service to which entry would be by competitive examination and in which promotion would be by merit. A Civil Service Commission, with the limited objective of examining the suitability of nominees for the service, was established in 1855, although it was not until 1870 that entry by open competition was instituted by another Order in Council. Following the report of the Playfair Commission of 1874 into the staffing of the civil service, the service was divided into four divisions: administrative officer (first division), higher division, lower division and boy clerks.

SPECIALISTS IN THE CIVIL SERVICE

The second special characteristic of the founding members of the Institution was that they were specialists, in the sense that the special skills which they were required to possess for their work were usually acquired in other employment outside the service of the state. The specialists have always combined a particular knowledge of one or more of the scientific, technical or professional disciplines with administrative skills.

The first state-supported scientific institution was the Royal Greenwich Observatory, founded in 1675, primarily for navigation purposes. Next came the Geological Survey and the Meteorological Office for the safeguarding of seamen. Science went hand in hand with the development of trade and the British Empire. In 1899 the Imperial Institute was founded and research bodies were developed to investigate tropical diseases. They included the Tropical Diseases Research Fund and the Sleeping Sickness Bureau, which was enlarged in 1912 into the Imperial Bureau of Entomology.

Between 1870 and the outbreak of the First World War the British government began to take a much stronger interest in scientific work. Although the earlier part of this period was one of British pre-eminence in many branches of industry, there were already indications that the United States and Germany were edging ahead in some of the new technologies. The state had to intervene in Britain to carry out research which private industry was failing to undertake. One very important British development was the establishment of the National Physical Laboratory (NPL) in 1900, following considerable agitation by the British

Association for the Advancement of Science and the Royal Society for Britain to have a national laboratory comparable to the Physikatisch-Technische Reichsaustalt in Germany. The laboratory fulfilled the double function of maintaining and improving methods of measurement of all physical qualities and pioneering and assisting in the application of physics to industrial problems.

In July 1915 the Advisory Council for Scientific and Industrial Research was appointed by Order in Council and the corresponding department, the Department of Scientific and Industrial Research (DSIR), was established in 1916. The National Physical Laboratory became one of its research stations and continued to play a pioneering role in research in various fields which were often hived off when further development would be more advantageously undertaken by the creation of an independent institution. In 1909 the Development Commission, to help British agriculture and rural industries, was established.

In the social and environmental field a wide range of specialists were recruited into the service of the state to deal with problems of health, industrial safety, sanitation, the supply of water, housing and the development of hygienic standards in the preparation, distribution and sale of food. For example, the first medical officer, Dr John Simon, was appointed in 1855 to supervise the development of vaccination programmes. The National Health Insurance Act, 1911, reinforced the concern of the state in matters of public health. This encouraged medical research and before long a Medical Research Committee of the Privy Council was formed, replaced in 1920 by the Medical Research Council (MRC).

The pollution caused by industry also prompted public measures to safeguard the community and hence the employment of scientists for this task. The chemical industry, centred on the north-east coast and on Merseyside, was reducing much of the surrounding countryside to wasteland. Sodium carbonate was needed for the manufacture of glass, soap and other items, but one of the by-products, when poured out from industrial chimneys, had a destructive effect on almost every living thing on which it descended. The Alkali Act, 1863, was passed in an endeavour to compel chemical manufacturers, largely against their wishes, to take remedial measures. Scientifically qualified inspectors were appointed for the purpose of implementing the Act (Parris, 1969, p. 241). In later years, new legislation was passed to strengthen the original purpose of the Alkali Act.

Some of the first excursions of the state into science and technology were associated with military purposes. Britain has always had, for example, a very strong interest in maritime technology, whether in the building of ships, the charting of the seas or the supply of weaponry for naval men-of-war. In 1854 the War Office appointed a young chemist, F. A. Abel (later Sir Frederick Abel), as 'War Department Chemist' to advise on and develop new types of explosives. Many of the present research and development establishments in the Ministry of Defence can trace their origins to the work of his small department. Sir Isaac Newton often advised the Admiralty and the Royal Navy has its own Corps of Naval Constructors whose work embodies the knowledge of scientists. The Admiralty's first full-time scientist was H. A. Madge, who in 1908 came from the Marconi organisation to develop wireless communication for ships at sea. Part of what had started life as the War Office's Balloon Equipment Store at Woolwich in 1878 later became HM Balloon Factory and later still the Royal Aircraft Establishment (RAE) at Farnborough. In 1904 the Woolwich Arsenal Research

Department was established, a sign that science and technology were becoming more important in the development of the means of war.

War is nearly always a forcing house for technological change. The First World War brought science to a new level of importance in public life. There was hardly an aspect of the war effort where science and technology could not be applied with great advantage. In the development of weapons, the use of metals, the employment of aircraft, the application of medicine, the stimulation of food production and the introduction of substitutes, science and technology were vital. Scientists were drafted into government service under the direction of specialist bodies such as the Munitions Invention Department, the Board of Invention and Research and the Optical and Glassware Munitions Department of the Ministry of Munitions. By March 1917 the Institute of Chemistry recorded: 'several hundred chemists have been engaged for assistance in the laboratories and in the works of Government and controlled establishments, to supply armaments, munitions and other materials of war' (Dobbie, 1918). Chief among these establishments were the Woolwich Arsenal, the Government Laboratory and RAE, Farnborough.

Although many of the scientists brought into the government service as part of the war effort left again after the end of the war, the number of scientists within the civil service by 1920 was considerable, estimated at approximately 1,200. Of these approximately 64 were in the scientific museums, 100 in the War Office research establishments, 470 in the Air Ministry scientific establishments, 164 in the Admiralty scientific establishments, 150 at NPL, 53 in the Geological Survey, about 70 in the various establishments administered by the Ministry of Agriculture and Fisheries and about 100 in the DSIR headquarters and research stations. In addition there were the staffs of such quasi-scientific institutions as the Patent Office.

Scientists, technologists and technicians by now formed a very vital part of the civil service and specialists as a whole numbered over 10,000. Nevertheless, despite their importance they were still everywhere regarded within the service as a subordinate group. The dominance of the administrators, the generalists and the 'educated amateurs' was as yet unchallenged. As F. A. A. Menzler (1937, p. 169) commented later: 'the specialist in the civil service has been in the past, and still is, regarded as an inconvenient intruder . . .' Compared with his administrative counterpart the professional civil servant suffered several disabilities. There were gross disparities between administrative and professional salaries; the professional staff for the most part answered to senior administrative grades; and there was no uniformity of pay and grading structure within the specialist classes.

> The chaotic grading of the specialist classes is convincing evidence that the experts have yet to be assimilated to the main service structure, and are in no sense regarded collectively as performing any distinctive generalised function. But this is not all. There is an unwritten law that specialists shall rarely be allowed to ascend to the highest administrative posts. The one or two exceptions do not dispose of the criticism that specialist officers have in practice been debarred from advancement to purely administrative posts. (Menzler, 1937, pp. 172–3)

If the interests of the specialist grades were to be protected, some form of collective organisation had to be created. The creation of the Whitley machinery in 1919 provided the means through which their collective grievances could be articulated. Indeed, it was the establishment of Whitleyism which made it imperative that some organisation to represent their interests should be formed.

According to Henry Parris (1973, p. 25) there were three preconditions for the establishment of Whitleyism in the civil service:

> Staff associations had evolved to the point where they could effectively represent the great majority of civil servants. Civil servants had achieved enough by negotiation within the administrative system for them to be prepared at least to try a procedure which contained no provision for appeal to the political level. The establishment side of the Treasury had developed in such a way that it was competent to take on the task of leading the Official Side.

THE GROWTH OF CIVIL SERVICE TRADE UNION ORGANISATION

The founding fathers of the Institution who met in London towards the end of 1918 were not, of course, the first civil servants who had expressed concern about their pay, conditions and career prospects and who had considered the possibility of forming a collective organisation to protect their interests. There was, in fact, a long history of trade union endeavour among sections of civil servants, particularly in the Post Office. One of the first recorded examples of collective representation took place as long ago as 1834 when a number of civil servants protested against the terms on which new pension arrangements were introduced. An Act of Parliament in 1834 sanctioned the principle that civil servants should make a financial contribution to their pensions. It also increased the number of pensionable posts. Unfortunately, it also discriminated against many civil servants by excluding them from the new arrangements. Even more important, some of them were expected to contribute but were excluded, for no apparent reason, from receiving benefit. Moreover the contributions apparently were much more than sufficient to finance the pensions. Also, 1834 was the year of the Tolpuddle Martyrs, when a small group of trade union pioneers, agricultural labourers in the Dorset village of Tolpuddle, were sentenced to seven years' transportation to the penal colony in Australia. They were convicted of the crime of administering unlawful oaths. The sentence evoked widespread protests. In the same year, 1834, following a period of unprecedented trade union activity in a number of industries, a new national body, the Grand National Consolidated Trades Union, came temporarily into existence.

The protest movement did not develop into a permanent organisation. Nevertheless, a Civil Service Committee was formed to give expression to the protest and it claimed to represent some 9,000 men. The movement was led by a senior civil servant, Richard Madox Bromley. It was eventually successful in securing the appointment of a Royal Commission headed by Northcote and Trevelyan which in due course reported, and this, in turn, led to the passing of a new Act in 1859 which abolished employee contributions to pensions, reduced the maximum age of retirement and extended pension rights to many more civil servants.

After the first protest movement around the issue of pensions, civil service trade union history throughout the rest of the nineteenth century was largely dominated by events in the Post Office. In an article published many years later in *State Service*, Mr F. A. A. Menzler wrote:

> All grades of the service owe much to the high courage and persistence of the postal workers. It was they who fought for nearly half a century, in season and out of season, in Parliament and out of Parliament, for the right of civil servants to organise for purposes of collective bargaining. The tale is too often a discreditable one of obstruction and victimisation.

Many postal workers were disciplined, punished and, in some cases, dismissed for trade union activity. But, though the movement frequently receded and was often pushed underground, it eventually proved successful. Whenever there was a high peak of activity in the trade union movement in British industry it was nearly always reflected in new activity in the Post Office. Thus there was a period of feverish activity just after 1870 and again in 1883. There was a strike of telegraphists in 1871 and in the 1880s there was continuous activity. Following the defeat of the 1890 strike many activists were dismissed or left the Post Office. However, new activists formed a postmen's federation which became increasingly active in the wider trade union movement, affiliating to both the TUC and the Labour Representation Committee. It also attempted to initiate the formation of a Civil Service Federation and supported a paper called *Civil Service Times*. By parliamentary pressure it succeeded in securing various improvements in pensions and wages and the abolition of unpaid Sunday labour. Pension entitlement was extended to men who hitherto had been on the unestablished list.

Efforts towards trade union organisation had been made sporadically in other parts of the civil service, although nowhere so widespread, or at that time so successful, as among the postal workers. Post Office engineering workers had begun to organise in the 1880s, groups of foremen in the Royal Arsenal at about much the same time or even a little earlier, second division clerks in the 1890s and the basic grades of clerical workers shortly after the turn of the century. Tax surveying officers had formed a committee as long ago as 1858, but it was not until the early twentieth century that they succeeded in establishing a permanent representative organisation. The first women in the civil service to become organised in trade unions were clerks and telegraphists in the Post Office. In 1892 the Tracers Association was formed. Most associations, apart from the Second Division Clerks Association, tended to follow departmental lines.

Although some departments had already conceded limited recognition to staff associations, 1906 marked a major turning point. In that year a new Liberal government was elected, pledged to introduce legislation more favourable to trade unionism. Sidney Buxton, the new Postmaster General, established for the Post Office the principle of trade union recognition by stating that 'the full right of representation and combination ought to be allowed in the postal service'. This caused an immediate increase in association activity and organisation throughout the service and coincided with a peak of trade union activity in the rest of the country. Trade unionists had been extremely active in the 1906 general election, first to secure the return of the first substantial body of Labour members to Parliament and, secondly, to secure the return of a Liberal government pledged to the introduction of new legislation to protect trade union rights, including, in particular, the right to strike without fear of legal liability.

There was a further strong burst of trade union organising activity in the civil service in the period from 1911 to the outbreak of the First World War. Again, it owed much to a rising tide of industrial ferment in Britain. This industrial ferment coincided with significant political controversies and changes. They included a constitutional crisis concerning the power of the House of Lords to throw out legislation approved by the House of Commons, the threat of armed resistance by a group of officers, supported by sections of the population in Ulster, to the demand for Irish Home Rule to which the elected Liberal government in Britain was pledged, and the introduction of very important new social measures such as old-age pensions, the provision of labour exchanges and unemployment benefit. From 1895 to 1912 the cost of living rose by 21 per cent while over the same period general money wages rose by only 13 per cent. Trade union membership increased from 1,955,704 in 1900 to 3,018,903 in 1911, and again to 4,145,000 in 1914.

The continued frustrations of trying to bargain with an unresponsive Treasury, together with the growing general discontent, caused, according to B. V. Humphreys (1958, p. 61):

a breakdown of the barriers between grade and departmental unions and brought all organised civil servants together in one federation for a common purpose, to force complete administrative reform . . . the same causative incidents plus staff reactions gave birth to an official view, reflected in the recommendations of the McDonnell Commission and House of Commons debates from 1912 to 1914, that a formal negotiating procedure should be established together with facilities for conciliation and arbitration.

The McDonnell Commission, appointed in 1911 after pressure from the civil service unions, reported in 1914 just as the war began. It recommended that there should be closer co-ordination between the educational systems of the country and the civil service examinations and suggested a new system of grading which would correspond with educational levels. It also supported the principle of open competition which should be adhered to and, wherever applicable, extended, and that promotion should be determined on merit. As far as the staff associations were concerned, the Commission stated (McDonnell, 1914, Vol. XVI, p. 98):

We do not doubt that generally such Associations serve a useful and worthy purpose in promoting co-operation amongst many individuals serving under similar conditions; and we are glad to find that the heads of public departments generally 'recognise' such Associations in the sense of receiving from them directly representations on matters affecting their interests.

They recommended that a special inquiry should be held to consider the whole question of trade unions in the service and the desirability of creating suitable machinery for considering civil service grievances, particularly pay and conditions. On the outbreak of war, however, the Treasury notified civil service associations that further consideration of pay and conditions would have to be suspended. The McDonnell Commission's report was not implemented and was overtaken on industrial relations matters by the Whitley Committee proposals.

However, the existence of the Royal Commission had stimulated the interest of civil servants in securing the right of representation. An article in *State Service* in 1927 by G. H. Stuart-Bunning, recalling this period, said that 'it was a remarkable one for civil service agitation . . . associations and societies were spangled all over the service . . . . journals began to appear, mostly monthly and bought at will, small offices were taken and it could be said there was a measure of organisation almost everywhere'. W. J. Brown, who was later to become perhaps the most widely known of civil service trade union leaders, first made his mark by the presentation of evidence on behalf of clerical workers to the McDonnell Commission. By the outbreak of the First World War more than seventy staff associations were in active existence among civil service clerical workers. Some specialised groups also began to organise into occupational associations. Among them, for example, were the managers of the newly established labour exchanges. Professional staff had hardly yet asserted their occupational identity and, apart from a few engineers based on the Admiralty, were slow to join the new movement among civil servants. Technicians, on the other hand, particularly in the Admiralty, were well to the fore. The Admiralty Draughtsmen's Association was formed in 1909.

CONCILIATION AND ARBITRATION

The establishment of conciliation and arbitration machinery in 1917 acted as a further stimulus to trade union organisation in the civil service and accelerated the trend towards internal negotiation procedures rather than political pressure as the main channel of representation for civil service unions.

At the outset of the First World War the civil service union leaders, like the great majority of trade union leaders, joined with the government in support of the war. Most British trade union leaders, like their German counterparts, turned their backs on their previous declarations of international solidarity and urged their members to observe industrial peace, to accept sacrifices for the war effort and to contribute in every way to the defeat of the enemy. In Britain the official leadership of the unions became integrated, with few exceptions, into the machinery of the state. Union officials took seats on a range of committees connected with the mobilisation of industry, and unions signed agreements for the relaxation of traditional protective practices.

Even so, the government of the day soon had to face the mounting problems of a wartime economy. These problems affected the mood of trade unionists. Prices began to rise and profits soared to new heights. Many of the dilutees and women brought into industry were not paid the rate for the job except under trade union pressure. A system of industrial leaving certificates was introduced, the effect of which was tie many workers to their particular jobs. This led to grievances and injustices which it was not always easy to redress. Strikes were virtually outlawed and replaced by a system of compulsory arbitration.

At first civil servants, other than those in the Post Office, not only faced the same problem of changing conditions of employment and a rapidly rising cost of living, but were denied the privilege of arbitration. The Treasury readopted its previous policy of refusing to hear the claims of grades as a whole and insisting on departmental approaches. It refused to grant wage claims as 'part of a deliberate policy of attempting to break the vicious circle of increases in wages, given on account of a rise in prices' (Treasury, 1930, p. 50).

Discussions on the desirability of a conciliation and arbitration procedure for the civil service had been continuing in Parliament and elsewhere since the turn of the century. They were given an added stimulus by the McDonnell Commission's report. On 2 November 1916 the government succumbed to pressure and it was announced that 'His Majesty's Government have decided to set up a standing arbitration tribunal to decide during the war questions of wages arising between the Government and its civil employees'. The Board was established in early 1917 with Sir William J. Collins in the chair, and acted as an immediate stimulus to union organisation, because claims could only be presented on a collective basis. Moreover, the Board's insistence on conciliation before arbitration and its requirement that departmental procedures must have been exhausted accelerated the development of departmental recognition of unions. The Board also allowed classes to be represented by non-members of the class, which included trade union officials. Contact between departmental officials and trade union officials, often avoided in the past, was required during the process of conciliation.

The direct impact of conciliation and arbitration machinery on trade union organisation was demonstrated by the fact that the extension of arbitration facilities in 1919 to civil servants on salaries up to £1,500 p.a. (the limit in 1917 had been set at £500 p.a.) was rapidly followed by the formation of three associations in the higher grades: the Association of Staff Clerks and other Civil Servants, the Society of Civil Servants and the Association of First Division Civil Servants. It probably also played some part in the establishment of the Institution. The operations of the Board had also pointed up the difficulty of dealing with claims on a departmental rather than a service-wide basis and the frequent differences of view between the Treasury and departments, thus laying the ground for the acceptance of full Treasury responsibility and the development of a single official side, another of the preconditions for the later establishment of Whitleyism.

THE WHITLEY COMMITTEE

Industrial unrest grew as the war continued. In some engineering and shipbuilding centres, and to some extent in coal-mining, a new rank-and-file leadership emerged to take the place of the official leadership. The official leadership, through its commitment to the war, found itself either unable or unwilling to take up vigorously many of the issues which were causing unrest among the working population. Many of these rank-and-file leaders were shop stewards in the big engineering factories and shipyards on the Clyde, Tyneside and in London. Some of them were not only industrial militants but were also strongly influenced by the traditional socialist opposition to what they believed was an imperialist war. On Clydeside in particular the rank-and-file leadership of the shop stewards' movement exercised very strong influence among tens of thousands of workers. They were a constant thorn in the side of the employers and of the government.

In the autumn of 1916 the government decided to set up a subcommittee of the Committee on Reconstruction to consider the problems of industrial relations. The subcommittee sat under the chairmanship of Mr J. H. Whitley, MP. The terms of reference of the subcommittee were:

(1) To make and consider suggestions for securing a permanent improvement in the relations between employers and workmen.
(2) To recommend means for securing that industrial conditions affecting the relations between employers and workmen shall be systematically reviewed by those concerned with a view to improving conditions in the future.

By the time the series of Whitley Committee reports was published, the first in March 1917 and the last in July 1918, the industrial unrest had in no way diminished and the revolution in Russia had added a new dimension of social ferment, stimulating widespread discussion among trade unionists and provoking fears of similar developments throughout the governments of Western Europe.

The main recommendation of the Whitley Committee was that joint industrial councils, representative of employers and employed, should be established in industries where national negotiating machinery did not exist. Thus industries with long-established machinery, such as engineering, were not directly affected by the main recommendation. The principal purpose of the proposed joint industrial councils was to promote closer co-operation between employer and employed by providing the means whereby matters of mutual interest could be considered.

The approach of the Whitley Committee was to seek what it described as 'a permanent improvement in the relations between employers and employed'. This, it said, required 'that any proposals put forward should offer the workpeople the means of attaining improved conditions of employment and a higher standard of comfort generally and involve the enlistment of their active and continuous co-operation in the promotion of industry'. To this end it urged that in each industry there should be an organisation representative of employers and workpeople to consider 'matters affecting the progress and well-being of the trade from the point of view of all those engaged in it, as far as this is consistent with the general interests of the community'. The scope of the suggested joint industrial councils was to be wide, not only including discussion of terms and conditions of employment but also involving employees more fully in the day-to-day running of their establishments. They were thus regarded as both consultative and negotiating bodies.

The Whitley scheme favoured trade union membership. The report stated that in the committee's considered opinion an essential condition of securing a permanent improvement in the relations between employers and employed was that there should be adequate organisation on the part of both employers and workpeople. The proposals outlined for joint co-operation depended for their ultimate success upon there being such organisation on both sides; such organisation was necessary also to provide means whereby the arrangements and agreements made in industry could be effectively carried out.

Despite this backing for trade unionism, the trade union movement was by no means unanimous in supporting the Whitley proposals. A number of members of the Whitley Committee, among whom was the union leader and later Cabinet minister J. R. Clynes, wrote a reservation to the main recommendations to the effect that whilst they welcomed the proposals for co-operation and improved conditions they felt that 'a complete identity of interests between capital and labour cannot thus be effected and that such machinery cannot be expected to furnish a settlement for the more serious conflicts of interest in the working of an economic system primarily governed and directed by the motives of private profit'. Some other trade unionists were much more critical. A number of strongly organised unions with long-established negotiating arrangements were suspicious of any kind of state intervention. Others regarded the entire Whitley exercise as a window-dressing operation, designed to divert the energies of trade union militants into ineffective schemes of class collaboration.

The civil service unions had no such reservations. They saw in the proposals a new opportunity to establish full trade union recognition and negotiating machinery. As Whitley himself said:

> When my committee had issued its first report, the people in the civil service were among the first to prick up their ears, and I had, very speedily, an enquiry from the ranks of civil servants as to whether or not what we had said was meant to apply also to the civil service.

THE STRUGGLE FOR WHITLEYISM IN THE CIVIL SERVICE

There is no doubt that at first the government intended that the Whitley proposals should not apply to the civil service. Indeed, the first report was circulated by the Ministry of Labour only to employers and unions in private industry, even though a further report from the Whitley Committee published in October 1917 contained a specific recommendation that the proposals should be brought to the attention of state departments and municipal authorities. The government argued that the civil service could not be regarded as an 'industry' in the sense to which the Whitley Committee referred. The civil service unions rejoined that if the recommendations of the Whitley Committee were sufficiently good to be commended by the government to private employers it was utterly inconsistent for the government to refuse to apply them to its own area of employment. At a conference of clerical associations held in November 1917 a resolution was passed suggesting that a board comprising equal numbers of persons appointed by the government and by the staff associations should be established to exercise general supervision over the general conditions of civil servants. The civil service unions mounted a campaign to influence public opinion and the Treasury.

In May 1918 the government convened a conference of departments employing large numbers of industrial (manual) civil servants to consider the possible application to them of the Whitley proposals. Shortly afterwards an interdepartmental committee, chaired by Mr J. H. Roberts, was established to consider the question, and was asked to consult Whitley. The committee appointed a subcommittee under the chairmanship of Sir Thomas Heath to draw up a draft scheme for application to non-industrial (non-manual) staff. At the TUC one of the civil service unions tabled a motion calling upon the government to apply the principles of the Whitley Report to all government departments. This motion was treated somewhat nervously by the Parliamentary Committee of the TUC because, although the Parliamentary Committee had in the previous year expressed general support for the Whitley proposals, regard had to be paid to the known opposition of some of the large unions. Nevertheless, the motion was carried. The civil service unions were supported by the majority at the TUC, including the general workers' unions who, like the civil service unions, saw in the Whitley proposals a new opportunity to establish collective bargaining in industries and undertåkings where hitherto the employers had been resistant.

The committee report on industrial staff closely resembled the Whitley proposals and was adopted by the Cabinet in 1918. However, the Heath Report was slower to emerge and there was a resurgence of agitation among the staff associations; representations to the Treasury were made and mass meetings held. The Heath Committee finally reported in March 1919 and recommended that a consultative scheme should be established embracing a national joint council, joint departmental committees and local committees. These committees were not to have executive functions because it was held that ministers could not be bound by decisions within such joint departmental machinery. The civil service unions protested against this interpretation of the Whitley proposals and pointed out that consultation was not a substitute for collective bargaining and joint agreement. Moreover, pay and conditions were not included in the subjects to be covered by such a procedure.

The Treasury circulated copies of the Heath Report to every union together with an invitation to attend a gathering at Caxton Hall on 8 April 1919. The Institution sent three representatives to the meeting. On the previous evening the unions agreed upon an amendment to the report calling for a joint committee made up of an equal number of official and staff side nominees to consider the application of the Whitley principle and to prepare an agreed scheme for the civil service. Mr Stuart-Bunning was deputed to move the amendment and it was agreed that in order to impress the Chancellor with the unanimity of the staff side's view after it had been formally seconded, no one else in the hall should join the discussion. The gathering proceeded as planned. The Chancellor of the Exchequer gave a speech commending the report to the meeting and was followed by Stuart-Bunning who, while welcoming the proposal to establish a Whitley system, made it clear that the report outraged one of the basic conceptions of the Whitley system, namely, that before a joint council was established there should be full consultation between employers and workpeople, and that there should be negotiation between equals, not simply consultation. After the amendment had been formally seconded there was silence in the hall.

No one in the crowded assembly rose to speak. Mr Chamberlain indicated that he had given up a whole morning in order to hear the views of the service. He asked if there was no one else who wished to express his view. Still there was silence. Stuart-Bunning says, 'Not a soul rose: not a sound, save the rustle and murmurs ever present at a conference. For once the service was not only solid, but silently solid.' (Callaghan, 1953, p. 4)

Eventually the Chancellor relented and accepted a proposal from the unions that a joint committee should be established to prepare a detailed scheme for the suggested national council and to formulate the main principles on which departmental and local Whitley bodies should be constituted. The significance of this proposal was that it provided for joint determination in the setting-up of the scheme and not merely for consultative arrangements. The provisional joint committee was duly established, consisting of fifteen official representatives and fifteen from the trade unions including three from the Institution, and was jointly chaired by Sir Malcolm Ramsay and Mr G. H. Stuart-Bunning.

The way was now clear for the acceptance of the Whitley scheme in the civil service. Further discussions were held very quickly and the Ramsay–Bunning Committee produced a unanimous joint report towards the end of May 1919. The vital principle was established that the new machinery was to be not merely advisory but could provide for agreed decisions which, after being reported to the Cabinet, would become operative. In effect, as the government subsequently explained, this meant that decisions would not be taken at the National Whitley Council except on issues where the government's representatives knew they were acting within a mandate received from ministers.

The Ramsay–Bunning Committee suggested that the new negotiating and consultative structure should have three tiers: a national council, departmental councils and district and office or works committees. The main objects of this system were:

> To secure a greater measure of co-operation between the State, in its capacity as employer, and the general body of civil servants in matters affecting the civil service, with a view to increased efficiency in the public service combined with the well-being of those employed; to provide machinery for dealing with grievances, and generally to bring together the experience and different points of view of representatives of the administrative, clerical and manipulative civil service.

The joint committee further recommended that the proposed National Council should consist of an Official Side and a Staff Side. It was made clear that neither the members of the Official Side nor those of the Staff Side need be civil servants, but that the members of the Staff Side should be appointed by specified staff associations. The Institution was one of the named associations. The committee recommended that civil servants who were members of the Staff Side of the National Council should be given special leave with pay when attending meetings of the National Council. The committee did not think it its duty to make any recommendations as to the allocation of seats on the Staff Side but it recorded that it had been informed of the proposed allocation. Of the twenty-seven on the Staff Side, two had been given to the Institution.

The committee also made recommendations for the constitution of departmental councils. It did not offer detailed recommendations but suggested in broad outline the principles on which the departmental councils should be constituted. The members of the Staff Side, it was urged, should be elected by the staff associations or groups of associations having members employed in the department. It would be open, said the report, 'to the electorate as constituted to choose as their representative any member or official of the association who is employed in the civil service or, if not a person so employed, is a full-time officer of the association. The election should in all cases be under the authority of the association concerned.' Among the functions suggested for the departmental councils were the application at departmental level of the general issues reserved for the National Council, the discussion of promotion cases in which it was alleged by the Staff Side that the principles of promotion accepted by or with the sanction of the National Council had been violated, and disciplinary cases. The report suggested that decisions of departmental councils should be reached by agreement between the two sides.

The establishment of Whitleyism gave trade unions in the civil service full recognition for the first time. Until that time civil servants who took an active part in organising their colleagues were likely to find their activities called into question and to incur official displeasure. The Treasury had refused to acknowledge their existence. Instead they had developed an 'alternative' to collective bargaining.

> Initially, the Treasury would ignore grievances until they mounted up: then they would become so acute that there would be considerable agitation among the staff, resulting in questions and pressure in Parliament: when the Government of the day could ignore the unrest no longer, they would set up a Royal Commission or a Select Committee of Parliament to clear away the accumulated grievances. The recommendations of these Commissions of Enquiry would be partially put into effect, and the pattern would repeat itself. Such an anarchistic system could not survive the influx of staff and new problems during the 1914–1918 war, and the Treasury found itself compelled to negotiate with some of the Staff Associations, which thus became 'recognised'. Nevertheless, the Treasury kept up an off-hand attitude towards these Staff Associations, and during the war grievances continued to pile up and discontent increased. (Callaghan, 1953, p. 2)

The establishment of Whitley machinery for the non-industrial civil service was thus the outcome of two main influences. The first was the radical demands voiced by active trade unionists in the factories, in the pits and in the railways during the First World War. It was this which led to the appointment of the Whitley Committee and strongly influenced the committee's recommendations. The second main influence was the development of trade union organisation within the civil service itself and the growing pressure from an increasing number of civil servants for a system of collective bargaining. The Institution was largely a product of these developments.

2 Thwarted Expectations, 1919–25

The establishment of the Whitley machinery, although a major step forward for civil service trade unions, did not of itself guarantee improved relations between management and unions. Indeed, the next twenty years were to be a severe test of the system. The constraints under which it was to operate were clearly laid down in January 1921: 'While the acceptance by the Government of the Whitley system as regards the civil service implies an intention to make the fullest use of Whitley procedure, the Government has not surrendered, and cannot surrender, its liberty of action in the exercise of its authority and the discharge of its responsibilities in the public interest.' Disagreement within the Whitley system could, if concerned with pay, be taken to arbitration, but in many cases disagreement could be broken only by executive action on the part of the government, as indeed it was on many occasions in the interwar years. The Official Side remained unconverted to the spirit of Whitleyism and conducted relations with the Staff Side at arm's length. In the words of Sir Albert Day (1953, p. 102):

> During the early years of Whitleyism relations between the two sides of the National Council were a blend of starch and dynamite. Each viewed the other with some distrust . . . Some meetings of the Council were chilly gatherings of about fifty men and women brought from overloaded desks to sit, most of them, mute and idle while more or less formal business was transacted; others were red hot rows.

THE REORGANISATION COMMITTEE

As soon as the Whitley scheme had been established in the non-industrial civil service, the National Whitley Council embarked on a thoroughgoing study of the organisation of administrative and clerical functions. At the second meeting of the Council, held on 14 October 1919, it was resolved 'That a special committee be appointed to consider the scope of the duties at present allotted to the clerical classes in the civil service; to report on the organisation most appropriate to secure the effective performance of these duties; and to make recommendations as to the scales of salary and methods of recruitment'.

The committee charged with this task became known as the Reorganisation Committee and it produced both an interim and a final report. In its interim report it said that an effective division of labour was the very essence of sound organisation. It therefore urged that within the service there should be four different classes for clerical and administrative work. They were to be known as a writing assistant class, a clerical class, an executive class and an administrative class. In addition there were to be two classes for typists and shorthand typists. The report made proposals for the assimilation of existing grades within the proposed new classes. It also went some way towards opening more opportunities for women in the civil service, though it fell well short of providing for equality.

The committee agreed that within the parallel classes of the civil service women should be given a status and authority identical to men and that the principles of training and promotion recommended for men should be applied equally to women. On the other hand the Official Side of the committee insisted that women should be selected temporarily by a system of impartial boards rather than by the open, competitive, written examinations which applied to men. Moreover, the pay scales for women stopped well short of the maximum for men in each class. The Federation of Women Civil Servants, represented on the Committee, fought hard against the inequalities embodied in the report and when the Staff Side refused to hold out on the issue the Federation withdrew from both the Staff Side and the Civil Service Alliance.

The final report of the Reorganisation Committee, published in 1921, dealt with the problems of assimilation, temporary staff and hours of work. On a number of issues, including overtime rates and hours of work, the committee was unable to reach agreement. The committee also did not deal with salary scales with maxima exceeding £500 per annum.

Within the National Whitley Council the representatives of the Institution sought to secure for professional and technical civil servants the same thorough-going investigation as had been secured for clerical and administrative grades. The proposal was made that a committee should be set up 'to consider the scope of the duties at present allotted to permanent (established or unestablished) professional, scientific and technical civil servants; to report on the organisation most appropriate to secure the effective performance of those duties; and to make recommendations as to scales of salaries and methods of recruitment'. This proposal was given support by the Staff Side of the National Whitley Council but was opposed by the Official Side. The view of the Official Side was that, whereas there was a common bond between clerical grades, who were recruited by a common examination, there was no similar bond between professional and technical civil servants. The view of the Institution and the view of the Official Side were in direct conflict.

PROFESSIONAL AND TECHNICAL CLASSES INQUIRY

Eventually, after a great deal of argument, the Official Side offered to establish three joint committees to consider certain professional groups. The three committees were to deal respectively with engineers and architects, valuers and analytical chemists. The terms of reference of the three committees were: 'To consider the scope of the duties at present allotted to professional, scientific and technical civil servants in the following category (there followed the names of the specified classes grouped under each committee); to report on the organisation most appropriate to secure the effective performance of these duties; and to make recommendations as to the scales of salary and method of recruitment.' It was agreed also that there should be a demarcation committee to consider into which group, if any, certain marginal professional, scientific and technical staff should fall; and a special committee to deal with general questions such as qualifications and recruitment but excluding remuneration and grading.

From the very beginning the work of the group committees was delayed by controversy. The Official Side showed marked reluctance to engage in a constructive inquiry. The first meetings of the three committees were delayed because of disputes within the demarcation committee. The Official Side insisted that certain categories should be excluded from the scope of the inquiry. The exclusions embraced all persons specifically appointed for and engaged in research, all persons possessing professional, scientific or technical qualifications but not engaged in work definitely involving the practice of those attainments (even though such qualifications were a prerequisite for appointment to the situation(s) in question), and all posts in respect of which the upper limit of the salary scale was in excess of £500 a year exclusive of bonus. The Official Side did agree, however, that the committees could consider any basic grade within the terms of reference if the £500 salary limit would otherwise exclude them from consideration. The Staff Side protested vigorously against these restrictive conditions but to no avail. The Staff Side also urged that further committees should be set up to deal with lawyers, medical grades, accountants, auditors and actuaries. They also proposed that the committee covering the analytical chemists should be extended to include other scientists. All these suggestions were rejected by the Official Side, although a committee on the legal classes was later established in June 1921.

The number of civil servants covered by the committee set up to deal with engineers and architects was far greater than the number covered by the other two committees. It included within its scope the large number of engineering and architectural draughtsmen employed in the Admiralty, the engineering department of the Post Office, the Office of Works, the War Office and the Air Ministry.

The lack of progress made by the committees soon led to protests. In July 1921 the Association of Valuation Office Valuers, a constituent part of the Institution, forwarded a resolution to the Council of the Institution expressing concern that no meeting of the group committee covering valuers had yet been held. This resolution was endorsed by the Council and it was agreed to write to the National Whitley Council drawing attention to the fact that for more than four months there had not been a single meeting of the professional classes committees. The resolution pointed out that a shorter period had sufficed for the Reorganisation Committee to make a detailed report on the clerical and administrative grades. The Council of the Institution urged that the time was now 'much overdue when these committees should proceed forthwith to deal energetically with the matters referred to them'.

The three group committees eventually started their work and continued through 1922 and 1923. By the summer of 1924, however, an article in *State Technology* (the Institution's monthly journal begun in April 1921) stated that the committees 'have reported practically no agreement' even though their work was drawing to a close. The Official Side, said the article, had resisted the bulk of the claims of the staff with irrelevant and evasive argument or by simple negation.

When the reports of the committees were published in the spring of 1925 the president of the Institution, Sir Richard Redmayne, said at the annual meeting that the direct result, as expressed in improved conditions and salaries, had been meagre. *State Technology* was more outspoken in its criticism. It said that the report of the committee covering engineers and architects was a remarkable exhibition of defensive play by the Official Side acting, of course, on Treasury instructions. They had succeeded in conceding practically nothing. Even though the joint committee had met on no fewer that fifty-seven occasions and the Staff Side on more than a hundred occasions, virtually no progress had been made. The report of the joint committee confirmed that from the outset the Official Side had refused to move on salaries. They informed the Staff Side that they did not acknowledge that the salary scales were inadequate. Even though evidence on the matter was called by the Staff Side, the Official Side did not think it necessary to produce any evidence in reply. The report stated 'the view of the Official Side was that no effective comparison was possible between the terms of remuneration appropriate to professional classes and to classes employed on clerical and administrative duties'. The order of the day, said the journal, was 'divide and rule'.

It was not only in respect of salaries that the work of the group committees proved abortive. The Official Side rejected the suggestions of the Staff Side designed to secure a common basis of recruitment among professional and technical grades. They also resisted any suggestions for the reorganisation of professional and technical grades in various departments. They maintained that any investigation of this kind must necessarily be a subject for departmental consideration.

The report of the committee covering engineers and architects was signed on 22 June 1925 and was formally received by the National Whitley Council some four days later. Many members of the Staff Side took the view that the committee had not carried out its terms of reference and had failed to agree upon any substantial measure of simplification and co-ordination of the grades and their pay. After a full discussion at its meeting on 4 December 1925 the National Whitley Council Staff Side agreed to move that the report should be referred back to the committee because 'this was the only procedure that would enable them to register their profound dissatisfaction with the report as a whole and to dissociate themselves from many of the extraordinary conclusions and expressions of opinion contained therein'. The committee, said the National Whitley Council Staff Side, had failed utterly to deal with the task entrusted to it. They made clear that this was not the fault of the Staff Side but was due entirely to the attitude of the Official Side.

REASONS FOR FAILURE

In explaining the dismal failure of the inquiry into the professional and technical classes, the Institution said that the Treasury had responded to a newspaper campaign for economy. The Whitley machinery, it stated, had failed in its first major test case put to it by the professional and technical civil servants. This feeling of dissatisfaction was so strong that the chairman of the National Whitley Council Staff Side, Mr George Middleton, wrote an article in *State Technology* designed to answer the question 'Is Whitleyism a failure?'. He acknowledged the grounds for dissatisfaction with the Whitley system, but argued that any withdrawal from it by the civil service trade unions would be unhelpful.

Clearly the attitude of the Official Side was influenced by developments in the economy at large. Mr A. O. Gibbon, who was the Staff Side secretary of the inquiry covering engineers and architects, pointed out in an article in the November 1925 issue of *State Technology* that the slump in the engineering industry had depressed the pay of professional and technical staff. The Official

Side, he said, had taken full advantage of the national position and were only too ready 'to apply the conditions at the bottom of the trough'.

This was, indeed, the major explanation for the failure of the professional and technical classes inquiry. The Reorganisation Committee was launched in 1919 when there were high expectations of significant improvements in salaries and working conditions. Britain was prosperous in the postwar boom and there appeared to be unlimited scope for the expansion of industry. After the shortages of the wartime years there was a huge backlog of unsatisfied demands. In addition, the population was in a buoyant mood. Peace had at last returned after the slaughter and privations of the war. The government, by its declarations, also contributed to the high expectations of the people. Britain, the electorate had been promised, would be a land 'fit for heroes to live in'. There would be a higher standard of living, prosperity, full employment and better social services.

The trade unions emerged from the war considerably stronger than they were in 1914. The affiliated membership of the TUC rose to about $6\frac{1}{2}$ million at the height of the first postwar boom and it was estimated that there were nearly another 2 million members in unions not affiliated to the TUC, including, of course, the Institution. The aspirations of working people, including millions of demobilised troops, were expressed in greatly increased trade union activity. In the early months of 1919, immediately following the formation of the Institution, improvements in pay and conditions were secured in many industries. In all the main industries unions were pressing for reduced basic hours of work, which at that time were between 54 and 56 hours per week. Agreements were secured in a number of industries for a 47- or 48-hour week, even though the claim in many cases was for the introduction of an 8-hour day and a 40-hour week. Everywhere the initiative was with the unions.

The clerical and administrative unions in the civil service had managed to take advantage of this favourable environment through the rapid deliberations of the Reorganisation Committee. The effort to establish a similar inquiry into the professional, scientific and technical classes had taken much longer and the deliberations of the committees once established had suffered considerable delay. By the time they reported in 1925 the economic climate had changed dramatically.

The reasons for the prolonged deliberations were several. The Treasury was not convinced of the need for such an inquiry, nor were the committees sufficiently familiar with the work of the classes under review. According to the 1922 Institution annual report,

> The Staff Side feels that one of the chief difficulties with which it has to contend is the ignorance, and one might say the indifference, of the Official Side (as a whole) with regard to the professional classes of the civil service, and the memoranda issued by the Official Side very clearly demonstrate this fact.

Moreover, whereas the clerical and administrative unions were well organised and had already articulated their views on administrative reform, for example, to the abortive McDonnell Commission in 1911, the Institution was but newly formed from an amalgam of individual associations and the Staff Side of the committees was composed of a number of different unions of which the Institution was only one. Only in the case of the valuers was the Institution the sole representative association.

One important lesson drawn by the Institution from the experience of the professional and technical classes inquiry, therefore, was that membership within the Institution should be strengthened. An article in *State Technology* commented:

> There will never be any appreciable improvement in the status and conditions of employment of professional and technical officers until all such officers band themselves together in one organisation for the protection of their common interests, acting through the National Whitley Council in close co-operation upon general service questions with organisations representing the other main branches of the civil service.

Constituent associations of the Institution were urged to recruit every member of the staff who was eligible by the rules, to establish contact with other professional and technical associations in the same department and to help form new associations where it was not practicable to admit staff to existing organisations.

COST-OF-LIVING BONUS

The automatic adjustment of civil service pay to take account of changes in the cost of living was first introduced during the First World War. The introduction of the principle of automatic adjustment was much delayed and, in the event, proved inadequate, particularly for non-industrial civil servants. Post Office workers were the first to gain a war bonus, but it was not until September 1916 that the government accepted that as from 1 July 1916, male civil servants earning up to 40s per week should receive a weekly bonus of 4s and those earning up to 60s a weekly bonus of 3s. Women and juveniles were to receive half these amounts. By 1 September 1916 the official index of retail prices registered a 50 per cent increase on the datum line of prices in July 1914. In August 1918 a very modest war bonus was given for the first time to civil servants earning over £500 per year.

Immediately after the war there was a resurgence towards improved conditions of employment, accompanied in many industries by strikes. For example, the miners were involved in a major strike in 1920 in which they were supported by the railwaymen and transport workers – the 'Triple Alliance' as it was called – and this was sufficient, despite the gathering clouds of industrial depression, to secure for the miners a temporary wage increase.

Early in 1920 a new cost-of-living bonus scheme was introduced which provided pay increases on a sliding scale for civil servants. The scheme was introduced as a result of a recommendation by the Joint Cost of Living Committee appointed by the National Whitley Council to consider the effect of the increase in the cost of living on the salaries of civil servants. The special committee was appointed in October 1919 and in its recommended scheme took as its standard for the cost of living the index figure of 130 for 1 March 1920, shown in the *Ministry of Labour Gazette* as the increase since July 1914 which formed the base line of 100. On the first £91 15s per annum of salary a full 30 per cent bonus was granted; for salaries between £91 15s and £200 only 60 per cent of the full bonus figure was paid; and for salaries between £200 and £500 per annum only 45 per cent was paid. The scheme also provided for increases or decreases in the bonus by ¹⁄₂₆ for every five full points the official index figure rose or fell below 130. The bonus was to be paid unchanged for four months from 1 March 1920 and was to be reviewed thereafter every four months during the first twelve months of the scheme and subsequently every six months. The civil service unions calculated that the effect of the bonus scheme, after taking into account price increases and income tax increases, was to reduce the living standard of every grade of civil servant in comparison with prewar days.

In the summer of 1920 the brief postwar boom came to an end. By February 1921 unemployment had reached the million mark and by June it was well over 2 million, 17 per cent of those eligible for employment.

In the spring of 1921 there was another major dispute in the coal industry. Following a lock-out which lasted until the early summer the miners were defeated and their wages were cut. This was the signal for wage reductions in many other industries, including engineering, building, cotton textiles, agriculture and seafaring. The depression continued through the winter of 1921–2, and in the opening weeks of 1922 the storm centre shifted to the engineering industry. The employers insisted on their right to enforce overtime as part of their managerial functions. The unions, on the other hand, argued in favour of a system of control under which some of their members would not be required to work regular and excessive overtime whilst large numbers of other members were unemployed. The dispute finally led to a national lock-out which lasted from early in March to the middle of June. The unions were defeated and their members returned to work with a resentment against the doctrine of managerial prerogatives embodied in the new procedure agreement which was to affect industrial relations in engineering for the next fifty years. At the same time the miners were again under attack from the mine-owners. Unemployment was high and by June there were further substantial cuts in miners' pay.

Many workers who were in regular employment, and this included civil servants, did not suffer the same acute cuts in living standards as the workers in the industries where there was heavy unemployment. The cost of living fell sharply in 1921 and continued to fall until well into 1923. The cost-of-living index was designed to measure living costs for working-class households and was not necessarily, therefore, an accurate indicator of changes in costs for other citizens whose pattern of expenditure might be different. The TUC, the Labour Party and the Co-operative Union therefore set up a Joint Committee on the Cost of Living, and in its report the committee said that the Ministry of Labour's cost-of-living index seriously underestimated the real increase in the cost of living since 1914. Where wages were tied to the index, as in the civil service, cuts were being enforced which were unjustified.

THE 'SUPER-CUT'

In July 1921 the government decided as part of a national economy campaign that the bonus received by civil servants earning more than £500 per year should be cut over and above the reductions in civil service bonus which were taking place as a result of the fall in the cost-of-living figure. Basic salaries of £500 but less than

£700 per year were to have an additional bonus reduction of 10 per cent. This bonus reduction was to be increased by 5 per cent for every additional £100 of basic salary up to a 60 per cent reduction on basic salaries of £1,600. No bonus was to be payable on salaries of £2,000 per year or more. This evoked a protest from the organisations representing the higher-ranking civil servants and particularly from the Institution. They felt that professional staff had a special grievance. Administrative and executive civil servants had benefited under postwar reorganisation so that the 'super-cut' in bonus, as it came to be known, was regarded by the Institution as to some extent a taking back from other higher-ranking civil servants of part of what had been given. Professional civil servants, in contrast, had not benefited under postwar reorganisation so that the 'super-cut' in bonus represented a real reduction in standards. They therefore urged in a separate memorandum to the Chancellor that the 'super-cut' should not be applied to professional civil servants until such time as regrading and reassessment of their remuneration corresponding to that accorded to other branches of the service had been effected.

This point of view did not go unchallenged. The Society of Civil Servants (SCS) sent a resolution to the Institution denying that only professional civil servants with salaries in excess of £500 per annum had not received substantial pay increases. The SCS asked the Institution to issue a statement accepting this correction. This the Institution declined to do, but agreed to publish the exchange of correspondence between the two organisations.

Some years later the Institution described the bonus 'super-cut' as an administrative act of appalling meanness perpetrated by the Coalition government in deference to a press campaign waged in 1921 against the civil service. The government argued that the National Whitley Council had no authority on the pay of civil servants whose salary exceeded £500 per year. The Staff Side said that this interpretation was in breach of an understanding reached at the time of the introduction of the bonus scheme. It had been understood, and this, it was pointed out, was confirmed in writing, that the scheme would 'be applied so as to include officers on rates of salary up to £1,000 per annum, and on scales of salary with maxima not exceeding that amount'. But for this understanding, said the Institution, the agreement for the bonus scheme would not have been signed.

Despite the protests of the civil service unions, the bonus 'super-cut' remained. Representations were made to successive governments but all proved abortive. Finally in November 1926 the issue was put to arbitration. The decision went against the unions. The tribunal accepted that there had been an 'honourable undertaking' regarding bonus payments on salaries up to £1,000 a year but pointed out that 'such undertakings could be withdrawn by the overriding authority of Parliament'. The tribunal commented, however, that 'it was only natural in the circumstances of the present case that feelings of resentment would be aroused when the "super-cut" was put into force without consultation on the Whitley Council'. In reply to the argument advanced by the Staff Side that the economic situation had improved since 1921, the tribunal stated bluntly: 'The Court are unable to find any such improvement in the financial situation of the country since 1921, when the "super-cut" was imposed, as would justify them in removing it now, and they therefore award against the claim of the applicants.'

ARBITRATION

Not much more than six months after the defeat of the miners in the 1921 coal dispute the government announced its intention to abolish the Civil Service Arbitration Board. The abolition was recommended by a Committee on National Expenditure, known at the time as the 'Geddes Axe'. The abolition was presented primarily as an economy measure, although the estimated saving was only £1,886 per annum. In its third report, dated 21 February 1922, the Geddes Committee stated:

> Whatever justification there may have been in time of war for setting up such a body, whose awards are final and who can thus authorise expenditure without the authority of the Chancellor of the Exchequer, we are very strongly of the opinion that the main justification for the existence of the Board has disappeared with the institution of the Whitley Councils in the civil service. It has now become the established practice in the civil service to consider on these Whitley Councils questions of remuneration, so far as they relate to posts carrying salaries not exceeding £500 per annum, and, in these circumstances, we are of the opinion that the need for a standing Arbitration Board no longer exists.

The Arbitration Board remained in existence for about another year to deal with cases already before it and its last official pronouncement was made in May 1923. During its period of existence it dealt with 222 cases. The Staff Side of the National Whitley Council protested against the abolition of the Board and affirmed its conviction that 'the existence of an independent court of appeal, such as a Board of Arbitration provides, is essential to the effective working of the Whitley system in the civil service'. The Staff Side called upon the government to replace the Board of Arbitration with another independent arbitration body.

In April 1922 a joint committee of civil service unions, formed to conduct a campaign for the restoration of arbitration, wrote to every member of Parliament with a reasoned statement protesting against the government's decision. In May the Chancellor of the Exchequer received a deputation from the civil service unions and confirmed that the Arbitration Board would not be restored. He indicated, however, that the arbitration provisions of the Industrial Courts Act, 1919, would be available on the joint application of the Official and Staff Sides. Arbitration would not be withheld in cases where the issue was susceptible to arbitration. The civil service unions did not regard this concession to their point of view as an adequate substitute for the arbitration machinery which had been abolished.

Towards the end of July the House of Commons debated the government's decision to abolish the Civil Service Board of Arbitration. The Labour opposition attacked the decision but the government survived the debate with a comfortable majority of fifty-nine. In the general election held towards the end of 1922 every parliamentary candidate was invited to pledge support for the restoration of arbitration in the civil service. Candidates were approached locally by civil service union representatives. Of those who were elected, 322 expressed support for arbitration.

The campaign of the civil service unions had been to good effect, and in May

1923 the Chancellor of the Exchequer told the unions that he accepted the principle of arbitration and was prepared to consider favourably any scheme which included necessary safeguards. These safeguards were that nothing should undermine the ultimate overriding authority of Parliament and that any decisions made by an arbitration body would be accepted by both sides. Both were acceptable to the civil service unions.

A joint committee was established to work out the details of a suitable scheme. It included Mr J. H. Salmon, who was then the honorary secretary of the Institution. Unfortunately, it was not found possible to reach agreement. The Official Side wanted, at first, to exclude salaries above £500 per year and they also wanted to restrict the right of the civil service unions to approach members of Parliament regarding service pay and conditions, on the grounds that they would be able to use arbitration as an alternative method. The Official Side modified their stand in subsequent discussions, but when a further general election was announced for the end of 1923 agreement on a civil service arbitration scheme had still not been reached.

The civil service unions then renewed their campaign among parliamentary candidates and this time received an even more favourable response than in the previous general election. The response was most favourable of all from among Labour candidates. More than 400 of the newly elected members replied favourably to questions submitted by the civil service unions regarding the restoration of arbitration. The new minority Labour government did not, however, prove as responsive to civil service union representations as the unions had hoped. The government insisted that, except in special circumstances, staff with salaries above £700 per year should be excluded from the scope of the proposed new machinery. At a Council meeting held on 23 June 1923 the Institution recommended that the proposed new machinery should be accepted, as it represented a 'distinct advance', though the Institution regarded the exclusion of civil servants with salaries exceeding £700 per year as 'unjust and illogical'. This point of view, reluctantly to accept the government's proposal, was shared by a number of other civil service union representatives, but there was still strong opposition from some unions. A joint meeting of the Executive of the Parliamentary Labour Party and the General Council of the TUC decided to support the campaign of the Civil Service Clerical Association (CSCA), the Union of Post Office Workers (UPW) and the Post Office Engineering Union (POEU) for an arbitration body with wider scope than that proposed by the government.

Before the campaign could be further developed the minority Labour government fell. Mr Baldwin became the new Prime Minister. Further representations were made to the government by the Staff Side, but continuity in government policy was maintained. On 2 January the Financial Secretary to the Treasury wrote to the Staff Side reiterating the government's view:

Dear Mr Stuart-Bunning,
I have now fully considered the representations which you and other members of the General Purposes Committee of the Staff Side of the National Whitley Council made to me last Wednesday on the subject of the proposed arbitration scheme for the civil service. I have also reported your recommendations to the Chancellor of the Exchequer.
I regret that I am unable to agree to the modification of the scheme so as to

provide for the application of the principle of compulsory arbitration to classes of civil servants on rates of salary in excess of that figure; or for the reference to arbitration of claims in respect of daily as distinct from weekly hours of work, and of questions of grading.

With regard to grading, whilst I would have been glad to meet the views of the Staff Side, I am afraid it is impossible to accept the terms of the formula on this subject proposed by the deputation or to assent to the inclusion of any such formula in the terms of reference to the Arbitration Board.

Yours sincerely,

(*sgd*) Walter Guinness

The Staff Side decided that further concessions were not now likely and on 14 January 1925 they accepted the proposed arbitration scheme. The full terms of the scheme were as follows:

(1) We are agreed that failing agreement by negotiation, arbitration shall be open to Government Departments on the one hand, and to recognised associations of civil servants within the scope of the National Whitley Council for the administration and legal departments of the civil service and of departmental Whitley Councils allied thereto on the other hand, on application by either party, in regard to certain matters affecting conditions of service, subject to the limitations and conditions hereinafter defined.

(2) We are agreed that the machinery for arbitration shall be the Industrial Court established by the Industrial Courts Act, 1919. In accordance with Section 1(3) of the Industrial Courts Act, the Court for the hearing of claims as hereinafter defined shall consist of such members of the Industrial Court as the President of the Court may direct; but it is understood that the Court will consist of a Chairman, who will be either the President of the Industrial Court or the Chairman of a division of the Court, together with one member drawn from a panel of persons appointed to the Industrial Court by the Minister of Labour as representing the Chancellor of the Exchequer for the time being and one member drawn from a panel of persons appointed to the Industrial Court by the Minister of Labour as representing the Staff Side of the National Whitley Council for the administrative and legal departments of the civil service.

(3) The members of the Industrial Court appointed as representing the Staff Side of the National Whitley Council for the administrative and legal departments of the civil service should hold office for three years and be eligible for reappointment.

(4) We are of opinion that for the purposes of this agreement civil servants and officials of associations and federations of classes of civil servants shall be regarded as ineligible for appointment as members of the Industrial Court.

(5) We are agreed that the Court thus constituted shall not be entitled to hear claims in respect of classes with salaries in excess of £700 a year exclusive of bonus (except in cases of classes for which the scale of pay commences at a figure of less than £700 a year but rises to a figure above £700 a year, in both cases exclusive of bonus) unless by the consent of both parties concerned in the claim.

(6) Claims eligible to be dealt with by the Court shall be claims affecting the

emoluments, weekly hours of work, and leave of classes of civil servants as herein defined, and cases of individual officers shall be excluded.

(7) The word 'emoluments', for the purpose of the foregoing clause, shall include pay, and allowances of the nature of pay, bonus, overtime rates, subsistence rates, travelling and lodging allowances. The term 'class' shall mean any well-defined category of civil servants who, for the purpose of a particular claim, occupy the same position or have a common interest in the claim.

(8) An endeavour shall be made by the parties to agree the terms of reference or the terms of the remit to the Court, but where this is not practicable the respective statements of claim shall be set out, and these will together constitute the terms of reference or remit.

(9) We trust that arrangements may be made to ensure that under normal conditions claims should be heard within one calendar month of the remit to the Court.

This statement was supplemented by a Treasury letter to the Staff Side in the following terms:

Dear Stuart-Bunning,
Thank you for your letter of 19 February, enclosing a signed copy of the report to the Chancellor of the Exchequer on the subject of arbitration.

As is clearly stated in Section 1 of that report, it becomes incumbent on Government departments to proceed to arbitration, if the associations concerned so desire, in the event of disagreement on matters affecting conditions of service as defined in the agreement.

With regard to your second question, subject to the overriding authority of Parliament, the Government would regard themselves as bound by awards of the Court.

Yours faithfully,
(*sgd*) R. R. Scott

The panel of Staff Side nominees for the Arbitration Board included Frank Hodges, former general secretary of the Miners' Federation of Great Britain; J. J. Mallon, Warden of Toynbee Hall, a former member of the Whitley Committee and Labour candidate in several general elections; Miss M. J. Symons of the National Union of General Workers and former member of the Executive Committee of the Labour Party; and Mr A. G. Walkden, the general secretary of the Railway Clerks' Association. Soon after the formation of the panel Miss Symons resigned. The Institution nominated Mr Harold Laski of the London School of Economics to fill the vacancy. The other nominee was Miss Margaret Bondfield, a trade union official, one-time Labour MP and Britain's first woman Cabinet minister. The voting on the Staff Side went in favour of the Institution nominee and Mr Laski was elected.

Despite the re-establishment of arbitration machinery, serious differences of interpretation continued to arise between the Official and Staff Sides. The Official Side refused to accept references to arbitration of claims involving retrospection. They held that the Arbitration Board was not competent to impose any charge on public funds in respect of a period prior to the date of its establishment. This interpretation was particularly resented by the Institution because it had hoped that the new Arbitration Board would deal favourably with some of the Institution's claims which had been considered and rejected by the Official Side during the inquiry into the scientific, professional and technical staff.

The second controversial issue concerned the refusal of the Official Side to refer to arbitration claims for improved salary which also involved claims affecting assimilation (i.e. the terms on which existing staff would enter the salary scales awarded by arbitration). The Institution argued that in such cases staff should enter any new salary scales at the point in the scale which they would have reached had the scales been in operation at the time of their appointment to these grades.

The third controversial issue concerned the insistence of the Treasury that claims could be referred to arbitration only if they affected broad categories of staff. The civil service unions held that arbitration was being refused on a number of claims in respect of what appeared to be well-defined groups of civil servants, even though they did not constitute a Treasury 'class'. All these difficulties of interpretation were indicative of the unfavourable political and economic climate in which trade union claims were being pursued.

THE ANDERSON COMMITTEE

On 29 March 1923 the Chancellor of the Exchequer announced that the government had appointed a committee of three to inquire into 'the present standard of remuneration and other conditions of employment' of the civil service and the armed services. The appointment of this committee was the outcome of a recommendation of the Geddes Committee that a thorough investigation should be made of the salaries of all public servants. Its three members were Sir Alan Garrett Anderson, who was a director of the Midland Railway and of the Bank of England; Sir Peter Rylands, who in 1919–21 had been president of one of Britain's main representative employers' organisations, the Federation of British Industries; and General Sir Herbert Lawrence, who had been Chief of Staff, HQ, British Expeditionary Force, in 1918.

The civil service unions were apprehensive about the purpose of the Anderson Committee. At the annual Institution dinner held towards the end of May 1923, the president, Sir Richard Redmayne, said that it was not surprising that civil servants were on their guard against schemes which were 'intended to form the basis of indiscriminate reductions in staffs and salaries'. In the House of Commons, in a debate initiated by the opposition, a Labour member suggested that the purpose of the Anderson Committee was 'to beat down wages'. The Prime Minister, Mr Baldwin, in reply, said this was not its purpose. It was appointed, he said, to report how, in existing circumstances, scales of pay in the civil service were related to scales of pay throughout the country and whether, when so compared, the scales of pay in the civil service were fair. He went on to say that he believed that close investigation would show that civil servants were not overpaid.

The Institution decided to give evidence to the Anderson Committee separately from the Staff Side of the National Whitley Council. This was because, in the Institution's view, the position of professional, scientific and technical civil servants differed materially from that of their colleagues. They had special grievances relating to pay, poor promotion prospects and the abolition of the prewar practice of giving professional men 'added years' for the purpose of superannuation calculation. The Institution memorandum urged that adequate steps should be taken to bring the position of professional men in the civil service into line with that of the remainder of the service. It was pointed out that owing to the delay in regrading, they had not received any benefits such as those enjoyed by other classes following the 1920 reorganisation report.

When the report of the Anderson Committee was published in the late summer of 1923 it proved disappointing to the Institution. The committee rejected the contention that there should be any direct relationship between the administrative and the professional civil servant. The latter, said the committee:

> should relate his pay and position with those of his professional brethren in the outside world, and in doing so he should remember all that the civil service offers in addition to its pay. Permanence of employment under the state and status have real value and when a highly qualified professional man of ripe experience has weighed the offer of the state against the prospects in private practice and has deliberately accepted service under the state he has no cause to complain because some other servant of the state, who is not a professional man and has been selected for a different kind of work at a different age and in a different way, seems to him to be better paid than himself.

The Institution sharply criticised the report of the Anderson Committee. The General Purposes Committee of the Institution described the report as utterly unfair and urged the Institution's Council to take steps to discredit it. A letter was published in *The Times* of 17 September 1923 on behalf of the Institution drawing attention to the different criteria set in the Anderson Report for the administrative and professional grades of the civil service. The relevant paragraph of the letter stated:

> On reading through the report one is struck by the different criteria set for the administrative and professional grades. That the commencing salary of an administrative officer is by no means high is shown by comparing it with that of an assistant master; but the fact that these careers bear no comparison at the age of 30, when the normal salary of an administrative officer is £700, plus bonus, is not considered worth mentioning. A very different attitude is taken up in dealing with the professional classes. The Committee does not agree that there is any direct relation between the pay of the administrative and professional officer; but apparently it does agree that they can both be compared with professional men in the outside world. Since this is so, surely it would be logical to compare these two classes with one another. The greatest differentiation in the treatment of these classes is seen when the Committee states, with regard to the professional class, that, as the present scales attract good candidates today, it sees no reason for an increase. This is certainly going back on the principle laid down in the beginning of the report – namely, that employees of the Crown would have a real ground for complaint if their pay were related to wages in industry only in the time of low wages. Further, is it just to relate the pay of one class only to the present state of the market? One wonders what would be the

commercial value of the administrative recruit in the market at the moment; but the Committee does not consider his salary in relation to the number of good candidates available today.

The letter subsequently drew a protest from the Association of First Division Civil Servants (FDA). The Institution's Council also decided to give publicity to the fact that under the American Classification Act of 1923, Congress had accomplished what the British Treasury had declared to be impossible, namely, the formulation and adoption of a properly co-ordinated scheme of salaries for the whole civil service – professional and clerical.

The keen disappointment felt by professional, scientific and technical civil servants at the report of the Anderson Committee and the failure to make any progress in the professional and technical classes inquiry proceeding at that time led the Institution to seek the support of the various professional institutions for a proposal that the pay of professional civil servants should be referred to arbitration. The professional institutions were informed that, in the view of the Institution, it had become impossible within the civil service to secure proper recognition for members of the professions.

The professional institutions responded sympathetically to the Institution's appeal. Early in 1924 the presidents of the Institution of Civil Engineers, the Mechanical Engineers, the Electrical Engineers, the Royal Institute of British Architects, the Surveyors' Institution, the Institute of Chartered Accountants, the Institute of Chemistry and the Institution of Naval Architects sent a joint letter to the Prime Minister pressing for improvements in the status of professional civil servants. They requested that the dispute about status and salary should be submitted to arbitration. A formal acknowledgement was received from the Prime Minister in response to this appeal and on 16 May the president of the Institution of Civil Engineers, acting as chairman of the meeting of the presidents of the professional institutions, sent another letter reminding the government of the urgency of the claim and the necessity for a speedy resolution of the problem.

When a reply was eventually received from the government it referred only to the pay of professional civil servants and not to the question of status. It pointed out that discussions were proceeding for the re-establishment of arbitration machinery in the civil service. On 1 September 1924 the presidents of the professional institutions sent a further letter to the government in which they pointed out that the reply earlier received made no reference to the policy of the government with regard to the promotion or appointment of scientific and professional men to the higher posts in the civil service. On 1 October a reply was received from the Treasury stating that there appeared to be some misconception as to the practice of the government. The Treasury letter pointed out that the Director of Naval Construction was invariably a fully qualified naval architect and the Director of Works at HM Office of Works was an architect and civil engineer. The Treasury letter stated that there was no bar to the appointment of any civil servant to be permanent head of any of the great public departments. The only object in filling these posts was to get the best man wherever he might be found.

The acute dissatisfaction felt both inside and outside the civil service about the treatment given to professional and scientific civil servants also resulted in an approach to the Institution from the National Union of Scientific Workers (NUSW) in the autumn of 1924 suggesting a separate civil service Whitley Council for professional, scientific and technical classes. The need for such a separate Council, said the NUSW, had been felt for some time because of the delay and unsatisfactory negotiations on the three professional subcommittees of the National Whitley Council. This proposal was seriously considered by the Institution and, although a report appeared in *The Times* of a revolt in the Whitley Council, the proposal was finally overtaken by the government's agreement to the restoration of arbitration.

SUPERANNUATION

From the date of its formation the Institution took a strong interest in superannuation. In 1921 the Institution gained representation on the Superannuation Sub-Committee of the National Whitley Council. Apart from the general claim for improvements in superannuation for civil servants there were two issues of special concern to Institution members. The first was a claim for 'added years' which had a long history, dating back to the repeal in 1914 of Section 4 of the Superannuation Act, 1859. Under this section 'years' could be added to the actual years served for purposes of calculating pension if necessary training for particular professional skills had been obtained in employment outside the civil service. The Institution's argument was that the provision for 'added years' was designed to assist professional civil servants who had to obtain professional training, often at their own expense, outside the service in order to enable them to fulfil the requirements of the Crown. By reason of their having to acquire such training they were precluded from joining the civil service at an age which would enable them to earn the maximum pension. The second was a claim for more favourable treatment for persons transferred from unestablished to established service – 'unestablished service to count for pension'. Both these claims, however, were ruled out for the time being because of cost.

However, early in 1922 the civil service unions did secure a major improvement in superannuation arrangements when, in response to long negotiations, the Treasury agreed that in future 100 per cent of the war bonus, instead of 75 per cent, should be added to salary for the purpose of calculating pension. The bonus so added was to be based on the average cost of living for the three months preceding the date of retirement and was to be subject to quarterly revision thereafter, but the bonus added was not at any date after retirement to exceed the amount assessed at the date of retirement. As the peak of the postwar inflation had by then passed, this restriction was, in practice, nowhere near as onerous as a similar restriction would have been in the years of continuing inflation following the First World War. It was also agreed that 75 per cent of the bonus should continue to be taken for purposes of calculating the gratuity to which civil servants were entitled on retirement.

3 The Development of the Institution, 1919–25

After the formation of the Institution the main internal tasks for the active membership were to extend organisation to an increasing number of professional, scientific and technical staff; to establish the necessary basis for a permanent, effective organisation including the employment of full-time staff; and to create a committee structure to enable the Institution to formulate its policies and to provide for democratic participation. Progress towards all these objectives was made in the early 1920s.

At the end of 1919 the nominal membership was not much more than 1,500. By the time of the Institution's annual dinner held in June 1920 the membership had doubled to 3,000, distributed among thirty different affiliated departmental associations. The associations in the Admiralty were, however, still by far the most active. The first formal annual meeting of the Institution was held on 21 March 1922 even though the Institution had by then been in existence for more than three years. The membership was recorded as 3,150 and the annual income as £2,594.

Between 1922 and the end of 1925 the membership of the Institution remained static. At the end of 1925 there were 3,046 members. The largest single constituent association was the Association of Valuation Office Valuers with 315 members. The second largest was the Office of Works Association of Architectural, Surveying and Civil Engineering Assistants and the third largest the Association of Engineering and Shipbuilding Draughtsmen. The latter organised draughtsmen both within and outside the civil service. It was affiliated to the Institution only in respect of those members who were working within the civil service. There were forty-nine constituent associations.

Early in 1921 Sir Richard Redmayne agreed to become the president of the Institution. It was a post he continued to hold for nearly thirty-five years until his death at 90 years of age on 27 December 1955. Sir Richard had for many years been HM Chief Inspector of Mines and had then vacated the office to take up private practice. He was one of the world's experts in mining technology. He started his working life as a mining apprentice, worked for many years in the industry, became professor of mining in the University of Birmingham and served on numerous commissions and committees concerned with mining.

In April 1921 the first issue of *State Technology* described the aims of the Institution as:

The advancement of efficiency in the civil service. The increase, promotion, teaching and extension of professional science, knowledge and practice, and its application for the good of the State. The improvement and maintenance of the position and status of civil servants . . . of the directing, administrative or higher grades engaged in professional, technical or scientific work. The protection of the rights and interests of such civil servants and the securing of adequate recognition of the importance of professional, scientific and technical work in the service. The provision of a central organisation to carry out these objects and to obtain proper representation of professional officers on or before the Whitley Councils and committees of the civil service, and on any other bodies dealing with matters which affect the interests of members and associates of the Institution.

A PART-TIME GENERAL SECRETARY

Towards the end of 1921 the first formal proposal was made that the Institution should have a full-time general secretary. As might be expected it came from the constituent associations in the Admiralty. Up to that time the secretary of the Institution was an honorary post, though a full-time assistant secretary, Mrs R. Miller, was employed at the office of the Institution in Victoria Street, London. The Council of the Institution referred the suggestion for a full-time general secretary to constituent associations. After considering the views received the Council agreed to appoint a part-time secretary and to seek new office accommodation to take both the part-time secretary and the full-time assistant secretary. By this time the salary of the assistant secretary had been increased to £300 a year. The advertisement for the part-time secretary to the Institution stated that the successful applicant would be required to attend at the office daily from 2 p.m. to 6 p.m. and to attend all Council and committee meetings, which were usually held in the evenings. Preference, said the advertisement, would be given to a man with professional experience who had a working knowledge of the civil service. All these arrangements were confirmed by the 1922 annual meeting.

The successful candidate for the part-time secretaryship was a Mr H. E. Weaver. He took up his new appointment in July 1922, but the office of honorary secretary was still retained by Mr J. H. Salmon who had held the office since 1920. Very little was said of Mr Weaver in the records of the Institution at the time of his appointment and it is clear from the minutes of committees that the honorary secretary still took the leading part in the Institution's proceedings. New offices for the Institution were also secured about this time in Buckingham Gate, London.

Early in 1923 the Council of the Institution agreed that the duties and salary of the full-time assistant secretary, Mrs Miller, should be related to those of higher-grade women clerks in the civil service. The outcome was that her salary was raised to £350 per annum. Within a few months, however, the suggestion was being voiced that the Institution needed not a part-time but a full-time general secretary. The principal advocate of this proposal was Mr F. A. A. Menzler, who by now was one of the most influential, and also one of the more radical, members of the Council. The Council did not accept Mr Menzler's suggestion, and his proposition for the appointment of a full-time secretary, moved at the March 1924 meeting of the Council, failed to find a seconder.

A few months later a problem of a new kind concerning the secretary precipitated an acrimonious controversy. At its October 1924 meeting the Council of the Institution considered a letter from Mr Weaver announcing his decision to stand for Parliament and asking for a fortnight's unpaid leave for the purpose. Though it was not mentioned in the official records at the time, Mr Weaver was, in fact, intending to stand as a Labour candidate, though in a constituency in which he had no chance of being elected.

The Council of the Institution strongly deprecated the action of Mr Weaver, but 'having regard to all the circumstances' accepted that his application be granted. They further agreed that in future a paid officer of the Institution should not be allowed to accept an invitation to stand for Parliament without first obtaining the consent of the Council.

After the general election Mr Weaver's action was again discussed at a Council meeting. Mr Weaver expressed regret that he had annoyed the Council by standing as a candidate but he did not think that the work of the Institution had suffered. He pointed out that he had worked overtime since his return and he reminded the Council that he was only a part-time employee. He reaffirmed that he had done what he thought was right and he had no intention in the future of giving up his political rights and activities. In discussing the issue the Council had before them resolutions from the Federation of Professional Officers' Associations, Admiralty and from the Royal Ordnance Factories Association of Professional Staff. Both deprecated the action of Mr Weaver and suggested that in future paid officials of the Institution should be required to refrain from public participation in politics.

The Council proceeded to pass three resolutions:

(1) That the Council dissociate itself from any responsibility for the action of the secretary in standing as a candidate for Parliament at the recent election, but, recognising that his action did not contravene the conditions of service then obtaining, accedes to his application for leave of absence and grants it without pay.
(2) That in future all paid officers of the Institution, whether whole or part-time, accept as a condition of service that they will not take any active and public part in politics.
(3) That this condition of service becomes operative on 1st June 1925.

Simultaneously with this controversy, and certainly influenced by it, the Council again considered the appointment of a full-time secretary. At the December 1924 meeting a decision in favour of making such an appointment was taken. The terms of the advertisement were drawn up and approved at the following meeting. The salary was to be £600 per annum and it was stipulated that: 'The secretary is required, as a condition of appointment, to give an undertaking that he will not engage in political activities of a public character.' This effectively excluded Mr Weaver. Having considered a request from two ordinary members of the Institution to do so the Council decided to postpone the appointment until after the annual general meeting.

At the annual general meeting of the Institution held on 7 April 1925 a considerable part of the time was occupied by debate on the Council's actions in relation to the secretary. The principal critics were Messrs Hume, Mead and Sellors. Mr Hume, who stated that he had worked and voted as a Conservative at the last three general elections, described the behaviour of the Council as 'most extraordinary'. He pointed out that only recently the Council had passed a resolution demanding full civil rights for civil servants. Could they, he asked, with any pretence to what was right, deny full rights to an employee? Mr Mead, too, underlined the contrast between the Institution's claim for full civil rights for civil servants and its treatment of their own secretary. Mr Sellors, who spoke on behalf of the civil service members of the Association of Engineering and Shipbuilding Draughtsmen (AESD) said that his Association had sent a letter of protest to the Institution about the action of the Council. They considered the Council's decision not to allow their secretary to take an active part in politics to be most unfair. They were later astounded to find that their letter of protest had not even been circulated to the Council.

Support for the Council was expressed by Mr Price and Mr Epps. Mr Price said that the Institution was involved in a political squabble and some of them felt strongly about it. Mr Weaver had come into the limelight and had put the Institution in a false light. Mr Epps said that a general meeting was not the place to discuss the appointment of a secretary. If the members did not like what the Council was doing they should send other representatives. Mr Menzler said that all were satisfied as to Mr Weaver's capacity but the real issue was the observance of the Council's policy as to the political activities of paid officers. He, Mr Menzler, had been in the minority when the Council had taken its original decision but he was now satisfied that a large majority of members were opposed to any suggestion that a paid officer of the Institution should be an active politician of whatever party.

Eventually Mr Hume agreed to withdraw the motion which he had moved regretting the virtual dismissal of Mr H. E. Weaver and requesting the Council to seek an understanding so that his services might be retained. Two speakers in the debate appeared to suggest that if the motion were withdrawn a suitable basis of accommodation might be found.

A few days after the annual general meeting the Council considered the report of the selection committee for the new full-time secretary. The successful candidate was Mr C. L. Leese. The son of a Staffordshire railway stationmaster, Leonard Leese went to Cambridge by his own efforts but left before graduating. His early career was unconventional, including a spell as secretary to a noble lord. He took up his appointment in May 1925.

Mr Weaver was informed that, if he so wished, his appointment could continue until 1 June 1925. This was a euphemistic way of giving him just over two months' notice. The report of the selection committee, however, met with strong opposition among a minority of the Council. By this time the critics of the decisions of the Council in relation to Mr Weaver's political activities had rallied their forces. The reference back of the selection committee report was moved but was defeated by twenty votes to eleven. The acceptance of the report was then carried, but by the narrower margin of sixteen votes to eleven.

Some thirty-five years later Mr Douglas Houghton, MP, general secretary of the Inland Revenue Staff Federation and by then chairman of the Staff Side National Whitley Council, referred in an article in *State Service* to the dismissal of Mr Weaver. He said:

He came on the Staff Side in 1923 and left in 1925, and thereby, I believe, hangs a tale. Weaver was a tall, pale and rather serious-looking man, much too upright and civilised for the intrigues and slanging on the Staff Side of his day. At the General Election in 1924 he surprised us all by standing as Labour candidate for the Isle of Wight. He stood no chance of getting in (he stood subsequently for East Surrey, another hopeless seat) but after the election the question of the civil rights of employees of the IPCS received attention from the

Council of that body. At that time, and for many years afterwards until the Masterman Report, a civil servant was required to resign on becoming a candidate at a parliamentary election. The Staff Side policy on this was clear – it was in favour of 'full civil rights' for civil servants. It wanted absolute freedom for a civil servant to stand for election and be granted special leave without pay for the period of the election, and also release for parliamentary duties if elected. What the Staff Side claimed for the civil servant, Weaver claimed for himself. He refused to compromise and ruined his chances of becoming the first full-time secretary of the IPCS by doing so. I admired Weaver; he was the stuff that martyrs are made of. He never got into Parliament. The last I heard of him was a story of struggle in an ill-paid teaching post.

Shortly after the events surrounding the dismissal of Mr Weaver the Institution lost its honorary secretary, Mr J. H. Salmon. He resigned because of the pressure of official business. He had held the post for more than five years and the Council paid a warm tribute to him for all the work he had done on behalf of the Institution.

On 30 June 1925 the Council elected Mr Freddie Menzler as the new honorary secretary. Mr Menzler had represented the Professional Officers' Association, Government Actuary's Department, on the Council of the Institution since February 1924 and almost from the beginning played a leading part in the Council's deliberations. In the following years he was to become one of the most prominent and influential personalities in the history of the Institution.

AN INSTITUTION OR A UNION?

Although both at the annual dinner of the Institution in 1921 and again at the annual general meeting in 1922 the president, Sir Richard Redmayne, had affirmed that the Institution was not a trade union, in its day-to-day activities it was already functioning as a union, albeit a union of professional civil servants. This dual identity, as both a trade union and an organisation of professional men, was reflected in its internal debates about the image of the Institution, particularly the necessity for remaining completely non-partisan on political issues, and in the relationships it forged or declined with other organisations. For example, in 1920 the Council considered and rejected an invitation to join the Middle Class Union on the grounds that its aims were purely political.

Mr Menzler was one of the first advocates of a change in title for the Institution. The term 'Institution', he argued, did not convey a realistic impression of the work and purpose of the organisation. Mr Menzler favoured the title Federation of Professional Civil Servants. Needless to say, his proposal was not adopted. He was, however, a little more successful in his advocacy of a change in title for the Institution's journal. The title should refer, he said, to professional civil servants. At the beginning of 1926 the Council agreed that the title should be *State Service* and that the new title should be introduced from April 1926.

Within the Institution there were also a number of advocates for changes in the content of *State Service*. Some of the more radical members wanted it to become a forum for lively contributions and controversy. In 1923, for example, the Council agreed that provision should be made for the publication of individual members' views in the journal, and this should include views opposed to the policy of the Institution. This attempt to enliven the journal was followed shortly afterwards by a decision of the Council that if the editor should be in doubt about the suitability of a letter for publication he was expected to refer the matter to the principal officers of the Institution. It was hardly the way to encourage journalistic vigour. Nevertheless articles of wider interest began to appear in the journal. In May 1923, for example, there was an article on political and industrial unrest in Germany. The article was first given as a lecture before an Institution audience. The author was a naval constructor who had been in Germany in 1919 and 1920. He described the rising of the Spartacists (left-wing socialists, many of whom later formed the German Communist Party, and whose two main leaders, Karl Liebknecht and Rosa Luxemburg, were murdered).

The Institution strengthened its links with other civil service unions and was a loyal constituent of the Staff Side of the National Whitley Council. It was reluctant to form alliances which might seem to detract from the unity of the Staff Side. Thus the Council displayed some caution when the Society of Civil Servants proposed the establishment of a joint consultative committee representing higher grades in the service, composed of the Society, the Institution, the Legal Society, the FDA and the Association of HM Inspectors of Taxes (AIT). The Institution's Council decided that 'the machinery suggested was of too rigid a character, but that . . . consultation should take place from time to time as occasion required'. In 1923, however, the Council did agree to appoint Mr Salmon as the Institution's representative on a committee to consider 'the establishment of definite machinery for bringing together organisations representing the higher grades of the civil service'. Draft rules of such a joint consultative committee were reported to the Council in September 1923 and it was decided to refer the matter to constituent associations. Many associations did not reply and of those that did the majority were unfavourable to participating in the proposed committee, particularly as it would be to some extent outside the Whitley machinery and would require constituent associations to reveal their plans on higher-grade matters in advance of normal Staff Side meetings. Indeed two members of the proposed consultative committee, the Legal Society and the FDA, had gone so far as to circularise their members on a suggested resolution that:

the Council instructs its Representatives on the JCC to report thereto that the Society is willing in conjunction with the other Societies represented on the Committee to withdraw from the National Whitley Council, provided that such a course does not prevent recourse being had to the Arbitration Court and that the formation of a separate council for the higher grades or the formation of a third side of the present Whitley Council proves impracticable.

A formal alliance was therefore considered undesirable, the Institution preferring to co-operate with other sections of the civil service when it was mutually advantageous to do so, but retaining its own independence of action.

The Institution also developed working relationships with unions outside the civil service. Both the AESD, affiliated to the Institution, and the NUSW had members within the civil service. The former had members in the War Department and the majority of NUSW members (400) were concentrated in six government establishments. Among the scientists most active in the formation of the NUSW in 1918 had been scientific graduates seconded to the NPL and Woolwich Arsenal. Among the first members of the NUSW Executive were Oscar Brady (Woolwich Arsenal), G. S. Baker (NPL), Dr C. C. Paterson (NPL), Richard Lobb (Woolwich Arsenal), J. W. Whittaker (Woolwich Arsenal) and Dr Alan Griffiths (RAE Farnborough). The NUSW was therefore particularly anxious to secure representation on the Whitley machinery. The NUSW suggested an arrangement for dual membership with the Institution whereby 'all members of the Institution would be accepted as members of the Union (NUSW) at a reduced subscription'; the Institution 'would continue to represent their sectional interests' while the NUSW would be prepared to back up those activities of the Institution while continuing to work for the improved recognition of scientific workers generally.

The Institution decided to explore the whole matter with NUSW representatives, aware of the possible danger that the NUSW might approach some other civil service union to secure Whitley representation and thus undermine the strength of the Institution among scientists. It was, however, reluctant to enter into a formal arrangement because the NUSW was a trade union and any alliance of that sort, it was held, might prejudice the Institution's relationships with professional bodies. The Institution therefore suggested that civil servants within the NUSW should form themselves into associations which could then affiliate to the Institution in the normal way. The matter rested there for the time being with each organisation agreeing to find out which of their own members were desirous of joining the other organisation.

In 1923 the Council declined an invitation from the National Federation of Professional, Technical, Administrative and Supervisory Workers to explore possible areas of co-operation. The Institution did, however, show rather more interest in an international congress of professional workers held in Paris in the spring of 1923, carrying a brief report of the proceedings in *State Service*.

The Institution continued to seek close working relationships with the professional bodies relevant to the membership. In 1919 the Council had established a special committee to prepare a scheme for the representation of the Council on professional and other societies. Mr Salmon approached the Surveyors' Association suggesting that the 500 surveyors in government offices should have direct representation. In 1922 under its new constitution the Council of the Surveyors' Institution reserved two seats for civil servants, and the Institution decided that Sir Richard Redmayne should fill one once he had become a 'fellow'. In 1921 the British Science Guild asked for the co-operation of the Institution in a committee they had instituted 'to consider and report on the question of the utilisation of science in government departments'. The Institution duly appointed representatives.

CIVIL RIGHTS

The controversy surrounding the decision of Mr Weaver to stand as a Labour candidate at the general election towards the end of 1924 coincided, by an irony of circumstance, with a campaign by civil service unions for the removal of some of the limitations on political activity imposed on civil servants by the state.

Following a deputation to the Chancellor of the Exchequer from the unions, the government announced that a committee was being appointed 'to enquire into existing regulations governing the candidature for Parliament and municipal bodies of persons in the service of the Crown, and to report whether any, and, if so, what changes should be made in the regulations'. Two of the six members of the Blanesburgh Committee were men with a trade union background. They were George Barnes of the engineers and Arthur Shaw of one of the textile unions.

At its meeting in June 1924 the Council of the Institution carried a resolution supporting the claim of the civil service unions for full rights of citizenship for civil servants. This point of view, however, was not supported by all constituent associations of the Institution and there were some who were conscious of the inconsistency between the Institution's claim for civil rights for its membership and the restriction which it sought to place on its own paid officials. In December the Association of Valuation Office Valuers sent a resolution to the Council of the Institution deprecating the movement for the extension of civil rights for civil servants and expressing the view that 'the present position in the civil service with regard to politics should remain unaltered'.

When the report of the committee of inquiry was published it recommended virtually no change for non-industrial civil servants. The committee was not unanimous in the exceptions to be allowed to the general rule that Crown servants must resign upon accepting a parliamentary candidature, but it agreed to recommend that industrial workers employed by the departments of the armed services should be exempt from the general rule. This did not satisfy most of the civil service unions. They wanted, at the very minimum, some of the non-industrial civil servants also to be exempt. The government shortly afterwards accepted the main recommendations of the Blanesburgh Committee. *State Service* stated that this decision would 'prove a great disappointment to the service as a whole', though it welcomed the ending of the privileged position of officers of the armed forces who, hitherto, had been exempt from the general rule requiring resignation on acceptance of a parliamentary candidature.

In September 1925 the Council of the Institution decided, after consultation with constituent associations and in the light of the government's decision on the report of the committee of inquiry, that the Institution should modify its support for the claim for full civil rights for all civil servants. Instead it decided to urge that, with the exception of certain administrative and analogous grades, civil servants should be able to stand for Parliament without prior resignation and should be able to return to duty if not elected. If, however, a civil servant was successful in the election he should then be required to resign from the service. Industrial civil servants and manipulative grades, it was urged, should, in addition, have the right of returning to the service if they were subsequently defeated at the polls.

THE REFORM OF STRUCTURE

The claim for the lifting of political restrictions on civil servants coincided with the voicing of criticisms by some of the civil service unions of the 'class' basis of the civil service. A conference of civil service unions carried a resolution in the following terms:

The reorganisation of 1919 was accepted by the civil service associations as a compromise, in the hope that, although founded on a class basis, it would in its administration abolish the class spirit previously existing in the civil service, and would secure to all grades an assured opportunity of promotion to the highest posts in the service. These objects have not been secured, and we consider the failure to be due to the essentially 'class' nature of the reorganisation and its administration. We are of the opinion that a spirit of co-operation in the service and an efficient performance of its duties cannot be secured in any organisation of which class division is a fundamental feature.

Many years later this call for a unitary basis of organisation, first made by the unions, found strong support from a committee of inquiry into the civil service under the chairmanship of Lord Fulton.

EX-SERVICEMEN

One of the difficult problems facing the civil service unions in the years immediately after the First World War was the introduction of special arrangements for the recruitment of ex-servicemen. On the one hand there was a strong case for such special arrangements, either because some ex-servicemen had not been available to qualify for entry at the normal recruitment ages or because they had a right to share in state employment opportunities after years of war service. There was also, of course, the special position of disabled ex-servicemen. On the other hand, the civil service unions had to have regard to the position and promotion prospects of the established staff, many of whom were themselves ex-servicemen. In a memorandum prepared in the early summer of 1923, the Staff Side of the National Whitley Council pointed out:

In 1920 the prospects foreshadowed in the National Whitley Council's Reorganisation Report, of a steadily increasing civil service, with its natural concomitant of an improved rate of promotion, were still generally anticipated.

These expectations have not, however, been realised, and many grades of the permanent civil service are now appreciably smaller than was at that time anticipated.

The Southborough Committee report on the employment of ex-servicemen in the civil service, published in June 1924, stated that on 1 May 1924 no less than 104,992 out of 187,098 permanent male staff in the civil service were ex-servicemen, and of this number 28,592 were disabled men. In all up to that time, from the date of the armistice, certificates of qualification for employment in a permanent capacity in the civil service had been issued in favour of 42,250 ex-servicemen.

A special problem for the civil service unions was that, whilst they were representative of the overwhelming majority of permanent civil servants, some of the ex-servicemen recruited as so-called temporary staff tended to look for the protection of their interests, not so much to the established trade unions, as to ex-service organisations and to sympathetic members of Parliament, some of whom had little appreciation of the problems of the civil service. This applied particularly to former officers in the armed forces. In time, however, despite some occasional controversies, these problems were overcome as ex-servicemen recruited in a temporary capacity were transferred to the permanent staff.

4 The General Strike and the Civil Service Unions

Events in the second half of the 1920s were mainly dominated by the General Strike of 1926; by the economic, industrial and political developments preceding it, by the strike itself and by its aftermath. The mining industry was at the centre of the dispute. In 1925, following the return to the gold standard by the Conservative government, the coal-mining industry faced a severe recession in trade. The coal-owners demanded that the pay of the miners should be reduced and that the working day should be extended. The miners resisted these demands and appealed to the Trades Union Congress for support. This support was forthcoming, and in the summer of 1925 the railwaymen and transport workers placed an embargo upon the transport of coal unless the coal-owners' demands for lower wages and longer working hours were withdrawn. The government intervened and provided a subsidy which was sufficient to persuade the coal-owners not to press their demands. These developments were regarded by the unions as a victory, and the day on which the solidarity action of the railwaymen and transport workers had brought these concessions came to be known as 'Red Friday'.

The victory was, however, more apparent than real and it proved to be short-lived. A new Royal Commission was appointed which, unlike the earlier Sankey Commission which had reported in favour of public ownership, was by its composition unlikely to be sympathetic to the miners' objectives. Its chairman was a prominent Liberal, Sir Herbert Samuel. When the Samuel Commission reported early in 1926 it recommended that wages should be reduced, though by less than the amount urged by the coal-owners.

With the slogan 'Not a penny off the pay, not a minute on the day' the miners rejected the Samuel Commission recommendations. The coal-owners, from their side, reaffirmed their demands for more drastic wage cuts and for a longer working day. Negotiations led only to deadlock and the miners then had to face being locked out from 1 May 1926 when the government's subsidy came to an end.

THE GENERAL STRIKE

The TUC General Council had undertaken to give support to the miners, and at a conference of the executive committees of affiliated unions held on 29 April 1926 overwhelming support was given to a call for sympathetic strike action. The unions were well aware, not least from the experience of the first postwar depression, that a defeat for the miners would lead to widespread attacks on wages and conditions in other industries. The General Strike started on 4 May 1926. It was precipitated by a breakdown in last-minute negotiations between the government and the TUC following a decision by print workers on the *Daily Mail* to refuse to print an editorial attack on the unions. This was, however, more a pretext for the government than the real cause of the breakdown.

The government had prepared for the dispute ever since the 'victory' of the unions on 'Red Friday' in the summer of 1925. Organisational plans had been made to meet the strike, including the recruitment of strike-breaking volunteers. Nevertheless, when on the first day of the General Strike the TUC called upon railwaymen, transport workers, iron and steel workers, builders and printers to stop work the response was overwhelming. It was the intention of the TUC to call out other workers as the strike continued but the first call evoked such a solid response that some TUC leaders felt it would hardly be necessary to do anything further to demonstrate the very firm support of the trade union movement for the miners. Indeed, some of the most influential leaders of the TUC were apprehensive of the enormous social power which had been released from below. Their fears were fed by strong propaganda from the government who spoke of the threat of revolution.

On 12 May, to the astonishment of millions of workers, the TUC General Council called off the strike. It claimed that Sir Herbert Samuel was suggesting a new compromise solution to the mining dispute, and said that it had reason to think that the compromise enjoyed the support of the government. The effect on the trade union movement was dramatic. The decision was denounced from many quarters. Many unions lost members, and disillusionment and cynicism were widespread. The weakness of the leadership was contrasted with the solidarity of the rank and file. The miners stood out for many months but they too were eventually and, in the circumstances, inevitably, defeated. Wage cuts followed in other industries and thousands of active trade unionists were victimised in some way or another for their support of the General Strike and of the miners.

THE PRESS CAMPAIGN AGAINST THE CIVIL SERVICE

In the months preceding the General Strike the civil service did not escape the attention of the propagandists who were wanting to attack pay and conditions. A sustained campaign was conducted in a number of provincial and national newspapers to suggest that the civil service was overmanned and that conditions were too soft. In September 1925, in response to this campaign of denunciation, the civil service unions, including the Institution, decided to set up a defence movement. A conference of civil service trade union executive committees was called at which all civil service grades were represented. The National Staff Side set up a defence committee to organise a campaign, and leaflets answering the press campaign were prepared and widely distributed. Resolutions in support of the stand taken by the Institution, jointly with other civil service unions, were received from many of the constituent associations of the Institution.

Local defence committees of the civil service unions soon followed. The December 1925 issue of *State Technology* noted that defence committee meetings had already been held in Southampton, Birmingham, Cardiff, Bristol, Liverpool, Portsmouth, Manchester, Glasgow, Leeds and Plymouth. The journal expressed the hope that the Institution members in the provinces would serve on local defence committees.

On 17 November 1925 the national Defence Committee organised a mass meeting in the Albert Hall to protest against the press campaign. The result exceeded all expectations. According to *State Technology*, 'Not only was the vast

Hall filled to its utmost capacity, but thousands remained outside to form overflow meetings, while thousands more were unable to obtain even this satisfaction. The officials at the Albert Hall state that the attendance surpassed all previous attendances in its history . . .'.

A resolution was carried at the meeting in the following terms:

This mass meeting of all grades of civil servants condemns the ill-informed and prejudiced attacks in certain sections of the press and elsewhere directed against civil service staffs and their conditions of employment; draws public attention to the fact that less than 50 per cent of the service receive full compensation for the rise in the cost of living, and that gross underpayment exists amongst large sections of the service; and pledges the civil service not only to resist to the utmost any attempt further to depreciate civil service standards of remuneration, but to prosecute by all available means the claim for reasonable standards of life for all those who serve the state.

In the course of the meeting one of the principal speakers, Mr W. J. Brown, said that of 300,000 civil servants half of them received a wage, including bonus, of 60s 6d per week or less. A series of mass meetings organised by local civil service union defence committees were held in the provinces in December 1925 and nearly all were well attended. One in Newcastle, for example, attracted an audience of more than 850 even though the weather was bad.

In the early weeks of 1926 the press campaign against the civil service concentrated on hours of work. If the civil service could be persuaded to accept longer hours it would, in the eyes of those responsible for the campaign, be easier to impose a longer working day on the miners. The February 1926 issue of *State Technology* carried an article under the title 'The attack on the service' replying to the demand of newspapers that civil service working hours should be increased.

Shortly afterwards the government published proposals for a number of economy measures. These proposals did not directly affect civil servants. The Institution stated: 'The National Staff Side and its Defence Committee deserve the congratulations of all ranks in the service for the success of their energetic action last autumn which has undoubtedly led to the present satisfactory result.'

In its annual report for 1925 the Council of the Institution said that the civil service defence movement was the most striking event of the year in civil service affairs, not least because of 'the inculcation in all grades of the civil service of a spirit of unity that has been somewhat lacking on previous occasions and your Council hopes that the present favourable atmosphere will not be allowed to be dissipated'.

It was indicative of the prevailing mood of unity that towards the end of March 1926 – only a few weeks before the General Strike – the Institution invited Mr W. J. Brown, then general secretary of the Civil Service Clerical Association, to give a lecture on Whitleyism at the Central Hall, Westminster. Mr Brown was at that time the best known of civil service trade union leaders and was regarded in some quarters as a 'bogey man' because of his left-wing views, although it was widely acknowledged that he was a man of very considerable ability. Mr Brown, who was always a stimulating speaker, did not disappoint his audience. His interest in the Whitley scheme, he said, was not that of a student but that of an agitator. The Whitley machinery had been created at the end of the First World

War, argued Mr Brown, as an insurance against revolt. This was why in the immediate postwar period the Whitley machine had produced some improvements in pay and conditions. This, however, had changed with the change in economic circumstances. 'When there is a conflict between two sides,' said Mr Brown, 'the ultimate result depends on the power of both sides. It is no good either cursing or blessing Whitleyism; what we have to ensure is that the power behind the machine is there.'

DIVISIONS WITHIN THE NATIONAL STAFF SIDE

This newfound mood of unity was rudely shattered by events during and after the General Strike. During the weekend before the commencement of the General Strike the National Staff Side convened a special meeting of its General Purposes Committee to consider whether any advice should be given to members of constituent unions on action to be taken during the strike. No prior notice of the meeting had been given and therefore Mr Menzler could not attend and the Institution was represented by Mrs Miller, the assistant general secretary. A number of unions were already pressing for assurances from civil service departments that civil servants would not be called upon to perform work outside the scope of their normal duties. Indeed, it was reported that an assurance to this effect had already been given to the postal unions by the Post Office.

The General Purposes Committee took two decisions. The first was that there should be an approach to the Treasury for an assurance, similar to that given in the Post Office, that civil servants would not be required to undertake duties outside their normal employment. This was subsequently endorsed by the Staff Side. The second was that civil servants should be advised not to volunteer for other work. This recommendation proved to be much more controversial and led to a bitter debate at the full meeting of the Staff Side. It was eventually adopted by sixteen votes to six with the Institution speaking and voting with the minority, consisting predominantly of the higher grades.

The Joint Consultative Committee (JCC), which consisted of the SCS, the Legal Society, the FDA and the AIT, then proposed an amendment: 'That the General Purposes Committee in issuing advice in the terms of their resolution of 3 May to civil servants as to their conduct during the recent crisis exceeded their powers and functions, and further that the advice which they tendered was improper and inconsistent with the obligations which civil servants owe to the State.'

This amendment was defeated. The members of the JCC then walked out while the Institution representatives remained. By sitting tight the Institution saved the National Staff Side from a damaging split and possibly total collapse. The National Staff Side was weakened but not rendered wholly unrepresentative.

The decision of the Staff Side urging civil servants not to volunteer for other work was welcomed by the trade union movement outside the service and warmly supported by many active trade union members in the service. On the other hand it was opposed by those who did not support the General Strike and by some who thought that the Staff Side should remain 'neutral' even to the point of indifference towards strike-breaking. After the General Strike the decision of the Staff Side evoked the hostility of sections of the press, particularly the *Daily Telegraph*.

The attitude of the majority of the Staff Side was that for civil servants to volunteer for work outside the scope of their normal duties amounted to 'blacklegging'. The effect, they said, would be to weaken the strike and thus to contribute to the defeat of the miners. This, in turn, would encourage employers in other sectors of employment to attack pay and conditions. The majority of the Staff Side felt that it would be highly inconsistent, and also selfish, for the civil service unions to remain indifferent to strike-breaking by civil servants when for months the civil service unions themselves had been campaigning, through their defence movement, to resist the press demands for a worsening of civil service pay and conditions.

The attitude of the Institution was that individual members of the civil service should form their own conclusions about the General Strike without accepting or receiving guidance from civil service unions. At the same time the Institution was strongly opposed to any suggestion that civil servants should be directed to undertake work which did not form part of their normal duties. Institution policy had been clearly laid down by Council at its meeting on 29 April 1921: 'That this Council puts on record its unanimous opinion that the present industrial dispute is a matter upon which members should form their own conclusions as individuals without accepting or receiving guidance from the Institution of Professional Civil Servants.' This resolution was reaffirmed at the Council meeting on 18 May 1926, a few days after the ending of the General Strike.

An editorial in *State Service* stated that in the opinion of the Council of the Institution the Staff Side had made a 'profound error of judgement . . . in adopting the resolution in which civil servants were advised not to volunteer'.

Immediately after the General Strike the Institution continued to play a crucial role in holding the Staff Side together. The representatives of the Institution, and Mr Menzler in particular, argued strongly for the maintenance of the unity of the Staff Side as a body representative of all civil service trade union members. Mr Menzler was among the stronger critics of those other associations, representing higher-grade civil servants, who wanted to dissociate themselves from the Staff Side and who had decided eventually to withdraw. As a member of the relevant subcommittee of the Staff Side, Mr Menzler was instrumental in securing a change in the standing orders whereby: 'On issues which are not primarily domestic service issues, but which are entirely or mainly national questions of a political or industrial character, the Staff Side shall not act except by the consent of all groups of the Staff Side.' The intention of this change, said *State Service*, was to prevent the recurrence of 'such incidents as the tendering of "advice" in regard to volunteering'.

In an article in the October 1926 issue of *State Service* Mr Menzler made it clear that in his view the overriding need of the time was to maintain the unity of the National Staff Side. He was therefore, he said, conducting a campaign on two fronts. On the one hand he opposed those who argued for the withdrawal of the higher-grade associations from the Staff Side and, on the other, he opposed those who now wanted to commit the National Staff Side to a policy of outright hostility to new legislation affecting the unions. 'The primary practical need of the moment for civil servants as employees,' said Mr Menzler, 'is to preserve intact the authority of the National Staff Side to speak on their behalf on matters of immediate concern that affect their status and conditions of employment.'

Early in November 1926 the Institution wrote to the National Staff Side asking for a definite ruling on the intention of the new standing orders. A reply was received in the following terms:

> I have to acknowledge receipt of your letter of the 4th instant, in which you ask on behalf of the Institution for a ruling as to whether it is the intention of Rule 11 of the National Staff Side standing orders to secure that in future the Staff Side shall take no action which can be construed as taking sides in political or· industrial disputes. The letter was before the National Staff Side at its meeting of the 5th instant, and I have to inform you that the Chairman gave the ruling which you asked for.

Shortly afterwards the Institution said that the overwhelming majority of the membership of the Institution would learn with relief of the formal adoption of the new standing orders by the Staff Side of the National Whitley Council.

Following this controversy the Institution took the initiative in establishing a Higher Grades Committee within the National Staff Side. It was confined to those earning over £500 p.a. and their representatives. As the body with the largest number of officers in this category (1,100), the Institution was allocated five out of the eleven seats on the Committee. Mr Menzler was elected secretary of the Higher Grades Committee. Shortly afterwards the committee convened a conference open to all higher-grade civil servants to discuss matters of mutual interest. As a consequence, relations between the National Staff Side and the Joint Consultative Committee were resumed.

FURTHER CONTROVERSY WITH THE PRESS

The controversy over the attitude of the Staff Side towards the General Strike continued for months. The *Daily Telegraph,* in particular, publicised the dissension within the civil service unions. The Institution officers felt that the *Daily Telegraph* had seized upon the events as an opportunity to make a general attack upon civil service trade unionism with a view to bringing about the dissolution of the National Whitley Council. The *Daily Telegraph* criticised the Institution for not withdrawing from the Staff Side, even though the Institution had dissociated itself from the advice given to civil servants by the Staff Side immediately before the General Strike.

Two letters were sent to the *Daily Telegraph* by the Institution's honorary secretary, Mr Menzler, setting out the Institution's views. The first was published on 2 June and the second on 12 July. The first protested against the systematic publication of the proceedings of the Staff Side – and not just its decisions – including the names of individuals and the actions they took. One paragraph in the letter stated:

> I do, however, venture to suggest that if the private proceedings of the Staff Side are to be systematically disclosed, together with the names of individuals and the actions they have taken, no civil servant who has any regard for his official career will be prepared to serve in a representative capacity, or to sacrifice his leisure in connection with staff association work. While urging that confidence should be respected, I of course raise no objection whatsoever to

public criticism of the decisions of the National Staff Side as distinct from the pillory of individuals for their actions at private meetings.

The experience of the Institution with another daily paper, the *Morning Post* (which later merged with the *Daily Telegraph*) was less satisfactory. Early in August 1926 the *Morning Post* published a series of articles under the title 'Civil servants and communism; by one inside'. The Institution was extremely critical of these articles. It was felt that their purpose was to establish some sort of connection between civil service trade unionism and communism while not furnishing any real evidence of the alleged connection.

In the middle of August Mr Menzler wrote to the *Morning Post* pointing out that the implication of one of the articles was that a number of unnamed civil service associations, including possibly the Institution, were 'tainted to a greater or lesser extent with "communism"'. Mr Menzler drew attention to the fact that the Institution had no political associations of any kind. Unfortunately, however, the *Morning Post* deleted from Mr Menzler's letter a paragraph which pointed out that the policy of the Institution was determined by its Council. 'The Council,' the deleted paragraph said, 'consists solely of civil servants representative of the various types of specialist officers in its membership.'

Some few days later the *Morning Post* returned to the attack with further hints of subversion. There was 'nothing definite', it said, about the posture but it was accused of 'trimming'. There was also, it claimed, a 'socialist leaven working from within'. The Institution was accused of taking no part in the protest against the 'disloyal action' of the National Staff Side in urging civil servants not to volunteer in the General Strike for work outside their normal duties.

The Organisation Committee of the Institution met immediately following the publication of this further article and it was agreed that this time a letter of reply should be sent to the *Morning Post* by the president. It was published on 28 August but again a number of sentences were omitted. The deletions were of sentences which underlined that the policy of the Institution was determined by its Council, consisting solely of civil servants. The officers of the Institution were particularly concerned that the *Morning Post* had deleted a statement from the president's letter confirming that the honorary secretary, Mr F. Menzler, had 'always most faithfully carried out' the policy of the Council. This was in reply to innuendos that Mr Menzler, as a socialist – he was, in fact, a Fabian – had not properly represented the views of the Institution.

The conclusion drawn from this unsatisfactory correspondence was set out in an editorial article in *State Service*.

From this example of the methods of modern journalism our readers will see clearly that it is a waste of time to attempt to carry on such unequal contests. The Organisation Committee has again considered the whole question and has decided to recommend to Council that in future no rejoinders to press attacks shall be issued and that any necessary comments on newspaper statements concerning the Institution shall be published only in this journal.

THE TRADE DISPUTES ACT

One important immediate outcome of the General Strike was the introduction by the Conservative government of new legislation, the Trade Disputes Act, 1927, affecting trade unions and industrial relations.

(a)   It declared illegal any strike which had any object other than or in addition to the furtherance of a trade dispute within the trade or industry in which the strikers were engaged.

(b)   It declared illegal any strike designed or calculated to coerce the government either directly or by inflicting hardship upon the community.

(c)   It removed the immunities of the Trade Disputes Act, 1906, from any act done in contemplation or furtherance of a strike which under the 1927 Act (i.e. the new Act) was illegal.

(d)   It changed the law on picketing so as to make it unlawful for persons to picket 'in such numbers or otherwise in such manner as to be calculated to intimidate any person . . . or to obstruct the approach thereto or egress therefrom, or to lead to a breach of the peace . . .'.

(e.)   It required that contributors to trade union political funds should 'contract in' whereas previously non-contributors had been required to 'contract out'.

(f)   It prohibited established civil servants from being members, delegates or representatives of any trade union organisation which was not confined in membership to persons employed by or under the Crown. It also prohibited any association between civil service unions and federations of unions embracing persons who were not established civil servants: and any association, directly or indirectly, between civil servants and any political party or organisation.

(g)   It declared it unlawful for any local authority or other public body to require employees or the employees of contractors to belong or not to belong to a trade union.

This Act was strongly opposed by the trade union movement. The unions argued that its effect was to outlaw sympathy strikes and thus to prevent supporting action by workers in one industry for workers in another industry whose wages and conditions were under attack from the employers. It also left to the courts, where most judges were unsympathetic to labour, wide scope for interpretation as to whether a particular strike was intended 'to coerce the government' or whether pickets were acting in a manner likely to intimidate others.

The unions regarded the change in law relating to political contributions as particularly unfair. They pointed out that firms could make political contributions without any provisions for the 'contracting in' or 'contracting out' of shareholders. Moreover, under the Trade Union Act, 1913, no union could even establish a political fund without first securing an affirmative vote in a ballot of its members. To impose a 'contracting in' requirement on top of this requirement under the 1913 Act was to erect obstacles against the implementation of democratic decisions.

The requirement that established civil servants should belong to unions consisting exclusively of civil servants and that civil service unions should not belong to trade union federations federations which included unions outside the service was seen as an invasion of the democratic rights of civil servants. After all, the unions argued, civil servants did not live in an occupational ghetto. Their pay and conditions were very much influenced by events and trends in industry and commerce.

Most of the civil service unions shared the criticisms voiced by the wider trade union movement. The Institution, however, took a much less critical view. It urged other civil service unions not to press the Staff Side to denounce the government's policy. The Institution urged:

> We accordingly appeal to those concerned not to put any strain on the loyalty to the National Staff Side of those organisations such as the Institution that are prepared to work strongly and devotedly for the cause of a united service, but the bulk of whose members hold very definite views as to the unwisdom, to use no stronger term, of the corporate intervention of civil servants in matters of public controversy in the industrial and political spheres.

The Institution also expressed support for the provision in the Act requiring civil service trade unions to have no direct or indirect association with political parties. This, said an article in *State Service*, undoubtedly commended itself to members of the Institution generally.

The campaign by a number of civil service unions against the new legislation nevertheless continued. Civil rights defence committees were set up by some unions with a view to explaining to the public and to other trade unionists that the new legal requirements represented an interference in the civil rights of civil servants. One or two newspapers, particularly *The Times*, suggested that the Institution, though not overtly associated with these defence committees, was nevertheless in sympathy with them. This caused considerable unease within the leadership of the Institution. There was no wish to embarrass other unions in the policies they were pursuing but at the same time the Institution wanted to make clear its own attitude. It was eventually agreed, with considerable reluctance, to send a letter to *The Times* pointing out that it was not true that the Institution was in sympathy with the purpose of the civil rights defence committees. The letter from the Institution which appeared in *The Times* on 30 November 1926 stated: 'The Institution has taken every opportunity to make it clear that it is a non-political organisation and is entirely opposed to political affiliation.'

The campaign against the Trade Disputes Act, 1927, continued for many years. The trade union movement regarded it as a vindictive measure and the civil service unions affiliated to the TUC were compelled to disaffiliate to comply with the law. When the first majority Labour government in British history was elected in 1945 one of its first measures was to repeal the 1927 Act. Most of the big civil service unions then rejoined the TUC.

REPRESENTATION ON THE STAFF SIDE

The controversy, following the General Strike, about the policies of the Staff Side gave added significance to a proposal that staff sides of departmental Whitley councils should be recommended to include in their rules a provision that representation should not be conceded to organisations which were not recognised by the National Staff Side or not affiliated to it through a federal organisation, such as, for example, the Institution. This proposal was first aired long before the General Strike but this did not prevent some commentators connecting it with the strike. The *Daily Telegraph* said that reprisals had been started by the Staff Side against non-political staff associations and that the move initiated by the Staff Side was an attempt 'to convert Whitleyism into a monopoly of socialism'.

In fact the case for the proposal of the Staff Side was a very strong one and the Institution was among its most ardent advocates. Organisations identified with the Staff Side were contributing, both financially and in manpower, to the maintenance of the national machinery of collective bargaining whereas some others were taking the benefits of national bargaining, paying nothing towards its expenses and confining their contribution to departmental machinery. The Institution took the view that if this were to continue indefinitely it would be an inducement to others to cease their national affiliation and representation and concentrate solely on cheap local representation. Such a trend would have been particularly dangerous for the Institution with its federal structure.

The National Staff Side did not seek to make its new proposal obligatory on departmental staff sides and it was accepted that in applying it, it would be necessary to safeguard the position of certain organisations which had 'not attempted to evade their responsibilities for selfish reasons'. The proposal was, it was argued, nothing more than 'an appeal to common decency'. The proposal was put to a conference of representatives of departmental Whitley councils held on 1 November 1926. The recommendation was moved on behalf of the Staff Side by Mr Menzler of the Institution and seconded by Mr W. J. Brown of the CSCA. There was some opposition to the proposal, particularly from some departments with specialist local organisations, but eventually the recommendation was carried by thirty-seven votes to twenty-four.

CAMPAIGN FOR ECONOMY

As the civil service unions had predicted, the defeat of the miners following the General Strike led to a renewed campaign for economies in the civil service. The defence movement which had come into existence in 1925 under the auspices of the Staff Side was kept in being and the central Defence Committee of the civil service unions met from time to time. The October 1927 issue of *State Service* reported that 'the season for the annual economy campaign opened at the Conservative conference at Cardiff when the usual crop of resolutions were considered'. Rumours were current that civil service staffs were to be cut by a fixed percentage. *State Service* urged that a watchful eye should be kept 'on the doings of the back benches who are worrying the government to do something spectacular'.

The campaign for economies in the civil service received support from a number of Conservative members of Parliament. One of them was Winston Churchill. He was reported as saying in a speech at Chingford that he agreed with the view that further efforts at economy must be made. He went on: 'Not for one moment must the effort be relaxed to reduce expenditure to cut down unnecessary charges, to dismiss unnecessary officials, to restrict the entry of officials who were thought not required, to suppress departments which were redundant, or functions of the state which could be dispensed with, and in every way to save the taxpayer money.'

The civil service unions pointed out that these calls for economy, though ostensibly addressed to the need to eliminate waste, could in reality only be met by either a curtailment of public services or by attacks on the standards of employment of civil servants. The possibilities of economies being made which did neither of these things were small. The demand for economies foreshadowed the cuts to be made in the forthcoming Great Depression of the early 1930s.

5 From the General Strike to the Tomlin Commission

One of the consequences of the Trade Disputes Act, 1927, and the proposed tightening-up of representation on the National Staff Side was to produce further rationalisation within the Institution's membership sphere. Some bodies outside the civil service had to cease their affiliation to the Institution while many associations within strengthened their ties with the Institution.

Towards the end of 1927 the Society of Post Office Engineers with some 400 members applied for and was accepted into affiliation to the Institution. In a ballot of the Society's membership more than 95 per cent favoured affiliation to the Institution, even though it meant an increase in annual subscription from 30s to £2. The Society of Post Office Engineers had a longer history than the Institution. It was formed at the turn of the century when many engineers employed on the then primitive telephone system were on the payroll of a private company, the National Telephone Company. The company's licence to operate was brought to an end in 1911 when the telephone system was brought under the Postmaster General. The Society of Post Office Engineers maintained a vigorous existence both before the First World War and during the years immediately following the war. Its decision to affiliate to the Institution was regarded by the Institution as a tribute to its efforts to bring about a united organisation of professional staff wherever they might be employed in the civil service.

The decision of the Society of Post Office Engineers to affiliate to the Institution also influenced other technical and professional staff in Post Office employment. In 1929 the 300-member Society of Post Office Engineering Draughtsmen and the Society of Post Office Engineering Chief Inspectors decided by overwhelming majorities to seek affiliation to the Institution. Meanwhile new staff associations covering professional, scientific and technical employees within the civil service continued to be formed and were admitted into affiliation.

As a consequence of the Trade Disputes Act, however, the affiliation of the civil service section of the AESD had to be dissolved. The AESD then assisted in the formation of the Association of Civil Service Designers and Draughtsmen (ACSDD) exclusive to the service. The new organisation was accepted into constituent membership of the Institution but remained on friendly terms with the AESD.

RELATIONS WITH THE AScW

A new agreement clarifying relationships with the Association of Scientific Workers (formerly NUSW) was also reached in 1928 in the light of the 1927 Act. Although the Association was directly represented on some of the local Whitley committees, the Institution felt that representation within the Whitley machinery for scientific staffs should be exclusive to the Institution. At the same time the

28 Broadway, Westminster, at which the meeting of representatives which established the Professional Alliance, HM Civil Service, took place on 1 January 1919

Sir Richard Redmayne, President of the Institution 1921–55

Institution recognised that its efforts to secure better conditions for scientists in the civil service would depend for their success partly on the support it was able to secure from scientists and scientists' organisations in the universities and in private industry.

A number of meetings were held between the two organisations and eventually in the summer of 1928 an agreement was concluded. At the time of the agreement 803 government scientists were in membership of the Institution, 316 in the AScW and 61 in membership of both organisations. The agreement recommended:

(1) That each body should encourage membership of the other body among those of its members who were eligible to join.
(2) That the Institution alone should deal with the civil service interests of scientists, not only in those departments where it was already fully representative of scientific staff but also in those departments where it was not at present fully representative.
(3) That in the local Whitley committees where both the Institution and the Association of Scientific Workers (AScW) held seats the AScW should retain its Whitley representation as a transitional arrangement. The negotiations were, however, to be conducted by the Institution.
(4) That in the one local Whitley committee where the Association of Scientific Workers held a seat but the Institution did not, the Association should retain its Whitley representation as a transitional arrangement but should transfer the representation to the Institution as soon as the Institution's representative capacity was adequately established.
(5) That machinery should be established for co-operation between the two organisations.

Mr Menzler was subsequently elected as the first chairman of the joint committee of the two organisations and six other Institution representatives were appointed. Meetings for scientific staff were held in each of the establishments where both organisations had membership. The Institution urged its scientific members to join the AScW whilst retaining their membership of the Institution for representational purposes within the civil service.

HIGHER-GRADES CONFERENCE

The Institution continued to press for the unity of the National Staff Side in relation to higher-grade representation in the aftermath of the discussion over the General Strike. It was determined to oppose the Joint Consultative Committee's proposal that there should be a separate autonomous body for the 'higher grades' which would have the power to deal not only with the purely higher-grade problems, such as the abolition of the 'super-cut' which was being pursued by the Higher Grades Committee of the National Staff Side but also with all general service matters whether peculiar to the higher grades or not.

At its September meeting in 1927 the National Staff Side passed the following resolution for the guidance of its representatives conducting negotiations with the Joint Consultative Committee:

That in any further negotiations with the Joint Consultative Committee, the representatives of the Staff Side shall be guided by the following principles:

(1) The primary object of the negotiations is to secure the return to the National Staff Side of the organisations represented in the Joint Consultative Committee on the basis of the *status quo* as it existed on 31 October 1926.
(2) Questions of recognition and representative capacity must be left for discussion on the National Staff Side if and when any or all of these organisations return to the National Staff Side.
(3) Any proposal for separate negotiating machinery for the discussion of problems peculiar to the higher grades must be subject to the preservation of the present single National Council and must be within the constitution of that body.
(4) The question as to whether any particular formula complies with (3) shall not be referred to any third party such as the chairman of the National Council.

Unfortunately the negotiating committee, consisting of the higher-grade members of the National Staff Side on the one hand and of representatives of the Joint Consultative Committee on the other, failed to reach agreement. In April 1928 discussions were broken off.

In the spring of 1929, however, the Institution agreed to enter a proposed higher-grades conference provided that it was given adequate representation within it. In taking this step the Council made it clear to the annual general meeting of the Institution held on 12 April 1929 that the purpose of this initiative was to re-establish the ultimate unity of all civil service trade union organisations. Speaking on behalf of the Council at the annual general meeting, Mr Menzler said that the Institution would take part in the higher-grades movement on the understanding 'that its policy will be to establish unity within the National Staff Side. We have made this perfectly clear, and we shall co-operate on the basis that this new movement will tend ultimately to restore the full representative capacity of the Staff Side as regards higher-grade civil servants.'

The higher-grades conference consisted of the Association of Executive Officers, the FDA, the AIT, the SCS, the Association of Intelligence Officers in the Department of Overseas Trade, the Association of Officers of the Ministry of Labour, the Civil Service Legal Society and the Customs and Excise Surveyors' Association. According to its constitution the object of the higher-grades conference was to promote the interests of higher-grade staff in the civil service. It was stipulated that action should be taken only with the unanimous approval of the members present.

At the instigation of the Institution a Unity Sub-Committee was established, of which Mr Menzler was a member, to consider the possibility of the return of certain sections of the higher grades to the National Staff Side. The Institution representatives had to exercise considerable pressure to ensure that this was seriously considered. Towards the end of December 1929 this committee issued a report stating that it was now satisfied that under its amended standing orders it was not possible for the Staff Side to take action on any matters not included in the constitution of the National Whitley Council except with the consent of all constituent groups. Following this report a number of the organisations representing higher-grade staff agreed to co-operate with the Staff Side of the National Whitley Council in the preparation of evidence for presentation to the Tomlin Commission.

MEMBERSHIP AND ORGANISATION

Despite the controversies surrounding the General Strike the membership of the Institution continued to grow. A membership of 4,000 was achieved by the early summer of 1927, representing a net increase of approximately 700 over the preceding twelve months. The occasion was marked by the publication in *State Service* of a number of congratulatory messages from other civil service union leaders and from men who had played a prominent part in the formative years of the Institution. In 1928 the membership reached 5,000.

The continuing growth and complexity of the Institution made certain organisational changes essential. The size of the Council had expanded, with the affiliation of new associations, to the point beyond which exhaustive consideration of important questions could be effectively carried out. The Council therefore decided, as an experiment, to enlarge the Organisation Committee which examined questions of policy in detail and acted in emergencies. The committee, established in 1925 and composed initially of the officers of the Institution and two members of the Council, was increased to twenty members including the officers and made as representative as possible of the different interests in the Institution. The Council was to meet less frequently and transferred the general responsibility for the business of the Institution during the intervals between Council meetings to the committee, subject always to confirmation of its actions by the Council. In addition, the growing number of scientists represented by the Institution stimulated Mr Menzler to suggest in 1926 that the Council should establish a standing committee to pursue their interests and to advise on policy. A Scientific Staffs Committee was accordingly established later that year composed of representatives from departments employing substantial numbers of scientists. In 1928 a similar committee was established for drawing office staffs.

The continued growth of the Institution and the diverse and pressing problems of the specialist classes with which it had to deal imposed a very heavy burden on the honorary secretary, Mr F. Menzler, and the small full-time staff. In the summer of 1927 it was decided that three additional assistant honorary secretaries should be appointed. As a result Messrs H. W. Monroe, A. W. Watson and E. Law were appointed to assist in matters relating respectively to scientists, salaries and grading and drawing office staffs. The appointment of additional honorary officials was intended to preserve the personal contact of the active lay membership with the day-to-day working of the head office and to maintain the tradition of the Institution that the control of policy should be completely in the hands of the Council and its lay officials. The growth of the Institution led also to the need for better head office accommodation. New premises were secured at 69 Victoria Street. The suite consisted of three good-sized rooms, together with a meeting hall which could comfortably seat fifty or sixty persons.

NEGOTIATIONS

It was indicative of the mood of the government in the aftermath of the General Strike that when the UPW decided to submit to arbitration a claim for wage increases, having been unable to persuade the Postmaster General to enter into negotiations, it was met by a counter-claim from the Official Side for a reduction in pay. The arbitration claim was taken before the Industrial Court in 1927 and, whilst the award did not concede the general claim of the union, it equally, with slight exceptions in the case of new entrants, rejected the government's claim for reductions of pay. The Institution noted these developments with some concern. It was felt that the decision of the Postmaster General to decline to negotiate before proceeding to arbitration was probably evidence of a Cabinet decision which had been strongly influenced by the disputes in other industries. On the other hand, the Court's decision meant that the standards of pay obtaining in a large section of the civil service had been vindicated by an impartial tribunal, despite the demands for 'economy' and within the context of external comparisons. In this sense, therefore, it was a useful defensive propaganda weapon.

The civil service unions also had problems in the operation of the Whitley machinery. The unions alleged that civil service departments on a number of occasions had broken agreements but that discussion of these infractions was refused by the Official Side. The unions were told at departmental level that it was not the function of departmental Whitley councils to discuss the interpretation of national agreements. But when efforts were made to ventilate the complaints nationally the Official Side ruled that discussion could not take place because by its constitution the National Whitley Council could not act as a court of appeal from departmental Whitley councils.

The civil service unions also complained that though the government had agreed to the conclusion of an arbitration agreement the agreement did not in effect provide for obligatory arbitration. Arbitration was denied, in the view of the civil service unions, to readily identifiable groups of civil servants because, according to the Treasury, they did not constitute a 'class' within the meaning of the arbitration agreement. The unions then proposed that differences of interpretation should be referred to the president of the arbitration court for decision. This suggestion was refused. After repeated representations from the civil service unions a compromise solution to those difficulties was reached. It was agreed that any disputed issue concerning a national arrangement could be referred to a special committee representing both the Official and Staff Sides of the National Whitley Council. The task of the special committee would be to examine the facts of the situation and to report to the Council.

COST-OF-LIVING BONUS

In 1927 prices fell to their lowest point since the end of the First World War. The cost-of-living index, which had reached a figure of 176 in November 1920, stood at 79 at the end of 1926. By June 1927 it had dropped to 63. It rose again in the autumn and early winter months but by the end of 1927, when it stood at 69, it was still 10 points lower than a year earlier. The fall in the cost-of-living index was of special significance for the cost-of-living bonus paid to civil servants. The civil service cost-of-living bonus was revised every six months in March and September. The figure was calculated by taking the average for the previous six months and then rounding it upwards to the nearest full five points. Thus if the average for the previous six months had been 66 the cost-of-living bonus payable to civil servants was calculated as though the average had been 70. The bonus payable for the six months beginning 1 September 1927 was calculated on the basis of an index figure of 70. Only six months earlier in March 1927 the cost of living bonus was calculated on the basis of an index figure of 80. The average monthly figure for the preceding six months had been 75⅙.

There was some pressure among civil service unions to press for the ending of the cost-of-living bonus agreement and to replace it by a consolidated salary. One of the arguments employed in favour of this course was that the cost-of-living index did not measure accurately movements in the cost of living for so-called middle-class households. It was a difficult case for the civil service unions to sustain. For years they had argued that many civil servants were receiving salaries very little higher than that of skilled manual workers. They could not now claim with any consistency that living costs for them were totally different from those for millions of other workers.

An article by Mr Menzler in *State Service* drew attention to the real source of the problem. It was not that the cost of living agreement was unfair but that many junior ranks had low basic salaries. For them a drop of a shilling or two a week in the cost-of-living bonus involved real hardship. 'What is wrong in their case,' said Mr Menzler, 'is not their bonus system but their basic pay.' He pointed out that the Staff Side had adopted a policy in favour of higher minimum rates and it was, he said, from this angle that the protection of the lowest-paid civil servants should be sought. 'To seek to overturn the bonus agreement,' he added, 'is more likely to harm than to help them.'

Nevertheless, despite this warning by Mr Menzler, the discussion which took place about the cost-of-living agreement both within the unions and by others outside, including politicians and press commentators who saw the opportunity to economise in civil service pay if the cost-of-living bonus payments could be consolidated at a low level, led to a proposition from the Official Side of the National Whitley Council that the existing cost-of-living agreement should be superseded by a new arrangement. Their proposal was that for the period 1 September 1928 to 31 December 1929 the bonus should be calculated at a cost-of-living figure of 67½. Secondly, they proposed that for periods after the 31 December 1929 the bonus should be revised annually on the average cost-of-living figure for the twelve months of the preceding calendar year. The bonus would continue to be based on a figure of 67½ so long as the average cost of living for the preceding twelve months did not exceed 72½ or fall below 62½. This proposal did not commend itself to the Staff Side. They urged that the proposed figure of 67½ should be increased to 70 and that all civil servants receiving an inclusive salary of £3 10s 0d per week or less should be exempted from any further fall. They also urged that more favourable special provision should be made for the very lowest-paid civil servants.

The Institution decided to call a special meeting of the Council to consider the Official Side's proposal. This was held on 11 September 1928. It was an indication of the interest aroused by the proposal for a revision of the cost-of-living agreement that there was a record attendance at the meeting. A resolution was adopted urging the Staff Side to accept the Official Side's proposition for a cost-of-living bonus on the basis of a figure of 67½ as a starting-point for negotiations. Most of the civil service unions, however, were much less disposed to accept the Official Side's proposal even as a basis for negotiations.

At the annual meeting of the National Whitley Council held in October 1928 by far the most important item on the agenda was the proposal for the revision of the cost-of-living agreement. Both sides presented their arguments at length but there appeared to be little prospect of agreement. Eventually it was decided to set up a joint committee to inquire into the operation of the cost-of-living agreement and to make whatever recommendations might seem desirable. One of the members of the committee representing the Staff Side was Mr F. Menzler of the Institution.

After holding eight meetings the special joint committee reported that it had reached deadlock. Within the Staff Side there was then a sharp difference of opinion. Some of the unions, including the Institution, continued to adhere to the view that the government's proposition to stabilise the bonus at a figure of 67½ should be accepted as a basis for further negotiation. On the other hand, the unions representing the main clerical grades in the civil service took the view that a public campaign for a more favourable settlement was now necessary and the Civil Service Confederation of clerical unions called a mass demonstration at the Albert Hall.

Events took a new and unexpected turn with the election of a Labour government in 1929. The Staff Side of the National Whitley Council made immediate representations to the new Chancellor of the Exchequer, Mr Philip Snowden, and urged that the partial consolidation of the cost-of-living bonus should be based on a figure of 70 and not 67½ as insisted by the previous Conservative government. Mr Snowden showed strong sympathy with the arguments put forward by the Staff Side and shortly afterwards announced that the government intended to change the cost-of-living agreement to provide for the continued payment of bonus at a rate based on a cost-of-living figure of 70, even though, according to the terms of the agreement, the bonus payable from 1 September 1929 would have fallen to a figure of 65.

Mr Snowden went on to say that the arrangement by which bonus was recalculated twice a year, on 1 March and 1 September, was open to serious objection. It meant inevitably that the pay of civil servants was higher in the summer when living costs were usually cheaper and their pay was lower in the winter when living costs were usually more expensive. Mr Snowden stated that after full consideration he had decided that the rate of bonus then payable at a figure of 70 should remain in operation for the six-month period beginning on 1 September. By that time the index had fallen to a figure of 61.

The Institution found themselves in some difficulty over this turn of events. Clearly the campaign conducted by the clerical unions had been partially successful, thanks largely to the replacement of the Conservative government by a Labour government. *State Service* commented, perhaps rather sourly, that it was now apparent that the days of automatic readjustments were over. If there was to be a sharp increase in the cost of living it would be difficult for the Staff Side to claim a corresponding increase in bonus. It seemed clear, said the journal, that the 1920 cost-of-living agreement was to all intents and purposes dead and that pending other arrangements the temporary stabilisation of salaries on the basis of a cost-of-living figure of 70 had taken place. The Institution journal felt that it was by no means impossible, nevertheless, that the cost of living would again rise sharply and that 'failing a permanent settlement of the bonus question the service may yet complain of the policy of pressing for the suspension of the September drop'.

THE 'ALL-SERVICE PROGRAMME'

The campaign for a revision of the cost-of-living bonus agreement was conducted simultaneously with a campaign for a general improvement in pay and conditions. A conference of executive committees of civil service unions convened by the National Staff Side unanimously decided early in 1928 to launch what became known as an 'all-service programme'. The programme covered four main points: (1) that there should be a minimum wage of £3 10s per week inclusive of cost-of-living bonus; (2) that all service should be pensionable; (3) that there should be equal pay for equal work; and (4) that the bonus 'super-cut' imposed on higher-paid civil servants should be abolished. Resentment against the 'super-cut' was particularly strong, not only because of the effect on the salaries of higher-paid civil servants, but because it was felt that the Official Side had broken an understanding with the unions and had imposed the cut without negotiation, a point highlighted by the Industrial Court in its award on the 'super-cut'. The Staff Side of the National Whitley Council conducted a vigorous campaign in favour of the 'all-service programme' which the Institution fully supported. In the summer of 1928 four pamphlets were published entitled, respectively, *The Super-Cut, All Service to Count for Pensions, Equal Pay for Equal Work* and *The Minimum Wage*. Copies of these pamphlets were circulated to Institution members.

The civil service unions had established an Equal Pay Committee, on which Mrs Miller represented the Institution, and it continued to press for implementation of the commitment to the principle of equal pay made by the government in 1920. Early in 1927 the Committee issued leaflets to all MPs asking them to support its request for a select committee to report on the application of the principle. A demonstration in favour of equal pay for equal work was also held in the Central Hall, Westminster, on 29 November 1928. The speakers were not only drawn from the civil service unions but also included Miss Margaret Bondfield, who had served in the 1924 Labour government and was the first woman Cabinet minister in Britain. Miss Bondfield was also a prominent leader of the National Union of General and Municipal Workers.

Early in 1929 the government rejected a claim for the immediate introduction of equal pay for equal work. The spokesman for the government was Mr Winston Churchill. He said that the government had given consideration to the matter in view of the representations recently made on the subject. It had, however, found it 'impossible to depart from the decision already announced both by this and by the late government that the present state of the country's finances will not admit of the great increase of expenditure involved in the application of the principle of equal pay for men and women in the civil service'.

When it had been announced that there was to be a general election in 1929 the civil service unions, including the Institution, urged their members to write to parliamentary candidates in support of the demand for equal pay for equal work. The Institution in a statement to the membership said that the House of Commons had repeatedly affirmed the principle of equal pay and the time had now arrived for it to give some evidence of its good faith.

Representations were also made to the party leaders about the introduction of equal pay and the abolition of the requirement in the civil service that women should be required to resign on marriage. The leader of the Labour Party, Mr Ramsay MacDonald, stated that his party was in favour of the principle of equal pay and opposed to the marriage bar. Mr Baldwin, on behalf of the Conservative Party, said that these questions would be investigated by a Royal Commission; and Mr Lloyd George, on behalf of the Liberal Party, stated that he accepted the principle of equal pay for equal work but that the method by which it should be achieved was one which any government in power would have to consider in relation to the financial condition of the country.

Though the 'all-service programme' launched by the civil service unions did not have an immediate effect in securing better pay and conditions it nevertheless helped to persuade the government that there was a case to be examined. Just before the 1929 general election the Prime Minister, Mr Baldwin, made public the government's decision to set up, if returned to power, a Royal Commission on the civil service. The method of announcement, however, annoyed the civil service unions. The announcement was not first made in Parliament, nor was the information first given to the National Whitley Council. It was given to a deputation of women's organisations on matters affecting women generally, including equal pay for equal work. There was some suspicion that the decision to set up a Royal Commission on the civil service was motivated more by a desire to delay action than to initiate reform. This suspicion found expression in Parliament. Replying on behalf of the government, Mr Winston Churchill stated that the object of the Royal Commission was not to shelve discussion but to undertake a dispassionate and informed examination of the civil service from the point of view of its efficiency as a national instrument and of its own well-being. The Commission's terms of reference and constitution would, he said, be announced when the new Parliament met after the general election.

The Institution welcomed the intention of the government to establish a Royal Commission. Indeed, earlier in the year Mr Menzler had written to *The Times* supporting a suggestion made in one of its leaders that a Royal Commission should be appointed. Mr Menzler suggested that the Royal Commission should consider increasing the efficiency of the service by giving greater scope to the technical expert.

THE ROLE AND PAY OF SPECIALISTS

At the same time the Institution had been arguing vigorously in favour of improved status for scientists in the civil service. It had no difficulty in pointing out that scientists had inferior status to that of administrators. 'It would be too much,' said an editorial article in *State Service* in February 1929, 'to expect the classical scholars who control the civil service to appreciate the necessity for a change of outlook.' The Institution was able to point out, for example, that in the NPL it required three or more promotions to reach the scale of £650 to £750 enjoyed by a principal scientific officer whilst among administrative staff a scale of £700 to £900 was obtained in one move. The Institution also pointed out that, while the permanent secretary of a first-class ministry received £3,000 and the secretary of a department of lower status £2,200 per annum, no head of a scientific department received more than £1,500. Even this figure was reached only after the operation of an incremental scale starting at £1,200.

The Council had first approved the principle of an inquiry into the professional, scientific and technical classes in 1926, but was reluctant to press the issue until suitable evidence had been collected and the Institution was fully representative of all scientific staffs, particularly at the NPL. By the end of 1928 the Institution felt sufficiently confident on both of these points to secure the support of the Staff Side for a proposal that there should be an inquiry into the employment of professional, scientific and technical staff in the civil service. At a meeting of the National Whitley Council the Staff Side proposed that a joint committee be appointed to inquire 'into the recruitment, organisation, duties and pay of the professional, scientific and technical civil servants employed in the scientific research and experimental branches of the public service and to make recommendations'. The Official Side refused to support the proposition but explained that the government had decided to set up an inquiry of its own to examine the organisation of the research departments. Shortly afterwards the Treasury announced an inquiry into the organisation and staffing of research and experimental establishments to be chaired by Professor H. C. H. Carpenter MA, PhD, FRS, professor of metallurgy at the Royal School of Mines.

MR MENZLER

In the late summer of 1929 the Institution suffered a serious blow with the departure from the civil service of the chairman of the Council, Mr F. A. A. Menzler. *State Service* described Mr Menzler's departure as a 'staggering blow from the standpoint of the professional and technical civil servant'. Mr Menzler left the civil service to take an appointment with the London underground railway group of companies, one of the organisations which some four years later was to form part of London Transport.

The Institution acknowledged that Freddie Menzler had done more than any other single individual to establish the Institution on a secure foundation. He first became a member of the Council of the Institution in July 1924. He was then a representative of the Professional Officers' Association, Government Actuaries' Department. Almost immediately he campaigned for the appointment of a full-time secretary and his efforts were rewarded when for the first time a full-time secretary was appointed in May 1925. In the following month Mr Menzler was appointed honorary secretary of the Institution. Almost from that date the Institution surged forward. The membership increase from 2,800 to 6,000 in little more than four years owed much to his personal efforts in recruitment. He also did much to reform the administrative structure of the Institution. In the months following the General Strike Mr Menzler played an outstanding part in maintaining as far as possible the unity of purpose of the civil service trade unions and worked to bring about a reconciliation between the higher grades Joint Consultative Committee and the rest of the Staff Side.

In January 1928 Mr Menzler had been elected chairman of the Council of the Institution. He initiated and saw through negotiations for co-operation with the AScW. This was an important practical step in moulding a relationship with a trade union representing scientific staff outside the civil service. Mr Menzler was tireless in attending meetings of the Institution in various provincial towns. He also took a leading part in the introduction of special schemes for assistance to Institution members, including library and dental services, the benevolent fund, and fire, motor car, sickness and accident insurance. He was prominent in the formation of the Civil Service Housing Association. In addition to all this he served as honorary editor of *State Service*. He rearranged the format of the journal and increased the advertising revenue more than fourfold in a period of four years.

Shortly after his resignation the Council of the Institution decided to invite voluntary contributions from members for a presentation to him. The presentation was made at the 1930 annual general meeting. The voluntary testimonial raised the sum of £353 7s 3d. Nowadays this sounds a modest sum but in 1930 it was a substantial amount. Moreover it was raised from a membership of less than 7,000. However, his services were not entirely lost to the Institution. Having been invited to continue to assist the Institution on a paid consultancy basis, Mr Menzler refused but agreed to continue to assist as far as possible in a purely honorary capacity. He continued to act as honorary editor of *State Service* on the same basis as before.

6 The Tomlin Commission and the Carpenter Committee

In the 1929 general election Labour emerged as the strongest single party. They won 288 seats to the Conservatives' 260. The Liberals, although increasing their vote from under 3 million at the previous general election to over 5 million, won only 59 seats. As a result of the election Labour formed their second minority government, with Ramsay MacDonald as Prime Minister. On 4 July 1929 the new Prime Minister confirmed in reply to a parliamentary question that it was the intention of the government to set up a Royal Commission to inquire into the civil service. He promised that the terms of reference would be so framed as to bring all matters of general importance affecting the civil service within the scope of the inquiry.

On 16 July 1929 a deputation from the National Staff Side met the new Chancellor of the Exchequer, Mr Philip Snowden, to discuss a number of issues of concern to civil servants, including the proposed Royal Commission. The Staff Side pointed out that they had not asked for a Royal Commission. Indeed, they said, they would have valued the opportunity of submitting their views on a wide range of matters before a decision had been taken on the proposed Royal Commission. There were a number of issues of concern to civil servants which ought to have been the subject of direct negotiations with the civil service unions. Had there been such negotiations, a Royal Commission could well have been superfluous.

The Institution had an additional point to put to the government. The Institution argued that the problem of the status of professional staff in the civil service could be considered properly only if the Royal Commission included among its members professional and scientific men of 'standing and administrative experience'. The Institution wrote to the Prime Minister stating that 'the problem of the structure of service organisations must be approached afresh in relation to the functions which should be accorded to the technical expert in the administrative machinery of the modern state'.

THE TOMLIN COMMISSION

The membership and terms of reference of the Royal Commission were announced on 1 October 1929. The chairman of the Commission was Lord Tomlin. The terms of reference were:

To inquire into and report on
(a) the structure and organisation of the civil service, including methods of recruitment;
(b) conditions of service in the civil service, with particular reference to (i) the general standard of remuneration of civil servants and the existing differen-

tiation between the rates and scales of remuneration payable respectively to men and women civil servants; (ii) machinery for the discussion and settlement of questions relating to conditions of service; and (iii) the position of ex-service civil servants in unestablished employment;

(c) conditions of retirement from the civil service, including the retirement of women civil servants on marriage.

Immediately after this announcement the Council of the Institution adopted a statement noting with concern that 'the Commission includes no representative of science, no representative of professions (other than accounting), and no person of eminence who has devoted study to the problems of public administration'. The Institution went on to say that in its view the presence of such representatives would have been of assistance to the Commission in its deliberations and it expressed the hope that steps would be taken to repair these omissions.

The Institution had been preparing since the spring for the sittings of the Royal Commission. A special committee was established to gather and prepare evidence, and the Council of the Institution decided to launch an appeal to the membership for a special fund to meet the cost of the additional work. This appeal for money was sent to all constituent associations and eventually nearly £1,000 was subscribed. In some of the constituent associations almost the entire membership contributed to the appeal.

The Council of the Institution was in no doubt as to the two main issues on which it wanted to make representations to the Royal Commission. The first was the contention of the Institution that professional, scientific and technical staff performed duties equal in importance to those of their administrative colleagues. The second was the need for greater uniformity of grading for specialist posts in the civil service. In the view of the Institution there were far too many different grading systems and salary scales for professional, scientific and technical staff.

Shortly after the announcement of the composition of the Royal Commission, the government indicated that the Commission's terms of reference had been so drawn as to bring the question of the cost-of-living bonus within the ambit of the inquiry. This was contrary to the wishes of the Staff Side who had asked the Chancellor of the Exchequer to ensure that the question of the cost-of-living bonus would be reviewed within the National Whitley Council and not by the Royal Commission. In reply Mr Snowden stated that as the issue was to be reviewed by the Royal Commission there would be no advantage, in his view, in resuming discussion of the subject within the National Whitley Council.

The 'super-cut' in bonus affecting higher-grade civil servants, first introduced in 1921, was also referred to the Royal Commission. The higher-grades conference of civil service organisations had asked the new government to abolish the 'super-cut' but in November the Chancellor of the Exchequer confirmed that the question was one which the government had decided should be left to the Royal Commission.

STAFF SIDE EVIDENCE

The evidence of the National Staff Side to the Tomlin Commission was wide-ranging. On the structure of the civil service it called for a review of the existing allocation of duties between various ministries and departments of state and suggested that more mobility of staff between departments was desirable. This, it said, would result in greater initiative and efficiency because of 'the interchange of methods, experience and personalities'. The Staff Side came out very strongly in favour of the general principle of recruitment by open, written, competitive examination. They complained that during recent years there had been serious departures from this method of recruitment.

In relation to conditions of service the Staff Side urged that there was no justification for employing anyone in the civil service above the age of 16 without an entitlement to pension, providing the employment was full-time and not of a casual nature. The Staff Side also called for the introduction of a 5-day working week.

On pay the Staff Side said that 'civil service remuneration should be based primarily upon the value of the work performed in the state service', and that it should provide for adequate amenities of life taking into due consideration all economic factors and the remuneration of relative professions. The evidence also placed great stress on 'the responsibility upon the state of being a model employer'. As far as the cost-of-living bonus was concerned the Staff Side said that the bonus was inadequate in amount and inequitable in its incidence. It suggested that fuller compensation should be given to civil servants and that the calculation should not rest solely upon the Ministry of Labour cost-of-living index. It went on to suggest that there should be some form of consolidation of bonus with basic pay throughout the civil service.

The Staff Side expressed opposition to any kind of provincial differentiation in pay. Civil servants in the general service classes should be paid the same, said the Staff Side, wherever employed. They urged that no full-time adult should receive a wage of less that £3 10s per week, inclusive of bonus. A call was made for the introduction of equal pay for men and women doing the same job. The Staff Side urged that unestablished service should count in full for pension, and they also suggested that for pension purposes provision should be made for 'added years' to the service of officers who by the nature of their duties necessarily entered the civil service late in life.

The Staff Side called for a number of improvements in the Whitley negotiating machinery. It was suggested that increased power should be given to departmental councils, that better facilities should be provided for staff representatives and that the salary limitation for negotiating purposes should be removed. The Staff Side also complained that on a number of occasions trade union representatives had not been given adequate opportunity to ensure that agreements were observed at departmental level. The Staff Side also argued for the powers of the arbitration court to be extended to include conciliation.

A considerable number of other issues were dealt with in the evidence of the Staff Side. One in particular caused some embarrassment among a number of active trade union members in the civil service. This was the call from the Staff Side that the existing requirement that women civil servants should resign on marriage should be maintained. The Institution and the Inland Revenue Staff Federation (IRSF) took a more enlightened view on the marriage bar and opposed its continuation. The attitude of the Staff Side was, however, strongly influenced by the largest of the civil service unions representing women workers, namely, the Civil Service Clerical Association. The CSCA balloted its members on the retention of the marriage bar and there was a substantial majority in favour of its retention. There was, however, an equally large majority in favour of the reinstatement in the civil service of women separated from or deserted by their husbands and from whom they were 'unable to secure any support'.

Though the evidence of the Staff Side was strongly influenced by the CSCA, as the largest of the unions representing civil service white-collar staff, the CSCA also submitted its own evidence. Much of it was on the lines of that of the Staff Side but it also included one very controversial point. This was that the executive class should be abolished. The CSCA claimed that the division between clerical and executive work was an arbitrary one, and that while the average level of work done by executive officers was higher than that done by clerical officers executive work was merely clerical work 'carried to a somewhat further stage'. In an editorial comment the Institution expressed disagreement with this evidence submitted by the CSCA. The Institution said that the suggestion that the new all-embracing grade should be recruited solely at ages 16 to 17 would be a retrograde step. It would deprive the civil service of men and women who had passed through a higher stage of secondary education. The Institution, nevertheless, expressed sympathy with the proposal that talented clerical officers should be able to look forward with some certainty to promotion to higher rank.

Once the Royal Commission began its sittings it soon became clear that there was little likelihood of any favourable outcome to the claim of the unions representing higher-grade civil servants for the abolition of the 'super-cut'. In one of the Commission's sessions Lord Tomlin indicated in unequivocal terms that in his view the real question was not what had happened in the past to the bonus but whether higher-grade civil servants were now being paid what they ought to be paid. Lord Tomlin went on to say that to refer to the history of the 'super-cut' was to confuse the past with the present. If the higher-grade staff were now receiving too much their pay ought to be reduced. If they were receiving too little their pay ought to be increased.

This exchange within the Royal Commission so upset the unions representing the higher grades that it was decided that a letter should be sent from the higher-grades conference to the Financial Secretary to the Treasury protesting against the point of view implicit in the statements of Lord Tomlin. As was to be expected this protest was, in effect, merely noted by the Treasury.

INSTITUTION EVIDENCE

The Institution submitted its evidence to the Royal Commission in the summer of 1930. The evidence was divided into five parts. Part 1 dealt with the Institution's representative capacity. Part 2 described the unsatisfactory status and organisation of the professional, scientific and technical classes within the civil service. The Institution argued that unless the expert was given fuller scope, was listened to with greater respect, and was given appropriate status and authority, administration could not be fully efficient and the public at large would suffer from the failure to apply the latest advances in professional and scientific knowledge. The existing situation, as presented by the Institution to the Tomlin Commission, was described later by Mr Menzler (1937, pp. 172–3).

The service being organised as it is, the chaotic grading of the specialist classes is convincing evidence that the experts have yet to be assimilated to the main service structure, and are in no sense regarded collectively as performing any distinctive generalised function. But that is not all. There is an unwritten law that specialists shall rarely be allowed to ascend to the highest administrative posts. The one or two exceptions do not dispose of the criticism that specialist officers have in practice been debarred from advancement to purely administrative posts. It is a commonplace that the possessor of administrative ability, that power of seeing facts in their perspective, of handling men, of modifying the technically sound judgement in the light of non-technical considerations, is a *rara avis*. Yet, despite official denials, service tradition has been practically to close the highest administrative posts in the service to specialist officers, and so to deprive the state of a valuable source of administrative talent.

The Institution submitted several proposals to remedy this situation. It was argued that the expert should be given wider powers of administration in his own department and the limits of his authority regarding expenditure and the handling of staff should be enlarged. The status of scientific and professional heads of department should be raised to equal that of administrative heads with similar responsibilities. Arrangements should be made for technical advisers to have direct access to parliamentary heads of department in cases where the Board was not in operation, and for the Board system under which the responsible technical officers would take their share in decision-making on equal terms with the administrators to be extended. Finally, it was urged there should be a graded technical service, based on equal remuneration with non-technical classes at equivalent levels, an adjustment of increments to enable officers to reach their grade maxima at a reasonable age, interchangeability of staff and improved methods of recruitment. Part 3 of the evidence concerned itself with general conditions of service, and Part 4 dealt with the machinery of negotiation, suggesting that there should be three sub-councils of the National Whitley Council to deal respectively with (a) administrative, executive, clerical and allied classes, (b) professional, scientific and technical classes and (c) manipulative classes. The final part of the evidence dealt with conditions of recruitment and, in particular, with the counting of unestablished service for pension, the provision of 'added years' for pension purposes, voluntary retirement, the retirement age and the marriage bar. On the last issue the Institution, dissenting from the Staff Side view, argued that whatever might be the rule for women in clerical employment, a strong case existed for women with professional and scientific qualifications and experience to be allowed to continue after marriage.

Unexpected support for the claim of the Institution for improved status for scientific, technical and professional civil servants came in the evidence submitted to the Royal Commission by the FDA representing the highest-grade administrative staff. The Association stated that it was in full sympathy with its professional colleagues in their claim for a level of remuneration adequate for their professional attainments and responsibilities. It recognised the growing importance of the part played by science in public administration and saw no justification for assigning to them a status which, measured by remuneration or otherwise, was inferior to that of their non-technical colleagues.

THE TOMLIN REPORT

The report of the Royal Commission was published in the summer of 1931. On the general standard of pay in the civil service, the Royal Commission stated that it was satisfied that 'the present general standard of remuneration of civil servants is reasonable in the light of the wage levels now prevailing and calls for no substantial revision'. The report further stated that in making comparisons with pay in outside industry and commerce the state should take a long view. Civil service remuneration, the Commission argued, should reflect the long-term trend both in wage levels and in the economic conditions of the country. The Commission regarded it as undesirable that the conditions of service of civil servants should be related too closely with factors of a temporary character. The Commission rejected the claim for a minimum wage and the argument that the government should act as a 'model employer'.

The Royal Commission regarded the continuance of the cost-of-living bonus as open to objection. It pointed out that the remuneration of analogous grades outside the civil service did not fluctuate in accordance with changes in the cost-of-living figure and that there was therefore no good reason why the wages of civil servants should be fixed on a basis different from that generally adopted. The Commission furthermore pointed out that it was unsatisfactory to relate the pay of all civil servants to a common cost-of-living figure which might be applicable to certain staffs but inapplicable to others. In the light of these considerations the Commission recommended that the bonus system should be abolished and that the bonus should be consolidated with salary.

On the employment of women the Commission endorsed the principle of 'a fair field and no favour'. A minority of the Commission favoured removal of the marriage bar, especially in the higher grades and the specialist classes, but for the sake of unanimity the Commission decided to recommend no change, except that the discretionary power to suspend its application should be more precisely defined. Opinion on the issue of equal pay was divided and the Commission therefore decided to make no recommendation.

The Royal Commission also argued that the existing rates of pay for specialist grades were adequate. Nevertheless it recommended some measure of improvement for higher grades and suggested that these improvements should be brought into effect 'as soon as conditions permit'. It rejected the demand for an extension of the Board system, remarking that there was no evidence that technical experts did not have the necessary degree of access to permanent secretaries and ministers. It also rejected any major restructuring of the specialist grades.

The report of the Tomlin Commission received a hostile reception from civil service trade unions. The National Staff Side at a meeting on 30 July 1931 passed a resolution condemning the report of the Commission 'for its total inadequacy to meet the considered claim of the service on the major problems which call urgently for solution'. The SCS organised a mass meeting at the end of July on behalf of all middle- and higher-grade civil servants. A resolution was carried expressing profound dissatisfaction with the report of the Royal Commission.

The Institution was no less critical. A statement was issued by the officers stating that the Institution viewed the report with 'profound disappointment'. It went on to deplore the failure of the Tomlin Commission 'to realise the function of scientific knowledge and method in the modern community'. The statement was reported in *The Times, Daily Herald, Yorkshire Post, Financial News* and *Daily Express*. An editorial in *State Service* stated that the report of the Royal Commission represented a serious setback to the hopes and aspirations of all members of the Institution. Special dissatisfaction was expressed with the Royal Commission's admission that it was not possible for it to review in detail the organisation of the various specialist classes. 'Nevertheless,' said the editorial, 'the Commission had found it possible without such an investigation to declare and even to emphasise that apart from a few of the top posts the remuneration of the professional, scientific and technical classes required no readjustment.'

To the Institution the crux of the criticism of the Royal Commission report was that very little attention had been given to the problems of the professional, scientific and technical grades organised in over 500 different classes. The Institution was also very critical of the proposal of the Commission that the cost-of-living bonus should be consolidated with salary at approximately the existing rate of bonus. The Institution argued that this recommendation represented not only a rejection of the case put forward by the Staff Side for a readjustment of the bonus, particularly in the higher ranges of salary, but was specially unfair as it called for the stabilisation of salaries at a time when the cost-of-living figure was at its very lowest level.

THE CARPENTER COMMITTEE

While the Tomlin Report proved largely abortive from the point of view of the specialist in the civil service, the Carpenter Committee report was regarded as a major breakthrough. It inaugurated the so-called 'Carpenter' technical and scientific officer classes, supported by the 'Carpenter' assistants, forming the beginnings of a unified scientific service. This lasted until the end of the Second World War.

The committee of inquiry had been appointed by the Treasury under the chairmanship of Professor H. C. H. Carpenter. Its terms of reference were:

To examine the functions and organisation of the undermentioned establishments in the government service and to report on the method of recruitment and conditions of service of the civilian, scientific and technical officers employed therein:

(a) the research and experimental establishments under the Admiralty, War Office and Department of Scientific and Industrial Research;

(b) the Department of Government Chemists and the establishments under the Admiralty and War Office concerned with chemical analyses; and

(c) the Meteorological Office.

When the membership of the committee of inquiry was announced it was found that it did not include a single person drawn from the trade union movement. The Institution protested against the exclusion of staff representatives from the committee of inquiry, but agreed that evidence should be submitted to it.

In its evidence to the Carpenter Committee the Institution concentrated on four main issues. First, it urged that there should be unification of the conditions of service of all employed in scientific departments. Secondly, that salaries should be increased because at the then existing level they were not sufficient to attract candidates of the requisite calibre. Thirdly, that if higher-grade men were to concentrate on higher-grade work heavier responsibility would also fall on technical assistants. For this reason improved conditions were also sought for them. Fourthly, all scientific staff should be brought under the Superannuation Acts.

The report of the Carpenter Committee was published in the early autumn of 1930. Although it did not endorse in detail all the points made in the Institution's evidence it went some way towards meeting them. In an article in the November issue of *State Service* Mr R. A. Watson-Watt, the chairman of the Scientific Staffs Committee of the Institution, said of the Carpenter Report that 'most of us would have liked it to go further, not all of us expected it to go so far: none of us think it has failed to go in the right direction'. His own view was that it was a good report.

One of the report's main observations was that the 'salaries and financial prospects are shown to be generally inadequate by the difficulty of recruiting and retaining officers of the high standard required for the work to be performed'. The state, the report pointed out, had to compete with private industry as well as with the universities for the services of research workers, and the committee made it clear that in its view steps would have to be taken to make the competition more effective. It said: 'We have come to the conclusion that the present schemes of grading and salary scales in the establishments under review are generally inadequate.' It also accepted over a wide range the Institution's proposals for uniformity of grading.

Much had still to be done, however, to secure the recommended improvements. At first, following the publication of the Carpenter Report, the Treasury claimed that it could not consider the report in detail because the Tomlin Commission was still sitting and its ultimate views on the proposals of the Carpenter Committee would have to be considered in the light of the Tomlin recommendations. Later, in the autumn of 1931, when Britain was overtaken by an economic crisis, the Treasury still declined to sanction the implementation of the recommendations because, it said, the times were not favourable to the introduction of improvements in staff conditions. The Institution made representations to the Treasury, and constituent associations were pressed to make representations through departmental Whitley councils.

At last, in the early spring of 1933, the Treasury stated that it was prepared to make some move on the Carpenter Committee recommendations. In a letter to the Institution the Treasury confirmed that some two years earlier it had accepted the Carpenter Committee's report in principle but that in the intervening period economic circumstances had prevented it from implementing it. It went on to say that 'the persistence of such circumstances sets serious limits to the extent to which action in the direction of implementing the report may be taken'. It had, therefore, decided that it was not practicable to undertake the reorganisation and regrading of the scientific and technical departments concerned on the lines proposed by the Carpenter Committee or to introduce the Carpenter basis of recruitment of scientific and technical officers. The Treasury stated that it was, nevertheless, prepared to introduce an assistant class in certain departments, organised and graded on the basis recommended in the Carpenter Report. It also proposed to make some slight improvement in the scales for staff in the officer class in the scientific departments.

The Institution considered these proposals at a meeting on 14 March 1933. It carried a resolution noting with extreme concern 'the grave situation arising from the implied rejection of the Carpenter recommendations' by the Treasury. The Institution also prepared a short historical statement on the delay in the application of the recommendations of the Carpenter Report and sent it to members of Parliament.

In the summer of 1933 proposals were introduced for certain departmental changes on the lines previously indicated by the Treasury. These were regarded as totally inadequate by the Institution. The Council then sent to the Treasury a letter conveying 'profound disappointment and resentment' at the decision of the Treasury to adjourn *sine die* the application of the Carpenter Report. The letter was signed by Mr R. A. Watson-Watt, then vice-chairman of the Council of the Institution. These protests had no effect.

In the spring of 1934 the Institution decided once again to press strongly for the implementation of the Carpenter proposals. A letter was sent by the Council of the Institution to the Treasury reminding it that it had not replied to the protest made in the previous year against 'the continued evasion of the major implications of the Carpenter Committee's report'. This was the strongest language so far used in the Institution's campaign. This time the protests were more successful. In October a letter was received from the Treasury announcing its decision to apply the recommendations of the Carpenter Report.

The controversy, however, was still not yet over. There were exchanges between the Institution, the Treasury and various departments about the interpretation of the Carpenter Report. In the autumn of 1934 the Institution became increasingly suspicious that under the guise of giving effect to the principles of the Carpenter Report the Treasury was attempting to downgrade the work of many of the staff in the scientific and technical departments.

Finally, in January 1935 after further controversy, an agreement was concluded on the implementation of the Carpenter Report recommendations. New scales were introduced for scientific and technical staff payable from 1 January 1935. The agreement also set out the main principles on which existing officers were to be assimilated into the new pay scales. This agreement was regarded by the Institution as a milestone in its history. For the first time an agreement covering a substantial number of members in a well-defined sector of the civil service had been reached by direct negotiations with the Treasury. In an article in *State Service* Mr R. A. Watson-Watt, who had played such a significant part in the campaign for the implementation of the Carpenter recommendations, said that the recommendations were a necessary preliminary levelling operation within the professional area but they must be followed by further efforts towards improved status for the professional, scientific and technical classes of the civil service as a whole.

THE BRIDGEMAN COMMITTEE

Meanwhile, in February 1932 the Postmaster General appointed a committee to inquire whether any changes in the constitution, status or system of organisation of the Post Office would be in the public interest. The chairman was a well-known Conservative land-owner and politician, Viscount Bridgeman. The Institution decided to give evidence to the committee because of the interests of its members employed in the Post Office. The Institution's evidence was based on the fundamental principle that the telephone business should be controlled by telephone men, and that the essentially technical telephone and telegraph services should be segregated from the mail-carrying and other non-technical activities of the Post Office.

The report of the Bridgeman Committee was published in August 1932. At least three of its recommendations followed closely the Institution's evidence, namely, the adoption of a Board of Management including the Engineer-in-Chief; an explicit recommendation that there should be no bar to the advancement of technical officers to controlling administrative posts provided they had shown themselves to possess administrative ability; and the continued utilisation by the Post Office of the appropriate services of the Stationery Office and the Office of Works. Indeed, certain passages from the Bridgeman Report neatly expressed Institution policy on the status of the expert. For example:

> We believe that engineering experience is insufficiently brought into the consideration and formulation of general policy . . . In an organisation such as the Post Office, which depends so much upon scientific discoveries and developments and their practical application, we consider it essential to bring engineering and research into more intimate touch with the general problems of administration. The object of this closer relationship is twofold; the engineer, on the one hand, will be in a position to visualise the picture as a whole, and thus to direct his activities into those channels where the need for progress and development is greatest; while, on the other hand, those who are charged with the day-to-day running of the administrative machine will be able to avail themselves of the scientific point of view to the fullest extent.

To this extent the Institution welcomed the report as a notable recognition of the soundness of the policy which it had consistently advocated on the place of the technical expert in the structure and organisation of the public service. It feared, however, that the failure of the committee to adopt the proposal that the telephone and postal wings of the Post Office should be separated and the committee's own proposal for provincial reorganisation under a single Post Office might negate the advantages gained. Accordingly the Institution sent a deputation to the Postmaster General who replied that its points would be considered by the Board of the Post Office once it had been established.

In 1933 the Institution had the satisfaction of seeing two of its main submissions to the Bridgeman Committee adopted. At the institution's dinner in November 1933 the Postmaster General intimated that it was his intention to make the highest appointments in the Post Office available to technical officers, and that at the beginning of the coming financial year he proposed to establish a functional board composed of civil servants.

7 The Years of Depression

Part of the explanation for the disappointing report from the Tomlin Commission and the procrastination in the implementation of the Carpenter Committee's recommendations was to be found in circumstances external to the civil service. Public employees could not escape the effect of the economic blizzard which started in the USA in 1929 with a stock market crash and swept over many countries in different parts of the world. By the summer of 1930 there were over 2 million unemployed in Britain and by the end of the year the figure had risen to some 2½ million.

One important effect of the world economic depression was that the prices of foodstuffs and raw materials imported into Britain fell more steeply than the prices of exported manufactured articles. This had a marked effect on the relationship between wages and salaries on the one hand and the cost of living on the other. The Ministry of Labour's cost-of-living index figure, which had reached a high point of 176 in November 1920, fell to a figure of 66 by January 1930. The fall had been uneven. It had declined sharply until 1923 and then, with some ups and downs, it fell more slowly until the beginning of 1930 when it reached the figure of 66. By the end of 1930 it had fallen to 55, by the end of 1931 to 48, and it reached a low point of 36 by the summer of 1933.

COST-OF-LIVING BONUS

Under the terms of the civil service cost of living agreement the bonus of civil servants was adjusted downwards with the fall in the index. These reductions were taking place regularly at six-monthly intervals and the effect on civil servants was disturbing. Many of them had standing commitments such as mortgages, and it was argued that the cost-of-living index, by giving a disproportionate emphasis to food, exaggerated the real decline in the cost of living of civil servants. The Labour government decided in the summer of 1930 to continue the concession introduced during the previous year whereby the cost of living bonus was based on a figure 5 points higher than the figure calculated by strict reference to the terms of the agreement. Even so, this still meant that there was a reduction in bonus because of the continued decline in the cost-of-living figure.

One or two of the civil service unions urged that the National Staff Side should protest to the government at the reduction in bonus payment. The UPW took a different view. It felt that a public campaign at a time when the government had already made a concession on the strict application of the cost-of-living bonus agreement would not secure public sympathy. It was supported by the Institution. The latter argued that any protest campaign would alienate public sympathy, particularly in view of the prevailing trade depression. This view was endorsed by the constituent associations of the Institution. In the end the recommendation of the UPW that a protest campaign should not be launched was carried within the Staff Side.

The National Staff Side did, however, write to the Chancellor of the Exchequer to express 'disappointment and alarm' at the decision to reduce the cost-of-living bonus although an even bigger cut could have been imposed by the strict application of the terms of the agreement. The Chancellor, Mr Philip Snowden, replied in strong terms. He regretted that 'this generous concession, which involves a very large addition to the taxpayers' burden for the benefit of the civil service should have been received in such a spirit of ingratitude . . .'. Mr Snowden's attitude was widely supported among those calling for cuts in government expenditure. Indeed the government was criticised for not imposing upon civil servants the full rigour of the cost of living agreement. The *Daily Mail,* in particular, in a leading article attacked the Chancellor for halving the bonus reduction of civil servants. It called for the full reduction to be imposed.

The Institution was less critical of the Chancellor of the Exchequer than most other civil service unions, even though, as constituent members of the Staff Side, they had been associated with the letter to Mr Snowden. An article in the September 1930 issue of *State Service* stated that 'it required considerable courage on Mr Snowden's part to go as far as he has gone and grant a concession of equal magnitude to that of twelve months ago'. The editorial article pointed out that there was a serious trade depression and that the Exchequer was in considerable financial difficulty.

The Staff Side nevertheless maintained their criticism of the Chancellor. In a further letter they argued that the bonus arrangement for civil servants, based upon the cost-of-living agreement of 8 May 1920, was obsolete and, at the very least, needed review and amendment. They acknowledged that if the agreement had been strictly followed the bonus would have been less than the amount conceded by the government. On the other hand, said the Staff Side, the bonus arrangement was totally inadequate to provide for the minimum needs of the lower-paid civil servants and, so far as the middle and higher grades were concerned, 'their salaries are neither in scale with the prewar civil service salaries nor the present-day remuneration of comparable professions'. On 29 January 1931 the Chancellor received a deputation consisting of the National Staff Side General Purposes Committee to urge the case for continuing the payment of the bonus on the figure of 65. In reply the Chancellor, having referred the question to the Cabinet, said that the government had decided that the cost-of-living bonus would be revised as from 1 March 1931 in strict accordance with the cost-of-living agreement of 1920 (as modified by the super-cut). In justifying this position Mr Snowden pointed out that civil servants did not have the nightmare of unemployment which was faced by industrial workers and they had not the same fears as industrial workers in regard to the effect on their jobs and living standards of illness, physical disability and old age. He pointed out that there were now over 2½ million workers without jobs.

The civil service trade unions were divided in their attitude toward the government's decision on the cost-of-living bonus. The Institution continued to express opposition to any campaign or protest against the decision, urging on the other civil service unions the point that it was dangerous to confuse opposition to the reduction of bonus, when these were warranted under the terms of the 1920 agreement, with opposition to the far more serious threats to civil service salaries represented by the campaign in the House of Commons by Conservative and Liberal members to consider further cuts in wages and salaries as a way out of the crisis. The UPW was also against a public campaign of opposition but felt that private representations should be made to the Chancellor. On the other hand, the unions representing civil service clerical workers favoured a campaign of public meetings to bring home to civil servants the threat to their living standards. The activities of these organisations gave rise to the fear that the government might be prevailed upon to give some concession to the lower-paid grades at the expense of the middle and higher grades. The Council of the Institution, therefore, had no hesitation in accepting an invitation from the SCS to a conference on 25 February 1931. As a result of this conference a statement, signed on behalf of the Institution and ten other organisations representing the middle and higher grades, was addressed to the Chancellor declaring that although higher-grade civil servants were just as willing as any other class to bear their fair share of sacrifices they were not prepared to be penalised. This action was successful in forestalling additional cuts in the bonus of the middle and higher grades.

THE MAY COMMITTEE

In February 1931 following a sustained campaign from the opposition parties, newspapers, bankers and industrialists, the Labour government appointed an economy committee composed largely of company directors, under the chairmanship of Sir George May, who had been one of the top men with the Prudential Assurance Company. The committee had the following terms of reference:

> To make recommendations to the Chancellor of the Exchequer for effecting forthwith all possible reductions in national expenditure on supply services, having regard especially to the present and prospective position of the revenue. In so far as questions of policy are involved in expenditure under discussion these will remain the exclusive consideration of the Cabinet, but it will be open to the committee to review expenditure and to indicate the economies which might be effected if particular policies were either adopted, abandoned or modified.

The May Committee reported in the summer of 1931. Of the £96 million to be saved as a result of the committee's recommended economies, no less than two-thirds was to be at the expense of the unemployed. It was this aspect of the report which eventually brought about a serious division within the Cabinet. Some members of the Cabinet felt unable to go along with the proposal for drastic cuts in unemployment benefit, although a number of them shared the prevailing view of the day that the way to economic salvation lay in curtailing government expenditure. At first some of the dissenting Cabinet ministers supported the proposal that all-round cuts should be made but when faced with strong trade union opposition they finally objected to the proposal that the biggest cut of all should be on unemployment benefit.

The TUC were emphatic in their opposition to wage cuts, the worsening of working conditions and reductions in unemployment benefits. In March 1931 the TUC General Council issued a statement which said: 'The Council are firmly convinced that no help whatever can be afforded by a policy of reducing wages. The application of such a policy can only intensify the slump by reducing the purchasing power of the community, thereby leading to further unemployment.'

In August 1931 the Cabinet continued to debate the proposed cuts in unemployment benefit. Towards the end of the month the Labour government resigned. A small number of its principal leaders, including the Prime Minister and the Chancellor of the Exchequer, joined with the Conservatives and some of the Liberals to form a National government. The new government made cuts in many directions. In October the new coalition of Conservatives, Liberals and a small minority of former Labour leaders won a substantial victory in a general election. The candidates supporting the National government received more than 60 per cent of the votes cast and Labour not much more than 30 per cent. In the new Parliament, Labour held only fifty-two seats.

Opposition to the cuts introduced by the National government in the autumn of 1931 was widespread. The most sustained was that of the unemployed and the most dramatic that of the naval ratings who participated in what subsequently became known as the Invergordon mutiny. The cuts in unemployment benefit meant that new lower rates of 15s 3d per week for an unemployed man, 8s for his wife and 2s for each child became payable. In addition a family means test was introduced for those who had been unemployed for six months or more. By the early part of 1932 it was estimated that only about half the total number of unemployed were drawing unemployment benefit. The other half had either been removed from the register by new regulations, were ineligible for benefit because of their former occupation, or had been eliminated by a means test.

In most industries where trade was very depressed the employers succeeded in reducing wages significantly. In coal-mining, where hundreds of thousands of workers were unemployed, the average cash earnings in 1932 were only 42s 1d per week. In the north-eastern coalfields workers employed for five shifts a week received only 32s 8d, and this for longer hours per day than they had worked only a few years earlier. In 1932 some 40 per cent of all coal-miners were unemployed. The textile industry also suffered badly. There was acute unemployment in the textile towns of Yorkshire and Lancashire. The employers attempted to reduce wages and to introduce more intensive working methods but they met with surprisingly strong opposition from hundreds of thousands of workers, the majority of whom were women. The example of the textile workers strengthened resistance to wage cuts elsewhere, and in other industries where trade was not so depressed the opposition of unions to wage reductions ensured that wages did not fall by very much.

IMPACT ON CIVIL SERVANTS

As far as public servants were concerned the May Committee had urged that the wages and salaries of all public employees, including civil servants, teachers, police and others, should be reduced. On civil service pay the committee said that 'having regard to security of tenure and pension rights the emoluments of civil servants (with the exception of the higher grades) undoubtedly compare favourably with the reward for corresponding posts in the majority of commercial and industrial undertakings at the present day'. The May Committee also said that the leave allowance of the administrative, executive and clerical branches of the civil service was unjustifiably generous. The committee recommended that the scale of leave should be cut by one-third. Two other recommendations of the committee were that the normal hours for the clerical classes in the civil service should be 8 per day, including three-quarters of an hour for lunch, and that the marriage gratuity paid to established women civil servants who were called upon to resign on marriage should be discontinued.

Civil servants fared better than many others, however, in that, despite the May Committee recommendations, the only economy actually made was the imposition of the cut in bonus from 1 September 1931 in accordance with the terms of the 1920 agreement. The Institution response was sympathetic. 'The overwhelming majority of our members,' said an editorial in *State Service*, 'recognise that no government could have reached any other decision than to allow the cost-of-living agreement to operate in the ordinary manner as from 1 September.' The majority of the civil service trade unions, on the other hand, were more hostile. A statement issued by the National Staff Side said that after the many cuts already suffered since 1921, amounting to over 30 per cent for the majority of civil servants, the civil service unions viewed the continuance of the unjust and inadequate basis of remuneration with deep anxiety and resentment. At a later stage the Staff Side urged that, whilst they would agree to the maintenance of the 1920 sliding-scale cost-of-living agreement as an expedient to meet the abnormal situation, there should be a minimum adult wage for civil servants. They also decided to convene a demonstration to be held on 21 October 1931 at the Albert Hall, to express their protest publicly.

At a meeting on 6 October 1931 the Council of the Institution decided that a letter should be sent to the Staff Side stating that the Institution was unable to support the proposed public demonstrations and that representations on civil service remuneration should continue to be made through the existing negotiating machinery. No action should be taken, said the Council 'which might add to the embarrassments of the state'. A note to this effect was also issued to the press.

The civil service unions were still apprehensive that, following the May Committee's recommendations, the government might ask them to make a further contribution to the economy drive. In December 1931 the Chancellor of the Exchequer received a deputation from the National Staff Side at which this point was discussed. The Staff Side asked whether the reduction in civil service bonus which took effect on 1 September was to be regarded as arising out of the normal application of the 1920 cost-of-living agreement or as an economy cut. In reply, the Chancellor of the Exchequer pointed out that the decision to apply strictly the 1920 agreement had been taken by the previous Labour government. The National government had since publicly announced, he said, that the reduction in cost-of-living bonus introduced from 1 September was to be looked upon as the civil service contribution to the general economy scheme. He assured the Staff Side that civil servants would not be asked for any further cut in respect of the economies demanded by the financial situation. The bonus agreement, he said, would remain in operation until it was replaced by another arrangement.

THE TOMLIN REPORT CONSIDERED

Detailed consideration of the Tomlin Commission's recommendations was delayed by the need to deal with the immediate problems generated by the national crisis and the report of the May Committee. In December 1931, however, the two sides began to prepare themselves for the opening of discussions on the Tomlin Report. Several joint committees of the National Whitley Council were established: Committee A to discuss the cost-of-living bonus and remuneration in general; Committee B to cover recruitment, classification, duties and future scales (including provincial differentiation); Committee C to cover promotion, machinery of negotiation, ancillary questions, and general principles to be observed in future in regard to the employment of temporary staffs; and Committee D to deal with superannuation. In addition, *ad hoc* committees to deal with the Commission's proposals on temporary clerical personnel (Committee E) and women's questions (Committee F) were established.

BONUS STABILISATION

In February 1932 the government proposed in Committee A that the existing cost-of-living bonus should be consolidated and that the cost-of-living agreement should be brought to an end in accordance with the Tomlin recommendation. This was strongly opposed by the civil service unions. They felt that the government was proposing consolidation at a time when prices were at their lowest level. Britain had left the gold standard a few months earlier and it was anticipated that prices would rise in the following months. The Staff Side said:

> The effect of the adoption of the Commission's proposals would be to rob civil servants of the advantages of a sliding-scale bonus system, with all its shortcomings, at a time when prices are expected to take an upward trend, after they have suffered its disadvantages over the long period of depression of prices during which a succession of automatic cuts has brought the remuneration of many thousands of them below that necessary to a decent subsistence, and seriously reduced the standards of living of all grades alike, lower, middle and higher.

The Staff Side pointed out that, according to official returns in February 1931, no fewer than 94,000 of the 300,000 non-industrial employees in the civil service received less than £3 a week. It was pointed out that a non-industrial civil servant who received a salary of £5 a week inclusive of bonus in March 1921 was receiving ten years later in March 1931 £2 19s 3d, representing a reduction of nearly 41 per cent.

Early in 1932 the Institution wrote to every member of Parliament drawing attention to the government's proposal to consolidate bonus with salary at a time when the cost of living was likely to be at its lowest point. The cost of living, said the Institution, was likely to rise as the cost of primary commodities rose. Feeling against the consolidation of the cost-of-living bonus at the very low level of September 1931 was running strongly in the civil service. Petitions were circulated in many departments and were submitted to departmental heads. In the Admiralty, for example, a statement was submitted by the Staff Side of the Whitley Council expressing to the First Lord the indignation of the staff at the government's proposals. In the Air Ministry a petition, accompanied by a memorandum showing the decline in civil service salaries, was submitted to the Secretary of State for Air.

By the early summer of 1932, however, the civil service unions were beginning to wonder whether they had been right to reject so strongly the government's offer to consolidate the cost-of-living bonus. Contrary to expectations, the level of prices did not rise after Britain left the gold standard. In fact, it continued to fall. By May 1932 the cost-of-living index had fallen to a figure of 43.

An editorial in the June 1932 issue of *State Service* pointed out that both the assumptions which had hitherto formed the basis of the policy of the civil service unions, namely, that prices were more likely to rise than to fall and that the government's offer of consolidation would remain, might prove to be unjustified. The world economic crisis was becoming ever more serious and one of the symptoms of the economic depression was the continued fall in prices. If this decline continued, was it unlikely, asked the journal, that the government would feel compelled to withdraw its offer to consolidate the bonus at the existing level?

On 30 June 1932 the cost-of-living bonus agreement for the civil service was finally brought to an end. The National Staff Side decided unanimously to accept an offer by the government to stabilise the cost-of-living bonus at its existing figure of 50. In view of the continued fall in prices this offer could be regarded as reasonably generous. If the offer had not been accepted it was almost certain that the bonus payment calculated by reference to the agreement would have fallen to a figure of 45 from 1 September 1932. Under the terms of the new agreement, which was to operate from 1 July 1932, total remuneration including bonus was to be stabilised. This meant that there would be no review at six-monthly intervals unless during the period of stabilisation the official cost-of-living figure fell to below 35 or rose above 60. The agreement provided that the period of stabilisation would be followed by eventual consolidation. Consolidation was, however, deferred until 1 April 1934. This deferment was made in response to the representations of the Staff Side who argued that the year 1932 was not an opportune time for consolidation. The agreement was accepted by the National Staff Side with the reservation that 'it did not regard the arrangement as meeting legitimate civil service grievances in relation to cost-of-living bonus and reserved to itself the right to press for a more equitable settlement of the problem at the end of the period of stabilisation'.

A NEW CAMPAIGN ON PAY

Towards the end of 1932 a proposal was put to the Staff Side that the civil service unions should organise a national campaign on pay. The object of the campaign would be to obtain the 'restoration' of the cut in pay imposed from September 1932 and in the second place to urge higher pay for all public servants. The Institution did not support this proposal. It felt that it would be injudicious to embark upon any agitation when there were millions of unemployed workers and when many others in employment had also suffered wage cuts. The Institution also felt that the Staff Side would be acting in a manner contrary to its own constitution if it embarked on such a campaign without the unanimous support of all affiliated civil service unions. It was pointed out in this connection that the standing orders of the Staff Side had been revised after the General Strike to make it clear that any action, other than that of negotiation and representation through the National Whitley Council, could be taken only by agreement between all constituent organisations.

When the issue of the proposed new campaign came before the Staff Side early in 1933 the Institution strongly opposed it. At a meeting on 14 March 1933 the Council of the Institution carried a resolution stating that the Institution was not only opposed to the substance of the proposals before the Staff Side but also that it considered them outside the scope of the constitution of the Staff Side. Strong support for the view of the Council was expressed by Sir Richard Redmayne in his presidential address to the annual general meeting of the Institution on 24 April 1933. He explained that the Institution was not opposed in principle to public campaigns on behalf of civil servants, but that if such a weapon was to be effective it had to be used with discretion. It must, he said, have the whole civil service behind it. This, he argued, did not obtain in relation to the proposed new pay campaign. He also felt that the weight of the civil service unions should be thrown into the negotiations for the new agreement on long-term consolidation and should not be dissipated in other campaigns.

The Institution's view was that the real issue facing civil service unions was not whether there should be a general pay increase but the rate at which the cost-of-living bonus should be consolidated into basic pay under the new long-term agreement which was due to be negotiated in 1934. This view was reinforced by the continued fall in the cost-of-living index. By June 1933 it had fallen to a figure of 36.

An editorial article in the July 1933 issue of *State Service* underlined the point that the question of consolidation was of overriding significance to civil servants. It pointed out that negotiations had to take place before April 1934 to determine the basis of consolidation. Stabilisation had been introduced related to the cost-of-living figure of 50 but meanwhile the cost-of-living index had fallen to 36.

Because of the opposition by the Institution and one or two other civil service unions to the proposal for a national campaign on pay, the unions favouring such a campaign decided to set up their own Civil Service Joint Committee whilst still maintaining their membership of the National Staff Side. In the light of this development the Council of the Institution decided to seek the views of all its constituent organisations on their attitude towards the proposed pay campaign. Replies were received from fifty-five constituent organisations. Of this number forty-two were in favour of the existing policy of the Institution, eleven were in favour of supporting the proposed campaign by the Civil Service Joint Committee and two were uncommitted. At a meeting on 20 July 1933 the Council of the Institution decided formally that, in view of the expression of opinion from constituent bodies, there should be no change in the Institution's policy. This decision was adopted by thirty-seven votes to six.

In October an article on civil service pay from Douglas Houghton, who was then general secretary of the Association of Officers of Taxes, was published in *State Service*. It emphasised that the real issue facing civil servants was the terms on which the consolidation of bonus was to be achieved. Mr Houghton set out at length the arguments for and against various alternatives, including an extended period of stabilisation, the consolidation of bonus at the existing level or the introduction of a new sliding scale relating wages to movements in the cost-of-living index. In the article Mr Houghton pointed out that though the index figure had fallen to a low point of 36 in the summer of 1933 it was now once again rising and had reached a figure of 41.

Within the civil service unions there were differences of view about the policy to be put to the Official Side in the negotiations for the new long-term agreement.

The main unions representing clerical grades were in favour of a claim for substantially higher pay. The Institution favoured a claim for consolidation based on a cost-of-living figure of 55, and a review of the settlement at the expiry of three years or earlier if the cost-of-living index figure rose above 65 or fell below 35 for six consecutive months. The Institution also felt that, if necessary, the stabilisation agreement should be extended to enable full negotiations to take place on the new proposals. The Council of the Institution also expressed extreme concern at the delay in the negotiations caused by the sharp differences of view between civil service trade unions and the consequent failure of the Staff Side to put forward agreed proposals. Because of these differences between civil service unions the negotiations for consolidation of pay did not begin until 1 February 1934. This left only two months before the period of stabilisation was due to expire.

BONUS CONSOLIDATION

In its claim to the Official Side the Staff Side referred to the drastic reductions in civil service pay made during recent years. It pointed out that there had been a succession of twenty-three cuts in the cost of living bonus amounting in all to more than 40 per cent of pay for thousands of civil servants. It further pointed out that, of the 300,000 non-industrial civil servants, about 35,000 received £2 a week or less, 183,000 received £4 a week or less and 219,000 received £5 a week or less. The Staff Side claimed that full compensation for the increased cost of living should be given to all civil servants on rates of pay of £3 a week or less and that in view of the obsolescence of the 1914 basis for the Ministry of Labour's cost-of-living index, a figure of 60, as against the figure of 50 in the stabilisation agreement, should be used as a basis for the new agreement. The Staff Side also urged that there should be increased pay for the lowest-paid grades in the civil service and that all adult men and women should receive equal pay for equal work. In making its claim the Staff Side had the benefit of evidence from inside and outside the civil service, collated by its own Statistical and Research Bureau, formed in 1933 to monitor general trends in pay outside the civil service.

The Institution took no direct part in these negotiations. Its representatives attended with only a watching brief, refraining from either associating themselves with, or dissociating themselves from, the Staff Side claim. The Institution Council took the view that the machinery for formulating policy on the Staff Side, despite the post-1926 reforms, was still not functioning satisfactorily in mobilising what they regarded as the 'middle' ground on major issues. The Council was therefore actively considering further measures to remedy the defects of collective decision-making on the National Staff Side.

By the date when the period of pay stabilisation was due to come to an end, 1 April 1934, no agreement had been reached on the new claim. The Official Side then proposed that a period of stabilisation should continue and this was accepted by the Staff Side. It was, however, understood that this was not to mean an indefinite extension. Meanwhile there was a fair amount of speculation in the press that in the forthcoming budget some of the cuts imposed in 1931 might be partially restored. The effect of this speculation was to make it more difficult to reach agreement in the civil service discussions. It was decided in the circumstances to await the details of the budget. In the budget the government announced that half the economy cuts in the salaries of public employees made in September 1931 would be discontinued.

Shortly afterwards the Official Side submitted proposals for consolidation of bonus with salary as from 1 July 1934. The proposal was that the consolidation should be on terms proposed by the Tomlin Commission or in relation to a figure of 55, whichever was the more favourable. In either case salaries were to remain subject to 'abatement at the appropriate rate in respect of the principle of maintenance of half restoration'. In other words, civil servants consolidated on Royal Commission terms would obtain immediately only half the difference between their existing salaries and the Royal Commission terms, and those who were consolidated in relation to a cost-of-living figure of 55 would suffer an abatement of 2½ points. The effect of the proposal would have been to give officers on salaries up to £140 a year slightly more than they would have received as a result of the removal of half the 1931 cuts, while those whose salaries were consolidated on a cost-of-living figure of 55 would receive for the time being only the budget restoration of the 2½ points. A further proposal from the Official Side was that from 1 July 1934 the uncut consolidated rate would be deemed to be the annual salary for superannuation purposes.

The proposals of the Official Side were considered by the Council of the Institution at a meeting on 1 May 1934, when a resolution was carried stating: 'That, in respect of the main features of the Official Side's proposal, the Council sees no reason to depart from its settled policy and instructs its representatives to vote for an acceptance, but to press for the insertion in any agreement of a provision for the review of pay arrangements.' The Institution was, however, in a minority on the Staff Side. Of the larger unions the CSCA and the Ministry of Labour Staff Association rejected the offer. The UPW also decided that the offer was unsatisfactory and instructed its representatives to press for further negotiations with a view to obtaining more acceptable terms. The Staff Side passed by a large majority a resolution stating that the proposals for consolidating bonus with pay were entirely inadequate.

The Post Office group of unions decided in June 1934 to put forward a compromise which they hoped would unite the Staff Side. They suggested that the government's main proposal for consolidation should be accepted but that further discussion should take place on a number of points of detail. This suggested compromise was strongly opposed by the unions representing the main clerical grades but was finally carried by twelve votes to eleven. The chairman of the Staff Side then ruled that the resolution was not effective because under the constitution a two-thirds majority was required on a matter of policy. Ultimately, in view of this division of opinion, the chairman of the National Staff Side wrote to the chairman of the Official Side on 26 June to state that he had no alternative but to indicate that the Staff Side was unable to enter into an agreement with the Official Side on the basis of the proposals which had been put forward.

On 3 July 1934, Mr Duff Cooper, the Financial Secretary to the Treasury, announced in the House of Commons that in view of the inability of the Staff Side to enter into agreement with the Official Side on the basis of the proposals which had been put forward it had been decided to put them into operation from 1 July. A Labour member asked whether this meant that the government proposed to apply the changes without the agreement of the Staff Side of the National Whitley Council. Mr Duff Cooper's reply was an emphatic 'Yes, Sir'.

WOMEN'S RIGHTS

The economic crisis, the economies introduced by the government and the campaign to restore the pay cuts culminating in the bonus consolidation in 1934 overshadowed all other issues in the civil service in the early 1930s. In February 1931 the Civil Service Equal Pay Committee was disbanded while the efforts of the unions were directed towards resisting wage cuts. However, following the report of the Tomlin Commission, Committee F had been established to consider the Tomlin recommendations concerning women's issues. The joint committee, on which Mrs R. Miller was the Institution's representative, reported in 1934. It dealt with three main issues. The first was the principle of 'a fair field and no favour', by which was meant that all posts in the civil service should be open equally to members of both sexes except when adequate publicly announced reasons existed to the contrary. The joint committee reported broadly in favour of this principle, making specific reference to its importance in specialist areas. The report also asked departments to review the position in the light of the committee's recommendations and recommended that within a period not exceeding three years a joint national body should undertake a central review of the position then obtaining throughout the service. The committee further agreed that it was desirable that women should be represented on selection boards for competitions for which candidates of both sexes were eligible. The second principle was that, as recommended by the Royal Commission, in any class or grade where both sexes were employed there should be aggregation of work and posts including common recruitment and promotion prospects.

On the 'marriage bar', the committee agreed that it should continue. However, the Institution's evidence in favour of abolition of the 'marriage bar', which had impressed the Tomlin Commission, was accommodated to the extent that where in the opinion of the appropriate authority 'any disadvantage which may arise out of the employment of a married woman is likely to be outweighed by her special qualifications or special experience' married women could be retained. The joint committee also agreed that regulations governing the recruitment of the administrative class and the tax inspectorate should include a reference to the possibility of retention after marriage and suggested that such a provision should be included in analogous departmental classes. The committee also considered the question of maternity leave and agreed that a married woman should in the event of confinement be allowed special leave, pre-natal and/or post-natal, on full pay for a period not exceeding two months and should be eligible for an extension up to three months if recommended by medical certificate.

The Staff Side also argued for the principle of equal pay which they regarded as indispensable to the achievement of 'a fair field and no favour'. The Official Side took the view that this was outside the terms of reference of the joint committee and the Staff Side therefore decided to press the issue through Committee A which was considering the Tomlin recommendations on remuneration. The Official Side later argued that the issue of equal pay was one of principle and therefore outside the terms of reference of Whitleyism, at which point the Staff Side decided that any action would have to be through a public and parliamentary campaign.

Although disappointed at the retention of the 'marriage bar' and the attitude of those civil service unions who supported retention, the Institution welcomed the joint committee's support for the principle of 'a fair field and no favour'. An editorial in *State Service* following the report, said: 'The principles upon which agreement has been reached respecting the employment of women in the civil service . . . must in course of time profoundly modify the status of women civil servants.'

In pursuit of the principle of 'a fair field and no favour' the Institution encouraged members at departmental level to ensure that the maximum number of posts were open to women and that the reference to waiving the 'marriage bar' which was to be included in the regulations covering recruitment to the administrative class should be rapidly incorporated in all regulations governing recruitment to professional, scientific, and technical classes for which women were eligible. The Institution's annual report for 1934 showed that this advice had already been acted upon in the Valuation Office, where the following provision was included in the regulations issued to candidates applying for posts in the grade of third class valuer:

> Women candidates must be unmarried or widows and will normally be required to resign their appointments on marriage; but exception to the rule requiring resignation on marriage may in individual circumstances be made where the employment of a married woman is considered advisable in the light of her special qualifications or special experience in relation to the duties required of her or of the special requirements of the department in which she is serving.

SUPERANNUATION

Committee D of the National Whitley Council completed its review of the recommendations of the Tomlin Commission relating to superannuation and presented a report which was adopted by the National Whitley Council in November 1934. From June 1935, provision was made for half the time spent in unestablished service after the age of 18, to be reckonable for superannuation purposes for all new entrants into the service. Unestablished service was defined as service in an unestablished capacity which was whole-time, civilian and remunerated directly out of monies voted by Parliament. The Superannuation Act, 1935, also gave statutory authority for the allocation of part of a pension to secure a pension for a spouse or dependant following the death of the pensioner. No progress was made, however, towards the aim of securing arrangements for 'added years', a cause particularly dear to the Institution whose members were often recruited to the service at a mature age.

MEMBERSHIP

The years of the depression brought a strengthening rather than a weakening of Institution membership. The cuts in the cost-of-living bonus and the threat of even further pay reductions and worsening of conditions served to underline the need for effective organisation. By the end of 1934 the membership had risen to over 9,100.

In the summer of 1930 the Institution had secured a major increase in

F. A. A. Menzler, Honorary Secretary 1925–8; Chairman 1928–9

Leslie Herbert, Chairman 1943–4;
General Secretary 1945–8

Stanley Mayne, General Secretary
1948–61

membership strength by the affiliation of the Society of Post Office Engineering Inspectors. It brought with it into the Institution a membership of 1,200 and in so doing completed the organisation within the Institution of all eligible Post Office engineering grades with the exception of a number of the superintending and staff engineers. The decision of the Society to become a constituent part of the Institution was taken as a result of a ballot vote of the membership. There was an extremely high poll in which 93·6 per cent voted in favour. The result was all the more remarkable because it was accompanied by a recommendation that there should be an increase in subscription.

The Institution was greatly encouraged by the admission of the Society of Post Office Engineering Inspectors. An editorial in *State Service* spoke of 'this breathless progress of the Institution', and pointed out that the total membership of the Institution had risen to more than 8,000. This, the editorial claimed, represented more than 80 per cent of those eligible to join. It pointed out, however, that the rapid growth of the Institution from less than 3,000 to more than 8,000 in no more than five years had led to a number of problems. First and foremost, it was argued, the organisation was inadequately staffed. Moreover, there might come a time when a higher subscription would become necessary.

8 The Second Half of the 1930s

In the mid-1930s Britain emerged slowly from the worst effects of the economic depression. But at no stage was prosperity attained. Even in the best period in the 1930s, which was the summer of 1937, unemployment was still not far short of 1½ million. This was much better than in 1931 and 1932 when the number of registered unemployed exceeded 2½ million, but it still represented a huge waste of productive manpower.

Although there was some expansion with new light industries in the midlands and the south-east and a general improvement in the economy in the mid-1930s, particularly a boom in house-building, there was still economic depression and social distress concentrated in the areas associated with the traditional basic industries of coal, steel, textiles and shipbuilding. The economic distress in the older industrial regions of Britain in the 1930s was accompanied by periodic social unrest. Many of the unemployed demonstrated for jobs and against any proposals to reduce the scales of unemployment benefit, particularly the proposed new scales and regulations towards the end of 1934. The size of these demonstrations in the depressed areas and the intensity of feeling which they expressed led the government of the day to retreat and to amend the proposals. There were also hunger marches of unemployed workers from the distressed areas. They evoked widespread public sympathy.

These events did not go unnoticed in the Institution, even though no official pronouncements were made on the policies needed to overcome the phenomenon of mass unemployment. In January 1935 *State Service* published an article on 'Civil servants and depressed areas' by Dick Gifford, general secretary of the Government Minor Grades' Association. He began his article by expressing pleasure that more and more civil servants were accepting the philosophy that they were their brother's keeper and had a responsibility to help succour the people of the depressed areas. He recalled that he had visited the north-east of England and had spent a day in the mining district of Seaham Harbour. He spoke of many men who were obviously undernourished and ill-clad. He continued:

They wore only a jacket – some had not one – a shirt and trousers. They wore no underclothes. Their flesh was visible through their threadbare garments. They had ridden on their bicycles eight miles from Sunderland and had worked four hours on the foreshore picking up coal. They were now pushing their 'finds' back to Sunderland – eight miles remember – where, after a rest, I learned they would 'peddle' the coal in the hope of getting a shilling for the larger bag and 8d for the smaller one. They would have worked an aggregate of about ten hours for one shilling and eight pence.

Some eighteen months later there was another article on the depressed areas published in *State Service*. This time it was about South Wales. The writer of the article, with the initials D. G., was probably the same Dick Gifford. In this second article the author said that he knew the South Wales valleys very well in the years 1919, 1920 and 1921. He had returned for the first time for fifteen years to Pentrebach, a little village a mile or so from Merthyr Tydfil. He wrote:

Throughout the district I saw pits closed down, buildings falling to pieces. On the way up the Merthyr Valley I passed shops empty and boarded up. I passed groups of men – waiting, waiting, waiting, waiting for work or, for all I know, death itself. As I passed them I noticed that in almost every instance their knees and elbows were discernible through their worn trousers and jackets . . . I felt it was almost wrong that I should be well fed and well clothed . . .

These articles were published in support of what was known as the Civil Service Social Service Movement. It was a voluntary organisation which raised money among civil servants to give assistance to voluntary organisations in the depressed areas. Those who organised this movement did not do so in the belief that it was a substitute for government action. Indeed, among the principal supporters of the movement were some of the strongest advocates of radical social measures for economic and industrial change.

In some five years the Civil Service Adoption Associations, as they were called, raised over £100,000. An article in the July 1938 issue of *State Service* said that the distressed areas of Northumberland and Durham offered the most obvious scope for this kind of voluntary assistance. Almost every village and all the large towns in the industrial parts of these areas, it pointed out, had their own social service clubs and practically every one of these clubs was receiving assistance in one form or another from the Civil Service Adoption Associations. Extensive assistance was also given to clubs and societies in the industrial areas of Yorkshire, Lancashire, Derbyshire, Staffordshire and South Wales.

The article went on to make a strong appeal for further assistance. It said that unemployed clubs provided opportunities for recreation and education to large numbers of unemployed workers. It pointed out that in many of the small towns in South Wales the rate of unemployment exceeded 40 per cent. In Blaina, for example, the unemployment figure was 66·9 per cent and in Ferndale 48·2 per cent. The highest percentage of all was 68·8 per cent in Brynmawr. In Lancashire there were 40·3 per cent unemployed in Hindley and 47·7 per cent unemployed in Westhoughton. In Yorkshire 32·7 per cent were unemployed in Haworth and 28·9 per cent in Dewsbury. The article was published above the signature of Sir Warren Fisher, the head of the civil service, and Mr Ewart Llewellyn, the chairman of the National Staff Side.

Even though the Institution studiously avoided any policy pronouncements on the economic issues of the day, there was interest among many active members in the debates which were then being conducted about social problems. In April 1937, for example, *State Service* carried a lengthy review of a book published under the title 'Britain without capitalists'. It was a study by a group of economists, scientists and technicians of what might be achieved in a socialist Britain.

This was also the period of the Left Book Club, a publishing venture launched by Victor Gollancz whose subscribing membership quickly grew to more than 50,000. One of its publications, *A Philosophy for a Modern Man* by the mathematician Professor Hyman Levy, was reviewed in *State Service* and described as 'brilliant'. Professor Levy had already become known to many active members of the Institution because of the forthrightness of his public expressions of opinion on the social responsibility of science and scientists. In March 1935 the Institution had invited him to give a public lecture open to the membership in

London on the subject of 'Science and social responsibility'. The hall was full and the lecture was subsequently published in *State Service*.

Another prominent scientist who did much to relate science to its social background was Professor Lancelot Hogben. His books *Mathematics for the Million* and *Science for the Citizen*, though both very long, became best-sellers. *Science for the Citizen* was given the most extensive review ever to appear in the pages of *State Service*. The author of the review was the distinguished elder statesman of the Institution, Mr Menzler. The main message of his review was that the book ran counter 'to the popular view, largely shared even by scientists themselves, of "science" as an intellectual activity apart from ordinary life, as something done "for its own sake", yielding fortuitous by-products in the form of practical applications to meet social needs'. The truth of the matter, said Menzler, following in the footsteps of Hogben, was precisely the opposite. Social needs inspired social advance.

The Institution's concern with the wider implications of science and technology was also manifest in its decision in 1936 to become a corporate member of the British Association for the Advancement of Science. The British Association was founded in 1931 'to give a stronger impulse and a more systematic direction to scientific inquiry; to promote the intercourse of those who cultivate science . . . to obtain more general attention for the objects of science and the removal of any disadvantages of a public kind which impede its progress'.

A leader in the May 1937 issue of *State Service* on 'The impact of science' stated the case for that decision:

> While every subject of scientific investigation, however academic and remote it may appear in the existing state of knowledge, has a potential bearing upon the welfare of the public, it is undeniable that the rapid advances of scientific discovery and invention in recent times have created a number of problems whose solution has become a matter of urgent importance. It is being recognised that, before the difficulties attendant upon the adaptation of man to his constantly changing material environment can be disposed of by legislative or administrative action, they must be elucidated by the application of the self-same processes of scientific inquiry and observation that have led to those environmental changes. There is no halfway house at which the scientist can hand over complete responsibility to the administrator, or the administrator seek to discharge the scientist from further participation in the march of progress.

In the months immediately before the outbreak of war in September 1939, reviews were published in *State Service* which commented sympathetically on books of social criticism. Mr Menzler, for example, reviewed at length a new book by Professor Harold Laski called *Parliamentary Government in England; A Commentary*, which contended that the neutrality of the civil service had been due to the fact that in the main the top posts had gone to the same class that constituted the ruling circles in society. Mr Menzler said: 'The assumptions upon which their ideas rest are the same as those of the men who control the instruments of production in our society.' Professor Laski's main criticism of the civil service was that he doubted whether it had the power to challenge fundamentals and whether it had that ultimate imaginative scepticism and the passion for constructive innovation which were demanded by the changing social environment.

RESTORING THE 'SUPER-CUT'

With the improvement in the economic situation the government decided that from 1 July 1935 the remaining half of the economy cuts introduced in 1931 should be abolished. For civil servants this meant that payment was to be made in full of the consolidated rates of pay introduced subject to abatement, as from 1 July 1934.

The unions representing higher-grade civil servants, including the Institution, were, however, unsuccessful in their effort to compensate for the 'super-cut' first imposed in 1921. A long statement setting out the history of the 'super-cut' was circulated to all members of Parliament by the Institution in August 1934. The statement was accompanied by a letter signed by Mr R. A. Watson-Watt, the chairman of the Council of the Institution. The letter stated that in 1921 the government had departed from what was described later by the Industrial Court as an 'honourable undertaking' and made special cuts from 15 to 60 per cent in the cost-of-living bonus of civil servants on basic salaries exceeding £500. The Institution said that vague promises had been made from time to time that the cuts would be reconsidered when the economic situation improved. The government, however, had not reversed the cuts.

The issue was finally determined by an arbitration decision in 1935. The Treasury had refused to agree to refer the claim to arbitration because it was a general issue. In order to overcome this difficulty the Staff Side were forced to submit the claim as a test case involving a particular grade, the district inspectors of the Ministry of Health. The Industrial Court rejected the claim on the grounds that civil service pay had been examined by the Tomlin Commission who, in recommending consolidated rates of pay, had taken the 'super-cut' into account. The Industrial Court said that the case had been put forward on the grounds that the financial condition of the country was such that the 'super-cut' should now be removed. This, however, would be to disregard the recommendation of the Royal Commission.

The Institution was critical of the grounds on which the issue had been fought. Unlike most of the other unions representing higher-grade civil servants, the Institution took the view that the real issue was whether the government had broken its initial undertaking to the unions and not whether the country could afford to pay. The Institution also argued that the main moral to be drawn from the 'super-cut' issue was that the organisations representing the higher grades should sink their differences and pursue a common policy. The vigorous handling of the 'super-cut' issue had been hampered by disunity. The higher-grades conference had been dissolved in November 1935 when the conference had initially decided not to associate itself with the National Staff Side in referring the 'super-cut' issue to arbitration. This refusal had led to delay in the submission of the case of arbitration. Indeed, some of the higher-grade staff had been more concerned to differentiate themselves organisationally from the main body of civil servants than to pursue the substantive claim in co-operation with the National Staff Side.

EQUAL PAY

The civil service unions also pressed, though unsuccessfully, for the issue of equal pay to be taken to arbitration. Early in 1935 the National Staff Side decided to establish a Civil Service Equal Pay Committee to launch a parliamentary and public campaign for equal pay for equal work in the civil service. The issue of equal pay had been ruled as being outside the scope of the Whitley machinery. Mrs R. Miller represented the Institution on the committee. In its campaign the National Staff Side recalled that as long ago as May 1920 the House of Commons had adopted a resolution stating that it was expedient that women should have equal opportunity with men in all branches of the civil service and should also receive equal pay. A further resolution on equal pay had been passed by the House of Commons in August 1921. This stated that although the House could not commit itself to equal pay because of the then financial position of the country, the question of the remuneration of women as compared with men should be reviewed within a period not exceeding three years. This review did not take place and in July 1924 the Chancellor of the Exchequer stated that it was impossible to grant equal pay to the service in view of the 'enormous increase in expenditure' involved. Similar replies were given on behalf of the government in 1925 and 1929.

A debate on equal pay took place in the House of Commons on 7 June 1935. The debate was introduced by Colonel Clifton Brown, MP, who suggested that the government should give a lead to industry by granting equal pay to its own staff. He was supported on behalf of the opposition by Mr George Lansbury. In his reply on behalf of the government Mr Duff Cooper, Secretary to the Treasury, said that the government was in no way pledged to the principle of equal pay for equal work. He argued that the words 'equal pay for equal work' were misleading and that the real issue was equal pay for work of equal value. Account had to be taken of sick leave among women and 'wastage' on marriage.

The issue, however, was not allowed to drop. On 1 April 1936 there was another debate in the House of Commons on an amendment moved by a Labour member of Parliament, Miss Ellen Wilkinson. This called for the introduction forthwith of equal pay for men and women in the common classes of the civil service. Before the debate the civil service unions urged their members to write to members of Parliament seeking support for Ellen Wilkinson's amendment. There was also a packed and enthusiastic public meeting at Caxton Hall, Westminster, in support of equal pay with speakers from all the main political parties. In the debate in the House of Commons Miss Wilkinson was opposed by the government but, nevertheless, with the support of Labour members of Parliament and a number of Liberals and Conservatives, her amendment was carried by 156 votes to 148. On the following day, however, the government announced that it was not prepared to depart from the policy it had hitherto pursued.

At its meeting on 29 April 1936 the National Staff Side viewed with concern the refusal of the government to implement the decision of the House of Commons in favour of equal pay for equal work. It carried a resolution of protest which it decided to send to the government. The resolution stated that equal pay was a matter on which the government had consistently refused negotiation to civil service staff and that for this reason civil servants had been obliged to seek a decision on equal pay from the House of Commons. The Staff Side pointed out that the refusal of the government to operate the decision of the House would, if adhered to, close to civil servants their only constitutional means of seeking redress of a grievance upon which negotiation had been denied to them.

In the meantime, however, the Staff Side were also pursuing two other lines of approach on the question of equal pay and opportunities for women. Having been debarred from negotiations on the question of equal pay, they decided to press for joint discussion on the differentiation which existed between men and women with a view to removing anomalies and to laying down some standard to which salaries should be related. In 1935 a joint committee on Sex Differentiation in Pay was established, on which the Institution was represented by Mrs R. Miller. The Staff Side submitted a claim that there should be no difference in pay in the recruitment grades until the marrying age, after which there should be a gradual differentiation up to a maximum of 10 per cent and that above a salary of £700 p.a. there should be no differentiation.

In support of the policy on equal pay the Institution sought in April 1936 to submit to arbitration a claim that the 'salary scale of women members of the various grades of the officer class in establishments, where the recommendations of the committee on the staffs of Government scientific establishments have been or may be applied, shall be the same as the men'. It argued that this was already the case in outside employment. The Treasury replied stating that it did not agree to such a reference. The Institution said that this refusal of the government to allow a claim to go to arbitration constituted an open breach of the arbitration agreement. By refusing arbitration and simultaneously by refusing to accept a vote of the House of Commons in favour of equal pay the government was denying to civil servants any constitutional means for the redress of their grievance.

Contrary to expectations, however, an agreement was reached in 1937 without prejudice to the Staff Side's general claim for equal pay for equal work. Under that agreement men and women were to receive the same salary on recruitment and the maximum women's salary in each grade should be not less than 80 per cent of the men's.

On women's rights in general within the civil service, the report of the joint committee on women's questions in 1934 had been referred to departmental Whitley councils with a view to its application on a departmental basis. A central review of progress was begun in 1937, which revealed that in a number of departments, and in particular the defence ministries, no consideration had been given to the committee's recommendations. It was only as a result of pressure by the central review committee that these departments commenced the review that should have been made in 1934. Although the Staff Side made a comprehensive review of the posts which continued to be reserved to either men or women, little progress had been made by the outbreak of war and negotiations were suspended.

ARBITRATION

The frustrations experienced in securing arbitration on the issues of the 'super-cut' and equal pay gave new impetus to the request of the civil service unions for changes in arbitration procedure. The Tomlin Commission had also commented adversely on certain aspects of the machinery, including the definition of 'class' and the maximum salary limit for the purpose of arbitration. There was marked reluctance on the part of the Treasury to go to arbitration on central claims affecting departmental grades, except when the claims were made department by department. On drawing office grades, for example, there was no provision for central negotiations. Each departmental group had to be negotiated for separately.

This was a problem which also affected the departmental clerical grades. Some of the departmental grades received lower pay than the general clerical class. For years the practice had been angrily denounced by the general secretary of the Civil Service Clerical Association, Mr W. J. Brown. The CSCA tried repeatedly to get central discussions on claims affecting the departmental classes, but its request was refused by the Treasury. Eventually in 1936 the CSCA found it possible to submit identical claims on behalf of six departmental classes. The union was able to persuade the Treasury to submit these cases to arbitration simultaneously on the understanding that all would be heard by the Court before it issued its award in any one case. As the Institution at the time pointed out, the Treasury thus 'saved its face' but the CSCA secured a tactical victory of the first importance. The union had secured, in effect, central consideration of the pay of the departmental classes. The outcome was favourable to the CSCA.

The Institution congratulated the CSCA upon what it described as its great victory, and paid special tribute to its general secretary, W. J. Brown. An editorial in *State Service* said that Mr Brown had never acquiesced in the Treasury insistence on separate treatment for the departmental classes. He had been unsparing in his condemnation of the Treasury and had shown burning indignation on the issue, which he had maintained at white heat year after year for the previous fifteen years. He never lost a single opportunity of denouncing the Treasury for its policy. This was a very warm tribute to pay to W. J. Brown because for years he had been a turbulent influence in civil service trade unionism. He was well known for his pronounced left-wing views both on trade union matters and in politics. He had been at the centre of the controversy in the civil service unions at the time of the consolidation of the cost-of-living bonus. Under his leadership the CSCA had wanted more vigorous opposition to the government and when this did not secure universal approval from other civil service unions W. J. Brown denounced both the government and some of his trade union colleagues in strident terms. In later years Mr Brown was to become an independent member of Parliament and he moved away from his previous left-wing views. He never ceased, however, to be a vigorous and independent controversialist.

Another objection of the Staff Side to the existing civil service arbitration arrangements was the developing practice for the Official Side member of the arbitration tribunal to be drawn from full-time members of the Industrial Court. The Staff Side objected because it was felt that such persons, being composed largely of private employers, were not necessarily suitable to deal with civil service cases. The unsuitability of the Industrial Court, as thus constituted, for hearing civil service cases was acknowledged by the government and the Official Side suggested that the machinery for arbitration on civil service cases should be divorced from the Industrial Court. Thus, in 1936 it was agreed that a separate Civil Service Arbitration Tribunal (CSAT) should be established consisting of an independent chairman, the president of the Industrial Court or, failing him, a person appointed by the Minister of Labour after consultation with the National Whitley Council, and two members drawn from panels nominated by the Official Side and the Staff Side. The Institution welcomed the new agreement which had the effect of removing civil service arbitration entirely from the ambit of the

Industrial Courts Act. Following the new agreement Sir Frank Goldstone, Professor H. J. Laski, Dr J. J. Mallon and Mr A. G. Walkden were reappointed for the period ending 7 April 1937 as the panel nominated by the Staff Side. In 1938 Professor R. H. Tawney and Mr L. S. Woolf were added to the Staff Side panel.

Discussions continued, within a subcommittee of the Joint General Purposes Committee of the National Whitley Council, on the definition of 'class' and maximum salary limit. The committee issued its report in June 1938 after a series of disagreements. The Staff Side failed to obtain any modification in the definition of a 'class' and was unable to persuade the Official Side that grading should be included within the scope of arbitration. Having claimed £860, the Staff Side finally settled for £850 p.a. as the maximum salary limit for arbitration instead of the existing limit of £700 p.a.

PAY

With the improvement in the economic situation in the mid-1930s the civil service unions began again to think of claims for higher salaries and better conditions. In the spring of 1935 a proposition was put forward that the National Whitley Council should explore the possibility of introducing a 5-day week in the civil service. This, however, did not find favour with the Official Side.

On salaries there was a difference of view between the unions. In 1936 the cost of living stood some ·4 points higher than in the previous year and there was a particularly sharp upward movement in 1937. The CSCA, with the support of some of the unions, wanted the National Staff Side to 'table forthwith a claim for *pro rata* compensation for the increase in the cost of living since the date of consolidation and for arrangements to provide for further increases as they arise'. This view was not supported by a number of other civil service unions who felt that it would be wrong to tie civil service pay too rigidly to the cost of living. There were a number of long discussions on the Staff Side but the majority view was against the submission of an immediate claim and in favour of keeping the matter under review.

The Institution strongly opposed any suggestion that civil service pay should again be tied to the cost-of-living index. An editorial in *State Service* said that there was 'an element of the grotesque in a proposal that civil servants should seek to entangle their remuneration once more in the uncertainties and instabilities of the moribund working-class index'. The adoption of such a course 'might well react to the lasting disadvantage of the whole body of civil servants; for it can be anticipated with certainty that even if, after a series of negotiations which, in the nature of the case, would inevitably be protracted, some temporary monetary advantage was secured, it would be accompanied by the stipulation that downward adjustments should be made in the event of a decline in the cost-of-living index'. This view was strongly endorsed by a meeting of the Council of the Institution on 7 December 1937.

In the months following this controversy the decision taken by the National Staff Side not to embark hastily upon a campaign for a new pay arrangement based on the cost of living was amply justified. By the second half of 1938 the cost of living had fallen from 60 to between 55 and 56. In that year the National Staff

Side decided to discharge the special committee set up in 1937 to report on what action, if any, should be taken in relation to the rise in the cost of living.

In addition to claims being pursued in conjunction with the National Staff Side, the Institution was also busy during the second half of the 1930s on a number of claims peculiar to its own members. There had rarely been a time during the first twenty years of the Institution's existence when some problem affecting draughtsmen was not under consideration. One of the earliest claims referred by the Institution in 1926 to the newly restored arbitration machinery concerned the salaries of architectural and civil engineering draughtsmen. The ensuing Industrial Court Award 1186 not only brought an increase in salary but also brought together the various departmental grades into a single service-wide structure. This was of crucial importance. The revised salaries, which had operated with effect from 1 July 1929, required urgent consideration in 1935 and a new salary claim for the grades was submitted. A satisfactory agreement was reached on new scales to operate from 10 November 1936.

Such uniformity of pay and grading did not, however, extend to mechanical, electrical engineering and shipbuilding draughtsmen. The Treasury continued to refuse to discuss a central claim for these grades and separate departmental claims had, therefore, to be submitted. The Institution tried to ensure, however, that as far as possible the claims were co-ordinated, and a series of new agreements were concluded along these lines.

By 1939, despite a large number of individual departmental settlements, the position of the specialist compared with both administrators within and professionals outside the civil service was still unsatisfactory. The salaries of the highest professional posts were still inadequate on whatever basis the computation was made. The Post Office, for example, in 1939 had to cover a field of technical activity much greater than could have been predicted at the time of the Tomlin Commission in 1931, yet a fixed salary of £2,000 p.a. attached to the post of chief engineer in 1939, £500 less than the amount recommended for the post by the Tomlin Commission before the great expansion of later years.

Following the announcement that the salaries of principal assistant secretaries and assistant secretaries were to be adjusted in accordance with the Tomlin recommendations as from 1 April 1939, the Institution wrote to the Treasury asking that effect should also be given to the recommendations of the Commission in relation to the salaries of the higher posts in the specialist area, both scientific and professional. The claim was unsuccessful.

EMPLOYMENT OF TEMPORARY TECHNICAL STAFF

When the Institution was founded in 1919 almost every specialist class had been inflated by additions of temporary staff to meet war requirements. In addition, returning ex-servicemen had to be placed in employment. While it was clear that the return of peacetime arrangements would result in many dismissals, it was equally clear that the prewar complements would be insufficient. The result was a large number of appointments classified as temporary and therefore unpensionable. The question of reorganisation was not effectively tackled, although it might have successfully been done during the shortlived postwar boom, and by 1925, despite the fact that some slight amelioration of the problem had been obtained for a number of classes, the problem of long-continued unpensionable employment remained applying to clerical and technical employment alike.

The problem was referred to the Tomlin Commission which, while refraining from specific recommendations, made the significant observation that it should be accepted policy that temporary employment in these classes should not be continued indefinitely. The Tomlin proposals, which referred only to the clerical grades, were reviewed by Joint Committee C established to consider that aspect of the Tomlin recommendations. In August 1932 the scope of established employment in the clerical and sub-clerical classes was widely extended.

The Institution, in consequence, pressed even more strongly its claim for pensionable employment for so-called temporary employees in its own area. It submitted to the Treasury a claim for temporary technical staffs to be established on the same conditions as those now granted to temporary clerical staffs. The Treasury replied that it did not consider the matter appropriate to central negotiations but asked the Institution to provide a list of those affected. This list showed that of 524 members in temporary employment 295 had served continuously for more than ten years, and 114 for more than fifteen years. Further discussions with the Treasury resulted in little progress, prompting a leader in *State Service* of February 1933 on 'The temporary staffs scandal'. It was clear, the article reported, that the Treasury regarded temporary employment for technical classes not as an aberration but as a central pillar of policy, facilitating flexibility in their deployment and enabling them to maintain a constant flow of new methods and new ideas. The Institution therefore decided to establish a special temporary technical staffs committee to consider the best way to pursue the issue. This committee decided after exhaustive consideration that the best course was to raise the question with the various departments concerned.

By April 1934, seventy-seven unestablished posts had been established and by 1936 major progress had been made. No sooner had the special committee been discharged in November 1936, however, than the problem reared its head again with a new temporary intake to meet booming war needs in 1939. On this occasion agreements were reached on a distinction between prewar scientific and technical staff, whether permanent or temporary, and similar staffs recruited as a result of war emergency. For example, in the Ministry of Supply it was decided that new staff recruited because of the war emergency would be designated experimental officers and experimental assistants in place of the normal 'Carpenter' titles.

SUPERANNUATION

Some progress was made in the 1930s in the improvement of superannuation arrangements for civil servants. From June 1935 provision was made for half the time spent in unestablished service to be reckonable for superannuation purposes. Unestablished service coming under this rule had to be continuous, whole-time, remunerated entirely out of monies provided by government and rendered after the age of 18. The Superannuation Act, 1935, also gave statutory authority for the allocation of part of a pension to secure a pension for a spouse or dependant following the death of the pensioner.

No progress, however, was made towards the Institution's aim to secure arrangements for 'added years' for pension purposes for scientists and technologists recruited at a mature age. Provision for added years had been contained in an Act of Parliament in 1859. Later official inquiries showed that the provision had led to abuses. Years could be 'added' not only for late entrants with particular professional skills but also for civil servants who were retired prematurely. The abuse had taken place mainly in premature retirement cases. A Royal Commission came down firmly against the provision of 'added years'. This has influenced official thinking on the subject right down to the present time.

ORGANISATIONAL CHANGES

With the rapid growth of the Institution in the second half of the 1930s there were a number of internal organisational difficulties and controversies. In 1935 the membership was less than 10,000. By the middle of 1939 it had grown to a figure exceeding 15,000, which represented 50 per cent of its potential membership.

Early in 1935 the Institution decided to change the designation of the two principal salaried officers. Instead of a secretary and an assistant secretary it was decided that in future there should be two officers, namely, a secretary (negotiation) and a secretary (organisation). The holder of the first post was to be the existing secretary, Mr Leese, and the holder of the second post, the existing assistant secretary, Mrs Miller. The main reason put forward for this change was that the Institution wanted to make clear what exactly were the duties of the two principal officers. Though it was unstated at the time in any of the publications of the Institution, the active membership were aware that there were differences of view between the two principal salaried officers on certain organisational questions. In addition, some of the honorary officers were concerned to ensure that their control over the Institution was not challenged by a too-powerful salaried officer. They felt that if there were two principal salaried officers of equal standing instead of one principal secretary it would be easier to maintain effective lay control.

The new system, as might well have been expected, did not work satisfactorily. Early in 1937 Mr Leese indicated to the honorary officers that in his opinion the new system of organisation, with two secretaries responsible respectively for negotiations and organisation, did not make for efficiency. He said that he was unable to work under this arrangement and he asked that his resignation should be put before the Council. The honorary officers decided that they would discuss with Mr Leese whether there was any way in which the organisational structure might be changed, on the understanding that the notice of resignation would be withdrawn while discussions were proceeding.

Mr Leese agreed to this proposal and for a number of months views were exchanged but without any firm agreement being reached. Finally the issue came before the Council. At this point Mr Leese stated that he could no longer withhold his resignation and he gave the Council the six months' notice required by his terms of service. At the same time, however, he let it be known that should his views as to the desirability of a change in the organisational structure be accepted he would be prepared to reconsider his resignation. Mr Leese argued strongly that there should be one principal salaried officer and that he should be responsible to the honorary officers and to the Council for all staff. Mrs Miller was known to favour the retention of the existing system of dual control, with certain modifications designed to meet the increasing complexity of the Institution's activities.

After prolonged discussion, including a special meeting convened for the purpose, a unanimous view did not emerge. There was, however, a majority in favour of the reintroduction of unitary control under a single secretary, although the overriding principle of control by honorary officers was to remain inviolable. At this point, after the change had been confirmed by the Council of the Institution, Mr Leese stated that he had decided not to withdraw his resignation. This was considered by a special meeting of the Council and it was decided to accept the resignation. It was agreed also that the vacant post should be advertised. It was learnt that Mr Leese was to become full-time general secretary of one of the constituent organisations of the Institution, the Society of Post Office Engineering Inspectors. In 1938 the Society gave notice to leave the Institution. Mr Leese retired from the general secretaryship of the Society in 1960.

Although Mr Leese left the Institution under a cloud, as had his predecessor Mr Weaver, he had given long and good service to the Institution. He joined the Institution in 1925 and served with Mr Menzler on the National Whitley Council through the difficult period of the General Strike. His term of office saw a huge expansion in membership which in its turn imposed an ever-increasing workload on the full-time secretary as well as on the honorary officers. The annual report on several occasions paid tribute to the work of Mr Leese; for example, it described his contribution to the Institution's evidence to the Tomlin Commission in these terms: 'his comprehensive knowledge and grasp of all matters affecting the conditions of employment of the members proved invaluable in the preparation of the Royal Commission evidence, and the Council wishes to pay its tribute to his work both in the actual preparation of the evidence and at the hearing of the Institution's witnesses by the Commission'.

He was also highly respected by his colleagues on the National Staff Side. Douglas Houghton, a contemporary on that body, said of him:

A presentable and likeable man with a *gravitas* brightened by frequent bouts of uproarious humour and laughter. He was fastidious in his use of the English language and he frequently drew attention to faults in NSS documents, being especially critical of the misspelling of the word 'judgment', and split infinitives.

He represented the Institution well and diligently: he was courageous on its behalf but never unfair. Looking back I think he held strongly but not inflexibly to the particular and difficult role in the NSS presented for him by the Council of the Institution. I liked him and he was an agreeable colleague. Considering the key position held by the Institution on the NSS for so long, the temptation to bully the Staff Side was never in evidence from Leese or anyone else.

The vacant post of secretary was advertised at a salary of £750 rising by annual increments of £25 to £900 p.a. and a minimum age of 30 years was stipulated. The successful candidate for the vacant post was Mr T. J. Hughes, an Irishman, who, after taking a BA degree at University College, Dublin, entered the British civil service in 1913 as a member of the staff of the Irish Department of the Ministry of

Labour. After the establishment of the Irish Free State Mr Hughes became a member of the Irish civil service and played an active part in staff association affairs, culminating in 1937 in his election as president of the Civil Service Alliance of Ireland. Mrs Miller was appointed deputy secretary and a Mr Engert was appointed assistant secretary.

The rapid growth of the Institution and the controversy surrounding the role of the salaried officers placed a heavy burden on the honorary officers. To accept honorary national office was, in the circumstances, to accept a very heavy workload which could not reasonably be asked of people working in their spare time. They were not only required to play a leading part in policy formation but they had to discharge administrative tasks which were now on a scale requiring full-time attention. The Institution was outgrowing its constitution. Moreover, a number of the dedicated lay members who had accepted national office were promoted to the higher grades which made full and active participation in the Institution more difficult.

One such member was Mr R. A. Watson-Watt, who first became nationally prominent in the Institution in 1929 when he was elected chairman of the Scientific Staffs Committee. He was later the Institution's principal witness before the Carpenter Committee inquiry. In 1932 he became vice-chairman of the Council of the Institution and in 1934 its chairman. Mr Watson-Watt found it necessary to give up his chairmanship of the Council shortly after he had been appointed to the post of superintendent of the new Air Ministry Research Station. Before his new appointment he had been superintendent of the radio department of the National Physical Laboratory from the time of its formation in 1933. At the 1937 annual general meeting of the Institution the president, Sir Richard Redmayne, described Mr Watson-Watt as a 'man of great and diverse qualities for whom I feel sure there is a very brilliant future . . .'. These were prophetic words. He was later to become renowned throughout the world for his pioneering contributions to the development of radar during the Second World War.

Other changes in honorary office-holders included the resignation of Mr H. W. Monroe and his replacement by Mr H. R. Lintern as honorary secretary in 1936. Mr Monroe, who was a representative of the Patent Office Examining Association, was one of the three lay members appointed to the newly created posts of honorary assistant secretary in 1927. He was responsible for the science grades and became joint honorary secretary following the retirement of Mr Menzler the following year. He became the sole honorary secretary in 1931 and one of the Institution's representatives on the National Staff Side in 1933. He served on several of its subcommittees. He continued the tradition, established by Mr Menzler, of regularly meeting members in London and the provinces. In March 1936 the Institution decided to appoint for the first time an assistant honorary secretary for women's questions. Dr S. G. Horner was elected to fill the post. At the end of 1937 the Institution lost one of its stalwarts in the resignation of Mr S. H. Bales as the honorary secretary for scientific staffs. He had been one of the original members of the National Union of Scientific Workers (later the Association of Scientific Workers) and acted as honorary secretary of the civil service section of the National Union of Scientific Workers. Following the negotiations in 1927 and 1928 between the Association of Scientific Workers and the Institution, Mr Bales became a very active member of the Institution. He did as much as anyone to improve the relationship between the two organisations.

In 1939 the Institution leased new offices on the second floor of the new Adelphi Building overlooking the Thames embankment. The opening of the new offices coincided with the decision of the Institution to extend the scope of its membership. It was agreed that laboratory assistants should be accepted as associate members.

The steady worsening of the international situation in 1939 and the danger of a new war led the Organisation Committee of the Institution to adopt a resolution stating that in the event of a national emergency the honorary officers should be given full authority 'to manage the affairs of the Institution on behalf of the Council and membership'. This resolution was unanimously adopted by the Council. The Council was very conscious of its unwieldy size and of the difficulty there would be in the event of war in convening a representative meeting. This was another example of the Institution outgrowing its constitution. It was the practice for the Council to meet approximately seven or eight times a year. It had the appearance of democracy but was becoming too large to exercise effective executive leadership.

Voices were already being raised for the introduction of a more rational structure. The danger of war and the need to provide emergency arrangements gave added weight to the call for reorganisation. The Institution had always pressed for a more closely knit and homogeneous civil service structure for professional staff and one result of such a structure would have been a considerable simplification of the Institution's working arrangements. The basis of representation on the existing Council was that all the diverse groups of professional, scientific and technical staff should have representation. At that time there were 160 representatives on the Council. At the same time all the constituent associations retained considerable autonomy. The machine was becoming increasingly unsuitable to meet the tasks facing the Institution.

THE THREAT OF FASCISM

Despite its firm commitment as a non-political association the Institution was influenced by the social and political currents of the second half of the 1930s. These found some expression within the Institution, both at meetings addressed by prominent speakers and in articles in *State Service*. In January 1939, for example, the Institution arranged a special lecture to be given by Mr Vernon Bartlett, MP, on the subject of the international situation. The chair was taken by the president of the Institution, Sir Richard Redmayne. A specially large hall was booked for the occasion and many hundreds attended. The meeting was packed to capacity.

Mr Bartlett, who was well known as a journalist of the *News Chronicle* – a liberal newspaper which was vigorous in its support of the principle of collective security and was generally sympathetic to the idea of a popular front of the centre and left against the National government – had recently been elected to Parliament in a by-election at Bridgwater, Somerset. Mr Bartlett stood as an independent progressive against the Conservative candidate and had not only won substantial support from Liberal and Labour voters but also gained the votes of many Conservatives who supported collective security and were deeply concerned at the appeasement policies of the National government. Mr Bartlett's lecture provided an extensive survey of the international scene. Extracts from it were published in the February 1939 issue of *State Service*. He said that with the abandonment of collective security, which was the basis of the League of Nations Charter, Britain had not done what ought to have been done to avoid war when Japan invaded China. The League of Nations Covenant had not been carried out and Britain's treaty obligations towards China had not been observed. The effect of Britain's attitude was to encourage Italy to intervene in Abyssinia. Mr Bartlett said that just before the invasion of Abyssinia the Italian papers were saying day after day that Britain would 'not mind because they did not mind the Japanese invading China'.

Mr Bartlett argued that the failure to defend international law had led to Italian and German intervention in the civil war in Spain. Furthermore, millions of Czechs and Slovaks had been placed under German rule as a result of the negotiations at Munich between Hitler and the British Prime Minister. He said that it would be only a matter of months before the whole of the wheat of Hungary and Romania, all the timber of the Carpathians and all the oil of Romania would be under German control.

Mr Bartlett spoke very strongly about the civil war in Spain. He referred to a recent visit which he had made there and said that he remembered many incidents that convinced him that the Spanish government was making a great effort to educate the Spanish people. The Spanish government was seeking to raise the people from a situation of poverty and misery which was a disgrace to Western Europe. He recalled that the Spanish government had been legally elected and that General Franco had taken an oath of allegiance to it. Subsequent action was clearly a case of open rebellion against a legally established government. Surely, asked Mr Bartlett, a better foreign policy for Britain would have been to afford the Spanish government its right to buy arms and to give it help in other ways. Instead the British government had adopted the policy of 'non-intervention'.

The plight of China, suffering from the invasion of the Japanese, evoked wide sympathy among the British people. In 1938 the National Staff Side decided to issue an appeal for all civil servants to contribute to funds organised by the China Campaign Committee for the alleviation of the suffering of the Chinese people. Regular weekly consignments of medical supplies were sent to China. The appeal was supported by the Institution and published in *State Service*.

CIVIL RIGHTS

In 1937 a member of the Institution, Major W. F. Vernon, who was employed on the staff of the Air Ministry, was convicted on two charges under the Official Secrets Act. There was no suggestion that Major Vernon had been engaged in any activity on behalf of a foreign power and his lawyer stated emphatically that he had not been engaged in any action of a subversive nature.

There were a number of unusual features about the case. Four men were charged with breaking into a bungalow near Farnham, Surrey, and stealing various articles including documents and papers belonging to Major Vernon. One of the defendants made a statement to the effect that the theft had been carried out with the object of showing up Major Vernon as a communist worker who had, among other things, undertaken subversive propaganda among soldiers in the Aldershot neighbourhood. On the following day the Chief Superintendent of the Royal Aircraft Establishment suspended Major Vernon.

Later Major Vernon was charged under the Official Secrets Act and the Institution put its services at his disposal and helped him in his defence. He was found guilty of having in his possession certain information 'relating to things in a prohibited place' and 'failing to take reasonable care of the information', and of retaining certain documents used in a prohibited place when he had no right to retain the documents. He was fined £50 and costs.

The National Staff Side took up the case with the Home Office and the Treasury, claiming that a line of defence appeared to have been allowed in mitigation during the trial of the four accused of burglary which implied that since Major Vernon was a member of a political party whose sympathies were broadly of the left, he could not be regarded as a faithful servant of the state and the burglary of his premises might, therefore, be judged by different standards from those normally required by the law. The letter to the Home Office continued: 'the Staff Side resent strongly the action of magistrates in permitting a line of defence which suggests publicly that, if his choice is exercised in a particular political direction, a Civil Servant is *ipso facto* disloyal to the state'.

In their letter to the Treasury the National Staff Side said: 'It may be that no political prejudice has entered into Major Vernon's suspension, but unfortunately a very large number of individuals in the Civil Service find that certain incidents in connection with the legal proceedings and elsewhere give colour to their apprehensions in the matter.' They therefore sought a statement to be issued to civil servants generally reaffirming their right, without fear of disciplinary action, to be members of any political party.

Major Vernon was subsequently dismissed from the civil service and the National Staff Side did not secure from the Official Side the clear statement on the political right of civil servants which they felt necessary. Instead a statement was made to a meeting of the National Whitley Council in December 1937 which emphasised that employment in the civil service implied a full sense of loyalty to the state. It continued that the general conception of loyalty to the state was well understood even though many of its implications were not capable of precise wording. The statement affirmed that civil servants were expected to maintain at all times a reserve in political matters and not put themselves forward prominently on one side or the other.

THE SHADOW OF WAR

With the growing threat of war the civil service unions began to give attention to the protection of civil servants as employees in the event of war. Two points were of special interest. The first was the need to protect civil servants who had to remain in London from the effect of high explosive bombs. The second was to make arrangements for the decentralisation as far as possible of the government's administration. This meant the organisation of administrative centres away from London.

In June 1938 the National Staff Side sent a deputation to the Financial Secretary to the Treasury to discuss these matters. The Staff Side pointed out that the questions they were raising affected not only civil servants but also the community at large. As employees of the state, however, they looked to their employer to take steps to provide adequate protection while they were at work.

They argued that there was no protection against high explosive bombs except by the provision of underground bomb-proof shelters, but there was no evidence that the government had any intention to provide such protection for civil servants. Most civil servants, it was argued, worked in old buildings in London which offered inadequate protection.

Mr W. J. Brown, who was a member of the Staff Side deputation, stated that it was quite clear that if the government provided bomb-proof shelters for civil servants and not for the public a situation would be created which would be indefensible. It was for that reason that it was impossible to deal adequately with air-raid precautions for civil servants without referring to the wider issue of precautions for the community at large. Mr Brown was critical of the government's lack of preparedness.

The views expressed by the National Staff Side on air-raid precautions were very close to those being publicly expounded by Professor J. B. S. Haldane. He wrote a book on the subject, entitled *ARP,* which said that the danger from air attack arose from three sources; gas bombs, incendiary bombs and high explosive bombs. The greatest danger, argued Professor Haldane, was not from poison gas but from high explosive bombs. Professor Haldane argued that the government had taken quite inadequate steps to cope with the possibility of extensive high explosive bombing. He urged that plans should be formulated for the evacuation of sections of the population and that deep underground shelters should be provided for those who had to remain for long periods of the day in the main centres of governmental, commercial and industrial activity. Professor Haldane's book was sympathetically reviewed in the October 1938 issue of *State Service.*

The Staff Side continued to press the Official Side for more effective air-raid precautions and expressed grave disquiet at the inadequacy of the government's plans. The policy of the Staff Side was summarised in three main demands. The first was to request complete information about the plans proposed by the government. The second was to press for the adoption of plans for the extensive decentralisation of staff from vulnerable centres if war should break out. The third was to urge the provision of underground bomb-proof shelters for staff who were to remain in London, and underground working accommodation for staff who would be required to remain on duty during air raids.

In response to frequent representations by the Staff Side the Official Side accepted that civil servants should be kept informed, within the limits prescribed by defence requirements, of the plans which were being made to enable the machinery of administration to continue to function during war. The Official Side also proposed to provide protection for civil servants against blast and splinter from high explosive bombs and from falling debris. It was explained that the Office of Works was surveying as rapidly as possible the buildings in which civil servants were working with a view first to selecting the accommodation which gave the greatest measure of natural protection and secondly to supplement that natural protection by the best means practicable. Basements and semi-basements would also be brought into use and would be strengthened. The National Staff Side regarded these proposals as inadequate and said they fell far short of those which had been put forward by the civil service unions.

9 The Early Years of the Second World War and a New Leadership for the Institution

With the outbreak of war in September 1939, immediate changes had to be made in the organisation of the Institution. The head office at the Adelphi in London was requisitioned and the Institution had to find temporary accommodation. A small office was found in Sutton, one of London's suburbs. In the expectation that there might be immediate heavy air raids on London all meetings were cancelled. In May 1939 the Council of the Institution had already decided that if war broke out full authority should be given to the honorary officers to manage the affairs of the Institution. The resolution, passed on 2 May 1939, stated:

> That in the event of a National Emergency arising within the next twelve months, this meeting of Council gives full authority to the honorary officers to manage the affairs of the Institution on behalf of the Council and membership, and instructs the honorary officers to do all things lawful which may be expedient to achieve the objects of the Institution as set forth in Rules 2–6 inclusive.

This provision was implemented. Economies were also introduced soon afterwards in *State Service*. The paper shortage compelled an immediate reduction in size.

NEW PROBLEMS

There was, however, no suspension of the negotiating tasks falling to the Institution. On the contrary, a whole new series of problems began to emerge almost within days of the declaration of war. A succession of Treasury statements was issued on such subjects as billeting arrangements for evacuated civil servants, the balance of civil pay for civil servants who either volunteered or were called up for the armed services, provision for civil servants who might be injured or killed in air raids, arrangements for evacuation, provision for the re-employment of civil service pensioners and for the employment of married women in the civil service, the promotion of staff to acting appointments during the period of the war, and the introduction of an earlier starting-time for civil service offices. In the closing months of 1939 and the opening weeks of 1940 further agreed arrangements were made on such matters as leave for evacuated staff, the treatment of unexpired season tickets for evacuated civil servants and payment for night work.

The Institution, together with other civil service trade unions, took the view that there were so many new issues arising and changes being introduced during the war that consultation and negotiations were essential if unnecessary difficulties were to be avoided. If the war machine was to function with as little friction as possible then Whitleyism had not only to be maintained in the civil service but strengthened. These views were put strongly to the Treasury who responded by affirming unequivocally that existing national agreements and arbitration awards would not be departed from without discussion through the appropriate central machinery. The Treasury also agreed to set up emergency standing committees of the National Whitley Council to deal with special matters arising from the war, and that new wartime departments should establish suitable Whitley machinery as soon as possible.

THE COURSE OF THE WAR

In April 1940 Germany invaded Denmark and Norway. In the months preceding this invasion Britain and France had been engaged mainly in preparing for intervention in Finland where the Finns were resisting Russian territorial demands designed to strengthen Soviet security in the Baltic against Germany. It was an odd international situation. Russia had signed a pact of non-aggression with Germany but in both Poland and Finland took territory which it argued would strengthen its defences. The potential aggressor was Germany. Britain and France were at war with Germany but the western front was quiet. Arms were being sent to Finland for her resistance to Russian demands. Later Finland was to fight on the side of Germany. This was the period when the phrase 'the phoney war' was coined. In March 1940 after a short war the Finns agreed to the Soviet demands and made peace. The British and French governments were caught unawares by the German invasion of Denmark and Norway and an attempt to resist the German occupation was defeated. One important result of the Norwegian campaign was the downfall of the British Prime Minister, Neville Chamberlain. He was replaced by Mr Winston Churchill. The new Prime Minister headed a government which included not only former supporters of the National government but also leading politicians from the Labour and Liberal parties.

In May 1940 the German armies invaded Holland and Belgium. Within days the Dutch army capitulated and only a few days later the Germans advanced well into northern France. The allied forces in Belgium were cut off. Before the end of the month the commanding officer of the British army was told that he should evacuate. In no more than a few days nearly 340,000 men were brought to England from Dunkirk. It was a great achievement in what otherwise was a disastrous phase. The collapse of France followed shortly afterwards. The ruling circles of France were rotten to the core in their so-called resistance to Hitler. Many of them were openly sympathetic to fascism and believed that it would have been far better if France had been allied with Germany in a war against Russia.

Following the invasion of the Low Countries the National Staff Side wrote to the Prime Minister affirming their loyalty and support to the state. The Staff Side said that it was their desire to use all their influence to ensure the most intensive and efficient participation by the civil service in the war effort. The new Prime Minister, Winston Churchill, replied stating that he much appreciated the message of loyalty and support received from the National Staff Side.

The Staff Side followed its message of support with an offer on behalf of the civil service to work whatever additional hours were necessary. It further offered to forgo any overtime pay until 44 hours had been worked in any week. On 25 May a statement was issued by the Treasury stating that the government had expressed appreciation of this approach by the National Staff Side and were arranging immediately to take full advantage of it. Following further discussion with the civil service unions it was agreed that the absolute minimum hours of attendance of all civil servants would be not less than 48 per week, but for the immediate future a working week of not less than 54 hours should be aimed at. It was further agreed that no payment for overtime need be made until 44 hours had been worked in any week.

The mood of civil servants was expressed in an editorial note in the June 1940 issue of *State Service*. Leisure, it said, fled the country when the Germans marched. It could only return at the cost of ceaseless effort. No man could now avoid fatigue. The note ended: 'We work to live, and the measure of our effort is the measure of our right to live.' Another article in the same issue of *State Service* struck a strongly political note. It spoke not only of the invasion of Holland and Belgium but saw these events as the culmination of previous acts of aggression including Abyssinia, Spain, China, Poland, Finland, Norway and Denmark.

One consequence of the desperate circumstances in which Britain now found itself was that civil service procedures were speeded up. This took place in response to a direct appeal from the new Prime Minister. All branches of the service were urged to take every possible step to avoid administrative delays, to accelerate decisions and to expedite executive action. Among the suggestions made were that there should be further development of oral discussion in place of written minutes with only the final conclusions being recorded. Once agreement on policy had been reached action should be taken immediately on the strength of oral instructions. These instructions were to be confirmed in writing if necessary but there was to be no delay in waiting for written instructions. The higher-grade civil servants were also urged to devolve responsibility and authority wherever possible. Where issues had to be submitted to higher authority it was suggested that an endeavour should always be made to put forward a specific recommendation rather than merely an analysis of the alternatives. Finally it was urged that the number of branches in a department or the number of officers who might be consulted on a particular question should wherever possible be reduced. They should be consulted only if they had a real interest in the question under consideration.

The effect of the war on all activities in Britain in the summer of 1940 continued to find expression inside the Institution. An editorial in the August issue of *State Service* said that life was now much fuller than a year ago. It was harsher and made more demands on citizens. Struggle, said the editorial, was a sign of life.

A Treasury ruling was issued at the time to the effect that civil servants technically qualified for work on munitions could be released, with an assurance of reinstatement and retention of superannuation rights. This was, of course, subject to the Ministry of Labour confirming that the civil servant concerned could be more usefully employed in munition work than in his civil service post. Similar provision was made for civil servants with special qualifications who volunteered for service in the merchant navy. One small practical sidelight of the changed situation was that the gardening notes in *State Service* were devoted each month to the growing of vegetables. The slogan of the day was 'Dig for victory'.

THE COST OF LIVING

The need to maintain negotiating arrangements in the civil service to meet changes in conditions as a result of war was underlined by the rapid rise in the cost of living in the closing months of 1939. At the outbreak of war the official Ministry of Labour cost-of-living index figure stood at 55. In the first month of the war it rose to 65. The National Staff Side decided in the light of this rapid increase in the cost of living to approach the Chancellor of the Exchequer with a view to inquiring how the government intended to deal with civil service pay.

At the beginning of December, by which time the cost of living index figure had risen to 73, the Chancellor of the Exchequer made a statement in the House of Commons in which he spoke of the possibility of 'fearful sacrifices', the need in a democracy for a 'willingness to sacrifice', and the impossibility of maintaining the prewar standard of living. He said that democracy could make a great contribution towards winning the war by citizens doing without rises in wages and by refraining from assuming that if costs went up remuneration must go up on a sliding scale.

The trade union movement was very much aware that sacrifices would have to be made but it was concerned that the sacrifices should be borne equally by all sections of the population and should not weigh unfairly on the working population and particularly on the lower paid. There was in existence at the time a National Joint Advisory Council to the Minister of Labour on which the TUC was represented. It was therefore possible for the trade union movement to express its views energetically and persistently to the government as to the manner in which the principle of equality of sacrifice should be observed. Unfortunately because of the 1927 Trade Disputes Act none of the civil service unions could be affiliated to the TUC and they were not therefore directly represented in the discussions on the National Joint Advisory Council.

Towards the end of 1939 the Chancellor of the Exchequer, Sir John Simon, agreed to receive a deputation from the National Staff Side to hear their views on the relationship between civil service pay and the cost of living. The meeting took place on 4 January 1940. An official statement was issued immediately afterwards which said that the National Staff Side had drawn the attention of the Chancellor to the rise in the cost of living since the beginning of the war and to the number of wage and salary increases which had taken place outside the civil service. The National Staff Side asked the Chancellor to set up a joint committee to work out a scheme of compensation to civil servants for the increase in the cost of living. The Chancellor, according to the official statement, reaffirmed the government's policy of reviewing civil service pay in the light of substantial changes in the level of remuneration outside the civil service but referred to the enormous financial strain on the country as a consequence of the war. There would be a grave danger of inflation if wages were automatically adjusted to prices. The Chancellor also said that the government was doing everything in its power to prevent unnecessary rises in prices. Finally, the Chancellor stated that he did not consider that the time had yet come to open negotiations on the question of adjusting civil service pay.

The reference in the official statement to the steps being taken by the government to prevent unnecessary rises in prices was a pointer to the introduction of a range of food subsidies. This policy had been strongly advocated by the trade union movement. By the end of the year food subsidies were running at a rate of approximately £50 million a year. They were concentrated on certain basic foods essential for working-class life and had the effect of stabilising temporarily the rise in the cost of living.

The refusal of the Chancellor of the Exchequer to set up a joint committee on pay and the cost of living was regarded as unacceptable by the civil service unions. The Institution view was that there should be some compensation for all civil servants for the rise in the cost of living but most of all for the lower-paid staff. The National Staff Side, after reviewing the results of the deputation to the Chancellor of the Exchequer, decided that a detailed claim for a cost-of-living bonus should be prepared, that a public campaign should be launched in support of the claim and that the campaign should be opened by the holding of a demonstration at Central Hall, Westminster, on Thursday 22 February 1940.

The response to the decision of the National Staff Side to launch a campaign in support of a cost-of-living claim was extremely vigorous. It soon became clear that the Central Hall would not be able to accommodate the large number of London-based civil servants who wanted to attend the demonstration. First one hall was booked for an overflow meeting and, when that seemed likely to be insufficient, another hall was booked for a second overflow meeting. More than 4,000 civil servants attended the main meeting in Central Hall and the two overflow meetings. The following resolution was unanimously adopted at all three meetings:

This meeting, representing all grades of civil servants, declares that a rise of 14 per cent in the cost of living since the outbreak of war has created a situation of great gravity for the lowest-paid staff; expresses its apprehension of the effect on the service generally of the further rises which are to be expected; repudiates the suggestion by the Chancellor of the Exchequer that the time has not yet come to consider the question of compensation in the service for the increased cost of living, although several millions of outside workers have already had increases in wages to meet it; and calls for the appointment forthwith of a joint body to negotiate a scheme of compensation for the service as a whole, with particular reference in the first place, as a matter of serious hardship and urgency, to the case of the lowest-paid officers.

In February 1940 the National Staff Side renewed their representations in favour of a joint committee to consider immediately the cost of living and the wages of civil servants. By 1 February the cost-of-living index figure had risen to 77. On 8 March 1940 the Chancellor of the Exchequer again turned down the request of the National Staff Side. His letter read as follows:

Dear Mr Day
In your letter of the 8 February you have laid before me the views of the Staff Side of the National Whitley Council on the question of the rise in the cost of living as it affects the salaries and wages of civil servants. You refer in the course of it to the deputation with which I discussed this subject on the 4 January. As you know, my reply to the deputation was that I did not think the time had come to open negotiations on the adjustment of civil service pay. Our discussions on that occasion covered much the same ground as your present

representations, and I have, therefore, had to consider whether the situation has changed so decisively as to call for a different reply.

After giving full weight to the arguments which are again put forward in your letter, and to the recorded facts as to the numbers and classes of workers who have received increases of pay since the outbreak of war – only a small proportion of whom, I may observe, can be regarded as closely comparable with civil servants – I am afraid I cannot agree with the conclusions you have reached. While the position generally has undergone some modification since I met the members of the Staff Side, there has not, I think, been any such substantial change as would justify me in modifying the views which I then expressed.

I am sorry, therefore, that I cannot agree that a case is made out for the appointment of a Joint Whitley Committee, as suggested in your letter, for the purpose of negotiating cost-of-living increases of pay for civil servants.

Yours sincerely,
(*sgd*) John Simon

8 March 1940

Despite this further rejection of the representations of the National Staff Side it soon became clear that something was going to be done about the pay of the more junior grades in the civil service. The Chancellor agreed to open discussions with the civil service unions, and on 10 May 1940 an agreement for the introduction of a civil service war bonus was concluded. The agreement provided for the payment of a war bonus from 1 February 1940 to all full-time non-industrial civil servants whose remuneration was 95s a week or less in London, 91s or less in intermediate centres and 87s or less in provincial centres. The amount of the war bonus was 1s 6d per week for staff under 18 years of age, 2s 6d per week for staff aged 18 and over but under 21, 3s per week for staff over 21 whose wage was less than 40s a week, 4s a week for staff aged 21 and over whose wage was 40s to 50s a week, and 5s a week for staff aged 21 and over whose wage was over 50s a week. The bonus was to be reckonable for overtime pay, but not for superannuation purposes. It was also agreed that the bonus would be taken into account for the purpose of calculating the balance of civil pay for civil servants serving with HM forces. There were two other important clauses to the agreement. The first said that the bonus 'shall be subject to withdrawal or modification at the conclusion of the present state of emergency'. The second said that the agreement was without prejudice to the Staff Side view that any war bonus should take the form of a percentage of the salary of each individual affected.

There were, of course, many members of the Institution whose salaries were well above the qualifying upper limit for payment. There was some criticism from these members but in general the agreement was regarded as acceptable. In particular the Institution said that it could not support in the circumstances then prevailing any claim for a cost-of-living bonus for people whose basic rate exceeded £500 per annum. An editorial article in *State Service* said that the international position of Great Britain dominated and overwhelmed the situation. Because of this situation the National Staff Side had refrained from pressing the government to extend the cost-of-living bonus to higher-paid staff.

In the summer of 1940 the cost of basic foodstuffs began to rise sharply. Between June and July there was a six-point increase in the cost-of-living index and a 10 per cent increase in the price of food. Civil service unions were concerned to do all that might be possible to assist the war effort but they could not be indifferent to the standard of life of their members. The Institution was particularly concerned about the men and women in professional, scientific and technical grades receiving between £250 and £550 a year. No compensation had been received by these civil servants towards the increase in the cost of living. Moreover, in the non-specialist grades many civil servants were receiving payment for overtime. As a result of a claim submitted in 1940 all assistant grades and the basic professional and scientific grades were receiving either overtime pay on the same basis as non-specialist staff or *ex gratia* payments, but this was by no means as comprehensive as the coverage for overtime payments in the non-specialist fields. The Institution pointed out that since the war began there had been an increase in the cost of living of some 17 per cent but that scientific, technical and professional staff receiving more that £250 a year had received no compensation at all. By the beginning of November the cost-of-living index had risen to a figure of 92 and by the beginning of 1941 to 96.

In October 1940 the National Staff Side decided to ask the Chancellor to receive a deputation to consider relating civil service wages to movements in the cost of living. The decision was criticised by the Institution. It was felt that there was very little possibility of the Staff Side achieving such a policy and that it would have been more sensible to concentrate upon securing salary increases for the higher-grade staff who so far had received nothing. The deputation was received by the Chancellor on 27 November. As the Institution expected, very little came of it. The Treasury was not prepared to relate pay to the cost of living but undertook to examine the points put by the deputation.

The circumstances were not favourable for a major move forward on salaries and this was well understood by the civil service unions. In September the heavy bombing of London had started and this had an extremely disruptive effect on working arrangements. Following discussions with the National Staff Side, the Treasury introduced new regulations for the attendance of staff during the winter months. Under the new arrangements a proportion of the staff were expected to work an 11-hour day and to sleep in the office during the night. They were then available for an early shift the next morning, finishing in the early afternoon. Office shelters with tiered bunks were provided by the Office of Works and blankets and mattresses were made available. Boxing Day was cancelled as a public holiday and in the spring this was followed by the cancellation of Good Friday.

Negotiations for a new cost-of-living agreement were continued during the opening weeks of 1941. No agreement was reached but the government decided to introduce certain improvements from 1 March 1941 by administrative action. For civil servants under 18 the bonus was increased from 1s 6d per week to 3s per week; for civil servants aged 18 and over but under 21 from 2s 6d to 5s; for staff aged 21 and over with remuneration of £250 per annum from 5s per week to 10s per week for men and 7s 6d per week for women. For staff earning over £250 but under £350 a new bonus payment of 5s per week was introduced for men but for women staff receiving over £250 but less than £300 the new bonus was to be only 4s per week.

The Institution was very critical of the new cost-of-living payments. The particular points of criticism were that there was still no payment for men receiving more than £350 per annum and for women receiving more than £300 per annum. In addition there was a significant departure from the principle of equal benefit to men and women embodied in the May 1940 cost-of-living bonus agreement. Sex-differentiated pay had now been introduced in relation to cost-of-living payments.

The National Staff Side decided to submit their case to arbitration, challenging the government decision on two issues. The first was on the differentiation between the amounts of bonus payable to men and women and the second on the different ceiling for the two sexes. The terms of reference submitted to the arbitration tribunal were that all civil servants of 21 years of age and over employed full-time whose remuneration did not exceed £150 per annum should receive a cost-of-living bonus of 10s per week. The award, which was made in September 1941, represented some improvement on the amount originally offered by the Treasury. The tribunal took the view that the maximum amount of pay up to which bonus should be payable should be the same for men and women but it retained the ceiling at £500 per year. The tribunal found against the Staff Side on the issue of the bonus differential between men and women civil servants. It confirmed this differential on the argument that this reflected the general trend in employment outside the civil service.

For lower-paid civil servants average earnings increased during this period because of the amount of overtime being worked. In June 1941, for example, the Treasury issued a circular stating that there should be an average 51-hour working week in government departments. The Treasury also decided that annual leave for civil servants should be reduced to one week for the year 1941. The Staff Side made representations about this drastic reduction in annual leave and suggested that an annual leave period of two weeks might contribute to greater productivity. The government rejected this suggestion but said it would keep the decision under review. Later it was announced that from 1942 a period of two weeks could be granted, plus an additional maximum of four separate days.

The following year the National Staff Side were more successful in their representations for an increase in war bonus. The 1942 agreement provided increases in war bonus for all civil servants with an annual salary up to and including £500. The bonus payable for staff under 18 years of age was increased to 4s a week, and for staff aged 18 and over but under 21 to 6s 6d a week. For staff over 21 the bonus payable to men receiving up to and including £250 per annum was increased to 13s 6d a week and to women 10s a week. For staff with salaries over £250 per annum and up to and including £500 the bonus was increased to 7s 6d a week for men and 6s a week for women. The bonus was to continue to be reckonable for the purpose of the balance of civil pay for civil servants in the armed forces and for the calculation of overtime pay. The increased bonus took effect from 1 June 1942.

TURMOIL WITHIN THE INSTITUTION

The 1940 annual general meeting of the Institution marked the twenty-first anniversary of the formation of the Institution. It also marked the twenty-first anniversary of the presidency of Sir Richard Redmayne. Though now 74 years of age he was still active in the affairs of the Institution. The AGM also marked, however, the first rumblings of discontent at the absence of democratic control within the Institution. There had been no meeting of the Council since the outbreak of war. This was in accordance with the terms of the resolution adopted by the Council in 1938 at the time of the Munich crisis and reaffirmed some six months later in the spring of 1939.

The annual report was moved at the meeting by Mr G. L. Pepler, the chairman of the Council, who said that the question of broadening the basis of responsibility for the carrying on of the Institution during the war was still an open one. He added that the honorary officers intended to confer together with a view to devising a scheme by which more members could be brought into participation. This issue was taken up strongly by a representative of the Estate Duty Office, Mr Leslie Herbert. He urged that it was the right and duty of all to collaborate in the work of the Institution and argued that there should be more democratic control of Institution affairs.

Following the AGM the Institution's solicitors expressed the opinion that the action of the Council in delegating its authority to the honorary officers had been *ultra vires*. To legalise the existing arrangements or to make other arrangements for the delegation of authority it would be necessary for the Council to meet and to submit to a special general meeting amendments to rules on the lines which the solicitors had drafted. Arrangements were made to convene a Council meeting in July 1940 but with the invasion and collapse of Norway, Holland, Belgium and France the war situation had become critical and the National Staff Side had advised their constituents to cancel or postpone meetings or conferences which were not absolutely essential. In these circumstances the solicitors were of the opinion that the honorary officers would be justified in continuing with the existing arrangements and postponing the proposed meeting until a more favourable time. Moreover, only 69 out of the total 129 constituent associations had so far appointed representatives to the Council and the meeting was therefore likely to be unrepresentative.

In the meantime correspondence had been received from the Estate Duty Office Association (EDOA) objecting to the action of the honorary officers in calling a Council meeting without first circulating an agreed statement setting out the views of the EDOA and the Association of Civil Service Designers and Draughtsmen (ACSDD) and of the honorary officers to enable associations to instruct their representatives before attending the meeting. The honorary officers, however, considered that there would be little purpose in circulating such a statement.

In February 1941 the honorary officers finally issued a circular to constituent associations containing a summary of the views of the EDOA and the ACSDD. The latter, dissatisfied with the actions of the honorary officers and with what they considered to be a misrepresentation of their views within the circular, issued a joint letter to all associations setting out their views about the need for greater democratic control within the Institution. Part of their letter included two proposals which they put forward for discussion among constituent associations.

Firstly, the Associations of which the Institution is comprised must have decisive control of policy. A small group of honorary officers is not reasonably representative of the great variety of interests within the Institution, and with all the good will in the world, cannot remain in contact with the views of the many associations or the interests of the many grades of the membership. In the present crisis, when this country is at war to defend democracy as something of itself worth defending, every effort must be made to keep fully intact the democratic machinery of our own organisation. In fact, the Institution is of little value, and, in the long run, cannot survive, unless it is democratically controlled and fully representative of the membership.

Secondly, the method by which this control of policy is secured must be simple, expeditious and efficient. Frequent meetings of a sovereign body such as Council consisting of over 100 members are impossible. The most likely solution would seem to be on the lines of a Council drastically reduced in size, composed of representatives appointed by the Associations, with direct reponsibility to make decisions on matters of policy in accordance with instructions from the Associations they represent. Most organisations of a similar character are governed by an Executive Committee elected on such a basis and have retained this form of control unimpaired since the war. If this suggestion meets with general approval, we would be prepared to submit detailed plans which have already been worked out and which can no doubt be improved in the light of suggestions put forward by other Associations.

The letter asked associations to submit their views and was signed by D. Manktelow, general secretary of the ACSDD, and F. Schaffer, honorary secretary of the EDOA. Prominent among those campaigning for a reform of the Institution in addition to the two signatories were L. A. C. Herbert of the EDOA and Reg Bartlett and A. M. Gunner of the Admiralty Association of Scientific and Technical Officers.

The president, Sir Richard Redmayne, when opening the 1941 AGM explained that after the business on the agenda had been dealt with a statement would be made on behalf of the honorary officers as to the reasons why the resolutions in question had not been placed on the agenda. He also said that an opportunity would be given to all concerned to comment on this decision. The EDOA then moved that the resolutions be put on the agenda. The president refused to accept the motion and a further motion was then moved that the chairman should leave the chair. The president declared the interrupter out of order and within five minutes the meeting had been abandoned. The president and honorary officers then left the hall. The meeting, which was the best attended of any general meeting in the history of the Institution, then proceeded to elect its own chairman and to discuss and pass the following resolutions:

(*a*) That this meeting of members and associate members of the Institution of Professional Civil Servants resolves that the resolutions recently submitted to the Institution by the Estate Duty Office Association for inclusion on the Agenda of the Annual General Meeting of 29 April 1941, and refused by the honorary officers, be placed on the Agenda of the adjourned Annual General Meeting.

(*b*) That adequate arrangements be made for notice to be given of the date of the adjourned Annual General Meeting and for the circulation of the views of the mover of the above resolutions prior to this meeting.

(*c*) Further that the adjourned Annual General Meeting be called for a date not later than five weeks from 29 April 1941.

The resolutions were forwarded to the honorary officers who decided that, since the meeting had no constitutional standing, no action should be taken on the resolutions.

The events at the annual general meeting led to the publication of a bitter editorial in the May 1941 issue of *State Service*. With the heading 'Crisis' it said that the Institution now had within it 'greater possibilities of dynamite and destruction than at any other time'. The editorial hinted strongly that the criticism which had been voiced was politically motivated and said that the Institution had maintained complete aloofness from the political arena. This, it said, reflected the views of the bulk of the membership. Critics, it went on, 'may call our civil service outlook a good many things; bourgeois, lethargic, conservative and reactionary . . . but the fact remains that our friends and foes alike have known where to find us and what to expect from us'. The editorial maintained that the criticism of the honorary officers was not general but had been developed by a persistent and vocal group whose spirit was 'indistinguishable from plain hostility to the honorary officers'. The editorial concluded with the warning that 'if a section of the membership persists in methods of thought and action which must result in the Institution ceasing to remain the professional body envisaged by its founders there must be a re-examination of membership and, if necessary, a parting of the ways'. The final sentence of the editorial said: 'The Institution serves the state; if there be any who are not prepared to accept that as the first and guiding principle of all our actions, let them go elsewhere.'

The critics responded vigorously to the charge made against them. The real issue, they said, was not their political opinions but the democracy of the Institution and the participation of the membership. If their political opinions led them to believe that democracy should prevail in the Institution and that the structure should be such as to encourage and not discourage maximum participation, then this reflected credit and not discredit on their individual political views. They pointed out that the demand for greater democracy and participation was not confined to members who held socialist or communist opinions.

A NEW LEADERSHIP EMERGES

The uproar at the annual general meeting prompted the honorary officers to call an early meeting of the Council. This was convened for 27 May 1941. The honorary officers, believing that they represented the majority of members, urged all constituent associations to be represented. In the May 1941 issue of *State Service* the honorary officers indicated that they 'will feel compelled to consider offering themselves for election. If all of them were to retire, it would indicate either that all were simultaneously overwhelmed with work or that they had developed communal cold feet.'

The meeting of the Council – the first to be held during the war – began in the Caxton Hall, Westminster at 2.30 p.m. on 27 May 1941. The meeting was crowded and the atmosphere tense. It was a lengthy meeting and did not end until 8 p.m. The election of honorary officers was deferred to enable discussion to take place on the motions submitted for the agenda put forward by the officers on the one hand and by the EDOA on the other. It soon became clear that the honorary officers had misjudged the volume of support for change in the Institution.

A resolution was adopted stating that control of the Institution's affairs by the honorary officers was not in the best interests of the Institution. The emergency resolution passed by the Council on 2 May 1939 and presented for endorsement by the honorary officers was accordingly rescinded. A further resolution said that the existing constitution of the Institution was not suited to wartime conditions and that for the duration of the war the affairs of the Institution should be managed by a representative emergency executive committee consisting of approximately twenty-five members. This was passed in preference to the honorary officers' suggestion that there should be an emergency committee of not less than five nor more than fifteen of whom at least two-thirds should be full members and the remainder associate members.

A third resolution adopted by the meeting of the Council set up a drafting committee of fifteen members, in addition to the chairman of the Council, who would be responsible for preparing a draft scheme for an emergency executive committee. The drafting committee included L. A. C. Herbert, Estate Duty Office Association; J. J. Jeffcock, Civil Aviation Telecommunications Branch; H. J. Curnow, Aeronautical Inspection Directorate Technical Staff; G. E. Carr, Society of Post Office Engineers; S. T. Brooks, Association of Civil Service Designers and Draughtsmen; V. Stott, National Physical Laboratory Scientific Staff Association; A. Liddle, Association of Scientific and Technical Assistants, Ministry of Supply; H. W. Monroe, Patent Office Examining Staff Association; L. Lanham, Association of Value Office Valuers; L. Bowen, Aeronautical Engineering Branch; F. M. Dean, Meteorological Office Branch; W. E. R. Wood, Association of Estate Surveyors, Ministry of Works and Buildings; H. Whittaker, Research Department Woolwich, Association of Scientific Officers; E. W. J. Mardles, Association of Scientific and Technical Officers, Royal Aircraft Establishment; and J. Fraser, Association of Civil Service Designers and Draughtsmen. It was agreed that the drafting committee should submit its proposals to each constituent association and that eventually the proposals should be submitted to a meeting of the Council and to a special general meeting of the membership.

The outcome of the meeting was undoubtedly a substantial victory for the critics. This victory was carried a stage further when in the June 1941 issue of *State Service* the honorary officers stated that the membership should regard as withdrawn the leading article which had appeared in the previous issue. This was the article headed 'Crisis' which hinted strongly that the call for more democratic participation was politically motivated by members with strongly left-wing opinions.

By the autumn of 1941 the drafting committee had completed its work. The proposals were circulated to constituent associations for comment and subsequently some amendments were made to the preliminary draft. Revised proposals were submitted to a special meeting of the Council of the Institution held on 15 November 1941. The proposals of the drafting committee were adopted by the special meeting with only minor amendments. The scheme provided for an emergency executive committee of twenty-five members. Each of the ten largest constituent associations was to be entitled to appoint one member to the executive committee. The remaining associations were to be divided into groups according to the profession represented. These were to be represented on the emergency executive committee roughly in proportion to their respective memberships (see Table 1). Provision was made for the election of representatives in the groups where there were more nominations than seats available.

Table 1 *Allocation of Seats on the Emergency Executive Committee*

Group	No. of Associations in Group	No. of Members in Group	Seats Allocated to Members	No. of Associates in Group	Seats Allocated to the Representation of Associates
1 Professional (General)	11	406	1	19	—
2 Architectural and Building	15	1,718	3	541	1
3 Engineers	18	875	2	614	1
4 Scientific	47	2,014	3	1,267	2
5 Inspectorates	11	671	1	279	—
6 Drawing Offices	8	58	—	698	1

The next step was to secure the endorsement of these changes by a special general meeting. On December 20 1941 a special meeting was convened, followed on the same day by the adjourned annual general meeting and a Council meeting. Full support was given to the changes in the structure of the Institution. The lead was once again taken by Mr Leslie Herbert of the EDOA.

The members of the newly elected Emergency Executive Committee were G. L. Pepler (chairman), G. C. Aubrey, H. Arram, S. W. Barker, I. Bowen, D. Briers-Hutchinson, S. T. Brookes, G. E. Carr, L. S. Cheeseright, A. E. Cotton, F. M. Dean, K. Ebbutt, P. D. Fairchild, J. Fraser, A. M. Gunner, L. A. C. Herbert, H. K. Kennedy, L. Lanham, J. H. Little, H. W. Monroe, S. W. Scott, V. Stott, J. C. Thomas, F. R. Thorpe and W. E. R. Wood. The first meeting of the Emergency Executive Committee took place on 19 January 1942. Subcommittees were set up to deal with finance and membership, salaries and grading, and the journal. The way was now clear for the operation of the new arrangements. The Institution had survived a period of turmoil and the old had given way to the new.

The opening of the new period was marked by an article in the March/April issue of *State Service* by Mr Menzler, the elder statesman of the Institution, on the problems and opportunities facing the new executive. He acknowledged that the successes and failures of the past needed scrutiny in the light of new conditions, but 'nevertheless, those who in 1942 feel the constructive urge would do well not to assume that nothing has ever been done in the past'. The new influential members of the Institution would be well advised, as preparation for endeavouring to formulate the 'New Institution Policy', to undertake a certain amount of research into the achievements as well as the failures of the past. He was under no illusions concerning the massive problems which would be faced in reconstruction after the war. 'After the war the central government, which means the civil service, will be faced with major and novel problems of administration, for the handling of which present traditional service methods and outlook require modernisation while, at the same time, the specialist classes must be enabled to make their full contribution, if an ordered social environment is to emerge and survive.'

In the same issue there was an article by the most influential of the new men who had been elected to lead the Institution, Mr Leslie Herbert. The article was published under the title 'What the Institution means to me'. Mr Herbert argued that the main function of the Institution was to protect its members' interests and to act as a medium through which the members could help to increase the efficiency of the state they served. He said that the cost of living was certain to be constantly in the news. He called also for an increase in membership, an expansion and reorganisation of the permanent staff, a less cumbersome structure in the Institution, a tightening-up of subscription payments, the elimination of the existing chaotic jumble of grades and the amalgamation of all associations covering similar grades.

Mr Herbert referred also to the 1927 Trade Disputes Act and made it clear that in his view Section 5, which prohibited the affiliation of civil service unions to the TUC, should be repealed. He pointed out that in relation to the pay of civil servants the government took the view that civil service remuneration must be related to wage trends in industry. This doctrine, he argued, if accepted, would put the civil servant in the position of trailing along behind all other employees. It was all the more reason for the maximum contact with the outside world. Clearly Mr Herbert's view of the role of the Institution was that it should act as a trade union and that it should acknowledge itself as such. The significance of the changes in the Institution were further marked by an editorial in the May 1942 issue of *State Service* under the title 'A new era'. Clearly, the new leadership was seen as the agent of change.

10 The War Effort and a New Social Role and Structure for the Institution, 1942–5

In 1941 the war took a dramatic turn. In the summer Germany invaded the USSR and in December the Japanese attacked the American fleet at Pearl Harbour, bringing the USA into the war. The year 1942 thus opened with the existence of a new and powerful anti-fascist alliance. These changes in the course of the war sharpened significantly the activity of the Institution on the role of scientists in the war effort and on related problems.

SCIENCE AND THE WAR EFFORT

The Second like the First World War brought about a massive increase in the specialist classes, from between 8,000 and 9,000 in 1939 to about 70,000–80,000 in 1945, while the size of the civil service as a whole doubled.

> In Britain the government reluctantly admitted the facts of life and felt itself bound to utilise any scientific straw floating on the waters. It did so tardily, and was saved only by the narrow margin of charmed muddling through. But just in time it undammed the tide which was to sweep the new experts into power, the 'boffins', who were able to combine scientific experience with a clear knowledge of operational needs. (Clark, 1962, p. 4)

All scientists within and outside the civil service were mobilised to cope with the problems of defence. Before the war Sir Henry Tizard was consulted by the Air Council; in its early stages Winston Churchill brought in Professor Lindemann, later Lord Cherwell, from Cambridge, as a private scientific adviser. When Churchill became Prime Minister, Cherwell was at his side. The armed services adopted scientific advisers such as P. M. S. Blackett and J. D. Bernal who worked alongside the controllers of operations, not only doing the necessary research but also becoming an integral part of the policy-making machine.

Towards the end of 1940 a new Scientific Advisory Committee composed of eminent scientists was established, directly responsible to the Lord President of the Council and the Cabinet. It included Lord Hanley (Chancellor of the Duchy of Lancaster), chairman; Sir William Bragg, president of the Royal Society; Dr E. V. Appleton, secretary of the Department of Scientific and Industrial Research; Sir Edward Mellanby, secretary of the Medical Research Council; Professor A. V. Hill, MP, physical secretary of the Royal Society; Sir Edwin Butler, secretary of the Agricultural Research Council; Professor A. C. Egerton, biological secretary of the Royal Society. Its terms of reference were:

> To advise the Lord President on any scientific problem referred to them; to

advise government departments on the selection of individuals for particular
lines of scientific inquiry or for membership of committees on which scientists
are required; and to bring to the notice of the Lord President promising new
scientific or technical developments which may be of importance to the war
effort.

The Institution welcomed this recognition of the major role which should be
played by the specialist in the war effort. A later editorial in *State Service* praised
the role of Robert Watson-Watt in extending this recognition.

The traditional treatment of the scientist in the civil service was to keep him on
tap in the background, to pick his brains up to the point where his advice
coincided with the wishes of the inquirer, and to offer him a local habitation
and a name, but the minimum of publicity and influence.

Once or twice an exceptional administrator or an exceptional scientist has
broken the stranglehold of tradition, but it has been left to Lord Beaverbrook,
on the one side, and Watson-Watt, on the other, to go the limit.

Robert Watson-Watt led the team which discovered radar, the weapon without
which Fighter Command would assuredly have been unable to win the Battle of
Britain.

While appreciating the role of such eminent scientists, however, the Institution, together with the AScW, conducted a campaign to attract public attention to
the part which could and should be played by science and scientists as a whole in
the war effort. The basis for co-operation between the Institution and the AScW
was laid by a working agreement signed in the summer of 1942 in which the
Institution acknowledged the Association's interest in wartime temporary staff in
the civil service and endorsed its public activities on the role of scientists in
society. In return, the Association recognised the institution as the one proper
negotiating body for scientific and technical staffs in the civil service. The
agreement was to be renewed at six monthly intervals. The AScW appointed a
representative to the Institution's Scientific Staffs Sub-Committee and Mr V.
Stott was appointed to serve as the Institution's representative on the corresponding committee of the AScW.

Leslie Herbert, the most prominent member of the new leadership in the
Institution, gave strong personal support to the campaign to underline the social
role of scientists. In an article in the July 1942 issue of *State Service* he called for
the full use of scientific power in the interests of the war effort. Strategy, he said,
could not operate in a vacuum. The closely related problems of manpower and
production would have a decisive influence on the course of the war. He pointed
out that it was now part of the strategy of the nation to open a second front in 1942.
This would be successful in proportion to the extent to which manpower was
harnessed to production. Mr Herbert's comment on the opening of a second front
referred to an agreement between Britain and the Soviet Union published in the
early summer of 1942. In this agreement Britain had undertaken to open a second
front in Europe in 1942 to assist the Red Army which in Russia was resisting the
onslaught of the Nazi war machine.

In the August 1942 issue of *State Service,* however, an editorial note suggested
that it would be out of keeping for the Institution to join in the popular clamour

for the opening of a second front in Europe. This aroused some criticism inside the Institution and letters were published in the recently established regular correspondence column arguing that scientists should not withhold their contribution from the discussion of major problems concerning the conduct of the war. A number of correspondents urged that a second front should be opened in Europe as the most effective way to bring about the defeat of German fascism. *State Service* returned to the subject of the second front in an editorial in the October 1942 issue. It said that it would be a pity if any misunderstanding of the position should arise. It was a very proper assumption, it said, that there was no need to stress the necessity of a second front. What was needed was blood, toil and sweat to make a second front possible. It ended: 'there can be no doubt about the need for a second front, there is doubt about the sufficiency of the means to mount it. A successful second front is the first necessity for the United Nations.'

Much of the correspondence and debate within *State Service* and the Institution at large concerned the problems of the utilisation of manpower in the war. Correspondents urged there should be more effective state planning. This demand for the effective use of manpower also found expression in a resolution adopted by the Emergency Executive Committee at a meeting in August 1942. The resolution said:

Realising the gravity of the present war situation to be such that the future outcome of the war may be decided in the next few months [the Executive Committee] considers that the Institution would be failing in its duty to the state if it did not emphasise now the need for manpower within the grades covered by the Institution's membership.

The Emergency Executive Committee urged all branches of the Institution to give these matters first priority in their day-to-day activities and called upon individual members to intensify their efforts in this direction. The resolution was adopted unanimously.

The Institution, in co-operation with the AScW, also organised a very successful meeting at the National Physical Laboratory to discuss the relationship of scientists to the war effort. The main address at this meeting was given by Professor J. D. Bernal. In it he said that the full effects of science on war could not be felt unless the scientific mind could be brought to bear on the war as a whole. This was not only a matter for 'higher-ups'; every scientific worker now had a widened social responsibility. Strong interest was also shown in the role of scientists in the USSR. In an article in the November 1942 issue of *State Service*, the Cambridge scientist J. G. Crowther explained that in the USSR scientific development was planned in a characteristically socialist manner. Planning was based on a general review of the needs and resources of the state.

In November a resolution received from the Woolwich branch of the ACSDD, and then endorsed by the executive committee of the Association, called for close bonds of friendship between the Institution and parallel organisations in the allied countries, particularly in the USSR and the USA. This was considered by the Emergency Executive Committee of the Institution and endorsed. The outcome of this resolution was that the Institution convened a meeting of allied scientists. It took place on 19 October 1943 and was addressed by Sir Stafford Cripps on behalf of the government.

The Institution also did much inside the civil service to stimulate the effective utilisation of scientific manpower. It was in the spring of 1942 that the Institution gave special attention to the question. Reports were called for from various groups of members and they were asked to classify the main problems which they had to face. These problems were then separated into various groups. Some were dealt with by local action, others by departmental action and others by central discussion within the National Whitley machinery. A report on these activities was given in the January 1943 issue of *State Service*.

As part of their growing involvement in the wider issues of science and its social responsibilities the Emergency Executive Committee in 1942 decided to rejoin the Parliamentary and Scientific Committee. The Institution had already been represented on the Parliamentary Committee of the British Science Guild which had merged in 1933 with the Parliamentary Science Committee initiated by the AScW in 1929, to form a combined Parliamentary Science Committee. At the time of the merged committee's inception the affiliated bodies were the Royal Institute of British Architects, the Institution, the British Science Guild, the Society of Engineers, the Institution of Mechanical Engineers, the Institute of Metals, the Institution of Naval Architects, the Joint Council of Qualified Opticians, the Oil and Colour Chemists' Association, the Pharmaceutical Society, the Institute of Physics, the AScW and the South Eastern Union of Scientific Societies. This committee suspended its activities at the outbreak of war and was replaced in November 1939 by a new Parliamentary and Scientific Committee with similar aims. These were:

(1) To provide members of Parliament with authoritative scientific information from time to time in connection with debates.
(2) To arrange for questions to be put in Parliament and other suitable action to be taken to ensure that proper regard is had for the scientific point of view.
(3) To examine all legislation with the above objects in mind and take such action as may be suitable.
(4) To watch in particular, the financing of scientific research from public funds, that such research is administered by persons of adequate scientific qualifications and that scientific and technical workers employed by the state and public bodies shall have adequate opportunities for advancement.
(5) To provide its members with a regular summary of scientific matters dealt with in Parliament.

TOWARDS VICTORY

By the summer of 1943 it had become clear that the early predictions of the collapse of the Soviet Union in face of the massive assault from the German war machine were to be proved false. The German advance was halted in front of Leningrad, Moscow and Stalingrad. It was, perhaps, the defence of Stalingrad which most captured the imagination of the British public. The Institution agreed to be represented at an Anglo-Soviet demonstration and it was decided that Leslie Herbert should be one of the speakers. In July 1943 a meeting of British scientists decided to show their appreciation of the Soviet defence of Stalingrad by donating a complete laboratory to a new Stalingrad hospital. The chair at the meeting was taken by Sir Robert Watson-Watt. The Institution agreed to participate in collecting funds for the hospital laboratory. By the spring of 1944 over £5,500 had been raised for the laboratory by the Joint Committee for Soviet Aid. Of this sum more than £1,300 was contributed by Institution members. From a membership of just under 30,000 this was a remarkable achievement.

With the possibility of victory thoughts were turning towards the shape of the postwar world. In February 1945 the AScW convened a two-day conference to discuss the subject of science in peace. Scientists from France and the Soviet Union were present and representatives of many scientific professional and trade union bodies, including the Institution, sent representatives. The proceedings of the conference were summed up by Professor Bernal who said that there would be no future for science except in an economy of growth and that an expansionist economy implied full employment. The economic practice of restriction and wage-cutting, he said, should give place to the expansion of production and improved standards of living. At the end of the conference a resolution was carried, with the support of the representatives of the Institution, which called for a progressive rise in living standards, an expansionist economic policy and the advance and efficient application of science under a central research and development council. The resolution also said that there should be close collaboration between organised scientists and the rest of the trade union movement, and that close collaboration must be maintained between the scientists of Great Britain, the USSR, France and the USA.

The Institution had also already been turning its attention to postwar problems for itself. Mr Menzler, in an article in the January 1943 *State Service* entitled 'Time presses', advocated the establishment of a 'reconstruction committee' to consider how to continue the prewar campaign for reform of the civil service to give a greater role to the specialist and secure equality of treatment in terms of pay, grading and other conditions of employment with other civil service classes. This article ended with a plea for quick and determined action.

The Institution, with its rapidly growing membership, has a great opportunity of making a distinctive contribution towards the drastic reconstruction of the Service, which is inevitable. All national institutions are in the melting pot and radical changes in service organisation, methods and outlook will have to be faced. Those who contend that scientific and technical knowledge and experience could be more effectively utilised in the general interest now have their opportunity, but the time is getting very short. The days are gone when these matters could be solemnly considered with all the dilatoriness associated with a Royal Commission, whose report might be ignored or, at the best, take years for its detailed recommendations to be applied. Postwar resettlement is going to present problems on such a scale and of such an urgency that the reorganisation of the service can hardly await even the termination of hostilities. The Institution must make up its mind about matters of principle well before the end of this year.

An article in similar vein by W. E. R. Wood, chairman of the Salaries and Grading Committee, appeared in the February issue. At its February meeting the Emergency Executive Committee decided to establish a Policy and Organisation Committee to consider these issues.

Consideration of the longer-term structure of the civil service as a whole had already begun in 1942 when the Sixteenth Report of the Select Committee on National Expenditure recommended, among other things, a staff college for the civil service and higher pay for temporary technical personnel. On the first point the Institution urged that there should be a scientist or professional man on the committee appointed by the Chancellor to consider this question. The Institution submitted its own memorandum to the Chancellor's committee and another one to the Parliamentary and Scientific Committee with special reference to the training of scientists in government service. The report of the Chancellor's committee on training in 1944, however, failed to deal with specialist training and the Institution advocated the establishment of a further committee to examine the general question of the training of scientific, technical and professional civil servants.

On salaries of technical officers the select committee emphasised that it was important that the civil service should pay adequate salaries to technical officers and that it was 'fundamental that there should be a reasonable relation between the salaries paid by government and industrial firms'. The committee pointed out that appointments made in wartime to the civil service were temporary and did not carry pension rights. It went on to say that persons who had proved themselves qualified to hold such temporary posts should receive rates of pay at least as high as those of established officers of equal rank. Following the publication of this report the Institution wrote to the Treasury expressing its support for the views of the select committee. It urged that technical officers should receive higher pay and that persons appointed to temporary posts should receive not less than staff in established posts. Further support for these views was also expressed in the House of Commons by Mr W. J. Brown, who was now an independent member of Parliament.

The Treasury replied to the Institution in March 1943. It rejected the view that in every case the range of salary payable to temporary officers should be identical with the permanent scales but accepted that the work of the wartime civil service should not suffer by reason of salaries insufficient to attract and retain competent staff. It said it had no evidence to show that in general the ranges of pay in force were inadequate to secure a reasonable proportion of the available supply of technical and professional staff. The Treasury agreed to send copies of the correspondence to the principal departments concerned, who, it said, would 'not hesitate to bring to the attention of the Treasury any cases in which recruitment can be improved without doing violence to general principles'.

Towards the end of 1942 the Institution was informed that an informal committee headed by Sir Alan Barlow, chairman of the National Whitley Council, had been established to consider what steps were necessary to make appointments to the scientific officer grades attractive to the best men leaving the universities and to secure their retention in the service. The Institution was invited to submit a memorandum. In March 1944 the Treasury invited the Institution to meet it for exploratory discussions on the postwar reorganisation of the professional, scientific and technical classes. The Institution chairman expressed the view that discussions prior to representations under the aegis of the National Whitley Council's Committee on Postwar Organisation would be very advantageous, and the Executive Committee appointed a small team of Institution representatives. It was agreed that the informal discussions with the

Treasury should be within the framework of the proposals endorsed by a special conference on postwar reconstruction held that month. From the latter had emerged suggestions for a three-class structure containing two grades each. These were a principal, an executive class (executive and assistant executive) and an ancillary class (assistants I and II); each grade title to be accompanied by the name of the discipline, e.g. chemist, engineer. It was agreed that at an appropriate stage the informal Postwar Organisation Committee of the National Staff Side should be involved.

The Institution also played its part in the general postwar reconstruction of the civil service. Leslie Herbert was a member of the Postwar Organisation (informal) and the Postwar Staffing (formal) Committee of the National Staff Side dealing with the immediate postwar staffing of the civil service. The first result of the negotiations of the formal committee was the government White Paper *Recruitment to Established Posts in the Civil Service during the Reconstruction Period*. The Institution was also represented by Leslie Herbert on the Committee of the Staff Side established later in 1944 to consider the postwar structure of the civil service.

WAR BONUS

In the summer of 1943 a new agreement was concluded between the Treasury and the National Staff Side for improved rates of war bonus to be payable from 1 June 1943. For the first time a bonus was payable to officers on salaries up to £850 a year. The bonus payment was regarded as inadequate by the National Staff Side who argued that it compared unfavourably with war bonuses granted in industry.

As a result of the strong representations made by the National Staff Side, and the increasing evidence that war bonus payments in the civil service were falling well behind those paid in industry, the Treasury agreed to introduce a higher rate of war bonus payment from 1 November 1943. The new payment was 19s a week for all men over 21 years of age with salaries up to £850 per year. The payment for women over 21 years of age was 15s 6d per week with a retainer up to £850. There was a proportionate scale of increases for men and women under 21.

The civil service unions welcomed the new war bonus payment, which had been introduced very largely as a result of their constant representations, and drew the attention of their members to two of its special features. The new agreement provided, for the first time since the war began, for a flat rate of war bonus for everyone over the age of 21 with a salary up to £850 per annum. Secondly, the new agreement had been concluded only a few months after the last agreement. This, the unions felt, was a vindication of the earlier protests they had made.

Early in 1944 further important gains were made. The Treasury agreed to accept the claim of the National Staff Side that war bonus should be regarded as part of pensionable pay. This was followed up by the Institution with an agreement applying pensionability of bonus to the special conditions of FSSU staffs. The ceiling for the payment of bonus was raised from £850 to £1000 with effect from 1 February 1944. A Bill was also introduced into Parliament providing for increased pensions for retired civil servants. It became law in the spring of 1944 and was made retrospective to 1 January of the same year. The increase in pensions was welcomed by the civil service unions but they regarded as obnoxious the introduction of a means test for pension increases.

A further general increase in war bonus was introduced on 1 November 1944 as a result of an agreement between the Treasury and the National Staff Side. The salary ceiling for the payment of war bonus was increased from £1,000 to £1,500. The war bonus for men aged 21 and over was increased from 19s to 23s a week and for women from 15s 6d to 18s 6d per week. Proportionate increases were given to civil servants under the age of 21.

THE REPEAL OF SECTION 5

The closer association which the Institution had developed with the wider trade union movement, particularly the AScW, in relation to the position of scientists during the war was also reflected in its approach to the repeal of Section 5 of the Trade Disputes Act, 1927. This Act had prevented civil service unions from affiliating to the TUC or any trade union federation which included unions from outside the civil service. The civil service unions maintained that a legal prohibition of this kind was inconsistent with the democratic objectives for which Britain and her allies were fighting in the Second World War. This was the view, not only of civil service leaders who were in favour of restoring the formal links with the rest of the trade union movement, but even of some active civil service trade unionists who were less persuaded of the need to affiliate to the TUC. They felt that this was an issue which should be decided by civil servants themselves. It was not something which should be regulated by law. To deny civil servants the right to associate with other trade unionists was to restrict their liberty of action.

Soon after the formation of the Coalition government under Winston Churchill, the National Staff Side decided to make representations at the highest level for the early repeal of the section of the Trade Disputes Act forbidding civil servants the right of free association with other trade unionists. It was well known that the new Minister of Labour, Mr Ernest Bevin, former general secretary of the Transport and General Workers' Union, was sympathetic to the view of the civil service unions. He received a deputation on the subject from the National Staff Side. There was, however, no agreement within the government for the immediate repeal of the objectionable section of the Trade Disputes Act. A number of Conservative ministers were strongly opposed to any such proposal.

When the new leadership of the Institution was elected in 1942 to constitute the Emergency Executive Committee, no time was lost in arranging for a discussion of the Trade Disputes Act, 1927. At the second meeting of the Emergency Executive Committee held in February 1942 it was agreed to write to all constituent associations inviting their views on the repeal of Section 5 of the Act, the section which denied civil servants the right of free association with other trade unionists.

The issue as to whether the Institution should support the repeal of Section 5 was debated in constituent associations during the summer months of 1942. At the September meeting it was reported that replies had been received from seventy-one constituent associations. This was just under half the total number in membership of the Institution. Of the seventy-one associations which had replied, forty-eight, with a total membership of 9,943, stated that they were in favour of repeal, and twenty-three, with a membership of 1,829, stated that they were opposed to repeal. In the light of this expression of opinion the Emergency

Executive Committee decided, with only three dissentients, that it should be the policy of the Institution to support the repeal of Section 5 of the Trade Disputes Act, 1927.

Early in 1943 the UPW, the largest of the civil service trade unions, decided in defiance of the 1927 Act to request affiliation to the Trades Union Congress. The UPW was eventually persuaded to withdraw its application not on legal grounds but on political grounds. It was put to it that if it pressed its application friction might be caused within the coalition which would impede the effective prosecution of the war. In a note on the decision of the UPW, *State Service* said that the union was to be congratulated on an action which left the situation in a fluid state so that further negotiations could take place. The journal went on to say that Section 5 of the Act was one of those laws which 'out-Hitlers Hitler'. It pointed out that the whole of the National Staff Side was united in demanding its repeal.

The controversy about the application of the UPW for reaffiliation to the TUC caused the Institution to look at its own relationship with bodies outside the civil service. It sought legal advice on its representation on the Salaries Committee of the Royal Institution of British Architects and on its affiliation to the Parliamentary and Scientific Committee. It was possible, and even probable, that the association of the Institution with both these bodies could have been declared illegal by the courts under the 1927 Act.

In the autumn of 1944 the Emergency Executive Committee of the Institution again took up within the National Staff Side the question of repeal. The request for further action came from one of the constituent associations, the ACSDD. This Association, it will be recalled, had been formed by the Association of Engineering and Shipbuilding Draughtsmen immediately after the 1927 Act had been placed on the statute book. The AESD, with a membership overwhelmingly in private industry, remained affiliated to the TUC.

The National Staff Side continued to make representations to the government for the repeal of Section 5 but the majority of the Cabinet were opposed to any suggestion of change. At the beginning of 1945 a number of civil service unions decided to campaign actively for the repeal of Section 5. A letter signed by fourteen members of the Institution appeared in *State Service* urging that the Institution should associate itself with the campaign. At about the same time it was reported to the Emergency Executive Committee that, despite representations made by the TUC itself in support of the civil service unions, the government, largely under the influence of Winston Churchill, had refused to change its view. The National Staff Side then decided that a campaign should be conducted with a view to influencing parliamentary candidates in the first general election after the ending of the war. A committee was established by the National Staff Side and it was given authority to organise constituency committees to make approaches to candidates. In the event the issue was not resolved until after the 1945 general election.

ORGANISATIONAL CHANGES

War is nearly always a forcing-house of change, and this was certainly true in the Institution. By the beginning of 1942 a new leadership had been elected. It was, however, with very considerable regret that the Council lost, through pressure of official duties, their chairman, Mr G. L. Pepler. Mr Pepler was chief technical officer to the Minister of Works and Planning. He had a very long record of service to the Institution and first became a member of the Council in 1921. He succeeded Mr Watson-Watt as vice-chairman in 1934 and became chairman of the Council in 1936. Mr Monroe, another long-serving member of the Council, was elected chairman to replace Mr Pepler. Mr Herbert was then elected vice-chairman.

The membership was rising and at the end of 1942 was in excess of 23,000, despite the fact that the Society of Post Office Engineering Draughtsmen had left the Institution in 1941 and the Society of Post Office Engineering Chief Inspectors, which had decided to amalgamate in 1941 with the Society of Post Office Engineering Inspectors, also left the Institution in May 1942 when the amalgamation was completed.

Much needed to be done to strengthen membership organisation. The difficulties of organising in wartime meant that there were very substantial arrears of subscriptions. A decision was taken to appoint an organiser to deal with recruitment, the amalgamation of associations and the collection of subscriptions. In February 1943 the headquarters were transferred back to London from Oxford, whence the Institution had moved in 1941. Premises were found in Chelsea but they were almost immediately requisitioned by the Admiralty. Eventually the Institution was able to find offices in Hans Place.

In the spring of 1943 Mr Monroe resigned from the chairmanship of the Council. Since first becoming a member of the Council in 1926, as a representative of the Patent Office Examining Association, Mr Monroe had served as assistant honorary secretary and joint honorary secretary. In 1931 he became sole honorary secretary and continued the tradition, established by Mr Menzler, of meeting members regularly in London and the provinces. He became one of the Institution's representatives on the National Staff Side in 1933 and served on several of their subcommittees. He became vice-chairman of the Council and its chairman in 1942. He also acted as honorary editor of *State Service* and was a member of the Emergency Executive Committee. He was replaced as chairman of the council by Mr Herbert.

The loss of Mr Monroe also coincided with the departure of the honorary secretary, John Fraser, who went into the armed forces. John Fraser was very much associated with the new leadership. He was a member of two constituent associations, the Association of Architectural Surveying and Civil Engineering Assistants at the Ministry of Works and the Association of Civil Service Designers and Draughtsmen. Leslie Herbert said of him that he was an outstanding officer.

In April 1943 Mr T. J. Hughes ceased to be the principal full-time officer of the Institution. His appointment as secretary had not been a successful one. Mrs Miller continued as acting secretary, ably assisted by one other full-time official, Mr Tom Profitt. The vacant post of secretary was advertised at a salary of £1,000 per annum, rising by annual increments of £50 to £1,250. The committee appointed to consider the applications recommended the appointment of Mr Stanley Mayne. At the time of this recommendation Mr Mayne was in the administrative class in the Ministry of Health. He had entered the civil service as a clerical officer and had been very active in the civil service trade union movement. He had served on the executive of the CSCA and was also actively associated with the National Council for Civil Liberties.

There was an attempt both on the Executive Committee and at a subsequent Council meeting to insist that the secretary should have 'no political associations'. Reference was made in this connection to Mr Mayne's association with the National Council for Civil Liberties. The restrictive move directed against Mr Mayne was defeated and the recommended appointment was ratified by the Council. Unfortunately for the Institution, Mr Mayne was not able to secure release from civil service employment. The Treasury was willing for Mr Mayne to be released but the Ministry of Health was not. This was a blow to the Institution, particularly as Stanley Mayne was known to be an extremely able and vigorous trade unionist. He was also fully in sympathy with the new leadership of the Institution.

The Institution continued without success to press for the release of Stanley Mayne. Finally it was decided towards the end of 1944 to offer the vacant position of secretary to Mr Leslie Herbert, the chairman of the Council. Mr Herbert was able to secure his release from the Inland Revenue Department and he became the secretary of the Institution on 1 January 1945. It was a fitting tribute to a man who had played an outstanding role in reshaping the Institution.

Leslie Herbert was born in 1912 and entered the civil service in 1930. He joined the Institution as soon as he became a civil servant and became a member of the Executive Committee of the Estate Duty Office Association in 1936. He joined the Council of the Institution in 1938. Apart from his many activities on the committees of the Institution he was also the initiator and author of *The Professional Civil Servants' Handbook* which had been published early in 1944.

A NEW STRUCTURE

In the period before his appointment as secretary of the Institution, Leslie Herbert was a strong advocate of measures for the reorganisation and unification of the Institution. He and others in the new leadership of the Institution urged that the smaller associations should be amalgamated and that eventually the Institution should be reorganised on a branch basis. This was not the first time that the issue had been raised. In 1926 the Council had recommended that constituent associations should consider calling themselves 'branches' of the Institution and arranging for their seats on the departmental Whitley councils to be held as Institution seats. The response from the associations had, however, been mixed and the matter was not vigorously pursued. They urged, too, that there should be an annual conference which would be the supreme policy-making body of the Institution and that between conferences responsibility should be vested in an executive committee. In brief, Leslie Herbert and his colleagues wanted the Institution to become a more effective trade union with an organisational structure similar to that of other trade unions.

In the summer of 1944, by which time the membership of the Institution had reached 30,000, the Emergency Executive Committee endorsed proposals to move towards a branch structure. It was agreed that, except in very special circumstances, no new constituent associations should be formed but that if they were they should be known as branches and not as associations. It was also agreed that each existing association should be recommended, whenever a suitable occasion arose, to amend its title to 'branch' and that amalgamations of associations or branches within departments should be encouraged. Two of the earliest groups to follow this advice were the nine associations representing 'Carpenter' staffs in the Ministry of Supply, who combined to form the Ministry of Supply Scientific Staffs branch, and the eleven associations representing similar staffs in the DSIR who formed the new DSIR branch.

Shortly afterwards, on the initiative of Leslie Herbert, the Emergency Executive accepted recommendations stating that ultimately the Institution should become a national organisation with departmental branches. Its governing body was to be an annual delegate conference which was to appoint an executive committee to carry on the normal business of the Institution between the conferences. Professional interests were to be safeguarded by professional group committees appointed by the main executive committee, and by branch committees. Four group subcommittees were established during the year: Professional (General), Architectural, Engineering and Scientific. It was also agreed that there should be a uniform scale of subscriptions payable to a central fund from which grants would be made to branches to cover local expenditure. A further proposal was that weekend schools should be held for honorary officials of branches.

These proposals stimulated a lively correspondence in *State Service*. One correspondent urged that the title 'Institution' should be dropped. It was, he said, incorrect and pretentious. Support for the proposals of the Emergency Executive Committee was expressed in a number of quarters, but there were others who asked for a scheme of organisation based upon professional identity rather than branch identity. The ACSDD, in particular, opposed the development of departmental branches on the grounds that they were an interdepartmental organisation and intended rejoining the AESD after the repeal of Section 5 of the Trade Disputes Act.

By the end of 1944 final proposals for a new structure and constitution of the Institution had been formulated by the Emergency Executive Committee. These proposals had been circulated to all constituent associations and subsequently considered at two meetings by the Council of the Institution. The Council approved the broad principles of the new scheme and the Emergency Executive Committee was authorised to submit new rules to a special general meeting of the membership. This special meeting took place on 11 January 1945 and the draft rules were endorsed. Unfortunately it was then ascertained that, because of the intervention of Christmas, the necessary statutory notice of the meeting had not been posted to all members. The decisions of the meeting had therefore to be declared null and void. Further difficulties then arose about arrangements for a further special meeting and it was not until approximately eleven months later, by which time the war had ended, that the new rules were endorsed at a special general meeting. They were carried by seventy-one votes to thirteen. Proxy votes were then counted and the final result was announced as 10,615 in favour of the new rules and 249 against.

The main feature of the new rules was the substitution of an annual delegate conference for an annual general meeting. The change was both necessary and inevitable in view of the growth of the Institution. When the membership rose to a figure of more than 30,000 an annual general meeting, which every member of the Institution was entitled to attend, was impracticable and therefore, in reality, undemocratic. Some form of representative government was required. The annual delegate conference was to consist of delegates elected by branches. The rules established that the delegate conference should be the governing body of the association and that the national executive committee should be its instrument for giving effect to decisions of the conference and for administrative purposes. As a means of overcoming the difficulty of transforming constituent associations into branches, the new rules provided that each branch would have its own constitution or regulations. Each branch was to consist of at least fifty members except by special decision of the annual conference or of the national executive committee. Those branches with less than fifty members not recognised by the new rules would be grouped together in a central branch.

The new rules also specified the objects for which the Institution was established. They included the maintenance and improvement of the position and status of members; the advancement of efficiency in the civil service; and the promotion, teaching and extension of professional science; and the interchange of views thereon. The national executive committee was given power to take common action with other societies in the civil service or with other professional institutions or bodies for the purpose of advancing the interests of members. It was, however, provided that there should be no affiliation to any other body without the consent of the conference. The new rules formalised the evolution of the Institution towards a normal trade union structure.

11   Postwar Reorganisation

The war in Europe came to an end in the summer of 1945. Japan surrendered some weeks later. In its comments on the ending of the war *State Service* emphasised the contribution made by scientists and technicians towards the defeat of fascism. Nazism, it said, was crushed and defeated but it had left in its wake the most appalling wreckage and misery that the world had ever known. During the war the brains and skill of scientists and technicians had been devoted to problems of war, and the technical civil service had co-operated closely with British industry. This partnership must not be allowed to lapse.

When the ending of the war appeared near Winston Churchill had proposed to the leaders of the Labour and Liberal parties that the Coalition government should continue in office at least until the end of the war with Japan. Some of the Labour leaders hesitated and a few were known to be sympathetic to Churchill's request. Aneurin Bevan, on the other hand, urged that there should be an early general election and his views were supported by the majority of the Labour Party. Winston Churchill resigned and the Conservative Party believed that because of the wartime prestige of their leader they would secure a comfortable majority in the general election.

The election took place on 5 July 1945. The announcement of the result had to be deferred for some three weeks to allow time for the troops to vote and for their votes to be counted. The result of the election was an overwhelming victory for Labour. The Labour Party secured 393 seats against 213 for the Conservatives and their allies. Twelve Liberals were elected and twenty-two independents. A number of civil service trade unionists were elected as members of Parliament. These included W. J. Brown (Rugby); Charles Smith (Colchester); H. E. Randall (Clitheroe); W. W. Wallace (Walthamstow East); W. R. Williams (Heston and Isleworth); L. John Edwards (Blackburn); L. J. Callaghan (Cardiff South). With the exception of W. J. Brown who was an independent, they were all Labour MPs. By the end of July Britain had its first majority Labour government.

The new government made early arrangements for the orderly demobilisation of the armed services and for the accompanying switch in public administration. There was an enormous amount of constructive work to be done. Many cities had suffered heavy damage from bombing, and there was a very large pent-up demand for durable goods of all kinds, including housing. Exports had to be built up and the social services developed. The new government was committed to an ambitious programme for the development of education, national insurance and a national health service. The mass unemployment which had been feared in the postwar period did not materialise.

One important immediate problem for the Institution with the ending of the war was to protect the interests of the many thousands of scientists and technicians in the civil service who might be affected by redundancy. In July 1945 a report was published, drawn up by the Civil Service National Whitley Council, on the release and discharge of redundant temporary staff in the civil service. It was particularly significant for the Institution because for the first time the scientific and technical grades were dealt with as a national group of civil servants and not as so many separate departmental grades. The report put forward a number of main principles for the programme of redundancy. The first to go, it suggested, should be those who volunteered to leave. They should be followed by other staff selected on the basis of 'least usefulness' in the higher grades and 'last in, first out' in the lower grades. The machinery for determining who was the 'least useful' was left for departmental discussion.

In December 1945 the National Whitley Council issued a report on recruitment to established posts for professional, scientific and technical staff. The Council urged that the general principles which it had suggested in an earlier report on the recruitment of civil servants should be adopted for the recruitment of professional, scientific and technical staff. The principles were:

(1) Normal recruitment should be by open competition of appropriately qualified persons and should be resumed at the earliest possible date.
(2) Special reconstruction competitions should be held over a period and should be designed to restore opportunity of entry to those who had lost it as a result of the war.
(3) Reconstruction competitions should be held under conditions which gave those who had served in the forces full opportunity to compete and should guarantee to them a generous proportion of the vacancies.
(4) Arrangements should be made for the permanent retention of exceptionally well-qualified temporary staff who were over the age-limit for reconstruction competitions.

POSTWAR RECONSTRUCTION

As far as the Institution was concerned, developments after the Second World War were very different from developments after the First World War. The professional and technical grades were largely excluded from the major advances made by the administrative, executive and clerical grades in the 1920 reorganisation. This time the Institution and the grades it represented were in the forefront. On 1 January 1946 nine new Treasury classes were created which transformed large areas of professional, scientific and technical employment from a chaotic medley of departmental grades into a coherent, tidy and compact group of Treasury classes. In contrast, in the twenty-five-year period between 1920 and 1945 only five such classes had been created, none of them in the specialist grades. By the end of 1947 over 90 per cent of the Institution membership had either agreed to or received proposals on a new structure. Furthermore, it was agreed that all changes on structure, whether finalised by that date or not, should be implemented with effect from 1 January 1946. Backdating on such a scale was unprecedented outside the professional and technical field. One of the major objectives of the Institution throughout its existence was thus achieved. The Institution also achieved a substantial improvement in the conditions of service of these classes both absolutely and also relative to other civil service classes, although the aim of complete parity with the administrative and executive classes remained to be won.

The first annual delegate conference of the Institution was held in 1946. Its success was a vindication of the decision to hold one. One hundred and twenty-one motions were on the agenda and for the first time branches had the opportunity to review the structure, policy and organisational machinery of the Institution. Among the important decisions made at that conference were the abolition of associate members and their inclusion as full members of the Institution. This was carried by 22,600 votes to 694. The posts of honorary secretary and honorary treasurer were abolished and the position of deputy vice-chairman created. The arrangement whereby branches fixed their own contributions was ended in favour of a standard scale of subscriptions, remitted to headquarters and from there dispensed to branches to meet their local expenditure.

A NEW DEAL FOR SCIENTISTS

In September 1945 the government issued its proposals for the reorganisation of the scientific civil service to be implemented from 1 January 1946, *The Scientific Civil Service: Reorganisation and Recruitment during the Reconstruction Period.* In the preamble to its recommendations the government recognised the great contribution made by science to the war effort and the need to maintain the quality of that contribution during peacetime.

1   The Government have decided that the Scientific Civil Service is to be reorganised. They are deeply conscious of the contribution made by science towards the winning of the war, a contribution which may have altered the whole course of the war and has certainly shortened its duration. They are equally conscious of the contribution which science can make during peace to the efficiency of production, to higher standards of living, to improved health, and to the means of defence. They are resolved that the conditions of service for scientists working for the Government shall be such as to attract into the Civil Service scientifically qualified men and women of high calibre, and to enable them after entry to make the best use of their abilities, in order that scientists in the Government Service may play their full part in the development of the nation's resources and the promotion of the nation's wellbeing.

In reaching its recommendations the government had taken into account the recommendations of the Barlow Committee, although it had carried many of the recommendations a good deal further than Barlow. The confidential committee on scientific staff, chaired by Sir Alan Barlow, KCB, KBE, of the Treasury, and comprising in addition Sir Edward Appleton, KCB, FRS, of the DSIR, W. F. Lutyens of ICI and Professor E. K. Rideal, MBE, FRS, of Cambridge University, had been established in 1942 and had been asked to consider three points in particular:

(*a*) The comparison between the initial salaries of administrative entrants and scientific entrants.
(*b*) The question whether the existing conditions of service for scientists provided adequate prospects for the average entrant.
(*c*) The question whether sufficient facilities existed for free interchange of scientific personnel, and in particular research scientists, between the government service on the one hand and the universities, industry and outside bodies in general on the other.

The committee approached the Institution informally and a memorandum of evidence was submitted. The report of the Barlow Committee, together with the Treasury memorandum commenting on it, was released at the beginning of December 1944. The Emergency Executive Committee circulated the documents to members and established an *ad hoc* committee to consider them.

The crucial recommendation of the Barlow Committee was that the scales and system of promotion of the scientific classes should ensure that the best scientific men should have equal prospects, pay and promotion with the best men in the administrative class, at least up to the top of the principal grade. The White Paper endorsed these principles but differed from the report of the Barlow Committee in certain details. It accepted that the salaries of the most highly qualified members of the scientific service should be brought into relationship with those of the administrative grades and that at the recruitment stage they should be aligned to them. A scale structure identical with that of the administrative grades, it argued, would not meet the requirements of the scientific organisation; but highly-qualified scientific graduates would be recruited, as scientific officers, to the same salary scale as assistant principals; and principal scientific officers would receive the same salary as principals. The Barlow Committee recommended that outstanding scientists should have a reasonable expectation of reaching the PSO grade in their early thirties, and the government agreed that staff complements should be so arranged as to ensure this.

The government also accepted the Barlow Committee's proposal that ultimate career prospects should be improved and proposed an expansion of posts above PSO, together with provision for promotion on the basis of the quality of scientific contribution, without necessarily expecting the staff concerned, as was usual before the war, to carry administrative responsibilities. To bring about better career prospects for high-quality scientists the government proposed that the existing assistant grades should be strengthened and some of the work done by scientific officers devolved to those grades. The assistant class was to be renamed the experimental officer class and an improved career structure implemented.

To ensure the maintenance of high standards throughout the service, the whole of the scientific service was in future to be recruited centrally through the Civil Service Commission. An interdepartmental scientific panel was to be created to maintain a uniform standard for promotions and special advancements. One of the first tasks of such a panel was to consider how a greater interchange of personnel and information between scientific civil servants and their colleagues outside could be implemented. This was one of the recommendations of the Barlow Committee.

The proposals were welcomed by the Institution who, within days of the publication of the White Paper, published its own pamphlet *A New Deal for Government Scientists?*. The extent of the suggested reorganisation, according to the Institution, was much more pronounced than in the case of the traditional administrative, executive and clerical grades. Mr Leslie Herbert, the secretary of the Institution, said: 'By far the most important organisational improvement is the introduction of central recruitment by the Civil Service Commission in place of the haphazard, hole-in-the-corner recruitment by departments which has hitherto held the field.' It was difficult to convey, he continued, how important this advance was. Previously the civil service had been sharply divided into Treasury classes (the administrative, executive and clerical grades) and 'the rest'.

The Institution also welcomed as vital the paragraphs of the Barlow Report, accepted by the government, which related to the general conditions under which the scientist should carry out his work, for example his powers of spending on equipment, his relationship to scientific colleagues in industry, and particularly the reduction of secrecy within government science which impeded the interchange of new ideas. It also welcomed the abolition of the artificial distinction between research and development grades.

The Institution accepted that the proposed salary scales were an improvement on former scales but protested that even so scientists would continue to lag behind the administrative and executive grades in status and remuneration. The gap had been narrowed but it still existed. The Institution also pointed out that much would depend on the manner in which existing scientific staff were assimilated into the new grades and scales of pay. The Institution also objected to the exclusion of laboratory assistants from the proposals.

In November a deputation from the Institution was received by the Financial Secretary to the Treasury to discuss in detail the structure of the scientific civil service. The Institution pressed for parity of status between scientific and administrative staff, and for the inclusion of several departmental grades within the White Paper scheme. A deputation from the Parliamentary and Scientific Committee to the Financial Secretary was also arranged to put forward the scientists' case.

The Institution's efforts to improve the status of scientists received powerful support from the publication in 1946 of a report of a government-appointed select committee, again under the chairmanship of Sir Alan Barlow, to consider the use and development of scientific manpower during the ten-year period following the end of the war. The report, *Scientific Manpower: Report of a Committee appointed by the Lord President of the Council*, was critical of the failure of Britain to meet the need for more scientists. It suggested that the government should accept an immediate aim to double through the education system the output of qualified scientists. In order to make the objective attainable, said the report, resources would have to be provided for increased and better teaching facilities.

At the beginning of 1947 Mr Leslie Herbert, the secretary of the Institution, underlined to the membership the main improvements which had been secured under the new scheme for scientists. In the first place, very substantial salary increases had been secured for scientific staff in the early years of service. Secondly, provision had been made for accelerated progress up the basic scale. Thirdly, there had been a substantial improvement in career prospects. Fourthly, there had been a significant levelling-up between different classes in various departments. Finally, although parity with administrative and executive staff had not been secured, there had been a notable improvement in the relative position of scientific staff.

In addition several departmental grades had been included within the White Paper proposals and in 1947 the government agreed to introduce a new assistant (scientific) class. Leslie Herbert described this as 'a new deal' for laboratory assistants. The establishment of this new class, he said, together with the salary scales and conditions applicable to it, could be regarded as an extremely satisfactory, if long overdue, settlement of the claims of a long depressed group of civil servants. The new class embraced a number of different departmental grades and numbered altogether some 5,000 staff.

By the beginning of 1948 Leslie Herbert was able to claim that a major objective of Institution policy, namely, the elimination of an enormous number of separate departmental grades covering scientific staff, had been very largely achieved. Within three years of the ending of the war, he pointed out, the whole specialist field had been reorganised into a small number of classes with common salary scales centrally determined. Substantial improvements in pay and career prospects had been achieved. This had been possible only because of the 'unification of the various specialist interests into a strong staff association covering most of the field'. The Institution he said, had insisted on 'central recruitment wherever possible and central negotiations throughout by all the strength of the staff concerned'. A survey conducted by the Institution revealed that the assimilation of existing staff into the new structure had proceeded on lines broadly to the satisfaction of the membership. Many appeals had been conducted and the Institution lost no opportunity in pressing the claims of its members.

PROGRESS ON OTHER PROFESSIONAL GROUPINGS

The reconstruction objectives of the Institution affecting other professional groups took rather longer to achieve. By the end of 1945 only the administrators, scientists and lawyers had received reconstruction proposals from the government. According to the Treasury at the time proposals for statisticians were imminent, and the accountants, drawing office staff, architects, surveyors, civil engineers and other engineers were all under investigation. Proposals had been framed by the Institution in consultation with the membership for all these and other major professional groupings, and were submitted to the Treasury. There were, however, special difficulties. Whereas for scientists and administrators common grading existed before reconstruction, for many other professional groups common grading throughout the civil service did not exist. The Treasury had little experience in dealing with their structure. The negotiations on structure were not completed until 1950.

In October 1946 proposals were agreed for central recruitment, service-wide grading and new salary scales for accountants and for professional architectural, civil engineering and allied classes who were henceforth to be known as the 'works group'. Although the scales for these grades represented a considerable improvement on prewar conditions they were not regarded as adequate by the Institution. A deputation to Sir Edward Bridges, head of the civil service, expressed the dissatisfaction of the Institution at the scales for the directing grades of the works group. As a result, and also following a claim on behalf of the administrative class, a special committee of inquiry was established by the government in 1948 to advise on the remuneration of the highest posts in the civil service. It was chaired by Lord Chorley.

In December 1946 it was agreed that there should be a Treasury class of mechanical and electrical engineers, covering staff in the Air Ministry, Ministry of Transport and Ministry of Works. Their salary scales were to be the same as the works group. Departmental variants of the Treasury class were established on the same scales in 1947. In August 1947, after complex and protracted negotiations, agreement was reached on architectural and engineering drawing office grades. Proposals on the technical classes were only forthcoming after strong pressure on the Treasury by the Institution, including a deputation to Sir Edward Bridges. It was finally agreed to accept parity with the drawing office scales only if there was parity in the number of hours worked. In the absence of such an agreement the Institution would not agree to be party to the reorganisation of the technical classes promulgated in 1948. The case on hours was eventually taken to arbitration in 1950 and only after considerable constitutional difficulties had been overcome with the assistance of Mr Albert Day, chairman of the National Staff Side. The main part of the claim was referred back by the Tribunal to the parties for negotiation.

New structures and scales for actuaries, statisticians and medical officers were agreed in 1947 and for cartographers and photographers in 1948. Supplementary negotiations took place on medical officers after the publication of the *Report of the Interdepartmental Committee on the Remuneration of Consultants and Specialists* (the Spens Report) in 1948. The Institution, jointly with the British Medical Association and the Medical Staff Association, which organised medical staff in the Ministry of Health and Ministry of Education, sought consequential increases for medical officers in the civil service. Increases were implemented from 5 July 1948.

In 1949 the information officer and librarian classes were established. The government information service had been the subject of a government committee, chaired by Mr J. I. C. Crombie, a Treasury official. The Institution disagreed with many aspects of the report, published in 1947, and with the Treasury view that information officers should be internally recruited and trained from the executive class. The Institution, together with interested bodies such as the National Union of Journalists, with whom the Institution had a joint membership agreement, argued that information officers should be drawn from professionally qualified staff with experience in the world of press and publicity. The National Staff Side supported the Institution and under their aegis the Institution's general secretary led negotiations with the Treasury. A deputation, which included the Advertising Association, the Incorporated Advertising Managers' Association, the Institution of Public Relations and the NUJ, as well as the Staff Side, met the Financial Secretary to the Treasury. The support of interested MPs was also secured. A compromise was eventually reached whereby information officers could be recruited both from within and, for candidates with appropriate experience, from outside the civil service. The agreement also virtually ensured that only qualified journalists would be regarded as eligible for promotion to higher posts requiring the special qualifications of a journalist.

THE CHORLEY REPORT

A White Paper on salaries of the higher administrative class posts was issued at the same time as that on the scientific civil service. This proposed modest increases in salaries, which were implemented without consultation and under protest from the First Division Association. Subsequently, as mentioned above, in 1948 the Chancellor of the Exchequer appointed a committee, under the chairmanship of Lord Chorley, to advise on the general level of remuneration of the higher posts of the civil service – administrative, professional, scientific and technical – and on any particular principles involved. The Institution submitted a memorandum to the committee and gave oral evidence, in which, among other things, it argued for greater career prospects for technical and scientific staff and for parity of technical and scientific directing posts with the administrative class. It also urged that there should be a general increase in the pay of the higher civil service to bring them into line with pay elsewhere. The First Division Association returned to the National Staff Side, having left in 1926, and co-operated with the Institution in relation to the Chorley Committee.

The submission of evidence to the Chorley Committee was another major milestone in the strategy for reconstruction of the specialist field. The *Report of the Committee on Higher Civil Service Remuneration* (the Chorley Report), published in 1948, recommended increases in salary but, more significantly for Institution members, it recommended that the pay for certain architectural and engineering posts should be improved relative to the administrators, and that career prospects for the professional and technical classes should also be improved. It also recommended that committees should be established along the lines of the Barlow Committee for scientists, to examine other specialist classes and most urgently the case of the works group and mechanical and electrical engineers and the professional accountant classes. Moreover it acknowledged the Institution's point that there should be a much greater control of specialists by specialists and integration of specialist classes across the service. It said:

> In the past, each department organised its own professional and technical work with little, if any, regard to what was going on in other departments. A good deal has recently been done in the direction of integration, and we gather that scientific work in particular has been tending to become an exception to the old rule and that a scientific civil service in the same sense is being gradually founded. We feel strongly that a similar development should be encouraged in the other professional and technical classes. Where the nature of the work permits it, we think it a good thing that someone should be generally accepted as the unofficial 'head' of each class and should be consulted in an advisory capacity on interchanges of staff, reorganisations of technical or professional work, etc.

On receiving the report the Institution established a professional staffs sub-committee to deal with negotiations arising from the report, and took the initiative in establishing a Chorley co-ordinating committee on the National Staff Side. The increases in pay recommended by Chorley and agreed with effect from October 1949 were caught by incomes policy and were to be deferred until October 1951, although the pensions of those retiring before the operative date were to be based on the recommended salaries.

The Chorley Report had determined only the salaries appropriate to the administrative grades, leaving the consequential increases in other grades to negotiation. Failing a negotiated settlement the issue went to arbitration by Sir Alexander Gray who awarded the Chorley co-ordinating committee substantially more than the Treasury offer. This was the first time that formal arbitration had been accorded to officers on such salary scales.

THE GARDINER AND HOWITT COMMITTEES

Although the Chorley Report in 1948 had said that 'Barlow' committees were urgently required, the two Gardiner committees on the works group and mechanical and electrical engineers and on the accountants were not established until early 1950. The composition of both committees, chaired by Sir Thomas Gardiner, GBE, KCB, LLD, was similar, as were the terms of reference: 'to consider and to advise on the future organisation, structure and remuneration on a common basis' of the classes concerned. At the same time a committee chaired by Sir Harold Howitt, GBE, DSO, MC, FCA, was established for medical officers with terms of reference similar to those of the Gardiner committees. The Institution submitted memoranda to each committee.

The reports of all three committees were disappointing to the Institution. The Gardiner Committee on the works group and mechanical and electrical engineers reported in September 1951, and recommended substantial increases in pay for those grades. Its proposals, however, fell short of the claim for parity with the administrative grades which the Institution had proposed in its evidence. Moreover, although the committee recognised the force of the parity argument at the level of the directing grades this was not reflected in its salary proposals. The report was also disappointing in relation to career prospects, where its main recommendation was that further work should be devolved to the supporting grades.

The Howitt Committee, which reported soon afterwards, proved even more disappointing and unsatisfactory. The Institution felt that it had not dealt adequately with the problems of organisation that confronted it and that it had not treated seriously the points put to it by the joint committee composed of the Institution, the BMA and the Medical Staff Association. The report suggested no improvement in salary scales, but merely minor adjustments in starting pay. The report also rejected the joint committee's view that a pay relationship with the administrative grades should be established.

The Gardiner Committee on Accountants, which reported in 1952, was also disappointing. Although it proposed increases in pay, the increases bore little relationship to the representations made by the professional accountants, including the claim for parity with the administrative grades.

TUC AFFILIATION

Although the Institution was heavily involved after the war in the internal reconstruction of the civil service, its horizons extended beyond the civil service to broader social and trade union issues. This wider social perspective had developed during the 1930s and was reinforced by the wartime experience. Specialists were directly involved in the war effort and there had been an influx into the civil service of men and women with a broader experience of outside industry. This concern was reflected in proposals for TUC affiliation, continued interest in the social responsibility of science and the issue of civil liberties.

One of the first measures taken by the newly elected Labour government was to repeal the 1927 Trade Disputes Act. The immediate effect was to lift the legal prohibition on the affiliation of civil service unions to the Trades Union Congress. The question of TUC affiliation soon became a subject of animated discussion inside the Institution. In the May 1946 issue of *State Service* an article was published outlining the objects, constitution and functions of the TUC. Another article set out arguments for and against affiliation. It was prepared by two members of the National Executive Committee who held opposing points of view. The arguments put forward in favour of affiliation were that there was a community of interest between members of the Institution and members of other organisations affiliated to the TUC; that most other civil service staff organisations were likely to affiliate; that if the Institution did not affiliate it would be open to other organisations such as the Association of Scientific Workers, the Association of Building Technicians and the Association of Engineering and Shipbuilding Draughtsmen to organise among professional, scientific and·technical civil servants and to speak on their behalf. It was pointed out that the TUC had no power of instruction over individual constituents and that affiliated organisations retained their autonomy. The argument against affiliation rested very strongly on the view that the TUC was associated with the Labour Party. The Institution, it was said, should stand apart from any association which might encourage anyone to think that it was biased in outlook when dealing with whatever government was in power from time to time.

With the repeal of the Trade Disputes Act, 1927, the National Staff Side accepted a statement from one of its committees that there was no justification for changing the basis of trade union organisation among civil service grades. This view was put to the General Council of the TUC. Acceptance of this view, it was said, was regarded as a corollary to the right of affiliation to the TUC of any *bona fide* civil service trade union. The clear implication of this statement was that the existing pattern of trade union organisation among civil servants should remain unchanged and that civil service unions should be free to affiliate to the TUC.

A proposal for affiliation to the TUC was submitted for the agenda of the first annual conference of the Institution in 1946 and was supported by the Executive Committee. The general secretary, Mr Leslie Herbert, threw his influence into the campaign for affiliation. He pointed out that of 480,000 civil servants represented by the National Staff Side, no fewer than 380,000, or roughly 80 per cent were already committed to affiliation to the TUC. He emphasised that the TUC was not an organisation solely for manual workers' unions. It included many white-collar workers, supervisory grades, technicians and professional staff. He also emphasised that the TUC was the voice of all organised employees and was consulted by the government of the day on issues of the highest importance. It included unions both with and without political affiliations. Although many active trade unionists were supporters of the political labour movement, there were no formal links between the TUC and the Labour Party.

The proposal that the Institution should affiliate to the TUC was keenly debated at the 1946 annual conference. Though supported by the National Executive Committee it was opposed not only by those who did not want the Institution to affiliate but also by a number of other delegates who said that they had not had the opportunity to consult their members. The outcome of the debate was a narrow defeat for the proposition. The vote for affiliation was 14,163, but the vote against was 16,103.

It soon became clear that the decision of the 1946 annual conference had not settled the issue. The controversy continued. The September 1946 issue of *State Service* said that the question to affiliate or not to affiliate had become the burning issue of the day. It reported that the National Executive Committee had again considered the question and had reaffirmed its support for affiliation. The NEC stated that many delegates at the 1946 annual conference had said that the membership had not been given sufficient time or information on which to reach a considered decision. The NEC considered this a valid point and decided to bring the facts and arguments to the attention of all members. They agreed that a verbatim report of the discussion at the conference should be published in *State Service*, that all branches should be urged to hold special meetings to consider TUC affiliation, that the editor of *State Service* should be encouraged to publish letters for and against affiliation and that a pamphlet should be prepared on the subject for circulation to the membership. The NEC decided that, despite the decision of the 1946 conference, they would continue to campaign in support of TUC affiliation. An editorial was published in the December 1946 issue of *State Service* supporting the point of view of the NEC and declaring that articles would be published in support of affiliation. The columns of the journal would also be open to those who opposed the policy. Many letters on the subject of TUC affiliation were received and a considerable number were published. The promised pamphlet was duly published and discussion on TUC affiliation took place in many branches.

Despite this campaign the amount of support for TUC affiliation at the 1947 conference was rather less than at the 1946 conference. A resolution was carried stating that no further action should be taken 'in connection with the proposal to seek affiliation to the TUC'. There were a number of reasons for the weakening of support for TUC affiliation. In the first place there had been a succession of very serious economic problems in the early part of the year which led at one stage to a near-disastrous fuel crisis. These problems were probably inevitable in the early aftermath of war. Nevertheless they served to stimulate criticism of the Labour government. Some of this criticism rubbed off on the wider trade union and labour movement. A strong campaign of criticism was also conducted by a number of national newspapers. Moreover, the mood of progressive reform and change, which had been uppermost in 1945 at the successful conclusion of the war against fascism, was already being replaced by the much different mood of the approaching 'cold war'. Relations between the Western Powers and the Soviet Union had already become strained, and within the trade union and labour movement there were serious divisions of opinion about the responsibility for the differences between the USSR and the USA.

SOCIAL RESPONSIBILITY

In the period immediately following the ending of the war there was a strong awareness among the membership of the Institution of the social responsibilities of scientists and engineers. It was symptomatic of the mood of the time that in December 1945 the Institution organised an engineers' conference to bring to public attention the contribution which engineers had made to the national effort during the war and, even more important, their potential contribution to the work of reconstruction. The Secretary of State for Foreign Affairs, Mr Ernest Bevin, agreed to open the proceedings. The chairman and speakers at the various sessions of the conference were drawn from a wide circle. They included an Air Vice-Marshal; the Director of the Royal Electrical and Mechanical Engineers; Mr John Edwards, MP, the general secretary of the Post Office Engineering Union;

the editor of *Engineering;* the Dean of Canterbury (himself an engineer); Mr Joe Scott, Executive Council member of the Amalgamated Engineering Union; and a speaker from the Women's Engineering Society.

Some two months later another conference on science and the welfare of mankind was held in co-operation with the Association of Scientific Workers, the British Association of Chemists, the Association of University Teachers and a number of other scientific organisations. Again the speakers were drawn from various walks of life, including Professors Blackett, Oliphant, Farrington and Bernal, Mr Arthur Horner, the general secretary of the National Union of Mineworkers, Sir Robert Watson-Watt and Dr Julian Huxley. The choice of speakers demonstrated the intention of the organisers of the conference to underline the social responsibility of scientists. A report of this conference was subsequently published and achieved a wide sale. The conference was described by the Institution as outstandingly successful.

In 1946 the Institution participated in a conference called to prepare the ground for a world federation of scientists whose main function would be to act as an advisory body to, and in co-operation with, the United National Educational Scientific and Cultural Organisation (UNESCO). In 1947 the Institution conference agreed to affiliate to the World Federation in respect of the Institution's scientific members. The association with the Federation was, however, short-lived; in 1949 the annual conference decided to disaffiliate.

Another indication of the mood of the time was the decision of the Institution to affiliate to the National Council for Civil Liberties. The Council had come to the fore in the 1930s because of its vigilance and campaigns in defence of civil rights at a time when democracy was threatened by fascism. The recommendation of the National Executive Committee that the Institution should affiliate to the NCCL was endorsed by the annual conference.

MEMBERSHIP CHANGES

The Institution underwent some significant changes following the war. The membership, which had expanded rapidly during the war, inevitably declined with the gradual exodus of those temporarily recruited, although new recruitment and the acceptance of several new branches partially offset the loss. Total membership declined from 30,278 in December 1945 to 29,785 at the end of 1947. There was also a very large turnover of membership.

The extension of public ownership in the immediate postwar period presented the Institution with a new problem regarding membership. Should the Institution organise in the nationalised industries or should it confine itself strictly to the civil service? There were certain areas where the distinction between the civil service and public industry was blurred. They included, for example, certain research associations, partly financed from public funds, where the Institution already had membership. The Institution took the view that it should not withdraw merely because of a change in formal organisation or structure. At the same time the Institution was anxious to maintain good relations with the AScW which also had membership in a number of areas of public employment outside the strict boundaries of the civil service. Following a 1946 conference resolution the NEC decided to initiate recruitment in certain nationalised industries.

The attempt was later abandoned when it was decided in 1947 to retain those already recruited but to cease further recruitment.

In September 1946 a new agreement was concluded between the Institution and the AScW to replace the previous agreement dating from June 1942. The new agreement stated that there should be the closest co-operation between the two organisations and that each would keep the other fully informed of its nego- tiations and activities. Arrangements were made for each of the two organisations to be represented on the appropriate committees of the other.

The AScW undertook to recognise the Institution as the sole organisation to undertake negotiations for scientists and technical staff in the civil service, and to encourage its members entering the civil service to join the Institution. Corre- spondingly the Institution recognised the AScW as the appropriate body to undertake negotiations for scientific and technical staff in non-civil service employment and to encourage those of its members who left the service to take up full membership of the AScW. The position in any particular section of the public service, as distinct from the civil service strictly defined, was to be the subject of consultation and agreement as the need arose.

Existing civil service members of the AScW could retain their full member- ship, but the AScW agreed not to accept as new members any civil service scientists not in membership of the Institution. All scientific staffs group members of the Institution were to become affiliate members of the AScW, subject to the right of the individual to 'contract out'. The Institution agreed to pay a sum of 7s 6d each per year for such 'affiliate' members. The Institution stated that 'if all scientific civil servants become members of the Institution, and through it, affiliate members of the AScW, they will ensure that their interests are fully safeguarded both in the civil service and national fields'. By the end of 1947 the number of members who had taken advantage of this new facility to become affiliated members of the AScW was 2,267. To prevent any misunderstandings the AScW agreed to reorganise on a geographical basis certain of its branches which hitherto had been organised by reference to civil service departments.

CONTROVERSY WITH DRAUGHTSMEN

Relations with some of the drawing office members in the Institution took a less happy turn. The problem had a number of facets. The drawing office grades represented an important minority within the membership of the Institution and their numbers had expanded greatly during the years of the war. Many draughtsmen felt that their pay and status in the civil service was inadequate even by comparison with the scientific grades, let alone by comparison with the executive grades. There was also some feeling that their interests had been submerged in a wider professional organisation catering for many different kinds of skill. The postwar negotiations for the restructuring of drawing office grades had not been completed as early as for scientific grades. Charge and counter- charge were levelled about the cause of this delay.

Negotiations on draughtsmen's pay continued through the summer of 1947. Agreement was reached in the early autumn and in a note in *State Service* the general secretary said that all concerned would breathe a sigh of relief that the long-drawn-out negotiations had at last resulted in new scales of pay. He said that although the new scales were less than those claimed by the Institution it would be agreed that very substantial benefits had been secured. In particular, provision was made for backdating the implementation of the new scales to 1 January 1946.

This, however, was not the end of the dispute about draughtsmen's pay. New scales were issued for draughtsmen in the Post Office and they were significantly less than for architectural and engineering draughtsmen in other departments. The Institution wrote to the Post Office pointing out that it had not been consulted about the new salary scales and it wished to protest about them.

Pay was not the only issue, however. A special problem arose from the circumstances in which the Association of Civil Service Designers and Draughtsmen had come into existence. The Association, which was a constituent of the Institution, was, it will be recalled, an offshoot of the Association of Engineering and Shipbuilding Draughtsmen, whose membership was drawn almost entirely from the privately owned sections of engineering and shipbuilding. When the 1927 Trade Disputes Act became law after the General Strike, the AESD found it necessary to arrange for the separation of its civil service membership. This it did by creating the ACSDD, which in turn became an affiliated constituent association of the Institution. The general secretary of the ACSDD, Mr David Manktelow, was also, simultaneously, a full-time official of the Association of Engineering and Shipbuilding Draughtsmen.

Some of the active members of the ACSDD never concealed that it was their wish, once the Trade Disputes Act was repealed, that the ACSDD should return to its parent body, the AESD. In their view the occupational identity of draughtsmen in all areas of employment was more important than the identity of civil service draughtsmen with other civil servants. A number of members of the ACSDD were also anxious that their organisation should rejoin the mainstream of the trade union movement through affiliation to the Trades Union Congress.

During the campaign for the democratisation of the Institution, in which the ACSDD, together with the EDOA, had played a prominent part, there had been an understanding, claimed the ACSDD, that the ACSDD should retain considerable autonomy and its interdepartmental identity. However, in the reorganisation of branches on a departmental basis following the war no exceptions were made for the ACSDD.

These problems came to a head in the summer of 1946. A special meeting of the National Executive Committee of the Institution was held in August to discuss a series of issues with representatives of the ACSDD. The ACSDD had affiliated to the TUC as an independent union. The Institution maintained that the ACSDD as a constituent of the Institution should have accepted the majority decision of the Institution conference against affiliation. The ACSDD had also formed a joint committee with the Society of Post Office Engineering Draughtsmen and the Association of Technical Assistants to discuss problems affecting drawing office grades. The former body had already seceded from the Institution in 1941 and the latter was continually attacking the Institution. Several other sections of draughtsmen within the Institution, on the other hand, had not been invited to join the joint committee.

The representatives of the ACSDD and the NEC failed to reach an accommodation, particularly because of differences in political views and conflicts of personality. In the early part of 1947 it was announced that the ACSDD intended to withdraw from the Institution from the end of March. The Institution announced in reply that it intended to continue to recruit draughtsmen. At the beginning of 1947 a strong attack on the Institution was made in the monthly journal of the Admiralty Draughtsmen's Association which had substantial numbers of engineering and shipbuilding draughtsmen in the Admiralty. The differences which had arisen concerned the policy being pursued on draughtsmen's salaries.

Draughtsmen themselves, however, were by no means united. Within the ACSDD there were some differences of view on whether the ACSDD should leave the Institution. Nevertheless a new organisation, the Society of Technical Civil Servants, was formed comprising the ACSDD, the Admiralty Draughtsmen's Association and the Society of Post Office Engineering Draughtsmen. Architectural draughtsmen, predominantly in the Ministry of Public Building and Works, who had never been members of the ACSDD or the AESD, remained with the Institution. Mr Cyril Cooper, who had been on the executive of the Institution during the debate with the ACSDD and who had personally favoured remaining with the Institution, became general secretary of the new organisation.

The STCS was able to maintain its representation on the Staff Side through its membership of the Federation of Civil Service Professional and Technical Staffs. This Federation had been formed after the split between technical and clerical associations within the Civil Service Confederation in the context of the establishment of the National Staff Side. The clerical associations had gone on to form the Civil Service Alliance.

By 1948 the Federation had a membership of more than 14,000 and comprised the Admiralty Technical Association, the ACSDD, the Association of Government Geographers and Allied Technicians (AGGAT), the Government Supervisors and Technical Staffs Association, the Association of Government Foremen, the Civil Service Radio Officers' Association, the Association of Civil Service Group Officers, the National Association of Admiralty Overseers, the Royal Navy Propellant Factories Sub Officers' Association and the Royal Navy Cordite Factory Technical Officers Association. All these associations could only achieve representation on the National Staff Side via the Federation of Civil Service Professional and Technical Staffs. The Federation was a constituent of the National Staff Side.

It was not until nearly twenty-five years later that the Society of Technical Civil Servants amalgamated with the Institution. Of the 30,000 members in the Institution at the beginning of 1948 about 3,000 were drawing office staff. When the STCS was formed it consisted of nearly 5,000 members from the ACSDD, about 2,500 from the ADA, about 2,000 from the SPOED and a few hundred others from departmental organisations. The STCS thus had a majority membership among draughtsmen.

For technical staff other than drawing office grades the Institution claimed sole negotiating rights. The Institution membership among non-drawing office technical grades was about 11,000, easily the majority. Various other organisations in the Federation of Professional and Technical Staffs claimed a total membership of less than 2,500. The National Staff Side endorsed the claim of the Institution for sole representation for non-drawing office technical staff. The Institution did, however, undertake to consult the Association of Government Foremen on matters concerning their members. Leslie Herbert pointed out that the Association of Government Foremen had co-operated with the Institution in departmental representation.

Friendly relations between the Institution and the STCS were later re-established, and early in 1950 a joint central committee was set up to ensure close co-ordination of activities on behalf of draughtsmen in both organisations. Indeed, a joint claim was lodged with the Treasury for improvements in the salary scales of draughtsmen and tracers, while the STCS also associated itself with the Institution's general 15 per cent claim in that year.

Following the establishment of the STCS there was some debate as to whether AGGAT should join the Institution or the STCS. The latter had some carto-graphic draughtsmen in small departments. In 1949 a ballot on amalgamation with the Institution was held and AGGAT's executive committee unanimously recommended its membership of 1,617 to vote in favour of amalgamation. An overwhelming majority of members agreed to the amalgamation by a vote of 1,358 for and 203 against, and the general secretary of AGGAT, Mr W. H. Stalley, became a full-time officer of the Institution.

The remainder of the technical associations within the Federation of Civil Service Professional and Technical Staffs gradually gravitated to the Institution in 1948 and 1949, following the restructuring of the technical classes. The rest of the organisations within the Federation gradually amalgamated or joined other organisations. The Government Supervisors and Technical Staffs Association and the Association of Government Foremen merged in the 1950s and later merged with the Civil Service Radio Officers' Association and the Barrack and Station Wardens to become the Association of Government Supervisors and Radio Officers (AGSRO). The Association of Civil Service Group Officers later joined the CSCA and the Society. The Federation continued and was only finally wound up after the STCS rejoined the Institution. By the time of its dissolution the Federation consisted only of the STCS and AGSRO.

THE DEATH OF LESLIE HERBERT

On 5 May 1948, the Institution suffered a serious loss with the sudden death of its general secretary, Leslie Herbert. He was then only 36 years of age. It was Leslie Herbert who probably more than anyone else was the driving spirit behind the reform movement in the Institution during the earlier part of the war years. The success of the reform movement led to far-reaching organisational changes which were to make the Institution, in fact if not in name, an effective trade union. Leslie Herbert never concealed his view that the Institution was wrongly named and that its prime functions were those of a trade union and not those of a professional institution. A Treasury spokesman described him as a man of 'quite exceptional talent'.

Leslie Herbert played a major role in the restructuring exercises in the professional, scientific and technical classes after the war. In the words of the chairman of the National Staff Side, these classes could fittingly be known as the 'Herbert classes'. Having pioneered the major changes in the constitution of the Institution during and immediately after the war, he continued to work for the establishment of a strong unified organisation and over his period of three years, first as secretary and from 1946 as general secretary, the number of branches decreased, as a result of rationalisation, from 123 to 64. Leslie Herbert helped to develop the services of the Institution and he took a particular interest in trade union education. The first weekend school for active members, at which he and Miss Molly Keith were the principal speakers, was held in October 1946.

A Herbert Memorial Fund was established to commemorate the major contribution made by Leslie Herbert. About £4,000 was raised and the Memorial Fund Committee decided that it should be used for the provision of a library, for which a sum of £500 was allocated, and for an annual one-week training course for Institution members. The first such course took place in January 1951. The speakers included a number of prominent scientists, civil servants, industrial leaders and trade unionists. The annual 'Herbert Memorial School' continues to this day as a vital part of the Institution's education programme.

12   From the 1940s to the 1950s: Some Basic Problems Remain

Between the second half of the 1940s and the mid-1950s Britain changed from conditions of postwar austerity to conditions which the Prime Minister of the day was later to describe as 'You've never had it so good'. In reality, the change was nowhere near so dramatic as these words might imply. Britain's fundamental economic problems of a slow rate of growth, substantial obsolescence in her industries, insufficient industrial development and a chronic imbalance in her international trade remained. At the beginning of 1948 Britain faced a large deficit in her international balance of payments and a considerable drain on her gold and dollar reserves.

This was the background to the proposals made by the government for wage restraint set out in a White Paper, *Personal Incomes, Costs and Prices*, published in the early spring of 1948. It was the first of a series of White Papers on incomes policy which has continued right up to the present time. The main argument of the White Paper was that Britain was faced with an acute balance-of-payments problem. Exports had to be increased to pay for essential imports and raw materials and for this reason it was essential that British prices should remain competitive in world markets. Wage increases unrelated to productivity would put up costs and would inevitably lead to higher prices. The government appealed not only for wage restraint but also for restraint in the distribution of dividends to shareholders.

The policy announced in the White Paper caused considerable controversy within the trade union movement. The TUC issued a statement generally sympathetic to the government's policy but pointing out that unions were justified in continuing to press for higher pay in return for higher productivity, or to meet a labour shortage, or to maintain necessary differentials for responsibility, skill and experience, or to raise the standard of low-paid workers to an acceptable minimum. With these qualifications, said the TUC, restraint was acceptable on condition that the government took firm and effective steps not only to stabilise but to reduce profits and prices.

This statement did not satisfy many of the critics within the trade union movement. They pointed to the high level of profits in private industry and their continued upward trend and they argued that it was a dangerous illusion to pretend that there was any likelihood that either profits or prices would be reduced by government action. A policy of wage restraint on the part of trade unions would lead to a redistribution of income in favour of the wealthy in society. Some of the critics also argued that the inflationary pressure in the economy was due in no small measure to the heavy arms programme of the government. Left-wing critics said that Britain was sacrificing its economic strength by its support for American policy in the 'cold war'. The marked deterioration in East–West relations and the development of the 'cold war' was a new feature to figure in economic debates in the next few years.

The government's proposals on incomes policy and the recommendations on them by the General Council of the TUC were considered at a special conference of trade union executive committees held in London on 24 March. The conference supported the General Council's recommendations, broadly in support of government policy, by a majority of approximately 3½ million votes. The TUC also supported the government in its acceptance of economic assistance from the United States of America under what was then known as the European Recovery Programme. This assistance from the United States was in the form of grants and loans.

On 18 September 1949 the government announced the devaluation of the pound sterling. This action was taken because, despite American aid, Britain's fundamental economic problem remained unchanged. There was still an acute balance-of-payment deficit. The General Council of the TUC supported the government's policy and urged unions to exercise even greater restraint on wage increases whilst at the same time insisting that the existing machinery of voluntary negotiation should be preserved.

Another special conference of trade union executive committees was convened on 12 January 1950 and a report submitted by the General Council of the TUC was endorsed by the relatively narrow majority of 4,263,000 to 3,606,000. By the middle of the year, by which time the cost of living had continued to rise, the TUC recognised that 'there must be greater flexibility of wage movements in future than was envisaged in the policy approved by the conference of executives in January'. They warned, however, that it would be folly to assume that the economic barometer was set fair for the pursuance of wage claims to provide for working people the standard of life the trade union movement would like to ensure for them.

At the 1950 TUC the General Council was defeated on wages policy. A motion proposed by the Electrical Trades Union and seconded by the Civil Service Clerical Association was carried in opposition to the General Council. It said that since the publication of the White Paper *Personal Incomes, Costs and Prices*, prices and profits had continued to rise and the living standards of large sections of the working community to fall. The resolution protested that no effective steps had been taken to prevent the continued increase in profits. It also called for the planning of the British economy and price control. The resolution was carried by 3,949,000 votes to 3,727,000.

REARMAMENT

In June 1950 war broke out in Korea between the north and the south. The prices of many raw materials rose throughout the world. The effect was to give a further upward twist to prices in the British home market. In addition, with the general deterioration of the international situation and in relations between East and West, the British government decided to embark on a substantial programme of rearmament. In conditions of near-full employment this extra demand on the use of resources inevitably increased inflationary pressures within the economy.

Those who took the view that the main responsibility for the worsening of the international situation rested with the East, and particularly with the USSR, generally supported the rearmament programme. There were, on the other hand, many critics. The acceleration of the inflationary trend, for which rearmament was a contributory factor, aroused considerable opposition among working people. Cuts were made in the social services and this led in 1951 to the resignation from the Labour government of Aneurin Bevan, Harold Wilson and John Freeman.

Aneurin Bevan developed his opposition to the introduction of health services charges into a much wider criticism of the policy of the government. He did not see the world situation in the same terms as those who were in support of United States policy and who attributed blame for the worsening of the international situation solely to the USSR. Mr Bevan argued that in many areas of the world ordinary people were pressing for radical social change, incompatible with traditional forms of land-ownership and aristocratic or capitalistic political rule. In many of these areas the policy of the Western Powers under the leadership of the USA was to resist these social changes and thus to thwart the efforts of millions of ordinary people for a better life. In a joint foreword to a pamphlet entitled *One Way Only*, the three ministers who had resigned from office, Aneurin Bevan, Harold Wilson and John Freeman, said: 'But it is our view that the vast war machines to which the Western World is fast committing itself will obstruct and not open the paths to peace and freedom.'

In its report to the 1951 Congress the TUC stated: 'The fact must be faced that the developing rearmament programme will, in the immediate future at any rate, mean a fall in the standard of living of the community as a whole.' The Congress accepted by a majority of 5,284,000 to 2,199,000 the view of the General Council that support should be given to the rearmament programme and that it was therefore impracticable to demand that living standards should be improved.

Towards the end of 1951 there was a further worsening in Britain's economic position. There was a grave deterioration in the balance of payments. Import controls were imposed by the government, investment in building was slowed down and credit was restricted by a number of measures, including the raising of the bank rate. Soon afterwards the government announced cuts in public expenditure, including education and the health service, and the reduction of investment in industry. In a statement on the economic situation presented to the 1952 TUC, the General Council stated that trade unionists could not contract out of the difficulties facing the community. Though it emphasised that there should be no interference with the existing machinery of wage negotiations, the clear message of the statement was that there should be continued adherence to a policy of wage restraint.

The Congress, however, adopted a resolution expressing opposition to the economic policy pursued by the new Conservative government. It said that the Conservative government was seeking to reverse the trend towards an equitable and just society. The resolution urged the Council to reject attempts to restrain justifiable wage increases necessary to ease the burden of rising living costs. A motion opposing the rearmament programme was defeated.

By 1953 the inflationary pressure in the economy had eased. The prices of raw materials were falling and were substantially lower than during the period of the Korean War. At the Trades Union Congress that year a resolution, moved by the Post Office Engineering Union, was adopted rejecting any form of wage restraint which might interfere with the freedom of collective bargaining and independent arbitration.

The extremely strained relations between East and West during the period 1948 to 1953 had a number of consequences for the British economy and for the trade union movement. The launching of a rearmament programme inevitably added to Britain's economic difficulties and contributed to the circumstances leading to the replacement of the Labour government by a Conservative government. The international political controversy was also reflected inside the international trade union movement. A number of Western trade union organisations, including the British TUC, withdrew from the World Federation of Trade Unions which had been established at the end of the war and which included trade union centres in both the East and West.

Inside the British trade union movement there was also controversy about the part played by communists. Towards the end of 1948 the General Council of the TUC issued a statement under the title 'Defend democracy' which said that communists were pursuing disruptive activities and, by opposing the European Recovery Programme, were opposing the policies of the British trade union movement. The opponents of the General Council's view said that the real threat to the living standards of working people came not from the communists but from the policies which were being pursued by the government. Military expenditure was being maintained at a high level in order to give support to the efforts of the United States to intervene in various parts of the world to prop up decaying social systems. Britain was involved in heavy overseas military expenditure at a time when the deficit in its balance of payments was dominating the economic scene at home. The anti-communist campaign, said the critics, was a diversion. Instead of discussing the real economic and social issues facing Britain, trade unionists were being encouraged to talk about mythical threats from a small minority of trade union members.

The civil service too was intimately affected by the developing 'cold war' and by the government's economic policies. With the publication of the White Paper *Personal Incomes, Costs and Prices* many inquiries were received by the head office of the Institution about its effect on scientific and technical civil servants. *State Service* reported that, judging from the number of inquiries received, this White Paper had created a bigger stir than any previous White Paper. The general secretary of the Institution, Leslie Herbert, emphasised in replies to inquiries that irrespective of any general salary claims, many professional and technical civil servants were affected by the implementation of postwar reorganisation proposals. These proposals did not constitute a normal salary revision. Leslie Herbert's general reaction to the White Paper was summarised in his statement published in *State Service* that 'it is safe to say that the National Executive Council is unlikely to place in cold storage any claim that it regards as reasonable'. Nevertheless, the government made it clear in Parliament that claims for pay increases by public employees would be dealt with in accordance with the principles laid down in the White Paper.

An equally serious product of the developing 'cold war', particularly for the Institution, was the 'purge' conducted within the civil service against those suspected of close association with the Communist Party. This is dealt with in detail in Chapter 13.

THE NEW GENERAL SECRETARY

The new general secretary, Mr Stanley Mayne, who had been appointed following the death of Leslie Herbert, commenced his duties on 1 September 1948. In his first article in *State Service* published in the October 1948 issue, Mr Mayne said that he would welcome invitations to attend branch meetings. This would help him to become better acquainted with people in the Institution and with the problems of the membership.

Some time after the death of Leslie Herbert a draft article was found among his papers. Its subject was the living standards of Institution members. Leslie Herbert said that as a result of the activities of the Institution in the postwar period substantial gains had been made for the membership. This improvement could be measured in three ways:

(1) the members were considerably better off in salary and prospects;
(2) they were considerably better off relative to other grades in the civil service in comparison with prewar;
(3) their salaries were now comparable to those paid to staff outside the civil service. Mr Herbert went on to point out that in the immediate postwar period Britain's national income in real terms was lower than it was before the war. Hence some groups had to do with less income than prewar. The answer as to how this burden should be shared, said Leslie Herbert, was the substance of political controversy. He held the view that the share of persons covered by the Institution and comparable organisations could and should be increased by reducing the share taken by profits and military expenditure. He acknowledged that this was a political matter. Those who said the Institution should not pursue political objectives ought not then to complain that the Institution was not doing anything about the factors which determined how much was available for salaries.

Stanley Mayne was similarly outspoken in his attitude to the main issues facing the Institution. He spoke forthrightly on the need for trade union action to defend the living standards of members. He also strongly opposed political discrimination in the civil service. He said that the 'purge' was a futile method of protecting the state because no one proposing to betray the state would attract attention to himself by belonging to a minority political party. Political discrimination, he said, was inevitably unfair. He also strongly rejected the argument advanced in some quarters that people who made demands for pay increases were likely to be 'communist-inspired'. He said that judging from the Institution membership this was nonsense.

THE IMPACT OF INCOMES POLICY

The first major civil service pay issue to fall foul of the government's incomes policy was the Chorley Committee, whose report (see Chapter 11), published towards the end of 1948, recommended substantial increases in pay. The government accepted the report but insisted that its implementation would have to be delayed. Eventually, after negotiation, it said that the first instalment of new salaries would be paid on 1 October 1949. In September 1949, however, following the devaluation of sterling, the Chancellor of the Exchequer announced that the promised salary increases to top civil servants would again be deferred.

Towards the end of October 1949 the Chorley Committee's second report was issued and recommended a substantial increase in salaries for assistant secretaries. The report was accepted by the government, subject again to deferment. The view of the staff associations representing high-ranking civil servants was that the civil service was being unfairly treated by the government. In a letter to *The Times* dated 9 January 1950, Stanley Mayne said that under the policy of pay restraint the government seemed to find it necessary to treat civil servants much more harshly than other employers treated their employees.

Early in 1950 the Association of First Division Civil Servants decided to submit a claim on behalf of principals and assistant principals to the Civil Service Arbitration Tribunal. The Treasury insisted, however, that the incomes policy of the day overrode whatever were the intrinsic merits of the claim. The Tribunal came to the conclusion that there was merit in the claim for an improvement in the salary scales for assistant principals and principals, but, in view of the Treasury's attitude, recommended that the claim be brought up again at a later date.

In December the National Staff Side established a special committee to consider the effect of the government's incomes policy on the civil service. The general secretary represented the Institution. The committee came to the conclusion that civil servants were being subjected to a more rigorous version of the White Paper policy than were outside employees. This conclusion was based on such facts as the withdrawal of firm offers of increases, the imposition of 'worse than White Paper' terms on civil servants, the denial to civil servants of the 'escape clauses' expressly designed to prevent a complete 'freezing' of wages, and undue pressure on the Civil Service Arbitration Tribunal.

In March 1950 the National Staff Side decided to write to the Prime Minister to protest about the government's attitude to civil service wages. The letter said: 'There is a widespread belief among civil servants of all grades that the government's policy of wage restraint is being applied more severely to them than to other workers.' The Staff Side said that, having examined the evidence, they were satisfied that the belief was well founded. They emphasised, however, that they were offering no challenge to the White Paper *Personal Incomes, Costs and Prices*. Their protest was against 'the singling-out of civil servants as a body for a more ruthless standstill on wages than the White Paper demands'.

In reply, the Prime Minister, Mr Attlee, said that he hoped that he had already made it plain why the postponement of increases of pay for higher-grade civil servants had taken place. This postponement was, he said, necessary if the wage stabilisation policy was not to be compromised at a critical juncture. Mr Attlee went on to say that the government was bound to observe towards its own employees the policy it hoped and expected that other employees would observe. The Prime Minister concluded by saying that he was glad to know that the Staff Side accepted the necessity for the maintenance in the national interest of stabilisation in wages, and he hoped they would agree on reflection that there was no question of discriminating against the civil service in the application of the policy. This exchange of correspondence was followed by a meeting between the Prime Minister and representatives of the National Staff Side. The Staff Side representatives again pressed their view that the government was discriminating against the civil service. The Prime Minister at the meeting said that he would give careful consideration to the points made by the National Staff Side.

The first official indication that the government might relax its attitude towards the Chorley Committee recommendations came in a statement from Sir Stafford Cripps, Chancellor of the Exchequer, on 3 July 1950. He said that the general situation in the country had improved and that a somewhat easier attitude could be adopted towards the pay claims. The co-ordinating committee of staff associations representing higher-ranking civil servants, in which the Institution took an active part and of which Stanley Mayne was the secretary, immediately made representations to the Treasury. The Chancellor of the Exchequer agreed to meet representatives of the co-ordinating committee.

On 10 August 1950, the Treasury wrote to the co-ordinating committee stating that it had been decided that 'while the need for restraint is still strong and the Government are still therefore unable to give full and immediate effect to the Chorley Committee's recommendations, they would not be justified in continuing completely to withhold adjustments in salaries which were agreed upon 18 months ago . . .'. The letter from the Treasury said that it had never regarded these recommendations as contrary to the principles laid down in the White Paper *Personal Incomes, Costs and Prices*. It proposed to begin the application of the new salaries on 1 October 1950. The recommendations of the Chorley Committee, it was explained, would be implemented by stages and would not become fully operative before October 1951.

FIFTEEN PER CENT PAY CLAIM

The attitude of the government towards the Chorley Committee recommendations for the pay of the higher civil service materially influenced the course of negotiations on other civil service pay claims. After the publication of the White Paper *Personal Incomes, Costs and Prices,* the government made it clear in the House of Commons that claims for wage increases by government employees would be dealt with in accordance with the principles laid down in the White Paper.

In the spring of 1949 the Institution decided to submit a claim for a 15 per cent increase in the salary scales of all Treasury and linked departmental classes represented by the Institution. The Institution also indicated that consequential claims would be made to departments in respect of departmental classes as soon as a settlement was reached on the main claim. In the initial letter submitting the claim, Stanley Mayne recalled that in paragraph 8 of the consolidation agreement of 31 December 1945 it was provided that the Staff Side should have the right to seek a revision in the event of substantial changes in the level of remuneration in the country as a whole. He said that the figures published by the Minister of Labour and National Service showed that wage-earners generally had been able to keep their earnings roughly level with the increase in the cost of living. This was not so with civil servants represented by the Institution.

The initial reply from the Treasury was not encouraging. It said that, according to information available to it, there was little support for the contention that there had been substantial changes in the level of remuneration for comparable work outside the civil service. In his reply Stanley Mayne said that between 1 January 1946 and 31 December 1948 wage rates had risen by 17 per cent and that during the same period earnings had risen by 26 per cent. He referred also to increases given to professional and technical staff employed on the railways and in the electricity supply industry.

The 1949 conference of the Institution gave full support to the salary claim. In his main address to the annual conference Stanley Mayne said that the salaries of civil servants were low. He pointed out that salaries for professional staff were determined from 1 January 1946. In the intervening three and a half years there had been a substantial increase in living costs. No one, said Stanley Mayne, welcomed the idea of entering into a spiral of salaries and prices but the fact had to be faced that it was prices and not civil service salaries which had risen. He examined various price indices and reached the conclusion that between 1945 and 1948 prices had risen by not less than 17½ per cent. He referred also to the general increase in wage rates and earnings and he described the claim for a 15 per cent increase in salaries as very modest. The conference adopted two resolutions expressing dissatisfaction with the application of government policy laid down in the White Paper on incomes and instructing the National Executive Committee to press for substantial increases in the pay of professional, scientific and technical staff.

The Institution did not have to wait long for the Treasury's official reply to the claim for a general increase of 15 per cent. The claim was rejected. The Treasury pointed to the provisions of the White Paper *Personal Incomes, Costs and Prices* and also contended that indications of changed pay levels outside the civil service were not relevant to this particular claim. Each class must be taken separately with its comparable staff outside the civil service. Following this rejection, the National Executive Committee of the Institution decided that the 15 per cent claim should go to arbitration and terms of remit were agreed in November. Shortly afterwards, however, the NEC changed its decision and agreed with reluctance to hold the claim in abeyance. In doing so it had in mind the fact that the arbitration tribunal had considered and rejected a similar claim by the CSCA and that it had rejected two other claims, one from the CSCA and another from the CSU, primarily on general economic grounds. It also wished to await the outcome of two important conferences to be held by the TUC in December and January to determine the course that affiliated unions ought to take. The position, said the NEC, would be reviewed again in March.

In an address to the 1950 annual delegate conference Albert Day, chairman of the National Staff Side, noted how quickly the first flush of reconstruction in the civil service following the war, for which the unions were grateful, had been superseded by the complete repression by the government of civil service pay claims. He continued:

It is quite true that devaluation to which this event is attributable has involved the rest of the community. But while it is true that we are all on hard times it would not be quite true to say that we are all in the same boat. Most of the community is in a boat on its own, not a very pleasant boat, with the exception of such people, perhaps, as the barrow boys and, if Mr Evans is to be believed, the farmers. But civil servants are in a boat of their own, and it is a boat which differs in a very important respect from the other one. They both have cracks in their seams and it is possible that for the occupants of both of them the rising tide in the cost of living may seep in. But the other is at least provided with some oars and a lifebelt or two and the facilities for baling out. Not so the civil service boat. Against the rising tide of the increasing cost of living the occupants of that boat have, as government policy stands at the moment, no protection at all.

The conference later passed a resolution instructing the NEC to press forward with the 15 per cent claim. Discussions took place with the Treasury following conference and disagreement was recorded for a second time in July 1950.

In view of the decision of the government to begin the implementation of the Chorley Committee recommendations the NEC decided that the time had arrived to press for arbitration. A date was arranged for arbitration to take place towards the end of February 1951. Before this date, however, the Treasury asked the Institution to defer the hearing to enable it to make an offer. Negotiations on the Institution's claim began and the arbitration hearing fixed for 26 February was postponed. These negotiations led to a settlement for some of the staff represented by the Institution, but the offer made for technical classes was regarded as inadequate. It was decided, therefore, to submit their claim to arbitration. The case was conducted jointly with the Society of Technical Civil Servants and resulted in an award significantly more favourable than the Treasury offer. The award was regarded by the two organisations as a victory. The increase for the various grades of draughtsmen varied between 8 per cent and 14 per cent and for other technical classes between 8 per cent and 15 per cent.

At its meeting in April 1951, following the settlement of the 15 per cent salary claim and the award of the Civil Service Arbitration Tribunal on technical classes, the NEC expressed appreciation to all who had contributed to the successful outcome. The general secretary, Stanley Mayne, was singled out for special praise.

OTHER ISSUES

In September 1945 the Institution submitted to the National Staff Side of the Whitley Council two motions calling respectively for the immediate return of prewar hours and leave conditions and for compensation for any extended hours of work by staff in civil service grades for which overtime payment was not normally made. As a result of this Institution initiative the National Staff Side took two important decisions. The first was to the effect that representations should be made with a view to securing a reduction in hours 'in the various establishments that their respective staffing positions allowed'. The second was in favour of a claim for the return to normal leave arrangements as from the beginning of the 1946 leave year. As a result of this pressure from the civil service unions the Treasury issued a circular in February 1946 stating that, whilst it was not yet practicable to return to normal arrangements, departments were asked to reduce standard hours to 45½ per week (inclusive of the lunch break) as soon as circumstances permitted. The circular said that because of the acute manpower shortage it had been decided that for the leave year covering the summer of 1946 leave should continue to be restricted, in the case of the higher entitlements, below the prewar level. The maximum annual leave allowance was to be 30 days. Civil servants were to be encouraged to take the leave to which they were normally entitled subject to a maximum of 30 days.

In 1947 the civil service unions continued to press for the restoration of prewar working hours and annual leave entitlement. In June 1947 the Treasury announced that the government had decided that it was essential in the national interest that the extended hours of work of 45½ per week, including lunch-breaks, which applied to staff whose normal entitlement was a 42- or 44-hour week including lunch-breaks, must continue. The Treasury informed the National Staff Side that it could not justify the restoration of prewar standards and must therefore institute a 'moratorium', which would be operative for the calendar years 1948 and 1949, on the obligation which the government had accepted at the beginning of the war that at the end of the war prewar conditions would be restored. The government did, however, agree that for certain middle grades, not entitled to full overtime payment in respect of hours in excess of 42 and 44, some financial compensation should be granted. A scheme was worked out and agreed with the National Staff Side.

On annual leave the response of the Treasury was more sympathetic to the views of the unions. The Treasury decided that all staff working a six-day week would be given their full authorised allowance of annual leave up to a maximum of 36 days each year. Provision was made for the abatement of the leave allowance for staff employed on a five-day week. Thus the maximum for staff employed on a five-day week was 30 days per year.

In November 1949 new overtime arrangements were introduced for staff employed in the technical, works, engineering and allied classes. Provision was made for back payment for rather more than one year. The negotiations which led to these new arrangements extended over a long period. Tom Profitt, who had been in charge of the negotiations, stated that they had been conducted in an amicable atmosphere and he doubted whether in the current year there had been many other discussions which had yielded such good results.

SUPERANNUATION

The Institution began the postwar period with two major superannuation objectives; that all service (except for officers specifically recruited for short-period temporary service) should be pensionable, either under the Superannuation Acts or FSSU, from the date of entry into the service; and the granting of 'added years' to late entrants. The Treasury had agreed to the latter for lawyers appointed to certain high legal posts, but so far had not approved it in the case of engineers and other professional staff who were similarly inevitably late entrants.

The 1946 Superannuation Act made some improvements in these two areas. On 'added years' the Act made provision for the Treasury to direct that a person who became an established civil servant after the age of 40 could be granted superannuation benefits on a special scale under which his service would be multiplied by eight-fifths for the purposes of superannuation. Anyone becoming a civil servant between age 35 and 40 could have his service before 40 disregarded and his subsequent service multiplied by eight-fifths. However, the provision was only to be used at the Treasury's discretion and was intended only for attracting to the civil service persons of high attainments and long experience outside the service. The Institution tried without success to widen the scope of this section of the Act and continued to pursue the matter through the Superannuation Committee of the National Whitley Council.

On 'unestablished service to count' some progress was also made. The Act provided that ex-forces recruits to the civil service during the period from 3 September 1939 to such date as might be appointed by the Treasury would be able to count their period of service with the forces as if it were unestablished service in the civil service. All unestablished service between 1919 and 1935 was allowed to count to the extent of one half for pension and in full for gratuity (the Superannuation Act 1935 already covered service from 1935).

Following the Act the Superannuation Committee of the National Whitley Council undertook a major review of superannuation questions and, despite the incomes policy restrictions on pay, the resulting Superannuation Act of 1949 made substantial improvements. It provided for widows' and orphans' pensions; dependants' pensions; voluntary retirement with pension rights after reaching age 50; improved pension and gratuity rights for officers retiring on ill-health grounds after more than ten but less than twenty years' reckonable service; the provision for civil servants after reaching normal retiring age to earn extra pension and extra lump sum gratuities; additional benefits under the injury warrants; the counting in full for pension purposes of any unestablished service rendered after the passing of the Act; and the payment of gratuities to unestablished staff upon termination of employment of seven years, irrespective of whether the termination was at the will of the department or the employee.

The Act represented some improvement on the initial agreement incorporated in the Bill. This improvement was largely the result of a campaign conducted by the Superannuation Joint Committee of the Staff Side. The Joint Committee included the FDA, AIT, Customs Federation, CSCA, POEU, SCS and the Institution. The Institution representative was Mrs Miller. MPs were lobbied during the passage of the Bill and civil service trade union members were urged to write to their own MPs. As a result of this pressure an amendment to the Bill was secured providing for the counting in full of temporary service performed after the passing of the Act.

In 1953 an important change was introduced in superannuation arrangements affecting some Institution members. Ever since the end of the First World War a number of professional entrants to the civil service had been enrolled for superannuation purposes in the Federated Superannuation Scheme for Universities. This was now abolished for new entrants to the scientific and statistician classes. Serving officers were given the option to transfer to superannuation under the Superannuation Acts. The Institution had for long pressed for changes because the FSSU scheme had resulted in many civil servants retiring on pension payments that were not only inadequate but were substantially less than would have accrued to them under the ordinary Superannuation Acts.

EXISTING PENSIONERS

One effect of the accelerated rate of inflation at the beginning of the 1950s was to create considerable hardship among civil service pensioners. Existing pensions were based on lower pay scales earned before the increase in the rate of inflation. The National Staff Side had no formal authority to make representations to the Treasury about the lot of civil service pensioners but they consistently appealed to the Treasury to help its former employees. The result of these representations was apparent in a number of Pensions (Increase) Acts passed by Parliament. The earliest of these Acts was dated 1944.

Pensioners who had retired before or soon after the outbreak of war in 1939 on a pension based on prewar salaries had to live through more than four years of continuously rising prices and increased taxation without any compensation for the falling value of their pensions. A further Pension (Increase) Act was passed in 1947 with effect from 1 December 1946. This increased modestly the scales of relief given by the 1944 Act and enlarged the pension limits within which increases could be given. Nevertheless the benefits given to civil service pensioners under both these Acts were made subject to various restrictive conditions.

In 1950 for the first time in the history of the civil service a number of civil service pensioners came together to form a Civil Service Pensioners' Alliance. It enjoyed the goodwill of the civil service trade unions. Partly as a result of the agitation which the Alliance conducted, supported by the efforts of the civil service unions, and partly, too, as a result of the support of the wider trade union movement and of a number of members of Parliament, a further amending Act was introduced in 1952. The benefits were again on a very modest scale but they established the right of civil service pensioners to look for some protection for the real purchasing power of their pensions.

EQUAL PAY

Another major issue during this period was that of equal pay. Towards the end of 1946 the report of a Royal Commission on Equal Pay provided much useful evidence to assist the civil service unions in their campaign for the introduction of the rate for the job. It pointed out that by 1944 the number of women in the non-industrial civil service was almost equal to the number of men, yet women represented only 4 per cent of the administrative class. Among the professional, scientific and technical staff only 1½ per cent were women. There was thus not only a problem of the rate for the job but of equal opportunities for women. The Commission stated:

> The civil service . . . presents as regards its non-industrial and common grades the conditions relevant to the application of equal pay in a highly simplified form. Such conditions include exact gradation of jobs, perfect interchangeability of men and women employees within each common grade, and again within each common grade, presumptively, equal efficiency of the two sexes, at least during the period when each is actively at work. Here over a big field are men and women doing identical jobs, doing them well, and doing them on unequal pay.

The Royal Commission did not recommend equal pay, partly because of the cost involved and partly because it gave some weight to traditional arguments against the introduction of the rate for the job. Nevertheless, in the words of the Institution at the time, it saw 'many reasons why it should be introduced in the civil service and comparable public employment'. A long article in *State Service* by Ruth Miller, now deputy general secretary of the Institution, stated that the reference of certain aspects of equal pay to a Royal Commission was a delaying tactic employed by the government. She pointed out that the principle of equal pay in the civil service had been confirmed again and again in the House of Commons and should have been applied long ago. The Labour Party was committed to support the principle of equal pay and it now remained for the Labour government to implement the policy to which the party had long been committed.

One blow for equal opportunities was struck, however, with the government's decision in 1946 to remove the 'marriage bar' in the civil service. This was greatly welcomed by the Institution who had consistently opposed the bar and had passed yet another resolution in favour of its abolition at its 1946 conference.

Before the publication of the Report of the Royal Commission on Equal Pay the National Staff Side had accepted an invitation to co-operate with other national organisations on an Equal Pay Joint Committee. The committee comprised representatives of the British Medical Association, National Staff Side, National Association of Local Government Officers, National Federation of Professional Workers, Medical Women's Federation, Educational Institute of Scotland and the National Union of Teachers. This Committee addressed a letter to the Prime Minister asking that, irrespective of anything that might emerge from the Royal Commission, the principle of equal pay should be applied forthwith in the public services. Following the publication of the Royal Commission's report, the Equal Pay Committee of the Staff Side made representations to the Chancellor of the Exchequer to ask for equal pay in the service. The joint committee sent a deputation to the Prime Minister and set up a subcommittee to ensure close co-ordination of the activities of the organisations represented on the committee. In 1948 the government accorded equal pay in the national health service.

With the approach of the 1950 general election the Equal Pay Joint Committee decided that the issue of equal pay should be put squarely before every candidate in the election. A pamphlet was issued entitled *Equal Pay for Equal Work – A Black Record*. The pamphlet surveyed the history of the claim for equal pay from 1914 to 1949. It recalled that in 1914 the McDonnell Commission had recommended that the Treasury should institute a general inquiry with the object of removing inequalities in the salaries of men and women not based on differences in efficiency and service. In 1918 the Haldane Committee had asserted that 'no discrimination can properly be enforced merely on the grounds of sex'. In the following year a War Cabinet committee on women in industry had recommended that the government should support the application of the principle of equal pay by applying it with the least possible delay in its own establishments. Further support for the principle of equal pay for work of equal value was contained in the Peace Treaty. It said that the principle was one of special and urgent importance.

In 1920 the House of Commons had accepted the principle of equal pay but in the following year the government said that it was not able to implement it because of the financial position of the country. In 1936 the House of Commons passed a resolution calling upon the government to implement the principle of equal pay which it had accepted in 1920. This resolution was then reversed when the Prime Minister made the matter one of confidence in the government. A similar situation arose in 1944. A resolution to abolish differentiation in the payment of men and women teachers solely on the ground of sex was carried by one vote, but again the Prime Minister secured a reversal by making the issue one of confidence in the government. In 1947 the Chancellor of the Exchequer on behalf of the newly elected Labour government stated that the government accepted as regards its own employees the justice of the claim for equal pay for equal work but was not able to apply the principle because it would be wholly inflationary in its results. The excuses for inaction remained unchanged for more than thirty years.

For the 1950 general election four civil service unions, the Civil Service Clerical Association, the Civil Service Union, the Institution of Professional Civil Servants and the Society of Civil Servants jointly produced a leaflet entitled *Equal Pay Now!*, designed to help branches and individual members to obtain pledges of support from candidates to the proposals for the introduction of equal pay in the civil service by instalments. The civil service unions were reinforced in their campaign by the terms of the Universal Declaration of Human Rights which had been approved by the United Nations Assembly in 1949. This declaration laid down that 'everyone without any discrimination has the right to equal pay for equal work'.

Despite the efforts of the trade union movement the government continued after the general election to equivocate on the issue of equal pay. In a statement to the International Labour Organisation (the specialised agency of the United Nations dealing with employment issues and industrial relations problems) the leader of the British delegation said in the summer of 1950 that the issue of equal pay was highly complex. He argued that real living standards depended on the maintenance of financial stability, and governments could not be expected to take positive measures to secure the observance of one particular principle of remuneration. He warned the conference of the danger of any formula which would have the effect of introducing undue rigidity into national wage and salary structures. This was an extremely disappointing statement because it was made by Britain's Minister of Labour and National Service, Mr George Isaacs. Before his elevation to the Cabinet Mr Isaacs had for many years been active in the trade union movement and had been a very long-serving general secretary of one of the printing unions.

On 3 January 1951 the National Staff Side sent a deputation to the Chancellor of the Exchequer, Mr Hugh Gaitskell, to press for the introduction of the principle of equal pay for equal work. These representations were equally unsuccessful. Later in the year Mr Douglas Houghton, MP, placed on the order paper of the House of Commons a motion which stated:

> That in the opinion of this House, further delay in making a start with the application of the principle of equal pay for equal work for women in the civil service will weaken the authority of Parliament and undermine public confidence in the repeated affirmation by this House of the acceptance of the principle of equal pay made during the past thirty years. This House therefore calls upon HM Government to announce a date by which a beginning will be made with the introduction of equal pay in the civil service.

Institution members were urged to get in touch with their members of Parliament to ask for support for this motion.

On 20 June 1951 the Chancellor of the Exchequer made a statement to the House of Commons on the government's attitude towards the representations made to it by the Staff Side on the question of equal pay. He said that the government reaffirmed its acceptance as regards their own employees and as a broad affirmation of the general principle of the justice of the claim that there should be no difference in payment to men and women for the same work. The

Chancellor then went on, however, to put forward a whole number of reasons why, in the government's view, equal pay could not be introduced immediately. They were no more than a restatement of objections which had been heard time and time again over many years. The Chancellor said that the government did not consider that it could proceed to extend the principle of equal pay at the present time and it could not therefore depart from the decision which it had previously announced. The Chancellor of the Exchequer, Mr Hugh Gaitskell, came under considerable criticism for his statement.

An immediate protest came also from civil service trade unions. The National Staff Side decided to hold a mass protest meeting in the Central Hall, Westminster. This meeting, held on Wednesday 18 July 1951, was packed to the doors with over 2,000 civil servants. Mr A. J. T. Day, chairman of the Staff Side, said that in all the long years of the fight for equal pay no statement by any government spokesman had had quite the infuriating quality of the speech made by the Chancellor of the Exchequer a few days earlier. It was not only a refusal to apply equal pay for the time being but it was also a statement of new reasons for not giving equal pay at all in the civil service unless and until other conditions were satisfied. At this protest meeting speakers on behalf of the main civil service unions, including Stanley Mayne of the Institution, pointed out that the statement made by Mr Gaitskell was in defiance of repeated decisions of the House of Commons, the Labour Party conference, the TUC, the Declaration of Human Rights, the considered judgement of the last Royal Commission on Equal Pay and of the ILO. In his speech Stanley Mayne recalled that in the voting on equal pay at a recent ILO conference there had been 105 votes in favour, 53 against and 40 abstentions. The government of the United Kingdom was included among the abstentions. Thus, said Stanley Mayne, 'we find ourselves in the disgraceful situation . . . of being one of the backward countries'.

The protest of the civil service unions was followed almost immediately by a statement of protest from the TUC. The TUC said that it was particularly concerned at the reasons given by the government for declining to make a start with the application of the principle of equal pay. The General Council, the statement added, 'regarded the government's attitude not only as reflecting opposition against the application of equal pay, but against the principle itself'.

The National Staff Side established a special subcommittee to organise a countrywide campaign to support the claim for equal pay in the civil service. The members of the committee were Miss R. Rowe (UPW), Mrs Kidd (IRSF), Miss Gilbert (CSCA), Miss Coult (CSCA) and J. Fraser (IPCS). The campaign was organised from the Institution headquarters. A campaign of fourteen provincial meetings was organised and information was distributed to members of each union suggesting action which should be taken to bring the equal pay issue before the notice of candidates in the coming election.

The general election of 25 October 1951 resulted in a Conservative victory, even though the Conservative Party received over 200,000 fewer votes than the Labour Party. The Conservatives won 321 seats compared with Labour's 295. The Liberals won six seats and there were three other members elected outside the main parties. The civil service unions urged members to write to the new members of Parliament to seek their support for the implementation of equal pay.

On 13 December 1951 the new Chancellor of the Exchequer, Mr R. A. Butler, received a deputation on equal pay from the National Staff Side. He made it clear that the new government was not prepared to agree to the introduction of equal pay in the then prevailing financial circumstances. Shortly afterwards it was announced that more than eighty members of Parliament had signed Mr Douglas Houghton's House of Commons motion calling for the implementation of equal pay.

The question of equal pay was again raised in a short debate at the House of Commons in March 1952. In reply to speakers from both sides of the House, the Financial Secretary to the Treasury, Mr John Boyd Carpenter, said that he had listened with a great deal of sympathy to what had been said but the substantial financial and economic considerations which the issue inescapably raised had to be looked at not only on their individual merits but against the background of Britain's economic difficulties. The question really boiled down, he said, to a matter of judgement as to when Britain's national financial position would permit actual steps to be taken to implement equal pay.

In another House of Commons debate on 16 May 1952 the government was asked to give an early and definite date by which the application of equal pay for equal work for women in the civil service, the teaching profession, local government and other public services would begin. Many MPs took part in the debate and a motion standing in the name of Mr Charles Pannell was adopted without a division. In replying for the government Mr Boyd Carpenter said that it was the wish of the government to start the implementation of equal pay in the public services as soon as it was possible without serious prejudice to Britain's national economic recovery. The full terms of Mr Pannell's motion read:

> That this House reaffirms its belief in the principle of equal work as between men and women; supports the doctrine universally accepted by the trade union movement of payment for all work at the rate for the job irrespective of sex; recognises, however, that the economic position of those with family responsibilities must be assured, which can be and is being progressively achieved by a combination of family allowances and other social services, and tax relief; that therefore in the opinion of this House there is no justification for continuing the 32 years' delay in implementing the motion of 19 May 1920, which declared that it was expedient that women in the public services should be given equal pay; and it now calls upon HM Government to announce an early and definite date by which the application of equal pay for equal work for women in the civil service, the teaching profession, local government and other public services will begin.

The first major advance in the campaign for equal pay in the public services came not in the civil service but from the Labour-controlled London County Council. In July 1952 the LCC decided that equal pay for equal work should be introduced for a wide range of jobs in the council's service.

The government continued its refusal to implement the principle of equal pay through the remaining months of 1952. Towards the end of November it also reaffirmed previous decisions that the claim for equal pay could not be put to the Civil Service Arbitration Tribunal. The civil service unions again called on their membership to write to members of Parliament in support of the immediate implementation of equal pay. Considerable publicity was also secured on St Valentine's Day, 14 February 1953, when a giant Valentine card, prepared for and carried by the members of the Civil Service Equal Pay Committee, was handed in at 11 Downing Street. The National Staff Side, together with the National Union of Teachers and the National and Local Government Officers' Association, also sent a joint letter to each member of the House of Commons. This letter recalled that nearly a year had passed since the House of Commons, on a motion from Mr Charles Pannell, had called upon the government to announce an early and definite date by which the application for equal pay for equal work for women in the civil service and other public services was to begin. Members of Parliament were asked to use any opportunity they might have during the forthcoming budget debate to press for action from the government.

Despite the efforts of the TUC and the civil service unions, the government remained unmoved during the first half of 1953. At the end of July there was yet another cause of delay. The government announced that there was to be a new Royal Commission on the civil service. In the debate on the appointment of the Royal Commission the Chancellor of the Exchequer said:

> The question of equal pay is within the terms of reference, but as the House knows, the government's policy in the matter has already been stated, namely, that we are in favour of the general principle, and that we hope to make progress on the matter as soon as the economic and financial circumstances of the country permit. I shall draw the attention of the Commission to this statement.

At its September 1953 Congress the TUC again protested at the continued failure of the government to implement the principle of equal pay for equal work in the public service. The resolution said that the General Council of the TUC should make the strongest representations to the government to acquaint it with the strong demand of the whole trade union movement for tangible progress to be made without delay.

INSTITUTION ORGANISATION

Between the end of 1948 and the end of 1953 the membership of the Institution rose from 31,491 to 43,176, an increase of over one-third. The highest point during this period was 1952 when the membership reached 43,801. During the following year there were redundancies in a number of departments affecting Institution grades and there was also an increase in subscriptions. At the end of 1952 the Institution estimated that its density of membership among the grades eligible to join was about 61 per cent. Potential membership, it was estimated, was more than 71,000.

The density of Institution membership among eligible grades was significantly lower than the density of trade union membership among the civil service as a whole. At the end of 1951, for example, it was estimated that of the total non-industrial civil service of 608,000, no fewer than 546,000 were members of unions affiliated to the National Staff Side. This represented a total density of membership of nearly 90 per cent.

National Staff Side membership at the end of 1952 rose to approximately 563,000 in conparison with 327,000 in 1939. The largest single group of unions affiliated to the National Staff Side were the Post Office group, with a total membership of nearly 230,000. Membership of the four clerical unions, constituting the Civil Service Alliance, namely, the Civil Service Clerical Association, the Inland Revenue Staff Federation, the Ministry of Labour Staff Association and the County Court Officers' Association, was almost exactly 200,000. Of the remaining organisations affiliated to the National Staff Side, the Institution was the largest. After the Institution came the Society of Civil Servants with 38,150 members, the Civil Service Union with 23,417, the Federation of Civil Service Professional and Technical Staffs with 13,050 and then a number of smaller organisations with a departmental identity. The Association of First Division Civil Servants, representing administrative grades, had just over 3,000 members.

In 1949 Mr Eric Widdowson resigned as chairman of the Institution. He had been an active member of the Institution for a number of years. He became a member of the Executive Committee in 1943, was elected vice-chairman in 1945 and chairman in 1947. He was chairman at the time of the death of Leslie Herbert and it was partly due to his energetic approach that Stanley Mayne was appointed general secretary. He served on many committees of the National Executive Committee and also served as chairman of the Civil Service Political Freedom Committee. Mr J. A. Nicol of the Ministry of Supply Accountants' Branch was elected to succeed Mr Widdowson as chairman of the Institution. Mr Widdowson was then elected one of the vice-presidents.

The year 1951 marked the retirement of the Institution's deputy general secretary, Mrs Ruth Miller. She had joined the staff in April 1920 soon after its birth when the membership was a mere 1,500. At the date of her retirement the membership had grown to 33,000. During that period she had taken an important part in the affairs of the Institution, stepping into the breach on the three occasions when the Institution was effectively without a general secretary. She had taken an active part in the affairs of the Institution and Staff Side but she was particularly remembered for her role in the campaign for equal pay. Following Mrs Miller's retirement the Institution appointed Tom Profitt as its new deputy general secretary. After leaving school at 14 years of age, Mr Profitt went to work in a steel mill in Yorkshire. From there he became a Post Office employee. Following continuous study in adult education schemes he secured an adult scholarship at Oxford University where he took a degree in philosophy, politics and economics. He had been appointed an assistant secretary at the Institution in May 1941.

In September 1949 there was a change of style in *State Service*. A competition was held for a new cover design and it attracted eighty-nine entries. The new cover was introduced with the September 1949 issue. Members were also asked to express their views on the contents of the journal. From the replies received it appeared that most members preferred the journal to remain much as it was.

By 1950 it was apparent that a further look at the organisation of the Institution was necessary. It had been six years since professional groups were established and four since annual conferences had taken the place of annual general meetings. These arrangements had been established in the very difficult and unsettled times towards the end of the war and since then the organisation had been varied by *ad hoc* changes as the need arose. Various conference resolutions had expressed dissatisfaction with the existing structure.

In 1949 and 1950 much of the time of the National Executive Committee was spent in drawing up a report on the organisation of the Institution. It was felt that the NEC should so organise its work that it would have more time to deal with long-term policy issues. It suggested that a Future Policy Panel, reporting to the General Purposes Sub-Committee, should be established. As far as the negotiating machinery was concerned the NEC felt that there was a need to represent adequately the various professional interests, that representation on such professional groupings should be directed from relevant branches and sections and that the machinery adopted should be flexible enough to permit minor variations without rule amendment. The NEC recommended that the existing four groups and fourteen panels should be replaced by a much larger number of professional groups (initially seventeen) including all the existing panels. They should report to the Negotiations Sub-Committee, which would replace the existing Treasury Negotiations Sub-Committee. Its terms of reference were to be widened to include all salary and grading negotiations and the consideration of recommendations from the various groups.

Changes were also suggested in branch organisation with a view to strengthening the democratic participation of the membership. Branches were urged to devolve as much as possible to section and subsection level. Provision was to be made for the co-ordination of views between branches, sections and subsections at each level of the departmental Whitley machinery. Amendments were also suggested to make conference representation more fairly weighted numerically as between departments. The report on organisation was submitted to the 1950 annual conference and, with one or two amendments, was adopted.

At the 1951 annual conference a very familiar face was missing. Because of illness the president, Sir Richard Redmayne, was not able to attend. In his letter to the conference, written in extremely warm terms, Sir Richard conveyed his good wishes to the delegates but referred to the possibility of his finding it necessary to resign because of ill-health. Sir Richard was persuaded not to resign and he was again present at the 1952 annual conference.

13 The 'Purge' and Civil Rights

The late 1940s and the early 1950s were the years of the 'cold war'. During this period the relationship between the wartime allies, Britain and the USA on the one hand and the USSR on the other, rapidly deteriorated. Basically, the 'cold war' developed from a confict of policy between the USA and the USSR.

Apart from its more general effect on economic and political life – for example, the growth of military expenditure and the implications for incomes policy – the 'cold war' had an indirect effect on the employment conditions of civil servants. Espionage was an instrument of 'cold war' policy and there were a number of examples in Britain of prominent scientists and diplomats who gave secret information to the Soviet Union. But in the drive for security suspicion sometimes fell, without evidence of personal unreliability, on persons known to hold strongly left-wing views, particularly if they had been or were members of the Communist Party or were associated with support for particular issues which were in line with current communist policies.

At worst these suspicions developed into witch-hunting campaigns. This was certainly the case in the United States. The witch-hunt was led by the late Senator Joe McCarthy and resulted in intimidation, fear and the dismissal of many people from jobs, in both the public and the private sectors, which were unconnected with security. The personal histories of large numbers of people were subjected to secret scrutiny and many who at some period in their lives, particularly in the 1930s, had been associated with left-wing and anti-fascist causes were victimised.

TRADE UNION CRITICISM

Though there were examples during the years of the 'cold war' of the betrayal of security by a small number of scientists, diplomats and government employees, those found guilty of espionage were not people who were active in the trade union and labour movement. The unions were highly critical of the assumption that persons engaged in left-wing activity were 'unreliable'. An atmosphere conducive to witch-hunting could easily be created which bore no relation to security but served to weaken the trade union and labour movement. Indeed, it was argued, the encouragement of this kind of intolerant hysteria, far from helping security, was likely to divert attention from the real problems facing Britain. Moreover, real espionage agents would be more likely to pose as pillars of the establishment than as political radicals.

One of the most serious cases of breach of security concerned the scientist Dr Nunn May. He was given a sentence of ten years' penal servitude. The National Executive Committee of the Institution adopted a resolution on the sentencing of Dr Nunn May which said that whilst the Institution in no way condoned his breach of the Official Secrets Act the sentence of ten years' penal service was 'harsh and unduly severe'. The resolution urged that the sentence should be reduced.

The resolution of the National Executive Committee on the Nunn May case was adopted in June 1946. By the early spring of 1947 the Institution had dealt with a number of other cases where action had been taken against members on security grounds. In two of these cases scientists who had been specifically recommended for certain work found their assignments cancelled at the last moment. No reasons were given and none could be obtained either by the scientists themselves or by the Institution. In the third case an unestablished scientist nominated for establishment by his department found his establishment cancelled. The Institution was not able to obtain any information on the reasons for the cancellation. The general secretary said that the scientist concerned was employed on purely civilian work and in a 'non-secret' department. The recommendation for establishment had also been accepted by the Civil Service Commission. In all three cases, according to the general secretary, there was reason to suspect that the current or previous left-wing activities of the officers concerned were factors in the action against them.

The Institution took up each of the cases of alleged victimisation of the scientists in the civil service. A satisfactory solution was secured in one of the cases and the civil servant concerned was subsequently given established status. In most of the other cases little satisfaction was achieved. The general secretary stated:

> the NEC maintains, of course, that civil servants should be treated alike, irrespective of their political views, and it cannot but regard these developments very seriously indeed. In view of completely unsatisfactory replies from the departments concerned and failure to obtain satisfaction from the Treasury, the matter has been raised with the National Staff Side.

In April 1947 the National Staff Side made representations to Sir Edward Bridges, the head of the civil service, urging that if nothing more was attributed to a civil servant than membership of a political party there was no justifiable ground for dismissal, for a refusal of establishment where this was otherwise justified or for interference in departmental posting. The Staff Side argued that if there were considerations to take into account other than membership of a political party and these considerations would have adverse results for the individual concerned they should be revealed to the individual.

THE PRIME MINISTER'S STATEMENT

Sir Edward Bridges undertook to consult the Cabinet and to give the National Staff Side a considered reply. Despite several reminders a reply was not forthcoming. Eventually on 15 March 1948 the Prime Minister made a statement on the subject. The substance of this statement was that a member of the Communist Party or a person 'associated with it in such a way as to raise legitimate doubts about his or her reliability' should no longer be employed on work vital to the security of the state.

The Prime Minister stated that it was not suggested that in matters affecting the security of the state all those who adhered to the Communist Party would 'allow themselves thus to forget their primary loyalty to the state'. But, he continued, 'there is no way of distinguishing such people from those who, if opportunity offered, would be prepared to endanger the security of the state in the interests of another Power'. The Prime Minister added that the same ruling would be applied to the employment of those known to be actively associated with fascist organisations. He affirmed that the state was 'not concerned with the political views, as such, of its servants', and that as far as possible alternative employment would be found on non-secret work for those deemed unsuitable for secret work. Where such employment could not be found, however, there might be no alternative to dismissal.

The Prime Minister's statement caused considerable concern in the Institution. The general secretary pointed out that because Institution members were concentrated in defence departments and were less transferable than non-specialist staff they were more likely to be directly affected by the 'purge'.

THE STAFF SIDE VIEW

Following the Prime Minister's statement to the House of Commons on the 15 March 1948 the Institution tabled a resolution for consideration by the National Staff Side. A special meeting was convened to consider it. The terms of the resolution were as follows:

> That this Staff Side, while supporting all appropriate measures against civil servants who are disloyal to the state, reaffirms its adherence to the principle that all civil servants should be free to join any lawful political party and to associate with persons freely chosen by themselves, regardless of political views or attachments of such persons. The Staff Side further reaffirms its views that any attempt to penalise on account of his or her political views (e.g. by transfer, dismissal, or refusal of establishment) a civil servant against whom there is neither evidence nor reasonable suspicion of actual or intended disloyalty, is inconsistent with this principle; and that where any charge of actual or intended disloyalty is made against a civil servant the grounds of the charge should be clearly stated to such civil servant and adequate machinery for appeal, with the aid of appropriate staff association representatives if desired, should be provided.

An addendum to this resolution, moved by the Union of Post Office Workers, was carried. It was incorporated in the main resolution which was then supported by the National Staff Side without dissent. The addendum read: 'Nevertheless, this Staff Side notes with satisfaction that the government intends to take appropriate action to safeguard state secrets, the unauthorised release of which might endanger the security of the state.'

The National Executive Committee of the Institution arranged for the publication in *State Service* of a fuller statement of its views on the 'purge'. In the first place, said the NEC, the Institution supported wholeheartedly any appropriate action against civil servants who were disloyal to the state. In the second place, the NEC declined to take steps on behalf of or against any political party whatsoever. In the third place, the NEC considered that action should be taken against civil servants only where there was evidence or reasonable suspicion of disloyalty, actual or intended. The NEC said that it could not agree that membership of any legal party was such evidence. It felt that civil servants should have the normal rights of a citizen to join any lawful political party they chose and to associate with persons freely chosen by themselves irrespective of the political connections of such persons. Where there was evidence or reasonable suspicion of disloyalty the facts should be stated to the civil servant concerned and he should have the normal rights of stating his case of appeal to an impartial body. In addition, said the NEC, he should have the right to call upon a staff association for aid if necessary. The NEC added that 'in so far . . . as the Prime Minister's statement indicated intention to take action against disloyal civil servants' it was whole-heartedly supported by the Institution. In so far, however, as it put forward a presumption that membership of any lawful political party was evidence of disloyalty and justified transfer or dismissal, the NEC said it was unable to agree.

The NEC concluded its statement by saying that it wished it to be known that it would use its best endeavours to prevent the penalising of any members of the Institution on purely political grounds. There must be, said the NEC, many members of the Institution of ten years, fifteen years or maybe even longer service who joined the Communist Party in circumstances in which the government had made it perfectly clear that they were entitled to do so and would not be penalised in any way. The NEC said that it felt it had a duty to defend members, and any member who was informed that action was to be taken against him in the light of the Prime Minister's statement was advised to write immediately to the headquarters of the Institution.

The National Staff Side decided to write to the Prime Minister expressing concern about the procedure for the implementation of the government's decision to remove communist and fascist civil servants from work of a nature vital to the security of the state. The letter protested at the failure of the government to consult the National Staff Side about points of procedure. The letter said that the National Staff Side 'were not invited to express an opinion on the safeguards which might be provided against the possibility of wrong or unduly harsh decisions'. No recognition was given to the existence of civil service staff associations and their appropriateness for representing civil servants when they were being heard.

As a result of these representations the Treasury made a number of changes in procedure. It was agreed that any officer appearing to be affected by the decision of the government should be given special leave with pay pending a final decision instead of being suspended from duty. The government did not, however, concede the right of representation by a staff association. The Staff Side therefore refused to agree to the new procedure until that point was satisfactorily settled, which it never was.

INSTITUTION RESOLUTION

At the 1948 annual conference of the Institution a lengthy emergency resolution on communists and fascists in the civil service was adopted. The resolution read:

1 That this conference, having considered the Prime Minister's statement of 15 March 1948, about civil servants who are employed on secret work and who are suspected of being members of, or of being associated with, the Communist Party or a fascist organisation, and having also considered the subsequent discussions on the National Whitley Council, the correspondence between the chairman of the National Staff Side and the Prime Minister and,

finally, the government statement issued to the press on 20 May 1948, refusing to allow 'suspects' normal trade union representation or appeal, places on record its profound disquiet.

2   Conference is of the opinion that the government's action has introduced into the British civil service deplorable principles and procedures from which it had until recently been unusually free. This freedom, from political discrimination, jobbery and injustice, had long been the pride of Britain and the envy of other nations.

3   In particular, conference is of the opinion that the use of information supplied by the security service (MI5, etc.) which cannot be examined, or challenged by any judicial process, carries with it the danger of grave injustice. This danger is most marked in cases where the 'suspect' is accused of association with either the Communist Party or a fascist organisation 'in such a way as to raise legitimate doubts about his reliability'. No attempt has been made to define the 'association' and the fact that officials of local Labour Party branches and individuals who resigned from the Communist Party in 1943 have been so accused indicates the reality of this danger.

4   Conference is also gravely apprehensive that the possibility of transferring 'suspects' to non-secret work will, in many cases in the professional, scientific and technical fields, prove to be largely illusory, and that the alternative of resignation or dismissal will be enforced. Experience has already shown that this is not the least danger; the security service has already prevented one industrial firm engaged on defence contracts from employing a 'suspect'. Specialists, in a scarcity category, may thus be compelled to seek new avenues of employment, for which they are not qualified, to the irreparable loss of both themselves and the state.

5   Conference is further of the opinion that the loss of superannuation rights, threatened in the government statement, would be the most obvious injustice, though not necessarily the most serious. To condemn a 'suspect' on such 'evidence', and by such a procedure, and to punish him by imposing a heavy 'fine' (the capital value of his superannuation rights, which may amount to some £10,000) as well as dismissal, would surely be such glaring injustice that it could not be upheld in British courts.

6   Finally, conference is of the opinion that the advisory committee can only be regarded as a face-saving device for the government if the present restrictions on trade union representation are maintained and if it remains within the power of a minister to overrule its findings on the evidence.

7   Conference therefore instructs the National Executive Committee to take all steps within its power to induce the government to reverse its policy of political discrimination or, failing this, to withdraw the present scheme and to institute a judicial procedure or so to modify the procedure that the possibility of injustice is removed.

8   In the event of failure of all these efforts, conference instructs the National Executive Committee to take all steps within its power to defend the rights of any 'suspects' in membership of the Institution.

THE EXTENSION OF THE 'PURGE'

In the summer of 1948 the Secretary of State for Air announced that special security precautions were to be taken covering staff in the Air Ministry headquarters. In the view of the Institution this meant that the Air Ministry headquarters were to be regarded as a 'purge' area. It was felt that this decision was contrary to the statement made by the Prime Minister in the House of Commons earlier in the year when he stated that 'there should be no general purge, no witch-hunt'. The Institution wrote to the National Staff Side asking that the extension of the 'purge' area should be raised with the Prime Minister. The Staff Side accepted this suggestion and wrote to the Prime Minister to express concern at the development.

This extension of the 'purge', as the Institution saw it, gave added significance to the establishment of a joint co-ordinating committee, known as the Civil Service Political Freedom Committee, of representatives of the Institution, the Civil Service Clerical Association, the Society of Civil Servants, the Civil Service Union and the Association of Scientific Workers to oppose the principle of the 'purge'. Mr E. J. Widdowson of the Institution was appointed as chairman of the new co-ordinating committee and Mr L. C. White, the general secretary of the CSCA, as secretary. In addition, the civil service branch of the National Council for Civil Liberties held a conference on 20 July at which the Institution's chairman was one of the principal speakers. Not all civil service unions opposed the principle of the 'purge', though all were concerned to ensure that it did not develop into a general policy of political discrimination.

The general secretary was forthright in his opposition to the 'purge'. In a comment on a letter published in *State Service* he said that the Institution had stated its clear opposition to the 'purge' because of the 'injustices involved and the fact that there is no evidence that the purge can serve a useful purpose'. An article in the November 1948 issue of *State Service* said that the procedure for dealing with civil servants affected by the government's new arrangements had been inordinately slow and in no case had any evidence been adduced of persons in the civil service having behaved improperly. There was not a single instance of a purged civil servant being subsequently prosecuted under the Official Secrets Act. In a further comment the general secretary said that political discrimination was a bad thing in the civil service. It was a futile method of protecting the state because no one proposing to betray the state would attract attention to himself by belonging to a minority party. (This point was confirmed when in 1949 Dr Claus Fuchs, who was a member of the Institution, was accused of espionage. It was an odd fact that, despite all the activities in purging civil servants, Dr Fuchs was not purged and, judging from press reports, it was only on the basis of his own confessions that his spying activities were brought to light. Dr Fuchs was expelled from membership when he was convicted.) Political discrimination, he maintained, was unfair in its incidence and method of operation. The Institution continued to complain vigorously that when civil servants were affected by the new security arrangements no provision was permitted for them to be represented by the staff organisation to which they belonged. The Institution pointed out that this offended against all established practice.

In reply to representations made by the National Staff Side, the Prime Minister maintained that particulars of complaints against civil servants had not, as they alleged, been consistently withheld. The Prime Minister said, however, that he had given instructions that even greater care was to be taken in future to see that a civil servant affected by security procedures was given all particulars that could be given without disclosing sources of evidence.

THE ADVISORY COMMITTEE

Before any final decision was taken on the suspension of a civil servant from work involving state security, the case was referred to three advisers appointed by the government. The advisers were Sir Thomas Gardiner, Sir Frederick Leggett and Mr J. W. Bowen. It was made clear in the terms of reference of the advisory committee that its task was to advise ministers in cases referred to it as to whether in its opinion a *prima facie* ruling that a civil servant was either a communist or a fascist, or associated with either the Communist Party or a fascist organisation in such a way as to raise legitimate doubts about his reliability, was substantiated. It was made clear that the decision on what employment was to be regarded as involving 'connection with work the nature of which is vital to the security of the state' was one not for the advisory committee but for ministers in charge of departments. It was also underlined that the functions of the advisory committee did not extend beyond advising a minister whether the *prima facie* case had or had not been substantiated. The committee was not concerned with the action which the minister might decide to take in relation to the case.

In further correspondence between the National Staff Side and the Prime Minister the civil service unions continued to maintain that the information supplied against civil servants affected by the security arrangements was so flimsy as to constitute totally inadequate evidence. This exchange of correspondence had no satisfactory outcome.

At the 1949 annual conference of the Institution the president, Sir Richard Redmayne joined in the criticism of the 'purge'. He observed that one of the most attractive things to him in the civil service was its freedom from political or religious discrimination. The advent of the 'purge' had troubled all in the Institution. 'Witch-hunting', he said, was a procedure repugnant to all men of goodwill. A form of political discrimination had in practice been extended to include a very wide circle of people. In presenting his report to the annual conference the general secretary said that colleagues who had been suspended under the 'purge' were in a very difficult and unfair position. The charges made against them had been extremely vague. Despite the representations made to the Prime Minister by the National Staff Side these vague charges continued to be made. A resolution was carried by the 1949 conference instructing the National Executive Committee to take every practicable step to ensure that the civil service was made free of any political or religious discrimination.

In the January 1950 issue of *State Service* there was an article by a member who had been a victim of the 'purge'. He described his experiences, and emphasised that the charges made against him were based entirely on information which he had himself volunteered. He recorded that he had been a member of the Labour Party, and engaged in minor local Labour Party activities, and before the war – and before becoming a civil servant – had subscribed to the Left Book Club. He concluded his article by saying that under the procedure of the 'purge' an entirely new feature had been introduced into public life. It meant that the government of the day or some hidden body of that government could, if it so wished, transfer or remove public servants without explanation.

By the spring of 1950, the government had removed forty-eight civil servants from their employment on grounds of membership of the Communist Party and one on grounds of membership of a fascist organisation. Twenty-five other civil servants had been moved on grounds of association with the Communist Party. At the annual conference of the Institution in 1950 the general secretary disclosed that of the total number of civil servants who had been 'purged' some thirty-six were members of the Institution. He said that in practically every case the senior officer of the particular department in which the victim was employed had no complaint to make against the victim and had expressed confidence in his probity. In not one of the thirty-six cases had any disciplinary action been taken against the accused and there had been no legal prosecution. A motion calling upon the Institution to take no further action in connection with the 'purge', other than to make representations on behalf of any member who might be affected by it, was defeated. The Institution continued to oppose the 'purge'.

NEW ARRANGEMENTS

At the beginning of 1952, there were indications of a new extension of the 'purge' procedure. The government decided to institute a new set of security arrangements for employees in atomic energy establishments and for some two or three thousand civil servants in other government departments. As part of these arrangements it was proposed that each officer should complete a questionnaire. The National Staff Side took very strong exception to a number of features of this new procedure. The general secretaries of the Civil Service Clerical Association, the Society of Civil Servants and the Institution issued a statement expressing concern at 'the nature of the interrogation which the government intends to impose on all civil servants employed in atomic energy establishments, and on some 2,000 to 3,000 civil servants employed on secret work'. The statement acknowledged the right of any government to safeguard itself against information being given to unauthorised persons. But it expressed grave doubts whether the new method of interrogation would achieve this end. It said that the new arrangements would encourage the creation of an atmosphere of suspicion between colleagues working together and this could only have harmful results.

These new security arrangements were condemned by the 1952 annual conference of the Institution. The main speaker in the discussion at the conference was the general secretary. He said that up to the time of the conference some sixty members of the Institution had been 'purged'. There was still not one case where any proceedings or disciplinary steps had been taken against a purged officer. It was obvious, he said, that there could have been no real suspicion attaching to any of the officers. A considerable amount of unhappiness and domestic disturbance had been caused. He was pleased to note that there were signs that the 'purge' was dying away and he therefore particularly objected to the new arrangements introduced at the beginning of 1952. He described the questions which staff were asked to answer and he ridiculed them. This sort of procedure, he said, would never catch a spy. Its effect would be merely to annoy and to irritate people and it did no real good. The conference adopted a resolution which said that the new arrangements were unlikely to ensure security but instead they encouraged malicious gossip and introduced a wholly undesirable atmosphere in the establishments concerned. Another resolution was carried advising members not to respond to the proposed new security interrogation where this involved giving information about colleagues.

The 1953 annual report of the National Executive Committee stated that, despite the great flourish with which the extension of the 'purge' had been introduced at the beginning of 1952, nothing very drastic seemed to have developed from it. Indeed, the number of new 'purge' cases was much reduced. At the 1954 annual conference it was stated that there had been 'no further developments' and no new cases of persons being suspended as a result of the operation of the new procedure. The Institution claimed that this decline in the 'purge' confirmed its view that the introduction of political discrimination in the civil service had, in reality, very little or anything to do with security but had been prompted by the prevailing political circumstances and the 'cold war' atmosphere in international relations. Civil servants with left-wing political views were particularly susceptible to victimisation, whereas any person who was really a security risk would be much more likely to pose as a 'pillar of respectability' and to express the most conventional views. The 'purge' procedure put a premium on malicious gossip and enabled politically motivated informers to pose as patriots. The Institution and other civil service unions pointed to the effect on members of Parliament and public opinion of their persistent representations to the government in defence of the civil rights of their members. They said that those representations had influenced the government.

THE MASTERMAN COMMITTEE

One other aspect of civil rights of concern to the civil service unions was the limitations imposed on the political activities of civil servants. Early in 1948 the government appointed a committee under the chairmanship of Mr J. C. Masterman to examine the existing limitations and to recommend any changes which might be desirable in the public interest. The other members of the committee were Sir Edward Cadogan, Miss Myra Curtis, Mr Graham White, Mr D. N. Chester, Sir Richard Hopkins, Sir Ronald Adam, Lord Dukeston, Sir William Cash, Jr, and Sir Miles Mitchell.

In their evidence to the Masterman Committee the National Staff Side pressed for the removal of restrictions on the political activities of civil servants. They proposed a new convention in the following terms:

> Civil servants are free to engage in party political activity and it is left to their discretion and good sense to do so with due regard to their rank, the functions of their department and their duties to it, on the understanding that an officer who by grossly negligent or wilful action or comment on a matter of party politics creates an intolerable position for his department will be liable to disciplinary action.

The Staff Side proposed that no civil servant should be prevented from standing as a candidate for election to the House of Commons. If elected he should then be given special leave without pay for the period of his membership. The civil servant, it was urged, should be free to return to his civil service career. The Staff Side also proposed that civil servants should be entitled to participate in local government affairs. If a civil servant wanted to stand for local government office he would be required to notify his intention to the head of his department. It would then be open to the head of the department to raise objections, particularly where there was a special relationship between the officer's work and local authorities. If this objection was not acceptable to the civil servant it would be open to the civil service trade unions to raise the matter within the Whitley machinery. The National Staff Side urged that civil servants serving on a local authority should be given reasonable time off to enable them to perform their local government duties.

The report of the Masterman Committee was published in the summer of 1949. It recommended that a horizontal line should be drawn through government service and that all above the line should not participate in party political activity. Those below the line would have freedom to engage in political activities. The line was drawn so as to exclude from political activity all but the so-called manipulative and industrial grades. Virtually the entire white-collar staff of the civil service, from administrative grades to clerical assistants and typists, were put 'above the line'. In national politics they were to be required to abstain from any public manifestations of their views which might associate them prominently with a political party. In particular they were not to hold office in any party political organisation; not to speak in public on matters of party political controversy; not to write letters to the press; not to publish books or articles or circulate leaflets setting out their views on party political matters; and not to canvass in support of a political candidate. The Masterman Committee even went so far as to 'draw attention to the tendency apparent over a number of years for the delegates of certain staff associations at conferences to make speeches of a political nature inconsistent, in the case of serving civil servants, with the existing rules of conduct'.

The National Staff Side reacted angrily to the recommendations of the report and the decision of the government to accept it. The National Staff Side said that it took away from many civil servants in junior grades rights which they had enjoyed since before the First World War. The civil service unions accepted that civil servants in more senior grades should exercise discretion in regard to party political activities but they argued that to extend this ban to many thousands of junior civil servants was unnecessary and, indeed, unhealthy for democracy.

As a result of the protest from the civil service unions the government retreated from its original decision to accept the Masterman recommendations. It agreed that the whole subject should be open for discussion within the National Whitley Council. The civil service unions wrote to all members of Parliament to acquaint them with the view of the civil service trade union movement and a leaflet in defence of the civil rights of junior civil servants was widely circulated. A conference on the implications of the Masterman Report was convened by the National Council for Civil Liberties and was supported by a number of civil service organisations.

The civil service unions welcomed the decision of the government to accept the recommendations of the Masterman Report applying to the government employees 'below the line'. The effect was to increase the civil rights of these public servants. For civil servants 'above the line' the government agreed, following the representations of the civil service unions, that,,pending further discussions, the existing rights of civil servants should not be reduced.

In the 1950 general election the Institution joined with other civil service unions in bringing to the attention of candidates the complaint of civil servants

about the proposed restrictions on their civil rights. The civil service organisations urged that, instead, the civil rights of the great majority of civil servants
should be extended.

Following lengthy discussions with the civil service unions within the National
Whitley Council the government announced in the spring of 1953 its decision on
the extent to which the recommendations of the Masterman Report were to be
applied 'above the line' in the civil service. The government accepted that there
should be not only an 'above the line' category but also an intermediate category
of staff who would be eligible, subject to permission, to engage in all national
political activities except parliamentary candidature. The granting of permission
would depend on a code of conduct. The intermediate category was to include
typists, clerical assistants and grades parallel to the general service grade of junior
executive officer. It was estimated that the intermediate class would include about
290,000 staff. The Staff Side pressed strongly that the intermediate class should
be extended to include executive officers and analogous grades. They also urged
that canvassing in elections should be excluded from the definition of political
activities. The government did not accept these suggestions.

The effect of these changes, in the view of the civil service unions, was that,
whilst they represented some improvement on the original recommendations of
the Masterman Report, they were in general more restrictive than past practice. A
number of departments up to that time had granted their staff a considerable
measure of civil liberty and some officers of senior grading had taken part in
municipal affairs and local politics. The National Staff Side passed a resolution
expressing regret that the government had refused to accept canvassing as a
generally conferred civil service right and had also refused to include the
executive class in the intermediate category for purposes of civil rights.

A resolution on the government's decision on the Masterman Report was
carried unanimously at the 1953 annual conference of the Institution. It condemned the decision of the government, and said that it prevented most
professional, scientific and technical civil servants from making their contribution to the public life of the country. The resolution also said that the government
had taken from some civil servants rights which had been exercised over a
substantial number of years without harm to the civil service and with benefit to
the community.

14 The Priestley Commission

On 30 July 1953 the government announced in the House of Commons that there was to be a new Royal Commission on the civil service. Its terms of reference were:

> To consider and to make recommendations on certain questions concerning conditions of service of civil servants within the ambit of the Civil Service National Whitley Council, thus
> (a) whether any changes are desirable in the principles which should govern pay; or in the rates of pay at present in force for the main catagories – bearing in mind in this connection the need for a suitable relationship between the pay of those categories;
> (b) whether any changes are desirable in the hours of work, arrangements for overtime and remuneration for extra duty, and annual leave allowances;
> (c) whether any changes are desirable within the framework of the existing superannuation scheme.

By this time it was becoming increasingly clear that the existing system of pay determination in the civil service was not working as it should. The Tomlin principles established in 1932 were not specific enough to obviate major disagreements between the parties. Intervals between pay settlements were too long. The disagreements between the Official and Staff Sides were becoming more frequent, as indicated by the huge workload of the Civil Service Arbitration Tribunal in the period 1950–6. In 1951 thirty-six cases were considered by the arbitration tribunal, in 1952 thirty-three cases and in 1953 thirty-one. Moreover, the Staff Side had been arguing for some time that the Treasury should abandon the fiction that each department should negotiate the pay of its employees. In an article in *State Service* in February 1952 entitled 'The dead hand', the general secretary argued that it was perfectly clear that the Treasury was in control of pay throughout the civil service.and quoted the evidence of the Treasury to the Committee of Public Accounts which said: 'As regards salaries (and wages), the Treasury exercises complete control over all departments in the sense that no salary may be paid by any department to anyone without the assent of the Treasury.' In such circumstances, the article concluded:

> can we now expect that they [the Treasury] will follow the logic and clarity with which Sir Edward Bridges has set out the position in dealing with the Committee of Public Accounts, by arranging that from now on negotiations on all pay and conditions will be with the Treasury and not with departments? It would be a relief to departments who are not allowed to more than act as a Treasury mouthpiece and are frequently forced to say things they know to be wrong but which are in pursuance of Treasury pay policy.

In setting up the Royal Commission the government indicated that it had no wish to disrupt the normal machinery for the determination of pay and conditions. Thus, the civil service unions were not precluded from taking claims through the ordinary stages of negotiation and, where appropriate, arbitration.

In the House of Commons debate on the appointment of the Royal Commission the Chancellor of the Exchequer confirmed that the question of equal pay was within the terms of reference of the Royal Commission. He added, however, that the government's policy on this matter had already been stated. The government, he stressed, was in favour of the general principle of equal pay and hoped to make progress towards it as soon as the economic and financial circumstances of the country permitted. He said that he would draw the attention of the Royal Commission to his statement.

The decision to appoint a Royal Commission was given a qualified welcome by the Staff Side. They pointed out, however, that if the Treasury had intended to solve the problems referred to the Commission it could have done so by the normal process of negotiation. Nevertheless, since the government had decided to establish a Commission the Staff Side could only make the best of the situation and settle down to the preparation of evidence on behalf of their members.

THE INSTITUTION'S ATTITUDE

The composition of the Royal Commission gave the Institution grounds for hope that it would be sympathetic to the claims of scientists and technicians. The chairman, Sir Raymond Priestley, was himself a distinguished scientist, whereas the chairman of the 1929 Commission, Lord Tomlin, was a judge, and the chairman of the 1912 Royal Commission, Lord McDonnell, was an administrator in the Indian civil service. Sir Raymond Priestley had had a distinguished academic career and had served as a geologist on the Shackleton Antarctic Expedition of 1907–9 and as a scientist with the Scott expedition of 1910–13. Another member of the Royal Commission was Mr F. A. A. Menzler, whose work for the Institution has already been mentioned. Other members of the Commission included Professor Willis Jackson, who had had a distinguished career as a technologist and educationalist, George Thorneycroft, the general secretary of the Transport Salaried Staffs' Association and a member of the General Council of the TUC, and Barbara Wootton, who had served for a time as a research officer with the TUC and was well known for her sympathy with the aims of the trade union movement. The other members of the Royal Commission were: the Countess of Albermarle; Sir George Robert Mowbray; Sir Alexander Gray; Hugh Lloyd Williams, MC; Stephen France Birman, MRE; William Cash; Noel Frederick Hall.

Following the announcement of the Royal Commission, the Institution got down to considering the evidence it should present. At its September meeting the NEC had before it a document of fifty foolscap pages prepared by the general secretary, and approved after minor changes by the General Purposes Committee, which reviewed all the points of Institution policy as a preliminary step to the preparation of detailed evidence. The National Executive Committee had to determine which issues should be given priority and the line which its representatives on the National Staff Side should take on questions affecting all civil servants. It invited the views of professional groups and branches. Two issues of particular interest to Institution members were already clear. One was the longstanding claims for parity between the scientific and professional classes on the one hand and the administrative classes on the other; and between the technical classes and the executive classes. The other was the question of 'added years' for superannuation purposes for late entrants.

The National Staff Side also began work on its evidence and established three committees to examine the three parts of the Commission's terms of reference. The Institution expressed regret that the Staff Side decided against giving evidence to the Priestley Commission on general pay issues, leaving each organisation to state its own particular case. The Institution felt that the difficulties that had been experienced in pursuing a centralised pay policy in the face of opposition by the Treasury would accentuate the need for presenting a united front on that issue.

The early meetings of the new Royal Commission were held during the hundredth anniversary year of the Northcote–Trevelyan Report which had favoured the then revolutionary idea of the introduction into the civil service of open recruitment and the abolition of patronage appointments. The civil service unions joined in the centenary celebrations of the Northcote–Trevelyan Report.

EVIDENCE TO THE ROYAL COMMISSION

In its evidence to the Priestley Commission the Civil Service Commission stated that there had been two major obstacles to the recruitment of scientists. Up to 1953 the starting salaries were slightly but perceptibly lower than the corresponding salaries in industry. Secondly, a large proportion of government scientific work was concerned with military purposes and accordingly was cloaked in secrecy and security. This was a deterrent to some of the best men. For engineering, architectural and allied professional and technical classes the Civil Service Commissioners stated that there was no shortage of recruits but there was a real shortage of quality applicants in some of the professions. The most serious difficulty was in the recruitment of draughtsmen. Civil service advertisements drew very few candidates from the outside market.

The Institution submitted evidence to the Priestley Commission. On the question of pay principles, the Institution pointed out that a variety of formulae had been devised, one of the least satisfactory of which was the 'Tomlin formula' which stated, although imprecisely, that civil servants should receive the current rates paid by the generality of outside employers to staff engaged on comparable work, taken over the longer term. The Institution suggested two major shortcomings of the 'Tomlin formula'; its meaning was not precise and where its meaning seemed precise it was difficult and sometimes impossible to apply.

For some occupations comparisons could be made. But often where it could be done, as for example with medical officers, the Treasury argued that internal relativities with other civil service grades were more important than comparisons with outside staff. In other occupations comparisons ought not to be made, for example, in the case of prison chaplains. In that case the low standard of remuneration of parochial clergy was due to the poverty of the church. This, said the Institution, should not influence the pay of prison chaplains. Other examples where comparisons were difficult to make were quoted. The Institution referred in particular to engineering draughtsmen and research scientists. In the case of draughtsmen it was the practice in private industry for the Association of Engineering and Shipbuilding Draughtsmen to determine a national minimum pay scale above which additional amounts were negotiated at factory level. National pay scales were therefore quite inappropriate for comparison. In the case of research scientists so many were employed in the civil service that it was the government rather than private employers who set the general standard of remuneration.

Another problem in achieving external comparisons, the Institution argued, was the prevalence of 'fringe' benefits in outside employment which formed a substantial part of remuneration. It was unlikely that comprehensive information on these could be obtained or that if obtained it could be clearly quantified.

As far as two other aspects of the Tomlin formula were concerned, the long-term trend in wage levels and the economic condition of the country, the latter, the Institution pointed out, was already indirectly incorporated in the notion of comparison with outside employment. The civil service should not be singled out for special treatment in this respect. As for the long-term trend in wage levels, the 'Tomlin formula' implied that civil service rates should be adjusted regularly in line with developments outside.

The Institution concluded that:

> it is not practicable to get proper evidence of what is being paid to particular groups of people outside of the civil service and that it is necessary, therefore, in circumstances such as have obtained in recent years, for general adjustments to be made to civil service salaries following a shape indicated as that being followed over the country generally.

In order to facilitate such regular adjustments the Ministry of Labour should be asked to provide evidence about movements in salaries in the same way as it already provided an index of the movement in wages.

The Institution concluded that the criteria which should apply to civil service pay in future should be as follows:

(*a*) That civil service pay should be maintained at its real value through national Whitley Council machinery on the basis of experience outside the civil service as disclosed by the wage rates index, so far as salary scales up to and including the maximum of the clerical class were concerned, and by other general statistical indications for classes on salary scales higher than that of the clerical class;

(*b*) that the pay of the various classes should

    i.   take full account of the responsibilities involved in and the character of the duties performed, the proper maintenance and development of the cultural and professional standards of the officers concerned, the social position of the officers as servants of the state, the capacity they show in performance of the work and the contentment of the officers;

    ii. where appropriate, and to the extent possible, be so determined as to take account of the pay and other emoluments given outside the civil service by the best employers of the kind of officer concerned;

    iii. take account of the levels of remuneration of officers in the civil service exercising similar responsibilities or in related classes.

In its evidence the Institution laid special emphasis on the need to improve the

Richard Nunn, General Secretary
1961–2

William McCall, General Secretary
1963–

Scientists march to a rally in Central Hall, Westminster, in August 1971, to protest at the Official Side's pay offer

Scientists march after their rally at Central Hall, Westminster on 6 March 1974, in support of an interim pay claim pending the Pay Board's report on scientists' pay

relationship between professional, scientific and technical civil servants on the one hand and administrative and executive civil servants on the other. Relativities needed to be reshaped on a basis which left no doubt as to the importance of the contribution made by professionally qualified staff within the civil service. Such a status would more accurately reflect the relationships obtaining between the administrator and the professional man outside the service, it would more accurately reflect the importance of the professional man in the life of the country as a whole, and would encourage young people to take up professional, scientific and technical careers.

The Institution said in its evidence that there were too many salary scales covering professional, scientific and technical staff in the civil service. It was pointed out that there were no fewer than 180 general service-linked departmental classes, each with its own set of salary scales in the part of the civil service covered by the Institution. The Institution suggested that there should be a much simpler set of salary scales for professional staff and that there should be a clear linkage of salary scales in the civil service between classes of similar educational standards and official responsibility. In particular, the Institution suggested that there should be a set of salary scales covering the works group of professional classes and their analogues, a set covering the scientific staff and a third covering the technical classes and their analogues.

On hours of work the Institution pointed out that certain groups of its members were employed on a basic working week longer than that normal for the civil service. The most important group in this category were the technical classes where there were up to 19,000 officers. Many of the technical classes were required to work a 49-hour week, including the lunch-break.

The Institution gave oral evidence to the Royal Commission on 1 and 2 July 1954. The Institution emphasised that it was seeking a re-evaluation of the contributions made by professional, scientific and technical staff within the civil service. Many scientists and technologists in the civil service, it was pointed out, carried administrative and executive responsibility and it was unfair and contrary to the public interest that they should have a status lower than their administrative and executive colleagues. The Institution drew the attention of the Royal Commission to some of the problems of recruiting adequately qualified scientists and technicians. The Institution also gave detailed evidence in support of its claim affecting particular groups.

EVIDENCE ON SUPERANNUATION

The terms of reference of the Royal Commission required it to consider whether any changes were desirable within the framework of the existing superannuation scheme. The National Staff Side submitted a number of proposals which they considered fell within the framework of the existing superannuation scheme. They urged that all unestablished service followed by established service should count in full for superannuation purposes; that temporary staff whose service by the time of their retirement on age grounds amounted to ten years or more should be superannuated as though their service had been in an established capacity; that there should be an improvement in the scale of gratuities payable to unestablished staff; and, a subject of special interest to Institution members, that there should be an extension of the existing statutory provision whereby late entrants to the civil service, who were recruited because of their specialised knowledge and experience, could earn a higher pension by receiving a credit for years over and above those actually served.

In oral evidence on the superannuation arrangements for civil servants, the National Staff Side concentrated on four main claims: that unestablished service when followed by established service should count in full for superannuation purposes; that the gratuities paid to unestablished staff who reached the age of retirement should be increased; that 'added years' for superannuation purposes should be given to late entrants whose work outside the civil service was essential for their civil service occupation; and that pension transfer arrangements between the public and private sector should be extended.

At one of its early meetings the Royal Commission decided to ask the Treasury for an estimate of the value of civil service superannuation as a percentage of salary. The reply was that the value of full superannuation rights for an average new entrant to the salary grades of the civil service was 15 per cent. For the manipulative and equivalent grades the corresponding figure was about 10 per cent.

To the disappointment of the civil service unions the Priestley Commission declined to receive evidence on the position of civil service pensioners. The Commission decided that the level of civil service pensions was outside its terms of reference. It argued that any changes in civil service pensions could not be confined to the civil service but would affect a far wider area. It would, therefore, as it saw it, be irresponsible for it to limit its examination to the civil service and not consider possible repercussive effects elsewhere, and it would be inappropriate for the subject to be considered by a Royal Commission on civil service pay and conditions.

ARBITRATION FOR HIGHER GRADES

Another issue in which the Institution had a special interest, and which was the subject of evidence submitted by the Staff Side, was that of arbitration machinery for higher-grade civil servants. The Staff Side drew the attention of the Royal Commission to the absence of any arrangement for submitting to arbitration questions affecting the pay of higher-grade civil servants. They recalled that the arbitration arrangements had been established by the civil service arbitration agreement of 1925. The agreement excluded claims in respect of classes above a specified salary limit, but provided that such claims could be submitted to arbitration with the consent of both parties. The original salary limit had been modified from time to time to take account of the revision of salary scales. At the time of the Priestley Commission claims in respect of grades having flat salary rates above £1,450 a year or scales with a maximum of £1,450 a year were excluded except with the consent of both sides.

Developments since 1925, the Staff Side argued, had produced a changed attitude to the whole question of arbitration at higher salary levels. First, the steady decline in money values had necessitated much more frequent pay claims and, secondly, there had been a change in the general conception of the place of arbitration machinery for those on higher levels of remuneration both inside and outside the civil service. Various procedures had been used to resolve claims affecting higher-grade staff. Sometimes an independent advisory body had been set up.

The Staff Side argued that it was necessary to determine the line between cases appropriate to the CSAT and those appropriate to any proposed advisory committee. They suggested that for the future the arbitration agreement should be extended to cover staff up to and including the equivalent of assistant secretary grade in the administrative class. The grade of assistant secretary, it was emphasised, was the main career grade in the administrative class. For staff above the grade of assistant secretary the Staff Side urged the appointment of a standing committee of three persons to be appointed at three-yearly intervals by the Chancellor of the Exchequer after agreement between the parties.

The Treasury in its evidence to the Commission agreed that a standing advisory body should be established for the pay of higher grades but argued that this should not be a matter for agreement between the parties but should be left to the initiative of ministers.

HOURS AND LEAVE

Strong representations on hours and leave were made to the Priestley Commission by the National Staff Side. A memorandum prepared by the Staff Side urged that the government should honour the undertaking given in 1942 to restore prewar hours of work and leave in the non-industrial civil service. These conditions were due to be restored by not later than the end of February 1948 but the Treasury had proposed a 'moratorium' on this obligation. The Staff Side also pressed for the elimination of the difference in hours of work between London and the provinces.

In the settlement on conditions of employment made at the end of the First World War, the hours of work, including the lunch-break, were less in London than in the provinces. The justification for this was that a provincial civil servant was supposed to be free to choose a convenient place of residence which involved him in no more travelling to and from his office than he was willing to undertake for his personal convenience. The Staff Side said that this justification had been deprived of its validity. Civil servants, in common with the rest of the community, had to live where they were best able to find accommodation suited to their needs, regardless of resultant disabilities in travel costs and length of journey to the office. In large towns and cities this could involve travelling on a scale comparable with that of London staff.

The Staff Side also pressed for the introduction of a 5-day week, and said that the hours of office staff should be compressed into a 5-day week wherever this could be done and into a 10½-day fortnight if for any reason in any area of the service a 5-day week was not practicable. The Staff Side also urged that the introduction of a 5-day week should have no effect on the leave allowances of the staff concerned other than the direct arithmetical adjustments rendered necessary by shortening the effective week, e.g. 48 days would be reduced to 40, 36 to 30, 30 to 25, 24 to 20, and so on.

The Royal Commission asked the Treasury to submit detailed proposals on hours of work and leave. The Treasury suggested that the prewar working week of 38½ hours in London, including the lunch-break, was too short. It urged that in London net working hours should be increased from the prewar figure of 69·5 to the figure of 72·3 per fortnight. Outside London net working hours per fortnight should be reduced from 80·5 to 78. The Treasury also suggested that there should be a redistribution of leave allowances to permit civil servants a number of Saturdays off. They also proposed that there should be a reduction in the annual leave allowances.

These proposals were less favourable than those offered by the Treasury to the civil service unions in 1949. The Treasury pointed out that the 1949 offer was an attempt to secure a settlement, taking account of the wartime pledge to restore prewar conditions, but it was not part of a comprehensive review of civil service remuneration and other main conditions of service.

PROTEST

The Staff Side protested strongly against the proposals of the Treasury. They recalled once again that the government was pledged to restore prewar hours and leave, and they said that strong feeling had been aroused in the civil service by the continued deferment of action either to redeem the pledge or to introduce revised arrangements which the staff could regard as a satisfactory discharge of the obligation imposed by the pledge. The Staff Side pointed to the significance of the failure of the Treasury to present proposals at least equal to those made in 1949. The Treasury, said the Staff Side, was proposing conditions which were appreciably less favourable in respect of both hours and leave than those which it had offered in 1949. It followed, in the unions' view, that the Treasury was seeking the Royal Commission's approval for a settlement which it knew would fall a good deal short of an honourable discharge of its obligation to restore prewar conditions.

An editorial in the November issue of *State Service* reacted strongly against the Treasury proposals. The one thing that seemed clear, said the editorial, was that the Treasury had really gone out of its way to make itself thoroughly disliked by the rest of the civil service. The proposals being made, it argued, were of a most reactionary character.

The publication of the Treasury proposals on hours and leave led to an outburst of protest from many sections of the civil service. To give expression to this protest the National Staff Side organised a central demonstration at the Central Hall, Westminster, on 16 November. The response exceeded all expectations and more than 4,000 civil servants sought entry to the main meeting. Overflow meetings were arranged but thousands more were unable to gain entry. They crowded into the open spaces outside the Central Hall and in Parliament Square.

In opening the Central Hall demonstration the chairman, Mr Len White of the Civil Service Clerical Association, pointed out that the demonstration was the culminating point of a fortnight of packed meetings in individual civil service departments. The general secretary of the Society of Civil Servants, Mr E. C. Redhead, moved a resolution which was adopted unanimously. It stated:

That this mass meeting of civil servants records its indignation at the breach of faith committed by the government, through the Treasury, in putting forward proposals to the Royal Commission for future hours and leave which:

1 represent a drastic worsening of the conditions of service to which existing staff were entitled;
2 lessen still further the attractiveness of the civil service as a career;
3 are contrary to the postwar trend towards improved holidays and shorter hours;
4 are a betrayal of the pledge given by the government to the Staff Side of the National Whitley Council to restore prewar hours and leave.

In seconding the motion Stanley Mayne of the Institution said that the Treasury's breaking of the pledge on hours and leave had to be seen as one of a series of moves each designed to worsen the working conditions of civil servants. He stressed that members of the staff association movement had to fight back to protect their working conditions and expressed the hope that the mass meeting would only mark a stage in a series of meetings and protests throughout the country.

The demonstration in central London was followed by similarly well-attended demonstrations in a number of provincial centres. Some 1,800 civil servants attended a crowded protest meeting in the City Hall, Newcastle, and nearly 1,000 civil servants were present at a protest meeting in Manchester. Other packed meetings were held in Cardiff, Southampton, Glasgow, Leeds, Liverpool, Bristol and Nottingham.

So great was the volume of protest against the Treasury proposals on hours and leave that the Treasury took the very unusual course of issuing a special statement. In this statement the Treasury acknowledged that the wartime undertaking about the restoration of prewar conditions was still binding, and that whatever recommendations the Royal Commission might make the introduction of any new conditions would have to be the subject of negotiations thereafter with the National Staff Side. The Treasury said that the restoration of prewar practices had to be considered together with the current practice outside the civil service for a reduction from the 5½-day working week to a 5-day week. In these changed arrangements, consideration should be given to the related questions of hours of work and leave. *State Service* said that the Treasury's reaction to countrywide indignation showed that it could be moved, but much more remained to be done if any substantial modification of its proposals was to be achieved.

EMPLOYERS' EVIDENCE

The Priestley Commission decided to receive no further evidence after 7 April. One of the last pieces of evidence put before the Commission was an attack by the British Employers' Confederation on the principle of fair comparison for purposes of salary determination. It stated that if comparison was to be made with remuneration in outside employment adequate account would have to be taken of differences in conditions of service other than pay. The only satisfactory way of doing this would be by careful job-by-job comparison between civil service posts and those in outside employment. Such a comparison could not, however, be undertaken through the machinery of collective bargaining. In private employment such comparisons were effected between one company and another by representatives of the management of the two companies discussing and examining the matter together on the spot.

The Confederation said that the most helpful suggestion it could offer the Royal Commission was that the linking of civil service salaries with salaries in outside employment should be abandoned. This was not to say that regard should not be had to such salaries in outside employment and their movement but that private employers could offer assistance to the Treasury in dealing with the problems of the civil service in the same way as one private employer helps another when dealing with salaries. Of necessity, said the Confederation, this precluded the possibility of information obtained by discussion between the responsible Treasury official and a private employer being made available to civil service staff associations. The Confederation said that comparisons should be made with representative employers rather than with employers selected for their reputation as 'good' employers.

The Institution saw the evidence of the British Employers' Confederation as 'one of the most reactionary statements made in recent years on relations with staff associations'. It was clear, said the Institution, that the British Employers' Confederation thoroughly disliked the idea of trade union organisation of clerical, administrative, technical or professional employees and wished to be as unhelpful as it could be.

THE PRIESTLEY REPORT

As the deliberations of the Royal Commission came to a close the Institution was becoming increasingly apprehensive not only about the recommendations which might appear but also about the financial atmosphere in which negotiations on the recommendations might take place. Some negotiations had been delayed while the Commission sat and, as a result, civil service conditions had deteriorated even further. There was a real fear that the current slogan 'Expand success and curb excess' might be put forward as a reason why any improvements which the Royal Commission might recommend should be at least postponed, as they were in the case of the Chorley Committee. The Staff Side took the view that the report of the Commission would be crucial in setting the status of the civil service in the community for years to come.

The Institution had stated its original fears to the Commission in its evidence. They were re-quoted in an editorial in the November 1955 issue of *State Service*:

> The very grave danger of the Treasury recommendations is that the general depression of the standard of the civil service will continue. For the moment the civil service can, in effect, live on the fat of the prewar years. With every year that passes that diminishes and will, in the not distant future, come to an end. It seems to the Institution that the Treasury is most ill-advised to follow such a shortsighted policy. It is the Institution's hope that the Royal Commission will restore the civil service to its proper place in the community.

The editorial went on:

> Subsequent events are showing, only too clearly, that the Institution's views were amply justified. It is now common ground in responsible circles that there is a near-crisis in civil service recruitment, that the civil service no longer offers sufficiently attractive careers to the younger men and women of the right

quality who are needed every year. This situation has developed all the more rapidly because the Treasury has, during the past two years, shelved its administrative duties in relation to recruitment, on the grounds that nothing should be done which could in any way be interpreted as prejudicial to the Commission's report.

The report of the Priestley Commission was published later that month. It urged that the primary principle of civil service pay should be 'fair comparison with the current remuneration of outside staffs employed on broadly comparable work, taking account of differences in other conditions of service'. For the purpose of making this comparison it suggested that a fact-finding unit should be established. It expressed the hope that individual outside employers would co-operate in the work of the fact-finding unit over the establishment of job comparisons and in the preparation of details of rates of pay and other conditions of service.

The Commission rejected the view that fair rates of pay could be defined as rates sufficient to recruit and retain an efficient staff. Financial considerations, it said, were not the sole or even always the principal incentive which attracted recruits to the civil service. Moreover, wastage was not a reliable indicator of the fairness or unfairness of rates of pay. It might sometimes be a symptom of the effect of pay, but the validity of a wastage test must be affected by the outside demand for particular skills. This varied a great deal at different times and for different classes. The Royal Commission also said that in conditions of near full employment, when all or most employers were likely to be conscious of the shortage of labour, the civil service could not be singled out for special treatment.

On hours of work the Commission recommended that the practice of regular overtime working should be brought to an end as soon as practicable. It accepted that hours of work in London should be shorter than in the provinces, but did not accept that the prewar length of the working week in London should be restored. It could not, it said, regard the prewar hours as 'other than short in the light of the evidence of outside practice'. It therefore recommended that hours of work in London should be even longer than those proposed by the Treasury. It was suggested that they should be 84 per fortnight, less lunch-breaks of 1 hour per day. In effect this was a proposal for a net 37-hour working week in London. The Commission did, however, recommend a rapid move from a 5½-day to a 5-day week wherever practicable, with a 10½-day fortnight as a transitional arrangement.

The Commission did not feel itself bound by the undertaking given by the Treasury in 1942 that prewar conditions would be restored. It said that whether its recommendations needed to be modified in the light of an undertaking which had been given in the past was a matter not for the Commission but for others.

A recommendation was also made for a reduction in leave. The Priestley Commission said it was in no doubt that the leave allowances enjoyed by civil servants – and still more so the leave allowances of prewar days – were much more generous than were found in comparable employment outside the civil service. It commented that if regard were had to this evidence and nothing more the case for drastic reductions in civil service allowances would be unanswerable. It agreed, however, that civil service leave should not be 'screwed down precisely and mathematically to commercial practice'. Nevertheless, it recommended that 'some steps should be taken in the direction of greater conformity with outside practice'. Detailed suggestions were put forward by the Commission. The only respect in which it suggested an improvement on leave allowances was in relation to Saturday leave. It said that Saturday leave taken outside the period of annual leave should be reckoned as half a day and not as a full day.

The Commission came down firmly in favour of pay differentiation between London and the provinces. It said that the arguments in favour of a form of differentiation were conclusive. Such differentation it found almost universal outside the civil service.

On superannuation the Royal Commission accepted the principle that unestablished service should be reckoned in full. It pointed out that the government's decision on retrospection taken in 1946 afforded a precedent and said that if 'a certain treatment is right at one point in time it is also right at others'. It was the view of the Commission, however, that 'the sole consideration is that of cost'.

The Commission rejected the claim for 'added years' for pension purposes. It was, however prepared to recommend that there should be somewhat wider use of the existing provisions of the 1946 Superannuation Act to provide for 'added years' in particular cases. The Commission also recommended an improvement in the scale of gratuities payable to temporary civil servants when they left the civil service either on grounds of age or for any other reason.

Of special interest to the Institution were the observations of the Royal Commission on the principle to be applied in dealing with the status and pay of specialist civil servants. The Commission rejected the views of the Institution. The relevant paragraph of its report stated:

> We have already said that for the civil service to give a lead to the country at large in matters of pay would endanger the non-political character of the service. In saying this we had in mind issues which are or may be the subject of political controversy. The question of the social and economic status of specialist workers is not, at present at any rate, a political issue. Even so, for the civil service to give a lead in altering the social and economic status of specialist workers (or indeed of any other group) would, we believe, be repugnant to public opinion. Moreover, if a deliberate departure from the principle of fair comparison were to be made in respect of some classes of the civil service it might well not be long before reasons were put forward for doing the same in respect of other classes.

'A BAD DOCUMENT'

The immediate reaction of the Institution to the Priestley Commission report was to describe it as 'a bad document'. The Commission, the Institution said, had run away from problems which were well within its scope of inquiry. It particularly criticised the recommendations of the Commission on pay. It said that the report in practically every line merely endorsed and underlined Treasury policy. The Institution was particularly critical of the failure of the Royal Commission to do anything about the specialist classes. It also expressed indignation at the Commission's disregard of the wartime pledge given by the Treasury to restore prewar conditions and the recommendation of the Priestley Commission on hours of work in London and on the proposed reduction in leave. Other unions were equally disappointed with the report.

Almost immediately after the publication of the report of the Royal Commission the Institution decided to organise a special series of meetings in all main centres where Institution members were employed to discuss the recommendations of the report. Nearly sixty meetings were held in different parts of Britain within the course of a few weeks. A large national demonstration was held in the Central Hall, Westminster. This series of meetings constituted the most intensive campaign conducted by the Institution since its formation. *State Service* said that the meetings not only served to disseminate information about the Royal Commission report but, in addition, had served 'the unplanned purpose of being an opportunity for members of the Institution to make clear not only their complete disappointment with the report generally but of their specific opposition to major sections of the report'.

The Institution made special arrangements with the Stationery Office for the purchase of copies of the report by branches of the Institution. No fewer than 4,500 were purchased by members through this special arrangement. This was an indication of the interest aroused by the report among the membership.

NEGOTIATIONS

Contrary to the fears expressed by the Institution, negotiations on the recommendations of the Priestley Commission report were opened at the beginning of January 1956 and were completed by May of that year. They were conducted intensively and meetings were held at not less than weekly intervals.

From the very beginning of the negotiations the Staff Side set out clearly their views on the principle which should govern civil service pay. They argued that comparisons with outside employment could only be fair where there was a reasonably wide field in which to make a comparison. Moreover, the Staff Side did not accept the Royal Commission's view that the absence of effective trade union organisation among some staff in outside employment must not be taken into account. The Staff Side also urged that outside comparison could only form a small part of the assessment of pay in cases where the state was the largest single employer.

The Institution convened a special delegate conference at the end of February 1956 to discuss the report of the Royal Commission. At this conference delegates expressed the views voiced by the membership at the large number of meetings held in different parts of Britain. The conference was notable for the very wide-ranging and lucidly delivered survey on the Royal Commission report given by the general secretary, Stanley Mayne. He paid tribute to the Treasury for the speed with which negotiations on the report had got under way. Two committees of the National Whitley Council were handling report matters; one a superannuation committee and the other a general committee. He indicated that already considerable progress had been made in negotiations on pay, hours and leave, but that on some of the issues concerning superannuation further delay might be likely. He drew attention to the decision of the government to introduce a new Pensions (Increase) Bill. The Institution welcomed the Bill. It removed the means test from pension increases given to civil servants under previous legislation and gave much-needed increases in civil service pensions.

The general secretary then proceeded to assess the major policy problem which confronted the Institution as a result of the report of the Priestley Commission. He attacked the Royal Commission view that the civil service should never give a lead in remuneration. He argued that 'unless the government takes it upon itself to give a clear and definite lead in altering the social and economic status of specialist workers then this country is dooming itself to destruction'. Several prominent people, including Sir Winston Churchill, had emphasised that the shortage of qualified scientists and technologists would damage the future economic and social progress of the country. Yet the Royal Commission had not only rejected the argument that the civil service should give a lead in raising the status of the specialist, it had made pay proposals which, if implemented, would worsen the position of scientific and professional civil servants in comparison with administrative civil servants. The Institution had a clear duty:

> our voice must be added to the clamant demand that something be done to make recruitment of technological manpower an issue of first importance. Great Britain must develop technically or Great Britain dies. Are we prepared to tackle this problem and, in serving the wider interests of the country, thus serve no less surely the direct interest of our members?.

AGREEMENT

By the spring of 1956 the Official Side and Staff Side of the Civil Service National Whitley Council had made sufficient progress in their negotiations to issue a joint statement outlining the basis of a possible new agreement affecting civil service conditions. On pay the Official Side indicated that they accepted the Royal Commission's recommendations on 'fair comparisons'. The Staff Side, while agreeing that 'fair comparisons' was a valid principle in civil service pay negotiations, recorded certain reservations. As a consequence an appendix to the proposed agreement, setting out the procedures to be followed in civil service pay and fact-finding, contained several modifications. It was agreed that 'fair comparisons', although a valuable principle, should not be the sole determinant in pay negotiations. In particular the appendix stated:

> Both sides agree that the principle of fair comparisons is not to be interpreted in a rigid and inflexible manner but as a broad guide in negotiations. It is, of course, of first importance that the facts on which 'fair comparisons' are to be made shall be obtained as widely as possible from both the public and the private sectors of employment and, within those sectors, from good employers.

In the appendix it was suggested that the fact-finding organisation recommended by the Royal Commission should be called the Civil Service Pay Research Unit and should be under the general control and direction of the Civil Service National Whitley Council. Control was to be exercised through a committee composed of six members from each side. The day-to-day control would be vested in a director to be appointed by the Prime Minister. Fact-finding, said the joint statement, involved two processes. The first was to establish job comparability, due allowance being made for differences in grading structure, and the second was the discovery of the pay and conditions of service attached to the jobs regarded as comparable.

On rates of pay the Official Side expressed willingness to accept all increases proposed by the Royal Commission. They further said that if a comprehensive settlement were concluded before 1 July 1956 the new scales of pay would be adjusted in the light of recent general pay movements outside and be brought into effect as from 1 April 1956. The Staff Side said they were not able to accept that the recommendations of the Royal Commission provided a satisfactory pay structure but, having regard to the desirability of reaching a settlement on the report as a whole, they accepted the application of the Royal Commission's scales on the understanding that the freedom of associations to renew their representations at a subsequent date would remain unimpaired.

The principle of provincial salary differentiation was also preserved with a modest widening of the existing differentials. The Staff Side said they were unable to agree with the view expressed by the Royal Commission and the Official Side on the reasons for provincial differentiation but they recognised that the Official Side regarded the increases in provincial differentiation as an integral part of the general settlement.

The joint statement said that both sides had agreed to the hours of work recommended by the Royal Commission. These were to be 42 gross in London and 44 elsewhere, with an allowance of 1 hour each day for lunch. Both sides agreed that the existing standard working week of 45½ hours gross should be abolished and that the civil service should proceed more quickly than recommended by the Royal Commission towards the introduction of a 5-day week.

On leave, a new system of allowances was suggested for new entrants. Staff already employed would continue to enjoy the leave entitlements (adjusted as necessary for a 5-day week or a 10½-day fortnight) which they had in their existing grade. The new leave allowances for new entrants rose from three weeks for staff on scales with maxima up to and including that of clerical officer (with three weeks and three days after ten years' total service), to six weeks for staff on scales with maxima above that of an assistant secretary.

The joint statement of the National Whitley Council on the outcome of the negotiations on the recommendations of the Priestley Commission report was reviewed by the National Executive Committee of the Institution. In a statement setting out its conclusions the National Executive Committee said that much as it disliked some of the features in the statement and much as it disliked being compelled to deal with various facets of civil service conditions as a 'comprehensive unity', it nevertheless recommended the forthcoming annual conference of the Institution to accept the document. The National Executive Committee pointed to a number of improvements which had been secured in negotiations, notably the introduction of the 5-day week, the retention of existing annual leave entitlements for staff already employed in the civil service, and certain improvements on the recommendations on pay and leave made by the Royal Commission. The attitude of the Institution towards the outcome of the negotiations was expressed in an editorial in the June 1956 issue of *State Service* which stated that:

nowhere in civil service association circles . . . is there general satisfaction with the substantive terms of the agreement. The attitude of members and of the National Executive Committee alike is that acceptance is better than the possible alternative of the application, by administrative action by the Treasury, of the precise terms of the Priestley Report, followed by months, or years, of negotiations which may, even then, only result in the amelioration offered in the proposed agreement.

At the 1956 annual delegate conference of the Institution the National Executive Committee tabled an emergency motion approving the proposals of the National Staff Side, which was carried by an overwhelming majority. It read:

That this annual conference has considered the report of the National Whitley Council Royal Commission Committee setting out the proposals for agreement on the points comprised in the 'comprehensive unity' in the recommendations of the Royal Commission on the civil service. It expresses the view that there is no justification for differentiation between the conditions applicable to new entrants and those applicable to existing staff but notes that the proposals must be accepted or rejected as a whole. This conference, whilst reaffirming its views expressed at the special conference, therefore instructs the Institution's representatives on the Staff Side National Whitley Council to vote in favour of adopting the document.

The National Staff Side at a meeting on Monday 18 June 1956 voted in favour of the package document and an agreement embodying the proposal was signed with the Treasury on the same day.

15 The Economic Climate Influences Negotiations, 1956–61

Although negotiations on the pay agreement following the Priestley Report were completed very quickly, this pattern was not to be followed in subsequent negotiations. The Treasury insisted that each class be taken separately, and argued that the pay research process would soon encompass each grade. As a leader comment in *State Service* in January 1957 said:

> The Institution, however, has so many classes, some of whom will present more than ordinary difficulties, that, even with the proposed increases in the staff of the Unit, there is little likelihood that all the classes will be considered within the next few years. The second question is whether the Unit's staff, as at present appointed, will be able sufficiently to appreciate the duties of some of the specialist classes in order to make adequate comparisons.

Although the Institution had no criticism to make of the first two completed reports of the PRU on the postal and telegraph officers and on postmen, both being painstaking and useful reports, it was clear that it would take a very long time for the majority of classes to be covered in the same detailed way. In the meantime the prospect that each class would eventually be covered provided the Treasury with grounds for delay in dealing with immediate pay claims.

By the end of 1957 the Pay Research Unit had completed twelve reports, none of which involved Institution grades. Towards the end of the year, however, work had begun on the survey of the technical works engineering and allied classes. In order to enable the Unit to cope with the specialised nature of the work of many Institution grades, the steering committee agreed in July 1957 to allow the appointment of technical advisers to assist the staff of the Unit. Such advisers were to be appointed by agreement of both negotiating parties and were to be involved, in an advisory capacity, at all stages of the surveys.

In March 1956 the government, faced with a continuous rise in prices, issued a White Paper entitled *The Economic Implications of Full Employment* which said that prices could be forced upwards either by an excess of demand in the economy or by 'pressure for higher income even when the level of demand is not excessive'. The conclusion drawn from this analysis was that it was up to the government to keep the pressure on demand at the right level but action by the people was also required in observing 'self-restraint in making wage claims and fixing profit margins and prices'.

'THE THREE WISE MEN'

In 1957, after largely abortive attempts to promote discussion with the trade unions on an acceptable incomes policy, the government set up a Council on Prices, Productivity and Incomes. It consisted of three members who came to be known as 'The Three Wise Men'. The three were Lord Cohen, Sir Harold Hewitt and Sir Dennis Robertson. It was nominally independent of the government and was given wide terms of reference. 'Having regard to the desirability of full employment and increasing standards of life based on expanding production and reasonable stability in prices, to keep under review changes in prices, productivity and the level of incomes (including wages, salaries and profits) and to report thereon from time to time.'

The government stated that the Council was not to concern itself with specific wage claims or disputes. Its purpose, in the words of the Chancellor of the Exchequer, was to 'create a fuller appreciation of the facts, both in the public at large and amongst those more immediately concerned with prices and cost matters'. In all the Council produced four reports. The first was published in February 1958 and the last in July 1961.

The trade union movement refused to co-operate with the Council on Prices, Productivity and Incomes. The TUC were wary of association with a body established by a government whose economic policies were in many respects at variance with those advocated by the trade union movement. The Conservative government had dismantled many of the direct controls for regulating the economy, and the unions were not therefore surprised that from one year to another the economic system in Britain lurched from expansion to stagnation. Instead of direct controls the government tended to rely on changes in interest rates, credit squeezes and taxation. The inevitable result, said the TUC, was a policy of stop-go.

In an editorial in *State Service* (September 1957) the Institution admitted to 'sharing the lack of enthusiasm in the trade unions for the government's latest Three Wise Men'. The editorial continued that it was not good enough for the government to hope that the Three Wise Men would help the public to appreciate the facts of inflation. All too often inflation had been attributed to rising wages. Unless the Three Wise Men could present the British people with convincing conclusions, *State Service* maintained, they would merely confirm the suspicion that their job was one of adding savour to unpalatable government policies.

'CORRESPONDING ECONOMIES'

The Minister of Labour, Mr McLeod, made it clear that the government as the largest employer in the country would ensure that where it was dealing with wage claims affecting its own employees it would apply and be seen to apply the most stringent tests. The government reinforced its intention by stating in establishment circulars in the civil service that in making provision for the cost of pay increases authorised by arbitration, departments would be governed by the general policy that 'pay increases are to be offset by corresponding economies'.

The National Staff Side protested against the government's declaration. They argued that it amounted to a direct interference with arbitration and that it was an administrative nonsense to decree that any pay increases authorised by arbitration should be offset by corresponding economies. This was likely to mean that pay increase had to be met by redundancies. The government replied by pointing out that it was the government's policy, as far as practicable, to prevent, both in the public and private sector, the provision of additional supplies of money to feed inflation.

In response the National Staff Side adopted unanimously a motion on collective bargaining in the civil service. Its terms were:

> The National Staff Side sincerely trusts that there will be no interference in collective bargaining in the civil service, including the Priestley doctrine of 'fair comparisons' or any action which might bring into question the impartiality of the Civil Service arbitration tribunal or any refusal to honour awards of the tribunal.

The Staff Side also expressed concern at the action of the Minister of Health in exercising his veto against an agreement reached at one of the Whitley Councils for the national health service.

Early in 1958 the threat of 'corresponding economies' was carried out. Following an arbitration award affecting 4,000 cartographic draughtsmen, steps were taken by the Official Side to arrange for the dismissal of temporary officers. Some 100 of the 116 temporary cartographic draughtsmen and surveyors were to be dismissed. The Institution protested strongly that the draughtsmen had been underpaid for a number of years. The tribunal had found in favour of the claim of the Institution but the Official Side had then decided for reasons unrelated to the efficiency of the service to dismiss a considerable number of temporary draughtsmen. In the event the Institution was unable to prevent the dismissal of eighty-five temporary cartographic draughtsmen. Fortunately, the indignation voiced in Parliament as well as directly to the minister appeared to have an effect. No further dismissals took place following pay awards to staff.

At the 1958 annual delegate conference the NEC tabled a successful motion roundly condemning the

> government instruction that pay increases shall be offset by corresponding economies. This policy, which must result in arbitrary cuts in staff and programmes, is an evasion of negotiation and arbitration, and the negation of sound administration. Conference therefore instructs the National Executive Committee to take all possible steps to combat this policy and to ensure that negotiated agreements and arbitration awards are properly and fully applied and not used as a basis for the imposition of penal economies.

In the debate delegates made it clear that they regarded the policy as a 'direct attempt at intimidation' of civil servants and that members did not intend to be intimidated by this sort of manoeuvre.

The most serious challenge to the government's pay policy in the public sector in 1958 came not from the civil service but from the London busmen represented by the Transport and General Workers' Union. An attempt was made to deny a wage increase to a section of workers, despite the increase in the cost of living since the last negotiated wage increase. If the Transport and General Workers' Union had accepted such a cut in real wages, a precedent would have been established which would have had a bearing on other wage negotiations in subsequent months, particularly in all parts of the public sector including the civil service. The strike of London busmen lasted for eight weeks. Ultimately the TGWU succeeded in winning a wage increase for all its members, including both central and Green Line services and maintenance workers. The outcome of this was seen at the time to have wide significance for the trade union movement.

CENTRAL PAY CLAIM

In 1956 and 1957 the National Staff Side succeeded in getting a general pay supplement covering all grades on the basis that similar increases had been given generally in industry. In November 1958 the National Staff Side decided to submit a further claim for salary increases. This claim covered all grades and classes except the higher ranks. It was clear that salaries in the civil service were again beginning to fall behind. Moreover, an article by Professors Alan Peacock and T. L. Johnston in the *Westminster Bank Review*, quoted in *State Service*, had reached the conclusion that:

> there seems to be enough evidence to support the assertions of the civil service employee organisations and unions that they have fallen behind in the wage race. The percentage of working population in public administration doubled between 1920 and 1950, the percentage of wages and salaries paid to them increased only slightly over the same period. In other words, over this period the remuneration of government administrators relative to the average must have decreased considerably.

On 31 December 1958 agreement was reached for a general 3·5 per cent increase. The general secretary commented that the increase was less than many would think warranted but on the whole it was gratifying.

THE COLERAINE COMMITTEE

Shortly after this central pay settlement substantial increases were secured for some higher civil servants as a result of a report by the Standing Advisory Committee, the Coleraine Committee. This committee had been established in 1957 to examine the pay of higher civil servants. It consisted of Lord Coleraine (chairman); Sir Alexander Carr-Saunders; Mr Geoffrey Crowther; Sir Alexander Fleck, KBE; Sir Oliver Franks, GCMG, KCB; and Lord Latham. The function of the committee had been outlined in general terms by the Priestley Commission. The grades to be covered by the Standing Advisory Committee were those staffs whose salary maximum or fixed rate exceeded the maximum of the principal. The committee was to be called into action in various ways:

(*a*) in the exercise of its general oversight of the remuneration of the higher civil service, to advise the government, either at the latter's request or on its own initiative, on what changes were desirable in the remuneration of those officers;

(*b*) where there had been a general pay settlement applicable to the lower and middle grades of the service, the fact would be reported to the committee who would then determine what, if anything, should be done for the higher civil service in consequence;

(c) when a major claim had been put forward by a staff association on the pay of a grade within the committee's sphere and it had proved impossible to reach a satisfactory solution.

The establishment of the Standing Advisory Committee was an important step forward. Before the Priestley Commission there had been no established negotiating framework for the pay of higher grades. Following the Priestley Report the establishment of a Standing Advisory Committee provided a mechanism for dealing with the pay of higher grades and meant that the National Staff Side could now speak authoritatively for staff at all levels in the civil service. As a consequence the Higher Grades Pay Co-ordinating Committee, in which the Institution had played a central role, was brought fully within the National Staff Side machinery.

The Priestley Commission had itself recommended rates of pay for the higher civil service. They were implemented. Before the Coleraine Committee had been established a further central pay increase had been awarded to other grades. Thus the first task which awaited the new committee was to advise whether that increase should be applied to the higher grades. It advised in the affirmative and the government complied. In 1958, however, the committee recommended only a partial consequential increase up to the £2,100 salary point. This was regarded by the Staff Side as an unsatisfactory decision.

For higher grades within the Institution there was a major setback in 1958. Two senior professional posts became vacant during 1958, the Director General of Works and the Comptroller General of the Patent Office. In the former case the director post was kept vacant and an under-secretary (administrator) put in as acting manager. In the latter case a new comptroller was appointed from the administrative class without qualifications in science or law. The Institution protested but without success.

The Institution also made representations to a number of departments about the pay of some top professional posts. It argued that these posts, which entailed wide professional responsibilities, were underpaid in relation to similar posts outside the civil service. It was important to obtain similar salaries inside the civil service not only to secure a proper status for the posts but also to set a sufficiently high ceiling for the intermediate managerial and technical staffs immediately below them. Having failed to convince departments, the general secretary wrote to the Treasury in early 1960 in the following terms.

It is our submission that if the Priestley doctrine of fair comparisons was applied to any of these top professional posts it would produce a salary substantially exceeding any other civil service salary. We doubt whether you would dispute this statement.

We have given careful consideration to the Royal Commission's view that it could envisage circumstances in which professional officers might receive more pay than a permanent secretary. This commends itself to the Institution.

As a matter of immediate politics, however, we accept other civil service salaries are a relevant consideration and, accordingly, our present claim is that the salaries of top professional posts should be limited to the remuneration of the permanent secretary. Examples of the posts we have in mind are:

Director General (Ships), Admiralty
Deputy Controller (Research and Development), Admiralty
Civil Engineer in Chief, Admiralty
Chief Scientific Adviser, Ministry of Agriculture, Fisheries and Food
Director General of Works, Air Ministry
Chief Valuer, Inland Revenue Department
Engineer in Chief, Post Office
Chief Scientist, Ministry of Aviation
Director General of Works, Ministry of Works

We have specified only top posts because it seems to us wrong to burden the Coleraine Committee with a mass of detail when the point of principle to be determined is simple. It is our assumption that if the Coleraine Committee determine the major principle, there should be no undue difficulty in our reaching agreement with you about the levels of the other directing posts.

The principle to be considered is that the pay of the top professional posts, as defined by illustration above, be reassessed on the basis of fair comparisons with industry and commerce, and should for the present be subject to an overriding limitation that it should not exceed that of a permanent secretary.

Some senior scientific posts, namely, the Chief Scientific Adviser, Ministry of Supply, and the Chief of the Royal Naval Scientific Service, had already been graded at permanent secretary level in 1957.

Early in 1958 the National Staff Side, against the opposition of the Treasury, succeeded in persuading the Coleraine Committee to undertake a review of higher-grades pay. On 30 January 1959 the Coleraine Committee made its report. According to the general secretary, writing in *State Service*, the effect of the review was simply to apply to the salaries recommended by Priestley the general pay increases given to the rest of the civil service in the intervening period.

PAY RESEARCH AND THE INSTITUTION

The attitude of the Treasury to claims put forward on behalf of individual classes was that they should await the outcome of pay research exercises. The Institution took a different view. It was not prepared to delay pressing claims, some of them outstanding during the period of the Priestley Commission, while the lengthy process of submitting each class in turn to the pay research process continued. Hence during 1956 the Institution tabled claims for several of its classes, both national and departmental. In February 1956 an interim claim had been submitted drawing attention to the erosion of differentials of the technical classes in relation to the industrial staff, whom many of them supervised. The Institution asked for the restoration of the relationship which had existed in 1947. The claim was taken to arbitration in January 1957 and a chairman's award went some way to restoring the differentials. By the end of the year arrangements were being made for the Pay Research Unit to start its investigation of the technical classes.

The success on the technical classes claim threw into sharp relief the unsatisfactory position of the works group. The arbitration award gave the technical class grade 2 officer the same maximum as the basic grade of the works group. If the basic grade were only a training grade for professional entrants that would have been satisfactory, but in fact many professionals remained on the basic grade for a long period. The Institution, therefore, submitted an interim claim on behalf of the works group. Failing agreement the case was taken to arbitration where it was thrown out, largely because the tribunal accepted the Treasury view that it would only be a short time before the works group had their first pay research exercise.

The Institution had more success with a claim on behalf of architectural and engineering draughtsmen. The claim, submitted jointly by the Institution and the STCS, sought to overturn certain recommendations of the Priestley Commission. It was partially conceded by the Treasury and on average gave the draughtsmen much the same increases as the Civil Service Arbitration Tribunal had awarded to the technical classes. By the end of 1958 preparations for a pay research exercise for A&E draughtsmen and for the works group were under way, and the PRU report on the technical classes had been received. A claim was made to the Treasury in March 1959, based on the PRU report. Towards the end of 1959 a joint claim by the Institution and STCS was submitted. This claim was based on the evidence provided by the Pay Research Unit report on architectural and engineering draughtsmen.

The work of the Pay Research Unit was by this time being slowed down with a large number of surveys. The frustration aroused by the delays was illustrated by the position of the assistant (scientific) class whose interim claim was heard by the arbitration tribunal in October 1957 and granted pending a full pay research survey. The class was referred immediately to the Unit for investigation but by October 1958 there was still no sign that even the preliminary work on the survey could begin. Indeed, it was realistically expected that the survey would not begin for another year. In an even worse position were those grades which had to be excluded from the pay research programme for the time being because there was no point in adding to the delays. At the same time the Treasury was staving off pay claims by referring them to the PRU even though there was no realistic possibility of an early outcome.

The implementation of the doctrine of fair comparisons was not only imposing strains on the Pay Research Unit, it also increased substantially the work of Institution staff, and members and officers directly concerned on the group committees and the NEC. It also necessitated changes in the arbitration procedures. The chairman of the tribunal pointed out that where Pay Research Unit material was under consideration rather more time than normal would be required for consideration of papers. It was, therefore, agreed that the time-limit for a hearing from the date of submission of terms of reference should be extended to six weeks; that the parties should have at least thirty-one days' notice of the hearing; and that the parties to the reference should supply six copies of their case to the Tribunal not later than fifteen days before the hearing.

It had already been agreed that there would be a review of the machinery of the Pay Research Unit in 1960. In the preceding year the Institution discussed its experience of the pay research process and of the principle of 'fair comparisons' itself. In January 1959 the general secretary addressed a meeting in Caxton Hall on the subject 'The Civil Service Pay Research Unit'. He reiterated the Institution's opposition to the 'fair comparisons' principle and its commitment to the view that the civil service should lead and not follow, especially in raising the status of specialists in society. He acknowledged that it was only fair to 'see how it works and judge the machine on the results that it produces'. The Pay Research Unit had for the most part done a thorough job, but in doing it thoroughly, which it must, there had been inordinate delays in settling pay. The general secretary suggested that

> both sides, the National Staff Side and the Official Side, must set out to ensure that claims are considered and dealt with in a period of months not years. If there is a thing that ought to be dealt with by the Pay Research Unit, one then recognises what is likely to be the period of time when it can be dealt with. You calculate that honestly and fairly. If that is going to be unreasonably far ahead, you do something about it of an *ad hoc* character in the same way as we did for years before the Pay Research Unit was invented.

The impatience of the membership over the long delays in the pay research procedure was manifested at the 1959 annual delegate conference when several motions on the subject, some criticising the process and some asking for its disbandment, were on the agenda. The attitude of the NEC speakers was to echo members' concern at delays but to caution against the too hasty abandonment of the new machinery. Other forms of pay negotiation might be more expeditious but they would not necessarily provide the right answer from the Treasury. This view carried the day.

At the 1960 annual delegate conference, however, a resolution was adopted which stated that the principle of 'fair comparison' was in fundamental contradiction to the longstanding belief of the Institution that the government should take the lead in improving the status and remuneration of scientific, professional and technical workers. This resolution was not as self-centred as it might at first appear. Throughout the 1950s increasing concern had been expressed in Britain at the shortage of scientists and technologists. In comparison with other leading industrial countries Britain was producing proportionately fewer scientists and technologists from her universities and it was felt that in Britain the educational system tended to belittle the role of science and technology in society. People from many walks of life drew attention to the very large number of scientists and technologists being produced by the educational system of the USSR. This, it was suggested, was one of the main reasons for the continued steady advance of Soviet economic strength. In other countries also, including the United States, Germany and Sweden, greater emphasis was placed upon the training of scientists and technologists.

The Institution urged that if this neglect of science and technology in Britain was to be overcome a special responsibility rested with the government. It was the government's duty not only to increase the output of scientists and technologists from the educational system but also to enhance their role in society. Policies of economic expansion had to be pursued to ensure that employment opportunities existed for the men and women coming from the universities. The Institution argued that if the government continued to pay its scientists and technologists on the principle of fair comparison with the pay of scientists and technologists in private industry then the required improvement in status would never be achieved. The only way to break out of this circle was for the government itself to give a lead. This was the reasoning behind the conference's rejection of the principle of 'fair comparisons'.

A CHANGING ECONOMIC CLIMATE

The general secretary, in his speech to the 1959 conference, had referred to 'a national neurosis of frustration' as far as the civil service was concerned. On pay, 1959 was 'a story of delay and, in my view, manipulated delay, that goes on in respect of all pay claims whether they affect a half-dozen or whether they affect thousands'. In the country in general, however, the economy was already beginning to expand and the outlook was brighter.

Despite the pleas of the government for restraint on wages the average increase in pay for all workers over the preceding four years had been significantly higher than the increase in retail prices. On the other hand, as the unions pointed out, the improvement in real living standards of working people was less than the proportionate increase in productivity, even though the expansion of industry had been repeatedly interrupted by stop-go deflationary policies. This improvement in living standards between 1955 and 1959 was a significant factor in the general election of 1959. The Conservative government was returned with 365 seats against 258 for Labour and 6 for the Liberals. At the previous general election in 1955 the Conservatives had 344 seats, Labour 277 and the Liberals 6.

The brighter economic outlook, which had already made for easier pay negotiations in the private sector, was reflected in the civil service during 1960. In the introduction to the annual report for 1960 the NEC stated:

> The year 1960 can well be described as a year of results, in contrast with 1959 as a year of frustration. In the nature of things, some of the results are more satisfactory than others. In every case it has been an advantage to get clear determination of salary issues and Institution members have benefited enormously in sheer hard cash as a result of Institution activities.

The first successes were the arbitration tribunal awards following Pay Research Unit exercises for the technical classes and architectural and engineering draughtsmen. Before the hearings the Institution had arranged meetings in many parts of the country at which members had expressed their anger and frustration at delays in securing a settlement. The technical classes case was heard on 16 June and for the first time special arrangements were made, since only forty seats were available in the court, for some three hundred members to listen to the proceedings by relay to an adjacent hall. Similar arrangements were made at the draughtsmen's hearing in August. The awards in both cases, showed substantial gains over the best that had been offered from the Treasury in negotiations.

The works group claim was heard in December 1960, the culmination of an extraordinarily long period of delay. The Institution had been seeking improved salaries for the works group since 1956. Negotiations on the claim, following a PRU survey, had begun in September and foundered within an hour. The award was satisfactory in that it took into account many of the special factors which the Treasury had refused to countenance. It paid attention to vertical and horizontal relativities, mobility and quality of work, and to some special factors derived from the nature of the work. Much of the work was unique to the civil service.

In addition to these major settlements there were also interim settlements for scientific officers, experimental officers, agricultural advisory service officers, librarians, information officers, cartographic draughtsmen and illustrators.

These interim settlements followed various other settlements for parent grades to which these other grades were linked.

The scientific assistants were omitted from such consequential settlements because, the Treasury claimed, their link with the clerical classes had been broken by the 1957 arbitration tribunal case. In March 1960 the arbitration tribunal rejected a claim for a second interim increase for scientific assistants. As a consequence scientific assistant members were urged to gather detailed evidence which would be helpful in the next round of negotiations. In November members at the Laboratory of the Government Chemist conducted a ban on overtime. The anger of the assistants (scientific) was brought home to the 1961 annual delegate conference of the Institution when members demonstrated from the gallery. They were greeted by loud applause from the delegates.

The brighter economic outlook enabled the National Staff Side to negotiate a 4 per cent central pay settlement at the end of 1960. In addition the Coleraine Committee recommended in July that the PRU settlement for the executive and administrative grades should be extended over the whole of the higher civil service. This was accepted by the Prime Minister. A development in the higher-grades area which was pleasing to the Institution was the Minister of Works' decision that the vacant post of Director General of Works should be filled again by a professionally qualified candidate.

REVIEW OF THE PAY SYSTEM

By 1961 the parties to the 1956 Pay Agreement were in a position to review the workings of the agreement and ready to propose changes where necessary. Although the Staff Side were in general satisfied with the work of the Pay Research Unit several practical difficulties had emerged. When several surveys were being conducted simultaneously it was not always possible to persuade outside companies to co-operate in every survey. Understandably, they objected to their own work being disrupted continually. Hence a company used in one survey could not easily be used for another. Moreover several companies flatly refused admission to the Pay Research Unit.

The lack of full evidence would not have mattered so much had the Treasury and the civil service unions been able to reach agreement on the interpretation of the results derived from the PRU reports. But there was often disagreement. The Institution took the view that the Treasury was committed to a mechanistic analysis of the evidence, and disregarded other relevant considerations. These were, for example, whether particular firms could be considered 'good employers', the extent to which account should be taken of the remuneration of partners and principals in professional firms, and the fact that certain government responsibilities could not be fully reflected in outside employment. Moreover, according to the Institution, the Treasury did not pay attention to internal horizontal and vertical relativities. The Treasury had also insisted in 1960 on quantifying and comparing annual leave and superannuation entitlements inside and outside the civil service, a move which the Staff Side had strongly resisted. All these points, together with the general problem of delays produced by the pay research system and by the attitude of the Treasury, were put before the Treasury in mid-1960.

As part of the central pay settlement in December 1960, a new agreement on arrangements for negotiations modifying that of 1956 was reached. It provided broadly for two things. First, that each November there should be a central pay settlement if the wage-rate index had moved more than 5 points since the previous central pay settlement. Second, pay research exercises on any major civil service class would not take place more than once every five years and general claims in respect of classes should be limited to not more than one in five years. The only circumstances in which reviews within the five-year period could take place would be if there were a general shortage of recruits in the class, a distortion of relativities within a hierarchy or chain of command and alterations in scale structure resulting from reorganisations in departments.

At the 1961 annual delegate conference there were several motions expressing hostility to the new agreement although in the event an NEC motion supporting the agreement, though with reservations, was carried. The conference voted, however, to abolish the pay research system and to prepare alternative schemes for achieving increases. The terms of the resolution were:

That this conference, having noted that recent pay awards within the civil service have been made in spite of, rather than because of the civil service pay research unit, proposes that steps be taken to abolish the pay research unit system and requests the National Executive Committee to prepare alternative schemes for the submission of pay claims, giving special consideration to a system following national vertical and horizontal relativities. With the increasing national importance of science and technology the Government should take a lead in improving the status and remuneration of such staff.

By July 1961 the first round of pay research negotiations had been all but completed. The only major classes which remained outstanding were the scientists whose pay research report had been received earlier in the year and on which analysis was proceeding. Although the process had not proved as deficient as the Institution had predicted it was clear from the 1961 annual delegate conference that the Institution's attitude was still basically hostile and nothing that had happened since 1956 had undermined the fundamental objection to the philosophy of 'fair comparisons' as it applied to scientists and professional and technical staff.

16 Some Other Issues in the Middle and Late 1950s

During the period of the Priestley Commission inquiry the Institution and the other civil service unions continued to use the normal negotiating machinery to advance the claims of their members. The biggest advance of all was made on the issue of equal pay. Early in 1954 a series of meetings was held in different parts of the country in support of equal pay for equal work. Equal pay poems, postcards, posters, cartoons, bookmarks and handbills were prepared to assist the campaign and 9 March was declared 'Equal Pay Day'. On the morning of that day a national declaration on equal pay was read in front of the statue of Mrs Pankhurst in Tower Gardens, Millbank, London, and at public places in many other towns. A first reading was given in the House of Commons to an Equal Pay Bill sponsored by Douglas Houghton. A mammoth equal pay petition organised jointly by the National Staff Side, the National Union of Teachers, the National and Local Government Officers' Association and the National Federation of Professional Workers was presented to the House. A mass rally was held in London, attended by over 6,000 people, and addressed by union leaders and MPs.

During his budget speech on 6 April 1954 the Chancellor of the Exchequer, Mr Butler, offered ·to meet the National Staff Side to discuss the possibility of implementing the principle of equal pay. This meeting took place shortly afterwards and agreement was reached that equal pay would be introduced by instalments over a period of years.

The Civil Service National Whitley Council set up a joint committee to devise a scheme by which equal pay for men and women might be introduced gradually in the non-industrial civil service. This committee recommended that all women receiving less than the men's rate for the same work should get an initial instalment towards equal pay and should then progress annually towards the full objective of equal pay over a period of six years. The initial instalment would be paid from 1 January 1955 and full equality of pay with men would not be achieved until 1 January 1961.

The civil service unions recognised that this deferment was one of the defects of the proposed settlement. Another was that special arrangements were not to be made for older women civil servants. Most women civil servants over 50 years of age would thus retire on pension terms less favourable than those provided if the principle of equal pay were to be fully observed. The scheme for implementation of equal pay was, nevertheless, a milestone in social progress, the outcome of thirty years' struggle not only by civil service unions but by the wider trade union movement. The eventual agreement for the gradual introduction of equal pay was dated 29 April 1955 and backdated to 1 January 1955.

At the 1954 annual delegate conference John Fraser was thanked for the major part he had played in the campaign as secretary of the National Staff Side Equal Pay Committee. An article in *State Service* stated:

It was in the person of John Fraser that the Institution was able to play a major part in carrying through a campaign that has finally achieved equal pay. All this was done on top of a very heavy load of Institution work. Only great interest in and enthusiasm for a job give rise to such willing expenditure of time and personal effort. John Fraser will have a special place in the record of the struggle to achieve equal pay.

AGE OF RETIREMENT

Towards the end of 1954 a new threat to civil service conditions of employment emerged with the recommendations of a committee of inquiry appointed to consider 'the economic and financial problems of the provision for old age'. The committee, chaired by Sir Thomas Phillips, a retired civil servant, suggested that the minimum age for the national insurance pension should be raised from 65 years to 68 years, and that minimum pension ages in occupational pension schemes should also be raised. The committee expressed the hope 'that the public services will bring their minimum retirement ages into line with those recommended for private schemes'. Two trade union members of the Phillips Committee published a minority report. They said: 'We find it impossible to agree with the majority recommendations for raising the minimum retiring ages.' They strongly opposed the recommendation for raising the minimum pension ages in occupational schemes.

Within the trade union movement, particularly among unions catering for white-collar workers, the report was strongly criticised. Richard Nunn wrote an article in *State Service* criticising the report, and arguing that it was based upon a number of economic fallacies. One was that, because of the increasing length of life of citizens, the non-economically active proportion of the population would grow significantly whilst the proportion of those in employment would decrease. The critics of the report pointed out that whilst it was true that the number of elderly people was increasing there were also fewer children in the population. The proportion of the total population engaged in full-time employment was not likely to change very much. An even more important fallacy, the article continued, was the implied contention of the report that changes in age distribution in the population represented an economic burden which could not be borne without serious consequences for the living standards of the country. The critics of the Phillips Report argued that this was not so. The expected rise in productivity was far greater than the expected increase in the cost of providing for old age.

A leading part in the criticism of the Phillips Report was played by the National Federation of Professional Workers. The Federation was able to show that even if the gross national product of the United Kingdom rose by no more than an average 1·5 per cent per annum it would far outweigh over a period of about twenty-five years the increased economic burden of catering for a growing proportion of elderly citizens. This criticism of the Phillips Committee report found endorsement at the 1955 Institution annual delegate conference and later at the annual congress of the TUC.

The campaign of the trade union movement against the recommendation to increase the normal retirement age to 68 proved successful. Despite an initial blaze of publicity in favour of an increase in retirement age, the economic fallacies on which the proposition was based were exposed.

PENSION INCREASES

At the beginning of 1955 the National Staff Side made representations to the Treasury in favour of further increases for civil service pensioners. In the spring the government gave a hint that these representations were being considered sympathetically. Civil service unions pointed out that since the beginning of the Second World War, Pension Increase Acts had been passed by Parliament in 1944, 1947 and 1952, but these Acts, said the unions, had been inadequate and were not designed to deal with the real problem of maintaining the value of a pension as at the time when the pension was awarded. A Pensions (Increase) Bill was published on 6 February 1956 and it represented a marked improvement over earlier similar Acts. The government proposed in the new Bill to withdraw the means test which had excited so much opposition on previous occasions. As a result of an amendment carried during a parliamentary debate the final terms of the Bill provided a uniform 10 per cent increase in pensions.

By 1959 inflation had again eaten away at the increases achieved in 1956. A public campaign was conducted to persuade the government to increase civil service pensions and as a result a new Pensions Increase Act was passed. The government, however, did not respond to the National Staff Side's view that civil service pensions should be taken out of the political arena by introducing a system of automatic periodic reviews.

UNESTABLISHED SERVICE TO COUNT

Throughout the second half of the 1950s and into the beginning of the 1960s the civil service trade unions continued to campaign for unestablished service to be counted in full for pension purposes. When in opposition in 1949 the Conservative Party, through its official spokesman Mr Peter Thorneycroft, had urged that unestablished service should count in full for pension purposes. The Labour government had compromised by agreeing that unestablished service after 14 July 1949 would count in full for pension purposes but that unestablished service before that date would count only for half. At the time Mr Thorneycroft had said:

I do not think anyone in private life with a servant who had served him faithfully for twenty years would turn round and tell him that he will get less pension because part of his service was on an unestablished basis. It would be regarded as a monstrous argument, and it would not be tolerated by members opposite in their private affairs . . . but every doing of justice of this character must cost money. I do not believe we are justified in saving money by doing less than justice to the servants of the Crown.

The Priestley Commission also said that there was no question of merit or principle outstanding. It said that it was now common ground that unestablished service should be reckoned in full. The sole outstanding consideration was that of cost. Nevertheless, despite Mr Thorneycroft's statement on behalf of the Conservative opposition in 1949 and the firm declaration of principle made in the Priestley Commission report, the Conservative governments of the 1950s continued to refuse to accept the principle of unestablished service counting in full for pension purposes. The cost, they said, remained the vital problem.

At the end of 1956 a public campaign on the issue was planned by the National Whitley Council Staff Side. But later the National Staff Side decided that it was inopportune to continue with the planned campaign of protest on unestablished service to count in full simultaneously with the very much bigger campaign of protest being conducted in Britain at that time against the policy of the British government in relation to the Suez Canal. The campaign was resumed, however, after an interval of some months.

In February 1957 a deputation from the National Staff Side, which included Douglas Houghton, MP, and Stanley Mayne, met the Chancellor of the Exchequer and the Financial Secretary to the Treasury to press the claim. It was estimated that at the beginning of 1957 some 475,000 serving civil servants were affected by the ruling that temporary service should not be counted in full for pension purposes. The number of retired civil servants affected by the same ruling was approximately 60,000. Douglas Houghton, MP, also played a leading part in securing parliamentary support for the claim of the civil service unions. He secured the signatures of nearly 250 members of Parliament for a motion on the subject in 1958. Of this number of supporting MPs, 225 were Labour members. The National Staff Side Superannuation Campaign Committee had also encouraged the establishment of constituency committees and these had also helped in mobilising the support of MPs. The government, however, still refused to move.

A small victory of significance to Institution members was achieved in 1958 with the implementation of the Priestley Commission's recommendation that the Treasury's powers to grant 'added years' should be extended and used more widely. The minimum age at which 'added years' could be granted was reduced from 35 to 30. The Institution submitted a detailed memorandum on the subject to the National Staff Side and asked them to press again the general case for 'added years'; this they agreed to do.

The National Staff Side renewed their campaign for unestablished service to count in full for pension purposes. A further deputation met the Chancellor in April 1959. At the Institution's conference that year delegates instructed the NEC to campaign actively on the issue. In July the government again rejected the demand and the Institution received many letters and resolutions of protest from members, branches and sections.

The impending general election in October 1959 presented the National Staff Side with a new opportunity to stimulate the campaign. The constituency committees were alerted and asked to consider possible action. It was realised that superannuation would not be a vital issue in the election but that the briefing of candidates would be valuable in any parliamentary campaign following the election.

In 1960 and early 1961 the National Staff Side arranged a series of protest meetings in different parts of the country, all of which were well attended. A new House of Commons motion was tabled, headed by Sir Lionel Heald, the Rt Hon. Jo Grimond and Mr Douglas Houghton. It included 372 signatures. Despite this support, the Chancellor of the Exchequer, Mr Selwyn Lloyd, in a letter to Sir Lionel Heald on 30 June 1961, reaffirmed the government's objection to the claim of the civil service unions. Mr Lloyd said that in the existing economic situation all his efforts as Chancellor 'must be directed towards containing, not adding to, the growth of public expenditure'. He said that acceptance of the claim would be incompatible with the demands of the economic situation.

OTHER ISSUES

Another issue had for some thirty-seven years caused dissatisfaction among civil servants; that of provincial differentiation. The National Staff Side had argued that provincial differentiation should be abolished and the Commission had recommended a modified version of that view. An agreement concluded in 1957, which the Institution welcomed as an enormous step forward, brought to an end the three-tier system of provincial differentiation. In its place there was to be introduced over a period extending from 1958 to 1962 a system of national rates with a London differential. In the first year of the period of transition the new national rate was to include towns with a population of 160,000 and upwards. From the second, third and fourth years the national rate was extended respectively to towns with a population of 120,000, 80,000 and 40,000 and above. From 1 January 1962 all remaining areas were to be brought up to the national rate. In addition, London rates of pay were to be given to all staff employed within a 16-mile radius of Charing Cross instead of the previous 12-mile radius. London weighting was to be pensionable for all civil servants.

The Institution also had some success in reducing the number of temporary staff by securing their transfer to established employment. The Institution pressed without success for a service-wide solution to the problem but some progress was made by increasing the established cadre in various departments. By 1959 the number of temporary officers in the professional and technical field had been reduced to a very low proportion, but among scientific staff there had been an increase.

A MINISTER FOR SCIENCE

During the 1950s the Institution continued to press its view that the status of scientists and technologists in society was too low and that as a consequence Britain was falling behind in economic and social development. This low status was reflected in the civil service.

In 1958 the new president of the Institution, Sir Graham Sutton, wrote an article in *State Service* reiterating the Institution's view that in a technological age specialists in the civil service should have a greater role in the management of their tasks.

> My own view is that in the future it is going to become increasingly necessary for professional civil servants to take a share in the functions which are now broadly classed as 'administrative'. In other words, I believe that the management of a research group, or any part of a ministry which is concerned with scientific and technical matters, should lie very largely in the hands of men who have professional knowledge.

He argued that just as it was no longer sufficient for administration to be carried on by men of outstanding intellectual ability but little specialist knowledge, so specialists could not expect to carry out administrative tasks without specialised training in administration.

As I see it, a main problem facing professional civil servants is how to ensure that an adequate knowledge of administration and management is passed on to the young professional man in his formative years. I believe that we must now recognise that training of this type is an essential part of professional education. The scientist must learn that there is an art of administration, the art of negotiating with other men, of putting a case moderately yet firmly, in fact the whole art of making the complicated machine work for you and not against you.

Hopes for adequate recognition of the role and status of specialists in the civil service and outside were raised by the appointment after the 1959 general election of a minister for science. Any euphoria engendered by such an appointment, however, was soon dissipated by the downgrading of scientific effort elsewhere in the government machine. While there were some signs of increased expenditure on scientific research, the DSIR, the department which would be expected to spearhead such developments, was under review. In 1955 the Lord President appointed a committee of inquiry to examine the organisation and functioning of the DSIR, chaired by Sir Harry Jephcott, chairman and managing director of Glaxo Laboratories. An interim report from the committee contained sweeping criticisms of the DSIR, which the Institution considered wholly unjustified. The report recommended that the department's advisory council should be replaced by a research council with executive powers and containing a substantial number of industrialists. There was a strong lobby that believed that there was no significant role for government-based industrial research, arguing that basic research should be done by universities and applied research within industry's own laboratories. The position was summed up in an article in *State Service*. 'Thus, over many fields, the government seems more concerned to push out to industry as much of the scientific research as industry can be bribed or bullied to take and at the same time to increase industrial control of research in the government service.'

Several laboratories within the DSIR were closed and some laboratories in the UKAEA reorganised with little consultation with either scientific staff or directors. The net result of these developments was less central co-ordination of government scientific effort, despite the creation of the post of Minister of Science.

In 1958 the Lord President of the Council established a committee under the chairmanship of Sir Claude Gipp, FRS, to examine the management of government research. Sir Claude died in 1959 but the committee continued its work under the chairmanship of Sir Solly Zuckerman. Its terms of reference were:

To inquire into the techniques employed by government departments and other bodies wholly financed by the Exchequer for the management and control of research and development carried out by them or on their behalf, and to make recommendations.

The Institution took the opportunity, in a memorandum prepared for the

Zuckerman Committee, to indicate disquiet at recent changes in the DSIR and elsewhere.

THE CAMPAIGN FOR THE LIMITATION OF SECRET POLICE POWERS

In March 1954 it was reported that, from the time of the introduction of the new security arrangements outlined by the Prime Minister in the House of Commons in 1948, twenty-four civil servants had been dismissed. Of this number seventeen were industrial and seven non-industrial civil servants. In addition, seventy-two civil servants had been transferred.

Towards the end of 1955, as the result of the defection of two foreign service officials, Burgess and MacLean, the government asked a committee of the Privy Council to report on security arrangements. The report of the committee recommended a number of changes. The full report of the Conference of Privy Councillors on Security, its official title, was not published because the government felt it would not be in the public interest to do so. A White Paper was, however, published in 1956 giving an indication of the substance of the report, including a number of specific recommendations. The report said that whereas 'once the main risk to be guarded against was espionage by foreign powers carried out by professional agents, today the chief risks are presented by communists and by other persons who for one reason or another are subject to communist influence'. It went on to argue that one of the chief problems of security was thus to identify not only members of the British Communist Party but 'that wider body . . . who are both sympathetic to communism, or susceptible to communist pressure . . .'.

Some of the recommendations of the conference dealt with the relationship between security risks and defects of character and conduct. Great importance was attached to character defects which might make a man unreliable or expose him to blackmail. There was therefore 'a duty on departments to inform themselves of serious failings such as drunkenness, addiction to drugs, homosexuality or any loose living that may seriously affect a man's reliability'. Supervisory officers, the report said, must regard it as their duty to know their staff and they must not fail to report anything which affected security. 'This covers both evidence which suggests communist associations or sympathies and also serious defects and failings which might jeopardise security of the section of the public service in their charge.'

The report also made a series of recommendations on persons of whom there was no evidence of Communist Party membership but where 'evidence exists of communist sympathies or of close association with members of the Communist Party'. This included individuals living with a wife or husband who was a communist or communist sympathiser. The report acknowledged that some of the measures outlined were 'in some respects alien to our traditional practices'. Decisions had sometimes to be taken without revealing full details of the supporting evidence and action sometimes had to be taken even although nothing might have been proved against a particular civil servant on standards which would be accepted in a court of law.

The 1956 conference of the Institution passed a resolution expressing opposition to the new procedures:

This conference notes the 'Statement on the Findings of the Conference of Privy Councillors on Security'. It deplores the fact that, while lip service is paid to the dangers of 'tale-bearing or malicious gossip', the tenor of much of the statement allows a willingness to accept, if not encourage, information detailed from such sources, which would not be acceptable in a court of law.

Conference reaffirms the emergency resolution of the 1948 conference on the civil service 'purge', and protests most vigorously at the proposed extension of security procedures in the statement. It considers that there has been nothing in previous failures in security that ordinary competent administration could not have prevented.

Conference instructs the National Executive Committee to take all steps in its power to oppose the improper procedures advocated and to demonstrate to the public that these security procedures are a serious threat to civil liberties in Britain.

Public attention was drawn to the new security procedures by the Lang case. According to a report in *State Service* the Minister of Supply had virtually compelled Imperial Chemical Industries to discharge Mr Lang, an assistant solicitor in the company, who had married in 1951 and whose wife had resigned from the Communist Party in 1949. *State Service* continued:

He is now turned out of his job and all that is said about him by the government is that Mr Lang's political association was one of a number of matters taken into consideration but not one single word as to what any one of the other matters was. This is political smearing of the worst kind. This is precisely the kind of treatment that some Institution's members have suffered. All that has been said to them is: 'You are believed to be associated with the Communist Party in such a way as to raise legitimate doubts about your reliability.'

Following the outcry over the Lang case, an *ad hoc* committee was established with the name 'The Campaign for the Limitation of Secret Police Powers'. It was an all-party committee and included a number of leading civil service trade unionists, among them Stanley Mayne and E. C. Redhead, MP. (Until his election to Parliament as a Labour member, Mr Redhead was general secretary of the Society of Civil Servants.) It also included, among others, Mr Benn Levy the dramatist and a former MP; Mr Christopher Fry; Mr J. B. Priestley; and the editors of the *Spectator, New Statesman* and *Tribune*.

The committee put forward a five-point plan. It was:

(1) Rules governing employment on security work should be approved by Parliament and made known to every person engaged upon it.
(2) No person should be removed from his employment on a mendacious charge; e.g. if security was the reason he should not be allowed to suppose it was inefficiency.
(3) Every person suspected of being a security risk should be advised in writing of the charges against him; of his right of appeal; and of his right to be supported by either a legal or trade union representative.
(4) In addition to or instead of the 'Three Advisors', the right of appeal should lie to three High Court judges who, sitting *in camera*, should examine the

security officers who had brought the charge, their evidence, their witnesses and their documents. The proceedings should be protected by the Official Secrets Acts.

(5) In the last resort, this court, if it had evidence of misconduct in the administration of security organisation, should report the matter, through the Lord Chancellor, to the Privy Council.

This programme was put to and endorsed by a very well-attended meeting at the Caxton Hall, Westminster, on 18 July 1956. Mr Stanley Mayne acted as secretary of the campaign committee. The campaign also produced a pamphlet entitled *The Secret Police and You* in an attempt to gain acceptance by Parliament of the code which it had suggested.

In the following months the campaign made spirited efforts to put its point of view before the public. A leading part in the campaign was played by Stanley Mayne. He made three principal criticisms of the security procedure then being operated by the government. The first was that there was lack of clarity in the accusations against suspended persons. Secondly, the procedure did not provide for the suspended persons to receive the help of trade unions or legal advisers in the course of interview. Thirdly, the procedure lacked any kind of judicial appeal tribunal. Stanley Mayne pointed out that under the procedure civil servants who had been subjected to the 'purge' had frequently found themselves up against very vague and general charges to which it was virtually impossible to provide a reply. The arrangement of the 'Three Advisers', he argued, was a facade which appeared to provide helpful arrangements but in fact did nothing of the sort. The 'Three Advisers' were unable to give the individual civil servant any more specific information on the causes of suspicion against him. They had no power to examine and to sift the evidence and there was no provision for a judicial hearing.

In April 1957 the Official Side informed the Staff Side of the number of staff who had been dismissed or transferred for security reasons up to March 1957. The total number of industrial and non-industrial cases was 159, of whom 81 had been transferred to non-secret work, 24 had been dismissed, 23 had resigned, 30 had been reinstated and 1 was on special leave pending a decision. At the 1957 annual conference of the Institution a resolution was carried reaffirming the previously declared policy of the Institution on security arrangements. The five-point proposals of the Campaign for the Limitation of Secret Police Powers were endorsed. Conference also expressed appreciation of Stanley Mayne's role in the campaign.

Towards the end of the year the Campaign for the Limitation of Secret Police Powers issued a second pamphlet, entitled *A Year with the Secret Police*. It was written by Mr Benn W. Levy, the chairman of the campaign. The booklet contained information about cases brought to light as a result of the campaign during the previous twelve months. It said these cases were of necessity 'only the tip of the iceberg', for the majority of the victims of underground security information rarely knew what had happened to them and only a few of those who did know cared to risk publicity. Secrecy, said the campaign, led to tyranny and potentially to blackmail. For these evils there was only one corrective, namely, the requirement that the secret police, MI5, should prove its case before independent judges in the presence of defendants who would be legally represented and who would hear the evidence against them and get a chance to

Professional and Technology grades arbitration hearing, 4 September 1974. Some members of the Institution team (left to right) R. Kitchen, W. Wright, J. Smith, W. A. T. Dorey, G. B. Vint, and C. Cooper

Members protest outside the arbitration court on 4 September 1974

The Institution's delegation to the 1976 Trade Union Congress in Brighton

cross-examine their accusers. The campaign, said the pamphlet, was in favour of arrangements which could ensure genuine security, safeguard liberty and actually improve the efficiency of security checkers.

The Campaign for the Limitation of the Powers of the Secret Police had the effect, so its sponsors believed, of restraining some of the worst features of the new licence granted to MI5. The Institution's annual report for 1958 stated that 'sweeping as were the extensions of the security arrangements, in practice little seems to have happened'. (The additional number of security cases between March 1957 and March 1958 was only three.) How far this was due to strong public reactions of the time or how far to a greater degree of common sense in administration, it was not possible to say. It was also reported that the National Staff Side had made yet further efforts to secure that persons subject to the 'purge' procedure should have the right to be accompanied at various stages by a staff association representative. The chairman of the Staff Side, Douglas Houghton, MP, wrote to the Prime Minister urging reconsideration of this point. His representations were unsuccessful but he received from the Prime Minister a long and careful statement on the government's attitude.

The Prime Minister set out what he believed to be the basic objection to the Staff Side proposal. He explained that the government had chosen as the 'Three Advisers' former senior civil servants and trade union officials whose attitude towards the individual would be fair and sympathetic.

We disclose to the three advisers all the sources of evidence and invite them to cross-examine the department's officers and the security service. In this examination it is the constant care of the advisers to ensure that no allegation is allowed to pass unchallenged. Equally in their examination of the civil servant the advisers frame their questions in their knowledge of the evidence, in the aim of giving him every chance to convince them that their suspicions are unfounded . . . The fundamental objection to your suggestion is this. The proceedings as they are now conducted unquestionably subject the government's secret sources of information to some risk. The presence of a 'friend' would increase this risk and might lead the advisers to having to abandon or severely curtail their attempts to give the individual the maximum chance to clear himself.

MEMBERSHIP AND ORGANISATION

In 1956 the Institution membership reached 50,000 and continued at around that figure for the rest of the decade. By the end of 1960 it had reached 53,923 which the NEC estimated represented 70 per cent of all eligible staff in the civil service. Of the large civil service departments the highest density of membership was in the Admiralty where it was estimated that 77 per cent of those eligible were in membership.

The Institution was strengthened during the 1950s by the accession of several small departmental specialist organisations. In 1954 the Association of HM Inspectors of Mines decided to amalgamate with the Institution. It had seceded from the Institution in 1945, a matter of particular regret in the light of the Institution president's association with the Inspectorate. It was therefore with great pleasure that the Association was received back into the fold. In 1955 the Insolvency Service Staff Association, the Ministry of Health Medical Officers' Association and the Association of State Veterinary Officers also joined the Institution. In the same year a membership agreement was reached with the British Airline Pilots Association, similar to that already established with the National Union of Journalists, whereby BALPA members employed in the civil service automatically became members of the Institution. The Institution conducted negotiations on their behalf while maintaining close consultation with BALPA.

Unhappily in 1956 relations with the STCS deteriorated as a result of the STCS trying to recruit drawing office staff who were members of the Institution. It was only with the greatest difficulty that a united front between the two organisations could be maintained in negotiations with the Treasury. Relations began to improve again in 1958 and the two organisations worked closely together in negotiations. This improvement continued in 1959 and the good relations were formalised in the establishment of a joint committee.

During 1960 the Society of Post Office Engineers branch decided to break away from the Institution. Members of this branch were executive engineers and senior executive engineers (departmental variants of the basic grades of the works group). The delay in securing a satisfactory pay increase for the works group, pending the completion of a pay research report, had resulted in a serious decline in differentials in relation to the grade immediately below them, assistant engineers, represented by the Society of Telecommunications Engineers. During the year the branch made two requests to the NEC to submit a special claim without waiting for the results of the pay research exercise. The NEC were unwilling to accede to this request, believing that the branch's proposal was unsound. As a result, at the biennial conference of the branch in November 1960, a resolution was carried instructing their Executive Council 'to withdraw the Society of Post Office Engineers from the Institution of Professional Civil Servants'. Several resignations from the Institution followed and despite further attempts by the NEC to explain that it was not in the long-term interests of the membership to seek to bypass pay research exercises, the Society of Post Office Engineers established itself as a separate organisation.

In 1954 a further edition of the Institution's handbook was published. That there was a real need for the handbook and that it was much appreciated was demonstrated by the fact that sales reached a record level with one in four of the members buying it. In 1958 a further edition was published. As an additional service to members a legal aid scheme was established in 1954 to assist members when legal action was necessary in connection with accidents or diseases arising from employment. The scheme was designed to deal with cases where negligence was involved and which therefore required action at common law. In 1957 the National Executive Committee decided to extend the scheme to cover members not only while they were at work but for the whole twenty-four hours of the day in relation to any accident in which the negligence of another party could be shown.

At the 1954 conference the Institution decided to affiliate to the Institute of Public Administration. At the same conference a motion to disaffiliate from the National Council for Civil Liberties was defeated. In that year the NCCL had joined the National Staff Side in protesting vigorously against the Masterman restrictions on the political activities of civil servants and this no doubt influenced the debate. Two years later, after speeches alleging communist domination of the NCCL, the conference decided to discontinue its affiliation to the NCCL, despite opposition from the NEC. At the same conference, however, it was decided to affiliate to the National Federation of Professional Workers and review the value of affiliation in 1958. In moving the motion to affiliate, the NEC speaker drew attention to the need to establish links with trade unions outside the civil service because of the system of fair comparisons with outside analogues.

At the 1958 annual conference a motion was moved to the effect that the Institution should disaffiliate from the National Federation of Professional Workers. The motion said that because of the Federation's direct association with the TUC the affiliation of the Institution was 'not now in accordance with the general wishes of members of the Institution'. The general secretary replied to the debate and acknowledged that there was a close association between the NFPW and the TUC. This ensured co-operation between the TUC and the Federation on matters affecting white-collar workers whilst in no way limiting the freedom of the Federation to take independent action where that course was thought necessary and desirable. The general secretary said that in his view the close relationship between the NFPW and the TUC should continue but this was in no way incompatible with the autonomy of the Federation. The motion to disaffiliate was defeated by 26,174 votes to 18,628. Two years later at the 1960 conference a similar motion was passed by a vote of 22,707 to 20,573 and the Institution disaffiliated from the NFPW. The mover of the motion argued that the NFPW was 'nothing more than a back door into the TUC' and that the affiliation had been of little material help in furthering Institution objectives.

NEW HEADQUARTERS

At the 1955 conference the War Department branch proposed that the NEC should negotiate the purchase of a permanent headquarters building for the Institution. The motion was amended to include the prospect of leasing a building if necessary. The motion, as amended, was passed. During the debate it was disclosed that the NEC already had a headquarters premises panel which could examine the details of possible schemes. By the end of the year premises were purchased at 3–9 Northumberland Street at a cost of £71,917. Before purchasing the building it had been estimated by professional advisers and by several members belonging to the relevant professions that the cost of converting the premises for use by the Institution would not exceeed £45,000. When tenders for the work were invited, however, it became clear that the cost would be not less than £70,000. The Institution was unable to secure a loan for this sum and in the circumstances the NEC decided to abandon the project and sell the premises.

The Institution was unable, however, to find other suitable property to rent and the NEC finally decided to retain the Northumberland Street property. At the 1958 conference there was a long and searching debate on the Institution's finances in general and the property proposal in particular. The NEC was subjected to many searching questions and critical comments and the Association of Value Office Valuers led the demand that the Institution should sell the property. The deputy general secretary, Tom Profitt, and the deputy vice-chairman, Bill Bowles, made a spirited defence of the NEC's proposals, stating that there was no feasible alternative. Eventually the conference approved the proposals and the associated recommendation that subscriptions should be raised to £3 3s for full members and £1 10s for members under 21. The NEC gave an assurance that there was a good prospect of negotiating the necessary loans by the end of the year. By December 1959 the demolition work had been completed and by January 1960 tenders for erecting the new building had been submitted. The Institution eventually moved into its new premises on 28 August 1961.

REFORM OF CONFERENCE ARRANGEMENTS

Something of a stir in the Institution was caused towards the end of 1959 by the publication of an article by John Beaton on what he regarded as the failings of annual delegate conference. Mr Beaton, who played the principal role in founding the Scottish branch in 1946 and had become a member of the first National Executive Committee in 1946, had been a prominent and colourful figure at the Institution's annual delegate conferences ever since their inception in 1946. He had served as a member and as chairman of the Standing Orders Committee of the conference and as a member of the NEC for a second period of three years from 1957. He had been chairman of the committee that prepared a revised version of the rules in 1950. His views, therefore, could not be disregarded.

His article in *State Service* was typically forthright. He said that it was unquestionably the fact that major issues which could put life and purpose into the conference were rejected before discussion. The conference showed timidity in dealing with major issues because of its fear that it might be labelled 'political'. Conversely, the agenda of the conference was overloaded with motions which related to the interests of only a handful of the Institution's membership. They had no bearing on general policy. The result of these deficiencies, according to John Beaton, was that conferences were boring. He suggested that the time had come for far-reaching measures to reorganise the proceedings of the conference. This article stimulated a considerable amount of discussion in subsequent issues. Most of the letters were sympathetic to the view expressed by John Beaton. An editorial in the May 1960 issue of *State Service* said that the discussion had been of value because it had ventilated the complaint that major issues tended to be submerged in a mass of detail.

After the 1960 conference, at which a few minor innovations had been introduced, the National Executive Committee decided to set up a small sub-committee to consider what changes, if any, should be made in the arrangements for running the conference. The report of the subcommittee made few radical suggestions. The main proposal was that branches should consider whether there were other ways in which their objectives could be furthered rather than by submitting them as motions for the annual conference. The report pointed out, for example, that suggestions could be forwarded by branches to the National Executive Committee or to a national officer responsible for departmental business. Other suggestions could be forwarded to professional group committees. The report on conference organisation also suggested that there should be an arrangement whereby certain motions of detail could be remitted automatically for consideration to the National Executive Committee. A proposal of this kind had been adopted at the 1960 annual conference. Other suggestions made in the report were that motions on like subjects should be composited and that the agenda should be arranged to ensure that the National Executive Committee could play a more prominent part in the proceedings. The arrangement of the agenda in this way, it was suggested, might help to ensure that attention was focused on the more important issues.

Despite these suggestions the report acknowledged that the subcommittee was not proposing any fundamental change in the procedure of the conference. It concluded that on the whole the procedure which had developed since 1946 was satisfactory and that the changes which had been suggested were really further stages in an already established development. The report ended by pointing out that the success of the conference proceedings depended very largely on the amount of effort put into the preparation of the conference by branches, by the NEC and by delegates. None the less, some ten years later events forced conference to adopt procedures not dissimilar to those advocated by John Beaton.

DEPARTURE OF FAMILIAR FACES

On 1 January 1959 the Institution celebrated the fortieth anniversary of its formation. It had grown from a handful of members to an organisation with more than 50,000 members. At the outset all the work had been undertaken voluntarily by active members. In 1959 the number of active members had grown to be counted not in dozens or even hundreds, but in thousands. They were assisted by a full-time negotiating staff consisting of a general secretary, a deputy general secretary and ten assistant secretaries.

Unfortunately, Sir Richard Redmayne, president of the Institution since its foundation, was not there to celebrate the anniversary. He had died on 27 December 1956 in his ninety-first year. At a memorial service held at St Margaret's, Westminster, the Institution chairman, Jimmy Fry, said that few men had lived such a full and active life. As president of the Institution Sir Richard attended every annual general meeting and annual delegate conference except two. These two absences were caused by severe illness. The Institution had joined with Sir Richard in celebrating his ninetieth birthday in 1955. This was his last activity with the Institution before his death. Sir Richard's obituary in *The Times*, reproduced in the Institution's annual report for 1955, indicated his valuable contribution to society and his wide range of interests. It said, in part:

> Although he will be best remembered as one of the most prominent experts on safety in mining, a man who did much more than anybody else to bring comparative security to the colliers below ground, this was only one of his many interests. He was a great mineralogist; an industrialist; and a director of companies; he knew much about agriculture; he was a graceful writer; and, what few people outside his own circle ever knew, a talented amateur artist. Above all he had a great zest for life. He was as keenly interested in affairs when well over 80 as he was when he was a young man, and he had that strong northern characteristic, a keen sense of dry humour, which was present almost as much and as often in his lectures as it was in his private conversation.

Following the death of Sir Richard Redmayne the Institution elected as its new president Sir Graham Sutton, director general of the Meteorological Office. He had been a vice-president of the Institution for many years.

In the previous year the Institution had lost another stalwart through the death in September 1955 of Frankie Dean. Affectionately known as a 'character' within the Institution, he had served in many capacities – as treasurer, editor of *State Service*, as a member and, later, chairman of the Scientific Staffs Group and as a member of the National Executive Committee. In addition, he had been, for many years past, chairman of the Staff Side of the Air Ministry Whitley Council, and of the Meteorological Office branch of the Institution. He was one of the small band of enthusiasts who, with Leslie Herbert, reformed the constitution of the Institution. He was the last of that band to remain active on the NEC which he had helped to create.

During the winter of 1955–6 there were important changes in the Staff Side of the National Whitley Council. The full-time chairman of the National Staff Side, Sir Albert Day, had decided to retire at the end of June 1955. He was to be replaced by an elected chairman who was to hold office for two years. There was also to be a secretary general who would act as the chief negotiating officer. The intention was that the new secretary general would be Mr L. C. White, the general secretary of the Civil Service Clerical Association. Unfortunately, he died on 11 May 1955. It was decided that Sir Albert Day should be asked to defer his retirement until new arrangements could be made. He continued in office until 31 March 1956. Sir Albert Day occupied the position of full-time chairman of the National Staff Side for a period of seventeen years. In a resolution of appreciation for his service the Staff expressed 'their deep sense of indebtedness . . . for his most distinguished and superlatively valuable services to the Staff Side and to the civil service staff movement . . .'. The newly appointed secretary general of the National Staff Side was Mr R. A. Hayward. He had already served on the National Staff Side as a representative of the Union of Post Office Workers for more than eight years. He entered the civil service in 1924 as a boy messenger in the Post Office and served at all levels as an active rank-and-file member of the Union of Post Office Workers. He was appointed an assistant secretary of that union in 1947 and he became deputy general secretary in 1951. The newly elected chairman of the National Staff Side was Mr Douglas Houghton, MP, general secretary of the Inland Revenue Staff Federation. He had served as general secretary of the Association of Officers of Taxes since 1922 and he became the general secretary of the Inland Revenue Staff Federation when that body was set up in 1938. Mr Houghton was also a member of the TUC General Council and the Labour member of Parliament for Sowerby.

At the end of June 1958 he completed his two years' chairmanship of the National Staff Side and withdrew from Staff Side activity after thirty-five years' service. The Institution marked the occasion by inviting him to contribute an article to *State Service* in which he made some interesting observations on leading figures in the history of the Institution. He said of Leslie Herbert that his early death in 1948 'was a great blow to us all'. It was incredible, Mr Houghton added, that the Institution should suffer such a loss with tragic suddenness. The warmest words of tribute, however, were reserved for Freddie Menzler who had played an outstanding role in maintaining the unity of the greater part of the National Staff Side in the crisis immediately following the General Strike of 1926. Douglas Houghton said: 'no praise can be too high for the wisdom and skill of Menzler's leadership of the Institution in those precarious years after the General Strike'.

In the early summer of 1956 Mr Laurie Sapper, who had been an assistant secretary of the Institution since 1951, left to become the deputy general secretary of the Post Office Engineering Union. (He was later to become general secretary of the Association of University Teachers.) He was replaced by Miss Ardene Hilton, an experimental officer in the Government Chemist's Department. She had served on the NEC since 1954 and was chairman of the Scientific Staffs Group in 1955. In 1956 the conference instructed the NEC to appoint a public relations officer on an experimental basis and later in the year a part-time officer, Mrs Frances Thomas, a Fleet Street reporter, was appointed.

In the summer of 1957 the editor of *State Service*, Mr Edwin Sykes, resigned because of family illness. He had been editor of the journal for four years. He continued to serve as a member of the NEC. At about the same time the Institution also lost the services of its finance officer, Miss Muriel Luntz. She had held the office since 1945. She resigned to emigrate to Canada where she had family ties. Mr Stalley took over Miss Luntz's duties as finance officer and a new assistant secretary, Mr John Lyons, was appointed to take over Mr Stalley's duties. Mr Lyons had taken an economics degree at Cambridge and worked for a time as a research officer with the Post Office Engineering Union.

In the autumn of 1958 two new assistant secretaries were appointed. One, Mr William McCall, was 29 years of age at the time of his appointment. He had been an active member of the Civil Service Clerical Association and had served on its Executive Committee before securing a scholarship to Ruskin College, after which he had joined the TUC staff. The other new assistant secretary was John Muir, a graduate of the London School of Economics, who had been an active member of the Society of Civil Servants, having served on its NEC. In 1960 he left the Institution to join the staff of the Society and was replaced as assistant secretary by Edward Hewlett, recently chairman of the Institution.

In 1959 the conference warmly thanked Jimmy Fry and Jim Watson for their services to the Institution. The former was retiring from the NEC after a long period during which he had been vice-chairman and chairman of the Institution. He was to remain as a trustee of the Institution. Jim Watson retired as an assistant secretary but was retained at headquarters in another capacity.

At the 1960 annual conference of the Institution a proposal to abolish the offices of president and vice-president secured a majority of votes but failed to secure the necessary two-thirds majority to change the rules. The proposition was moved by John Beaton who had written the controversial article on the need to change the procedure of the annual conference. Moving the motion Mr Beaton said that the offices of president and vice-president were appropriate when the Institution was a rather loose federation of associations. The offices had, however, outgrown their usefulness. He made it clear that his remarks were not in any way a reflection on the contribution made by the former president, Sir Richard Redmayne, or the present president, Sir Graham Sutton. The indications were, however, that the existing holders of the offices could not carry on after 1960/1 so that an excellent opportunity presented itself for bringing the structure of the Institution into line with current needs. He pointed out that under the rules the presidents and vice-presidents were not bound by the policies adopted by the conference. A number of delegates opposed the motion on the grounds that distinguished members of professions within the civil service should be able to give the

Institution the benefit of their advice, and the existence of the offices of president and vice-president provided such an opportunity.

MR STANLEY MAYNE

In April 1960 it was announced that the general secretary, Mr Stanley Mayne, who was then 59 years of age, would be retiring from the Institution's service after the 1961 conference. Mr Tom Profitt, the deputy general secretary, had indicated that because of ill-health he did not wish to be considered as a candidate for the office. He hoped, nevertheless, that he could continue to serve the Institution as a deputy general secretary. Towards the end of the year it was announced that the National Executive Committee had appointed Mr Richard Nunn as general secretary designate. Mr Nunn had been an assistant secretary of the Institution since January 1953.

The appointment of a new general secretary coincided with the election of a new president – Verney Stott – a name long connected with the Institution. He had been made an honorary member of the Institution in 1954. At the 1961 conference of the Institution, the chairman, Mr W. F. Bailey, said in his opening speech that a cloud overshadowed the proceedings. It was Stanley Mayne's last conference as general secretary. He said that the Institution owed a great debt to Stanley Mayne for his wise guidance and devotion. Later during the conference the delegates unanimously endorsed a resolution placing on record deep gratitude to Stanley Mayne, 'for his untiring work on behalf of the Institution during his period of general secretaryship . . .'. The motion was moved by Ted Lawson in a speech in which the sadness of Stanley Mayne's departure was made less keen by the humour of Ted Lawson's presentation of his tributes.

An article of appreciation on the contribution of Stanley Mayne was published in the August 1961 issue of *State Service*. Its author, John Beaton, recalled that Stanley Mayne had brought wide experience of civil service trade unionism to the Institution. His devotion to trade unionism never changed. John Beaton said that Stanley Mayne was a man of inexhaustible energy and had done ten men's work inside the Institution. His capacity for work, he said, was immense, his energy inexhaustible and his physical strength and stamina herculean. He had an ability to master detail and at the same time he had a broad vision of the strategy needed for the success of the Institution.

These tributes to Stanley Mayne were no more than he deserved. Everyone who knew him spoke of his enormous energy and capacity for work. This, together with his high intellectual gifts, made him a powerful figure by any standards. He had a strong personality and, on most issues, pronounced views. He made no secret of his left-wing political convictions but he never sought to inflict them on to the Institution in defiance of any of its policies or declarations. If he showed his convictions it was in his devotion to trade unionism and to the interests of the Institution, and in the energy and skill he brought to bear on issues vitally affecting the Institution's membership, such as, for example, pay, the training and status of scientists and technologists and the effect of the 'purge'. It was typical of him that even in his closing months with the Institution he was already preparing himself for new activities during his 'retirement'.

In February 1961, for example, he acted as chairman at a special meeting for civil servants called by the Campaign for Nuclear Disarmament. After his retirement Stanley Mayne became active elsewhere in the Labour movement. He was a member of the Inner London Education Authority, vice-chairman of its Further and Higher Sub-Committee, vice-chairman of the Bromley Hospital Management Committee and chairman of the Finance Sub-Committee. He became an alderman of the Greater London Council and, in addition, was a member of the governing body of the Chelsea College of Science, the Furzdown College of Education, chairman of the Governors of Acland Burghley Comprehensive School and a member of the governing body of the Avery Hill College of Education. He was also a member of the management committee of the Beckenham Constituency Labour Party and was active in local politics. Stanley Mayne was one of the commanding figures produced in the history of the civil service trade union movement.

17 The Pay Pause and Radcliffe, 1961–4

On 25 July 1961 the Chancellor of the Exchequer, Mr Selwyn Lloyd, announced that it was the government's intention to institute a pay pause. The government felt this to be necessary because in the years 1960–1 there had been an increase of £1,450 million in incomes compared with an increase of only £650 million in production. The pressure of demand at home had meant rising prices, rising costs, more imports and greater difficulty in selling exports; and the effect of this on the balance of payments had been so adverse that the government had to make arrangements to draw £1,500 million from the International Monetary Fund. The government's view was that unless drastic action was taken the maintenance of the living standards and level of employment already attained in Britain would be in danger.

TRADE UNION CRITICISM

The government's policy was strongly criticised by the trade union movement. They said that government policies had made a substantial contribution to the economic crisis. No attempt had been made to plan the economy, and industry had been left to the free operation of market forces. This had been shown to be a failure. The government, said the TUC, were not prepared to intervene except by the manipulation of interest rates and credit terms. The effect of this was to propel the economy from periods of expansion into periods of contraction. It was, they said, a 'stop-go' policy. Because of the failure of government policy Britain's investment in industry was lower than in other competing countries and the growth in national output and in productivity was correspondingly less.

Many trade unionists also criticised the arms programme of the British government. They pointed out that whilst other countries were devoting resources to industrial expansion Britain was devoting resources to an arms programme, including nuclear weapons, which it could not afford. The British economy was being weakened by pursuit of military strength. This, it was argued, was a wrong policy because there was no possibility of Britain attaining parity with the two Great Powers, the USA and the USSR. Moreover, the need in international relations was for an end to the arms race and the relaxation of tension. Nothing except economic weakness was to be achieved by support for 'cold war' policies in alliance with the United States.

An editorial in *State Service* in August 1961 reflected the criticisms of government policy made by the trade unions: 'Once more the hue and cry is raised against wages and salaries. Once again the technique of the "big lie" is being used to "prove" that wage increases are the cause rather than the effect of inflation.' The cutting back of purchasing power, the editorial argued, was a twofold folly. First, it undermined the thriving home market on which export business depended for its base. Secondly, the holding down of the cost of labour impeded the technical developments on which British industry depended. 'The greatest spur to the desperately needed re-equipment of Britain's industrial potential is the expense of using a man where a machine would do.'

The 'pay pause' began on 1 August 1961 and was to be reviewed at the end of February 1962. The terms of the 'pause' were conveyed to the National Staff Side in a letter from the Treasury, dated 10 August 1961, which said:

> The existing negotiating machinery will continue to function and pay research surveys should be undertaken as may be agreed; but, during the period of the pause, any offer of increased pay which it may be thought reasonable to make will be made for implementation when circumstances permit, with no retro-spection. It follows that in the event of arbitration the government must, on grounds of public policy, withdraw from the scope of the arbitration tribunal, and retain in their own control the timing (and if necessary, the staging) of the putting of an award into effect. Therefore in all proceedings before the Civil Service Arbitration Tribunal which take place in the period of the pause, whether or not terms of reference have already been agreed, the operative date of any award will not be arbitrable.

The government hoped that by implementing this policy in respect of its own employees, it would persuade private employers to do the same.

The introduction of the 'pay pause' met with resolute protest from the civil service unions. The National Staff Side adopted a resolution resenting 'the selection of public servants for the imposition of policies which the government wished to see adopted throughout the community'. They strongly deprecated the action of the government in 'interfering with the normal practice of arbitration machinery in order to further government policy'.

The National Staff Side decided to call a demonstration of protest in London on 30 August to be followed by similar meetings in other large cities. The central London demonstration was so well attended that two overflow meetings had to be arranged. This was only the start of a countrywide campaign to rally MPs in every constituency to support the demand for the withdrawal of the limitations on arbitration.

SCIENTIFIC ASSISTANTS

One group of Institution members who felt particularly aggrieved over the 'pay pause' were scientific assistants. They were due for a pay increase as a result of negotiations following an investigation by the Pay Research Unit. It appeared at one stage as though the increase might be deferred. At a meeting of the committee representing scientific assistants held on 1 August 1961 a resolution was carried recommending assistants throughout the civil service to strike for one day 'in the event of the government refusing to pay any award resulting from negotiations in progress since 1957'. The strike took place on 22 September and some 5,000 participated. Some 500 assistants with banners and balloons bearing slogans marched to the Treasury. At the time the Institution was reluctant to describe the stoppage of work as a strike. It preferred instead to call it a 'work pause' in response to the 'pay pause'. The scientific assistants lost a day's pay as a result of their strike but this was made up as a result of voluntary contributions by scientists throughout the civil service.

A prominent part in the campaign was played by Miss Brenda Webber, who was the leader of the scientific assistants' action group. The action group was brought into existence because of what she and other scientific assistants felt was the reluctance of the National Executive Committee to give a firm lead. Miss Webber said: 'I thought that the Institution was being "toffee-nosed" about this but since I have taken such an interest in things I can see that although individual members of the NEC were sympathetic to our action as a committee it had to express the feelings of the annual delegate conference.' At the conclusion of the campaign the action group was wound up but Miss Webber explained that she hoped the Institution would be empowered to take much stronger and more vigorous action when faced with similar situations in the future.

The pressure exerted by the Institution, supported by the membership, soon brought a favourable outcome. On 17 October an agreement on the pay of scientific civil servants was concluded. The Institution said that, whilst the agreement did not secure everything which had been requested, it was neverthe-less 'a good deal better than at some stages in the negotiations seemed possible'.

The pay research evidence had demonstrated what the Institution had argued all along; that outside companies usually knew what the civil service paid and that the career structure outside was different from that of the civil service. For these reasons the Institution had argued that pay research was inappropriate for the scientific classes. The Treasury analysis of the pay research results had in fact implied a reduction for some grades in the scientific officer class, the experimental officer class and the senior scientific assistant grade. Only the scientific assistant grade emerged well from the process.

Nevertheless, even in the context of the 'pay pause' and as a result of hard bargaining, the Institution salvaged something from the negotiations. It managed to retain interim salary increases already granted and to secure increases for the scientific assistants. The Treasury made it clear, however, that from then on it did not regard the pay of the scientific and experimental classes as in any way linked with the administrative and executive classes. The Institution's annual report for 1961, referring to the agreement, said: 'it should be stressed that the agreement for the scientific classes was one which would certainly not have been made but for the circumstances existing at the time'.

FURTHER PROTEST AGAINST THE 'PAY PAUSE'

The National Staff Side continued to protest against the government's policy and said that there would be the strongest reaction from their membership against interference with the accepted methods of settling civil service pay questions. In a letter dated 27 September 1961 the National Staff Side said: 'the Staff Side bitterly resent this unilateral breaking of an agreement and they must make it clear beyond any possibility of misunderstanding that they place upon the Official Side full responsibility for any deterioration that may follow both in staff relations and in service to the public'. After a further exchange of correspondence the National Staff Side wrote to the Treasury stating that in their view the government had abused its special position as an employer by imposing on civil servants penalties which it was able to inflict only because of its dual role of employer and government.

On 22 November the National Staff Side sent a deputation to the Minister of Labour to protest about the government's interference in the civil service arbitration procedure. The Staff Side made it clear that the dispute derived directly from the Chancellor's statement of 25 July 1961 and the later decision of the government to withdraw from arbitration both the operative dates and the payment of any element of an award over and above an offer from the Official Side. This, said the National Staff Side, was a direct interference with the freedom of arbitration tribunals and if unions proceeded to the Civil Service Arbitration Tribunal they would be doing so under duress. It was made clear to the minister that in the view of the National Staff Side the agreement for arbitration had been broken both in word and in spirit. The meeting proved abortive. The Minister of Labour reiterated the government's policy.

The action of the government in interfering with the normal negotiating and arbitration machinery in the civil service led to unprecedented actions by a number of civil service unions. The Civil Service Clerical Association, the Union of Post Office Workers and the Post Office Engineering Union all organised some form of protest action including 'working to rule'. In the Institution the scientific assistants had already taken action against the 'pay pause', and members among the DSIR staff pledged themselves not to work in future parliamentary elections for any candidate who supported the 'pay pause'.

In the spring of 1962 the government restored the normal functioning of the civil service arbitration machinery but insisted that no retrospective payments should be made earlier than 1 April. At about the same time the government also invited the Trades Union Congress to join with it in working out a longer-term incomes policy. The government issued a White Paper, *Incomes Policy: the Next Step*, which said that it was not possible to lay down hard-and-fast rules by which any given proposal for a wage or salary increase should be judged, but set a 'guiding light' and stressed the need for increases in incomes to match an estimated increase in productivity of some 2–2·5 per cent. Moreover, the White Paper also said that some criteria which had been used over the years to justify pay increases should not be given the same weight as hitherto. Among these criteria was comparability, of crucial importance to the civil service.

With the restoration of normal facilities for arbitration the National Staff Side submitted to the Civil Service Arbitration Tribunal a claim for a 5·5 per cent general increase. The claim was heard on 21 May 1962. The basis of the claim was that since the 1961 settlement there had been increases in wages and salaries in employment outside the civil service. The Staff Side case rested upon the principle of fair comparison. In their reply to the claim the Official Side concentrated almost entirely on the incomes policy of the government. The Treasury argued that the increase in personal incomes should be kept in proper relationship with the growth of national production, and that it would be wrong for the government in respect of its own employees to contract out of the policy which it was urging upon the nation. The Civil Service Arbitration Tribunal awarded a 4 per cent general increase to non-industrial civil servants with effect from 1 April 1962. The Institution described the award as 'a signal success for the Staff Side claim, bearing in mind the very heavy government pressure levelled against the argument both in the Tribunal itself and outside'. Following hard negotiations a further general pay increase of 3 per cent was agreed from 1 January 1963.

The 1962 annual conference of the Institution was extremely critical of the government's incomes policy. Typical opening words of motions on pay negotiations and arbitration in the preliminary agenda were: 'This conference notes with grave concern the contents of the Government's White Paper Cmd 1626 on *Incomes Policy: the Next Step*'; 'This conference deplores the basis of the government's White Paper'; 'This conference condemns the government's interference with civil service arbitration machinery'; 'This conference takes the very strongest exception to the action of the government during the period of the "pay pause"'; and 'Conference resents the selection of public servants for the imposition of policies which the government wishes to see adopted throughout the community'. There were twenty-eight motions in this section of the agenda all critical of government policy, followed in a later section by another twelve critical motions on particular applications of pay policy.

At the conference a resolution was adopted opposing the views expressed in the White Paper *Incomes Policy: The Next Step* that labour shortages, cost of living and fair comparison factors should be given less weight in determining civil service pay. The conference reaffirmed its view that these factors, together with internal relativities and the need to encourage scientists and technologists to come into the civil service, remained important considerations in pay determination. Another resolution was adopted taking 'the very strongest exception to the action of the government during the period of the "pay pause" in imposing upon the civil service rigid pay freeze conditions which were not, and could not be, applied outside the public service, and particularly its interference with civil service arbitration machinery . . .'.

THE NATIONAL INCOMES COMMISSION

On 26 July 1962 the Prime Minister announced the setting up of a national incomes commission. He said that it would be given terms of reference to inquire into and to express views on claims of special importance. In so doing it would take into account not only the circumstances of each claim but also the wider considerations of the national interest, such as the need for increases in incomes to be matched by increases in production.

The TUC strongly opposed the creation of the National Incomes Commission. They argued that the NIC had been set up essentially to control wages and salaries and that it was in no position to determine what the national interest was as a background to judgement about the value of any particular wage or salary negotiations. The TUC continued to argue for a policy of economic expansion and urged that such a policy would require effective planning. There was no evidence, in the TUC's view, that the government intended to depart from the policies which had contributed so much to Britain's economic difficulties. It was in this context that the proposal to set up a National Incomes Commission had to be judged.

The TUC did, however, agree to co-operate in the National Economic Development Council which was set up by the government at about the same time. The purpose of the NEDC was to bring together representatives of employers and trade unions, together with ministers, to discuss particular problems of economic policy and to help in the integration of policy between one section of industry and another. The TUC agreed to participate in the NEDC because they felt that they might be able to influence policy in a direction favourable to the interests of workpeople. In particular they wanted to avail themselves of every opportunity to press upon the government the need for economic expansion.

COPPSO

One effect of the decision by the government to introduce a 'pay pause' was to encourage a number of white-collar public service unions to come together to express their protest. Mr W. F. Bailey, in his opening address to the Institution conference in 1962, said: 'one good result of the pay pause has been the bringing about of a closer liaison between the non-industrial organisations. The Institution has taken part in a number of conferences of professional and public service organisations to discuss the many problems which affect us all.'

At the end of August 1961 the initiative was taken by the National Union of Teachers (NUT) to convene a conference of a number of public service white-collar organisations. The Institution decided to attend, as did the National and Local Government Officers' Association (NALGO), the Association of Scientific Workers (AScW), the London County Council Staff Association and four additional teaching unions. The conference adopted a resolution stating that it wished to register on behalf of the 683,000 employees which it represented strong opposition to the Chancellor's imposition of the pause in the public sector. The conference rejected this policy 'as being unjust, unreasonable and seriously damaging to good staff relations'.

The conference arranged a deputation to the Chancellor, representing its strong views against the imposition of the 'pause' over the whole of the public service. The response was unsatisfactory, however, and the organisations represented at the meeting with the Chancellor appointed a small working party, of which the general secretary of the Institution was a member, to prepare a report for a reconvened conference. As a result of this conference a new organisation was established, the Conference of Public and Professional Service Organisations (COPPSO), in which the Institution took an active part. A decision was later taken to set up machinery so that organisations could be brought together if need be to deal with any difficulties that arose from the application of government pay policy to the public service.

At the end of May 1962 COPPSO wrote to Sir Robert Shone, the director general of the National Economic Development Council, requesting consultation facilities for the conference which represented 600,000 salaried staff. A deputation from the conference met Sir Robert Shone on 10 July 1962. The deputation explained that they were concerned about the effect of the deliberations of the NEDC on incomes policy and, hence, on the pay of public service employees not represented in the TUC. The director general said that for the present the NEDC would not be concerned with incomes policy. The request for representational or consultative facilities for the Conference of Professional and Public Service Organisations was firmly refused. It was emphasised that the NEDC had no intention of encouraging the fragmentation of employee representation, and that the interests of employees were represented on the NEDC by the Trades Union Congress.

Following this rebuff COPPSO's activity gradually declined. It did little work in 1963 and no meeting was held after May 1963. Towards the end of that year, the Institution decided that the time had come to suggest that the conference review its future and functions. At a meeting of COPPSO on 5 February 1964, the general secretary of the Institution led the discussion by saying that if the organisation was to continue it should be for a real purpose and on a more effective basis. The meeting resolved that COPPSO should continue and that a conference should be convened, should the need arise, at the request of any constituent or of the chairman and secretary. The Institution's NEC considered the outcome of the meeting and decided that the Institution should resign from COPPSO as it appeared to be serving no useful purpose. COPPSO was disbanded soon afterwards.

TUC AFFILIATION – FURTHER DEBATE

As a result of the 'pay pause' and of the experience with COPPSO the question of TUC affiliation became a live issue in several of the unions which had been associated with COPPSO. In subsequent years all the main unions involved in COPPSO, including the NUT, NALGO, the Society of Civil Servants and eventually the Institution, joined the TUC.

At the 1962 conference of the Institution various proposals were submitted by branches concerning co-operation between the Institution and other organisations. They included immediate affiliation to the TUC, reaffiliation to the NFPW and a request that the NEC should prepare a report on possible affiliation to the TUC for consideration at the 1963 conference. The last suggestion was carried.

In October 1962 an editorial in *State Service* said that the membership faced important decisions on external affiliations. It said:

> One thing we cannot afford to do with recent events and developments on the economic front so fresh in our minds is to drift along on our own in the hope that all will be well. Active participation by each member is urgently needed to see that the scientific and technical worker begins to reap his share of the rich rewards his fruitful endeavours have already given to a larger section of his fellow countrymen . . .

Following the publication in January 1963 of the NEC's statement on affiliation to the TUC, which was essentially factual, the NEC wrote to the TUC and to the three main political parties to invite their observations on it. The TUC, in reply, said that they were obliged to the Institution for letting them have a copy of the report but they had no particular comment to make. They emphasised that the TUC did not intervene in any way in the domestic affairs of either an affiliated or a non-affiliated union. The Labour Party said in reply that it saw 'nothing at all in the affiliation of the Institution of Professional Civil Servants with the TUC which would prejudice in any way the Institution's traditional party political neutrality and independence'. The Liberal Party replied similarly. It said: 'We ourselves certainly do not consider that you would in any way prejudice your position of party political independence and neutrality by affiliation to· the TUC.' The Liberal Party went on to say that it welcomed affiliations to the TUC because that would help the TUC to represent more truly the organised employees in Britain. The reply of the Conservative Party was less clear-cut. It said that different associations of civil servants and public employees had reached different conclusions on the question of TUC affiliation and it thought it would be wrong for the party to try to influence the members of the Institution one way or the other. A lively debate followed in the correspondence column of *State Service*.

At the 1963 annual conference of the Institution, the chairman, Mr W. J. Bowles, made a strong plea in favour of the affiliation of the Institution to the TUC. He said that it was essential that civil service and other white-collar unions should be in a position to take an active part in the deliberations of the National Economic Development Council. The fact had to be faced that in Britain more white-collar unions were already in the TUC than remained outside. He speculated – prophetically as it turned out – on the possibility of the Society of Civil Servants, the National Union of Teachers and the National and Local Government Officers' Association deciding to affiliate to the TUC. The annual conference decided that there should be a ballot of the Institution membership and that no further action should be taken unless the majority were in favour of affiliation to the TUC.

Another consequence of the need felt by the Institution to associate itself with other salaried organisations to discuss the effect of the government's incomes policy was a decision by the 1963 conference to reaffiliate to the National Federation of Professional Workers. It had disaffiliated in 1958. The NFPW included among its ranks white-collar unions both in and out of the TUC. The NFPW maintained its friendly working relationship with the TUC whilst at the same time preserving its organisational independence and autonomy. By the end of 1963 the NFPW had extended its affiliated membership to more than 1 million aided by the affiliation of the Institution and of the 315,000-strong NALGO.

The debate on TUC affiliation continued while preparations for the ballot were being made. In a letter to *State Service* in November 1963, Mr R. G. Fall, the vice-chairman, sought to dispel the assumption, which he felt might have arisen from the chairman's statement at conference, that all the members of the NEC were in favour of affiliating to the TUC. He proceeded to make clear his personal views against affiliation, adding, however, that 'this is not a decision for NEC but for conference'.

In 1963 two other civil service unions debated the issue of TUC affiliation. The Society of Civil Servants rejected affiliation on a ballot vote by 19,677 votes to 14,969. This represented a considerable shift of opinion in favour of affiliation in comparison with the result of a ballot conducted among the Society's membership in 1947. In that year 31 per cent voted for affiliation whereas in 1963 it rose to 43 per cent. The Customs and Excise Federation, on the other hand, decided to affiliate to the TUC. It became the ninth civil service organisation to do so.

The result of the Institution ballot on TUC affiliation was announced in March 1964. It was:

For affiliation	11,913
Against affiliation	25,887
Abstentions	24
Invalid votes	19
Percentage voting	65·8

At the Institution's annual conference in 1964 a motion resolving that no application for affiliation should be made to the TUC was carried without dissent.

THE RADCLIFFE COMMITTEE

While the Institution was opposing the government's incomes policy and discussing associated policies and affiliations, another major issue emerged which was to cause considerable embarrassment, internal upheaval and conflict of views within the Institution. It centred on the report of the Radcliffe Committee and its consequences within the civil service trade union movement.

In May 1961, following the conviction of a British official, George Blake, on a number of charges under the Official Secrets Act, the government appointed a committee of inquiry under the chairmanship of Lord Radcliffe to examine security procedures. George Blake had served with the RNVR during the Second World War and in 1948 was temporarily employed as vice-consul at Seoul in Korea. He was interned by the Chinese during the Korean War and held for nearly three years in captivity. During this period of captivity, according to the Prime Minister, Mr Harold Macmillan, he voluntarily became a convert to communism. Mr Macmillan added that this was not the result of brainwashing or intimidation. Nor did he receive money for his services. He was never at any time a member of the Communist Party or any organisation associated with it. In its terms of reference the Radcliffe Committee was asked to review security procedures and practices followed in the public service and to consider what, if any, changes were required.

A section of the report was devoted to civil service staff associations and trade unions. The committee said that it was disturbed at the number of communists and communist sympathisers holding positions in civil service staff associations and trade unions either as permanent full-time paid officials or as unpaid officers or members of executive committees. The committee said: 'we regard this presumably deliberate massing of communist effort in the civil service unions as most dangerous to security . . .'. It recommended, therefore, that 'it would be reasonable to establish the right of any department in respect of establishments or staff employed in secret work to deny access to or to refuse to negotiate (either by correspondence or face-to-face) with a named trade union official whom it had reason to believe to be a communist under the definition used in the purge procedure'. It also suggested that civil servants who took part in staff negotiations should be warned in general terms that communist representation among civil service union officials was disproportionately high.

Within the civil service unions there was a good deal of criticism of the Radcliffe Report. It was argued that the recommendations affecting communists and those described as communist sympathisers were not consistent with the evidence produced by the Radcliffe Committee. The Radcliffe Committee said, for example: 'No evidence has been brought to our knowledge that communist union officers, whether serving on a paid or unpaid basis, have been detected in any form of espionage.' The contention of the Radcliffe Committee that there had been 'presumably deliberate massing of communist effort in the civil service unions' was contradicted in another passage of the Radcliffe Committee report in which it was said: 'We understand that there is no evidence that the communists have made any exceptional effort to gain control of these unions . . .'.

Nor was the Radcliffe Committee able to provide any evidence that it was the policy of the Communist Party to encourage or to undertake espionage. The report stated: 'It is not the policy of the Party, according to our information, to give its members, open or secret, any encouragement to undertake espionage, although this policy might, of course, be changed in changing conditions.' The committee also pointed out that the Soviet Intelligence Service did not necessarily or essentially choose its agents on ideological grounds.

In considering the Radcliffe Report the NEC took into account two resolutions from the 1960 and 1961 conferences; one reiterating opposition to any form of racial, religious or political discrimination; the other saying that security should not be made a cover for the unreasonable restrictions of civil liberties. In May 1962 the NEC sent out a circular to branches giving its views on the Radcliffe Committee report. It included the following paragraph:

The NEC recognising the need for an efficient security organisation would not wish an officer of a civil service staff association to be treated differently from a civil servant in the matter of security. Equally we could not tolerate interference in our right to appoint or elect our own officers and would resist objections to negotiators engaged on matters which have no security aspect. To keep things in perspective it should be noted that non-secret work represents the bulk of Institution activities. There is ample provision in existing machinery for dealing with negotiations for grades engaged on secret work and the NEC and the National Staff Side see no difficulty in dealing with work of a secret nature as distinct from the general broad run of civil service staff negotiations.

The Institution's annual conference in 1962, which *State Service* described as being 'overshadowed by the hovering clouds of the "pay pause" and the Radcliffe Report', had before it no less than twenty-nine emergency resolutions on the report and its possible implications for the Institution. In addition there were at least sixty amendments to the emergency motions. At first the Standing Orders Committee, chaired by Miss B. Baker, whose 'clear-headed explanations . . . given calmly and with disarming charm, were one of the highlights of the conference', according to Verney Stott, suggested that the emergency motions, together with the amendments, should be debated during a 1½-hour period at the end of the Friday afternoon session of the conference. Clearly, this time was inadequate. There was then a procedural debate about how and when the debate on the Radcliffe Report should be taken. Eventually it was decided to take the whole of Saturday morning for the debate and to deal only with the substantive motions but not with amendments.

The conference adopted two emergency motions moved by the NEC. Emergency motion 14 said:

That this conference notes the Radcliffe Report and wholeheartedly supports the need for security as set out in the report. It notes in particular paragraphs 33–7 and wishes to place on record its appreciation of the long and efficient service of the honorary and paid officers of the Institution. It directs attention to the statement of the Radcliffe Committee that no evidence had been brought to its knowledge to indicate that union officers had been detected in any form of espionage. Conference affirms its determination to ensure that the Institution cannot possibly be used as a vehicle to assist subversive activities and instructs the National Executive Committee:

> 1   To ensure that if any Institution officer is challenged as a negotiator by a department he shall be given every facility to appeal against any such challenge.
> 2   If any officer is confirmed as a security risk to take whatever steps are necessary to protect the security of the state, the integrity of the Institution and the financial welfare of the officer which could include financial compensation.

Emergency motion 15 said:

> That this conference, in the light of the publicity given to the Radcliffe Report, reaffirms its belief that there should be the maximum political freedom for civil servants and paid officers of staff associations compatible with the security of the state.

A further emergency motion, which said that in the light of the adverse publicity generated by the press following the Radcliffe Report the Institution would welcome investigation by the security services, was supported by the NEC. Two other emergency motions were carried, however, which went further than the NEC would have wished. They suggested that the NEC should ascertain whether any of the paid officials of the Institution constituted 'security risks' without waiting for them to be 'named', and suggested that those who did constitute a security risk should be dismissed. Three emergency motions which proposed a less harsh line were lost, as were other motions which wanted to see a ban on communists and sympathisers holding office and an extension of 'positive vetting' to include trade union officers. After these motions had been considered time ran out and it was agreed that the remaining seventeen emergency motions should be expunged from the record.

The concern felt by the delegates at the annual conference, manifest in the number of emergency motions and amendments, had been partly stimulated by reports in the press to the effect that among the Institution's officers were a number who were known to have left-wing views. The conference debate was closely followed by the press and the outcome of the debate on the Radcliffe issue was well summed up in a report which appeared in the *Sunday Times*. It said that the Institution had decided to support the government's campaign against communists and communist sympathisers in the civil service but had refused to take part in any kind of witch-hunt against any colleagues who fell foul of state security investigations. The Institution envisaged the possibility of dismissals among the officials but agreed that adequate compensation should be paid to them. The *Sunday Times* reported that the general secretary of the Institution, Richard Nunn, had declined to hazard an estimate of how many Institution staff might have to receive compensation but had conceded that it might well involve some officers of the union.

In subsequent issues of *State Service* there was a lively exchange of correspondence on the Radcliffe Committee report. In one issue it was reported that a far larger number of letters had been received than on any issue hitherto, and it was regretted that because of lack of space it had not been possible to publish many of them. One letter of special interest came from the retired general secretary, Mr Stanley Mayne. He described the Radcliffe Report as an ill-considered, illogical and unreasonable document. He also argued strongly against those who were urging that any officer of the Institution who fell foul of the government's ruling on security should not be compensated.

Stanley Mayne pointed out that over very many years the Institution made it clear to itself and to the world at large that it had no political attachments. In appointing officers the Institution had made it known that there was no political or religious restriction upon them. Thus if one or more of the Institution's officers fell foul of a government rule, but not an Institutional rule, then in common fairness the Institution should treat that individual in the full light of the fact that he was appointed without political discrimination and that if he had been in the civil service and employed on work requiring 'positive vetting' he would almost certainly have been transferred to other work. The Institution had not the same opportunity as the civil service to transfer such officers to other work but it had, nevertheless, no less responsibility to its officers.

MR RICHARD NUNN

In November 1962 it was announced that the National Executive Committee had received a request from Mr Richard Nunn for permission to terminate his contract as general secretary. The National Executive Committee accepted this request in principle and reported that it was considering suitable financial arrangements under which his contract could be terminated. The announcement was published above the signatures of the chairman and deputy general secretary of the Institution.

Because of various reports in the press and pressure upon the NEC for information it was decided to issue a further statement to the members. It was emphasised, however, that full details of the reasons for the resignation would have to await a closed session of the 1963 annual conference.

On 11 December 1962 the NEC sent a letter to all branches, sections and subsection secretaries about the termination of the general secretary's contract of employment. It said that they had 'initiated the action which resulted in the request from Mr Nunn for permission to terminate his contract'. It was emphasised that the action of the NEC had not arisen out of the way in which Mr Nunn had performed his duties as general secretary. At the meeting of the National Executive Committee on 26 November a resolution was carried and recorded in the following terms: 'The National Executive Committee then asked that the minute should record their appreciation of the past services given by Mr Nunn to the Institution and that this appreciation should be conveyed to him by letter.' In a final message to the membership Richard Nunn stated:

To all my colleagues and friends in the Institution and civil service movement I bid a reluctant and regretful farewell. I have had such great joy from the work I have done over the last ten years in the Institution and I am very sad it must end. My warmest thanks and best wishes to all those whose companionship had made the job so worthwhile. All strength to the future work of the Institution.

In February 1963 the membership was informed that at the request of the NEC Miss Molly Keith had submitted her resignation as an assistant secretary. The NEC recorded its high appreciation of Miss Keith's efficient services to the Institution over a long period. The NEC promised a detailed explanation of the circumstances of her resignation at the closed session of the 1963 conference should the delegates so wish.

A NEW GENERAL SECRETARY

At a special meeting held on 14 January 1963 the NEC appointed Bill McCall to the vacant post of general secretary. He was only 33 years of age, and his duties since his appointment as an assistant secretary in 1958 had included responsibility for negotiations in the Ministry of Supply, Stationery Office, Ministry of Aviation, Ordnance Survey and a number of other departments. He was also responsible for legal and superannuation matters.

It fell to the new general secretary to defend the actions of the NEC in dealing with the resignation of Richard Nunn, and later of Molly Keith, an assistant secretary. The conference in 1963, as an article in *State Service* pointed out, 'could have been as much under clouds, and fraught with as much potential dynamite as last year', but, in fact, it proceeded smoothly under the chairmanship of Bill Bowles and with the general secretary's report to the closed session on the effect of the Radcliffe Report on the Institution.

The closed session began on the Tuesday morning with a statement on behalf of the NEC, given by the new general secretary, Bill McCall, in which he recalled the terms of the various emergency resolutions passed at the 1962 conference. In accordance with emergency resolution 12 the NEC had informed the Treasury that they would welcome any investigation by the security services. The Treasury had replied that the Radcliffe Committee had not suggested that such investigations were called for and that the Government would follow the recommendations of the Radcliffe Committee.

The NEC had taken expert legal advice on the implications of the other emergency resolutions. The advice was that the cumulative effect of the three resolutions was that a 'named' official must cease to serve as an official of the Institution, that this might involve dismissal, and that if dismissal took place, the official was to be paid a reasonable sum in compensation in addition to the preservation of his pension entitlement.

Counsel's advice was that mere 'naming' by itself did not provide grounds for dismissing an employee and should the Institution do so it could be sued for breach of contract. Counsel outlined the possible damages which might be awarded. The NEC sought an agreement with the assistant secretaries on a formula under which any officer who was named would resign and accept proper and adequate compensation, but agreement could not be reached. The NEC therefore decided that any officer 'named' should be offered, on a without prejudice basis and on receipt of his resignation, an annual amount which would be the same as he would have received under abolition of office terms plus a lump sum payable immediately which would be the same as he would have received under abolition of office at age 60. At age 60 he would then be paid his superannuation pension but no further lump sum. The NEC had decided that in any future contracts with staff it would be specifically stated that any officer would be dismissed without compensation in the event of his being 'named' on security grounds.

Following the statement, conference endorsed the NEC's actions and placed on record, as the NEC had already done, its deep appreciation of the work done by Mr Richard Nunn and Miss Molly Keith. Two of the motions complaining about lack of information were withdrawn as a result of the explanation. A motion that alternative employment should have been considered before dismissal was lost.

A NEW NATIONAL PAY AGREEMENT

During and after the internal trauma generated by the Radcliffe Report the Institution continued to deal with issues concerning the pay and conditions of members. It also gave much attention to proposals affecting the policy and organisation of scientific activities in government employment.

The National Staff Side regarded the 'pay pause' as a unilateral abrogation of the provisional agreement on pay reached in December 1960, thus freeing the National Staff Side from the obligation to ratify it. This provisional agreement had been much criticised. Some constituents had not ratified it at their 1961 conferences and the Institution itself had serious reservations about the operation of the existing pay research system.

The National Staff Side submitted revised proposals for a national pay agreement in November 1961 but did not receive a reply from the Treasury until June 1963. Negotiations began and a new agreement was reached in February 1964. In common with the trend towards long-term pay agreements outside the civil service, the agreement was to run until 31 December 1966. Thus, it was agreed that the central pay increases for the following three years would be 3 per cent from 1 January 1964, 3·5 per cent from 1 January 1965 and 3·5 per cent from 1 January 1966. The pay research cycle was reduced from five to four years, and pay research exercises were to be limited to the main classes and to the key grades within those classes. It was to be open to each side, exceptionally, to propose the survey of a grade which was not itself a 'main' or part of a 'main' class.

OTHER ISSUES

On 23 June 1964, the National Staff Side took to arbitration a claim for a reduction in hours of work of two per week. In support of the claim the civil service unions were able to show that average basic hours of work in British industry and commerce had been reduced. Despite this, the Treasury was opposed to any reduction in hours for the civil service and argued that hours of work were already less than the average hours worked by clerical and administrative staff in British industry and commerce.

The arbitration tribunal awarded that as from 1 October 1964 the weekly conditioned hours of office staff in the non-industrial civil service outside London should be reduced to 43 gross. One year afterwards, that is from 1 October 1965, the weekly conditioned hours of work were to be reduced to 41 gross in London and 42 gross elsewhere within the United Kingdom. Although the award did not grant the claim in full for staff in the London area it represented complete success for all staff outside London. Excluding the lunch-hour the award meant that the normal hours of work were to be reduced to 36 in London and 37 outside London.

In 1964 there was a major development in the campaign to secure establishment for long-serving temporary officers who had given efficient service. An agreement reached at the beginning of May secured establishment for those temporary officers with twenty years reckonable service on reaching minimum retiring age. Provision was also made for those who had retired already to be re-engaged between the ages of 60 and 65 to complete twenty years' service. The agreement marked the end of a phase of negotiations which had been continuing for many years. It contained a provision for a review after three years. The National Staff Side gave notice that the question of shortening the qualifying period would then be raised.

On the longstanding claim for unestablished service to count for pension purposes the National Staff Side were not so successful. In 1960 the National Staff Side renewed their campaign on this issue and some 400 MPs signed a motion on the Order Paper of the House of Commons calling upon the government to grant 'reckoning in full for pension of the service of temporary officers'. Sir Lionel Heald led an all-party deputation to see the Chancellor. The Chancellor, however, rejected the claim on the grounds of economic difficulties and the 'pay pause' and made it clear that there would be no Whitley discussions on the matter. The Institution's general secretary referred to this treatment in his address to conference as both unfortunate and 'shabby'.

Higher-grades pay was also a casualty of the 'pay pause'. In 1961 Sir Oliver Franks replaced Lord Coleraine as chairman of the Standing Advisory Committee. The National Staff Side pressed the Advisory Committee for a further major review of higher-grades pay and for an immediate interim increase. The higher grades had not received an increase since the last major review in 1958. In February 1963 the Franks Committee advised and the government agreed that an interim tapered increase of 8 per cent should be awarded for salaries up to and including the level of under-secretary, and that there should be a new general review.

The National Staff Side also pressed that the Institution's longstanding claim relating to top professional posts should be considered within the next general review. Eventually the Treasury acceded to the request and the Institution submitted a memorandum based on evidence commissioned from the Economist Intelligence Unit. This was in addition to a National Staff Side memorandum on higher-grades pay to which the Institution was party.

The Standing Advisory Committee completed its deliberations in July 1963. It awarded considerable increases to all the higher grades and widened internal vertical differentials which had been steadily compressed since the previous review. Nevertheless, in three major respects the Institution found the report disappointing. The report assumed that civil service salaries would lag permanently behind salaries outside; it did not envisage regular reviews to prevent any further falling behind and compression of differentials; and it did not feel that any special recommendations needed to be made in respect of top professional posts. On this last aspect the Institution concluded that it would have to continue pressing the claims of individual top professional posts as the opportunity arose, as part of the general campaign by the Institution to secure public recognition of the importance of science and technology.

Another significant development during 1964 was the completion of the joint working party review of progress in training since the Assheton Committee report of 1944 on training in the civil service. Ardene Hilton represented the Institution on the working party which had recommended several ways in which training could be improved. Many of the recommendations were aimed at giving greater priority to training. There was also a plea for more detailed consideration to be given to the possibility of establishing a central institution for the advanced training of civil servants.

SCIENTISTS' PAY

The issue of scientists' pay, which had not been fully or satisfactorily resolved in 1961 following the pay research exercise, again came to the fore. The issue began in April 1962 with a £54 'Franks increase' for the administrative principal grade, and for chief and senior executive officers. This increase was given arising from the resolution of a difference of opinion about evidence in the pay research reports for administrative and executive classes. The Institution argued that the principal and senior scientific officers and the chief experimental and senior experimental officers should also receive the £54 increase because they were still linked to the administration group, following the settlement reached in 1961 which retained the traditional relationships between the science and administration classes. The Treasury, on the other hand, refused to meet the £54 claim because to concede the claim would involve it in an open acceptance of the doctrine of parity between the scientific and the administrative and executive classes. The matter was referred to arbitration.

The arbitration tribunal awarded in favour of the scales claimed by the Institution except for senior scientific officers. In doing so, however, it stated that it

[did] not endorse any link between the scientific officer class and the administrative class, or between the experimental officer class and the executive class, but [took] the view that the evidence before them [was] insufficient at this time to disturb the relativities between these classes which [had] in fact existed following the Report of the Royal Commission on the Civil Service, 1953–5.

At about the time of the £54 claim public concern was beginning to be expressed about the 'brain drain' to North America of a substantial number of the most able and highly qualified scientists and engineers. As an article in *State Service* remarked, this was a drain which was only too familiar to Institution members but attention was being focused on it by the publication of factual information. The government's contribution to the issue, said the article, was to play down the extent of the problem, and within government service to depress still further the salaries of scientific personnel. Thus, for example, in the Atomic Energy Authority, the administration had worsened the career prospects of the scientific officer class. Moreover, the Treasury's refusal to grant the £54 increase would, if sustained, have worsened the relationship between the administrator and the scientist. The article continued:

> Government policy on remuneration for the scientific civil service is narrow-sighted and illogical. The government is easily the largest single employer of scientific manpower and it exercises a marked influence on pay levels outside the civil service on the basis of 'fair comparisons' with these outside rates. Obviously if we are to survive in this modern age the government must do what the Institution has consistently pressed it to do, which is to give a lead on scientific pay and remove the discrimination in favour of the administrator against the scientist . . .
>
> The government is constantly expressing its appreciation of the value of the scientist and the engineer in this technological age. It is time it paid something more than lip service to these sentiments.

The Institution sought to protect the relative pay of scientists in government service by urging the Treasury to omit scientists from a further round of pay research, and to grant them increases corresponding to those for the administrative, executive and clerical class. In support of this claim the Institution argued that an earlier exercise in pay research had showed that outside employers tended to follow the civil service. Thus the process had become a largely circular and meaningless exercise. The Treasury agreed to the general proposition although it did not commit itself to accepting the arguments behind it. It rejected, however, the specific claim for any relative improvement for scientists. At the 1964 conference a demand was made that in respect of the rejection of the scientific assistants' claim the NEC should take all possible steps by means of intensive propaganda to discourage the recruitment of temporary scientific assistants in all areas of the scientific civil service.

Subsequently the general secretary sent a letter asking local section committees to inform local careers and youth employment officers and the local press about the unsatisfactory salaries and careers for scientific assistants. Eventually an agreement was reached which restored the senior scientific officer to his relative position before the Franks award and gave worthwhile increases to scientific assistants. The maximum of the scale fell short of that of the clerical officer by only £15. The Treasury did not concede some other aspects of the Institution's claim.

THE ZUCKERMAN REPORT

The organisation of government scientific research was the subject of two inquiries during the 1961–4 period. The first inquiry was on the management of government research. The committee responsible for the inquiry was appointed by the Lord President of the Council in 1958. Its chairman was Sir Claude Gibb. He died in 1959, but the committee continued its work under Sir Solly Zuckerman. It reported in December 1961.

The Institution submitted a memorandum dealing with the scope and organisation of government research and gave supplementary oral evidence. It stressed the view that the scientific needs of government and the scientific needs of the country itself could be adequately met only if government were fully responsible for much of the research work. Moreover, in the interests of scientific detachment, the research work should not be done within executive departments but in separate research organisations such as the DSIR. There was also, the Institution argued, a need for groups of scientific staff within executive 'customer' departments to determine their future research needs and interpret relevant research findings. The Institution also advocated a greater transfer of scientific staff into administrative posts on a temporary or permanent basis. Active encouragement for close liaison between government research laboratories and research staff in industry, technical schools and colleges was also urged.

Among the recommendations of the committee were:

that research councils and government departments should examine the possibility of amalgamating or grouping small isolated establishments;

that those in charge of government research organisations should consider with university authorities means whereby the two could achieve closer liaison;

that the practice of employing research staff in a temporary capacity before they became established should be extended;

that directors should be given greater powers to recruit staff up to principal level on short-term contracts;

that the number of research fellowships to be filled by scientists from outside the service should be increased;

that greater use should be made than in the past of procedures whereby the above average research worker could be encouraged;

that there should be more secondment between government research organisations and industry, the universities or colleges of technology;

that everything possible should be done to encourage interchange between posts in the scientific officer class and in other civil service classes, including the administrative class.

The recommendations of the report received a mixed reception from the Institution. In particular the Institution expressed concern at the proposal to extend recruitment on a short-term contract basis. Concern was also expressed at the proposal to employ research staff in a temporary capacity before establishment, and at the proposal on research fellowships. As Jimmy Fry, in his comments on the report in *State Service*, said:

A temporary fringe by any other name is still something the Institution must oppose. It took a long time and a lot of effort to create a real scientific civil service out of the hotch potch that once existed and these proposals cut at the root of the whole thing.

On the other hand, the Institution was very pleased with the recommendation that scientists should be given opportunities to transfer to administrative posts.

During 1962 the Scientific Staffs Group prepared a memorandum commenting on the Zuckerman proposals. In addition to the points already made by the Institution the memorandum also criticised the Zuckerman view that 'pure' basic research, i.e. that which is undertaken to satisfy the tasks and intellectual curiosity of the scientist, should be left to the universities, and 'objective' basic research, i.e. that which is done to fill in gaps in the scientific knowledge required to further some particular technological development, should be the concern of government research. However, it welcomed the recognition by the committee that 'objective' basic research, the predominant business of government research, was as intellectually demanding as 'pure' basic research. The Institution urged that the number of special merit promotions should be increased to reflect this fact.

The government proceeded with the Zuckerman proposals, especially those concerning quality control and the greater use of temporary posts, despite opposition from the Institution. Towards the end of 1962, however, the government began to explore possible ways of increasing the interchange of scientists with the administration class. A small number of administrative principal posts were opened to the scientific officer class.

THE TREND REPORT

The second inquiry on government scientific research was initiated in June 1962. A committee was established under the chairmanship of Mr B. St J. Trend to review the organisation for the promotion of civil science by government agencies. Its terms of reference were:

(1) whether any changes are desirable in the existing functions of the various agencies for which the Minister for Science is responsible concerned with the formulation of civil scientific research and whether any new agencies should be created for these purposes;
(2) what arrangements should be made for determining with appropriate scientific advice the relative importance for the promotion of civil scientific research in the various fields concerned;
(3) whether any changes are necessary in the existing procedure whereby the agencies concerned are financed to account for their expenditure.

The Institution welcomed the setting-up of this committee and submitted evidence arguing strongly for a Minister of Science whose function would be to survey the problem of national research requirements and to set up, administer and co-ordinate functional research institutes. The Institution said that it would be necessary to change the existing organisation of the civil service and to introduce into the staff of the ministry a large number of experienced scientists. The Science Ministry, it was suggested, would be able to co-operate with the Ministry of Education to ensure that the best possible use was made of the resources available for the education and training of scientists.

The Trend Committee published its report in October 1963. It recommended that no major change should be made in the organisation of the Medical Research Council or the Agricultural Research Council, but that the Department of Scientific and Industrial Research should be abolished and replaced by three new agencies organised as non-civil service research councils comparable with the Agricultural Research Council. The three new research councils were to be the Science Research Council, for science projects in pure and applied science; a Natural Resources Research Council, for all work on natural resources; and an Industrial Research and Development Authority, for the support and encouragement of industrial research. The Minister of Science would become responsible for all the research councils and it was suggested that he should be advised by a body of independent members, half of whom should be scientists, while the research agencies should be directed by professionally qualified full-time chairmen. The office of the Minister of Science should be strengthened by an increase in scientific staff who would then be interchangeable between the ministry, the headquarters of the agencies, and the research stations operated by them.

The Institution found some of these recommendations 'ill-considered and largely illogical'. It reiterated its view that responsibility for the civil service should be vested in a minister of Cabinet rank supported by a major scientific department. The Institution also opposed the recommendation that the DSIR should be dissolved. Its work, said the Institution, should be expanded in the new Ministry of Science. The Institution did not favour the reorganisation of research agencies and argued that the effect would be to disrupt applied research and development.

The views of the Institution were sent to the Prime Minister. In his reply the Prime Minister, Sir Alec Douglas-Home, said that it was not the government's intention to break up individual research stations of the DSIR to conform to some arbitrary division between basic and applied research. In any proposals for reorganisation the interests of the staff would be taken fully into account. The Prime Minister indicated that it was the government's intention to accept the main recommendations of the Trend Report. The DSIR was thus to be divided broadly as suggested in the report but with one or two minor amendments. The Institution replied that the government's decision had caused wide dismay in the professional, scientific and technical civil service and asked the Prime Minister again to reconsider his decisions.

At the 1964 annual conference of the Institution two resolutions critical of the government's decision on the Trend Report were adopted. The first said that a single ministry charged with responsibility for education, universities, civil science and some aspects of defence science was wholly wrong and revealed a fundamental misconception by the government of the whole problem of the promotion and application of science to the needs of the community and industry. The motion urged that the organisation of civil science should be the sole responsibility of a minister of Cabinet rank. The second motion attacking the Trend Committee report criticised the transfer of government scientific institutions to bodies of the research council type.

In his presentation of the annual report to the 1964 conference the general secretary devoted most of his speech to science policy and the effect of government policy on the emigration of scientists. He said that it was unfair to attempt to apply 'fair comparisons' to the pay of scientists when the government was in fact the major employer. Government pay scales exerted a profound influence on the behaviour of employers outside. He said that the career prospects of scientists and technologists were inferior to those of administrators and that the role of specialists needed to be changed from one of subordination to administrators to one of equal responsibility.

On the Trend Report he said:

The recommendations of this report have, regrettably, been accepted by the government despite widespread criticism, and representations which we have made both to the Minister for Science and to the Prime Minister. The major recommendation was that the Department of Scientific and Industrial Research should be broken up. In our view this recommendation was paltry, irrelevant and seriously damaging. The intention, apparently, is to separate the basic research from applied research and its industrial exploitation. This decision has been almost universally deplored by those most competent to judge.

The Brundrett Committee, established in 1962 to consider the government research function and organisation in the geological and mining fields, reported in May 1964. Representations by the Institution on that report became interwoven with representations on the Trend Report. The government decided to transfer the extraction of metals group of the National Chemical Laboratory to the Warren Spring Laboratory. This decision and the way it was implemented caused an upsurge of bitterness in the NCL. Neither the director nor the steering committee of the laboratory was consulted before the decision was made. As a result the director and half the group of staff concerned in the transfer resigned.

Further representations on the Trend Report were postponed because of the imminence of a general election. In the meantime the government announced the appointment of yet another committee in the scientific field. This committee, under the chairmanship of Sir Mark Tennant, was to review the organisation of the scientific civil service. This arose from a recommendation of the Zuckerman Committee that the scientific classes needed review, a view with which the Institution disagreed.

OTHER ISSUES AFFECTING INSTITUTION MEMBERS

The scientists were not the only group of Institution members to keep the Institution busy preparing memoranda and making representations. In 1962 a separate telecommunications technical officer class was established following pressure from the Institution beginning in 1959. The response had been long delayed, partly as a result of the 'pay pause'. During 1963 the Ministry of Defence and the Ministry of Public Building and Works were reorganised and in 1964 the air traffic control officers (ATCOs) were contemplating militant action over their pay.

The reorganisation to form a new Ministry of Defence, which involved bringing together four departments, Defence, Admiralty, War Office and Air, and which took effect from 1 April 1964, had a substantial impact on the Institution's members. Approximately 25 per cent of the membership were to be in the new ministry and the reorganisation led to considerable upheaval. Co-ordinating arrangements had to be made within the Institution and Staff Side.

The reorganisation proved beneficial to the Institution's members in so far as it gave the chief scientific adviser and his staff a much-enhanced part in the formulation of defence policy.

The implications of the Ministry of Public Building and Works reorganisation were less beneficial. The reorganisation, which amalgamated the three service works departments and the old Ministry of Works, started in 1963. The Institution hoped that the professional staff would have maximum control over their relationships with clients. In the event the traditional civil service attitude of employing professional and specialist staff in a subordinate capacity reasserted itself. Thus by October 1964 morale was exceedingly low, resulting, said an editorial in *State Service*, from the fact that the minister and his officials showed

a lack of understanding of the place of the technologist in a modern world; a lack of will to consult with the staff upon changes fundamentally affecting their status and their future; and a lack of desire to communicate their plans and intentions to their officers.

With a general election imminent, the minister concerned said that he did not have time to meet a deputation from the Institution to hear their views.

THE RADLEY COMMITTEE

On 25 June 1964 a committee of inquiry under the chairmanship of Sir Gordon Radley, KCB, CBE, PhD, MIEE, and including Stanley Mayne, was appointed 'To examine and report on the structure, conditions of service of the air traffic control officer class and the basis on which its pay should be determined in relation to its duties'. The immediate prelude to the committee was a withdrawal of goodwill and a work to rule by ATCOs to begin from the 3 July and to continue until a committee of inquiry was established. The Institution wanted remedial action to overcome the low morale and serious discontent which had existed in the class over a long period.

This was not the first time that ATCOs had taken industrial action over their poor pay, career structure and superannuation arrangements. The Institution had submitted claims to arbitration in 1951, 1955, 1959 and 1962. In 1962 some 95 per cent of ATCOs had asked for a day's leave on the same day to demonstrate their dissatisfaction. In April 1964 the branch council passed a resolution calling for a referendum on militant action. In the referendum 549 voted in favour of militant action and 188 against. This expression of discontent could not be ignored either by the Institution or the department and the committee of inquiry was established before the threatened action actually started.

The committee got down to work quickly and reported by the end of the year. Its report fully vindicated the Institution's decision to press for an inquiry. Following negotiations on the basis of the report salaries were increased by between 10 and 30 per cent and were in future to be clearly linked to the executive class. Hours were to be reduced to those normal in the civil service; a new class structure closely modelled on that proposed by the Institution was introduced; the 'temporary fringe' was abolished; there was to be an urgent review of training arrangements; and personnel management was to be improved along the lines indicated by the report.

INTERNAL CHANGES IN THE INSTITUTION

The membership of the Institution through this period remained stable at just under 58,000. Rising costs made it inevitable, however, that subscriptions should be increased. The previous rise in subscriptions had been in 1959. Since that time the average take-home pay of Institution members had risen by more than 20 per cent. A new subscription rate of £4 4s per annum was recommended by the NEC and accepted by the conference. An attempt to introduce an intermediate rate for members over 21 years of age on lower rates of pay was defeated.

The new Institution headquarters were finally occupied on 28 August 1961 and the chairman, Walter Bailey, officially opened them in the presence of representatives from all the branches on 21 September. This was the first time in its forty-two years of life that the Institution had its own permanent headquarters offices.

There were also several changes in the full-time and honorary officers over the period. There was a succession of editors of *State Service*. This was a clear indication that the duties constituted a heavy burden on any lay member who undertook to act as editor. In July 1962 Neil Reid, who had succeeded Edwin Sykes, resigned as editor and Ron Window took over. Within a year, however, Ron Window resigned from the NEC to take up an appointment at the Pay Research Unit. Dennis Papworth of the NEC became the new editor, but again within twelve months there was a further change. Pressure of other Institution business led him to resign and become assistant to Miss Helen Lindlay who became editor.

In 1961 Verney Stott succeeded Sir Graham Sutton as president of the Institution and John Beaton and Stanley Mayne became the new vice-presidents. These were to be the last of the breed, however, for at the 1964 annual conference of the Institution it was decided by a substantial majority to abolish the offices of president and vice-president. The Institution thus brought itself into line with nearly all other trade unions whose principal officers are drawn from among the active membership. In the formative years of the Institution the support given by distinguished scientists and professionals was extremely helpful and it was fitting that they should occupy titular offices without being drawn into day-to-day activity, but, with maturity, the Institution found it more in keeping with normal trade union practice to change its organisational arrangements. It was, however, emphasised that the contribution made by Sir Richard Redmayne, who for so many years had occupied the presidential office, would always be honoured in the Institution.

In 1963 Margaret Platt and Tom Clifton, who had both been active members in the Institution, were appointed assistant secretaries. The former entered the civil service as an examiner in the Estate Duty Office and had served as a member of the Standing Orders Committee. The latter was, at the time of his appointment, a senior experimental officer in the Meteorological Office and deputy vice-chairman of the Institution. They were joined by Stuart Johnson who came to the Institution after retiring from the overseas civil service. They replaced assistant secretaries Molly Keith who had left following the Radcliffe Report, Bill McCall, who had become general secretary, and Peter Whittaker, who had retired on medical grounds. Early in 1964 Mr Brian Stevens, previously head of the social insurance department of the National Union of Mineworkers, joined the staff as finance officer replacing Mr A. W. Stalley who had retired on medical grounds. Later Mrs Judith Lawson came from the Institute of Personnel Management to become research officer, replacing Mr Geoffrey Walker who had resigned to take up a post in the civil service. Mr Jimmy Watson finally retired, having served in a dis-established capacity since his retirement from an assistant secretary post in 1958.

Towards the end of 1964 the Institution appointed two extra assistant secretaries, following a review of internal staffing needs. They were Mr George Janeway and Mr Colin Waters. Mr Janeway was a civil servant in Northern Ireland and at one stage served as the chairman of the Staff Side of the Whitley Council for the Northern Ireland civil service. Mr Colin Waters came from the London County Council Staff Association, where for over four years he had served as deputy secretary. Before that he was on the staff of the Union of Post Office Workers.

RELATIONS WITH THE AScW

Co-operation with the AScW on major matters affecting scientists continued during the period 1961–4, but difficulties arose in 1963 over the membership of staff in the Scottish Institutes and the Agricultural Research Council. As a result of strong pressure from the 1963 annual conference the Institution entered into discussions with the AScW in an attempt to modify the 1946 demarcation agreement to enable the Institution to recruit into membership staff employed by the Agricultural Research Council and Scottish Agricultural Research Institutes. These discussions proved abortive.

The NEC regretted the failure to reach agreement with the AScW but in view of the 1946 agreement it proposed to the 1964 conference that no further action be taken. The general secretary, in putting forward the view of the NEC, emphasised the need for demarcation agreements between trade unions if competitive recruitment was to be avoided and trade union organisation was to be effective. If agreements were to be ignored there would be chaos between unions. The general secretary stressed that the closest possible co-operation was needed between all organisations representing scientists but this could not be done if the Institution were to indulge in a membership war with the AScW. The critics of the NEC, who included the MAFF, Scottish and DSIR branches among others, said that they regretted that it had not been possible to reach a negotiated settlement with the AScW but that the views of scientists employed by the Agricultural Research Council and the Scottish Research Institute could not be ignored. Over 1,200 staff had written to say they wanted to join the Institution. In the outcome the NEC were instructed to recruit into membership staff employed by the Agricultural Research Council and the Scottish Agricultural Research Institute, providing that they were not already members of the AScW. The successful resolution pointed out that the AScW had less than 450 members in the Agricultural Research Council service.

After the conference the NEC decided to give notice to the AScW to terminate the 1946 demarcation agreement and to recruit staff of the ARC and the Scottish Institutes. By the end of the year the matter was settled amicably. The AScW indicated informally that it accepted the facts of the situation in SARI and the ARC and hoped co-operation could continue. It was suggested by the Association, and agreed to by the Institution, that representatives of the two unions should meet to try and formulate a new agreement on spheres of influence.

18 Prices and Incomes Policy, 1964–70

For the Institution the period 1964 to 1970 was dominated by three main developments. The first was the effort of the Labour government to implement a prices and incomes policy in broad agreement with the trade union movement. The second was the appointment of the Fulton Committee to examine the organisation of the civil service. The third was the further strengthening and expansion of the Institution by the decision of the Society of Technical Civil Servants to amalgamate with it.

In October 1964 a Labour government was elected with a very narrow majority. It took office with Mr Harold Wilson as Prime Minister. The new government was pledged to develop an incomes policy which took account not only of wages and salaries but also all other forms of income including dividends, interest and rent. The Labour Party emphasised also – and in this it was expressing a view strongly held by the unions – that what was needed was not only an incomes policy but a policy which would increase productivity and, as far as possible, hold down prices. The basic requirement for such a comprehensive policy it was urged, was that there should be economic expansion. It was to this task that the new government addressed itself.

JOINT STATEMENT OF INTENT

The government sought to develop the new policy in association with the employers and the unions. Discussions with employers and unions were initiated and by December 1964 a *Joint Statement of Intent on Productivity, Prices and Incomes* had been agreed and published. It said that the government's economic objective was to achieve and maintain a rapid increase in output and real income combined with full employment. The social objective was to ensure that the benefits of faster growth were distributed in a way that satisfied the claims of social need and justice. The joint statement emphasised that the major objective of national policy must be to increase productivity and efficiency so that real national output could increase. In this way it would then be possible to maintain stability in the general level of prices and to hold increases in wages, salaries and other forms of income in line with the increase in productivity.

The joint statement was considered by the National Staff Side at a meeting on 7 January 1965. It was decided to write to the Treasury stating that in the view of the Staff Side the pay principles which operated in the civil service were not in conflict with the statement of intent. These principles, and the machinery to implement them, had been well tried and did no more than ensure that in general civil service pay did not fall behind outside pay movements. The Staff Side also said that they readily subscribed to the undertaking given by the signatories to the joint statement of intent to 'encourage and lead a sustained attack on the obstacles to efficiency'. They pointed to one of the declared objects of the National Whitley Council, which was 'to secure the greatest measure of co-operation between the state in its capacity as employer, and the general body of civil servants in matters affecting the civil service, with a view to increased efficiency in the public service combined with the well-being of those employed . . .'.

On productivity, the National Staff Side took the initiative in suggesting that there should be a joint standing committee to consider ways of improving efficiency in the civil service so that more effective use could be made of the knowledge and experience of the staff. On 23 March 1965 it was agreed that a joint Civil Service Efficiency Committee should be established, with ten representatives from the Treasury and an equal number from the Staff Side, whose terms of reference would be 'to promote the broadest measure of co-operation between the state in its capacity as employer and the general body of civil servants in matters affecting the civil service with a view to increased efficiency in that service combined with the well-being of those employed'.

The new productivity, prices and incomes policy received the support of the majority of the trade union movement. The TUC summoned a special conference of executive committees of affiliated organisations and a report in support of the joint statement of intent was endorsed by 6,649,000 votes to 1,811,000. The report said that the economic circumstances of the country and the wider interest of workpeople had established the imperative necessity of the measures proposed by the government. In reaching this conclusion the TUC said they were guided by two major considerations. The first was that the government had declared its clear commitment to a plan for the revival of the British economy, and the second was that the stated social objective was to ensure that the benefits of faster growth were distributed in a way which satisfied the claims of social need and justice.

The prices and incomes policy lasted right through the period of the Labour government from 1964 until 1970. The policy was developed in detail in a series of White Papers. The instrument for the implementation of the policy was a National Board for Prices and Incomes (NBPI), established under the chairmanship of Mr Aubrey Jones, a former Conservative Cabinet minister. Mr Jones was a man of liberal inclinations and a strong supporter of the concept of an incomes policy. The NBPI consisted of persons with management, trade union and academic experience.

CAUTIOUS SUPPORT

In April 1965, after the publication of a White Paper entitled *Prices and Incomes Policy*, the National Staff Side issued a statement emphasising that they expected the government to honour in letter and spirit both the Whitley Council agreement on the principles of settling pay in the civil service and the three years' pay agreement of 1964. The Staff Side again stressed their view that the methods and machinery for settling civil service pay were not inconsistent with the principles of the government's incomes policy. The Staff Side went on to say that they could not be a party to any arrangements which had the effect of depressing civil service pay in relation to that for comparable work in outside employment. They said they would expect civil servants to be treated fairly in relation to other salary- and wage-earners and not to be singled out for special treatment.

Among white-collar employees one of the early expressions of detailed criticism of the incomes policy, though within a general statement of support for the policy, was contained in a successful resolution at the annual conference of the NFPW held in the spring of 1965. Delegates from the Institution participated in the conference and supported the successful resolution. It approved the aims set out in the joint statement of intent but drew attention to three factors which it said had been omitted from the White Paper and without which an incomes policy would be unlikely to be accepted by unions representing non-manual workers. These were:

1 the need to maintain and improve differentials for specialised training and expertise;
2 the need to honour existing agreements on wages and salaries;
3 difficulties involved in restraining incomes derived from profits and business expenses.

At the Institution's 1965 conference cautious support was given to the new incomes policy. A resolution was adopted, moved by the NEC, which noted the joint statement of intent but made support for it conditional on three considerations. The first was that the incomes policy should be applied fairly and equitably to all sections of the community. The second was that it should not be applied unilaterally by singling out the civil service for particular restrictions. The third was that it should not preclude consideration of the merits of any special claim which might be submitted. The general secretary, in speaking to the motion, acknowledged that an incomes policy was an important factor for economic progress providing it was related to an expanding economy. The government, he suggested, was entitled to a cautious measure of support for an incomes policy with the three conditions set out in the proposition of the NEC. The policy was challenged by the delegates from the DSIR and from the EDO but the conference supported the NEC. Another successful resolution, this time carried unanimously, instructed the NEC to ensure that the Civil Service Arbitration Tribunal remained independent of any political pressure from the government.

HIGHER-GRADES PAY

The first sharp difference of opinion between the government and the civil service unions on the implementation of the incomes policy came towards the end of 1965. A report of the Standing Advisory Committee on the Pay of the Higher Civil Service (Franks Committee) had recommended new rates for the higher grades to take effect from 1 September 1965. The contents of the report were not divulged to the Staff Side until 22 November when the government decided to refer the report to the NBPI. The Staff Side protested strongly against this decision, pointing out that the Standing Advisory Committee in its report had stated that it had paid regard to the general economic situation. They could not see, therefore, why further consideration needed to be given to these matters. It also pointed out that civil service pay did not set a lead to outside industry. On the contrary, the recommendations made by the Standing Advisory Committee were based on movements in salaries which had already occurred in outside employment. Civil service pay had fallen behind the salaries already being paid to others.

The government rejected the National Staff Side protest and said that, whilst it was aware that the Standing Advisory Committee had paid regard to the economic problems confronting the country at the time when making its recommendations, the situation had since changed. New measures on prices and incomes had subsequently been announced. It had, therefore, concluded that the NBPI should examine and report on the Standing Advisory Committee's recommendations in the light of the considerations set out in the latest White Paper on prices and incomes.

The NBPI's report *Pay of the Higher Civil Service* was published in January 1966. It concluded that the recommendations of the Franks Committee were in accord with the White Paper and should therefore be implemented with effect from 1 September 1965. It also recommended that in future the Franks Committee should take account of the government's White Paper when framing its recommendations. The government accepted the NBPI report and the increases for the higher civil service were promulgated in February 1966. The Staff Side accepted the position but noted that the new rates recommended by the Franks Committee did not fully reflect their assessment of what would constitute fair and reasonable remuneration. They warmly welcomed the committee's declared intention to review the salaries of the higher grades earlier than would otherwise have been the case.

During 1965 and the early part of 1966 wages and salaries in British industry and commerce continued to increase at a faster rate than national output. The civil service unions were becoming increasingly restive at the extent to which civil service pay was falling behind. The effect of the current long-term agreement in the civil service was sufficient to keep pay abreast of the cost of living but not, in the view of the unions, sufficient to keep pace with the general movement of wages and salaries in outside employment.

CONFERENCE DEBATES

At the 1966 Institution conference the main interest was centred on a debate on incomes policy. A motion was moved by the general secretary seeking to establish three important principles in relation to pay. The first was that there should be determined opposition to any incomes policy which singled out the civil service for particular restrictions; the second was that the civil service unions should press for a further long-term pay agreement similar to that negotiated in 1964, and the third was that specialists in the government service should be fairly rewarded for their services. The motion came under attack from several branches. Delegates argued that the 1964 pay agreement had been anything but fair and that in outside employment many workers had secured pay increases in excess of the norm of 3 to 3·5 per cent. The general secretary, however, stuck firmly to the view that annual increases could only be achieved by central arrangements and that the long-term package had been honoured despite the very difficult circumstances. Eventually the delegates accepted the policies proposed by the NEC but only after they had deleted any reference to the 1964 pay agreement. They were not prepared to describe it as 'fair'. Another amendment sought to delete that part of the motion advocating a further central pay agreement. The amendment was defeated on a card vote by 33,023 votes to 20,391. The conference supported the NEC proposal.

In another resolution on pay the conference expressed concern at the decision of the government to refer the recommendations of the Standing Advisory Committee on the Pay of the Higher Civil Service to the NBPI. It said that the decision created a dangerous precedent which might lead to the destruction of the long-established negotiating procedure for civil service pay.

Pay research also came under attack. A number of speakers on succeeding motions emphasised that fair comparisons were anything but fair to specialists and that the process was costly and time-consuming. The Land Registry branch wanted alternative methods to pay research explored and conference agreed. Others argued that professional, technical and scientific staff should be withdrawn from pay research if their pay and status was to be improved. Their negotiations, it was suggested, should be based on such factors as qualifications, training and difficulties of recruitment. This proposition presented the Institution with a dilemma. Certain specialist classes had done well out of pay research and there was evidence that the position in outside employment was changing in their favour. It was essential, the general secretary said, to have a detailed alternative policy worked out. On the promise that the NEC would present a full and comprehensive report on the subject to conference in 1967 the motion was remitted to the NEC.

The general mood of discontent over incomes policy and the delay in settling claims was also reflected in a successful motion on militant action. The resolution proposed that support be given to some militant action in order to expedite claims. The action proposed included:

(i) Ban on all travel in own time,
(ii) 'Work to rule',
(iii) Ban on performing any clerical work,
(iv) Lobbying of MPs,
(v) Full statements to the press to publicise the action,
(vi) Simultaneous leave arrangements.

STANDSTILL AND SEVERE RESTRAINT

By the end of 1965 the incomes policy was beginning to run into difficulty elsewhere. The hoped-for acceleration in economic growth was not being achieved and the balance-of-payments deficit persisted. In November 1965 an early warning system for the notification of intention to raise prices or to claim increases in incomes was introduced by the government. It secured the co-operation of the TUC for this policy.

The balance-of-payments and inflationary problems were, nevertheless, not overcome, and in the middle of 1966 the government introduced a 'prices and incomes standstill' to be followed after six months by a period of severe restraint. The norm for wage and salary increases was put at nil, and there was to be a ceiling for increases of not more than 3·5 per cent except where it could be shown that there had been exceptional increases in productivity.

Whilst the new legislation was being submitted to Parliament the annual conference of the NFPW took place. This was the only annual occasion on which representatives of the Institution had the opportunity to join with other unions to discuss the economic situation. Delegates from a number of unions strongly criticised the new proposals and said that the declaration of intent had not contained any mention of coercive legislation to enforce a pay standstill. Delegates from one or two unions spoke in favour of the new development in incomes policy and argued that it was very much in the public interest. The conference, however, was in a critical mood, and went on to record that it opposed 'any kind of legislation which would provide for penalties to be imposed, in circumstances to be determined by the government or any of its agencies, on workers or trade unions for the submission or prosecution of a claim affecting wages, salaries or working conditions'.

The standstill was announced by the Prime Minister on 20 July 1966 just as pay research negotiations for the Institution's grades were on the point of completion. At the beginning of 1966 pay research negotiations were in progress for no less than nine Institution classes, including the works, technical, drawing office and TTO classes and some associated departmental grades, with an operative date of 1 January 1965. All the pay research reports had been received in 1965 and a formal claim on behalf of the A&E draughtsmen was submitted in October 1965. An unacceptable response from the Treasury was received in January 1966 but by May 1966 agreement had been reached. For all the other classes negotiations continued but were brought to an abrupt halt by the standstill. The Institution did not oppose the standstill but expressed reservations about it. The NEC said that the Institution was willing to play a full and fair part with other members of the community in meeting the nation's economic difficulties but it had always been and would remain firmly opposed to any policy which singled out the civil service for special treatment.

In a letter to the Treasury the NEC said that the policy on which the government had embarked contained obvious dangers of injustice and inequity. The professional and technical classes in the civil service had last had a substantive pay review as long ago as 1958. To disregard the merits of the case for substantial improvements for professional and technical classes would, therefore, not only create a serious injustice between them and their counterparts outside the civil service but also between them and other civil servants who had had a pay review in more favourable economic circumstances. The NEC expressed grave concern at the possibility of the government seeking to apply the freeze in such a way as to diminish or suspend pay increases which should have operated from a date (1 January 1965) well before the announcement of the standstill.

The letter included the following paragraph:

Technologists and technicians – for whom in its general policy pronouncements the government has so frequently expressed such concern as the people who hold the key to the plans for expansion and productivity – are badly treated in the civil service. Their pay and careers are far inferior to those in other classes with similar or lesser qualifications and responsibilities. Over the last decade their position has been getting worse rather than better. The last substantive review of the pay of these classes dated from 1958. They have been exceedingly patient. But owing to these long-drawn-out pay reviews they have, understandably enough, been getting exceedingly anxious. Apart from a conviction that they were badly treated they were, at the same time, subjected to heavy pressure because of the severe shortage of staff and the chronic and serious failures in recruitment. They were supported by constant assurances on the operative date of the pay reviews and by the hope and belief that they could now expect a fair deal. If this hope is shattered by the government and they do not receive a fair deal, there will be a profound and long-term reaction.

At the same time the NEC laid plans for a campaign including the possibility of militant action along the lines envisaged at the 1966 conference. A circular was sent to all branches, sections and subsections to obtain their views on the action to be taken.

In replying to the Institution the Treasury referred to representations from the National Staff Side which were already under consideration, and stated that the specific case posed by the Institution would have to await the outcome of those deliberations. At a meeting between the National Staff Side and the Official Side immediately following the announcement of the standstill the Staff Side had made four major points: that the civil service should not be singled out for prejudicial treatment; that pay negotiations in progress before the standstill should continue on their existing bases; that awards made but not yet paid should be allowed through; and that the position of those about to retire should be protected.

The Treasury said in reply that it had conveyed these views to ministers and stated: 'Ministers appreciate . . . that some pay reviews had been taking place for a long time and were on the point of conclusion when the standstill was announced. They appreciate too the apprehension and concern of the staff who are affected. Our aim is that these negotiations should be completed as soon as possible.' However, the Treasury made it clear to departments that negotiations were not to go beyond the point of establishing the facts, and offers were not to be made until the government issued its White Paper giving guidance on policy for the period of severe restraint.

On 22 November 1966 the government issued a White Paper on the policy to be pursued during the period of the severe restraint for the six months following the pay standstill. In response to Staff Side representations the government agreed that the negotiations on outstanding pay research surveys for 1965 and 1966 could continue on the normal basis and settlements could be reached as soon as possible during the period of severe restraint. The operative dates, however, were deferred by six months to take account of the standstill period. The government also stated that the increases, if substantial, should be payable in instalments, the first of which would be paid on 1 July 1967. All these arrangements were conditional on Staff Side acceptance of a limitation of retrospection to six months in future surveys. Although there was no disagreement between the parties on the need for the pay research process to be speeded up, the Staff Side regarded the making of the settlement of outstanding reviews dependent on the acceptance of the proposal on retrospection as a disgraceful and deplorable tactic on the part of the government. Nevertheless, they had little alternative but to accept it.

The Staff Side protested vigorously at the instalment arrangements and the provisions of the White Paper, in which the criteria used appeared to discriminate against the civil service and its pay system based on comparability. The Institution decided, after considering all the circumstances, that it would be best to press on with negotiations to achieve the best settlement possible. It was unlikely that public support for a campaign against the terms of the White Paper would be forthcoming. There were already a large number of ill-informed protests about the fact that annual increments were still being paid within the civil service. Nor was it realistic to expect the loss of six months' retrospection to be recovered, since the six-month standstill on which it was based applied to all.

A NEW AGREEMENT ON PAY RESEARCH

Immediate arrangements were made with the Official Side to undertake a joint review of pay research and negotiating procedures to minimise the effect of the six-month limit on retrospection. A new agreement was concluded in February 1967 in which the six-month limit was incorporated, with an additional month for consequential claims, and an extension of six weeks beyond the limit if a case was taken to arbitration. The agreement also confirmed the arrangement made in 1964 to limit pay research to the main grades and classes. The timetable for the conduct of the pay research process was shortened and the process simplified. The position of technical advisers was also redefined.

After the conclusion of the agreement the way was open for negotiations on the outstanding 1965 pay reviews to be completed. In April agreement was reached for revised salaries for the works group and technical classes complex of grades, and agreements on the rest followed soon after. The agreement provided for increases ranging up to more than 12 per cent on top of the interim 3·5 per cent 1965 central pay settlement. The 1966 3·5 per cent central pay increase was also paid. The negotiations, which had been long and arduous and disrupted by incomes policy, nevertheless provided a substantial increase and went some way to improve the unsatisfactory salaries of the professional and technical classes. The first instalment, giving increases of up to 5 per cent, was authorised for June 1967 and the rest for December 1967.

In an article in the May 1967 *State Service* the general secretary said that the pay agreement was a satisfactory one in many respects, given the difficult circumstances of the time. It had improved the relative position of the seriously undervalued professional and technical classes; the system of fair comparisons had survived unparalleled difficulties and had been improved by the new agreement on procedures; and for the first time in major negotiations for many years agreement had been reached without recourse to arbitration.

The agreement did, however, have three unsatisfactory features which the general secretary highlighted in his report to the 1967 conference. The government refused to do anything to make good the effect on pensions of the lost six months during the standstill. It refused to grant the normal consequential increases to the illustrators, cartographic and recording draughtsmen, and reproduction A grades which were linked to the A&E draughtsmen. Finally it refused to pay the sixty A&E draughtsmen in the office of the Receiver for the Metropolitan Police the increases paid to the other draughtsmen in the civil service. On this last aspect the Institution took legal action.

LEGAL ACTION

To secure the increase for the draughtsmen the Institution took two individual test cases to Lambeth County Court. In one case the plaintiff, Mr John Joseph Phillips, had been offered employment to commence on 1 August 1966 on the newly agreed scales but as a result of the standstill he was told that he would not be paid the salary entered in his contract but the earlier rate. Accordingly Mr Phillips sued for the difference. The other plaintiff, Mr Douglas Henry Griffin, who was a senior draughtsman with many years service and whose position was representative of the rest of the sixty draughtsmen, claimed that, but for an administrative hitch, their awards, following the rest of the civil service, would have been paid before the standstill and that he was therefore entitled to payment.

The action in court was successful, but subsequently the government issued a Part IV Order under the Prices and Incomes Act. This did not affect Mr Phillips and other new employees, but affected Mr Griffin and the other similar staff. Their court victory was, in effect, reversed. The Institution decided to take legal action to test the validity of the Part IV Order. In the meantime a debate in the House of Commons in January 1967, initiated by the opposition, aired the case but, with the Whips on, the motion to withdraw the ministerial order was lost by sixty-one votes.

The county court found against the Institution's claim. The Institution decided to appeal. In explaining the decision to take this action the general secretary said:

> We are not challenging the incomes standstill or the period of severe restraint. The Institution has taken this action because the Metropolitan Police draughtsmen have been victimised by the government. They were not paid increases under an agreement which covered draughtsmen in the civil service. All the other draughtsmen covered by the agreement were paid their increases before or after the income standstill was introduced. This is a principle which has been applied by the government both inside and outside the civil service; where some people covered by an agreement have properly received their payments before the standstill the remainder received the increases in full. This principle has not been applied in the case of the Metropolitan Police draughtsmen.

The appeal was successful.

THE PRESS COUNCIL

Not only did the incomes policy bring the Institution into contact with the courts, it also brought conflict with the press. The Institution had been worried for some time about the number of scurrilous articles on the civil service appearing in the press. A particular example of this was a long article by Colm Brogan in the *Sunday Express* on 4 December 1966, in which he declared that the incomes standstill and the period of severe restraint did not apply in the civil service because civil servants continued to receive scale increments. The general secretary immediately wrote a reply in which he dealt with the question of the payment of fixed increments both inside and outside the civil service. He pointed to the difference between scale increments and other pay increases. The letter was not published. After a further exchange of correspondence with the *Sunday Express* the editor indicated eventually that he would be prepared to consider a letter which did not exceed 200 words. This letter was sent but was also not published.

The Institution referred the issue to the Press Council and pointed out that the article by Mr Brogan was intended to deal with a matter of public importance and to influence public opinion. The Institution argued that a responsible newspaper had an obligation to give some space to criticism of such articles and to correct inaccurate statements; in respect of Mr Brogan's article the *Sunday Express* had failed on both counts. In his defence Mr John Junor, the editor of the *Sunday Express*, said that Mr Brogan's article put forward the simple point that civil service increments were still being paid at a time when most other workers were denied a pay increase. He said that Mr McCall's letter did not answer this basic point.

In its statement rejecting the complaint the Press Council concluded that 'the question of whether the proposed letter of reply was of suitable length and dealt with the basic points in issue was a matter within the discretion of the editor'. Commenting on this adjudication the general secretary said:

> The *Sunday Express* published a long and vitriolic attack on the civil service which contained numerous inaccuracies. The editor did not publish any reply. The Press Council has taken the view that this was a matter for the editor's discretion. I therefore deplore the way in which the editor exercised his discretion . . .

DEBATE ON PAY

At the 1966 conference the NEC promised a policy statement on pay procedures. This statement, together with twenty-five motions on pay policy and a further twenty-six motions raising miscellaneous points about pay, dominated the proceedings of the 1967 conference.

The NEC's detailed policy statement traced the history of pay policy in the Institution, examined current issues and eventually came to the somewhat unexciting conclusion that each case had to be approached on its merits and in the situation prevailing. In introducing the paper for conference approval the general secretary emphasised that flexibility was essential. He said: 'If you bind our hands by any single doctrinaire pronouncement then you could put us into an extremely awkward situation and frustrate the very progress that you are so anxious to see.' There was, he went on, no single magic formula; there was no magic wand that could be waved which would ensure that members received increases as soon as they asked for them and which would delight them.

A number of delegates found this conclusion disappointing and felt that there should be some formula or set of principles which could be applied to determine any particular pay claim. Nevertheless, the NEC paper was finally approved by a fairly large majority. During the debates on pay, tribute was paid to the achievements of the Institution and its general secretary in securing the recent settlements for the works group and related classes.

THE MIXTURE AS BEFORE

In the spring of 1967 the government issued a new White Paper, *Prices and Incomes*

Policy after 30 July 1967. The two main objectives set out in the paper were to create conditions favourable to sustained economic growth and to seek voluntary agreement with the Confederation of British Industry (CBI) and the TUC to secure this objective. There would be a need, said the White Paper, for continuing moderation during the next twelve months. In its discussions in June the National Staff Side decided that in the light of the incomes policy the most pressing claim was that for the lower-paid, for whom provision for exceptional treatment was made within incomes policy. A central pay claim for all would then be pressed.

A claim for the lower-paid was made for 5 per cent on a salary of £750 p.a., or 15s in cash. TUC approval was sought for this claim. Negotiations were extremely difficult, despite the modesty of the claim, and in the end agreement was reached in November that there should be an increase of 12s per week with effect from 1 August 1967 for full-time adults whose basic pay did not exceed £11 15s per week and tapered increases for adults whose basic pay was between £11 15s and £14 per week.

In the same month agreement was reached on an increase in London weighting. The claim for £50 for inner and £25 for outer London was submitted in 1966. Before the Official Side could reply the standstill had intervened. At the beginning of 1967 the Staff Side resubmitted the claim and the Treasury decided with reluctant Staff Side agreement to refer it to the NBPI. The report of the Board, *London Weighting in the Non-Industrial Civil Service*, which was seriously delayed, was published in November 1967. The Board took the view that the most appropriate basis for calculating London weighting both inside and outside the civil service was the difference in the cost of living between London and the rest of the country. This difference could in part be objectively measured by movements in housing and travel costs, using a formula recommended by the Board and special indices prepared by the Ministry of Labour. In future rates should be adjusted at three-yearly intervals in accordance with movements in travel and housing costs for inner London and housing costs only for outer London. For the present the Board recommended a new rate of £125 per annum for inner and £75 per annum for outer London to be operative from 1 November 1967.

In response the Staff Side were prepared to accept the increase suggested, and, for the time being, the proposed method of review. They thought, however, that three years was too long an interval and the operative date too late. Further representations were made on both these issues.

DEVALUATION

Between the end of 1964 when the Labour government came into office, through 1966 when it was re-elected with an increased majority, until the end of 1967, no fundamental improvement took place in Britain's economic position. The deficit in the balance of payments, which the Labour government inherited from the previous Conservative government, was still there and the rate of economic growth was still low. The necessary stern measures to deal with these problems at an early stage were not taken. The attempt at economic planning was little more than a system of prediction with a few spurs and curbs to encourage activity in some directions and discourage it in others. Basically, however, the 'planning mechanism' relied on market forces. This meant that there was very little real control of the economy. Nor were any effective measures taken to deal with the balance-of-payments deficit either by drastic cuts in overseas spending for military purposes as advocated by many trade unionists or by devaluation.

Finally, in November 1967, the government, faced with continuing economic difficulties, decided to devalue the currency. This led inevitably to price increases. Devaluation was also accompanied by various restrictions designed to reduce the balance-of-payments deficit. The government's policy was to hold down domestic demand and to divert resources into exports. In his subsequent budget the Chancellor of the Exchequer, Mr Roy Jenkins, put forward the strategic aim that total demand in the economy should be reduced by 1 per cent. In this way the incomes policy, which had been commended to the trade union movement as a policy for the planned growth of real incomes, became an instrument for enforcing a policy designed to prevent any improvement in living standards for the majority of working people.

In commenting on these developments the 1968 annual report of the Institution stated:

With the developing economic crisis culminating in devaluation, the position at the end of the year was even more acute. Incomes policy considerations are factors with which the Institution in common with other trade unions will have to deal, whether we like it or not, for as long ahead as can be foreseen. It is in the interests of the members of the Institution as well as other sections of the community for the economy to be placed on a sound and progressive basis free from periodic crises.

At the beginning of April 1968 the government published a new White Paper, *Productivity, Prices and Incomes Policy in 1968 and 1969*. Although it declared its firm intention to proceed on a voluntary basis, in consultation with the CBI and the TUC, the government strengthened its powers by introducing a ceiling of 3·5 per cent per annum on wage, salary and dividend increases after 20 March 1968 except where agreements were negotiated which genuinely raised productivity and efficiency and helped to stabilise or reduce prices. The White Paper also envisaged introducing legislation, when the relevant sections of the existing Prices and Incomes Act, 1967, expired on 11 August 1968, lengthening the maximum delaying power on price and pay increases to twelve months in the context of a reference to the NBPI. All increases in pay, or other significant improvements, would need to be justified against the criteria and considerations of the policy.

Throughout 1968 the civil service unions and the government continued to argue about the effect of incomes policy on civil service pay. One particular aspect of the policy continued to exercise their attention; it was the doctrine associated with the policy that comparability was not acceptable as justification for pay increases. According to this doctrine, if comparability was to be given full weight then a pay increase for one group of workers might ultimately be extended throughout the entire labour force of the nation. Thus, it was said, comparability was highly inflationary in its effect. This doctrine, however, was in flat contradiction to the principle on which civil service pay was determined. This principle was that civil service pay should bear fair comparisons with that in outside employment.

The conflict between the doctrine of the incomes policy and the principle of fair comparison for the determination of civil service pay was never satisfactorily resolved during the period of the prices and incomes policy. The civil service unions maintained constant pressure on the Treasury to adhere to the principle of fair comparison and, though this pressure succeeded in maintaining the operation of the Pay Research Unit and the implementation of its recommendations, the civil service unions felt, nevertheless, that they were constantly engaged in a catching-up operation. Moreover this delay in making pay adjustments was accentuated by the government's insistence that certain increases should be staged over a period of time.

Despite these difficulties pay increases were secured for virtually all Institution members during 1968. At the beginning of 1968 the Staff Side re-opened discussions on a central pay claim and a new agreement was reached providing for an increase of 5 per cent on 1 January 1966 rates of pay where the last increase was from 1 January to 1 July 1966; and for an increase of 3 per cent where the last increase was from 1 July 1967 for staff whose flat rates of scale maxima were at or below £3,107 at 31 December 1967. The operative date was 1 July 1968. The civil service unions regarded the settlement as unsatisfactory but felt they had no option but to accept it. They argued that the increases offered by the Treasury were significantly less in percentage terms than the general movement of wages and salaries in outside employment. The Treasury, on the other hand, said that the government had to be seen to be operating its own incomes policy strictly to its own employees.

Staged increases were also implemented for administrative and executive grades, based on pay research evidence, and the government accepted a recommendation from the Franks Committee that consequential increases should be paid to the higher grades, staged where necessary. There was further good news for the higher grades in that the Franks Committee decided that the time was ripe for a new substantive review of higher-grades pay. It wished, however, to await the report of the NBPI on the pay of top jobs in the country generally, before making its own recommendations.

At the 1968 conference the general secretary said that the policy of restraint – dull, dreary, wearisome and negative – had gone on for far too long. Incomes restraint was not the panacea for Britain's economic problems. A policy for incomes was only one element, and not necessarily the most important element, in determining economic progress. If a policy for incomes was to be successful it could not be based on any rigid arithmetical exercise or legal sanction. It involved bringing together a wide range of factors relating both to the general economic position and the circumstances of the particular case. Adequate recognition should be given to skill, qualifications and responsibility.

A fraternal address, critical of the government's incomes policy, was also made to the 1968 conference by Mr John Dutton of the Association of Scientific, Technical and Managerial Staffs. ASTMS was the new organisation created by the amalgamation between the Association of Scientific Workers and the Association of Supervisory Staffs, Executives and Technicians. Mr Dutton delivered a sharp attack on the prices and incomes policy. In reporting his speech, *State Service* said that the initial reaction to Mr Dutton's views was 'something remarkably like shocked silence' but that he finished triumphantly to considerable applause.

The conference carried unanimously a resolution which opposed any incomes policy which (*a*) did not apply fairly to all sections of the community, (*b*) did not help to provide conditions to enable real improvements to be obtained in salaries and conditions, (*c*) froze the salaries of professional, scientific and technical staff, (*d*) failed to provide reasonable differentials and incentives and to reward extra responsibilities, and (*e*) unreasonably delayed operative dates of agreed new scales either in whole or in part. In the discussion reference was made to the very serious shortage of staff in many scientific and technical grades in the civil service. The general secretary recalled that in 1963 the Prime Minister, Mr Wilson, who was then in opposition, had called for a much greater valuation to be put on the work of professional, scientific and technical staffs.

THE BELLINGER AND MALLABAR COMMITTEES

On 31 July 1968 the government announced in the House of Lords that it had decided to seek the help of a panel of experienced people from business, industry and the trade unions to join in an investigation into particular areas of work in the civil service, where large numbers of staff were employed, and where there might be scope for savings. In a letter to Leslie Williams, secretary general of the National Staff Side, the Treasury said: 'It is not proposed to lay down detailed terms of reference, or particular targets for staff savings. Ministers are anxious that those concerned should feel at liberty to ask whatever questions they would like about the way in which work is done and indeed why it is done at all.'

The move was a further manifestation of the lack of confidence in the civil service, fuelled particularly by the press and certain politicians. The Staff Side protested vehemently at the lack of consultation over the proposal which had emerged 'out of the blue'. Efficiency was already under discussion, they argued, by the Joint Civil Service Efficiency Committee, established in 1965 on the initiative of the Staff Side. Despite the protests, the new panel was established under the chairmanship of Sir Robert Bellinger, GBE, DSC.

Although the Staff Side were united in condemning the lack of consultation they were divided in their reaction to the appointment of the panel. The Institution and some others felt that good could come from the appointment of the Bellinger panel provided certain conditions were met. First, the Staff Side should be fully involved from then on; secondly, the review should be comprehensive, embracing areas of staff shortage as well as suspected overmanning; thirdly, they should look critically at the cost of contracting out work to private industry; and finally, they should not put arbitrary ceilings on manpower but relate it clearly to the work to be done.

At the same time as it announced the Bellinger panel to look into the non-industrial civil service, the government also announced the appointment of a committee under the chairmanship of Mr J. F. Mallabar, chairman of Harland & Wolff, to look into the efficiency of the industrial civil service. They were to look primarily at the Royal Ordnance Factories and the Royal Dockyards. The Institution established a subcommittee to prepare evidence jointly with the STCS.

ARBITRATION

Unlike during the period of the pay pause, arbitration had survived the Labour government's incomes policy. As usual the Institution was by far the major customer. Thus, for example, in 1966 and 1967 eight cases were taken, all for small classes, and in four of them the Institution was 100 per cent successful.

In 1968 Sir George Honeyman retired as chairman of the arbitration tribunal after sixteen years. In his last case he awarded an increase on the existing clothing allowance paid to Meteorological Office experimental officers who gave the weather forecast on BBC television. This was an Institution case and it doubled the Official Side's offer.

Since Sir George had taken over the chair in 1952 the Institution had taken ninety-five cases to arbitration. His chairmanship was highly respected for its consistency, fairness and independence. While in theory he was only concerned with each individual case, in practice he tried to bear in mind the relationships within the civil service as a whole. He resisted government interference during the difficult period of the pay pause. Stanley Mayne paid tribute to his chairmanship in the *Whitley Bulletin,* concluding with the words: 'With Sir George Honeyman leaving us we pay tribute to a man who was always honest and fair in his dealings with the parties that appeared before him and dealt with them as equitably as was possible within the circumstances as he saw them. He brings lustre to the list of Civil Service Arbitration Tribunal Chairmen.' Professor H. A. Clegg was appointed chairman in his place.

THE FINAL PHASE OF INCOMES POLICY

The first steps in defining the criteria for the sixth and final period of incomes policy came in October 1968. Mrs Barbara Castle, Secretary of State for Employment and Productivity, invited the CBI and TUC to begin discussions on the future of the policy. By this time, however, it was clear that the policy was of declining usefulness. Indeed, the Chancellor in April 1969 announced that 'less emphasis' would be put on prices and incomes policy in 1969.

An incomes policy which had begun with the objective of increasing real incomes and redistributing them in a spirit of social justice had been carried out in economic circumstances which entailed its use largely as a weapon to control and eventually to depress living standards. The lower-paid were worse off in both relative and real terms than they had been at the beginning. Although the policy had theoretically applied equally to all, the public sector had been more harshly dealt with than the private, because it was more visible and more directly amenable to government control.

In these general circumstances the civil service had not emerged unscathed but pay research increases, although phased and later staged, had eventually been paid. The machinery had not been abrogated altogether. The position of the professional and technical staff had been marginally improved. Moreover the two NBPI reports on higher grades pay and on London weighting had been helpful.

Nevertheless, at the 1969 conference discontent on pay was mounting. The dissatisfaction of delegates with the effect of incomes policy on pay determination in the civil service was expressed by the passing of a motion calling for an investigation as a matter of urgency into alternative methods of determining salary levels. This led to a lively debate and the motion was adopted by 198 votes to 29. The sponsors of the motion drew attention to the shortcomings of the Pay Research Unit. One speaker described the PRU as a time-wasting farce. The Unit was trying to compare 'unlike with unlike', and had introduced new league tables, analogues and masses of words to describe the simple fact that some people in industry were paid differently from some in the civil service. The National Executive Committee opposed the proposal. It acknowledged that the pay research machinery was imperfect but there was no magic formula by which the Institution could secure everything the members wanted. The government, said the NEC spokesman, would be pleased to do away with the principle of fair comparison if it was given an excuse to do so. Despite this opposition from the NEC the majority of delegates were clearly unhappy about the manner in which the principle of fair comparison was being eroded by the effect of the incomes policy.

In the first half of 1969 incomes policy was continuing to bite in the public sector. As a result civil service pay was well behind that of its counterparts in private employment. The NBPI Report No. 107, *Top Salaries in the Private Sector and Nationalised Industries,* had indicated that the higher grades in the civil service were lagging behind their counterparts outside. The works group and associated classes, for whom negotiations on the basis of pay research reports were continuing, were also far behind. Increases since 1965, the date of the last major pay review, had averaged 2 per cent per annum, while pay outside had moved by at least 20 per cent. Substantial increases were therefore clearly due.

After extremely difficult negotiations, agreement was reached on 5 June for central pay increases from 1 July 1969 of 5 per cent for those whose last pay settlement was on 1 January 1968, and 3·5 per cent for those whose last settlement had been on 1 July 1968 with an underpinning minimum of 10s per week. This, although subject to staging and still lagging behind the general movements in salaries, was the best that could be achieved within incomes policy. It reinforced the Staff Side's determination to seek as soon as possible a review of the pay agreement. The discussions on revised pay arrangements began in the autumn of 1969.

Agreement on a pay-research-based settlement for the works group and associated classes was reached on 19 June. The settlement produced substantial increases ranging from 20·6 to 27 per cent on the 1965 pay scales, and from 11·2 to 16·9 per cent on the 1 July 1968 interim rates. The agreement resulted in improvements in the relative position of certain grades, in particular the senior engineer and the technical grade I, in relation to other grades in the civil service, thus contributing to a longstanding aim of Institution policy. The agreement was satisfactory not only in that it produced substantial increases within the time-limit for retrospection but also because it was achieved by negotiation and had demonstrated a willingness by both sides to compromise in order to reach agreement despite the constraints of incomes policy. The agreement, however, had to be staged in order to satisfy incomes policy and the final instalment was not paid until 1 January 1970.

Higher-grades pay was also settled during 1969 following the report in July of the Standing Advisory Committee, now under the chairmanship of Lord Plowden. The committee concluded on the basis of advice from several quarters, including the NBPI report *Top Salaries in the Private Sector and Nationalised Industries*, that although other elements of remuneration and conditions of employment such as superannuation were roughly equal, civil service pay was below that of the commercial sector. The committee went on to recommend substantial increases which should be paid in three stages. The government, while accepting the report in principle, rejected the recommendations on staging. Instead it agreed to pay the following rates (the Plowden Committee recommendations are in brackets): under-secretary £6,000 (£6,750), deputy secretary £7,100 (£9,000), permanent secretary £9,800 (£14,000), head of the civil service, permanent secretary to the Treasury and secretary to the Cabinet £10,400 (£15,000). The government said that it would consider the implementation of the outstanding amounts in the light of incomes policy.

During the second half of 1969 there was a substantial improvement in Britain's balance of payments. This helped to create a mood among many that the pay policy could be relaxed. In particular, there were signs of serious unrest among groups of low-paid workers. The revolt was led by dustmen. They broke through the policy. In response to this pressure a White Paper, *Productivity, Prices and Incomes Policy after 1969*, was published in December 1969. It urged that special attention should be given to the position of low-paid workers. It said that a real improvement was needed 'in the position of those low-paid in the context of particular situations, of particular needs, and of particular systems of pay negotiations'.

At the end of 1969, following further discussions between the National Staff Side and the Treasury on the arrangements for determining pay in the civil service, a statement was issued by the National Staff Side which said that fair comparison should continue as the primary principle for determining civil service pay. The National Whitley Council was, however, they said, reviewing existing procedures with a view to reducing time-lags which occurred in bringing the pay of civil servants into line with their outside analogues. Pay research surveys were organised on a three-year cycle and investigations were now going on with a view to moving to a two-year cycle of pay research surveys.

During 1970 there was an upsurge in wage and salary claims. The rate of pay increases accelerated and there were many indications that the formal policy had broken down. Among millions of trade unionists there was the feeling that there had not been any significant improvement in living standards for a number of years. A general election was also impending and neither the government nor the opposition considered it politically opportune to urge that wage and salary claims and settlements should be kept at a level commensurate with the increase in national output.

With the general breakdown in the implementation of the incomes policy the civil service unions shared in the trend towards much higher rates of pay settlement. At the 1970 annual conference the general secretary recorded that in twelve months the Institution had secured increases for virtually the whole membership ranging from 14 per cent for the scientific and related classes to 18–22 per cent for the technology classes. He added that some increases had been even higher.

At the 1970 annual conference of the Institution delegates endorsed the policy of the National Staff Side to secure pay reviews not less frequently than every two years. They also urged that there should be annual central pay settlements to provide realistic interim pay increases between pay reviews. Delegates expressed concern about the extent to which pay in the civil service had fallen seriously behind that in industry and commerce.

There was a particularly lively debate at the 1970 conference on a motion moved by a former branch of the Society of Technical Civil Servants – now amalgamated with the Institution (see Chapter 21) – stating that as a last resort the National Executive Committee should be prepared to take militant action in support of claims advanced by the Institution. The movers and supporters of the motion made it clear that they did not think the policy of militant action was a substitute for good negotiating machinery but it was a necessary 'last resort'. If the Institution did not express its readiness to take strike action it would be toothless.

The proposal met with opposition from a number of delegates but the turning-point in the debate came with the presentation of the NEC's view by the general secretary. He said that in extreme circumstances the NEC would be prepared to take some form of militant action but only with the approval of the membership and the authority of the NEC. If the conference passed the motion it did not mean that there was going to be an outbreak of strikes in the civil service. The NEC did not intend to depart from its traditional attitude of depending on the normal negotiating machinery, but it did not rule out industrial militancy as a final weapon. The proposal was carried.

The main lesson of the period 1964 to 1970 was that the success of a prices and incomes policy depends not only on the terms of the policy and the machinery with which it is implemented but on the economic framework in which it has to operate. This was precisely the point put by the general secretary of the Institution to successive annual conferences of the Institution. Economic expansion provides the basis for higher living standards, but if this expansion does not take place a prices and incomes policy will inevitably run into difficulty. It will be seen as an instrument for holding down the living standards of trade unionists.

It was the achievement of the 1964–70 Labour government that during its period of office a substantial balance-of-payments deficit, which was inherited from the previous Conservative government, was converted into a substantial balance-of-payments surplus. This was secured, however, not so much by a drastic reduction in overseas spending or by economic expansionism, but by restraining the economy. In this way the demand for imports was held down. The policy pursued made it impossible to fulfil the expectations aroused by the 1964 joint declaration of intent on productivity, prices and incomes.

During 1969 the government published a number of White Papers setting out its proposal for a new earnings-related social security system. These proposals were bound to have an effect on the civil service occupational pension scheme and long discussions about them took place between the Treasury and the National Staff Side. In these discussions consideration was given not only to the implications for the civil service occupational scheme of the proposed earnings-related state scheme but also of a recommendation from the Fulton Committee report (see Chapter 20) that all civil servants should be pensionable and that pension rights should be preserved or transferred when a civil servant changed his employment.

At the end of 1969 the Secretary of State for Social Services stated in the House of Commons that the government had no intention of dismantling public service pension schemes and that benefits earned by previous service in existing schemes would not be subject to retrospective change. He added that there was no intention to change the retirement ages in public service pension schemes and that any necessary changes in occupational pensions arrangements would be fully discussed with trade union representatives. He also indicated that the new proposed arrangements for public service pension schemes would be even more comprehensive than the old arrangements.

Agreement in principle was reached between the Treasury and the National Staff Side, subject to parliamentary approval, that the civil service superannuation scheme should be put on a non-statutory basis under general enabling powers. This would enable changes in the superannuation scheme to be made without legislation. The scheme could thus become more flexible.

In 1969 a new Pensions Increase Act was passed by Parliament designed to give increases in civil service and other related public service pensions.

19 Exploiting Technology

Considerable emphasis had been given during the 1964 election campaign to the important role of science and technology in the British economy. The Institution made it clear to the incoming government that it expected to see those words and aspirations translated into concrete action in 1965 and the years that lay ahead. After the election an editorial in the December 1964 *State Service* gave clear warning:

> To create a scientific revolution, which commands the respect and co-operation of all, requires sound judgement, imagination and detailed planning. It requires a knowledge of what science can do and what it cannot do.
>
> Sound organisation is essential. Reorganisation may be necessary, but decisions must be taken for sound technological reasons. Merely to shift those who serve the state from one ministry or public authority to another is not technological progress. The proposal to split the DSIR has evoked strong technical opposition. To be effective, the organisation of science must have the whole-hearted co-operation of those on whose efforts the success of the scientific revolution depends.

A NEW STRUCTURE FOR SCIENCE AND TECHNOLOGY

The new structure for science and technology was announced as soon as the new government took office. A Ministry of Technology was established to accelerate the process of modernisation and innovation by stimulating a more rapid application of scientific and technological advance in British industry. The Ministry of Technology was to form a small advisory council on technology, consisting of industrialists, scientists, economists and trade unionists. It was to be chaired by the minister, with Professor P. M. S. Blackett, FRS, as deputy chairman. The Ministry of Technology was to take over the work of the DSIR concerned with industrial research, with most of the research stations, and to assume responsibility for the UKAEA. The position of the National Physical Laboratory and the National Chemical Laboratory was still being considered.

The Secretary of State for Education and Science was to retain responsibility for the other functions of the DSIR, and for two new research councils – a Science Research Council (SRC) and a Natural Environment Research Council (NERC). The advice of both these councils would be available to other ministers in relation to research on matters within their field of interest. In particular, the newly created Ministry of Land and Natural Resources would be interested in some of the work of the NERC which would incorporate the Nature Conservancy and the Geological Survey and Museum. In addition the Secretary of State for Education and Science would appoint a council for scientific policy to advise on his general responsibilities for the government's civil science programme, and more specifically on the scientific and financial balance of the programmes of the Medical Research Council (MRC), the Agricultural Research Council (ARC), the SRC and NERC.

The Institution's response was swift. In a letter to the Prime Minister the general secretary said that the Institution was no less dismayed by the present government's proposals than it had been by the previous government's response to the Trend Report. He also objected strongly to the lack of consultation. The letter reiterated the Institution's fear that by splitting the DSIR basic and applied research were being separated. The letter continued:

Basic and applied research cannot really be divided; each stimulates the other and they flourish together. Moreover, while basic research has great attraction for young graduates, applied research is vital to the nation's economy and must attract a full share of the best scientists. It must not, therefore, be put in a position where it will be regarded as a second-class occupation.

These problems can be overcome if the DSIR is transferred as a whole to the Ministry of Technology. We strongly advocate this. Moreover, since the essential problem is to achieve the optimum use of limited reserves of capital and scientific manpower, there should be within the Ministry of Technology a central committee with overall responsibility for the development of scientific resources.

In reply the Prime Minister said that he had already taken account of the views expressed by the Institution on the Trend Report and that in making major changes in the machinery of government on assuming office it had been impossible to consult all the many interests involved. Towards the end of the year the Institution made further representations on the reorganisation. It also established a committee to represent the views of all the different groups of staff who were to be transferred to the new research councils.

THE TENNANT REPORT

In his address to conference in 1965 the general secretary returned to the theme of the poor status of scientists and technologists in government employment and in society in general. He referred to the Committee on Scientific Manpower which documented the grave shortages of scientific and technological manpower. Within the civil service in 1963 62 per cent of vacancies for architects and maintenance surveyors were unfilled at the end of the year. For civil, structural and public health engineers the shortfall was 41 per cent, and for mechanical and electrical engineers it was 44 per cent. To alleviate these shortages the Treasury had tried to lower the standards of entry and had resorted to recruitment above the basic grades.

The general secretary recalled that in the debate in the House of Commons on the Feilden Report, *Design in the Engineering Industry,* the government had welcomed the opportunity which the debate gave to re-emphasise the importance of engineering in the country's economy, and had said that the status of engineering needed to be raised. He stated that the time had come for the government to take action on the serious problems which existed. On the scientific front that opportunity would be presented by the review undertaken by the Tennant Committee whose report was soon to be published.

The report of the Tennant Committee in October 1965, *The Organisation of the*

Scientific Civil Service, however, turned out to be a grave disappointment. In its evidence to the committee the Institution had said that the structure and career values of the scientific classes in the civil service were inadequate. The promises made at the end of the war in 1945 had not been fulfilled. At a time when the major political parties were committed to extending the application of science throughout industry and to expanding the nation's scientific manpower to make this possible, it was necessary that the government should adopt a new principle and give a lead in the recognition and status accorded to scientists. The scientific staff in the civil service should be given more rewarding career prospects and improved salaries independently of the fair comparison principle. The Institution also urged that management training and experience should be made available to scientists in the civil service so that managerial posts at the highest level should be freely open to them. These posts, it was argued, should not be kept as the special preserve of the administrative and executive classes.

The Institution described the report as superficial. The committee had concluded that in general the civil service was attracting to the scientific officer class its fair share of graduates. It was, however, it said, rather less successful in attracting really outstanding young scientists. The Institution disagreed with these conclusions. It produced figures to demonstrate that the civil service had considerable difficulty in recruiting scientists. The Institution also criticised the Tennant Committee for not making any real examination of the reasons why the civil service was less successful in recruiting outstanding young scientists.

The Institution prepared a response to Tennant in two parts. The first dealt with the inadequacy of the report in general. The other made detailed proposals on each of the subjects in the committee's recommendations, and repeated the demands made in the Institution's evidence to the committee. In the meantime, however, the Fulton Committee was appointed and the issues raised were subsumed in the wider context of the Fulton Committee's examination of the whole civil service structure.

THE BRAIN DRAIN

Concern continued to mount both within and outside the Institution about the growing shortage of scientific and technological manpower, and the low pay and status of science and technology which the Institution was convinced lay behind it.

Confirmation of the arguments being made by the Institution in favour of improving the status of scientists and technologists came in the early summer of 1966 from Lord Snow, Joint Parliamentary Secretary to the Ministry of Technology. He said that unless the status of the engineer in Britain was raised to a level more in keeping with his importance to society, economic damage would result. He maintained that engineers got the 'rough end of the stick' in most countries with the exception of Russia. In Britain the position was less favourable than in the USA or in Continental Europe and far less favourable than in the USSR. Lord Snow pointed out that pure science continued to be remarkably successful in the United Kingdom. Scientists enjoyed a high status but the same could not be said of technologists.

Towards the end of 1966 official reports pointed to the scarcity of scientists in industrial employment. One of the reports, the *1965 Triennial Manpower Survey of Engineers, Technologists, Scientists and Technical Supporting Staff*, revealed that during the preceding years a high proportion of those obtaining first class degrees had taken courses leading to a higher degree and had then remained in academic research or had entered government research establishments. Few of them had entered industry. The second report, *The Interim Report on Manpower Parameters for Scientific Growth*, compared the pattern of demand for employment with the flow of graduates into jobs. It pointed out that since 1962 universities and further education establishments had increased their stock of engineers and scientists by 35 per cent but there was a much lower growth rate for engineers and technologists in the chemical and the electrical and mechanical commercial fields.

The shortage of scientists and technologists was being exacerbated by emigration to countries which paid more for their services and offered better opportunities. An editorial in *State Service* in January 1967, 'Time to put the stopper in', said:

> The very people on whom we shall ultimately depend are seeking fresh outlets for their energies and imaginative ideas. Discouraged to the point of exasperation by the lack of interest shown in their careers, they can be seen in ever-increasing numbers comparing conditions in Canada, Australia, America and elsewhere. Anywhere, it seems, but here.

The 'brain drain' was debated at the Institution's 1967 conference. A delegate from the Science Research Council pointed out that there were 105 pages of recorded debate on the 'brain drain' in *Hansard* but there was no indication anywhere of the role of the government in this field. In spite of the Prime Minister's avowed intention of forging ahead in the white heat of a technological revolution, there had been no hint of any intention by the government to raise the status of scientists and technologists.

The seriousness of the problem was graphically illustrated by the report of the Working Group on Migration published towards the end of 1967. The report stated: 'From a near numerical balance in 1961 we have moved to a position in 1966 which represented a net loss equivalent of 19 per cent of the 1963 output of newly qualified engineers and technologists and 9 per cent of that of scientists . . . This trend could have disastrous consequences for British industry and the economy within ten to twenty years if it were to continue at the present rate.' The report rejected the 'Berlin Wall solution' of physically trying to stop migration or imposing penalties on those who emigrated. Instead it drew attention to the poor pay and opportunities of scientists and technologists, a line of argument directly paralleled by the Institution's policy and its submissions to Fulton. The report stated quite plainly: 'The level of salaries offered to qualified manpower in British industry is clearly an issue central to the whole brain drain situation.'

The report was marred, in the Institution's view, by a suggestion that civil service pay should lag permanently behind industry in order that the attraction of industry could be increased. In attacking this aspect of the report the general secretary, in an article in *State Service*, said that it appeared to reflect the pressures of industrialists. To depress the pay of the civil service was directly contrary to the Priestley principles and would do nothing to solve the problem. A paramount need, he continued, was for effective trade union representation for scientists and technologists in industry. For its part the Institution would try to ensure that the government gave a lead in raising the pay and status of such staff.

THE SELECT COMMITTEE ON SCIENCE AND TECHNOLOGY

Public research and development issues also continued to engage the resources of the Institution during the period. One major issue concerned the future of the UKAEA and the future reactor programme; another concerned the organisation and role of the defence research establishments, and finally the Institution issued a major policy statement on public research and development – *Exploiting Technology*. All these developments followed the appointment of the Select Committee on Science and Technology in 1967, a body whose formation the Institution welcomed and with whom it was to have close relations in the coming years. The committee chose for its first investigation the nuclear reactor programme.

ATOMIC ENERGY

In 1965 a new law, the Science and Technology Act, extended the powers of the Atomic Energy Authority to include research work outside the nuclear field. The intention was to apply, where practicable, skills and devices developed for or primarily associated with nuclear energy to the wider needs of industry. This development was welcomed by the Institution which had long been pressing for such diversification. The United Kingdom Atomic Energy Authority was one of the biggest employers of scientists, engineers and other technical staff in the country. Initially atomic energy work in the United Kingdom was mainly for military purposes but in the 1950s it was recognised that there was a need for a large and concerted effort on the development of nuclear power for civil use. Under the Atomic Energy Authority Act, 1954, provision was made for the setting-up of the United Kingdom Atomic Energy Authority as a body financed from public funds and subject to ministerial direction on major issues of policy, but free of direct ministerial control on day-to-day matters. In 1965 the Authority employed about 34,000 men and women, of whom just over 18,000 were non-industrial staff. More than half of this 18,000 were in grades represented by the Institution.

At the invitation of the Select Committee the Institution submitted four written memoranda and also gave oral evidence. The main memorandum was divided into three parts. The first dealt with the nuclear reactor programme and the organisation of the nuclear power industry. It made suggestions for change in both which would make the United Kingdom more competitive in the export market. The second part considered the effect of the suggestion made in the first part which would entail a reduction in the Authority's effort on nuclear work because the basic groundwork had already been completed. In the third part it went on to discuss the redeployment of the staff who would be affected. It suggested that the Authority should be permitted to follow the example of the United States Energy Commission which had recently decided to extend the boundaries of its industrial co-operation programme to include non-nuclear work.

The report of the Select Committee in November 1967 contained, in the eyes of the Institution, a mixture of good and bad recommendations. The Institution congratulated the committee on its comprehensive analysis of the fundamental problems of the nuclear power industry and on its main proposal that there should be a single organisation for the design and construction of nuclear boilers. On the other hand, its recommendation that the UKAEA should be split and certain functions 'hived off' was criticised, together with the suggestion that there should be a review of the functions and staffing of the UKAEA. The Institution continued to urge that a single organisation should cover the whole spectrum from basic research to production and sale; the Select Committee's proposals entailed a split between basic and applied nuclear research.

In the summer of 1968 the government announced its intention to reorganise the nuclear power industry. The Industrial Reorganisation Corporation was asked to assist in the creation of two design and construction organisations, each with a minority government shareholding, in place of three existing commercial firms and design teams working within the Atomic Energy Authority. The Institution was opposed to this development. It felt that the skills and resources of those engaged in the design and exploitation of nuclear reactors should be brought together within a single organisation. It seemed clear to the Institution that the Authority, an outstandingly successful public enterprise, was being dismembered in deference to sustained pressure from commercial organisations which had themselves failed to exploit the lead established by the UKAEA in the provision of competitive power from nuclear energy.

The Institution also put it strongly to the government that it was dismayed that no reference had been made to the welfare of the staff, whose future would be so vitally affected by reorganisation. The Institution wanted to know what steps would be taken to ensure the continued employment of staff affected by the proposed organisational changes.

In the autumn of 1969 the Select Committee on Science and Technology published a supplementary report on the UK nuclear power industry. In this report the committee considered the progress made on the reorganisation proposals announced by the government in July 1968. The Institution submitted two memoranda to the Select Committee. Many of the points put to the committee by the Institution were subsequently endorsed in the report. The Select Committee criticised the lack of progress that had been made, and said that very little had been achieved to rationalise, strengthen and make the nuclear power industry more competitive in world markets. The committee also criticised the inadequate attention to staff consultation. The Select Committee suggested that it would be worthwhile for the government to consider increasing the shareholding of the UKAEA in the two design and construction companies. The committee concluded:

However much it may be desirable that there should be a division of work between the Authority and the companies on the lines of generic research on the one hand and commercial development on the other, the fact is that existing facilities of the Authority, their involvement in programmes of development already running, their control of fuel development and production – and the need for public financial support – all make for a blurring of this theoretical distinction . . .

The Institution saw the report of the Select Committee as a broad endorsement of its own views. On the publication of the report the Institution said that it remained convinced that it was wrong for the UKAEA to be excluded as a matter of policy from seeking and, when required, managing export orders for reactors. The Institution came out firmly in support of public enterprise in the development of the nuclear power industry.

EXPLOITING TECHNOLOGY

Because of the appointment of the Select Committee on Science and Technology and because of numerous statements made during 1967 by ministers and other public figures about the future of public research and development, the NEC decided to undertake a special review of the subject. At the end of September 1967 the NEC devoted a weekend to it and was addressed by various speakers including Mr I. Maddox, controller (industrial technology) of the Ministry of Technology; Sir Richard Way, former permanent secretary of the Ministry of Aviation and the War Office; Dr J. V. Dunworth, CB, CBE, director of the National Physical Laboratory; Mr W. R. Smith of the National Agricultural Advisory Service; and Mr John Maddox, editor of *Nature*. Following that weekend the NEC appointed a subcommittee to prepare by the end of the year a paper reviewing the situation in the public research and development establishments and setting out the Institution's policy for the future.

The results of the review were published in a booklet, *Exploiting Technology*, in March 1968. The booklet took the view that the research and development capacity of the government should be retained but more closely linked with the needs of industry. Such a development was far preferable to the view which was being put forward by some that scientists and technologists should be 'shaken out' of the government service and spread within industry. The essential message lay in the following quotation:

> The Institution accepts that there is need for change in the public sector; indeed, we have accepted this for longer than some of its present critics. We realise that there will be structural change and that change will involve cutting back in some areas and expansion in others. Not all these changes will be in the immediate interests of our individual members but it is clear to us that reform is necessary. But reform must be realistic and must respect the facts. Prime among these is a recognition that the public research and development facilities are valuable national assets, capable of making a much greater contribution than in the past. Our own proposals involve a radical change of attitude, considerable reorganisation and the creation of a new and intimate partnership with industry. We believe that they will give a new dynamic to public research development, are realistic and capable of speedy implementation.

Copies of the document were widely circulated within the Institution, and outside the Institution copies were sent to all MPs and to a wide variety of organisations interested in research and development problems. It was widely reviewed in the technical press and had some notice in the national press. It was also very well reviewed by a variety of influential companies, organisations and officials.

The general themes expressed in *Exploiting Technology* were taken up again in the Institution's evidence to the Select Committee on Science and Technology when it came to look at the organisation of defence research during 1968. It said that in addition to its traditional functions of providing advice to ministers and undertaking functional roles directly related to ministerial responsibilities, the civil 'spin-off' from defence research should also be taken into account.

As part of *Exploiting Technology* the Institution had advocated a detailed review of the research establishments engaged in defence research. This should be aimed at producing a rationalised organisation which would enable the defence research establishments to fulfil their traditional functions and to provide a research service to industry. The Select Committee reported in May 1969. It did not accept the Institution's basic proposal that the defence research establishments should be used to make a major contribution to technological development in the country. The committee took the view that the execution of development projects should as far as possible be left to industrial contractors and not undertaken within government R&D establishments. At the same time, however, it recognised that there were certain types of work which were not attractive to civil industry and which the government establishments would need to undertake.

OTHER REORGANISATIONS AND COMMITTEES OF INQUIRY

In addition to the reorganisations specifically concerned with research and development there were several other major changes which concerned the Institution's members during this period. There were wide-ranging changes in defence. The Labour government came to power in 1964 committed to a major review of defence. As a result of that review it was estimated that by the mid-1970s there would be a reduction in the active strength of the armed forces of about 75,000 with a consequential reduction of civilian staff of the order of 80,000. The timetable for these reductions was brought forward by devaluation. The rationalisation of various common functions continued throughout the period.

There was also the issue of 'civilianisation' on which a special committee under the chairmanship of Sir Henry Wilson Smith, KCB, KBE, was appointed to consider the desirable balance between military and civilian personnel. The committee made few reports and those which it did make the Staff Side found completely unsatisfactory. It was agreed in 1968, therefore, that the issue of civilianisation should be raised again in the context of the reorganisation of the Ministry of Defence and the wider reorganisation which would follow Fulton.

A major area of reorganisation during the period was the Post Office which left the civil service and became a public corporation on 1 October 1969. From the White Paper announcing the change in 1967 until and beyond vesting day the unions on the two Post Office Staff Sides sought to ensure that the new agreements on pay and conditions of service were at least as good as those prevailing in the civil service.

The publication of the document *Exploiting Technology* was a continuation of the tradition of concern within the Institution over the role of public research and development and the relationship between science and society. That concern had been particularly manifest during the 1930s and during the Second World War and in the immediate postwar period. The renewed interest in the exploitation of science and technology and the concern over the shortage of scientists and engineers after 1964, and the establishment of the Select Committee on Science and Technology, provided a context in which the views of the Institution, which represented members forming the largest single concentration of research and development personnel in the country, carried considerable weight. The Institution was to continue and develop its interest in the area of public research and development over the next decade, and was to be a major force in the campaign to achieve the status and rewards for scientists and technologists which befitted their crucial role in a technological age.

20   The Fulton Committee

In February 1966 the government appointed a committee under the chairmanship of Lord Fulton to 'examine the structure, recruitment and management, including training, of the home civil service and to make recommendations'. Lord Fulton was the vice-chancellor of the University of Sussex. One leading trade unionist, Mr Walter C. Anderson, the general secretary of the National and Local Government Officers' Association, was appointed to the committee. The membership also included Sir James Dunnett, permanent secretary at the Ministry of Labour; Sir Norman Kipping, formerly director general of the principal employers' organisation, the Federation of British Industry; Mr Norman Hunt, lecturer in politics at Oxford; Mr John Wall, managing director of EMI; Lord Simey, professor of social science, University of Liverpool; Sir Edward Boyle, Conservative member of Parliament; Sir Philip Allen of the Treasury; Sir William Cook, deputy chief scientific adviser at the Ministry of Defence; Mr Robert Nield, economic adviser to the Treasury; and a Labour MP, Mr Robert Sheldon.

In a statement in the House of Commons announcing the setting up of the committee the Prime Minister said that the decision was reached in view of the changes which had taken place in the demands placed upon the civil service and of the changes in the country's educational system. The time had come, he said, to ensure that the service was properly equipped for its role in the modern state. He indicated that the government's willingness to consider changes in the civil service did not imply any intention on its part to alter the basic relationship between ministers and civil servants. Civil servants, however eminent, would remain the confidential advisers to ministers who alone were answerable to Parliament for policy. The terms of reference limited the inquiry to the home civil service and thus excluded the diplomatic service.

The major catalyst in establishing the Fulton Committee was the Sixth Report of the Estimates Committee which had been looking into recruitment difficulties in the civil service. In evidence to the Select Committee, the Institution had made three basic recommendations.

The government should:
(a) Exploit to the full the training and talents of its scientists, technologists and technicians and ensure there is full employment in terms of the quality of work they are given to do.
(b) Make clear that specialists are full and equal partners with other staff and that they have an equal opportunity to gain promotion to the top posts.
(c) Offer pay and careers which demonstrate that scientists, technologists and technicians are no longer regarded as inferior or second and third rate.

In its report, *Recruitment to the Civil Service*, the Select Committee found that in many classes there was a shortfall of recruits. In the case of specialists in science and technology, it was partly a reflection of the general shortfall in the supply, but in the case of the administrative class the civil service was attracting a decreasing proportion of an increasing supply. The Select Committee made some detailed recommendations for improving the process of selection and recruitment but also recommended a much more wide-ranging review:

(5) (i) A committee of officials, aided by members from outside the civil service on the lines of the Plowden Committee, should be appointed to initiate research upon, to examine, and to report upon the structure, recruitment and management of the civil service.

(ii) The position should be reviewed by the government immediately upon the receipt of the report; the government should report to Parliament the action it proposes to take; and if a further inquiry by a Royal Commission be then found to be necessary, such Commission should be appointed forthwith.

The Institution strongly supported a review of the kind suggested in the report and was gratified to find that the proposal excited wide public interest and was the subject of extensive comment in the press. A particularly welcome feature of the press comment was the emphasis placed on the need for a greater role for the specialist. The response of the government was to establish the Fulton Committee.

The Select Committee report, however, was only the final stage in a developing demand both outside and inside the civil service, particularly on the part of the Institution, for civil service reform. Looked at from the Institution's point of view, much of the concern was crystallised in a series of two articles based on a lecture given in October 1964 by Dr Stephen Toulmin, director since 1960 of the Nuffield Foundation Unit for the History of Ideas and previously professor of philosophy at Leeds University, a fellow of Cambridge, and a government scientist early in his career. In this he made a threefold distinction in the relationship of science to government. Science could be either (i) the servant of policy formation – giving technical advice to the policy-maker, (ii) an object of policy formation – as when the DSIR advises on the allocation of research funds, or (iii) an instrument of policy formation – as when analytical work, whether in the physical or social sciences, contributes to the solution of political problems.

He argued that traditionally the government structure in Britain had been specifically adapted to deal with science in the first of these three roles. He said:

the attitude of the decision-makers towards the experts has – with a few exceptions – been that of Lady Catherine de Burgh towards the Reverend Mr Collins. The experts have appeared a regrettable necessity: one is compelled to employ them for certain practical purposes, but only as one might employ a dentist or a mechanic – one is not obliged to ask such people into the drawing room.

Instead, Toulmin argued, the great need in modern administration was for the use of science in role (iii). Only with a fresh grasp of the social role of scientific research and technological development could the contribution of science in sense (ii) and in public affairs in general be achieved. A major barrier to the achievement of the integration of science with general policy-making was the administrative class.

The deficiencies of the administrative class had been described by R. H. S. Crossman, among others, in an article in *Encounter*, quoted by Toulmin, where he said that they remained predominantly arts men from Oxford and Cambridge with scarcely a handful of men with an understanding of science. The same point was made in a leader in the *Guardian*. Commenting on the report of the Select Committee, it said:

> There must be something wrong with an organisation, the civil service, which admits to a pressing need for more specialists but which debars them, as a matter of policy, from the highest positions. The administrative class of the civil service is inexpert in the many specialised disciplines of modern government, and proud of it.

The role of the specialist and the position of science and technology in government were of major concern to the Institution and figured prominently in its evidence to the Fulton Committee. There were, however, a wide range of other issues which had been causing concern and on which some aspects had already been reviewed or were in the process of being so. For example, on training, the existing pattern of civil service training, stemming from the Assheton Report of 1944, was reviewed by a joint working party chaired by Mr S. P. Osmond. Subsequently, on its recommendation a committee, chaired by Osmond, was established 'to consider the training needs for middle and higher management in the civil service . . . and the desirability or otherwise of setting up a Civil Service Staff College'. Discussions were also taking place on the removal of obstacles to mobility between the civil service and other employers.

THE INSTITUTION'S RESPONSE

The Institution welcomed the Fulton Committee and in his address to the 1966 conference the general secretary said: 'It will be our business to do all we can to see that it provides answers relevant to this technological age.' A subcommittee, under the chairmanship of the Institution chairman, R. G. Fall, was set up to prepare evidence. It also proposed to sponsor and undertake wide-ranging research. The Institution's professional groups and branches were asked to submit their views. In preparing the Institution's evidence the Fulton Subcommittee took into account the Fulton Committee's desire not to be overwhelmed with a mass of detail. The strategy, therefore, was to state the general principles of the Institution's evidence and to illustrate this with examples from the main professional, technical and scientific classes. Arrangements were agreed with the Fulton Committee that further detailed evidence would be submitted as appropriate and the Institution would have the right to reply to evidence submitted by the Treasury and other civil service departments.

A decision was also taken to commission a symposium on the relationship between professionals and administrators in Britain and in civil services abroad. The symposium was under the editorship of Professor F. F. Ridley, professor of political theory and institutions at the University of Liverpool. The papers, which covered the civil services of Australia, France, West Germany, Sweden and the USA, clearly influenced the Fulton Committee.

The Institution arranged for the contributors to prepare their studies and findings in a form suitable for wider publication. To them were added an initial chapter by the Institution's deputy general secretary, Tom Profitt, setting the

British scene, and a concluding chapter by Professor Ridley dealing with the wider aspects of the problem of the relationship between generalists and specialists. The symposium was then published as a book entitled *Specialists and Generalists*. Its commercial publication was handled by Allen & Unwin but a special clothbound edition at a reduced price was made available to Institution members.

The symposium, published after Fulton reported in the autumn of 1968, received excellent reviews. The Institution was also congratulated on its initiative in producing such a symposium. Thus, for example, said *The Economist*: 'In preparation for the Fulton Committee, the Institution of Professional Civil Servants, a highly sophisticated trade union, did more than make its case; it commissioned from a group of academics . . . a series of studies on the position of professional civil servants in various countries . . .'

TREASURY EVIDENCE

The Treasury submitted its evidence to the Fulton Committee in May 1966. It envisaged only minor changes in the structure of the service which included merging the administrative and executive grades and opening up greater opportunities for suitable officers in the scientific and professional classes at the senior levels of management. Commenting briefly on the evidence when it first appeared, the Institution said: 'It is not unfair criticism to say that the paper does little more than preserve the concept of a civil service governed by a *corps d'élite* of administrators and executives drawn primarily from the arts side.'

The Institution prepared a considered reply to the Treasury's evidence which it submitted to the Fulton Committee. It said that the major changes in the role of the government since the Northcote–Trevelyan Report, and the increasing use of scientific, technological, economic and social policies which these, activities entailed, demanded a radical reorganisation of the civil service, not a minor modification of the present system as suggested by the Treasury.

> Over the last century the government has become involved in the complex economic, technological and social problems of modern society. Despite this, the top structure of the civil service has changed hardly at all. Management and administration at the higher levels are still almost exclusively the monopoly of the administrative class. Implicit in the Treasury's proposals is the view that this state of affairs will continue. A major question for the committee, however, is whether or not the near-monopoly of top management by the administrative class should be perpetuated.

The Institution pointed out that under the Treasury's proposals there was no realistic prospect that the careers of specialists would approach those of the administrative and executive grades, and that only a very few would reach the senior management levels where the Treasury's more 'open' structure would apply.

INSTITUTION EVIDENCE

The NEC spared no effort in the preparation and submission of the Institution's evidence to the Fulton Committee. In all, nine written submissions were made and oral evidence was given on two occasions. The preliminary evidence to the committee was submitted in November 1966; in this the Institution drew attention to some of the important problems with which it hoped the committee would deal. Following this the Institution gave oral evidence. In January 1967 the Institution submitted its main evidence.

The evidence began by outlining the changing relationship of the civil service with the community. It said that the main defect of the existing civil service was that it was supposed to fill a positive role in the community with an organisation and atmosphere inimical to that role. It added that the process of government was shrouded in secrecy and should become more open.

> Our thesis is that if government is to fulfil its new role then the machine in the government's hand is inadequate. It is inadequate in a number of ways; but the underlying reason is that it was designed in the nineteenth century for the *laissez-faire* state in which the least government was the best government. Its structure and management are still basically those of the nineteenth century.

It recommended that professional staff should have more responsibility placed on them and that their relationship with the general civil service classes should be changed. There should be completely unified hierarchies. The Institution not only argued in favour of a unified higher civil service but urged, in addition, that all posts above the broad level of administrative principal should be included within this higher group. Posts should then be filled by those best able to do the job.

The Institution urged that at lower levels in the civil service the class structure should be simplified. The three classes dealing with scientific matters should be merged and there should also be a merging of the works, technical and drawing office classes. It was suggested that within this lower structure there should be greater flexibility and easier movement from one group to another.

The Institution recommended that within the reformed civil service provision should be made for recruitment at several levels. Entrants with equivalent qualifications, whatever their class, should have similar career expectations. Much greater emphasis, it was urged, should be placed on management training and facilities should be provided for civil servants to acquire qualifications within the service.

At the 1967 conference there was a major debate on the Institution's main evidence. Some felt that the evidence had gone too far in setting out suggestions for integrating classes. Others felt that it should have gone further and advocated an entirely unified grading structure. Others again felt there were some elements of the evidence which they could not support. However, despite these reservations the overwhelming mood of conference was of support for the proposals put to the Fulton Committee and congratulations on producing the document.

Later in 1967 the Institution submitted supplementary evidence on the creation of a social scientists group. In its main evidence it had referred to the recent formation of the economist class whose qualifications were often similar to those in the research officer class. The Treasury later submitted a note dealing with the economist, statistician and research officer classes in which it proposed no change. The Institution therefore took the opportunity to expand on the brief reference in the main evidence. It proposed that a new group be formed comprising the research officer, economist and statistician classes, and some other individuals or classes, including the psychologists and departmental classes such as the planning grades in the Ministry of Housing and Local Government. The social science group, it was suggested, should be graded in parallel with the administrative group to provide similar career prospects. The Treasury submitted further evidence against the Institution's proposal and the Institution submitted a rejoinder.

A supplementary paper was also submitted to the Fulton Committee on the particular problems of professional accountants in the service. Again, account was taken of a note by the Treasury to the committee on the same subject. The Institution felt that the Treasury had merely tinkered with the problem. The Institution evidence contrasted the wide role in higher management levels of accountants outside the service with their limited role in the service where they were engaged mainly in financial and cost investigation. In its main evidence the Institution had noted the absurdity whereby

> posts in the vast field of general financial management and control are currently restricted to members of the administrative/executive class. Professional accountants are not even allowed to apply for these posts – simply because they are members of the professional accountants class. We are not saying that such posts should in future be reserved for accountants: instead, we propose that a man should not be debarred from a middle or higher post of financial control simply because he is a professional accountant.

The most urgent need, said the Institution, was for a fundamental reappraisal of the role of the professional accountant in the civil service. The paper stated that they should be used on financial policy and its implementation, management accounting, commercial accounting, internal audit and insolvency services, and should be eligible for general management posts. Their career expectations should match those of the administrative class.

Early in 1968 the Institution submitted supplementary evidence to the Fulton Committee comparing the career values of the administrative, works group and scientific officer classes. The Institution suggested that the academic or professional qualifications required for direct entrants to these three classes were much the same. They then went on to calculate the amount of salary earned in each of the three classes by a direct entrant over a normal career. The calculations were based upon statistics issued by the Civil Service Commission and the Treasury's Central Statistics Department. For the purpose of 'a normal career' the Institution took the median ages of those promoted to each of the various grades. Each career was taken to last from age 23 years to 60 years. The figures calculated by the Institution showed that for the administrative class the career expectation of earnings ranged from about £125,000 to £131,000. For the scientific officer it ranged from just over £84,000 to just under £96,000, and for the works group it ranged from just over £92,000 to just over £94,500.

The Institution also produced figures on the percentage of the three classes reaching the higher grades in their particular class. In the administrative class nearly 47 per cent reached the grade of assistant secretary or above. Among scientific officers the number who reached the same minimum level was only

23·6 per cent, and among the works group it was as low as 8·7 per cent. More than 15 per cent of the administrative class reached the grade of under-secretary or above. The equivalent figure for scientific officers was 2·3 per cent and for the works group 0·2 per cent. These figures, said the Institution, told only too clearly of the few opportunities to reach the highest grades of the civil service offered to the scientific officer and works group classes. The Institution pointed out that the calculations were not foolproof, but the comparisons had a common source in official statistics. While the calculations might not have been accurate to the last pound they pointed clearly to the inferior career prospects and earnings of the works group and scientific officer classes in comparison with the administrative class.

The Treasury replied to this supplementary evidence from the Institution. It agreed that the administrative class entrant had the prospect of earning more and of reaching a higher level in the civil service, but it did not believe that such a comparison had much validity or relevance. It saw no inherent reason why the career prospects of those qualified at professional or graduate level ought to be the same. It was not the qualification of the entrant which determined prospects but the nature of the work performed. The Treasury also said that the selection process was different. In the case of the administrative class it was designed to test the candidate's potential for general management. The Treasury also challenged the view that the academic standards required for professional qualifications by the Council of Engineering Institutions were as high as those required for the administrative class.

OTHER CIVIL SERVICE EVIDENCE

The view that class barriers in the civil service should be eliminated was also put forward to the Fulton Committee in evidence submitted by the SCS, representing the executive class, and by the CSCA, representing the clerical class. The Society said that the barrier separating the administrative and executive classes should disappear and suggested that the old distinction between administrative and executive functions was no longer realistic. The merger of two classes into a new management grading structure would facilitate the more flexible use of staff. The Society also urged that there should be a merger between the Civil Service Commission and the management and pay divisions of the Treasury. It saw no justification for separating responsibility for recruitment from the central management of the civil service. The CSCA suggested that better opportunities should be offered to clerical class recruits. Opportunities for promotion should be improved and more extended facilities should be provided for training.

The First Division Association, representing the administrative class, had something rather different to say to the Fulton Committee. The administrative class, it said, was uniquely able to perform its function because of its broad background, intellectual capacity and experience in operating in government. The essential function of the staff it represented, said the FDA, was to bring together the disparate issues involved in taking major decisions of policy, to advise on what these decisions should be and subsequently to put them into effect. The FDA was not sympathetic to the suggestion that top posts should be opened to specialists. The role of the specialist in decision-making was, it argued, to speak with professional experience on the scientific or technical merits and implications of a particular course of action. It did not believe that this role could be combined with the administrative work of bringing to bear, on all or any major issue, all the wider considerations that were necessary. A specialist who became fully able to perform the administrative role thereby ceased to be a specialist and would in time need other specialists to provide the element of expert knowledge that was essential to the dialogue. The FDA concluded its evidence with a firm statement of its belief that the administrative class provided a basis on which to build the future management of the civil service. It also reaffirmed its belief that even at the higher levels of the civil service there was a distinction between the function of general management and the contribution of specialists.

THE FULTON REPORT

The report of the Fulton Committee was published in June 1968. It was very critical of the civil service. It said that the structure and practices of the service had not kept up with changing tasks and the service was now in need of fundamental change. It listed six main defects.

First, the service was still essentially based on the philosophy of the amateur (or 'generalist' or 'all-rounder'). This was most evident in the administrative class. This concept had most damaging consequences. The cult of the generalist was obsolete at all levels and in all parts of the service.

Secondly, the system of classes in the service seriously impeded its work. There were forty-seven general classes whose members worked in most government departments, and over 1,400 departmental classes. Each civil servant was recruited to a particular class and his membership of that class determined his prospects. Such a rigid compartmentalism led to the setting-up of cumbersome organisational forms and seriously hampered the civil service in adapting itself to new tasks. It also prevented the best use of individual talent, contributed to the inequality of promotion prospects, caused frustration and resentment, and impeded the entry into wider management of those well fitted for it.

Thirdly, many scientists, engineers and members of other specialist classes were given neither the full responsibilities and corresponding authority which they ought to have nor the opportunities which ought to be provided for them. Too often they were organised in a separate hierarchy while the policy aspects of the work were reserved to a parallel group of generalist administrators. The access of the specialist to higher management and policy-making was restricted. In the civil service a wider and more important role should be opened up for specialists trained and equipped for it.

Fourthly, too few civil servants were skilled managers. Few members of the administrative class actually saw themselves as managers. They tended to think of themselves as advisers on policy to people above them rather than as managers of the administrative machine below them. Scientists and other specialists were also open to the same criticism. Not enough of them had been trained in management.

Fifthly, there was not enough contact between the service and the rest of the community. Most civil servants spent their entire working lives in the service and it was not surprising, therefore, that they had little direct and systematic experience of the daily life and thought of other people. Another element in this remoteness was the social and educational composition of the civil service. Direct recruitment to the administrative class since the war had not produced the widening of its social and educational base that might have been expected. The public interest suffered from this isolation, which hindered a full understanding of contemporary problems and restricted the free flow of men, knowledge and ideas between the service and the outside world.

Finally, the Fulton Committee said that to some extent the urgent need for fundamental reform had been obscured by the very considerable strengths of the civil service, notably its capacity for improvisation. There were also exceptionally able men and women at all levels of the service with a strong sense of public duty. The integrity and impartiality of the civil service were unquestioned and the country did not fully recognise how impressively conscientious many civil servants were in the personal service they gave to the public. It was of high importance, said the Fulton Committee, that these and other qualities should be preserved. The basic guiding principle which should govern the future development of the civil service was the simple one: look at the job first. The civil service should continuously review the tasks it was called upon to perform and the possible ways in which it might perform them. It should then think out what new skills and kinds of men and women were needed and how these people could be found, trained and employed.

In addition to its main criticisms and suggestions for a unified classless structure, the Fulton Committee made a number of other important recommendations affecting existing civil servants. It called for greater flexibility of movement between the civil service and other areas of employment, much more developed training facilities inside the service, the establishment of a civil service college to provide major training courses in administration and management for both administrators and specialists, more short-term appointments for fixed periods, the further development of transferable pension arrangements to facilitate mobility between the service and outside employment, pensions for temporary staff, and wider powers to retire on pension those who had ceased to give satisfactory performance. The committee also recommended the setting-up of a new Civil Service Department to take over from the Treasury its pay and management functions in relation to the civil service. The head of the new department would be the head of the civil service and would be responsible directly to the Prime Minister, but on day-to-day matters the Prime Minister should have the assistance of a Cabinet colleague.

RESPONSE TO THE FULTON REPORT

The report of the Fulton Committee was welcomed by the Institution. The general secretary said that it provided confirmation of principles and policies which the Institution had advocated throughout the fifty years of its existence. Most of the recommendations should be accepted without ado. Rigidities which the existing class system had created in the civil service should be removed at once. The principle of the best man for the job should be introduced immediately. The general secretary then introduced a note of caution. Not all civil servants were equally happy with the proposals and some of the criticisms were resented. The immediate aim should be to secure a joint report of the National Whitley

Council before the end of the year setting out a blueprint and a timetable for action. In the autumn of 1968 the Institution arranged for a large number of meetings to be held in many different provincial centres to discuss the Fulton Report. A special meeting for the London membership was held in Caxton Hall, Westminster. STCS members were invited to all these meetings.

Soon after the publication of the Fulton Report, the National Whitley Council began its examination of the various recommendations and the possibility of implementing a number of proposed changes as soon as possible. In particular, priority was given to the implementation of the principle of accountable management, the abolition of class barriers and the simplification of the class and grading structure. The Official Side also indicated that they proposed to establish a new Civil Service Department (CSD). The new department came into existence on 1 November 1968. The Civil Service Commission was integrated with it, but it was decided by the government that the Commissioners would continue to be independent on all matters relating to the selection of individuals. The government also said that the Commission would continue to make its own annual report to the Crown.

In a debate on the Fulton Report in the House of Commons held in the second half of November 1969 the Prime Minister said that the government, in addition to setting up the new CSD, had also accepted the recommendation for the establishment of a civil service college. Another important recommendation already accepted by the government, said Mr Wilson, related to the abolition of the class system in the civil service.

In the spring of 1969 the National Whitley Council Joint Committee on the Fulton Report published a statement of the progress made in the first six months in the consideration of the various recommendations. It outlined the decisions already taken by the National Whitley Council. Ten thousand copies of the report of the joint committee were distributed to members of the Institution. The circulation of this record of activity on the Fulton Report helped to make possible an informed discussion on the subject at the 1969 annual conference of the Institution.

In his main address to the 1969 annual conference the general secretary said that members would be deceiving themselves if they thought that all that was now necessary was to sit back and wait for beneficial change. The Fulton Report could be the herald of a new deal, but it would only be so if civil servants themselves made it possible. For the Institution it was vital that action should be taken on the finding that scientists, engineers and other specialists were frequently given neither the full responsibilities and opportunities nor the corresponding authority they ought to have. The conference proceeded to welcome in principle the Fulton recommendations and urged their rapid implementation. It called on the government to ensure that reform was not impeded by lack of manpower or finance.

21 Trade Union Structure – a Time of Change

The many developments in the Institution's environment, including incomes policy, the Fulton Report and changes in the machinery of government, had profound implications for the Institution's internal structure and for its relationships with other unions. Incomes policy forced the issue of TUC affiliation once more to the forefront, while the reorganisation of major departments and the establishment of the Post Office Corporation produced organisational changes in the Staff Side and within the Institution.

MEMBERSHIP GROWTH

During the period the Institution also experienced a massive growth in membership from 55,142 in 1964 to 85,617 at the end of 1969, 9,000 of which was attributable to the transfer of engagements of the STCS. The Institution also gained members from the decision to recruit in the ARC and the Scottish Research Institutes. By the time of the annual conference in 1965 there were already 1,000 members in the ARC alone.

The growth in membership, however, did not simply reflect new areas of recruitment and the amalgamation; it also was the result of a sustained effort to improve organisation and membership. In 1966 discussions were held with a number of large branches which appeared to be having recruitment difficulties, concentrating on a detailed analysis of their problems and consideration of specific proposals to assist them in overcoming them. Moreover, in September of that year all branches were asked to consider their organisation and recruitment activities against certain criteria. Among these were that each branch should have a membership officer, should identify and approach all potential members, should have a representative in every office and building, check communications to the membership and see that 'membership and recruitment' was a regular item on the agenda.

Another important factor in maintaining and increasing membership was the introduction of the 'check off'. In 1965 the Treasury entered into an agreement with the Staff Side to enable members of recognised civil service unions to pay their union subscription by monthly deduction from pay. The scheme started from 1 January 1966. It proved to be of great help in reducing the number of members who at the end of each financial year had to be 'written off' because of non-payment of subscriptions. In the Institution, for example, it was normal for some 8,000 or 9,000 members to be written off only to be reinstated subsequently. This was a time-consuming and expensive procedure. By the end of 1968 more than 70 per cent of the membership had agreed that their subscriptions to the Institution should be deducted monthly from their pay.

The rate of subscriptions was also, as always, a factor in membership growth and in 1965 the NEC tried to reform the subscription rate structure. At the

1965 conference an attempt was made to introduce a range of subscriptions based upon the grading of the membership according to their subsistence allowance entitlement under civil service regulations. Up to that time there were only two rates of subscription in the Institution, one for members over 21 years of age and another for members under 21 years of age. The proposal that differential subscriptions should be introduced based on subsistence classes was narrowly defeated on a card vote by 27,814 to 24,238. Another proposal to introduce a student rate subscription, equivalent to half of the existing lower rate of subscription, was, however, adopted. It was agreed that the new student rate of subscription should be offered immediately to all student and apprentice draughtsmen. During the course of the debate it was pointed out that the STCS had been much more successful in recruiting young draughtsmen than the Institution. The STCS was able to recruit approximately three out of four of all young draughtsmen under 21 years of age. The proposal that there should be a lower student rate subscription was designed partly to make the Institution more attractive to young draughtsmen.

At the 1968 annual conference the delegates agreed to increase the rates of subscription. The rate for members over 21 years of age was increased from 1 January 1969 from 7s to 9s 6d per month. The rate for those under 21 years of age was increased by 1s 2d from 3s 4d to 4s 6d per month. The increase in subscriptions was overdue. Expenditure had exceeded income in 1967 by more than £6,000 and in 1968 this annual rate of deficit had risen to more than £20,000. The subscription rates were unaltered between 1964 and 1969.

The Institution's conference the following year, 1969, decided to introduce an intermediate subscription rate. The new rate came into effect on 1 January 1970 and applied to members aged 21 and over who were in grades entitled to the class C subsistence allowance under civil service regulations. The new intermediate subscription was 7s 6d a month.

CLOSER WORKING

With the proposed changes in the civil service following the Fulton Report, increasing attention was given by the active membership of the Institution to possible changes in the structure of the trade union movement within the civil service. In an article printed in *State Service*, the general secretary said that ever since the Fulton Report was published it had been obvious that the time would come for a fundamental review of staff associations in the civil service. The organisation of staff associations was very much based on the traditional class organisation of the civil service. With the abolition of classes a new situation was being created and the staff associations would serve their members badly if they were not as ready to reform their own organisations as they were to see changes in the structure of the civil service itself. The most important organisational change affecting the Institution during the second half of the 1960s was the amalgamation with the STCS.

During the second half of the 1960s, however, before the Fulton Report, the Institution was already making a determined attempt to improve its relations with the few civil service organisations where there were still areas of friction. These were principally the STCS, AGSRO and the CSU. On 10 December

1965 an agreement on demarcation and closer working was signed with the CSU. The agreement stated that both organisations accepted that it was essential to have unity among officers in the same class or grade. Each undertook, therefore, to recommend strongly that any officer in membership in a class or grade which, according to the demarcation agreement, was appropriate to the other organisation, should transfer his membership. They also agreed to keep each other informed of negotiations or activities which might affect the other's membership.

Relations with AGSRO proved more difficult. The irritation centred on the recruitment and representation of radio technicians and telecommunications staff. In 1965 discussions with a view to amalgamation took place but the proposal was rejected by the AGSRO conference. In 1966 the Institution offered to open formal discussions if the AGSRO executive agreed. Discussions, however, never really got off the ground. Early in 1967 AGSRO sought to recruit telecommunications technical staff in civil aviation where the Institution had recognition for TTOs and the CSU for radio technicians. The Institution therefore withdrew the invitation to amalgamation talks. Later in the year further disagreements occurred in the Navy Department where AGSRO sought to represent chargemen and recorders who were graded as technical class III and therefore within the Institution's field of representation.

In the meantime close and friendly relations continued with the CSU and in 1967 agreement was reached on a demarcation issue which formed an appendix to the main agreement of 1965. The agreement referred to radio technicians and telecommunications grades. Both organisations agreed on the desirability of having a single organisation representing radio and telecommunications grades in the Air Force Department and the Board of Trade (Civil Aviation) and the CSU agreed that in those departments the Institution would recruit radio technicians who were not members of the CSU. In return the Institution continued to accept the CSU's rights on national recognition for radio technicians in the Treasury, and existing departmental recognition. A standing joint committee was set up to co-ordinate the policies of the two organisations in those fields. In 1968 the CSU abrogated part of the demarcation agreement although friendly co-operation continued in other areas. During that year the CSU also reached a comprehensive demarcation agreement with AGSRO.

The Institution's relationship with AGSRO improved during 1968. Differences between the two organisations in the Navy Department and in the Board of Trade were resolved when AGSRO achieved sole recognition for radio technicians. Informal discussions also began on the possibility of reaching agreement in the broader radio technician and TTO area. Some argued that the proposed agreement would, in the long run, favour AGSRO. On the other hand, it was argued that an agreement could pave the way, and was intended to do so, for further developments with AGSRO which could eventually lead to amalgamation. In this respect the agreement had to be seen in the Fulton context.

Thus in 1969 an agreement was concluded between the two organisations to form what was described as a consortium. This consortium was vested with authority for negotiating on all matters affecting telecommunication technical officers and radio technicians. The agreement said that both organisations recognised that it was essential for them to act together. They also agreed to observe the TUC Bridlington principles in relation to the recruitment of new members. This meant that both organisations undertook to inquire of applicants for membership whether they were or had been members of the other organisation. Where the answer was yes, the consent of the other organisation would be sought before recruitment took place.

In 1968 the Institution also initiated discussions with a number of unions representing industrial grades in the civil service with a view to providing closer working relations. Towards the end of the year an agreement was signed with the Boilermakers, Painters and Decorators, the Woodworkers, the Engineering Workers, the General and Municipal Workers' Union and the Transport and General Workers Union. Closer working was essential because of the reorganisation of the industrial grades following the NBPI report *The Pay of Industrial Civil Servants*, and because of the likely changes in the structure of the non-industrial grades following the Fulton Report. It was also thought at that time that the 'industrial' and 'non-industrial' distinction might be abolished. The agreement stated that the industrial unions would represent craftsmen grades up to and including first-line supervisors. Grades above first-line supervisors were to be represented by the Institution. The agreement also dealt with certain special but limited areas where the distinction was not so clear. The agreement said that the types of work in question involved 'construction, maintenance or inspection of novel or complex equipment, often without close supervision, and required the ability to apply theoretical principles derived from a systematic knowledge of science or technology in addition to the exercise of craft skills'. Provision was made for determining the trade union membership of such staff. The agreement also provided machinery for dealing with disputes and for arbitration on them. Any issue which might arise during the transitional period before the long-term pattern of organisation was determined was to be settled by discussion within a newly formed joint liaison committee.

AMALGAMATION – THE STCS

By far the most important development, however, during this period was the growing close and friendly relationship between the Institution and the STCS. This relationship led ultimately to amalgamation but was preceded by long negotiations.

A first attempt at agreement on arrangements for closer co-operation was made in 1965 but was turned down by the STCS annual conference. The Institution, however, persisted in its efforts to establish a good working relationship with the STCS and further discussions were opened.

Both organisations were conscious that the Fulton Committee might recommend changes in the structure of classes which would make much closer working inevitable. Indeed, the Institution NEC had passed a resolution at its meeting in April 1966 which stated:

The general secretary, in consultation with the drawing office group, be authorised to continue exploratory discussions to seek an arrangement whereby, if the Fulton Committee indicated a merger of the technical classes, drawing office class or any other classes represented by the two organisations, there should be a serious attempt to consider amalgamation. There should be no final commitment without further reference to the National Executive Committee.

For the STCS, however, the issue was a complex one. It was clear that the STCS could not survive for long as an independent organisation. Yet many STCS members were still opposed to rejoining the Institution for deep-seated historical reasons. Some were reluctant to join an organisation which in their view represented the 'management' grades in the drawing office context. More important, however, was the fact that the prospect of eventual re-entry into the Draughtsmen's and Allied Technicians' Association (DATA), originally cut off in 1927, was still a live one and formed a much more attractive option for many members of the STCS.

Fundamentally the real issue, as Mr Cyril Cooper, the general secretary of the STCS, later pointed out, was 'the fairly straightforward trade union one, as between those who wanted one union to cover a broad field of employment and those who saw the future in one union for all those having a skill in common'. At the time of the eventual amalgamation between the Institution and the STCS Mr Cooper generously commented that it was interesting to note that the current trend in Britain, with which the STCS would be conforming, was in accord with the former concept, which the Institution had been supporting throughout.

There were, however, two specific factors which brought home to the STCS membership the realisation that amalgamation with the Institution was the only viable option. The first was that DATA was in the process of entering into a loose form of amalgamation with other engineering unions, principally the AEU, to form the Amalgamated Union of Engineering Workers. This meant that DATA itself was following the 'industrial' rather than the 'craft' option. This made DATA a much less attractive merger proposition for the STCS; for it emphasised that the focus of DATA's membership and activity within the new amalgamation would be in the private engineering industry rather than the public services. Civil service draughtsmen in that context would be an exceedingly small minority interest. The second major factor was the report of the Fulton Committee which, if implemented, would herald the end of the drawing office class and their merger with the technical and professional classes within the civil service.

At the 1967 conference of the Institution a resolution was carried instructing the NEC 'to do all in its power to bring to a successful conclusion amalgamation with the Society of Technical Civil Servants'. A joint committee was established with the STCS to explore the future relationship of the two organisations and shortly before the 1968 conference it produced a report which recommended amalgamation and set out the basis on which it should take place. The conference then carried the following resolution.

That this conference approves the principles and suggestions contained in the report of the Joint Committee on the future of the Society of Technical Civil Servants and the Institution of Professional Civil Servants regarding the proposed amalgamation of the two bodies.

Conference, subject to guarantees that the staff of the Society are fully and freely deployable within this Institution's field at the time of the amalgamation, accordingly

(a) directs the National Executive Committee to proceed with the discussions on the basis of this report with a view to reaching an early agreement on terms for a transfer of engagements;

(b) confirms the authority of the National Executive Committee to approve and accept this transfer of engagements;

(c) notes that under Section 3 of the Trade Union (Amalgamations, etc.) Act, 1964, the National Executive Committee is empowered to alter the Institution's rules so far as is necessary to give effect to the Instrument of Transfer and instructs the National Executive Committee to exercise such powers as requisite.

At a special conference of the STCS in December 1968 a resolution in favour of amalgamation with the Institution was carried by ninety-seven votes to twenty-three. The amalgamation proposals were subsequently put to a referendum of the STCS membership which produced a substantial majority in favour – 5,603 votes for and 1,350 votes against.

Under the terms of the Instrument of Transfer the members of the Society became members of the Institution on 23 June 1969. For an introductory period of three years the former STCS members constituted a separate division within the Institution. During this period the Executive Committee of the STCS division continued to deal with matters of direct concern to the membership of the division and the division held its own annual conference. It also remained affiliated to the TUC for this period. The NEC of the Institution and the Executive Committee of the STCS division then proceeded to arrange for the integration of the division within the Institution. The Society brought an increase in membership to the Institution of more than 9,000. It represented by far the most significant amalgamation in the history of the Institution.

UNION REORGANISATION IN THE POST OFFICE

In the White Paper on the transfer of the Post Office to independent corporation status the government made it clear that it was seeking and expecting a rationalisation of trade union structure in the Post Office. At that time there were twenty unions with members in the Post Office. The first response was for the four largest and exclusively Post Office unions to make a bid to represent all staff in the Post Office. This move, not surprisingly, disturbed the other unions, particularly those such as the Institution who represented middle and senior management grades.

The same four unions, the Union of Post Office Workers (UPW), the Post Office Engineering Union (POEU), the Post Office Management Staffs Association (POMSA) and the Association of Post Office Executives (APOE), some of whom had already amalgamated with other sections of Post Office staff, considerably modified their approach in 1968. They joined together to form the Council of Post Office Unions (COPOU), which then replaced the existing Post Office staff sides. Invitations were sent to other unions, including the Institution and the STCS, who formed a joint committee to look after the interests of their drawing office members in the Post Office, inviting them to become members of COPOU on certain conditions. The most important of the conditions was that each union should present to its members the option of transferring to a COPOU organisation within a period of two years from September 1969.

These proposals were put to the Post Office group of the Institution and the Post Office Section Committee of the STCS, and both accepted them. Thus both the Institution and the STCS achieved a seat on COPOU although without the right to vote for officers or to have membership of the finance and general purposes committee. In 1968 the Institution and STCS were recognised by the new Post Office 'Board. Towards the end of 1968 informal discussions on closer working were being arranged between the Institution and the SPOE and later with the POEU.

RELATIONS WITH THE AScW

Outside the civil service the signing of a new agreement between the Institution and the AScW in 1966 brought to an end an unhappy period in relations between the two organisations. It provided for close co-operation and defined the respective spheres of influence of the two unions. The AScW was recognised as the appropriate body to undertake negotiations for scientific and ancillary scientific staff in private employment. The Institution was similarly recognised as the sole body to undertake negotiations for professional, scientific and technical staff in the civil service. In certain areas of the public service, as distinct from the civil service strictly defined, the two organisations agreed to divide spheres of influence. These were clearly laid out in two appendices to the agreement, Appendix A covering those non-civil service bodies whose specialist staff would be represented by the Institution, and Appendix B those similar bodies whose staff would be represented by the AScW. The new agreement, which replaced that of 1947, was strengthened by a provision for resort to independent arbitration in the event of a dispute.

In 1968 the AScW merged with ASSET to form the Association of Scientific, Technical and Managerial Staffs (ASTMS). Together they represented 85,000 members. The Institution's general secretary welcomed the move as an excellent development. He hoped that it would lead to much more effective trade union organisation outside the public service which at that time was painfully weak. The chairman of the Institution, Dan Dorey, also referred to the amalgamation with hope at the 1968 annual delegates conference and described how

> Too often in the past and especially since Priestley, the lack of organisation of employees similar to ourselves has reflected itself in the evidence obtained by the Pay Research Unit. It is not going to be easy for those in the private sector to become organised. There is a definite policy against such organisation in many enterprises. We must therefore ensure that we are strong enough to give assistance to the specialists in the private sector whenever we are able.

The agreements made with the AScW in 1966 continued with the ASTMS.

TUC AFFILIATION – FURTHER DEBATES

After the rejection by ballot vote in 1964 of the proposal to affiliate to the TUC the issue was not formally raised again until the 1966 conference. For supporters of affiliation, however, the case for affiliation appeared to be becoming stronger. Thus, for example, during the debate on incomes policy at the 1965 conference the general secretary pointed out that the Institution had played no part whatever in the formulation or development of the proposals agreed between the government, the employers and the unions. This, he said, placed the Institution at a serious disadvantage. The Institution was the largest organisation catering for scientific, professional and technical staff in the country and it was important that the Institution's voice should be heard directly in the most influential councils of the nation. The fact that the Institution had not been able to participate in these developments was due to the decision of the membership not to affiliate to the TUC. In working out the new policy the government, understandably, had sought consultation with the main representative organisations of employers and employees and not with the very many separate bodies representing employers and workers in different trades and occupations.

This, however, did not convince the opponents of affiliation. In his opening address to the 1966 conference the chairman, Mr R. G. Fall, made it clear that in his view the introduction of a formal incomes policy with TUC support had strengthened rather than weakened the case for opposition to affiliation. He suggested that during the pay pause civil service staff associations not affiliated to the TUC had fared no worse than those that were affiliated. Secondly, under an early warning system for pay claims the necessity for affiliated unions to submit claims first to the TUC would bring more delay but no more support.

As at the 1966 conference the Metropolitan Police Receivers Office Professional Association urged that there should be a further referendum on the TUC affiliation. Their spokesman said that since the previous referendum several important matters affecting the interests of the membership of the Institution had fallen within the area of influence of the TUC. It was also significant that certain other unions, for example, NALGO, had decided to affiliate to the TUC.

The general secretary, speaking on behalf of the NEC, said that the time had now come to give a lead on the question of affiliation. The case for affiliation was stronger than it was three years ago. There were many factors that had contributed to the change, but by far the most important were the significant and substantial developments in economic organisation and incomes policy. The general secretary said that he did not believe that a referendum was the best way to decide the issue. He invited conference to reject the proposal that a further referendum should be held and instead to support a proposal that a statement on affiliation be prepared by the NEC for consideration by the 1967 conference. In the vote both the proposal that there should be a referendum and the proposal suggested by the NEC were defeated. The voting against the proposal put by the NEC was 33,042 to 20,369.

In the February 1967 issue of *State Service* the general secretary returned to the question of TUC affiliation. He said that at meetings during recent months and in correspondence a considerable number of members had asked for an explanation of the views of the NEC. He recalled the substance of the speech he had made at the previous conference when he indicated that the NEC believed that the time had come to give a lead on the question of affiliation to the TUC. The general secretary also recalled that in his speech to the conference he had put forward arguments against deciding the issue by a referendum. In the first place, many members, indeed one-third of the members on the occasion of the last referendum, did not vote. In the Institution there was a carefully devised democratic machine and this machine was not just for the purpose of voting. Speaking for the NEC, he said:

We believe that it should, and that it does, and that it is absolutely vital for it to, provide for discussion at every level in the Institution . . . We believe that machinery is the right one on which to take decisions on any important policy issue. We believe that the proper authority for taking the decision should be conference, and that there is no better method than the one which has been evolved through the years for conducting our business. We believe therefore that there ought not to be a referendum either now or later. We believe that the referendum is an unsatisfactory and unnecessary expense.

This statement brought a letter of dissent from the former chairman of the Institution, Mr R. G. Fall. He said that TUC performance during the period of pay restraint had reinforced his opposition to affiliation. The TUC had not pressed their criticisms of the government 'for fear of rocking the political boat'. Mr Fall also objected strongly to the general secretary's views on a referendum. The members, said Mr Fall, should have a direct say in determining whether or not the Institution should affiliate to the TUC.

At the 1967 conference a major debate took place on the question of TUC affiliation. The first issue was whether the Institution was, in principle, in favour of affiliation. The second issue concerned the method by which the decision should be taken; whether by referendum or by the conference. The viewpoint of the NEC was that the conference should take the decision but the decision should be open to reaffirmation or rejection by the 1968 conference. This procedure, it was argued, would allow the issue to be discussed thoroughly by the membership through the Institution's normal democratic procedures. After considerable debate the conference rejected the motion calling for a referendum and accepted the NEC view. However, on the substantive issue of whether the Institution should affiliate to the TUC the motion was lost by a very small margin, 27,292 to 27,017, on a card vote.

Such a close vote served not to close the issue but to stimulate further discussion inside the Institution about the advantages and disadvantages of TUC affiliation. The result was that the NEC decided to prepare and publish a special report setting out the arguments for and against affiliation. This was circulated to the membership towards the end of 1967. The report not only outlined the main arguments of those in favour and of those opposed to TUC affiliation but also described the structure and work of the TUC. It also listed the many public service and non-manual trade unions already affiliated to the TUC.

Following the circulation of this special report the NEC issued its own recommendation in favour of affiliation. The principal argument in favour of affiliation, it said, was that through the TUC the Institution could have a voice with the government on the many national policies which affected the interests and well-being of members. There were a number of organisations which the government had established through which the interests of employees were represented by the TUC. The NEC also said that it was satisfied that the Institution's sovereignty would be unimpaired by affiliation to the TUC. Other organisations, including civil service unions, had shown that affiliation was possible without party political bias. The conclusion of the NEC was

(1) There is a strong case in favour of the Institution affiliating to the TUC.
(2) (*a*) This can be done without prejudice to the fundamental principle that the Institution must remain completely free of party political bias.
   (*b*) To dispel any possible doubt, the Institution's position should be made clear in any application for affiliation and on any occasion should the need arise.
(3) The Institution should therefore seek affiliation provided a motion to that effect is carried by conference by a two-thirds majority, or by succeeding conferences with simple majorities.

The NEC also publicised a statement made by the Conservative spokesman on labour matters, Mr Godber, on the occasion of the affiliation of NALGO to the TUC. Mr Godber said:

NALGO's recent affiliation to the TUC is of great significance for the trade union movement. It is also important for all of us interested in trade union organisation and the present and future role of trade unions in this country. Conservative policy is to encourage and support democratic trade unionism 100 per cent; and over the past thirteen years actions have shown that this support is not a matter of words. We certainly welcome any move which will produce greater cohesion and co-ordination with the trade union movement.

In recent times successive Conservative governments have worked closely with the TUC on many problems of national importance. There have been new links in the economic sphere through NEDC; the continued co-operation on the Ministry of Labour's National Joint Advisory Council; and we have worked together in many fields of industrial activity. NALGO's affiliation to the TUC will undoubtedly help to link its members closely with many collective activities of government and industry, and should thus prove of value to all concerned.

At the 1968 conference the issue was debated again. This time the conference passed by 34,965 card votes to 29,391 an NEC-sponsored resolution that consideration should be given to affiliation to the TUC. However, an amendment proposed by eleven branches was also carried by 37,225 card votes to 27,356 that a referendum should be held.

THE REFERENDUM

The terms of the referendum were drawn up in association with National Opinion Polls Ltd. Instead of a simple question for or against TUC affiliation, the ballot form included six questions:

Question 1   Do you agree or disagree that it is 'desirable and important' for the IPCS to have more influence over the formulation of national policies which affect the interests of its members?

Question 2   Do you think that affiliation to the TUC will increase the influence of the IPCS, or reduce it, or make no difference?

Question 3   Do you think it is possible or not possible for organisations which are affiliated to the TUC to maintain their political neutrality?

Question 4   Do you think the IPCS would or would not maintain its political neutrality if it were affiliated to the TUC?

Question 5   Are you for or against the IPCS affiliating to the TUC?

Question 6   How strongly do you feel about the question of affiliation to the TUC?

In replying to these various questions members were given a range of alternative answers. They could indicate that they felt very strongly, quite strongly, not very strongly, not at all strongly or 'did not know' about the issue. Presumably the intention of this complicated referendum was to conduct an attitude survey rather than to find a straight answer to a simple question.

When the results of the ballot were announced the figures were analysed in considerable detail. The vital result was that 27 per cent of those who had voted were in favour of affiliation to the TUC and 71 per cent were against. The remainder were undecided. A clear majority of members, 72 per cent, were in favour of the Institution having more influence over the formulation of national policies affecting the interests of members. Only 25 per cent felt that affiliation to the TUC would increase the influence of the Institution; 30 per cent felt that the influence of the Institution would be reduced; 39 per cent felt it would make no difference. Only 29 per cent thought it possible for organisations affiliated to the TUC to maintain their political neutrality; 64 per cent thought that it was not possible; 7 per cent said that they did not know or they did not provide an answer. Of those voting 51 per cent said they felt very strongly about the question of affiliation to the TUC. The total number of valid ballot papers received was 24,632. The number eligible to vote was 72,248. Thus only slightly more than one-third of the membership exercised their right to vote.

INTERNAL ORGANISATION

Several changes and attempted changes in the internal organisation of the Institution took place over the period. Reorganisation in the MPBW and MoD necessitated consequential changes in both the Institution's branch structure and in the staff sides. The reorganisation of these and many other government departments into larger units after 1964 produced a situation in which over 50 per cent of the Institution's membership were in six large departments out of a total of forty-six. The NEC therefore suggested that the upper limit on the number of NEC members from any one department should be increased. This suggestion was, however, decisively defeated at the 1965 conference only to be accepted by the 1966 conference which then asked the NEC to review the position.

Comments were also made from time to time on the need to reform the conference procedures to ensure that major issues were fully debated and that the conference was not swamped with issues of little significance. In an article in *State Service* in May 1966 the deputy vice-chairman, Philip Middleton, emphasised the point:

> There is no disguising the fact that in recent years annual delegate conference has been in the doldrums. The reason is simple. Every year the conference agenda becomes more congested with motions and amendments on the minutiae of everyday working conditions . . . The real issue is whether conference is to be regarded as a resolution-carrying machine, getting through the maximum number of resolutions in the time available, or a deliberative body which lays down policy on issues of major importance. The very process of debate, with the opportunities it gives to hear every point of view expressed, is an essential part of major decision-taking.

The 1966 conference agreed to a small step towards this end by passing a resolution seeking to place non-controversial motions in a special section of the agenda which could be voted on as a single motion without discussion.

In 1968, an attempt by the standing orders committee to reduce the number of motions at the conference ended in uproar. The SOC suggested to the conference that some motions should become amendments to other motions and this was adopted. As the conference proceeded, however, attempts were made to suspend standing orders for one reason or another. The NEC, in discussing these developments afterwards, agreed that whilst the efforts of the standing orders committee should be supported the real problem was how to achieve its objectives, especially when issues were controversial. It decided to circulate branches on the desirability of modifying conference procedure along the lines sought by the standing orders committee.

At the same conference, however, delegates did respond to a call from the Scottish branch for a more interesting and stimulating conference with a concentration on issues of major importance, and with routine matters being left to the NEC. The conference, they said, wanted 'fizz pop and jam' throughout, the bread and butter being left to the NEC, a view which appealed to the vast majority of delegates.

STATE SERVICE

During the second half of the 1960s a number of trade union journals went over from a magazine-style format to a newspaper format. The possibility of introducing such a change for *State Service* was considered by the NEC in 1964 and 1965, but there were divided opinions about it. Some of the criticism of the existing journal, however, arose from the fact that it had as editors Institution members who did the job part-time. The burden was too much to expect of any member who had to perform his normal job during working hours. Some members of the NEC suggested that the journal should be turned over to a newspaper format but others felt that this would not be satisfactory. Serious articles, it was argued, could be published more suitably in a magazine than in a newspaper-style publication.

When the issue was debated at the 1965 conference the view of the majority of delegates was that *State Service* should remain a magazine. A delegate from the Central Office of Information made a telling point when she said that *State Service* in a newspaper format would be disastrous because newspapers had a life of no more than a few hours and this influenced the attitude of the reading public towards newspaper-style publications. Prestige goods, she said, would not be sold with cheap publicity. Another delegate said that he thought there was a danger of the journal deteriorating into a publication consisting of headlines and little else.

Following the conference the NEC decided to make no radical change in *State Service* pending a full report to the 1966 conference on communications but that in the meantime the present *State Service* should be improved as far as possible. It was also decided to publish a new monthly bulletin mid-way between the issues of *State Service* which would contain establishment circulars and other items of special interest to branch officers.

The 1966 conference debated the NEC's report on communications. Of its seventeen recommendations, five had been singled out by branches for debate. The attack focused particularly on the suggestion that there should be a professional editor, both on the grounds of cost and because many feared it could be a threat to the independence of the journal. The attack failed. Conference decided in favour of a new-look journal and a professional editor. It endorsed the report with one minor exception; it did not want a coloured title for *State Service*.

In the autumn of 1966 a new full-time editor and public relations officer, Terry Pitts Fenby, was appointed. He had previously been editor of *Industrial Society* and for seven years had been chairman of the National Conference of British House Editors. Before that he had worked as a journalist with Northcliffe Newspapers.

PERSONNEL

During the years from 1965 to 1969 there were a number of changes in the full-time staff of the Institution. In 1965 two new assistant secretaries were appointed, Mr W. Wright and Mr F. R. Mullin. Mr Wright was appointed successor to Mr Stuart Johnston who had resigned to take a post in industry. Mr Wright came to the Institution with a long record of trade union activity in the civil service, in both the CSCA and the SCS. Mr Mullin had a different background. For the previous eleven years he had been assistant general secretary of the National Society of Electrotypers and Stereotypers. In 1966 the

Institution created a second deputy general secretary post and Mr John Lyons was promoted to the new post. Early in 1969 Mr Edward Hewlett was promoted to deputy general secretary in anticipation of the retirement in that year of Mr Tom Profitt. The latter had served during the periods of office of five general secretaries and had been an efficient and extremely popular official. At the 1969 conference it was said of Tom Profitt that he had the power completely to disarm opponents with his charm, logic and wit.

The 1969 conference also saw the retirement from the NEC of Mr Ted Lawson who had served continuously for the twenty-three years since its inception. He was the last honorary treasurer and the first new-style chairman. As Mr J. C. McLaughlan said in nominating him for honorary membership, 'mention any job on the NEC and Ted had not only filled it, but had distinguished himself carrying out its functions'. His one-man shows at conference evening cabarets were a delight, and he was also one of the moving spirits behind other concerts given by groups of members of which perhaps the most memorable was that given by the Scottish branch on the departure of Stanley Mayne as general secretary in 1961. After leaving the NEC he served as chairman of the Civil Service Housing Association and continued his official duties as assistant director of the Advisory Accounts Section in the Inland Revenue.

Mr Ted Lawson was joined by four other long-serving members who were elected honorary members at the 1969 annual delegates conference. They were Walter Bailey, who had been on the NEC for eighteen years and was the first representative of the technical classes to become chairman of the Institution; Mr R. G. Fall, who was chairman from 1964 to 1966 and chaired the team which produced the Institution's evidence to Fulton; Mr Tom Profitt, who had been with the Institution since 1941; and Mr James Watson, one of the Institution's assistant secretaries appointed in the early 1940s. The new honorary members were added to a distinguished line which had begun in 1965 with the election to honorary membership of Mr Verney Stott, Mr John Beaton and Mr Stanley Mayne. They had been respectively president and vice-presidents of the Institution when those offices were abolished in 1964.

Towards the end of 1968 Freddie Menzler, one of the great personalities in the history of the Institution, died. He was 80 years of age. In a tribute to him Mr Douglas Houghton, MP, said that 'he was the man who saved the National Staff Side from complete disruption and the whole Whitley system from breaking up in 1926'. Freddie Menzler had the strength to withstand the pressures and to endure the strain because he was a man of strong political conviction. In the words of Douglas Houghton, 'he was a Fabian and a socialist, and knew where he stood in the nine days that shook the world'. He concluded his tribute by saying that if there were any survivors of the breakaway consultative committee after the General Strike of 1926 he hoped to see them bowed in penitence at Menzler's tomb.

A similar very warm tribute to Freddie Menzler was paid by Stanley Mayne. He recalled that Freddie Menzler had joined the Council of the Institution in July 1924 as the representative of the Government Actuary's Department. Within twelve months he was the Institution's honorary secretary. Its membership at that time was only 2,800. When he became honorary secretary Freddie Menzler devoted tremendous energy and all his very great ability to building the Institution. He travelled the length and breadth of Britain to address meetings, making frequent visits to Scotland for which he was still remembered with gratitude by the older generation. His lifelong interest in the civil service was recognised by his appointment to membership of the Priestley Commission. Stanley Mayne concluded by saying that Freddie was 'a man among men'.

22 Industrial Relations Legislation

The year 1969 was the Institution's Golden Jubilee. In an article in *State Service* the general secretary reviewed the issues that were likely to be facing the Institution for the next decade. The Fulton Report, he said, constituted a watershed in the Institution's history and there was no doubt that the major work of the next decade would be associated with the findings of the Fulton Committee. This would have major implications not only for the nature of the civil service but also for the organisation of the civil service trade union movement. Superannuation was also likely to be a major issue. A review had already begun in 1969 and had been given impetus by the recommendations in the Fulton Report. The machinery of government was also singled out by the general secretary as an area of major concern, together with relationships with Parliament and, through more open government, with the community. Pay principles and the status of scientists and technologists were also high on the list of priorities for the coming decade. The Institution would also continue to make a major contribution to the debate about the scope and purpose of public research and development.

THE GOLDEN JUBILEE YEAR

The jubilee year opened with many messages of congratulation from other unions in the civil service and the Post Office. On 20 November the Institution held a Golden Jubilee reception at which some 600 guests were present including representatives of the Institution's branches, the heads of government departments and senior members of the scientific and professional civil service. The year was also marked by the formal amalgamation with the STCS which took place in June 1969.

The same year, 1969, also marked the Golden Jubilee of Whitleyism in the civil service and in a memorial lecture to celebrate the occasion Sir William Armstrong, the head of the civil service, looked back on the beginnings of Whitleyism and then looked forward to the next fifty years. In speaking of the future he said: 'we are by extraordinary coincidence, embarking not merely on the second fifty years of Whitleyism but also on an entirely new era in the civil service'. He was referring particularly to the report of the Fulton Committee and the fact that in 1969 the Post Office would cease to be a government department.

IN PLACE OF STRIFE

The year 1969 was also marked by the publication of the government's proposals for new legislation in industrial relations in a White Paper entitled *In Place of Strife*. In the first half of the 1960s it became fashionable in sections of the press to suggest that the system of industrial relations in Britain and with it the trade union movement were in need of overhaul. Although the amount of time lost through industrial disputes in Britain represented only an extremely small fraction of the total working time there were a number of commentators who suggested that industrial disputes in Britain were a prime cause of the nation's economic difficulties. Britain was becoming increasingly aware that its rate of economic growth compared unfavourably with those of many other industrial countries. The Labour Party was pointing to the alleged wasted years of Tory rule, with low industrial investment and 'stop-go' policies. Right-wing spokesmen, on the other hand, complained of the alleged lack of control of members by certain unions and of the outdated structure of the trade union movement.

In 1965 the government appointed a Royal Commission on Trade Unions and Employers' Associations under the chairmanship of Lord Donovan. The terms of reference called for an examination of the role of trade unions and employers' associations in promoting the interests of members and in accelerating the social and economic advance of the nation.

The Donovan Report was published in 1968. One of its conclusions was that the central defect in British industrial relations was the disorder in factory and workshop relations and pay structures which were outside the control of formal national level negotiating procedures. The Commission recommended changes in the law but its main emphasis was on the need for reform within an essentially voluntary system. It urged that there should be more orderly factory-wide agreements, and that industry-wide agreements should be limited to those matters which they could effectively regulate.

The trade union movement, including unions in the public sector, welcomed many of the conclusions and recommendations of the Donovan Commission, particularly those relating to the need to retain the essential characteristics of a voluntary system, though it criticised the extent to which the report had been influenced by evidence drawn from manufacturing industry and had neglected the system operating in the greater part of the public service, including the civil service. The proposals in *In Place of Strife* came as a surprise to the trade union movement. There were various proposals to assist unions and promote trade union objectives but there were also proposals which the unions strongly opposed and which were not consistent with the findings of the Donovan Report on the need for reform within an essentially voluntary system. The government proposed to take discretionary powers to require a union to take a ballot before a strike which, in the minister's opinion, threatened economic damage. These powers would be backed with the threat of financial penalties. The government also proposed to take discretionary reserve powers to impose a conciliation pause in certain disputes. These powers were also to be backed by threat of financial penalty. Another proposal was that the Secretary of State for Employment should have power in inter-union disputes to impose financial penalties on an employer or union which refused to comply with a recommendation by the Commission on Industrial Relations (a body established following the recommendations of the Donovan Report) that a union should be excluded from recognition. Yet another proposal was that there should be obligatory registration of trade unions and that unions should be required by statute to ensure that their rulebooks covered certain defined objects.

The TUC said that whilst they welcomed some of the government's proposals they were emphatically opposed to any proposal which envisaged financial penalties on unions and workpeople. They asserted that the government proposals were unworkable and that to threaten unions with financial penalties unless they could impose discipline upon their members was to misunderstand the relationship between a union and its membership. Unions were answerable in the ultimate to their members; not the members to the union. Union discipline rested upon the willingness of rank-and-file members to accept it. It could not be imposed on large numbers of workers who had reached their own decisions.

In April 1969 the government announced that it had decided to introduce into the current session of Parliament a short interim Bill to deal with some of the main proposals in *In Place of Strife*. The government regarded the immediate problem as that of unofficial strikes. The new Bill was to include provisions for enforceable recommendations in certain circumstances on questions related to recognition of trade unions and inter-union disputes and the ordering of a conciliation pause in unconstitutional stoppages.

Trade union opposition to the government's proposals continued to grow and a special TUC was convened in June 1969. At this congress a motion affirming the trade union movement's unalterable opposition to the imposition of financial penalties on trade unions and workpeople was adopted by an overwhelming majority. The General Council of the TUC was authorised to take further action for the purpose of assisting in the improvement of procedures and the settlement of disputes by voluntary means.

At a succession of meetings between the government and the TUC, the representatives of the trade union movement continued to express vehement opposition to the government's proposals. It also became clear that a substantial number of Labour members of Parliament would not support the government's proposals. A compromise was inevitable and the government finally withdrew its proposals. In return, the General Council agreed to a solemn and binding undertaking to give urgent consideration to disputes which led or were likely to lead to an unconstitutional stoppage of work involving directly or indirectly large bodies of workers and to give advice to the union or unions concerned with a view to promoting a settlement. In cases where, in the General Council's view, there should not have been a stoppage of work before the procedure was exhausted, the General Council undertook to place an obligation on the union or unions concerned to take energetic steps to secure an immediate resumption of work. This undertaking was set out in detail in an agreed statement between the government and the General Council and was subsequently accepted by congress.

This controversy for the most part had little direct effect on the Institution. It did, however, find an echo in an article written by the general secretary in the March 1969 issue of *State Service*. In this article the general secretary indicated that he disagreed with some of the suggestions in the White Paper but that taken as a whole the government's proposals would be of benefit to unions, particularly to white-collar unions outside the public area of employment. He pointed out that the White Paper sought to strengthen collective bargaining, and he drew particular attention to one paragraph which he described as an excellent statement:

> Collective bargaining is essentially a process by which employees can take part in the decisions that affect their working lives. If it is carried on by efficient management and representatives of well-organised unions, negotiating over a wide range of subjects, it represents the best method so far devised of advancing industrial democracy in the interests of employees and employers. It offers the

community the best opportunity for securing well-ordered progress towards higher levels of performance and the introduction of new methods of work.

The article went on to say that the most effective way to prevent strikes or other industrial action was to ensure that the system of collective bargaining was so effective that sensible solutions were produced. So long as there was a reluctance on the part of any employer to deal reasonably with a claim there would be a tendency for those who had the power to take militant action.

THE INDUSTRIAL RELATIONS ACT

When the Conservative government was elected in 1970 it was pledged to introduce a comprehensive Industrial Relations Act which would 'provide a proper framework of law within which improved relationships between the management, men and unions can develop'. In its manifesto the Conservative Party claimed that its objective was to strengthen trade unions and the official leadership of the unions by providing deterrents against unofficial minorities. The new Act, it said, would lay down what was lawful and what was not lawful in the conduct of industrial disputes. A new Registrar of Trade Unions and Employers' Associations was to be established and his task would be to ensure that 'rules were fair, just, democratic and not in conflict with the public interest'. The Act would also provide for a secret ballot in the case of a dispute which would seriously endanger the national interest and for a 'cooling-off' period of not less than sixty days.

The Industrial Relations Act, 1971, which was passed by Parliament after long and heated debate, followed broadly the lines set out in the Conservative Party election manifesto. It introduced a number of new features and liabilities. It listed a number of 'unfair industrial practices', a new concept in British law, which gave rise to legal liabilities. The Act also laid down a legal requirement that before a union could call itself a trade union and thus enjoy certain limited legal advantages it had to register. The new Registrar of Trade Unions would have substantial power to determine and alter trade union rules. The right to trade union membership was to be balanced by a right not to join a trade union. Any collective agreement would be presumed to be legally binding unless an express provision to the contrary was included in the agreement itself.

The trade union movement strongly opposed the new Act. The TUC had organised a national petition against it when the Bill was going through Parliament, had held a national demonstration of opposition at the Albert Hall and had organised one of the largest ever protest demonstrations in Trafalgar Square. Leaflets had been distributed in cities and large towns, and full-time officials of many unions attended training programmes for the campaign of opposition. A special Congress on the Industrial Relations Bill was called by the General Council who said that 'the fiction that the British economy had been threatened by industrial disputes pervades the government's whole approach'. The congress accepted the view of the General Council that the Bill was designed to reduce the power of the trade union movement, to limit the right to strike, to undermine the freedoms won by working people over many generations and to enforce all these limitations by the courts.

The TUC's objections to the government's measures were summarised in a booklet which they issued entitled *Reason*. They said that the government's measures would undermine and disrupt union organisation, jeopardise trade union funds and surround legitimate trade union activities with a morass of legal obstacles.

> Far from improving industrial relations these proposals would create innumer-
> able new sources of friction in industry and generate the most widespread
> bitterness and anger.
>   Far from strengthening voluntary agreements they would bring confusion to
> established voluntary procedures and undermine both the will of employers
> and the power of unions to bargain freely and realistically.
>   These plans do not stem from any proper study of industrial relations
> problems, but from prejudice and political dogma.

The STCS division of the Institution, which was still affiliated to the TUC, participated fully in the TUC campaign against the proposed new legislation. Publicity about the campaign of opposition was carried in the section of *State Service* devoted to news of the STCS division.

At a special congress held in March 1971 the General Council strongly advised affiliated unions not to register under the Industrial Relations Act. The Amalgamated Union of Engineering Workers (AUEW) urged that this was not sufficient. It pressed strongly that unions should be required not to register. The General Council's recommendation was accepted by the relatively narrow majority of 5,055,000 votes to 4,484,000 votes. At the regular congress of the TUC held in September 1971 this decision was reversed. The AUEW secured a majority for a resolution instructing the General Council to support all unions in their fight against the legislation and in turn to instruct affiliated unions not to register under the Act. This resolution was carried by 5,625,000 votes to 4,500,000.

THE INSTITUTION DECIDES TO REGISTER

It was anticipated that the impact of the Industrial Relations Act on the Institution would be largely neutral. On the one hand it was felt that it was unlikely to suffer unduly from the penal provisions of the Act since most of the 'unfair industrial practices' were directed at the activities of those unions for whom industrial action was a more common occurrence and whose negotiations tended to be much more decentralised than in the civil service. On the other hand, it was unlikely to benefit to any great extent from the provisions for gaining recognition since the issues of recognition and areas of jurisdiction between unions in the civil service were already largely settled. Indeed, at its meeting in October 1970 to consider the consultative document on the Industrial Relations Bill the NEC had concluded that the proposals in the consultative document were largely irrelevant to the circumstances of the Institution and the public service.

Nevertheless the NEC did oppose the Bill in principle on the grounds that the proposals were potentially dangerous and likely to damage the effective system of industrial relations developed in the civil service and in other organisations where the Institution had members. The NEC considered that the recommendations of the majority of the Donovan Commission were to be preferred. The National Staff Side, too, in their submission of views on the consultative document, emphasised that the Whitley system could develop effectively only on a voluntary basis without legal enforcement.

While suspending judgement on the detailed implications of the Industrial Relations Bill, however, the NEC decided in the spring of 1971 that the balance of advantage was in favour of registration. They proposed therefore to register under the 1871 Trade Union Act. This would enable the Institution to be entered on the provisional register under the new legislation and would put the Institution on a similar footing to most trade unions.

This view was endorsed by the 1971 conference, though a number of speakers expressed opposition to the new industrial relations legislation. One of the deputy general secretaries, Mr Cyril Cooper, spoke strongly on the subject and said that the problems of industrial relations could not be solved by legislation. The majority of delegates were not, however, prepared to declare total opposition to the Act.

A more critical attitude was taken towards the draft code of industrial relations practice prepared by the government later in the year. It was so vague, said the NEC, as to be meaningless in places, and in others it set standards which fell well below these already established. The Institution made the point that representation by responsible trade unions was essential for good industrial relations and it could not comprehend the possibility, mentioned in the foreword to the proposed code and in the code itself, of industrial relations arrangements covering all workpeople at work 'whether or not they are organised in trade unions'. The code, said the Institution, should state explicitly that good industrial relations depend on representative and responsible trade unions, and all employees should be encouraged to join trade unions. A responsibility should be placed on management to encourage employees to join the appropriate trade union and management should give full facilities for recruitment to that union.

Certain sections of the Industrial Relations Act, 1971, came into effect from 1 December of that year, including the section stating that all written agreements were automatically legally binding unless there was an agreed provision to the contrary. The NEC considered that the collective bargaining arrangements of the civil service depended on the continuation of voluntary procedures and a circular was sent to all branches advising them to take steps to ensure that agreements were not legally binding. This decision was consistent with the policy of other civil service unions. Agreement was reached with the CSD early in 1972 on the arrangements for ensuring that agreements made in the civil service were not legally binding, although a mutually acceptable standard disclaimer clause was not finalised until the middle of 1973.

FURTHER DEBATE ON THE ACT

At the 1972 conference of the Institution the delegates approved by a very large majority a report from the NEC recommending that for the time being the Institution should remain on the register. The NEC undertook, however, to explore all the implications of the new Act for the Institution's rules and to report in detail to the next year's conference. The NEC was apprehensive that the requirements of the Act relating to registered unions might impose rule changes on the Institution which would introduce practices alien to its tradition. In particular, branch and other local lay representatives might find themselves with legal liabilities and responsibilities for the action of their colleagues. Such legal liabilities on rank-and-file honorary office-holders had never been envisaged in the essentially voluntary structure and history of the Institution. In this very practical way the Institution's active membership were coming up against the underlying philosophy of the Industrial Relations Act which had aroused so much antagonism within the trade union movement.

The NEC recommendation that the Institution should in the meantime remain on the register came under spirited minority criticism from a number of delegates at the conference including one delegate from the Office of Population Censuses and Surveys branch who argued that the Institution lacked a positive policy towards the Industrial Relations Act. It should not be necessary, she said, to convince a court of the right to represent certain types of staff. What was necessary was to convince the members and potential members themselves. If a union could not do this it did not deserve their loyalty. The Institution would have to prove its fitness to represent its members should the necessity arise. It should not seek to get the legal profession to do the job for it. In reply to the debate the general secretary said that he accepted completely the mover's basic point that a union was representative if, and only if, it proved its fitness and the members supported it. On the other hand, there was no reason why the Institution should give an unnecessary advantage to some upstart competitor. The competitor might claim an advantage because it could show that it was registered.

The 1972 conference instructed the National Executive Committee to make legally binding agreements where such agreements would be in the best interest of the staff. The mover of the successful resolution, from the Science Research Council, said that he thought the Institution was in danger of becoming politically motivated. Mr Cyril Cooper, deputy general secretary, said that the NEC was in general opposed to legally binding agreements because legal procedures could undermine the system of voluntary negotiations. The NEC recognised, however, that there were rare cases where legally binding agreements might be helpful.

Another proposal before the 1972 conference was that the NEC should take action to ensure that all non-members in grades represented by the Institution should be required to make a donation to the union's funds or to a nominated charity as described under the provisions for agency shops in the Industrial Relations Act. This suggestion was the subject of a spirited debate. The NEC speaker said that if what was really wanted was an agency shop – a legalised form of obligatory union membership with certain exceptions – then this proposal should have been put forward in a straightforward manner. The motion was defeated on a card vote by 51,258 votes to 35,008 votes.

UKAPE, APST AND ASTMS

As feared, the Institution was threatened in some areas by the intrusion of other organisations, particularly the United Kingdom Association of Professional Engineers (UKAPE) which had sprung into life following the Industrial

Relations Act. Under the Act any staff association which could pass the Registrar's test of independence could apply for recognition in a specified bargaining unit or apply for withdrawal of recognition from an established union provided it could show sufficient support. Unregistered unions could not initiate the mechanism for recognition although they were not precluded from being chosen as the bargaining agent.

These provisions resulted in a mushrooming of independent staff associations, particularly among professional and other higher-paid staff where it was envisaged that 'professional' bargaining units could be carved out of larger areas and 'professional' staff separated from their colleagues even where they were engaged on similar work. UKAPE, for example, claimed to represent the interests of professional engineers and made a bid to organise such staff in the civil service, who were already represented by the Institution. In his address to the 1972 conference the chairman, Mr McLauchlan, regretted the poaching activities of UKAPE, adding that 'if they wished to use the dubious weaponry of the Industrial Relations Act then let them turn it on those employers, and there are too many of them, who refuse to recognise any trade unions, rather than poaching on our reserves'. The attempts made by UKAPE to poach members, however, were shortlived and the threat to the integrity of the Institution soon subsided.

Another independent association, the Association of Professional Scientists and Technologists (APST), emerged following the Industrial Relations Act. It had similar objectives to UKAPE in mind for organising professionals. In this case, however, an understanding with the Institution was reached in the early stages and it was agreed that the Institution was the appropriate body to represent scientists and technologists in the civil service and associated areas of employment. The APST intended, unlike UKAPE, to concentrate on areas where scientists and technologists were not already well organised.

The other threat to the Institution's sphere of influence came, strangely, not from newly emerging associations, but from a union affiliated to the TUC, ASTMS. The decision of the Institution to register and its continued non-affiliation to the TUC provided ASTMS with an excuse for its policy of recruiting in the civil service. The Institution did not have the protection of the Bridlington agreement, which laid down rules of conduct in disputes between unions affiliated to the TUC.

ASTMS began its encroachment on civil service territory in a blaze of publicity in 1972. Its main target was the SCS but it also made some headway in the Institution's area, especially in the Estate Duty Office (EDO) and the museums. ASTMS as an unregistered union was precluded from using the institutions of the Industrial Relations Act to claim recognition. Instead, it used the technique of encouraging an individual member, as provided for in the Act, to apply to the National Industrial Relations Court (NIRC) for the sole bargaining rights of the Institution to be revoked in respect of the EDO.

The NIRC referred the claim to the Commission on Industrial Relations (CIR) who conducted a survey and later published, in confidence to the parties, their conclusions. The Institution found these totally unsatisfactory, and despite some amendments the final report was still considered distorted and harmful. The Institution therefore issued a writ in the Chancery Division challenging the right of the CIR to publish the report. The Institution was able to sustain its claim that the CIR had no statutory authority to publish a report, despite the fact that it had done so on every other reference under the Act, a finding which itself threw the Act into greater disrepute. More important for the Institution, however, the NIRC then (July 1974) ordered a ballot in which the staff voted by a substantial majority in favour of the Institution rather than ASTMS. Later, under TUC auspices, an agreement was reached between the civil service unions affiliated to the TUC and ASTMS, that ASTMS would not seek to recruit in the civil service. The agreement covered the Institution even though it was not affiliated to the TUC.

PROTEST CONTINUES

Meanwhile, outside the civil service the trade union campaign against the Industrial Relations Act reached a new level. In a railway dispute in the spring of 1972 the government used its new legal power to apply to the National Industrial Relations Court for an order requiring the railway unions to discontinue their industrial action. The application was granted and a 'cooling-off' period took effect. At the end of this period the industrial action by the unions was resumed. The government then applied to the NIRC for a compulsory ballot of railwaymen. The result of the ballot showed overwhelming support for the unions. The effect of the whole procedure was to strengthen rather than to weaken the resolve of the majority of railwaymen to support the claim submitted by their respective unions. This particular provision of the Act was not used again in any other dispute.

In July 1972 five dockers were imprisoned following their refusal to comply with an order of the NIRC relating to the 'blacking' of work at a company in Hackney. As a result of their imprisonment there were immediate stoppages of work in many industries. The TUC protested vigorously against the imprisonment and said that the Industrial Relations Act was worsening industrial relations. They pointed out that the policy of registration had failed, that a strike ballot had failed in the railway dispute and the decisions of the NIRC were creating widespread hostility. The objectivity of the entire judiciary, they said, was thus being brought into question by the actions of a special court which was widely regarded as politically motivated.

Despite the representations made to the government by the General Council of the TUC, no progress was made for the release of the imprisoned dockers and towards the end of July the TUC called on all affiliated unions to organise a one-day stoppage of work. The effect of this call for a one-day general strike was immediate. On 26 July 1972 the dockers were released from prison under a legal device which was almost universally regarded as politically contrived.

The AUEW in particular took an uncompromising line towards the NIRC. It refused to recognise the authority of the court. It was particularly angry at the court's intervention in a case concerning trade union recognition at a small engineering firm in the south of England. The employer claimed that he was being subjected to an 'unfair industrial practice' because the union refused to call off the dispute after it had been referred to the CIR. Fines were imposed on the AUEW and, when the union refused voluntarily to pay, its funds were seized. The effect was to provoke bitter feeling in the union and strikes took place in many engineering factories.

DE-REGISTRATION

The mounting opposition to the Industrial Relations Act affected the mood of many active members of the Institution. At the 1973 conference the NEC recommended that the Institution should de-register. In moving this recommendation the general secretary said that the really crucial question concerned the constitution and management of the Institution. Registration required a precise definition of the powers of the NEC, of branches, sections and subsections, and of officials at headquarters and of lay officials at every level. This meant that the Institution would have to set out in the rules precise guidance on who had authority to give instructions to whom. It would be necessary to lay down a disciplinary procedure together with a complaints procedure which would open the possibility of challenges to the voluntary decisions taken by the Institution and its representatives, both lay and full-time. The general secretary said that the Institution was proud of the accountability which it demanded from the NEC. Under the Institution's procedure this accountability was concerned with policy issues rather than with whether or not a particular authority had been exceeded. The general secretary believed it was more fruitful to be accountable in policy than in legalistic terms.

The general secretary recalled that when the Institution decided to register only one advantage of registration had been claimed, namely, that it might help to repel marauders. That danger in the civil service had now passed. It would be unwise to embark on a wholesale rewriting of the rules which would put all the Institution's procedures on a highly legalistic basis. This recommendation was opposed by a number of delegates but was eventually accepted by the conference. The Institution thus joined the overwhelming majority of the trade union movement as an unregistered organisation under the Industrial Relations Act.

The Act was finally repealed in 1974 when a new Labour government was elected. It did, however, have two positive developments in the civil service to its credit. The unfair dismissals provisions embodied in the Act survived largely intact. The civil service had provided its own alternative procedures and constitutions as it was entitled to do under the Act, and established the Civil Service Appeal Board in 1972 to consider appeals from civil servants who were to be dismissed or prematurely retired. This replaced the previous arrangements under which civil servants had the right to appeal only to the heads of their departments. The Board had a chairman, Sir Harvey Druitt, KCB, a deputy chairman, and two panels composed of Official Side nominees on the one hand and Staff Side nominees on the other. The existence of the Board did not preclude a civil servant from taking his case to an industrial tribunal under the state scheme.

The Board continued to function and in 1977 Stanley Mayne, in an article in *State Service* assessing the record of the Board, said: 'the Civil Service Appeal Board is a high spot in the joint efforts to ensure that individual civil servants get a fair crack of the whip in disciplinary and dismissal matters'.

The other positive development was the effect of the provisions relating to shop stewards' facilities of the code of practice on industrial relations. This provided the ammunition for the Staff Side to open negotiations with the CSD on a new facilities agreement for union representatives. For some time Institution conferences had been asking for a review of facilities available to the Institution's representatives and in 1972 a resolution was passed asking specifically for the application of the code. After considerable delay, and the submission of inadequate initial proposals on the part of the Official Side, a new facilities agreement was finally reached at the end of 1974. The agreement, wrote the general secretary, represented a major step forward, providing for official recognition of the value and importance of trade union work, encouraging active participation and minimising the fear of victimisation.

23 Incomes Policy and the Scientists' Pay Dispute

The new administration elected in June 1970 announced that there were to be changes in incomes policy. The NBPI was brought to an end and the machinery for the formal implementation of an incomes policy was disbanded. The government took the view that its influence on pay should be exerted primarily through the negotiations for which it had a direct responsibility, a carbon copy of its 'pay pause' policy of ten years earlier. This meant that it sought to influence negotiations in the public sector, including the civil service. The government believed that this would then affect negotiations and settlements in the private sector. The government's policy became known popularly as 'N minus one'. The idea was that each succeeding major settlement should be 1 per cent less than the preceding settlement. In this way inflationary pressure would eventually be brought under control without the necessity of a formal incomes policy or statutory intervention in the collective bargaining process.

The impact on the civil service, however, was not immediate. The government responded to pressure from the Staff Side for full implementation of the 1969 recommendations of the Standing Advisory Committee on higher civil service pay and the full award was paid from 1 January 1971. In November 1970 the government announced that it was going to change the arrangements for determining higher-grades pay by the establishment of three review bodies with interlocking membership. One, later designated the Top Salaries Review Body (TSRB), was to advise on the remuneration of the boards of nationalised industries, the judiciary, senior civil servants, senior officers of the armed forces and such other groups as might be appropriately considered with them; another was to advise on the pay of the armed forces; and a third was to advise on the remuneration of doctors and dentists in the national health service. The new review bodies were to be serviced by the Office of Manpower Economics.

DIFFERENTIALS AWARD

The other major pay development of interest to the Institution which took place in the early months of the new administration was a major award on differentials. In April 1970 the NBPI produced its second report (No. 146) on *The Pay and Conditions of Industrial Civil Servants*. It called for new and improved rates of pay for industrial civil servants to be achieved primarily through the development of incentive payment schemes and productivity or efficiency agreements. These developments, together with the implementation of new systems of accountable management as proposed by the Fulton Report, entailed major changes in the role of the Institution grades supervising industrial staff. They also produced acute pay problems; joint examination of the facts had revealed that there had been a distortion and in some cases a total inversion of differentials between industrial and non-industrial employees.

This presented the Institution with both short-term and long-term problems. In the short term a temporary allowance would have to be achieved to bridge the gap until the major pay and grading review took place in 1972 for the professional, technical and related grades. In November 1970 the Institution submitted its claim for a differentials allowance for the technical and drawing office classes, in conjunction with the AGSRO who represented the process and general supervisory and stores supervisory classes. Negotiations on the claim failed to secure a settlement and the case was submitted to arbitration on 19 February 1971.

In a cogently argued and well-presented case, the general secretary, on behalf of both organisations, referred to the claim as a very modest one which even if granted in full would still leave very tight differentials. He told the tribunal, chaired by Professor Hugh Clegg, that since the beginning of 1969 the industrial grades had received increases of over 30 per cent whereas the technical classes, even taking into account the proposed allowance, would be no more than 25·5 per cent better off, decreasing to 10 per cent at the maximum of the technical grade I. It was made clear that even if the Institution's proposals were accepted by the tribunal they would still fall short of the relativities established in 1969. Views were quoted from the NBPI Report No. 146 on the role of supervisors and the need to maintain differentials. In concluding the case the general secretary said:

> There is a great strength of feeling at the situation which has arisen. The Institution has been under great pressure in restraining members and it is a measure of the sense of outrage felt by the members that people who have given years of dedicated service should feel compelled to consider militant action. No arguments heard today in this court can adequately convey the feelings of the members towards the situation which presently exists.

The CSD argued, on the other hand, that the problem would be resolved in the next pay research exercise and that there was justification for only a small allowance of £75 at the age of 26 scale point of the technical grade III and basic draughtsman, tapering to nothing at the maximum of the scale. This, they argued, was 'where the shoe pinched. We consider that a modest adjustment for first-line supervisors is all that is needed.'

On 22 February 1971 the arbitration tribunal made its award which came much closer to meeting the Institution's case than the CSD's. It awarded £200 annual allowance for the technical classes grade III and II and the basic and leading draughtsmen, tapering to nil at the top of the technical class grade I and draughtsmen equivalent. This compared with the claim for an allowance of £250 per annum tapering to nil. The award was to date from 1 July 1970 and to end at 31 December 1971, as the Institution had claimed.

'SACKING THE REF'

In November 1970 the National Staff Side submitted a central pay claim for 13 per cent and an underpinning cash minimum to operate from 1 January 1971. Because of the government's pay policy, negotiations were particularly difficult and the case was referred to arbitration. Shortly before the claim was due to be heard the Official Side made a revised offer and agreement was reached in March. The agreement was for 9·5 per cent and an underpinning cash minimum of £1·75 per week for officers aged 21 and over. Although the increase did not match the general movement in wages and salaries of 13·3 per cent, the Institution accepted the agreement because it also contained assurances that pay research would continue to operate, subject to any requirements of an overriding national policy of general application. At the beginning of April agreement was also reached on London weighting with revised allowances of £175 for inner and £90 for outer London from 1 January 1971.

In the meantime the government's policy was running into serious difficulties outside the civil service. Workers in the public sector, some of whom were among the lowest paid in the community, resisted the attempt to enforce the policy at their expense. There were disputes with local authority employees and with electricity supply workers. Independent inquiries were established and increases recommended which were higher than the amounts previously offered in negotiations.

One of the consequences of these developments was that the government refused to reappoint Professor Clegg as chairman of the CSAT when his period of office came to an end in March 1971. The government's refusal was, they said, based on Professor Clegg's acceptance of the union nomination to the Scamp Inquiry into the local authority dispute in 1970.

The Institution and the rest of the National Staff Side protested strongly and the Institution NEC adopted a resolution deploring the refusal of the government to reappoint Professor Clegg. They pointed out that Professor Clegg was appointed by agreement of the two sides of the National Whitley Council and had acted with the strictest impartiality throughout his period of office. The NEC deplored the fact that the government's decision appeared not to have been based on these facts. Rather it appeared to be a petty and apparently personal reaction to the report on local authority pay by the Scamp Inquiry of which Professor Clegg was a member. His appointment as a union nominee on that committee had not been opposed when it was first made but only when the results of the inquiry were known. The NEC went on to say that the implied requirement that the chairman of any arbitration tribunal must agree with the advice of the government on economic and incomes policy matters was incompatible with independent arbitration.

CONFERENCE DEBATE

The Institution joined the general public sector protest against the government's pay policy. At the 1971 conference the general secretary said that there could be no doubt that the government's policy had involved discrimination to the disadvantage of the public sector. This was in complete violation of the recommendations of the Priestley Royal Commission which had specifically recommended that pay in the civil service should be based on pay for comparable work in outside employment. The Priestley Commission had advised against the civil service being used to give a lead to others. It was apparent, the general secretary said, that the views of the Priestley Royal Commission were now being disregarded. The criticisms expressed by the general secretary were strongly supported by the delegates and a resolution was adopted asking the NEC to publicise wherever possible the feelings of civil servants on the issue.

In his address to the 1971 conference the chairman, Mr J. McLauchlan, said that morale was very low in the civil service and in the public service in general. Part of the reason was the discrimination in relation to pay, but there was also the general unpopular image of the public service. This reflected a loss of public confidence and esteem which was essential to the job satisfaction of public servants. The civil service – its pay, efficiency and size – had remained an election issue ever since the Second World War with the service being 'kicked around as a sort of political football'. He continued: 'And so it is that dedication and integrity have come to be rewarded by parsimony and denigration . . . The central pay award was mixed up with a new procedure – a kind of ministerial brinkmanship with a final offer that was more final than final, and a new arbitration formula which one paper called "sacking the ref".'

SCIENTISTS' PAY

One of the most serious issues the Institution had to face during the 1970s was the issue of scientists' pay. From the date when scientists went into pay research in 1970 for the first time in ten years, the claim was to absorb a large part of the energies of the Institution. The fact that the pay-research-based review coincided with a government policy of pay de-escalation in the public sector made matters even more difficult, but it was a dispute which went far deeper, and concerned the major question of whether the system of fair comparison was appropriate at all to government scientists. The Institution had argued before the Priestley Commission and subsequently that fair comparison was inappropriate, and had successfully kept scientists out of pay research for ten years. The Official Side, having been pressured by some employers of scientists who said that civil service pay was too high, were equally firmly of the opinion that scientists should be the subject of pay research.

The scientists' pay claim affected some 17,000 scientists and others in the civil service scientific classes. In negotiations the Official Side offered to increase the pay of some grades but offered nothing to almost half the scientists. The total cost of the Official Side's offer was about 2·5 per cent on the existing pay bill. The Institution claimed up to 15 per cent and regarded the offer as totally unacceptable. The pay talks finally collapsed on 2 July 1971 after an hour-long meeting between the Institution and Lord Jellicoe, the Lord Privy Seal. It was agreed that the case should go to arbitration. The general secretary said after the meeting, 'the government has proved to be completely obstinate as well as unreasonable. By this act it has forfeited the confidence of the scientific classes in the civil service and the scientific community and has created deep bitterness and distrust.' In disputing the offer the Institution was not simply concerned about obtaining more money for scientists; equally important was the need to find a fair basis of assessing pay for civil service scientists in the future.

A couple of days before the case was due to be heard on 12 and 13 August 1971 a massive protest meeting on scientists' pay was held in London, which was the culmination of a series of meetings over the previous two months in various provincial centres. The protest meeting, which was attended by 4,300 members, was preceded by a march, with banners and placards, from Waterloo Station to Central Hall, Westminster. The following resolution was carried unanimously at the protest meeting:

That this meeting of over 4,300 Institution members expresses its deep disgust at an 'offer' which would substantially cut the standards of living of many thousands of scientists and devalue their position in the community. The meeting expresses its grave concern at the frustration of the Fulton reforms which application of this offer would involve. The meeting also expresses its anxiety at the effect the offer would have on the pay of scientists generally and on the longer-term implications for British science which is of profound importance for the well-being of the economy. The meeting therefore requests the National Executive Committee to communicate these views to the Prime Minister and to take all appropriate action after the award of the arbitration tribunal to establish a satisfactory long-term basis for determining the pay of scientists and to ensure continued and early progress with the Fulton reforms.

The resolution was conveyed to the Prime Minister and was formally acknowledged by a private secretary, a response which showed an incredible lack of interest, if not downright contempt for government scientists. This response incensed the Institution.

The arbitration tribunal sat under its new chairman, Mr Michael Mustill, QC, who had succeeded Professor Clegg. The scientists' case was his first. The proceedings started, as always, with the Staff Side case. The general secretary told the tribunal that the case was one of the most important it was ever likely to hear and that certainly it was the most important one that he had ever brought to the tribunal. He went on to draw the attention of the tribunal to the deep sense of resentment among scientific members as shown by the very many letters and telegrams received at the Institution's headquarters and the very big attendance at the London protest rally. The offer, he said, was an affront to scientists.

The general secretary proceeded to outline the Institution's case in detail. He said that the pay research report indicated marked differences in age structure of scientists inside the service and those outside. The opportunities presented in industry for scientists to move into administration, production and sales in pursuit of satisfactory careers were much greater than inside the service. Most important, almost all the outside organisations included in the survey took some account of civil service pay in determining scientists' salaries.

The general secretary made reference to the Priestley doctrine that where pay research could not produce valid comparisons, vertical and horizontal relativities within the structure could be used as a secondary factor. He argued that because the career structure of scientists within and outside the service differed so widely and because the government, being the largest single employer of scientists in research and development, influenced the pay of scientists outside, pay comparisons were invalidated and therefore horizontal and vertical relativities should play a substantial part in the determination of scientists' pay.

Detailed arguments were presented which related to the vertical differentials with the industrial grades and horizontal relativities with the technology classes. Attention was drawn to the practice which had developed over the past few years of cross-classifying posts between the scientific, professional, technical and drawing office classes, leading to the conclusion that there was sense in providing a close pay relationship between these classes. The general secretary also argued that the examination of structure at the principal level, which was being conducted for Fulton purposes by the CSD, had already indicated the value of maintaining a close relationship between all classes at principal level.

The CSD rested its case on the fact that the Pay Research Unit claimed that it had been able to find adequate analogues based on functional job comparisons. There was no reason, therefore, why scientists should not submit to pay research in the same way as the other major classes within the service and why the reports should not carry the same weight for scientists as for other classes. Given that fair comparisons had been established, the CSD offer was a fair one based on the evidence.

A 'PERVERSE' AWARD

The CSAT award was a significant improvement on the Official Side's offer. It awarded 5 per cent to those who had previously been offered nothing and for the scientific assistant grade the increases ranged up to 25 per cent. The total cost of the award was 7·5 per cent but the average increase was 9·5 per cent.

Nevertheless, the award disappointed the Institution, and the general secretary described the decision of the CSAT as 'perverse'. The Institution, he said, would accept it because it honoured its agreements and the arbitration agreement prescribed that an arbitration award would be accepted by both parties. It was not, however, required to like it. The basic defect of the award was that it failed to resolve the major issue in dispute. The tribunal said that in making its award it had paid attention to pay research, to the special features of the scientific civil service and to internal relativity considerations. However, it gave no guide to how scientists' pay was to be determined in the future. This marked the beginning of a new stage in the dispute rather than its end.

The Institution was concerned that the new structure of the science category, agreed in principle before the tribunal hearing, should not be based on the unsatisfactory scales which had emerged from the CSAT award. The general secretary said that a heavy onus rested on the CSD and the government to clear up the mess which they had done so much to create. In mid-September the Institution agreed to a new pay and grading structure, subject to a number of improvements and conditions. First, some modest improvements were made on the scales awarded by the CSAT which, together with favourable assimilation terms, produced worthwhile improvements for many members. Secondly, the pay scales in the new structure were agreed without prejudice to any argument that the Institution might put forward for a better scale structure in the future. Thirdly, there was to be a joint review of the criteria for determining the pay of the scientific grades which was to be completed if possible by the end of the year. Fourthly, scientists were to be included in the central pay increase from 1 January 1972 without prejudice to any subsequent developments arising from structural changes affecting the science group, including any associated pay changes. Finally, decisions on unified grading at principal level were to be reached early in 1972 and 'Project ST', concerned with restructuring at the lower end of the scientific, technical and drawing office hierarchies, was to be completed and decisions were to be made as soon as possible. There was no guarantee that any of these developments would have the outcome desired by the Institution but they did at least give prospect of some early change in the existing unsatisfactory situation.

The fact that agreement was reached so quickly after the tribunal award was due to the CSD adopting a more flexible and reasonable approach than it had done in the pay negotiations preceding the reference to arbitration. In the view of the Institution the attitude of the CSD in the review of pay criteria would be the acid test of its real intentions towards scientists.

JOINT WORKING PARTY

A joint working party consisting of five representatives of the CSD and six from the Institution, led by the general secretary, held its first formal meeting on 1 December 1971. It was agreed at an early stage that, although some information was already available from official and other published sources, it was essential to obtain additional information about the deployment of scientists in organisations outside the civil service. Two members of the working party, Mr C. Waters from the Institution and Mr B. Mills from the CSD, were delegated to undertake the review of outside organisations, using the good offices of the Pay Research Unit to make the initial contacts. Their findings, subsequently known as the 'Mills–Waters' Report, were accepted by the joint working party in June 1972 and the conclusions were agreed. The report showed that there were substantial differences in scale between the employment of scientists in research and development within the government service and those employed in any single organisation outside the civil service. There was also a substantial difference in the age-spread of civil service scientists and those in outside employment. Only a very small number of organisations outside the service provided a career in research and development along the lines of the provision within the civil service. In none of the organisations visited by the team was there any apparent distinction, of a kind existing in the civil service, between staff engaged on research, production and general administration.

The Mills–Waters Report thus confirmed the Institution's case that the career structure of scientists inside and outside the civil service were very different, though it did not fully support the Institution's secondary submission that the civil service actually determined outside rates.

The Institution's Scientific Staffs Group took the view that on the basis of this evidence pay research should be regarded as inappropriate in their case and that alternative criteria for determining scientists' pay should be agreed. They decided that the immediate objective should be to secure a formal link on the basis of parity with the professional and technology grades. The NEC approved this approach.

The CSD did not dispute the conclusions of the Mills–Waters Report but it would not agree that, except in the case of differences in age and career patterns, the facts shown had any significance for pay comparisons. They did not, therefore, agree that the facts invalidated fair comparisons, nor could the two sides agree any formula for taking those factors which the CSD considered significant into account in the pay research process.

Thus an impasse was again reached in mid-1972 and in yet another attempt to solve the problem the Institution suggested that an independent committee should be set up to advise the government on pay criteria for scientists and that it should report by the end of 1972 so that its recommendations could determine the basis on which the substantive review of scientists' pay due at 1 January 1973 would take place. Further consideration of this suggestion by the government was, however, overtaken by the announcement of the government's programme for controlling inflation.

OTHER PAY ISSUES

In 1970/1 the government policy of pay 'de-escalation' ran into difficulty. It had had its first major victory in the defeat of the postal workers' strike in 1971, which was accompanied by increased bitter feeling within the public services.

Early in 1972 the government's policy suffered its most serious setback. The government encouraged the National Coal Board, in response to a claim from the miners, to stand firm within the limits of its incomes policy. A strike took place and a court of inquiry, chaired by Lord Wilberforce, was appointed. Following the publication of its report, a settlement was secured on terms well in advance of anything originally sanctioned by the government. The TUC said that the mining dispute was precipitated by 'the government's negative attitude and . . . its attempt to impose rigid restrictions on collective bargaining in the public sector . . .'.

Within the civil service a central pay agreement was concluded early in 1972. For the first time in the history of the National Whitley Council, the agreement was opposed by the Institution's representatives. Nevertheless, the agreement was accepted by the National Staff Side by the required two-thirds majority, sixteen votes to eight. The Institution opposed the agreement because the increases which it provided were both less than the increases in the cost of living and, more relevantly, less than the increases in pay outside the service. The agreement provided for increases of 7 per cent for staff with salaries exceeding £2,000, and 7·5 per cent for staff with salaries of £2,000 a year or less, with an underpinning minimum of £1·65 per week for all adults, with correspondingly smaller amounts for younger staff.

In January 1972 agreement was reached for an improvement in annual leave. In reporting this improvement to the Institution's 1972 conference it was said that the agreement met the claim in terms of the number of days granted but fell short of the claim in respect of the qualifying length of service for the various leave entitlements. Nevertheless, the agreement was a satisfactory one since although there was clear evidence that leave entitlements were improving outside they were still significantly less than those which existed in the civil service.

Pay was high on the agenda at the 1972 Institution's conference. In his address to conference the general secretary deplored the attempts by the government, yet again, to influence the process of arbitration. In November 1971 the Chancellor of the Exchequer had said in the House of Commons that 'the government decided that the most effective way to stop the runaway inflation was to impress on all those responsible the paramount need for the progressive reduction in the level of pay settlements, and the government remains resolved to stand firm on reasonable pay offers where our own employees are concerned'. The Chancellor's speech, said the general secretary, was sent to the arbitration tribunal, presumably for some purpose. Moreover, continued the general secretary, it was difficult to believe that it was not also conveyed as an instruction to Official Side negotiators. It was quite impossible to reconcile this guidance with the specific assurances given in 1971 by the government that civil service pay would be settled in accordance with the agreed criteria. Later in the conference the delegates passed an NEC motion which instructed the NEC to continue to oppose any policy on incomes which by intention or application discriminated against the public sector of employment.

From the debate on scientists' pay it was clear that the Institution's members regarded the unsatisfactory situation on pay as part of a general attack on scientists and the scientific civil service. This view was strengthened by developments in the organisation of science, particularly the Rothschild Report (see Chapter 24). This report seemed to be suggesting short-sighted decisions which would have a negative impact on the essentially long-term basic research to which government science had always made a major contribution.

Another major issue on the agenda of the 1972 conference was the pay research system. In seeking support for an NEC motion which called for a review of the criteria and procedures for determining civil service pay, the general secretary made a balanced argument for retaining what was good and changing what was harmful in the pay research procedures as they currently operated. One good feature of the fair comparisons principle was that, as intended by Priestley, it had isolated the civil service from the economic and political implications of leading rather than following outside pay. The civil service had had staging, phasing and delays but the pay research increases had eventually been paid. It would have been infinitely worse if the civil service were among the leaders and had to bear the full brunt of the government's economic and incomes policy doctrines. There were other sections of the community better equipped and more able to fight on those issues. On the other hand, argued the general secretary, the pay research system had become inflexible and was interpreted by the Official Side in a mechanistic way. The importance of a sensible salary structure and of internal relativities was seriously devalued under the existing arrangements and some nonsenses had been created by the over-slavish devotion to pay research evidence. The existing system had to be speeded up and improved in these respects.

In July, much against the odds as they appeared in certain stages of the negotiations, agreement was reached on revised pay scales for the new professional and technology category. The agreement produced increases from 1 January 1972 on the last full pay-research-based review in 1969 of 31·3 per cent at principal professional and technology officer (PPTO); 28·6 per cent at PTO I; 30·8 per cent at PTO II; 33·5 per cent at PTO III; and 35 per cent at PTO IV. The percentage figures for the TTOs and RTs were 30·4 per cent at TTO I and TTO II; 31·1 per cent at TTO III; and 35 per cent for the RT. These figures compared with increases in the retail price index of 23 per cent and in the weekly wage-rates index of 33·8 per cent over the same period. The Institution formally entered a caveat that it did not think the revised scales fully reflected the merits of the argument, but had taken account of the prevailing economic climate and the powerful pleas by the government for moderation.

Following representations by the Staff Side the government also accepted the report of the TSRB which recommended increases on an annual compound basis since 1 July 1969 averaging 6·8 per cent per annum, pending a full substantive review of top salaries.

INCOMES STANDSTILL

In 1972, after the government's incomes policy had suffered a further setback following a dispute on the railways, there was an exchange of views between the government, the CBI and the TUC about the measures needed to secure economic growth, ensure full employment and reduce inflation. No agreement was reached in these discussions and in November 1972 the Prime Minister announced that the government intended to bring in statutory measures on prices and incomes. There was to be an immediate standstill on prices, rates, dividends and pay. Under the second stage of the policy announced later a Price Commission and Pay Board were established to implement a price and pay code drawn up by the government.

In the autumn of 1972, when the government had been discussing with the CBI and the TUC proposals for a voluntary prices and incomes policy, the Institution issued a statement emphasising that there should be no discrimination between the public service and other sections of the community. The Institution also said that it expected the government to observe the assurance given to the National Staff Side in 1971 that, subject to any requirements of an overriding national policy of general application, the government intended to continue to reach and implement settlements on the basis of surveys by the Civil Service Pay Research Unit in accordance with existing procedural agreements.

In October 1972 the Official Side sent a circular to departments instructing them to defer making offers or entering into any new commitments – but not to suspend negotiations – until further guidance was issued or until there had been further consultation with the Civil Service Department. The Staff Side protested at the issue of this circular without consultation. They pointed out that it meant the imposition on civil servants of limitations which did not apply to the rest of the community.

With the announcement of the pay standstill of three months until 31 March 1973 the National Staff Side made immediate representations against any interference with incremental pay scales about which there had been considerable adverse comment in the press and Parliament. As a result of these representations there was no interference with incremental progression within the civil service. It was pointed out that incremental progression did not add to the total pay bill. The cost of increases given to those ascending the scales was balanced by the savings secured as a result of those retiring at the top of the scales.

In January the National Staff Side made representations to the Prime Minister putting the case for fair treatment of the civil service under Phase 2 of the incomes policy. There was already discontent among civil servants at the extent to which their pay had fallen behind and the standstill prevented any catching-up settlements in January 1973. Those concerned had therefore been denied pay increases to reflect the substantial changes in outside pay which had occurred during 1972. The civil service was already in a turbulent state, militancy was growing, and this, said the Staff Side, would be intensified if civil servants were discriminated against further. There were growing internal anomalies which required solution, not least of which was the case of the scientists for whom there had been no response to the Institution's suggestion of an independent inquiry.

The standstill and subsequent phases of the government's incomes policy were strongly opposed by the wider trade union movement. The TUC convened a special congress in March 1973 which adopted a resolution calling upon the General Council of the TUC to lead co-ordinated action in support of affiliated unions in dispute. The unions were also invited to join in a day of national protest stoppage against wage control and the increase in prices. The retail price index had risen by 10·6 per cent and the food prices index by 19 per cent over the period November 1972 to November 1973.

STAGE 2

In its White Paper *The Programme for Controlling Inflation: The Second Stage* the government laid down a pay code for the second stage of incomes policy from 1 April to 6 November 1973. There was to be a limit of £1 plus 4 per cent on the annual pay bill of each negotiating group. The distribution of increases within each negotiating group would be for negotiation but regard should be had to improving the relative position of the lower-paid. No increases of more than £250 per annum per individual would be allowed. Progress towards equal pay was to be exempt up to one-third of the male/female differential existing at 31 December 1972. Increases in holiday entitlement, provided these did not exceed three weeks in total, were exempt, as were reductions in hours to not less than 40 per week. The White Paper also stated that as part of the consultations which the government would have with the CBI and the TUC and other bodies the government would be considering the policy in the third stage to be pursued on problems of anomalies and relativities produced by the standstill and the second stage. It would seek the help of the Pay Board in an advisory capacity on these problems.

The first decision taken in relation to Stage 2 by the National Staff Side was a unanimous one that all the money available in Stage 2 should be used for increasing basic pay. The second decision was that the whole of the non-industrial civil service should be treated as a single group for pay purposes. The third decision was that there should be an element of redistribution from the higher- to the lower-paid. Finally, the Staff Side decided that there should be time for each constituent organisation to consult its members before any final decision was taken.

The Institution's membership, after extensive consultation, decided by a slim majority to support an agreement providing from 1 April 1973 for minimum increases ranging from £1·60 per week at age 16 to £2·15 per week at age 21 and above, which would require abatement from the strict application of the £1 plus 4 per cent formula for those with salaries above £2,500 per annum, tapering from nil at £2,500 to an abatement of £50 per annum for those with salaries of £4,708 or more.

In March it was agreed that the two major issues of the criteria determining scientists' pay and the restoration of the civil service pay agreement should be referred, separately, to the Pay Board. The reference of science pay criteria to the Pay Board was the government's response to the Institution's request for an independent inquiry. The Institution was therefore concerned to ensure that the Pay Board would not be influenced by short-term incomes policy considerations. It was agreed that detailed arrangements for the review and the procedures to be adopted would be the subject of consultation between the Pay Board, the Official Side and the Institution, aimed at reaching arrangements which were acceptable to the parties concerned. The aim was to try and complete the review by the end of Stage 2. The terms of reference were agreed in July.

To consider the criteria and methods which should determine the pay of the science group in the civil service, bearing in mind the provisions of the National Whitley Council agreements for determining the pay of civil servants, and having regard, *inter alia*, to the pay history of the civil service scientists and the dispute which has existed between the Civil Service Department and the Institution of Professional Civil Servants since 1971, and to report to the Minister for the Civil Service.

Both sides bound themselves to honour the outcome.

A YEAR OF TROUBLE AND TURMOIL

In his address to the 1973 conference the general secretary drew attention to the general state of crisis in industrial relations in the civil service. The existing position of scientists, he said, was outrageous in every respect. Apart from the assistant scientific officers, scientists were worse off in real terms than they had been five years earlier. Their salaries were now lagging 20 per cent behind the general movement in earnings. There were gross internal anomalies between scientists and other groups with whom they often had to work. 'Injustice' had 'run riot'. The reference to the Pay Board was a belated and less than satisfactory response to the Institution's demand for an independent inquiry. The Board would be very much 'on test' as an instrument for securing a just and long-term solution.

Other grades in the civil service were also lagging well behind the rest of the community. Those who were due for a substantive review in 1973 were particularly hard hit. It was vital, said the general secretary, that the Pay Board, in its reference on civil service pay under the general provision for dealing with anomalies and relativities arising from incomes policy, should provide the basis for the restoration of the civil service pay agreements in Stage 3.

The general secretary also referred to the Stage 2 general civil service pay increase which had been dubbed the 'Robin Hood' agreement. The agreement had produced acute divisions of opinion within the Staff Side and within the Institution. On the various pay issues during the last year the National Staff Side had come perilously close to breaking-point. The agreement which was reached was the only one which could retain the unity of the National Staff Side.

The concern of the members over the pay situation was clearly manifest at the conference. First, it took the unusual step of setting aside the NEC's motion on pay policy and of carrying, instead, five motions from branches. It was not so much a revolt as a difference of opinion. Delegates wanted to emphasise individual aspects of pay policy in such a way as to determine priorities, such as the establishment, as quickly as possible, of a fair and permanent method of determining pay, the submission of a substantial claim under Stage 3 and a policy for the lower-paid. One of the motions, moved on behalf of the Ministry of Agriculture, Fisheries and Food branch, which welcomed the NEC's opposition to discrimination against the public sector and instructed the NEC to take any necessary action including militant action to secure a substantial award in Stage 3, was carried.

There were fourteen emergency motions on the 'Robin Hood' agreement, five of which were discussed. They dealt not only with the principle involved in redistribution to benefit the lower-paid but also the manner in which it was reached and the way in which members were consulted. In replying to the criticism the general secretary re-emphasised the point that a decision had to be taken by a two-thirds majority of the National Staff Side. Without the Institution's support for the compromise which favoured the lower-paid there would have been no agreement. The Institution could not have 'gone it alone' because many of its members were linked for pay purposes to other constituents of the Staff Side. The NEC also believed that it was right in principle to help the lower paid. Two of the motions, one of which was submitted by the NEC, were carried and the delegates endorsed, by very large majorities, both the action taken and the method used to determine the views of members.

There were two emergency motions concerning the reference of the scientists' case to the Pay Board. The first was submitted by the Ministry of Defence Procurement Executive Scientific Staffs branch and urged that the Institution should not agree to abide by the outcome of the reference to the Pay Board unless categorical assurances were obtained that it would not be influenced by incomes policy. The motion was lost. Another motion from the Department of Environment, Directorate General of Research branch, which expressed disappointment at the fact that the independent committee to review criteria was to be the Pay Board, was, however, carried against the advice of the NEC.

THE WIDER ISSUES REVIEW

The application of incomes policy continued to provide a steady source of discontent for civil servants. The absurdities and restrictions of Stage 2 became steadily more irksome as the months went by. Thus, for example, in August 1973, the general secretary commented on three cases affecting small pockets of the

Institution's membership. The Official Side had refused, on grounds of incomes policy, the claim for a grant for prison chaplains towards the cost of providing themselves with cassocks. The Pay Board had refused to allow a lump sum payment to House of Lords *Hansard* reporters agreed before the incomes standstill. The reporters had therefore decided to strike on Friday mornings, but decided to work normally following a promise by the Institution to test the decision in the courts. Acting on behalf of the Institution, Mr Peter Pain, QC, secured leave to issue a writ which would be heard in the autumn. Before the hearing took place, however, the issue was settled by negotiation. The third group to suffer from the absurdities of the pay restrictions were the fingerprint officers of the Metropolitan Police. The inversion of differentials associated with the absence of any long-hours' gratuity and overtime payments for higher-grade officers had produced much discontent resulting in the banning of overtime. Normal working was resumed following the establishment of a basis for negotiation as soon as incomes policy permitted.

These expressions of frustration in small areas within the Institution reflected the general discontent felt among Institution members, although for the majority no militant action had been taken. In other unions on the Staff Side, however, frustration had led to a one-day stoppage earlier in the year in protest at the abandonment of the civil service pay agreements. These more widespread outbreaks of militancy and the general expression of discontent emerging continually from union conferences persuaded the government that some initiative should be taken on issues which were causing widespread dissatisfaction but which were not directly attributable to incomes policy.

In a letter dated 6 April 1973, proposing a review of wider problems, the Lord Privy Seal suggested that the National Whitley Council should consider whether the concern which had been so widely expressed about civil service pay might be symptomatic of problems going both wider and deeper than the immediate issue of pay. The National Staff Side, while making it clear that they would in no circumstances regard the review as a substitute for the restoration of confidence in the pay system, accepted this opportunity for dealing with some of the outstanding problems and sought assurances that the necessary resources would be made available to deal with them. By September each constituent had forwarded its views to the secretary general of the National Staff Side on the subjects to be covered.

The Institution, while making it clear right from the outset that such a review should not be allowed to detract from the need to reach a satisfactory conclusion on the pay issues, forwarded a list of items which it considered important. All aspects of pay were covered, including the need to secure a fair settlement of all the 1973 pay reviews, the problems of distorted differentials and changing relativities, long pay scales and the need for urgent action to protect the position of civil servants who retire during periods of pay restrictions, as well as the special position of scientists. In the longer term the paper called for a coherent pay and grading structure and far greater co-ordination between constituents of the Staff Side on pay research reviews. Career prospects and recruitment policies, job satisfaction, the meeting of the claim for unestablished service to count for pension purposes, and the improvement of facilities for trade union work were also mentioned. The Institution also emphasised the need to ensure that the review was an effective one including consultation at all levels.

Scientists and supporting staff at the Central Veterinary Laboratory, Weybridge, walk out on 9 July 1977, in support of their claim for London weighting (*Surrey Herald*)

Members of the Directorate of Overseas Surveys protest, on 16 November 1976, against their projected dispersal to Glasgow (*M. Taylor*)

Focal point of the DOE Directorate General of Research branch demonstration, on 10 May 1978, to protest against manpower cuts in their research establishments, including the Transport and Road Research Laboratory

Opposite: The Institution in action during the one day strike for full restoration of pay research on 2 April 1979

In June and July 1979, after the history of the Institution had been completed, the Institution took militant action of a scale and duration never previously contemplated. The photographs show (a) a section of the audience at the national rally at the Wembley Conference Centre on 22 June, which began the campaign to secure fair pay for scientists and technologists and (b) the march to a regional rally in Bath on 17 July 1979 (*L. W. Router*)

This exercise achieved little beyond giving further impetus to office improvement schemes. As the Staff Side had originally feared, the resources to implement proposed changes were not forthcoming and action on the final report was quietly dropped by the Official Side.

ANOMALY TREATMENT

In its Advisory Report No. 1, *Anomalies*, published in September 1973, the Pay Board confirmed the soundness of the civil service pay research system and recommended that 'anomaly' treatment should be given to grades entitled to a pay research review with effect from 1 January 1973. The effect of the recommendation was that negotiations based on pay research for 1973 should proceed but that details should secure the approval of the Board before implementation, and that the operative date should be 7 November 1973, the beginning of Stage 3. The Board also recommended that the government should consider imposing some limitation on large increases by either staging or tapering. It made no recommendation about scientists. In addition the Board recommended that pay research should be on an annual basis and that 'outsiders' should be associated with the pay research exercise to stress its independence.

The Institution was very disappointed with the report. The pay of the professional and technology grades was already well behind that of their outside counterparts at the end of 1972. If no action was taken to secure pay-research-based increases from 1 January 1974, very serious anomalies would arise not only between the civil service grades and their outside counterparts but also between those grades and others within the civil service.

Following the report the Staff Side made further representations to the government, culminating in a meeting with the Prime Minister, to obtain anomaly treatment for scientists and anomaly treatment for the 1974 pay research reviews, for retrospection of anomaly treatment for the 1973 cases to 1 April, and for no tapering or staging to be applied. As a result of these representations the government agreed that the 1974 pay research reviews should be entitled to anomaly treatment. Large increases would be staged but not tapered. Increases for those whose basic pay exceeded £5,000 per annum would be staged and paid in two equal amounts; one on 7 November 1973 and the other at least twelve months later. It was agreed that the question of anomaly treatment for scientists should be referred to the Pay Board.

STAGE 3

During the closing stages of the Conservative government's incomes policy in January 1974, agreement was reached for the application of Stage 3 salary increases of 7 per cent to civil servants, subject to an underpinning minimum of £2·25 a week and an overriding maximum of not more than £350 per annum. The operative date was 1 January 1974. For those subject to a pay research review effective from 1 January 1974, and for the science grades, for whom a special review was in process, together with their related grades, the Stage 3 increases were paid on an interim basis.

The Stage 3 pay code also permitted increases in pay and improvements in conditions over and above the main settlement amounting in total to not more than 1 per cent of the salary bill. The civil service unions took advantage of this provision to open negotiations on a number of issues including overtime arrangements and starting pay on promotion. The improvements were secured.

Stage 3 of the pay code also permitted agreements to be made providing for threshold payments related to movements in the retail price index. An agreement was made in the civil service under this provision in May 1974. By the terms of the agreement successive extra payments of 40p per week became payable related to increases in the retail price index above a certain minimum level. The first of these payments was triggered by a rise in the retail price index in May 1974. When the agreement ended in November 1974 a total of eleven threshold payments had been authorised, providing additions to pay of £4·40 per week.

An increase was also secured in the London weighting payment. An agreed review of London weighting had, at first, been delayed by incomes policy restrictions, and the subject of London weighting was referred to the Pay Board. Pending the review of the Pay Board an interim agreement was reached for increases from 7 November 1973. The new rate for inner London was £228 per annum and the new rate for outer London was £110 per annum. This represented increases of £53 in inner London and £20 in outer London.

The report of the Pay Board on London weighting was published in July 1974. It suggested a basis of calculation which pointed to an increase in existing London weighting allowances. Following negotiations with the Official Side agreement was reached on revised arrangements for London weighting in the civil service payable from October 1974. The agreement provided for an increase of inner London weighting to £410 per annum and an increase in the outer London weighting to £260 per annum. The boundary for inner London weighting was extended from a 4-mile radius to a 5-mile radius from Charing Cross and the outer London boundary of 16 miles was extended to approximately 18 miles from Charing Cross. The operative date for the changes was 1 April 1974.

Other improvements negotiated by the Staff Side included a revised overtime and long-hours gratuities agreement and the provision of Saturday premium payments. Agreement was reached on these issues in June 1974.

The final breakdown in the new phase of the government's policy came at the beginning of 1974 in a confrontation with the miners. The miners said that the National Coal Board, under instructions from the government, was not permitted to negotiate a settlement which took into account the need to secure adequate manpower for the industry and to pay miners a satisfactory wage. There was a strike in the industry and the government then asked the Pay Board to undertake an examination of the claim of the miners for a pay increase larger than that permitted in the pay code. The effect of the mining dispute on British industry was extremely serious. Industry was reduced to three-day working and the economy deteriorated rapidly. The government decided to call a general election. In this election it was defeated and a new minority Labour government was returned. Labour won 301 seats out of a House of Commons of 635 members. The Conservatives won 297 seats even though their total vote was slightly more than that given to the Labour Party.

SCIENTISTS' PAY

The scientists' pay dispute continued. The Pay Board did not report by the end of Stage 2 as initially planned. Indeed, the terms of reference were not agreed until September. The Institution submitted its written evidence to the Board on Friday 19 October 1973; it was published in booklet form for wide distribution among the membership. The first part set out the background to the dispute, dealing briefly with the National Whitley Council pay agreements, the Priestley Commission report, the work and structure of the scientific civil service, its pay history, and the activities of the joint Institution/CSD working party. The second part presented the Institution's case against pay research and in favour of internal relativities.

In concluding its submission, the Institution, having drawn attention to the Priestley Commission's clear statement that the aim in pay negotiations should be to provide remuneration thought fair by members of the civil service and the community, said:

The Institution must leave the Board in no doubt about the feelings of scientists. Their present position within the service violates every notion of equity and justice. There is deep bitterness and resentment at the way in which every effort of the Institution to bring the dispute to an early end has been frustrated. The delay has become quite intolerable. And there is an intense and burning sense of injustice throughout the scientific grades who are now so seriously underpaid in comparison with their colleagues in other groups.

The situation cannot be justified on the basis of the Priestley Royal Commission report, frustrates the implementation of many of the Fulton reforms, militates against good management and affronts all feelings of justice.

The Institution therefore invites the Board to find in favour of its submission that:

(i)   pay research is inappropriate in the special circumstances of the science group;

(ii) the pay of the science group should be determined on the basis of internal relativities; and

(iii) these internal relativities should be with the professional and technology group.

The CSD evidence was submitted on 9 November and the Board was subsequently provided by each party with written notes on the other's case and with a number of supplementary factual memoranda. By the end of the year there had been three hearings at which the Institution, the CSD and the secretary general of the National Staff Side gave evidence. On the occasion of the CSD's presentation of its case Institution members demonstrated their solidarity behind the Institution's submission by sending many telegrams and letters of protest to the head of the civil service and departmental management.

THE SCIENTISTS' STRIKE

The expectation that the Pay Board would report early in the New Year was rudely shattered when the chairman of the Pay Board, Sir Frank Figgures, made it clear to the parties in the second week in January 1974 that the Board was finding it extremely difficult to come to a decision and would therefore be making further investigations which would take a considerable time. The Institution made immediate protests to the chairman of the Board and the head of the civil service and followed this with a claim for an immediate interim increase in the pay of scientists to restore broadly the relative position which obtained in 1971.

The CSD's view, expressed in an open letter to scientists published in *State Service*, was that by refusing to subject themselves to pay research scientists had brought the present situation on themselves. It said: 'They have therefore no formal procedure for determining their pay, and have not benefited, as have large numbers of non-industrial civil servants, from special treatment under the Stage Three Pay Code.'

The NEC gave official support to demonstrations organised by scientists at local establishments in support of the interim claim. The exact nature of the demonstrations was left to members at each establishment to determine. At establishments all over the country half-day strikes or mass walk-outs were staged. They were generally preceded by mass meetings at which resolutions were adopted calling upon local management to recognise the frustration of scientists and to communicate the fact to the CSD. Concurrently with these actions about forty groups of staff decided upon a policy of non-co-operation. This took a variety of forms including withdrawing agreement to Saturday working relating to the three-day week, overtime bans, refusal to travel outside official hours and the use of official transport only. The first round of demonstrations was brought to an end on 8 February, pending developments.

On 7 February, Airey Neave, MP for Abingdon, a constituency in which there were many civil service scientific establishments, introduced an adjournment debate on scientists' pay. Mr Neave said the CSD was entirely to blame for the sad situation on scientists' pay. He had never been satisfied about the government's attitude to scientists. By permitting the gap between the pay of scientists and administrators to arise the government had stamped itself as being anti-science and given credence to the view that the civil service administrators did not favour scientists at all. Several other MPs supported Airey Neave.

None of this pressure, however, secured a response from the CSD. Therefore, the Institution NEC called a half-day strike for scientists on 6 March. The NEC also decided for the first time in its history to authorise strike pay at the rate of £2 per half-day and later appealed to members for financial help towards the cost of the dispute. The strike call met with an enthusiastic response, and rallies and protest meetings were arranged in major establishments and provincial centres. A rally at the Central Hall, Westminster, was attended by 4,000 members and filled to overflowing. After the rally a march, led by a jazz band, stretched the whole length of Whitehall and a deputation called at 10 Downing Street to deliver letters of protest and the unanimous resolution of the meeting. The strike received widespread press and TV coverage.

The strike action was rapidly followed by discussions on the interim claim with the Minister of State for the Civil Service in the new Labour government formed in March, but these were overtaken by the publication of the Pay Board's report on 9 April.

THE PAY BOARD'S REPORT

The report of the Pay Board, *The Civil Service Science Group*, recommended as follows:

(a) The science group should continue to be treated as a single entity for pay purposes and should be subject to the normal pay research process. Differences between the civil service and outside employments which cannot be taken into account in making comparisons should be treated as unquantifiable factors in the negotiations.

(b) The parties, together with the PRU, should review pay research procedures for the science group with a view to ensuring that the full range of factors making up the jobs which are to be compared are identified.

(c) The negotiations on pay research findings for the PSO should take account of internal relationships as well as the unquantifiable factors.

(d) The adjustment for both these factors should be such as to ensure that the PSO salary, at the minimum and the maximum of the scale, does not differ by more than 5 per cent from that of the principal.

(e) As a corollary to (c) and (d) there should be a review of PSO posts to ensure that they are all of an equivalent level of responsibility to principal, bearing in mind the range of tolerance in salary recommended above.

(f) The maximum of the SSO scale should be adjusted if pay research does not produce an appropriate differential with the minimum of the PSO scale. This adjustment should be regarded as also taking account of the unquantifiable factor of differing career patterns for older SSOs.

(g) All possible steps should be taken, by regrading if necessary, to ensure that posts are correctly graded as between the science group and the P&T group.

The Institution's immediate reaction to the report was summed up in its statement to the press:

The Institution is severely disappointed by the formal recommendations of the Board in the light of all the evidence which was submitted during the inquiry. The recommendations are by no means straightforward. They will require discussions with the government and management and they will take a considerable time to implement. In these discussions the Institution will aim for an agreement using the Board's report as a basis. Given goodwill on the part of the government there is no reason why an agreement satisfactory to both parties should not be reached.

The Board's report makes plain the imperative need for an immediate and substantial increase in the pay of scientists. This cannot await the long-term solution. Negotiations must start at once and we hope the government will agree that they should be concluded by the end of this month.

The Board's report was disappointing to the Institution primarily because it did not accept that pay research was inappropriate for scientists, although it did suggest considerable modifications in its operation. It did accept the need to take internal relativities into account, particularly at PSO level, but offered, in recommendation (*d*), a quaint formula to carry this into effect. The Institution was at a loss to understand why a 5 per cent margin of tolerance had been chosen when the administration principal and PPTO had never diverged by more than 1 per cent when their reviews were most nearly in phase. These issues, and particularly the need for reviews stemming from recommendations (*b*), (*e*) and (*g*) of the report, were for resolution in the long term.

In the short term there was an immediate need for an increase and to determine the basis on which the pay of the science grades was to be fixed until long-term arrangements could be agreed. At a lengthy meeting with the minister of state on 18 April the Institution commented in detail on the Pay Board report, indicated how the issues left unresolved could best be tackled and presented an immediate pay claim for scientists. On 6 May the government announced that it had decided to give its consent to enable immediate pay increases to be given to the science group and those in related employment in the civil service and other public bodies.

Discussions on the size of the increase proved to be more difficult, and it was not until a deputation had been taken to the Prime Minister that an offer was received which the scientific staffs group (SSG), with only one dissentient, felt able to recommend to members. Members were extensively consulted on the offer which, although it did not meet the Institution's claim in full, made substantial improvements on the relativities with the administration group established in 1971. A substantial majority favoured acceptance, subject to certain reservations. Formal agreement was reached on 13 June, but in its letter of acceptance the Institution made it clear that the offer was accepted most reluctantly and only because of the extremely difficult economic and industrial relations situation.

For the settlement of the pay of scientists in the medium term, pending the resolution of the outstanding long-term problems, it was finally agreed in October that any form of pay research was impossible for 1975 and that the pay of the science group should be adjusted in that year by interpolation from any adjustments made to the administration group's pay at the current equivalent pay levels.

The frustration and disappointment of the scientists that their longstanding pay dispute had still not been satisfactorily solved was reflected in the debate at the 1974 conference. Two of the motions censured the general secretary, the NEC and the SSG. The motion condemning the general secretary for his 'abject failure' to maintain the pay and status of scientists over the past three years was moved by the Atomic Weapons Research Establishment branch, but was heavily defeated by conference. The second motion, moved by the same branch, censured the scientific staffs group and the NEC for lack of leadership during the scientists' pay dispute. The general secretary, defending the NEC and the SSG, said that conference should not be deceived as to who was the enemy. The dispute would have been settled long since had it rested on the decision of the Institution alone. The opposition had been from the government. The motion was defeated. Another motion, moved by the Atomic Energy branch, seeking the dissolution of the SSG, was also defeated.

Four emergency motions were carried by conference. One endorsed the actions of the SSG and the NEC and authorised the NEC to take all appropriate action to secure an agreement and to obtain acceptable pay criteria and a satisfactory pay structure for the science group for the future. Another said that in the event of scientists being submitted to pay research, modification of the procedures to ensure fair results was essential. Another asked for a national public campaign demonstrating the inequality between the science and administration groups. The final emergency motion suggested that the NEC should make the implementation of Fulton a prime aim of the Institution.

So ended the second major episode in the fight for scientists' pay. The long-term resolution of the dispute was still to come, but in the medium term arrangements had been secured that would ensure that scientists did not fall too far behind their equivalents in other grades within the service.

24 The Machinery of Government Changes

The Conservative Government came to office in 1970 committed to achieving substantial changes, both qualitative and quantitative, in the organisation of the civil service. It was committed to cutting the number of civil servants and streamlining the machinery of government.

In reviewing the 'new regime' after a month in office the general secretary drew attention to the government's intentions but noted that it was too soon to say what the effect would be. Any new government, he said, was entitled to the goodwill of the civil service but

> At the same time, it is necessary to speak frankly about the problems which face the service. It is, I believe, true that the civil service is in a highly sensitive state because of the way it has been treated, examined and re-examined over recent years. This is not intended as a condemnation of the previous government. As an employer it made serious mistakes and errors of judgement but it also has much to its credit. The fact nevertheless remains that unless there is manifestly fair treatment of the service there is a likelihood of a major collapse of morale.

This warning was prophetic. The cuts in civil service, together with the controversies over civil service pay, were to bring civil service morale to its lowest ebb for many years. Morale in the Institution was affected by these general developments but also by the problems of scientists' pay and further reorganisations in research and development, which, together, were interpreted by members as a specific attack on the scientific civil service. The Institution was also affected by redundancies among the membership, and by growing disappointment arising from slowness in implementing the recommendations of the Fulton Report.

PROGRESS ON FULTON

In February 1969 the Joint Committee of the National Whitley Council issued its first report on progress, *Developments on Fulton*. Soon afterwards the NEC issued a circular to branches and professional groups reviewing the Fulton recommendations on structure. The circular indicated that the NEC intended to press for early interim action on the abolition of class barriers, the creation of a unified higher civil service above the level of administrative principal, PSO and senior grade engineer, and the simplification of the present class structure by amalgamating as many as possible of the existing classes. A decision had already been taken in principle for the creation of a unified structure at the level of under-secretary and above.

The NEC took the view that in preparing proposals for interim steps in reorganisation the Institution should adhere to the basic proposals which it had submitted to the Fulton Committee. One of the first issues which needed to be decided was whether to propose combined or separate science and technology categories. The Professional (B and E), Technical Classes, and Drawing Office Groups and the STCS Executive Committee were all in favour of a combined science and technology category. The Scientific Staffs Group, however, rejected the proposal for a combined category by a vote of seventeen to thirteen, and by a vote of eighteen to ten urged the NEC not to put such a proposal to the CSD.

In July 1969, a year after the publication of the Fulton Report, an agreement on the 'timing of interim changes in the grading structure of the civil service' was announced. The agreement said that it was intended to establish a common structure from the top of the service down to under-secretary and below that it was intended to introduce one or more continuous grading structures from top to bottom in the field covered by the scientific, works group and supporting classes, and that there was to be a merger of the administrative, executive and clerical classes as soon as practicable. Certain departmental classes were also to be included in the merged structure. The joint committee of the National Whitley Council on the Fulton Report affirmed the principle of free lateral movement between different occupations within the civil service.

The interim structure closely resembled the proposals which the Institution had submitted to the Fulton Committee. Moreover the common structure at the top, the creation of continuous grading structures from top to bottom below that and the removal of class barriers were three of the five points which the Institution had singled out for early action. A great deal of work was also done on the implementation of the principles of accountable management, another of the items to which the Institution had given priority.

On the day chosen for the Institution's Golden Jubilee celebrations, 20 November 1969, the NEC brought together 250 branch representatives at Caxton Hall, London, to discuss the Fulton diagnosis and its many implications. The programme was divided into sessions on training, personnel management and structure. On the latter the general secretary had this to say:

> The first principle in reorganising the structure of the civil service is to implement the normal career expectations which we have been advocating for every year of our fifty years of existence. In our evidence to Fulton we emphasised how very far behind are all the areas of our membership compared with those in the administration grades. Any structure that emerges that does not improve the careers of the professional classes and bring them up to the level of the administration classes will be unacceptable to us, and we ought not to have anything to do with it. This is a crucially important period and if we settle for less than our basic aims now then we will be in mischief for the next fifty years.

In March 1970 the joint committee of the National Whitley Council published its second progress report, *Fulton: A Framework for the Future* which reported on the developments in staff structure envisaged following Fulton. It was largely a record of the studies being pursued following the agreement on the interim developments which were jointly accepted as desirable. The report also gave the Official Side's proposals for an interim merger of the administrative, executive and clerical classes. The report ended with a reminder of what the objectives of the Fulton Report were:

> our objectives are to eliminate the obstacles to the flexible deployment of the human resources on which the service depends, and to provide those at present in the service and those who join it in the future with the fullest possible opportunity to develop their talents. In particular it is essential that there is clearly seen to be 'an open road to the top'.

Some progress was made in 1970 but it was neither as fast nor as extensive as the Institution was anxious to achieve. Shortly before the end of the year agreement was reached on the interim merger of the administrative, executive and clerical classes to form the general category but progress on the interim merger of the science and technology classes was not satisfactory. Agreement was reached on the wide extension of job appraisal interviews, and good progress was made on producing new annual report forms but much work remained to be done on the introduction of satisfactory career management arrangements. In the spring the Official Side had acknowledged the need to improve career prospects for the professional classes but little progress was made in securing improvements.

It was becoming increasingly clear by this time that developments following the Fulton Report were not at all satisfactory from the Institution's point of view and disillusionment was developing among the membership. By the publication of the third report by the joint committee of the National Whitley Council, *Fulton: The Re-shaping of the Civil Service – Developments during 1970*, there were a few satisfactory developments to report. The disagreement between the CSD and the Institution over whether the proposed science category should have six grades or five had finally been resolved in favour of the Institution's point of view. Work had also begun on 'Project ST' which was to investigate the grading structure at the lower end of the science and technology classes and their relationship to supporting staff in both the industrial and non-industrial grades. Agreement was also reached on 'lateral movement and opportunity posts', whereby movements of staff between different occupational groups could be more easily achieved. Little progress was made, however, on improving the career prospects of specialists in comparison with the 'generalist' grades.

The 1971 Institution conference carried a resolution sponsored by the NEC which asked the Institution to make a determined effort to improve the situation, particularly on career prospects, and to make a special report for consideration by branches by December. The speaker for the NEC reminded delegates that the Official Side were themselves administrators and that 'the leopard does not change his spots overnight'. Real progress on career prospects was only likely to be made with the early implementation of the Fulton proposals on accountable management and integrated hierarchies so that specialists would have the authority to match their responsibilities and the experience needed to compete in the 'open structure at the top'.

A new science category was agreed in October 1971 and a new professional and technology category was introduced from January 1972. The agreement for the setting up of the latter category included a number of other welcome features.

From January 1972 the hours of work of the technical classes were reduced to those which were normal in the civil service. Staff who were formerly in the works group, main and basic grades, were also made eligible for long-hours gratuities. The establishment of the new professional and technology category on 1 January 1972 was also made to coincide with the pay research review of the pay of the grades involved in the merger. The Institution was able to persuade the Civil Service Department that the pay negotiations should aim at producing pay scales for the five combined grades.

In an article in *State Service* the deputy general secretary of the Institution, Mr Cyril Cooper, said that the setting-up of the P&T category was a very important step forward. It was not so much that in itself it created improved career opportunities but that it provided the essential framework within which improvements could become possible. Career opportunities for professional and technological grades should be equal to those in the administration group.

DISAPPOINTMENT ON FULTON

These welcome developments, however, were matched by disappointment on other fronts. In March 1972 the government indicated that it had decided not to pursue the Fulton open structure recommendation 'by the further extension of unified grading (below under-secretary) at this juncture'. The Institution saw this as ensuring the continued hold of the 'administrative mandarins' on the top posts in the civil service, and as a move which would inevitably restrict the career opportunities of specialists. The study of posts below under-secretary, down to and including senior principal level, had shown that it would be possible to devise a workable scheme for carrying unified grading down to that level, but the Institution was almost alone in arguing that this should in fact be done. However, it was agreed that above principal level the civil service would remain, as it was then, a single entity for purposes of pay determination. It was also agreed that in the immediate future attention should be concentrated on the possibilities of simplifying grading structures between the principal and under-secretary levels and on the reduction of the number of pay and grading structures.

By the time of the 1972 annual conference morale in the Institution on the Fulton issue had reached a low ebb. The final report from the joint committee of the National Whitley Council, *The Shape of the Post-Fulton Civil Service*, published before conference, seemed to imply by its title and its content that the major work had been completed. The first paragraph stated: 'While much still remains to be done in reaching decisions and while the work of implementing them has in many areas only just started, the report shows that a clear indication of the shape and substance of the post-Fulton Civil Service is emerging.'

For Institution members the progress they had expected to see from the Fulton recommendations had hardly begun. As the general secretary remarked in his address to conference:

It is manifest that there is throughout the Institution a deep disappointment and concern about the present position. Reports come of gleeful whispers in the corridors of power that Fulton is dead. There are mournful complaints from some members that if this is Fulton they want nothing to do with it.

The general secretary's view was not entirely pessimistic. He reminded conference that the Fulton Committee had said that the reforms would not be easy to carry out, that they would require a great deal of prolonged, difficult, and complicated work, and that full implementation would take a good many years to achieve. Progress had been made on several fronts although these were not necessarily immediately beneficial to every individual. There had been some progress on introducing accountable management. Management training had been improved but, unfortunately, there was a reluctance among Institution members to take advantage of the new training opportunities. There had been developments in the procedures for career management. On the other hand, the membership were right to be concerned about the lack of progress in improving career prospects.

On structure the situation was unsatisfactory. Although there was now a unified grading structure at under-secretary level and above, very few members had a direct personal interest at that high level. For there to be a real 'road to the top' as far as specialists were concerned, it would need to be brought down much lower and the Institution would continue its campaign for this to be done. Mr McCall acknowledged that new categories had been established for the purposes of pay and grading and that they were very much along the lines desired by the Institution. Nevertheless, not enough progress had been made in the grouping of other classes within the various categories and a great deal of work remained to be done.

The chairman, in his address to conference, made it clear that in his view if the Institution was to make progress on aspects of the Fulton Report which they held dear, particularly the issue of unified grading down to principal and equivalent level, then it would have to 'go it alone'. It had become clear to him that the view taken after the publication of the Fulton Report that the best prospect of rapid progress lay in joint rather than unilateral representation was a mistaken one. The FDA and the Society were opposed to the extension of unified grading and to other changes which would increase the competition from specialists.

Sir William Armstrong, the head of the civil service, also addressed the 1972 conference. The delegates gave him a friendly welcome and listened with close attention to his speech. The content of his speech, however, in which he said that after long and earnest study it had been decided that the further extension of unified grading was not the most advantageous way forward, did not please conference. Immediately following Sir William Armstrong's speech the conference discussed the latest developments in the implementation of the Fulton Report and a very critical resolution was adopted. The conference noted with regret the change in the Official Side's policy to one of opposition to the extension of unified grading. The delegates instructed the National Executive Committee to continue to press for the extension of unified grading.

At the 1973 annual conference frustration at the slow progress on Fulton was mounting. In his address to conference the general secretary reported a lack of progress on many fronts but some progress on others. Project ST had been completed in April 1972. The inconsistencies and anomalies which it revealed had been the source of indignant protest and bitterness for many years and both sides had accepted that it should be dealt with urgently. The Institution had proposed that the report should be used as the basis for a comprehensive rationalisation and simplification of the grading structure but despite Institution pressure there had been no comprehensive discussions. Progress had been made in developing career management systems for the newly integrated science and professional and technology structures but on the crucial issue of career prospects progress had again been disappointingly slow.

Membership feeling at the lack of progress in implementing Fulton was strongly expressed by the delegates. The first seventeen paragraphs of the NEC's annual report, which dealt with progress on the Fulton recommendations, were 'referred back'. The reference back of the first sixteen paragraphs was moved by a delegate from the Ordnance Survey branch. He recalled that there had been jubilation in the Institution following the Fulton Report. Today, the only jubilation which could be found was in the corridors of the CSD, inhabited by the FDA and the Society. They danced their triumphal jig on the Fulton grave and the joyous cry of 'Fulton is dead, victory and long life for tradition, privilege and the philosophy of the all-round amateur' could be heard. He added that the CSD was supposed to implement and administer government policy and not to obstruct and frustrate it. He urged that the Institution should take action where it would be effective and he deplored the apologetic content of the NEC report.

Speaking on behalf of the NEC, the deputy general secretary, Cyril Cooper, said that in Fulton lay the salvation of the specialist grades and it was quite disgraceful that Fulton had not been operated to any real extent in the way that was intended when the report first appeared. He said that the Institution would continue to make strong representations in support of the policy determined by the annual conference.

The reference back of paragraph 17 on career opportunities was moved by a delegate from the DoE Directorate General of Research branch. He argued that paragraph 17 was misleading in that it did not reflect the lack of progress which had been made on the issue. In reply, Cyril Cooper, for the NEC, said that it was not the intention of the paragraph to suggest that there was now equality in career prospects between generalists and specialists, but valuable achievements had been gained. In both cases the reference back was carried.

THE MELVILLE–BURNEY REPORT

In its evidence to Fulton the Institution had drawn particular attention to the plight of the professional accountants in the service and they were one of the three specialist groups on whom the Fulton Report had made specific comments. A working party on accountants 'to examine the problems of accountants in the civil service in the light of the Fulton Committee's report and to make proposals for dealing with them to the appropriate Fulton subcommittee' was one of the first working parties to be established following Fulton. Little progress was achieved and a new inquiry was established in 1971.

Sir Ronald Melville, a recently retired permanent secretary, and Sir Anthony Burney, a senior partner in a prominent firm of chartered accountants, were appointed in October 1971 to consider (i) to what extent the civil service would benefit from employing the services of more professional accountants and particularly those of high calibre; (ii) how the needs could best be met; (iii) whether there was any scope for improving the use made of professional accountants already in the civil service; and (iv) whether any changes should be made in the arrangements for the recruitment of professional accountants to the service and their subsequent management.

The Institution's Accountants Group, together with the District Auditors' branch, submitted evidence to the inquiry, pointing out a number of fields where professional accountants could be used to considerable advantage. It also pointed to the poor career prospects of accountants and the existence of a severe 'age blockage'.

The Melville–Burney Report on the use of accountants in the civil service was published in 1973. Its main recommendations were: (i) the creation of a strong accountancy service comprising the existing professional class, the district audit service and additional accountants brought in on secondment or contract terms; (ii) the appointment of a high-calibre head of profession, with second permanent secretary status, with responsibility for the accountancy service and for the professional standards and career of all its members; (iii) the introduction of flexible recruitment arrangements, including direct recruitment at all levels for some years at least; and (iv) the improvement of career opportunities for accountants, including faster promotion for the best people within the accountancy service, interchange with outside employers and the possibility of movement to administrative posts.

The Institution welcomed the report and was anxious to make progress as quickly as possible. It was agreed with the CSD that the first priority must be to find a suitable head of profession. This proved very difficult and a suitable candidate was not found until 1975, when Mr Kenneth Sharp, immediate past president of the Institute of Chartered Accountants in England and Wales, was appointed.

The other two groups in the Institution's membership to be singled out for special mention by the Fulton Committee were the research officers and the lawyers, among whom the Institution had members (although the majority of lawyers were represented by the Civil Service Legal Society). By 1972 progress was well advanced, following advice by Sir Edmund Compton, on the creation of a legal career service, the appointment of a head of profession and the introduction of an appropriate degree of central management.

Agreement on the future of the research officers was not achieved until 1976 when in place of the former linked departmental class of research officer there was established a research officer category comprising two occupational groups – a social science research group and a resource and planning research group. The previous lower three grades in the research officer class were retained but renamed, and two extra grades were added at senior principal and assistant secretary level.

THE MACHINERY OF GOVERNMENT

In a speech opening the Civil Service College, shortly after the 1970 general election, the new Prime Minister referred to the section of the Conservative Party manifesto for the general election which stated:

There has been too much government interference in the day-to-day workings of industry and local government. There has been too much government; there will be less . . . and we also said that we would reduce the number of civil servants, and that the functions and responsibilities of all departments and government agencies will be systematically rationalised with cost reduction plans for every single ministry in Whitehall.

The Prime Minister went on to say that the size of the civil service was largely the result of the tasks it was called on to perform by the government and that there would, therefore, need to be a reduction in those tasks. He also referred to the government's intention to introduce businessmen into Whitehall, in consultation with the Staff Side.

During the summer of 1970 informal consultations took place and the government undertook a review of functions, the outcome of which was published in October in a White Paper, *The Reorganisation of Central Government*. It outlined the government's proposals for the immediate reorganisation of departments, and its intention to review certain functions, and to consider 'hiving off' work from the civil service. The Board of Trade and the Ministry of Technology were brought together in the Department of Trade and Industry (DTI), and the Ministry of Housing and Local Government, Ministry of Public Building and Works and the Ministry of Transport were combined to form the Department of the Environment (DoE). By the end of the year steps had been taken to abolish the Land Commission.

ACCOUNTABLE MANAGEMENT AND 'HIVING OFF'

The Institution had supported the notion of 'accountable management' in its evidence to Fulton and had been gratified to see it supported by the Fulton Committee. The creation of large departments and the emphasis on efficient management in the White Paper on the machinery of government gave the Institution great hope that accountable management and the associated notion of integrated management hierarchies comprising both specialists and generalists would be widely adopted in the service.

The Institution was less keen about 'hiving off' functions entirely from the civil service. In some cases, the Institution argued, this was right. Thus, the general secretary in his address to the 1971 conference referred to the example of the Civil Aviation Authority which had been created in 1970 as a result of the recommendations of the Committee of Inquiry into Civil Air Transport, chaired by Sir Ronald Edwards. In that case the way that civil aviation had been passed from department to department in a virtually non-stop series of changes since the end of the war had been thoroughly unsatisfactory and damaging to efficiency. But, he argued, 'hiving off' was not the right answer in most cases. It could increase the number of staff and complicate procedures and could never be justified simply as an artificial device for reducing the number of civil servants.

Support for accountable management in the form of which the Institution approved came from two reviews flowing from the White Paper, one in defence and one in the DoE. Mr D. Rayner, a member of the top management team in Marks & Spencer, was asked by the government to assist with its inquiries into the functions of government. His report on the organisation of the procurement executive responsible to the Secretary of State for Defence proposed an organisational structure

> aimed at strengthening line management and at getting away from the exist-ence of parallel hierarchies within defence procurement . . . This would result in the creation of accountable units of management with all their attendant advantages, one being that there would be a sharper focus of responsibility than is possible under the present system.

The Institution had high hopes that the inquiries within the DoE would have similar results. One was an inquiry into the structure, organisation and management of the constructive responsibilities of the former MPBW, appointed in 1971 and headed by Mr Herbert Cruikshank, a businessman and deputy chairman of Bovis Holdings. Another was the inquiry into property management in government, also appointed in 1971 and chaired by Mr Timothy Sainsbury of J. Sainsbury. Finally, there was an inter-departmental working party on accountable management for the supplies division. The Institution gave evidence to all three inquiries, including the need for accountable management units managed by integrated hierarchies including professionals.

The inquiries resulted in the establishment of a Property Services Agency (PSA) in September 1972, which was to include the bulk of the former MPBW organisation, including the supplies division, together with the defence lands service of the Ministry of Defence. The initial organisation of the PSA provided for a management board, headed by a chief executive, Mr John Cuckney, a banker who had previously chaired the Mersey Docks and Harbour Board. The Board also included four deputy chief executives and three under-secretaries. The Institution was disappointed to find that only one member of the manage-ment board was a professional officer, and a deputation was taken to the chief executive to express the Institution's concern at the diminution of professional influence in the higher management of the PSA's activities which had resulted from the top appointments.

The Institution urged that there should be clearly understood machinery under which, on matters affecting the whole range of work of the Agency, the collective views of heads of professions could be reported direct to the man-agement board. Informal arrangements to do so were in consequence made. It also urged that there should be some form of machinery for identifying talented professional staff early in their careers so that they could compete on equal terms with administrators for top management posts in the future. Towards the end of 1972 two part-time appointments of professionals from outside the service, Mr Herbert Cruikshank, a professional engineer who had headed the inquiry, and Sir Hugh Wilson, a former president of the Royal Institute of British Architects, were made. The Institution made it clear that external appointments of professionals could be no substitute for serving professional officers sitting on the management board by virtue of their line management responsibilities.

In May 1973 the government published a Government Trading Funds Bill which was to provide for certain quasi-commercial services within government to be financed through trading funds rather than directly from votes. The Bill named six Crown services for which trading funds would be established, although others could be included later if their operations were found suitable for trading funds. Those named were the Royal Ordnance Factories (ROF), the Royal Dockyards, the Royal Mint, Her Majesty's Stationery Office (HMSO), the Ordnance Survey and the Supplies Division of the PSA. The Institution welcomed this development which was in line with its general policy of support for accountable management.

In the event the Ordnance Survey was excluded from the Government Trading Funds Act, 1973, but cost and budget centres were introduced by agreement with the Staff Side. HMSO established a trading fund as did the ROF organisation within MoD (PE). The Royal Dockyards in MoD (PE) and the Supplies Division within PSA and the Royal Mint also developed similar arrangements.

Several areas in which the Institution had an interest were 'hived off' from the civil service. The Water Research Centre was created in 1974 and the Water Pollution Research Laboratory was transferred out of the civil service to its control. Negotiations on behalf of the staff secured a contract which compared favourably with civil service conditions. Towards the end of 1972 the trustees and director of the British Museum announced the formation of a new company, British Museum Publications Ltd, to handle work hitherto carried out by the publications department of the museum. Before there was any consultation with the Staff Side the posts of managing director with 'profit participation' and an accountancy secretary were advertised in the press. The Staff Side reacted strongly and the proposed new arrangements were suspended. The new company began in 1973 and agreement was reached that no individual should participate in profits and one board member should be nominated by the British Museum Staff Side. Apart from five senior posts it was agreed that the company should be staffed by indefinite secondment from the British Museum. The government also decided in 1972 to 'hive off' a small amount of work of the Overseas Survey Division of the Overseas Development Administration and hand it over to private enterprise. Despite protests from the Institution the move went ahead.

The Institution also feared at one point that the Manpower Services Commission and its agencies, the Employment Services Agency and the Training Services Agency, newly created in January 1974, would be completely 'hived off' from the civil service. In the event they remained within the civil service.

In 1971 the decision was taken to establish the British Library as a fringe body and to include within it the British Museum Library, the National Reference Library for Science and Invention, the National Science Lending Library, the National Central Library and the British National Bibliography. Its establishment followed the report of the National Libraries Committee, under the chairmanship of Dr F. S. Dainton, vice-chancellor of Nottingham University, which had been asked to consider how a comprehensive national library service covering all categories of library-users might most efficiently be provided. While welcoming the proposal that the main national libraries should be brought together under one administration, the Institution opposed the separation of the British Library from the civil service. The Institution played a leading part in the consortium of seven staff associations which negotiated conditions of service in the British Library. As a result of representations to the Secretary of State for Education and Science a statement was included in the British Library Act of July 1972 which safeguarded the conditions of those who had previously been employed in the civil service or by the trustees of the British Museum. It ensured that the terms of employment taken as a whole would be 'not less favourable in the case of each person than those on which he is employed at the time when an offer is made to him of employment with the Board'.

THE NEWTON AND MELVILLE INQUIRIES

In December 1970 the Prime Minister invited Sir Gordon Newton, editor of the *Financial Times,* to lead a review of the Central Office of Information (COI). The terms of reference were: 'To review the aims and functions of the Central Office of Information, its relationship to departments and whether its functions and status accord with general government policy set out in the White Paper on *The Reorganisation of Central Government;* and to report on these matters and their organisational implications.'

The Institution was apprehensive about the review in the light of the long history of reviews and cuts in the COI since its inception in 1946. As recently as 1969 the Duncan Committee on overseas representation had questioned the effectiveness of existing methods of publicity and proposed a reshaping of the government's overseas information services. The Institution's evidence to the Newton Committee made a strong case for the COI remaining as a single integrated organisation. It argued against 'hiving off' which would have the effect of making relationships with its client departments within the civil service more tenuous, could create difficulties with the Official Secrets Act, and would damage the existing intimate understanding of the way in which government policy was formulated. The Institution's evidence argued strongly for the information officer class to be used in the Foreign and Commonwealth Office and for an extension of career prospects for COI staff.

The Newton Report was not published. Shortly afterwards the Prime Minister decided that the COI should continue in being but that its trade fairs work should be transferred to the DTI. He also announced that a further review of activity in the COI, headed by Sir Ronald Melville, formerly a permanent secretary in the Ministry of Aviation Supply and seconded to the CSD for special duties, was to be set in hand. The review was to be aimed at cutting out any overlap and at reducing those activities which departments asked the COI to undertake by relating such activities more directly to specific objectives. Special attention was to be paid to the overseas information effort, and the information work in departments was to be examined.

As a consequence of the Newton Report some ninety-eight staff, eighty-four of them within the information officer class, were transferred to the newly created British Export Board. The Board, though strictly speaking outside the civil service, was to be staffed by civil servants from the DTI, although later, against Staff Side opposition, some twenty-four British National Export Council staff were offered established civil service posts with the Board.

The Melville Report was issued in 1972. It recommended an extension of 'contracting out'; reorientation and reduction in the information effort directed overseas; and the transfer of the low-priced-books scheme from the COI to the British Council. Other suggestions were put forward regarding overseas dispatch arrangements and the setting-up of a research unit in the COI for greater research into the home and overseas programme. There was a possibility that the Central Film Library would be transferred to a commercial agency. Sir Ronald's recommendations amounted to a further reduction in the COI complement.

The Institution opposed any redundancy that might arise from the report but was prepared to discuss future manning requirements on their merits. The Institution did not agree that COI work should be contracted out unless it was clearly cheaper and more efficient for the work to be done outside, and unless the work was of an appropriate character to be done outside. In the event the recommended manpower reductions did not result in any redundancy.

THE MATTHEW–SKILLINGTON INQUIRY

In 1972 the Secretary of State for the Environment announced the setting-up of a two-man team of inquiry to advise him on the best possible means of promoting high standards of design in government buildings, in the conservation of the built environment and in new physical developments falling within his purview. The inquiry team consisted of Sir Robert Matthew, a former president of the Royal Institute of British Architects, and Mr W. P. D. Skillington, a deputy secretary in the Department of Environment in charge of the housing and construction industries group.

The Institution submitted evidence to the inquiry in October. It set out the need to establish the PSA in a leading design and construction role within the industry and pressed for the appointment of a first-class design architect on the staff of the Agency at management level. It stressed the need within the DoE to ensure satisfactory co-ordination and control of the department's responsibilities for 'the built environment' across the full range of professional activities, and recommended the creation of a post of director general of the built environment which would include the functions of a chief architect for DoE Central. It restated the case for integrated team-working to replace the system of parallel 'works' and 'secretariat' hierarchies in the PSA. It also pressed for provisions for the advancement of professional staff to senior levels on the basis of high professional competence. The evidence also criticised the amount and quality of work which was put out to external consultants and the extensive use made of contract drawing office staff.

The Matthew–Skillington Report became available in July 1974. The Institution welcomed its proposals to appoint a chief architect at board level in the PSA and at deputy secretary level in DoE Central. It opposed, however, the report's preference for parallel rather than integrated hierarchies in the management structure below those levels. The Institution also regretted the omission by the inquiry team of any recommendation in respect of training and career development, and its failure to deal with the problem of outside contractors and consultants. In March 1975 the secretary of state published proposals, without prior consultation with the Staff Side, which further diluted the impact of the report's recommendations and further reduced the likelihood of achieving the Institution's objectives.

REDUNDANCY AND STAFF CEILINGS

As a result of the government's declared intention to cut the number of civil servants and the reviews of the machinery of government which it had set in motion, it was clear that for the first time in many years there were likely to be redundancies in the civil service.

Early candidates for such redundancies were likely to be Institution members in the Ministry of Agriculture, Fisheries and Food (MAFF), where a special committee had been established to consider reductions in the ministry's advisory work. This was done without consultation with the Staff Side. The Institution held a press conference to protest publicly at the investigation which, according to the Institution, did not seek to examine the case on its merits but was concerned to find some means of bringing about cuts in staff. This approach said the Institution, was exemplified by the Minister of Agriculture, who had said when justifying cuts,

I am a member of a government which sincerely believes that we have over-governed in the past . . . we aim to reduce the amount of government activity so cutting back public expenditure and the number of civil servants. It is against this background that I am reviewing the functions of the department to determine which should be discontinued.

The cuts in MAFF were focused on the staff who provided technical and scientific information to improve the productivity of the farming industry. It was initially envisaged that 500 to 800 of these advisory posts would have to go, representing about 25 per cent of the agricultural advisory service. The process was to begin by cutting the retirement age to 60 years and dismissing temporary staff. During 1971 the Institution conducted a campaign both against the cuts themselves, claiming that the impartial professional advice supplied by the advisory service in MAFF could not adequately be replaced by private industry as the government envisaged, and against the methods being used to implement the cuts.

The cuts proceeded, however, and over a three-year period up to March 1974, 478 staff had to be made redundant. This was achieved through volunteers, as the Institution had requested, but also by natural wastage and the compulsory discharge of officers over 60 years of age. This last action was strongly resisted by the Institution on the grounds that wastage and volunteers were providing the required rundown, but MAFF was adamant in discharging all these officers at the end of July 1972. It was only as a result of strong Institution pressure that they were not discharged much earlier. The over-sixties were informed that they could appeal to the Industrial Tribunal against their discharge and some of them did so. The Institution decided to give financial and legal backing to an initial group of over-sixties for a test case at the Industrial Tribunal, but was unsuccessful in getting the dismissal defined as 'unfair'. As a result of pressure from the Institution, however, all officers who wished to accept re-employment at a lower grade were offered the opportunity of doing so.

On 4 November 1971, a new premature retirement agreement was signed in the civil service eleven months after the first proposals were put by the Official Side. The agreement marked a significant improvement in the existing 'abolition of office' terms in both scope and amount of compensation. The agreement provided for the division of staff into 'mobile' (executive officer and above) and 'immobile' (below EO) categories. The latter, who hitherto had been unable to receive compensation under 'abolition of office' terms, were now to receive compensation for redundancy if there were no alternative posts available within daily travelling distance. The agreement also provided improved compensation terms for premature retirement for those in mobile grades.

The agreement was also significant, however, in that it introduced the possibility of premature retirement on structural grounds. This provision, on which the Official Side was most insistent, gave rise to acute difficulty and was opposed by the Staff Side. As a result of negotiations it was agreed that premature retirement on structural grounds could only be used at senior principal grade equivalent and higher grades. It was also agreed that there should be consultation with the Staff Side and a search for 'willing victims' before any compulsory retirement on these grounds was decided. The agreement also provided for premature retirement on grounds of 'limited efficiency', but it was agreed that this would only take place exceptionally in the case of grades below the level of senior principal, and that there would be carefully devised procedures to ensure that staff affected would have every advice and assistance in improving their performance before a final decision was taken. Appeals against any form of premature retirement could be taken to the newly established Civil Service Appeals Board.

During negotiations the Staff Side expressed fears that the new agreement would alter the whole character of employment in the civil service and was the prelude to large-scale redundancies, but the Lord Privy Seal gave an assurance that this was not the government's intention. Provision was made to review the operation of the scheme after two or three years and the National Staff Side said they would be watching closely to see how it operated in practice.

In the autumn of 1972 the National Staff Side tabled proposals for a new national redundancy agreement for the civil service, intended to determine principles which should apply in any potential redundancy situation. The proposals covered, for example, the order of discharge which would need to be followed when redundancy occurred and also laid down a series of measures which should be taken before redundancy was contemplated. It also outlined measures which should be taken after people had been declared redundant to see if alternative appropriate employment within the civil service was available.

A new model redundancy agreement was not agreed until October 1975. It set out lines of action to avoid redundancy, including such measures as suspension of recruitment, intra- and interdepartmental transfer and voluntary premature retirement. It also provided for defined units of redundancy, which in the case of mobile staff could be all the members of the grade concerned in the department affected. It produced an order of discharge, starting with casual and contract staff, those over 65, those who volunteered for premature retirement and those who already had forty years' pensionable service.

Apart from the redundancies among members in the MAFF, the other redundancies among Institution members during the period 1970–4 were not as great as feared. The only other substantial redundancy involving Institution members was at the Nuclear Power Group, which being outside the civil service did not qualify for the new premature retirement terms. Some 250 staff were given notice during the summer of 1971, and a redundancy scheme suited to the particular requirements of the situation and much better than those usually found in industry was negotiated by the Institution. The Institution also put a set of proposals to the Secretary of State for Trade and Industry which, if acted upon, might have materially changed the company's prospects and perhaps have averted some of the redundancies.

Another method used by the government to limit the growth of the civil service was to impose 'staff ceilings'. This usually led to an increase in overtime and more contract work. Thus, for example, in the DoE the number of contract staff employed on drawing office work increased from 352 in April 1969 to 579 in February 1972. At the 1972 conference of the Institution a motion was carried calling for an agreement that staff should not be called upon to work regular overtime whilst staff complements were being reduced. It further asked that until such an agreement was reached the Institution should advise members in the relevant areas not to work regular overtime. Another motion carried at the same conference asked the NEC to take a more positive line of resistance to the government's policy of placing work out to contract, and to seek guarantees that the economics of 'contracting out' were demonstrated by the Official Side. Similar motions were passed in 1973.

Another problem on manpower which was beginning to affect Institution members at this time was the employment in increasing numbers of overqualified staff. During 1972 unemployment had risen and with it, for the first time in postwar years, came the phenomenon of unemployment among graduates. As a consequence, particularly in the scientific area, directors of establishments were recruiting first and second class honours degree graduates for what were essentially scientific assistant vacancies. This, said the Institution, was creating severe career problems for the longer term and was in no way reducing the total number of unemployed.

THE ROTHSCHILD REPORT

With the advent of the new Conservative government the Institution was apprehensive that since it had been elected pledged to cut public expenditure and to encourage industry to 'stand on its own feet', arbitrary and short-sighted decisions might quickly be made on government research and development without its real role and importance being adequately considered. Some cuts in the planned expenditure on research and development work were announced in the autumn budget in 1970 but they were not large and were part of the wider programme of cuts in government expenditure. The government made it clear that research and development would form part of the review of all government activities and functions and several reviews were immediately set in train.

One of the most important of these reviews was that conducted by Lord Rothschild, head of the Central Policy Review Staff. Lord Rothschild's report, *A Framework for Government Research and Development*, was published in Green Paper form at the end of November 1971, together with the Dainton Report, *The Future of the Research Council System*. In Lord Rothschild's own words the report was

> based on the principle that applied research and development, that is research and development with a practical application as its objective, must be done on a customer/contractor basis. The customer says what he wants; the contractor does it (if he can) and the customer pays.

Unlike the Dainton Report which distinguished between tactical, strategic and basic research, Lord Rothschild recognised only two kinds, basic and applied, and of these only applied research should be governed by the customer/contractor principle. In each department with major research responsibility there should be a chief scientist to represent the customer and a controller of research and development to represent the contractor, i.e. the department's research establishments. There should be close liaison between the two, and between their respective staffs, but they should be in formally distinct lines of command.

The report recommended a substantial strengthening of the chief scientist's organisation in a number of departments and supported the concept of a general research surcharge, on average 10 per cent of the operating expenditure, to enable laboratories to undertake programmes not directly commissioned by customers. Lord Rothschild also supported the concept of multi-functional laboratories and wished to see a strengthening of the scientific element in the administrative class. The report went on to apply the same principles to the research councils. It wished to see all the applied research carried out by research councils paid for by those government departments which had the overall responsibilities in the various fields of their applied research. Thus, he proposed that MAFF should be responsible for £4·5m. of the total of £18·7m. spent by the ARC; that the DHSS should be made responsible for £5·6m. of the £22·4m. paid to the MRC; and that £7·6m. of the total expenditure of £15·3m. by the NERC should be made the responsibility of the DoE, DTI and MAFF. No proposals were made to alter the basis of funding the SRC and SSRC because they were concerned wholly with basic research.

In an introductory note to the Green Paper the government endorsed the 'customer/contractor' principle and considered 'that it should be implemented in respect of applied research and development carried out or sponsored by the government, whether by research councils or elsewhere'. Before reaching decisions on the detailed application of the principle, the government allowed until the end of February 1972 for wide public debate about the issues involved. The Institution, among others, was specifically asked for its views.

RESPONSE TO ROTHSCHILD

The Institution published its comments on the Rothschild Report at the beginning of March. It was produced in the light of branch comments and the advice of the Public Research and Development Committee. Copies were sent to the Lord Privy Seal and the Select Committee on Science and Technology and distributed widely within and outside the Institution. The Institution preferred the three categories of science outlined by Dainton (i.e. tactical science, strategic science and basic science) to the distinction between basic and applied research made by Rothschild, and Dainton's terminology was used throughout the Institution's submission.

The Institution agreed that the objectives of tactical science should be customer-determined but that in determining them the research interest should also be involved. It was vital to appreciate that the research scientist had a creative, not merely a passive, role to play in developing and determining the lines of research to be followed. Provided the scientists' central role was recognised, the Institution envisaged satisfactory arrangements being developed along the following lines:

(i)   each department would define its own customer interests

(ii)   broad areas of customer interest would be vested in a board(s) consisting of representatives of customer interests, including the chief scientist's interest plus a representative(s) of the relevant research establishments, either as permanent or *ad hoc* members depending on the circumstances. There could be several customer interests represented on any one board, not all of which would necessarily be from within the same department

(iii)   the boards would determine the fields of work and the research and development objectives, but responsibility for the execution of the programmes would belong to the directors of research establishments

(iv)   research establishments should be able to put proposals to the boards for consideration, either directly or through a representative of the research establishments' interest on a board

(v)   if they are not already members, directors of research establishments, or their representatives, should have a right of access to boards concerned with research in their fields of responsibility

(vi)   scientists in the research establishments should continue to have the right to the publication of the results of their research where neither state nor commercial security is involved

(vii)   there should be regular interchange of staff between the chief scientist's organisation and the research establishments, and continuous informal dialogue between all the parties involved.

The Institution welcomed the importance attached by Lord Rothschild to the need for strong chief scientist's organisations in departments with research responsibilities. It did not agree, however, that there should necessarily be a separate controller, research and development, except in very large R&D organisations such as MoD (PE). In most departments the Institution said that it would prefer to see a unified scientific organisation under the chief scientist. The chief scientist's headquarters organisation should be relatively small and staffed with senior scientists of standing. The Institution also welcomed the support for multi-functional laboratories and for a research surcharge, although it thought that a range of 10–15 per cent would be better than the 10 per cent of total expenditure suggested by Rothschild.

On the research councils the Institution contended that the Rothschild proposals cut across the basis on which the councils were established by Parliament, with all-party agreement, in 1965. Research councils were particularly concerned with strategic science and it was necessary that they should continue to be able to conduct or supervise strategic research in those areas of science for the development of which they had an overall responsibility. It was not a central function of research councils to take on applied research work. It should be a matter for research councils themselves to decide how much contract research work they should do, whether for departments or other organisations. In the case of serious disagreement between a research council and a department over whether a particular piece of research should be undertaken, it should be resolved at ministerial and if necessary Cabinet level.

The Institution strongly disagreed with the allocation of research council income laid down in the Rothschild Report. It represented, the Institution argued, an arbitrary division of the strategic research responsibilities of the research councils, and if implemented would leave the research councils without reliable criteria on which to base their future work.

The Institution strongly supported Lord Rothschild's recommendations for putting chief scientists on to research councils as full members. It equally strongly supported the proposals for a better two-way interchange between science and administration. The Institution also said that it would like to see common conditions of employment introduced for all research staffs.

At the 1972 annual conference the general secretary described himself as well pleased with the manner in which the Institution's representations had been received by the government and the way in which consultations were proceeding. Many of the Institution's submissions, he said, had also been endorsed by the Select Committee on Science and Technology. The Institution's proposals had been designed to improve the organisation within government departments so that decisions on priorities could be taken with the full knowledge of all relevant factors including scientific possibilities and the economic, social and political considerations. For the research councils the central question which had to be determined was the role which the government wished them to undertake for the future. In the Institution's view the research councils should be responsible to the government for the development of science in areas of national importance; should undertake or sponsor basic and strategic science as necessary to discharge that responsibility; should finance scientific research and postgraduate training in the universities; and should provide specialist and expensive research facilities for university use.

In July 1972 the government published its views on the Rothschild Report and the ensuing public debate in a White Paper, *A Framework for Government Research and Development*. It endorsed the main Rothschild recommendations but conceded to a considerable extent the Institution's main point that an essential part of the customer/contractor approach should be the provision for continuing discussion and partnership between customers and contractors, and that 'in practice many of the ideas for research and development to meet the customer needs come from the scientific staff in the contractors organisation'. The government agreed to the establishment of new chief scientist's organisations in the DHSS and MAFF where they had not previously existed.

On research councils the government decided to transfer a total of £20m. of research council income from the DES to departmental votes over a three-year period commencing in 1973/4. The Institution viewed this as too large a sum but agreed that the new system should be given the chance to work. The Institution welcomed the government's decision that there should be a reconstituted Council for Scientific Policy which would not only advise the Secretary of State for Education and Science on the allocation of the science budget of her department but would 'know and be able to take into account the size and nature of the work to be commissioned by customer departments'. The Institution objected, however, to a decision to split nature conservancy, a part of the NERC, with its research functions remaining with NERC but the rest being put under a new statutory Nature Conservancy Council, under the Secretary of State for the Environment. That decision was put into effect in 1973.

INTERCHANGE OF SCIENTISTS

The White Paper's acceptance of the view that movement of scientists into administration and management should be encouraged was welcomed by the Institution. So too was the government's decision to set up a task force under Sir Herman Bondi, chief scientific adviser to the Ministry of Defence, to consider in the widest context the question of interchangeability of scientists between occupations. These developments were also in line with the recommendations of the Fulton Report. Its remit was to encourage the interchange of scientific talent between the civil service on the one hand and the research councils, universities and industry on the other. The Institution gave evidence to the committee.

The Bondi Committee eventually reported in 1974 in favour of interchange and the CSD set up a unit to monitor transfers. Although in favour of interchangeability the Institution was doubtful whether the inducements held out by the report would result in many transfers. This proved to be the case and the unit was eventually wound up. New initiatives on encouraging interchange with industry for all civil servants were developed in early 1978.

The Institution was also asked to give its views to the Bessborough Committee on the interchangeability of scientists between research associations, government and industry. This committee had been established in 1972 to inquire into the future of research associations. In its submission to the Bessborough Committee the Institution contended that interchange was desirable both as a means of producing cross-fertilisation of ideas and of opening up wider career opportunities and greater job satisfaction for the staff.

The Institution said, however, that promoting interchange would not be easy and was unlikely to take place on a large scale. It could not, therefore, be considered as a panacea for the solution of otherwise intractable problems. The Institution outlined the many obstacles to mobility; for example, differing pay and conditions and the restrictions on transfers of civil service scientists to industry in situations where the individual might obtain personal reward from the exploitation of knowledge gained as a civil servant. It expressed the view that measures would be needed to promote interchange and outlined several methods by which this could be done.

OTHER RESEARCH AND DEVELOPMENT ISSUES

Apart from the general issues raised by the Rothschild Report, the Institution was also involved in other specific issues relating to public research and development. The Institution gave evidence in 1971 to the Vinter Committee which was looking into the Central Electricity Generating Board's plans for future nuclear reactors. One of the Institution's main concerns was to try and assess which of the various types of reactor available was most economic to use in Britain. It came down in favour of the British steam-generating heavy water (SGHW) reactor.

The reorganisation of the nuclear industry also continued to occupy the attention of the Institution. The two new commercial companies, British Nuclear Fuels and the Radiochemical Centre, were established on 1 April 1971. UKAEA staff in the areas concerned were transferred automatically and the Institution was formally recognised for negotiating purposes. Some other staff, together with relevant staff from the MRC, were transferred to the new National Radiological Protection Board on the same date. In August 1971 it was announced that the Atomic Weapons Group of the UKAEA would be transferred to MoD (PE).

In August 1972 the Institution welcomed the government's announcement of its intention to encourage the consolidation of the nuclear design and construction industry into a single strong unit. The Institution, however, was disappointed with the method, announced in the spring of 1973, by which this was to be achieved. The major share of the new company was to be made up of private share capital, 50 per cent from the General Electric Company, 35 per cent by other companies within the industry and only 15 per cent by the UKAEA. The Institution felt that the immense contribution made by the UKAEA to the development of nuclear power and the continuing need for substantial government support necessitated a much larger public shareholding. This view was supported by the Select Committee on Science and Technology, who argued that the public shareholding should be at least 30 per cent.

Rationalisation also took place in the MoD research and development effort. As part of the White Paper *The Reorganisation of Central Government* it was announced that Mr D. Rayner was to head an inquiry into how best to organise the integration of all defence research and development activities under the reponsibility of the Secretary of State for Defence. The Rayner Report suggested that the controller of research and development establishments and research should prepare a plan for rationalising the research and development establishments with a view to its earliest implementation. Six working parties were established covering different research areas and proposals were drawn up for closures of certain establishments. There was no consultation with the Staff Side and no Staff Side representation on the working parties. A paper detailing the Staff Side's objections to the proposed first stage of rationalisation was put before the minister of state, but it was clear that there was no intention to amend the proposals.

On the review of the work of the research establishments within the DTI the Institution was more successful. The review, again foreshadowed in the government's White Paper, *The Reorganisation of Central Government*, concerned the DTI's research stations and also those of the UKAEA involved in non-nuclear industrial research. The Institution argued that the continual reviews of research establishments 'which had undoubtedly led to a serious drop in morale among the scientific staffs concerned' should cease and that policies emerging from the present review should be based on criteria likely to be enduring for the next decade. The Institution said that it would like to see a recognition of the need to make much more and better use of government research establishments in the future. It accepted that government industrial research should aim to achieve a 'pay-off'. Some work could be done on an immediate contractual basis for industry, but there was other work which was vital to industry in the long term which could not attract a repayment from industry. There was also other work which needed to be done in the national interest, such as work on environmental pollution.

The minister of state in the DTI declared himself impressed by many of the Institution's arguments. The report of the Select Committee on Science and Technology on the same issue found that the industrial research establishments 'should continue to provide those supporting scientific services and technical facilities which industry cannot or is unlikely to establish on its own account . . .'. The Institution welcomed these sentiments with the hope that they marked a turning-point in public opinion about government-supported industrial research.

Following the review, the DTI decided to introduce a series of requirements boards which would bring together the major customer interests within the department and which could review their research requirements. They could then commission research within the department and outside it. At the same time the industrial research establishments of the DTI and the UKAEA were to be allowed to develop the research which they did for private individual firms. By the autumn of 1973 the new requirements boards had been established in full agreement with the Institution.

A working party on fisheries research organisation was set up in 1971 and reported in 1972. It recommended a fisheries research board to co-ordinate research programmes undertaken in the various departments concerned. It also recommended, closely following the Institution's evidence, that there should be a controller of fisheries research responsible to the new research board, and that the board should have responsibility for the development of the careers of fisheries research scientists. Following the Rothschild Report the Institution argued that there should be a chief scientist for the fisheries research board rather than a controller, research and development, but this argument was rejected by the departments concerned.

SUPERANNUATION

In 1971 big improvements were secured for civil service pensioners. The Pensions (Increase) Act, 1971, passed in July provided for all pensions issued before 1969 to be brought up to date in terms of purchasing power at April 1969 prices. In addition the Act gave an increase of 18 per cent, with effect from 1 September 1971, on all pensions dating from before 1 April 1969 and proportionately smaller increases for those issued after that date. For the future there were to be biennial reviews of all public sector pensions. The increases were to follow changes in the cost-of-living index. The Institution and National Staff Side welcomed the proposals as the successful outcome of two decades of negotiation. They would, however, have preferred to see annual reviews tied to the standard of living rather than the cost of living. At the end of the year the government agreed to annual reviews.

The campaign for unestablished service to count in full for pension purposes did not meet with the same success. The claim was again turned down in 1971. In 1972, however, a further major improvement was achieved with the decision to free the civil service pension scheme from detailed parliamentary control by allowing it to be set out in non-statutory documents instead of Acts of Parliament and statutory instruments.

The first Act of Parliament laying down general provisions for civil service pensions was passed in 1810, and for the following 160 years every change in civil service pension arrangements required an Act of Parliament to authorise it. The Institution, together with other civil service unions, had for long urged that civil service pension arrangements should be freed from control by Act of Parliament. The effect of making civil service pensions subject to legislative control had been to build into the civil service pension scheme a strong inertia against change even when the Official Side and the Staff Side had agreed about the need for change.

Another very important development affecting civil service pensions was the publication in 1972 of a report of a committee to review superannuation arrangements in the civil service. This committee, representing both the Official Side and the National Staff Side, was appointed towards the end of 1968. In the course of its work it conducted the most fundamental review of the civil service superannuation scheme since it was first established on a statutory basis. Although many of the changes did not have their origins in the Fulton Report, many were at least recommended and strongly supported by the Fulton Committee. The timing of the review owed much to the added impetus given to the question by the Fulton Committee.

The main proposals of the joint committee were:

The scheme should remain non-contributory.
Pension benefits should be based on pay in the best of the last three years of service.
Service should be reckoned by completed days and not by completed years.
Preservation of pension benefits should be introduced for all those leaving before the retirement age with five or more years' service.
The qualifying period for pension should be reduced from ten to five years.
Short-service gratuities should be introduced for those leaving with between two and five years' service.
The marriage gratuity should be abolished, except that staff in post should have an option in certain circumstances to the gratuity in respect of past service.
Wider transfer arrangements should be introduced to cover moves between the civil service and the private sector.
The pension scheme should be extended to unestablished full-time staff and to part-time staff who work eighteen hours a week or more.
There should be improvements in ill-health retirement pensions, widows' benefit and family benefit.
Civil servants who would not otherwise be able to reckon forty years by the minimum retirement age should have an option, subject to certain conditions, to buy added years of pension credit.
There should be a legal entitlement to the main pension benefit.

The 1972 annual conference of the Institution unanimously approved the proposals for the new civil service superannuation scheme. Similar approval was given by the annual conferences of all the other civil service unions. The National Staff Side formally agreed to the new proposals at its meeting on 1 June 1972 and the new scheme came into effect from that date. Certain features of the scheme were made retrospective. From the same date it was agreed that all unestablished staff in the civil service with five years' service on 1 June 1972 would be automatically established by a process of nomination. Those with less than five years' service would become established after five years or before if they were successful in open competitions or were nominated by their department. In future all appointments, with a few exceptions, would be established.

EMPLOYMENT OF WOMEN

In the summer of 1970 the CSD, without prior consultation, announced that it had set up a small working party under the chairmanship of Mrs E. M. Kemp-Jones of the DHSS to study all aspects of women's employment in the non-industrial civil service. Although both the Priestley Report and the Fulton Report paid some special attention to women civil servants, the last full investigation of their problems had been made in 1934. Since that time progress had been made on several fronts.

The Institution simultaneously undertook research among its own members into the problems of women. Although it found no evidence of discrimination in promotion, it found that there were certain jobs still confined to men. The Institution suggested that they should be opened to women. It also suggested that provisions should be made for full reinstatement within five years of leaving and that there should be greater provision of part-time work. These points were submitted to the working party.

The report of the CSD working party, *The Employment of Women in the Civil Service*, was published in the autumn of 1971. It made many proposals to increase opportunities for women in the civil service, by opening up to both sexes certain jobs until then confined to one sex, and by encouraging the extension of part-time employment. It also made many recommendations to ease the problems of combining a career with domestic responsibilities, including the provision of nurseries and greater flexibility in granting special leave, in taking annual leave, in the hours worked and in the provision of training facilities. It also made recommendations for reinstatement for those leaving the civil service for a period for child-rearing or other purposes. Agreement between the CSD and the Staff Side was reached on virtually every recommendation and plans were laid for two nurseries on an experimental basis. The first civil service experimental nursery at Llanishen was opened on 8 October 1973.

RELATIONS WITH OTHER UNIONS

The Fulton Report and the machinery of government changes continued to create organisational problems for the Institution and other civil service unions. There was a need for simplification and rationalisation. The amalgamation with the STCS was a significant move in this direction. The last conference of the STCS division took place in Folkestone on 5 May 1972 and the division ceased finally to exist from 26 June 1972. From that date onwards the STCS became a fully integrated part of the Institution.

With the separation of the Post Office from the civil service and the creation of an independent Post Office Corporation, the Institution, with the support of its STCS division, agreed that the drawing office grades in the Post Office should have the opportunity to opt for transfer to the Post Office Engineering Union or the Association of Post Office Executives according to the grade of each particular member. Both the POEU and the APOE were willing to make transitional arrangements if the members of the Post Office branch of the former STCS wanted to transfer their membership. It was exlained that there would be no question of compulsory transfer of membership but that if the majority of members wanted to transfer then it was in the interests of good trade union practice that all should be encouraged to do so. A ballot was taken among the drawing office members and the result confirmed that it was the clear wish of the overwhelming majority that they should be given the opportunity to transfer to the POEU and the APOE. As a result of this arrangement 2,778 drawing office members of the Institution were transferred to the two Post Office unions.

In April 1970 the NEC submitted a report to branches and conference delegates on the reorganisation of civil service staff associations and in particular on the question of relationships with the FDA and the SCS. The report recorded that agreement had been reached on a resolution adopted by the executive committees of the FDA, the Society and the Institution. It said:

Having regard to the agreement in principle to the introduction of a senior policy and management group on the basis of common grading right across the service with jobs filled using the principle of 'best man for the job', the Official Side's proposal to introduce common grading throughout the service in the area between the senior policy and management group and the principal maximum, the difficulties which will inevitably be created or exacerbated if the various organisations in this area of the Service continue to retain their separate existence, the need to ensure that these changes and others following on the Fulton Report are carried out in such a way that they are in the interests of the Associations' members, [the FDA, the Society and the Institution] resolve that:

all possible steps shall be taken to improve relations at Branch level, areas of common interest shall be examined with the aim of working out common policies, ways shall be considered of drawing the three Associations closer together, and in earnest of this Resolution agree together to establish a Joint National Committee to carry these matters further, and to establish where appropriate Departmental Co-ordinating Committees to work out common policies on matters of common interest arising at Departmental level.

At the same time it was agreed that the FDA should affiliate to the Society.

The NEC submitted an emergency motion to the 1970 conference seeking endorsement of the agreement. Because of a procedural arrangement the emergency motion fell, following the passing of a more comprehensive resolution instructing the NEC to explore, and to report on, the possibility of the Institution working more closely with other civil service staff associations with the eventual aim of reorganisation. The general secretary intervened to state that the NEC would continue to operate the agreement but would also, as instructed, make a comprehensive report to the 1971 annual conference.

At the 1971 annual conference an attempt to refer back that section of the annual report which dealt with the formation of the Joint National Committee (JNC) on the grounds that the interests of FDA members in relation to Fulton reforms were incompatible with those of the Institution was lost. On the more general issue of reorganisation the general secretary talked of the overlapping interests of the Institution, the Society, the FDA and the AGSRO, but emphasised that it would not be practicable in the foreseeable future to have a 'grand national union of all civil service unions'.

The debate was revived at the 1973 annual conference when the general secretary moved the NEC-sponsored motion welcoming the decision of the National Staff Side to undertake an examination into the future trade union organisation of the civil service. The motion also called upon the NEC to prepare a report on the subject. The general secretary pointed out that in the National Staff Side there were no less than twelve organisations. They did not exist, he said, in their present form on any rational basis. They were a product of history and did not reflect either the machinery of government or the structure of the civil service. Some departmental organisations were out of date. He pointed out that the IRSF overlapped with the Society and with the CPSA in the typing and clerical fields. The CPSA overlapped with the Society in respect of clerical officers promoted to executive officer. There were also problems in terms of recognition rights between the Society and the FDA. The Institution also had overlapping interests with the AGSRO, the CSU, the Society and the FDA.

The structure of the civil service trade union movement, the general secretary said, was as out of date as the class structure of the civil service which the unions had condemned. He was under no illusion, however, about the likelihood of introducing changes. It would be very difficult. The NEC, he explained, had put the motion in very broad terms because it believed it was right to put the problem to the annual conference.

Although the motion was carried by a very large majority there were a number of delegates who spoke against it. One said that one of the myths in trade union thinking was that bigger meant better. There was no evidence to show that this was so. Mergers did not mean increased efficiency. A larger organisation was almost invariably less democratic and less efficient.

Another issue debated at the 1973 conference was TUC affiliation. Debate on the issue at the 1972 conference had been cut abruptly short by a successful motion for moving 'next business'. This time the issue was fully debated. Considering the history of the subject and the importance attached to it, including the fact that most delegates had come to conference mandated by their branches to vote one way or the other, it was surprisingly open and without rancour. The motion debated was a simple one asking conference to affiliate to the TUC. It was moved by a delegate from the MoD (Navy) Drawing Office branch who began his speech by congratulating the SCS on its decision taken the previous day to affiliate. This action meant, said the mover, that the only worthwhile union now not affiliated was the Institution. As in the past, the government was having discussions with the CBI and TUC to determine the framework in which the Institution would have to negotiate; discussions from which the Institution was excluded. The NEC speaker continued with the point that there was a substantial and leaderless white-collar vote within the TUC for which the Institution could supply the leadership. The NEC was convinced that the Institution could have an influence far in excess of its size.

The opponents of affiliation largely argued on the basis of the need for a referendum and the fear that the issue would split the Institution. The main drift of the debate was in favour of the motion but when it came to the vote the motion was lost.

Although the Institution was not yet prepared to affiliate to the TUC it did broaden its links with other trade unions by two other affiliations. In 1971 the Institution affiliated to the Ruskin Trade Union Research Unit, which had been established earlier that year for the purpose of undertaking research of common interest to its affiliated members and producing commissioned research for individual affiliates. This brought the Institution, in particular through its research officer, into closer contact with other unions both inside and outside the civil service. Of greater import was the decision taken at the 1972 conference to affiliate to the Public Services International, an organisation which comprised 150 public service unions in 66 countries with a total membership of over 4 million. Besides providing a useful forum for the exchange of information and ideas, the Institution was concerned to achieve greater co-ordination between public service unions within Europe following Britain's accession to the European Economic Community (EEC). During 1972 a European Regional Advisory Committee was established within the PSI to play a part in encouraging closer working relations and exchanges of information on problems of public servants in Western Europe.

INTERNAL MATTERS

At the end of 1969 the paid-up membership of the Institution was 85,617; by the end of 1973 it had risen to 97,234 despite the loss of some members to the Post Office unions, and despite increases in subscriptions which became necessary with the accelerating rate of inflation. The 1971 conference agreed to increase subscriptions from January 1972. The existing rate of subscriptions had been unchanged since 1968. The new subscriptions were 70p per month for the higher rate, 50p per month for the intermediate rate and 30p per month for the lower rate for members under 21 years of age. Two years later subscriptions were again increased. The new rates from 1 January 1974 were 80p per month for the higher rate, 60p per month for the intermediate rate and 35p per month for the lower rate.

Acting on the instructions of the 1969 conference the NEC appointed a subcommittee to review the Institution's internal organisation in the light of Fulton and developments in the machinery of government. Branches were invited to submit their views and a report was presented to the 1972 conference. On the basis of that report certain changes were accepted. Among the most important of the changes was the establishment of a Professional and Technology Category Co-ordinating Committee, made up of representatives from the professional B&E, technical officers and drawing office professional groups, to co-ordinate issues of concern to the P&T category. The organisation of other professional groups was to be reviewed in the light of relevant post-Fulton developments. A substantial reorganisation of branches, especially in the new mammoth departments, was also envisaged.

With the continued growth of the Institution there were more frequent changes in the full-time officers and an increase in the number of full-time staff. In 1970 Judith Lawson transferred from her post as research officer to become an assistant secretary. In July 1973 she left the Institution to take up an appointment with the Monopolies Commission. Her place as research officer in 1970 was taken by Valerie Ellis. Mrs Ellis (she became Dr Ellis while working for the Institution) came to the Institution from the Commission on Industrial Relations, before which she had been a university lecturer.

In 1970 the Institution introduced a new grade, negotiations officer, to help assistant secretaries in servicing branches and professional groups. Two of the new appointments were from the STCS ranks, Peter Downton, editor of *Right Angle,* the STCS journal, and a draughtsman at Portsmouth Dockyard until his full-time secondment to the STCS in 1969, and Peter Ellison, a draughtsman in the Post Office in Bradford, and an active member of STCS and prior to that of DATA. The other two appointments were George Giles, a senior scientific assistant in the Meteorological Office and an active member of the Institution, and John Sheldon, previously a technical officer within the Post Office and an active member of the POEU who, at the time of his appointment, was completing a two-year diploma course at Ruskin College.

At about the same time the NEC appointed Mr David Cook, an engineer and active Institution member for almost twenty years, for a period of three years as an assistant secretary. The post was a temporary one, created by the NEC to assist in the work on issues related to the structural changes and the introduction of job evaluation schemes resulting from Fulton.

Early in 1971 Mr Terry Pitts Fenby left the Institution to become the secretary general of the British Association of Industrial Editors. Mr Pitts Fenby had served the Institution for four years as its journal editor and public relations officer. Miss Pauline Clark was appointed to fill the vacancy. She was a journalist with the *Guardian.* Miss Clark left, however, by the end of the year and Mr Peter Downton was appointed in her place.

Towards the end of 1971 the Institution appointed two additional negotiating officers. One was Mr David Davies, who was an active member of the Institution and a graduate of the University of Keele. The other was Mr Roy Maynard, a former draughtsman and active member of the STCS. He was first elected to the Executive Committee of the STCS in 1964.

Early in 1972 the Institution appointed four more negotiations officers. They were Mr Peter Carew who, after graduating from the University of Newcastle, worked in Canada as the research director of the Canadian Labour Association; Mr Ron McDowell who, after attending Liverpool University, became an active member of the Institution whilst working for the United Kingdom Atomic Energy Authority; Mr Keith Good, who was an active member of the Inland Revenue Staff Federation; and Margaret Niles, who joined the Institution's headquarters' staff as a secretarial assistant in 1966, was promoted to the newly created grade of assistant negotiations officer in October 1969 and promoted again to negotiations officer on 1 March 1972.

In the late spring of 1973 further appointments were made to the assistant secretary grade. Mr Peter Carew and Mr George Giles were promoted from the negotiations officer grade. Mr Cliff Crook, an engineer with the UKAEA and member of the NEC, and Mr Peter Robinson, who had held both lay and full-time office in the NUT, were also appointed. Later that year four new negotiations officers were appointed. They included Elizabeth Stallibrass, who was promoted from assistant administration officer, and Elizabeth Jenkins, an active Institution member from the Office of Population Censuses and Surveys. In addition there were two outsiders: Robert Aitken, who had been employed for twenty-six years in the HMSO press at Harrow and was an active member in the Society of Graphical and Allied Trades, and Robert Price, a research associate at the University of Warwick.

By the beginning of 1974 both Mr Carew and Mr Robinson had resigned their appointments. Mr David Davies was then promoted from negotiations officer to assistant secretary and a new assistant secretary was appointed, Mr W. H. Brett. Mr Brett had been a divisional officer of ASTMS and before that time he had worked for the Transport Salaried Staffs' Association and the National Union of Bank Employees.

The end of 1971 marked the retirement of Tom Clifton, who had been an assistant secretary since 1963, and Mr John Fraser. Mr Fraser had been a full-time official since 1947 and before that had been an extremely active lay member of the Institution. He served at one period as its honorary secretary. The general secretary paid a very warm tribute to him on his retirement. He said that as an organiser he had 'no peer'. He had boundless energy and enthusiasm and his work was characterised by meticulous attention to every detail. The general secretary said that John Fraser had done a superb job for the Institution and had shown kindness and consideration to all with whom he worked. At the 1973 conference he was made an honorary member of the Institution.

Early in 1973 there were changes among the senior full-time staff of the Institution. After more than fifteen years with the Institution Mr John Lyons resigned his post as deputy general secretary to become the general secretary of the Electrical Power Engineers' Association. The general secretary said that John Lyons had made a valuable and distinguished contribution to the work of the Institution. He expressed regret that he was leaving but he carried with him the best wishes of the Institution for success in his new post.

Shortly afterwards Mr Cyril Cooper, the former general secretary of the Society of Technical Civil Servants, was appointed senior deputy general secretary of the Institution and thus became the immediate deputy of the general secretary. This was a fitting tribute to a talented official whose qualities had been recognised when the STCS was a separate organisation and who quickly made his mark after the amalgamation.

With the appointment of Mr Cyril Cooper as senior deputy general secretary, the Institution also decided to create two new assistant general secretary posts. Margaret Platt and William Wright were promoted to these positions.

On 5 December 1973 the world learned of the death of Sir Robert Watson-Watt. Sir Robert had achieved a worldwide reputation as the man who more than anyone else was responsible for the development of radar. It was a measure of the contribution he made during the war years that he received an *ex gratia* award of £50,000 for his 'invention of radar and his contribution to the development of radar installations'. He was knighted in 1942. Throughout his career Sir Robert Watson-Watt had strong sympathies with trade unionism and played an active part in the Institution. He was the chairman of the Institution from 1934 to 1936.

25 The 'Social Contract' and After

Following the general election of February 1974, brought about by the confrontation between the Conservative government and the miners, and the return of a minority Labour government, new policies were introduced. The miners' strike was settled with substantial improvements for miners, and normal working was restored throughout British industry after the enforced three-day week caused by the mining dispute. The new government also announced its intention to bring to an end the statutory incomes policy of the previous government and to replace it with a voluntary policy on the lines previously discussed between the Labour Party and the TUC. These earlier discussions had resulted in the publication in February 1973 of a joint statement from the TUC/Labour Party Liaison Committee entitled *Economic Policy and the Cost of Living*. The statement said that the problem of inflation could be properly considered only within the context of a coherent economic and social strategy. The strategy should be designed both to overcome Britain's grave economic problems and to provide a basis for co-operation between the unions and the government.

The TUC and the Labour Party in their joint statement urged that there should be direct statutory action on prices to influence the climate of collective bargaining. There was need also, they suggested, for a new approach to housing and rents, a large-scale redistribution of incomes and wealth, greater spending on social priorities and an immediate commitment to a pension of £10 a week for a single person and £16 for a married couple. All these policies, explained the TUC and the Labour Party, had to be underpinned by agreed policies on investment, employment and economic growth.

The TUC and the Labour Party also called for the repeal of the Industrial Relations Act and its replacement by new legislation to provide for voluntary collective bargaining and the voluntary reform of the system of industrial relations. It was urged that a new independent conciliation and arbitration service should be established.

NEW POLICIES

Almost immediately on taking office the new Labour government introduced a budget which fulfilled a number of these pledges. Pensions were increased to £10 for a single person and £16 for a married couple. Tax changes were also introduced to help the less well off through increased allowances. Higher taxes were imposed on the better off and a number of tax loopholes from which the wealthy had benefited were also closed. The government stated that it would introduce a wealth tax and a gift tax. Additional funds were allocated for food subsidies and an early decision was taken to freeze rents. A Royal Commission on the Distribution of Income and Wealth was established some time afterwards.

The government also carried out its election programme in relation to the reform of industrial relations. The Industrial Relations Act was repealed and a new measure, the Trade Union and Labour Relations Act, 1974, was passed by Parliament. It restored the essential features of the voluntary system which had been changed by the Industrial Relations Act. The National Industrial Relations Court and the Commission on Industrial Relations were abolished. So, too, was the Pay Board. A new body, the Advisory, Conciliation and Arbitration Service, was established, independent of the normal machinery of government, to provide conciliation and arbitration in industrial disputes and to help, where necessary, in the reform of collective bargaining machinery. The government later introduced another important measure affecting the trade union movement. It was the Employment Protection Bill which finally became an Act of Parliament towards the end of 1975. The new Act introduced a number of specific measures to promote collective bargaining and also introduced a number of new minimum rights for all employees, including, for example, the right to trade union membership, time off for trade union duties and activities, maternity leave, time off to look for work or arrange training in the event of impending redundancy and consultation on redundancy. The Advisory Conciliation and Arbitration Service was also put on a statutory basis and charged with the duty of promoting the improvement of industrial relations and the extension of collective bargaining throughout all areas of employment.

Crown employment was excluded from certain enforcement provisions of the Employment Protection Act on the grounds that ministers must remain ultimately responsible to Parliament. The civil service unions were, however, given assurances in Parliament that the government would abide by the spirit of the legislation even though it would not be legally bound to follow all its provisions.

This new legislation, together with other measures for equal pay, the elimination of discrimination against women in employment, and the promotion of better safety and health arrangements in industry, represented, in all, the most favourable legislative framework for the development of industrial relations and workers' rights in the history of Britain.

Not surprisingly, these developments affecting industrial relations and workers' rights were strongly supported by the trade union movement. The unions were also sympathetic to the policy of the government in dealing with the very serious economic problems facing the nation. Steep increases in oil prices had contributed in large measure to the growth of the deficit in the balance of payments. Prices were rising but in many countries industrial output was slowing down. The United States, Japan and Western Europe were in recession and unemployment was rising in all these countries.

THE 'SOCIAL CONTRACT'

In June 1974 the General Council of the TUC issued a statement entitled *Collective Bargaining and the Social Contract* which said: 'Although the groundwork is being laid for increasing consumption and living standards in the future, the scope for real increases in consumption at present is limited, and the central negotiating objective in the coming period will therefore be to ensure that real incomes are maintained.' This, said the General Council, would entail claiming compensation for the rise in the cost of living since the last settlement, but threshold agreements (on the lines previously negotiated in the civil service) were to be taken into account. The General Council urged that there should be a twelve-month interval between major increases and that priority should be given to attaining reasonable minimum standards. This policy was endorsed by the 1974 TUC.

Speaking in the House of Commons on 29 July, Mr Edward Short, Lord President of the Council, said that all negotiators should strive to settle pay claims within the TUC guidelines. Whilst some exceptional action would be necessary in extreme cases, the government could not condone settlements which went beyond the TUC guidelines. That would also be the policy of the government in negotiations for which it was directly responsible, such as the civil service.

ARBITRATION ON P&T PAY

In 1974 no sooner had the Pay Board report on scientists' pay emerged than the Institution was involved in a sharp difference with the CSD over the pay of professionals and technologists. By the summer of 1974 the Institution was saying that there was no point in disguising the seriousness of the disagreement with the CSD on the pay of the professionals and technologists. It was not possible at that stage to announce to the membership the precise details of the difference because confidential discussions were continuing, but the Institution said it was clear, nevertheless, that the intention of the CSD was to hold the pay of the P&T category down to a level well below that which the staff concerned considered reasonable. Hundreds of messages were received at the headquarters of the Institution, and the general secretary wrote in the September issue of *State Service* of the 'ridiculously small increases' offered by the CSD.

Among the messages received at headquarters were many which said that members would support any militant action the NEC decided to take. Others decided to withdraw goodwill and took other actions without waiting for the NEC to suggest it. Thus, one message said, 'the members at the Royal Radar Establishment are thoroughly disgusted with the way in which the CSD is attempting to avoid its obligations under the principle of fair comparisons and this disgust is expressed by the immediate withdrawal of goodwill until a time to be decided by the NEC of the Institution'. Another message said: 'In view of the derisory offer made to the P&TO grades by the CSD – and the absence of any realistic negotiations – the Aircraft Department (Naval) call for concerted action throughout the civil service to work-to-rule, hold mass demonstrations and lobby MPs.'

As a result of this pressure the NEC called upon P&T members to take industrial action short of a strike from 30 July. P&T members organised a series of protest meetings throughout the country and industrial action was taken in a variety of ways. On the assurance by the CSD that advance payments, based on the arbitration award, would be made with September pay, and that final payments would be made in October, the NEC called off the protest action. Arbitration was fixed for the 4 September.

The Civil Service Arbitration Tribunal made an award on the Institution's claim substantially higher than the offer made by the Civil Service Department. The award provided increases of 10·2 per cent on the rates of pay which were current on 1 January 1974 and nearly 18 per cent on the figures current at 1 April

1973. The award effectively doubled the amount of money which the Civil Service Department had offered to the Institution in June 1974 and which the Institution had rejected. In a press statement the Institution said: 'This award confirms that the attitude adopted by the Civil Service Department was unreasonable and proves the value of independent arbitration.' The award also provided for a substantial shortening of the pay scale of the PTO IV. This too was welcomed by the Institution.

MILITANT ACTION DEBATE

Following the protest action taken by both scientists and P&T grades during 1974, which in both cases had been taken for the first time and at very short notice, there were several motions on the 1975 Institution conference agenda dealing with militant action. Five motions, and an additional four which were composited with them, formed the basis of a common debate in which each of the five motions were moved before the whole question was thrown open to debate.

The first motion, moved by the delegate from the MoD Navy Scientific Staffs branch, called for all members to move towards internal unity and to express the Institution's solidarity by supporting fellow members in future disputes even when they were not personally involved. The mover said that in the past when a group had been driven to take militant action over a claim members in other groups had remained on the touchline. The second motion, moved by the MoD Navy Engineering branch, was critical of the handling of the two sets of protest actions and instructed the NEC to carry out a review of organisation to ensure that an effective militant action campaign could be mounted at short notice. While hoping that the need for militant action would not arise again, the Institution should be fully prepared for that eventuality.

The third motion, moved by the MoD Air, former STCS, branch, asked conference to instruct the NEC that no decision regarding the introduction or withdrawal of militant action should be taken in future without full consultation with the membership. In the P&T industrial action in 1974, the delegate argued, there had been a lack of clarity in the instructions from the NEC on how the action should be taken and a lack of consultation in deciding to halt the action. The Agricultural Research branch went further by demanding in its motion that any call for strike action in future should be put to a ballot of affected members through the branches and that no such action should be taken unless supported by a simple majority of votes. This, the delegate argued, would avoid the patchy response engendered in the scientists' strike and make it easier to ensure support from the waverers.

The final motion asked that industrial action, once started, should continue until all affected members had been advised and consulted. The mover pointed out that industrial action on the P&T claim had begun in August, but was called off at the end of August, while headquarters officers were still touring the country raising support for the action. This had resulted in confusion and disillusionment among the membership.

In replying to the debate on behalf of the NEC, the general secretary said that it was right for conference to discuss and review in detail what had happened in the first two instances of major militant action taken by Institution members. He said that the NEC supported the first motion on the need for unity but that the guidance would need to be used with discretion. The NEC could not ask all members to take industrial action in every case, however small the number of members involved. On the second motion the NEC accepted the need for a review and one had already begun within headquarters. On the last three motions the NEC agreed that there should be full consultation but not necessarily by ballot. On the one hand the NEC was being criticised for not consulting members and on the other for not showing authoritative leadership. A balance needed to be struck between the need for full consultation and the need for the NEC to be able to take immediate and decisive action as the situation required. After the debate the conference followed the general secretary's advice and the first two motions were carried, the second two remitted and the final one was lost.

NEW NATIONAL PAY AGREEMENT

A major agreement was concluded just before Christmas 1974, after negotiations lasting since 1972, on the terms of a new national pay agreement defining criteria and procedures for determining pay in the non-industrial civil service. During the course of the negotiations meetings were held by civil service trade union representatives, not only with the Lord Privy Seal but also with the Prime Minister. The new agreement provided for annual reviews of pay in the civil service, for a new operative date of 1 April, with negotiations being concluded by that date, though extra time could be taken for arbitration if necessary, for the updating of information relating to outside organisations, and for compensation for increases in the cost of living between the date of the outside settlement and the operative date of the civil service settlement. The new agreement represented a substantial improvement on the old arrangements and was designed to lessen the severe problems caused by the rapid rate of inflation.

During the latter half of 1974, following the abandonment of formal incomes policy restrictions on the accession of the Labour government, earnings outside the civil service rose steeply. This continued in early 1975. These developments were reflected in the 1975 pay review for the civil service and this, together with the improvements embodied in the new 1974 pay agreement, combined to produce the biggest all-round pay increase for all non-industrial civil servants ever secured.

The overall annual increase was approximately 26 per cent but this included threshold payments already received. The total increases amounted to more than 30 per cent but these related to a period of 15 months because of the shift in the date of operation under the new agreement to 1 April rather than 1 January.

The general secretary pointed out in *State Service* that it was to the credit of the government that it had decided to honour the agreement for the application of the fair comparison principle in the determination of civil service pay, despite its desperate anxiety to limit the rate of inflation. Civil service pay, the general secretary emphasised, was determined on the basis of fair comparison with the pay for jobs in industry and commerce. What this meant was that civil service pay, under the terms of the new agreement, was no more than a reflection of pay among the rest of the community. He also paid tribute to the CSD for playing its full part in enabling negotiations to be concluded so speedily.

The 1975 pay review was also notable for being the first time that the separate pay reviews for administration and P&T grades had been conducted simultaneously. There was a high degree of co-operation between the various unions involved throughout the negotiations. In the working party stages on the analysis of the pay research reports there was close consultation between the research departments of the various unions. In the final stages of negotiations there were many meetings with senior negotiators from the CSD in which the general secretaries of the constituent organisations combined together. By doing so invaluable improvements were secured for each group.

THE £6 LIMIT

In the summer of 1975 the government decided that there needed to be greater restraint on earnings. Britain's rate of inflation, which had reached 30 per cent during the winter of 1974–5, was higher than in other competing industrial countries and Britain's economic stability, it was argued, was dangerously dependent upon the goodwill of foreign creditors. If the rate of inflation continued to exceed that of other countries the balance-of-payments deficit would grow even larger and foreign creditors might transfer their balances from London to other financial centres. The international value of sterling would then fall precipitously with disastrous effects on import prices and employment.

It was also part of the government's case that the rate of inflation was contributing to unemployment. Accelerating inflation, it was pointed out, caused uncertainty amongst industrialists, and their confidence in future prosperity was so low that they were not prepared to invest in British industry. Employers claimed that soaring costs were eroding the funds necessary for industrial investment. Britain's problems were made even worse by the deepening recession which had overtaken Western Europe, Japan and the United States.

The government entered into urgent discussions with the TUC to explore the possibility of securing agreement for a tougher policy. The result was an agreement for a limit of £6 a week on wage and salary increases with no increase for those earning more than £8,500 per year. The TUC had urged that there should be a flat rate increase which would protect the lower-paid.

The new policy was endorsed at the 1975 congress of the TUC. A report by the General Council entitled *The Development of the Social Contract* was adopted by 6,945,000 votes to 3,375,000. In its report the General Council set the problem of inflation in a wider social context. It recalled that the government had repealed the Industrial Relations Act 1971 and introduced new legislation favourable to trade unionism. The report spoke of the factors contributing to inflation, including wages and salaries, and explained that the situation had developed in the summer to the point where there was urgent need to bring down the rate of inflation. There had been pressure on sterling and if the situation had continued to deteriorate mass unemployment would have been the likely result.

The General Council called for support for the new policy, together with determined measures designed to reduce unemployment and to provide higher investment in industry. It was urged that there should be selective import controls because certain important British industries were being undercut on the British home market by imports from abroad. The TUC did not call for such new restrictions as a permanent feature of Britain's international trade, but argued that temporary relief was essential if even more unemployment was to be avoided. Time had to be given to enable British industry to recover by new investment and hence greater productivity.

Whereas at the 1974 congress the critics of the General Council's policy on the social contract had been few in number, at the 1975 congress they were more numerous. A critical resolution had been withdrawn after debate at the 1974 congress but at the 1975 congress the critics secured 3,375,000 votes against the General Council's report. The essential point of their criticism was that, whereas in the first stage of the social contract it had been said that living standards should be maintained, the new form of the social contract provided for a reduction in the living standards of millions of working people. The critics said that military expenditure was still running at a high level but industrial investment was at a low level. They also alleged that the government had retreated on a number of issues, including, for example, on the provisions of the Industry Bill. It was, they said, mistaken to believe that British capitalism could be restored to prosperity with the goodwill of the capitalists. What was needed, they said, were socialist measures. Public investment was essential to increase the efficiency of British industry and with this public investment should go public accountability. Those who were critical of the General Council's policy also argued that measures which held back the living standards of millions of working people would increase rather than reduce unemployment.

In the second half of 1975 the new incomes policy of the government, with its £6 per week limit and cut-off point at £8,500 per annum, was almost universally observed. There was little doubt that it carried a wide measure of public support, including the support of the majority of trade unionists. By the end of the year there was evidence that the rate of inflation, though still high, was beginning to slow down. A substantial reduction was also secured in the balance-of-payments deficit. Unemployment, on the other hand, remained at a level which the trade union movement regarded as unacceptably high.

One particularly disturbing feature of the situation was that Britain's industrial base was continuing to contract. Fewer people were employed in industry and Britain's relative place in world output continued to fall. The trade union movement repeatedly emphasised that there was gross under-investment in British industry. British workers, it was said, had to work with poorer and less efficient equipment than workers in other advanced industrial countries.

IMPACT ON THE INSTITUTION

The Institution and the civil service as a whole were better placed in facing the new restrictions on incomes than they had been on previous occasions. For the first time all civil service staff were not already lagging behind the rest of the community because of the updating contained in the 1975 pay review.

Moreover, in addition to the major pay review several other improvements in terms and conditions of employment had been achieved during the brief breathing space between the end of the second stage of the Heath policy and the imposition of the £6 limit. The agreements on anomaly treatment and overtime achieved early in 1974 were the prelude to further agreements of long-term significance, such as revised arrangements on starting pay on promotion, and night duty and shift disturbance allowances.

There had also, however, been disappointments. No progress was made on the Staff Side's claim for allowances and improved conditions for staff in Northern Ireland. The government argued that it would be unacceptable to treat civil servants as a privileged class in Northern Ireland. The Staff Side argued that other employers were already granting a wide range of benefits to employees in a similar position and therefore they were not seeking privileged treatment. The Staff Side, after consultation with members in Northern Ireland, modified the claim. But this too met with a negative response.

There was disappointment, too, on the issue of unestablished service to count in full for pension purposes. In addition to the familiar claim by the government that such a step would be too costly, the Official Side also produced a new argument. They said that to grant the claim would be to undertake a retrospective improvement in pension benefits to which they were opposed in principle. To overcome this objection the Staff Side replied that a favourable response on this issue would be without prejudice to any other case. Nevertheless the Official Side refused to move.

The Institution NEC took the view that the £6 limit should be supported because of the need to bring inflation down, the danger of savage cuts in public expenditure and the prospect of much worse unemployment. There were, however, several disquieting features of the policy over which the Institution and the rest of the Staff Side had reservations.

For the first time the civil service was singled out for special treatment. The White Paper *The Attack on Inflation* announced the suspension of pay research and the work of the Top Salaries Review Body for the duration of the policy. Increments were to be paid only to staff earning less than £8,500 per annum. They were to be notionally awarded to staff above that level for pension purposes only. This caused serious anomalies. The second stage of the increase recommended by the TSRB in early 1975 for certain grades above under-secretary level were not to be paid except notionally for pension purposes.

The incomes policy had an impact on the civil service in several other respects. There could be no increases in allowances or improvements in non-monetary benefits such as annual leave or conditioned hours. There could be no improvements in superannuation schemes. Sectional claims not settled by August 1975 were to be held in abeyance, and progress on restructuring exercises was suspended.

The Institution supported the National Staff Side in its representations to the CSD and the Lord Privy Seal, which were concerned with three key issues. These were the need to restore pay research for determining civil service pay and to keep the Pay Research Unit in being in the meantime; the need to continue with the payment of increments; and the importance which the Staff Side attached to no worsening in the working environment or conditions of service as part of an economy drive. In reply the Lord Privy Seal failed to give assurances on these issues. Later in the year, however, the Minister of State for the Civil Service, in reply to a parliamentary question, stated that 'the government remains committed to the "fair comparisons" principle. But in order that its own employees shall be treated consistently with the rest of the community, the settlement of civil service pay must obviously be considered in relation to the development of our counter-inflation strategy.'

TUC AFFILIATION

Throughout this period, when the government and the trade union movement were engaged in continuous discussion about the economy, the Institution had virtually no influence at all on the shape of the national incomes policy. This was not because the Institution was deliberately excluded from any discussions but because of its self-imposed isolation. Unlike all other principal unions in the civil service, the Institution remained outside the TUC. Yet the incomes policy affected Institution members no less than it affected others.

At the 1974 annual delegates conference the issue of TUC affiliation, like that of militant action, was dealt with by a common debate. The common debate embraced nine motions, which ranged from one put by the NEC calling upon the conference to agree to affiliation to one put by the British Nuclear Fuels branch (BNFL) which expressed opposition to affiliation. Between these extremes lay several motions calling for a referendum of one kind or another. Three other motions were incorporated in the debate by a decision of conference which in general terms sought to instruct the NEC to cease compaigning for affiliation to the TUC. When delegates were asked to vote after hearing all the arguments, the NEC's motion to affiliate was rejected and the BNFL motion opposing affiliation was carried by 245 votes to 175. The motion calling for a referendum to decide the issue was also carried by 244 votes to 178.

In the January 1975 issue of *State Service* a statement was published giving facts about the constitution of the TUC and advancing arguments for and against affiliation. The result of the referendum was announced in the early spring. It was as follows:

For affiliation	14,676
Against affiliation	26,302
Spoilt papers	349

The total number of valid votes cast was 40,978, representing approximately 43 per cent of members eligible to vote.

With the further developments on incomes policy in the summer and autumn of 1975, the question of the influence of the Institution on matters affecting members' interests was bound to be raised again. In the November issue of *State Service*, the general secretary put the point directly.

For the foreseeable future, negotiations in accordance with the civil service pay agreement are not in prospect. The economic crisis and the incomes policy this year – and its likely successors – have created a completely new situation.

The difference in circumstances from the settlement of the civil service pay earlier this year to the current situation cannot be overstated.

It is against this background that the National Executive Committee has been giving careful and comprehensive consideration to the policy which the Institution should adopt. It is true that this is not the first incomes policy which has interfered with civil service pay agreements, but the circumstances of the present incomes policy constitute not only a change in degree but a fundamental difference in character.

For the Institution there is a simple question. Could we influence, and should we seek to influence, the development of the incomes policy? Are we fulfilling the function of protecting and promoting our members' interests if we do not try to do so? Quite obviously we now need to take a wide range of factors into account in determining pay policy to which we have paid no – or little – attention in the past when we were able to shelter behind the civil service pay agreement. We are no longer able to do so.

Towards the end of the year the National Executive Committee circulated a consultative paper for discussion by members on the implications for the Institution of the government's policy of incomes restraint. Branches were asked to discuss the document and a series of weekend schools was arranged on the subject. The NEC paper said that the government's policy was the latest in a long line of such policies which had interfered with the operation of the civil service pay agreement. It would be wrong to suppose that the pay research system would be quickly or easily restored.

The NEC paper said that the circumstances of 1975 were so different from those of earlier times as to represent change of a fundamental kind. The economic position was particularly serious. There had been more extensive consultations than ever before between the government and the TUC and the CBI. For the first time specific reference had been made in a White Paper on inflation to the civil service pay agreement and the need to suspend pay research. Normal incremental progression had been under attack and there was criticism from various quarters of civil service conditions and agreements. In the press civil servants were constantly criticised for being overpaid, pampered, arrogant, secretive, and much else besides.

The final part of the paper was concerned with how the Institution could protect its members' interests in the new circumstances. The NEC was in no doubt about the answer. It was only by affiliation to the TUC, it said, that the Institution could hope to have any influence on the development of incomes policy. The incomes policy, rather than ordinary pay negotiations, would determine members' pay and standards of living for as long ahead as could be foreseen. Quite simply, said the NEC, without affiliating to the TUC, 'We cannot fulfil the basic aims of the Institution in the ensuing period'.

The NEC paper pointed out that with a membership of more than 100,000 the Institution would be one of the larger organisations affiliated to the TUC. The paper also explained, as had been done so often before, that affiliation to the TUC did not compromise the strictly neutral party political stance of the Institution. There were a considerable number of other unions already affiliated to the TUC which were similarly not associated with any political party.

The debate in branches began and the correspondence columns of *State Service* were full of letters on the TUC issue in the period leading up to the annual conference. By the time the issue was debated at the conference, there had been plenty of opportunity for members to discuss it and for delegates to take the measure of the members' views. The agenda carried fourteen motions in favour of affiliation, an identical number in favour of settling the issue by referendum, one for a postal ballot, one for a referendum requiring a two-thirds majority for acceptance and two opposing any move to affiliate. The motions in favour were composited, as were those favouring a referendum and those opposing affiliation. The two variants on a referendum stood on their own and the entire set of motions was taken in a 'common debate'.

This time those supporting a referendum were on much weaker ground for, as one of the speakers in favour of TUC affiliation said, each branch could have held its own referendum during the consultative process, and indeed some branches had. The delegate from the Office of Population Censuses and Surveys, who moved the lead motion in favour of affiliation, echoed the theme of the consultative paper. She said the Institution had a bald choice between affiliation and impotence. If the Institution did not affiliate, no matter how reasoned and well-informed its voice was, it would not be heard in 'the consultative desert of our self-imposed exile'. On a card vote at the end of the common debate the OPCS motion in favour of immediate affiliation was carried by 54,434 votes to 38,246; the rest of the motions therefore fell. The Institution affiliated to the TUC.

The first congress at which the Institution was officially represented was the special conference of the TUC held on 16 June 1976 to decide the trade union movement's attitude to *Social Contract 1976–77*. The general secretary, like many others, failed to get to the rostrum to speak, but the Institution, in common with the other civil service unions and the majority of delegates, endorsed the report of the General Council, *Social Contract 1976–77*.

The Institution had its first chance to speak at the TUC Congress in September 1976. The Institution had submitted two motions, one on incomes policy and the other on the Health and Safety at Work Act. In moving the latter motion, Don Downton, the chairman of the Institution, became the first Institution speaker at the TUC. The former motion was composited but the general secretary eventually caught the president's eye and was able to explain the Institution's view that there should be an orderly return to free collective bargaining but that the benefits gained from current restraint should not be dissipated.

To both these conferences the Institution took its full entitlement of delegates. In the autumn the NEC consulted branches on future arrangements for appointing delegates and a motion based on the results of these consultations was passed at the 1977 conference providing for the twenty-one seats to which the Institution was entitled to be distributed on the following basis: five delegates nominated by branches and elected by the conference; the three honorary officers; seven elected by the NEC; and six from headquarters' staff. Any future reductions in the size of the delegation should be decided by the NEC by reducing the numbers in the NEC and/or headquarters quota.

Once affiliated, the Institution began to play a growing part in TUC activities. Margaret Platt, assistant general secretary, represented the Institution on the Fuel and Power Committee, being thus able to influence the debate on the role of nuclear power in the context of the continuing energy crises. During 1977 the Institution was also allotted a place on the Transport Committee in respect of its members in civil aviation. An Institution member, Dr Ellwood, was appointed as one of the TUC's nominees on the Genetic Manipulation Advisory Group. Dr R. T. Ackroyd, a member of the Atomic Energy branch, was appointed as one of the two TUC nominees on a new committee on the safety of nuclear installations which had been established by the Health and Safety Commission to replace the

Nuclear Safety Advisory Committee. Mr V. C. Moores, the deputy vice-chairman, was appointed as an adviser to the TUC delegation to the International Labour Office Tripartite Committee on Civil Aviation. In 1978 Institution member Ms Philippa Bignell, a research assistant at the Science Museum, was selected to serve on the newly created TUC Advisory Committee on the Arts, Entertainment and Sport.

In 1977 the Association of First Division Civil Servants voted by 57 per cent to 43 per cent to affiliate to the TUC. This meant that all the civil service unions were now in the TUC. Among all significant employee organisations only the British Medical Association and the Royal College of Nursing remained outside.

INCOMES POLICY CONTINUES

Provisional agreement was reached between the TUC and the government on the incomes policy to be pursued from August 1976. The intention was to achieve a further halving of the inflation rate by December 1977. To that end the government was prepared to agree to tax reliefs if there could be a very low limit on pay increases over the next twelve-month period. It was agreed that the pay limit should be on average about $4\frac{1}{2}$ per cent, with a minimum increase of £2·50 per week and a maximum of £4. The £6 increase was not yet to be consolidated into basic pay rates nor were there to be any special exceptions to the pay limit for productivity or for the rectification of serious anomalies. The TUC insisted that there should be control on prices during the new period of incomes policy and continued to press for further measures to reduce unemployment and boost industrial training. These proposals were considered and endorsed at a special conference of the TUC on 16 June 1976.

In January 1977 the NEC issued a new consultative document to members outlining the Institution's views on incomes policy and on economic strategy. Thus the 1977 conference would be able to take an informed, democratic decision on the Institution's policy for the third stage of incomes policy for the period 1 August 1977 to 31 July 1978. Early in April 1977, following protracted argument and negotiation with the CSD as to whether salary increments within the scale were 'self-financing', and in which Institution representatives played a very prominent part, the National Staff Side concluded an agreement which provided the maximum allowable pay increases for civil servants under the second stage of the government's incomes policy.

In the light of the extensive consultations within the Institution a consensus emerged at the 1977 conference that the Institution should support a third stage of incomes policy based on the following provisions:

(1) For the period from August 1977 until July 1978 there should be a general percentage increase in pay to provide some compensation for increases in the cost of living. There should be an underpinning cash minimum to help solve the special problems of the lower-paid. This increase should be negotiated taking into account changes in income tax which, together with the general percentage increase in pay, should provide improvements in differentials and greater incentives for effort, skill and responsibility.

(2) There should be scope for negotiating genuine productivity agreements and restructuring exercises designed to improve efficiency.

(3) Some provision should be made to deal with anomalies. It would not be possible to solve every anomaly but some progress was essential. It was also essential that any special arrangement should be generally recognised as fair and acceptable. This would require independent investigation either by a special body along the lines of the old Prices and Incomes Board, or by the Government/TUC/CBI. The National Executive Committee considered that some such arrangement was necessary to deal with the genuinely exceptional cases in the short term.

(4) Any outstanding awards of independent bodies held up by Stages I and II, such as those from the Top Salaries Review Body, should be implemented with effect from the beginning of the next stage, i.e. August 1977

The Institution was to seek to have that policy adopted at the TUC in September.

In introducing the motion on behalf of the NEC the general secretary said that all employees had experienced a savage reduction in their standards of living during the first two stages of incomes policy and serious anomalies had developed. While not wishing to throw away the sacrifices of the previous two years there must be some provision for the worst injustices to be eased; nor should there be any discrimination against the public sector. He also attacked the CSD for using incomes policy as an excuse for refusing to make progress in preparing restructuring exercises, even though it was agreed that no payments from these exercises could be made during incomes policy. The delegates who opposed the motion did so largely on the grounds that the suggested policy would do very little to prevent the further erosion of differentials which were already severely compressed. On the other hand, a delegate from the British Museum made a plea for more help for the lower-paid in the form of a 'flat rate' increase for all.

At the end of July the government issued a new White Paper, *The Attack on Inflation after 31 July 1977*, and the TUC issued a statement, *The Economic Situation and Pay*. Both supported the objective of an orderly return to normal collective bargaining but they differed on the means by which it was to be brought about. The only point on which both were equally firm was that the 'twelve-month rule', whereby there should be a twelve-month gap between major pay reviews, should be maintained.

For the rest, the government laid out the implications of various levels of wage settlement for the rate of inflation and argued that if inflation was to be reduced below 10 per cent the average of pay settlements would need to be well within single figures. The government stated that it would do everything possible to ensure that full account was taken of this guidance throughout the public sector. In addition, the government stated that it intended to use sanctions against private sector companies which broke the broad guidelines. It stated: 'Where a firm has reached a settlement which is quite clearly inconsistent with the policies set out in this White Paper, the government will take this into account in public purchasing policy and the placing of contracts, and also in the consideration of industrial assistance.'

The TUC argued that there should be a return to 'responsible' collective bargaining, in which unions should take account of the economic and fiscal policies of the government designed to reduce inflation and to promote growth in real incomes. It said that the emphasis in bargaining should be on looking forward to what could be genuinely gained in terms of real living standards, not looking backwards in an attempt to recoup the losses in standards of living suffered for the previous two years. To attempt to regain lost ground would be self-defeating.

At the TUC in September 1977 the Institution's motion on incomes policy, based on the resolution passed at the 1977 conference, was composited with others. Unfortunately the general secretary was not called in the debate. The composite called for an immediate return to free collective bargaining with confirmation of the twelve-month rule. At the end of a lively and hard-hitting debate, congress passed, by a majority of 2,780,000, the composite motion:

> This congress, recognising the sacrifices and self-restraint shown by workers during the past two years in their commitment to the social contract, instructs the General Council to call for an immediate return to free collective bargaining at the end of the second stage of the social contract, with a confirmation of the twelve-month rule between principal settlements.
>
> Government action is urgently required if the necessary climate for an orderly return to free collective bargaining is to be established and achieved, requiring further reflation of the economy to reduce unemployment and allowing living standards to rise again.

This effectively ended the period of the 'social contract' and voluntary agreement on incomes policy. In the debate at congress the general secretary of the TUC said that there would be no agreed third stage. Clearly, however, as the Institution's general secretary said in an article in the October 1977 issue of *State Service*, there could still be an incomes policy applied unilaterally to government employees. The government's failure quickly to restore the 1974 civil service pay agreement was the first major indication of its hard line towards civil service pay.

RESTORATION

At the Institution's 1977 conference a resolution was passed calling for the restoration of the 1974 civil service pay agreement not later than April 1979. Similar resolutions were passed at other civil service union conferences. The National Staff Side made representations first to the CSD, then to the Lord Privy Seal, and finally, on 14 July, to the Prime Minister, seeking the immediate restoration of the pay agreement and the operation of the pay research unit. The Prime Minister referred to the criticisms which had been made of the pay research system and said there were a number of proposals the government would like to put to the Staff Side before restoring the pay agreement. The Staff Side made it clear that they thought that the agreement should be restored unconditionally, but agreed to consider any proposals.

The negotiations on the restoration of the 1974 pay agreement were completed by the end of 1977. The 1974 agreement remained unchanged in all its essential characteristics but a number of supplementary arrangements were introduced. First, there was to be a Pay Research Unit Board, which, it was claimed, would help to rebut public criticisms and misconceptions. Secondly, there were new proposals affecting senior P&T grades and the whole of the science group. The CSD insisted on the inclusion of the superintending grade and the director grade B in the professional and technology pay research surveys. This was to take effect from 1980. These grades had been excluded by agreement after the first round of pay research, seventeen years previously. To insist on their inclusion, without argument to justify the proposal and as a condition for the restoration of the 1974 pay agreement, was, in the opinion of the Institution, an action lacking in principle. The Institution was very critical of the attitude of the government and the CSD.

For scientists, the problem of the criteria for determining their pay had not yet been resolved and the government insisted that its agreement to the restoration of the 1974 pay agreement depended on the National Staff Side's acceptance that all groups of 2,000 or more staff, and in particular the science group, should be the subject of pay research. The Institution was determined that under no circumstances would the position of the scientists be sacrificed to the need to restore pay research for other groups. The National Staff Side agreed unanimously to support the Institution's resistance to the inclusion of scientists in pay research.

While negotiations on the remaining elements in the agreement were gradually completed, the problem of the scientists was left outstanding. It was not until after a series of meetings with the CSD and ministers, including the Prime Minister, that a formula emerged which was acceptable to the National Staff Side and the Institution. This was to refer the issue to the newly created Pay Research Unit Board.

CVL WEYBRIDGE

The restoration of the pay agreement was one major achievement in 1977. For the Institution a successful claim at arbitration for outer London weighting for the Central Veterinary Laboratory (CVL) at Weybridge was another. This came at the end of a three-year campaign to secure payment of outer London weighting.

The 1974 agreement on London weighting provided that certain listed towns on the 18-mile boundary measured from King Charles I statue in Whitehall should be included in the outer London area. These towns included Weybridge and Chertsey, but the CSD argued that the CVL was in neither town. The non-industrial staff, predominantly Institution grades, could not understand why they should be excluded when members of the industrial staff at the CVL site traditionally received London weighting. Non-industrial staff in establishments farther away than Weybridge also received it.

The National Staff Side had failed to persuade the CSD of the CVL's case following the 1974 London weighting agreement. New hope, however, came with the Employment Protection Act of 1975. Schedule 11 of that Act, which came into effect from 1 January 1977, seemed to provide the opportunity for taking a claim to the Advisory, Conciliation and Arbitration Service. The CSD refused to allow the case to go to ACAS on the grounds that the Employment Protection Act excluded Crown servants, despite the fact that when the Act was passed the Minister of State for the Civil Service had stated that it was the intention of the government to stick to the spirit of the Act in relation to its own employees.

On Wednesday 6 July 1977, 600 scientists and support staff at the CVL walked out, marched to a local centre and held a meeting where it was decided unanimously to impose a work-to-rule, withdraw co-operation with effect from the following Monday and to seek a meeting with the Minister of Agriculture.

The latter promised to raise the matter with the Lord Privy Seal. The staff also had the support of the local MP, Mr Geoffrey Pattie, who accompanied the march on 6 July and spoke at the mass meeting. His attempt to sponsor an adjournment debate on the matter on 29 July was thwarted when MPs decided to dispense with the final day of the parliamentary session.

On 24 October the industrial action was stepped up by instituting selective strike action in certain departments at the CVL with a view to putting pressure on the MAFF and thence upon the CSD to secure arbitration. The decision was made on the understanding that there would be no suffering to animals and that it would be aimed at bringing the issue to a speedy conclusion. The meeting also agreed that there would be an intensification of the work-to-rule and overtime ban in support of the small number of members who would actually be on strike. Hopes were raised just before the strike was due to begin when the Minister of State for the Civil Service conceded the principle that the dispute could go to the CSAT, but were dashed again when the CSD insisted on terms of reference which were unacceptable. The strike went ahead, with the full backing of the Institution, and a 24-hour picket was mounted. By the end of the second week of picketing the industrial action, and the co-operation of other unions in not crossing the picket lines to deliver supplies, was so effective that the laboratory was down to one day's supply of oil.

As a result of the action, acceptable terms of reference were agreed and the industrial action was called off. The case, put by the secretary general of the National Staff Side, was heard on 23 February. The arbitration tribunal awarded the CVL claim in full, and the long campaign thus ended in complete success. In commenting on the CVL case at the 1978 conference the general secretary said 'that justice was ultimately done but it was only accomplished because of a persistent and brilliant campaign conducted by the committee at CVL with the full support of all the members there'.

PAY IN 1978

The restoration of the pay agreement for 1979 did not solve all the outstanding problems on pay. Leaving aside the case of the scientists (see below), there was still the problem of deciding what criteria should govern civil service pay in 1978. Moreover, the civil service unions were likely to face a government determined to impose its incomes guidelines on the public services.

The National Staff Side had asked for an emergency pay research survey for 1978 and in support of that demand meetings of members of all Staff Side unions were held all over the country in December. Nearly 3,000 London-based members of civil service unions attended a meeting at Central Hall, Westminster, on 29 November, addressed by the secretary general of the Staff Side, Bill Kendall, and attended by all the general secretaries of Staff Side unions. The meeting passed a resolution demanding an emergency pay research exercise for 1978.

The government, however, refused to contemplate emergency pay reviews. The National Staff Side was unable to reach a consensus on how they should proceed in the light of this refusal. The SCPS and CPSA produced their own calculations of the movements in pay in comparable employment since the last full pay review in 1975 and based their claims on that.

The Institution's NEC, pursuing the principle approved by the annual conference that there should be no discrimination against the civil service, decided that the formulation of the April 1978 claim should be deferred until the last possible moment in early 1978, so that account could be taken of the developing situation for Stage Three settlements in the country as a whole. Early in 1978, the Institution invited all other constituents of the National Staff Side who shared its view of the situation to form an *ad hoc* consortium to pursue a claim for a substantial increase. The *ad hoc* consortium, which included all members of the National Staff Side except the SCPS and CPSA, submitted the claim to the CSD on 31 January 1978. After their initial differences of approach, all the members of the National Staff Side came together at the final stages of negotiation. This resulted in a 9·5 per cent increase in basic salaries, with the remaining 0·5 per cent used to make up a wide variety of improvements, the most important of which was the consolidation of the 1976 and 1977 increases into basic rates.

In January 1978, the NEC had decided to support a request for assistance from the Fire Brigades Union which was then involved in a strike. A donation of £1,000 was made to the FBU. The NEC did this in the belief that the FBU's long-drawn-out strike over pay was part of the campaign to oppose discrimination by the government against the public services. The success or failure of the firemen's strike would have considerable repercussions for pay in the rest of the public services. Simultaneously with sending the donation, the NEC sent a letter to the TUC putting its view that discrimination against the public services should be strenuously opposed.

The donation caused considerable controversy among the membership, reflected in the correspondence columns of *State Service* and in sixteen critical motions for the conference agenda. In his address to the conference the general secretary defended the NEC decision and claimed that events had already confirmed the validity of the decision. The pattern set by the firemen's settlement was followed in the recommendations of the review body on armed forces pay, of the review body on doctors and dentists' pay, and in the settlement for university teachers. The 'common debate' on the NEC's donation ranged from opposition on the grounds that the government guidelines should be supported, to criticism of the way the decision was taken. Those supporting the donation referred to the need for solidarity with the public service unions in the fight against discrimination. From the CVL came the argument that the Institution should repay in kind the solidarity it had experienced from other unions in its own recent dispute. In the end the debate was brought to a close by the moving of next business.

In his speech to conference the general secretary also referred in more general terms to the need for an agreement backed by the TUC to oppose any attempt to discriminate against the public services. The firemen's dispute had highlighted that need. He mentioned that David Basnett, the general secretary of the General and Municipal Workers' Union, had taken the initiative by suggesting the creation of a public services committee within the TUC, and had written to the Institution asking for support. This proposal deserved support, he said, but it was right at the outset to recognise a basic difficulty. It would require the support of the whole TUC to ensure that the public services did not remain the Cinderella of the economy and to ensure full and equal treatment for all sectors of employment. The caution in the general secretary's speech was reflected in the decision by conference to remit to the NEC the motion which called for the NEC to pursue the Basnett initiative, so that the full implications could be studied.

The NEC responded to David Basnett's first approach by explaining that the Institution recognised there were common problems for unions in the public services sector but it was not entirely happy with the terms of reference suggested for a public services committee. It felt that any proposed terms of reference should be more fully explored before the Institution could commit itself.

In July a further approach was made by David Basnett inviting the Institution to join in preliminary discussions. The NEC responded favourably. By the end of the year the General Council of the TUC embraced the idea and a TUC Public Services Committee was established composed of the fifteen General Council members with an interest in the public services sector together with representatives from other interested unions who were not on the General Council. The general secretary represented the Institution on the committee.

At the 1978 conference a number of resolutions had been carried on incomes policy for the period 1 August 1978 to 31 July 1979. The general consensus was that there should be a return to free collective bargaining, that there should be normal unfettered negotiations on pay research reports following the restoration of the pay agreement and that there should be no discrimination against the public service in their pay settlements. This sentiment was reflected in the Institution's motion submitted to the TUC, which became part of a broader composite motion. The latter, while recognising the need to limit inflation, felt that after three years of restraint trade unions should negotiate freely in their members' interests. The motion recommended certain bargaining priorities and urged the General Council to ensure that public sector workers were not discriminated against in wage bargaining.

The motion was carried overwhelmingly. The general secretary, Bill McCall, was called in the debate. He emphasised that the composite motion was not a 'licence for irresponsibility', as the Prime Minister had suggested to congress the previous day, but a means of recognising the multiplicity of circumstances and the need to deal with them on merit. It also recognised that the economic circumstances, the need to limit inflation and the objectives of congress had to be taken into account. These objectives included the need to achieve higher standards of living and to deal with low pay and anomalies, as well as the need to reward skill, effort and responsibility.

The 1978 congress set the scene for a return to free collective bargaining in the absence of any agreement with the government. The latter had already made it clear in the White Paper *Winning the Battle against Inflation* that the increase in earnings over the period from 1 August 1978 should be limited to no more than 5 per cent except in cases where self-financing productivity deals or incentive schemes were included.

The civil service unions took some comfort from the fact that the White Paper suggested that there was a small number of cases in which some exceptional increase might be possible, as in the case of firemen, the police, the armed forces, others covered by review bodies, and university teachers, where 'the pay of the groups concerned was determined very largely by external comparisons and this process was interrupted by the introduction of the £6 policy in July 1975'.

This provision seemed to fit the circumstances of the civil service with the restoration of pay research, but there was some concern among constituents of the

National Staff Side about the government's policy. At the beginning of July the SCPS tabled a motion for consideration by the Staff Side:

> This meeting of the National Staff Side notes with concern that the government has still not given an absolute assurance that the 1979 civil service pay settlement will be based on the full implementation of the pay research evidence. It is agreed, therefore, that preparations should now be made so that a united civil service-wide campaign of industrial action can be mounted speedily if at any stage it becomes clear that civil servants will be denied full, fair comparison pay increases on 1 April 1979.
>
> Committee A are instructed to prepare detailed contingency plans for united action and to report back to the October meeting of the full Staff Side.

After a detailed debate the motion was remitted to Committee A and all constituent unions were then asked to determine their policies.

The Institution responded to the Committee A request by setting out the Institution's normal approach to suggestions for militant industrial action. Such action, it was emphasised, should be taken only as a very last resort. It must have the support of the members concerned and be authorised by the NEC. The Institution was clear that before militant action was contemplated all the normal channels of negotiation should be exhausted and a traditional campaign aimed at influencing ministers, MPs and the public should be mounted.

If industrial action became necessary the Institution was prepared to play its part and to participate in machinery for financing and co-ordinating the action. It was clear that Committee A would be the obvious organisation to carry out the work of co-ordinating the campaign and they could set up *ad hoc* machinery as required. The Institution, however, would not be prepared to cede its autonomy in such matters.

The Institution's views, together with those of other unions, were considered by the National Staff Side meeting on 2 November 1978 at which a number of broad decisions on future action were taken. It was agreed that an immediate task was to get Pay Research Unit reports delivered in mid-November so that the process of detailed interpretation could begin; that there must be maximum informal contact with ministers and CSD officials to warn them of the major industrial relations and management problems ahead; that all settlements in April 1979 should reflect the criteria in the Civil Service's National Pay Agreement; that there should be a maximum exchange of information about progress in negotiations; and that there was a need for co-ordinating machinery if central action of any kind was considered desirable.

It was agreed that the traditional National Staff Side machinery should continue to deal with the normal negotiating and campaigning process but that special arrangements would be made should co-ordinated industrial action prove necessary. There would be an obligation on all unions to consult other members of the National Staff Side over any proposals they had relating to industrial action. An attempt would be made to reach agreement since united action was essential. Unions should be considering what action was possible in their own areas and should submit their initial ideas as soon as possible. Expenses associated with action approved centrally should be met from a central campaign fund, which would initially contain £1 million in earmarked contributions by individual unions.

The Institution NEC considered the Staff Side policy and agreed to support it in principle, subject to there being tight control and individual sanction by the Institution of any of its money which might be needed to support militant action by others.

In the event a staged implementation of the pay research reviews was agreed in April 1979 without the need to resort to the full co-ordinated campaign agreed the previous November. Some unions, however, organised militant action independently. On 2 April 1979 many Institution members, with permission granted from the NEC, joined a one-day strike which had already been planned by the CPSA and the SCPS. The strike was a protest at the recent offer from the government and had the desired effect of rapidly producing a better one.

There were three other major pay issues in 1978: London weighting, which concerned the Staff Side as a whole, the differentials claim, which concerned the Institution and the AGSRO, and the scientists' pay issue, which concerned the Institution alone.

The claim for a revised London weighting allowance was submitted in July 1978 as soon as the Department of Employment's indices for use in the 1974 Pay Board formula were available. These indicated substantial increases for inner London and lesser increases for the outer London area. The Official Side eventually made an offer to the Staff Side in October of an increase to £524 for inner London (12·7 per cent) and no increase for outer London. The offer was firmly based on the 10 per cent Stage Three limit. The offer was unacceptable to the Staff Side who then decided to refer the question to arbitration. The government informed the Staff Side that it could agree to arbitration only if it was accepted beforehand that if the award exceeded 10 per cent the excess would be deducted from the April 1979 pay settlement. Further representations failed to move the government and in 1979, amid protests from the Staff Side, the government's offer on London weighting was implemented by administrative action.

DIFFERENTIALS CLAIM

A claim for a differentials allowance for the professional and technology category amounting to £375 p.a. at all points of the scale for the PTO IV, the grade closest to the industrial interface, and tapering to £25 at the PTO I maximum in respect of the period 1 July 1977 to 1 April 1978 was submitted to the CSD in December 1977. The basis for the claim was that the differentials between industrial civil servants and their immediate supervisors in the P&TO grades had been severely compressed and in some cases inverted since the last major pay review in 1975. That claim, however, fell foul of incomes policy. The TUC advised that although the claim could not be regarded as a major review it, nevertheless, violated the twelve-month rule. They also advised that the twelve-month rule would not be an inhibition after April 1978.

The April 1978 pay settlement gave a measure of temporary relief, and it was decided to pursue the issue again following the settlement of civil service industrial pay in July 1978. Although the Institution met the CSD in July to stress the severity of the problems at the interface between industrial and non-industrial grades, further progress was delayed by the length of time it took to conclude the industrial settlement and to get full details of the earnings of industrial grades following the settlement. Full information on the extent of the differentials problem did not become available until the very end of 1978 when a new claim for a differentials allowance to cover the period from 1 July 1978 until 31 March 1979 was in an advanced stage of preparation.

SCIENTISTS' PAY

One of the conditions for the restoration of the 1974 pay agreement was, as already described, that the new Pay Research Unit Board should examine the issue of how scientists could be included in pay research in 1980. Following the Pay Board report on scientists' pay in 1974 the general secretary had emphasised in a meeting with the Minister of State, Civil Service Department, that the Pay Board had not produced a solution to the problem of scientists' pay and it was the responsibility of the parties to find one. He said that the Institution intended to take a constructive attitude in which the main elements would be:

(i)   The National Whitley Council pay agreements must apply to all grades.
(ii)   There should be full parity between the PSO and the principal.
(iii)   The Institution would be prepared to accept and participate in a review of the PSO, principal and PPTO grades to confirm and ensure a common level of responsibility.
(iv)   Urgent progress should be made on the outstanding structural issues as a preliminary to regradings.
(v)   Subject to the National Whitley Council agreements and to agreement on the other aspects the Institution would be prepared to accept pay research for some grades whether they were in the science group or some other structure.
(vi)   An urgent and comprehensive review of pay research procedures for scientists should therefore take place.

Following this meeting it was agreed with the CSD to proceed jointly with the three reviews recommended by the Pay Board. These were: the review of pay research procedures; the review of PSO posts; and the review to ensure correct grading between the science group and the professional and technology group. It was agreed to deal first with the pay research procedures.

A joint working group was established comprising representatives from the Institution, the CSD and the Pay Research Unit. After an exhaustive investigation of the problems which had occurred in the past, it was recommended that the full range of factors making up the jobs to be compared could only be identified after a comprehensive survey of the way in which outside employers employed and managed their scientific staff. An agreed questionnaire, based on the Mills–Waters inquiry, was prepared for this purpose and it was agreed that the survey should be undertaken by the Pay Research Unit. The parties would be supplied with full details of the returns. There was subsequently only one meeting with the CSD to consider the implications of the Unit's report before all discussions on matters relating to pay were terminated by the government on the introduction of the incomes policy restrictions in July 1975. However, the Pay

Research Unit's survey, later to be referred to as the career pattern inquiry, was to form a crucial element in the arguments before the Pay Research Unit Board. The issue remained dormant from July 1975 until 1978 when it was referred to the PRU Board.

The exact terms of reference submitted to the PRU Board in May 1978 were:

> Both sides agree that there should be a general return to pay research for 1979. The timetable is now very short, especially as new arrangements are to be introduced by agreement by the Official and Staff Sides. A particular problem concerns scientists who have not been in pay research in recent years. The Official Side and Institution of Professional Civil Servants agree that they will ask the new Pay Research Board as soon as it has been constituted to investigate the problems of applying pay research to scientists and produce its own recommendations (which both the Official Side and the IPCS agree in advance to accept) as to how pay research for scientists should be applied in 1980.

The PRU Board was established on 27 February 1978 with the appointment of its chairman, Lord Shepherd of Spalding. The rest of the Board included Sir Derek Rayner; Professor J. R. Crossley; Mr L. A. Mills, general secretary of NUBE; and Baroness Pike of Melton. The remaining members were the director of the Pay Research Unit, two representatives of the Official Side and two representatives of the Staff Side of the Civil Service National Whitley Council. The scientists' pay case was the first task confronting the PRU Board. Since the two Official Side representatives were a party to the scientists' dispute, and it was recognised that this would give them an advantage over the Institution, they agreed to withdraw from all discussions on the Board relating to the formulation of recommendations. The Staff Side member, Bill Kendall, secretary general, and Percy Avery, chairman, of the National Staff Side, although not directly parties to the dispute, also agreed to withdraw on the same basis. Care was taken to ensure that no information was obtained by the Official Side members of the Board which was not also given to the Institution. The director of the Pay Research Unit sat in throughout the deliberations but only the chairman and independent members of the Board were responsible for the conclusions and recommendations.

The Board received evidence, written and oral, from the Institution and CSD. It also took evidence from the MoD, DoE, DoI and the UKAEA. The Board decided to seek the views of a number of major employers of scientists outside the service and asked them particularly to comment on the practicability of making job comparisons between scientists in different organisations on career development for scientists and pay relativities between scientists and other staff. The chairman and deputy chairman between them also visited five civil service research establishments to see at first hand the work being carried out by civil service scientists.

INSTITUTION EVIDENCE TO PRU BOARD

The Institution's submission to the PRU Board rested firmly on the basic parameters established by the Pay Board. The Pay Board had confirmed the Institution's view that there were two basic features of scientific employment which made it difficult to apply normal pay research comparisons – the effect of individual scientific merit and performance and the differences in career patterns of scientists inside the civil service and outside.

The Institution did not, therefore, repeat these arguments in detail, since they were covered in the Pay Board report. Instead, it concentrated on three important implications of the Pay Board's findings and the career pattern inquiry which had subsequently been conducted.

First, there was the issue of 'unquantifiables'. The Pay Board had argued that in principle the difference in the nature of employment of scientists inside and outside the civil service could be taken into account as 'unquantifiables'. But neither the Pay Board nor the two parties to the dispute could find any way of giving a measurement to them. They differed in scale and complexity from any 'unquantifiables' taken into account in other pay research surveys. It was for this reason that the Pay Board had turned to internal relativities, particularly at the PSO and SSO levels where the difficulties were most acute.

Secondly, while agreeing with the Pay Board's view that internal relativities should be the primary criterion at PSO level, the Institution disagreed with the Pay Board's formula which proposed 'that the adjustment for unquantifiable factors . . . should be such as to ensure that the PSO salary . . . does not differ by more than 5 per cent from that of the principal'. The Institution could not understand why the Pay Board had suggested the figure of 5 per cent since when they were in phase the maxima of the scales for the PPTO and principal had 'never differed by more than 1·1 per cent either way'. Thus, for all practical purposes they were the same. Indeed, in 1975, the first year when the principal and PPTO were in pay research at the same time, they had identical maxima.

Thirdly, the career pattern inquiry had, in the Institution's view, confirmed the Pay Board's view that the pattern of employment inside the service and outside was substantially different. Moreover it showed that there were insufficient companies whose employment of scientists was similar to the civil service to constitute an adequate external sample. The agreed purpose of the career pattern inquiry had been to establish whether there were sufficient firms with a pattern of organisation similar to that of the civil service to form a satisfactory field for pay research purposes. It was also agreed that: 'While a perfect match at all points was unlikely to be found the aim should be to eliminate all those organisations that diverged too far from the civil service pattern and thus to avoid having to make substantial allowances for the differences between the two.'

The working group had agreed that the inquiry should be confined to those firms likely to have a structure similar to the civil service and that for this reason:

(a)   they should employ at least 200 staff on work similar to that of the science group;
(b)   they should employ staff up to at least senior principal scientific officer level;
(c)   they should retain at least some of their scientists on research and development up to retirement age.

The CSD argued that thirty-five of the seventy-seven organisations approached by the Pay Research Unit were acceptable in that they did not differ too far from the civil service pattern. The Institution argued, on the other hand, that only five firms satisfied the agreed criteria and a further nine were borderline cases. The remaining twenty-one organisations provided a career structure markedly different from the civil service. An external field of fourteen companies was quite inadequate to establish fair comparisons. The first pay research survey for the scientific classes had contained forty-nine and the second thirty-five organisations.

The career pattern inquiry also showed that of the thirty-five organisations acceptable to the CSD, twenty-nine had common grading structures covering administrative, technical and scientific staff. Thus in outside organisations a major role in pay determination was played by internal relativities. In its proposals to the PRU Board, therefore, the Institution relied heavily on internal relativities within the service, particularly for the higher grades.

The Institution's proposals to the PRU Board were that the pay of the PSO should be based on parity with the principal and PPTO grades. The ASO and the SO, where the career pattern differences were not significant, should be included in pay research so long as a close watch was kept on the 'circularity' argument, i.e. that outside companies did not look to the civil service in establishing their own pay levels. The pay of the HSO and SSO, the Institution suggested, should be based on internal horizontal and vertical relativities.

CSD EVIDENCE TO THE PRU BOARD

In its evidence to the Board the CSD swept aside the report of the Pay Board. It argued that pay research could provide true and fair rates for all civil service scientific grades and that no problems arose for them which could not be dealt with through the established processes of fact-finding and negotiation. There was no evidence, it claimed, that any differences which might be encountered in a pay research survey of all grades of scientist were of a different order from the differences encountered in pay research surveys for other civil service groups. Any suspicion that the pay research system was being manipulated to suit any particular civil service group would be damaging to the integrity of that system.

The CSD relied heavily in its case on the evidence collected in the career pattern inquiry and on its own estimate, with which the Institution disagreed, of the numbers of civil service scientists engaged on R&D. It argued that only approximately 45 per cent of the staff in the science group were actually engaged on R&D at any one time. It also alleged that when external R&D scientists were compared with this 45 per cent the evidence available did not reveal any marked differences in career patterns.

The CSD argued that it would be wrong to overturn pay research evidence of external rates of remuneration in order to maintain internal horizontal relativities. In its view the civil service internal relativities must shift in the light of pay research. Moreover, none of the different factors, which the Institution suggested invalidated pay research, taken individually, justified any change to the normal pay research procedures, nor was it necessary to modify the process to take account of the cumulative effect of these factors.

In the oral evidence the Institution's general secretary cast doubts on several aspects of the CSD evidence. The Institution did not accept, for example, the CSD's estimates of the proportion in the science group engaged on R&D, nor the definitions which it had used to reach its 45 per cent figure. Circumstances had not significantly changed since the Mills–Waters Report when it was agreed by both parties that two-thirds of the science group were employed on research and development. The general secretary said that he had no hesitation in describing the CSD's evidence as a 'disreputable case containing a farrago of misrepresentations. It disowned much of what the CSD had previously admitted and it did not contain a constructive thought or suggestion for solving what had been the major industrial relations problem in the civil service in recent years.'

PRU BOARD REPORT

The Board reported in November 1978. It recommended that:

(a) The normal processes of pay research should apply to ASO, SO and HSO grades subject to a continuing check on the influence of civil service pay scales on outside pay rates. The pay for the SPSO and DCSO grades should also be based on the normal processes of pay research but special care must be taken to assess the weight of outside evidence before changing long-established internal relativities.

(b) The pay of the PSO and SSO grades should be interpolated between the rates settled for the grades above and below them on the basis of horizontal and vertical relativities, taking account of the outside evidence on such relativities. The Pay Research Unit should provide pay information on outside analogues for the PSO and SSO grades, and on the pay relativities in multi-discipline organisations for scientist and engineer analogues at PSO and PPTO level.

(c) The pay research survey should cover a wide range of outside organisations to produce an adequate number of comparisons at all levels and to provide the information referred to in (b) above.

(d) The Pay Research Unit should ensure that its internal survey covers all significant work functions undertaken by civil service scientists and that comparisons are made for all these work functions. The survey should cover the major proportion of work undertaken by civil service scientists.

(e) CSD and the Institution should reach an understanding on the principles and practice of fluid grading and this should be applied consistently in all departments.

(f) When reporting pay information for scientists the Pay Research Unit should take particular care in giving all the available evidence on the means used by outside organisations to reward individual scientific merit.

The Institution was disappointed with the PRU Board's report. However, having agreed to abide by the recommendations of the Board the Institution began to prepare for a pay research survey for scientists in 1980.

26 Government Policies and the Institution

Apart from the incomes policies pursued after 1975, other policies of the Labour government had a significant impact on civil service staff and the public services in general. There were manpower cuts, cash limits and general attacks on the civil service from sections of the media which were also supported by some MPs. At the 1977 conference a motion was carried deploring the misinformed and scurrilous campaigns against the civil service and asking the NEC to counter them by publicly demonstrating the value of public services to the community.

On the positive side the government's policies in relation to health and safety and industrial democracy were welcome. There were, however, considerable difficulties in getting them properly implemented in the civil service. This was partly because of the reluctance of the government to make any allowance for extra expenditure in a period of financial stringency but was also a reflection of the attitude of the CSD.

Other government policies which had implications for the Institution and other civil service unions during the period were dispersal and devolution. Neither of these eventually came to pass during the period of the Labour government, although both were important elements in their strategy. Towards devolution the Institution was neutral, towards dispersal the Institution's attitude changed from one of support in principle subject to certain conditions to one of almost total opposition because of its impact on Institution members and the degree of enforced bulk removal which it was bound to imply.

Several other issues also affected the Institution and its members. These included the Armitage Committee on political rights for civil servants, and the Select Committee on Expenditure's review of Fulton developments which gave the Institution an opportunity to air its disappointment at lack of progress and raised hopes of new initiatives.

There were also major developments in the internal organisation of the Institution and the civil service movement. New alliances were forged and attempts made to improve on the processes of consultation within the Institution and the Staff Side as a whole.

PUBLIC EXPENDITURE CUTS AND CASH LIMITS

Incomes policy was not the only way in which the government sought to reduce inflation; it also embarked early in 1976 on severe cuts in public expenditure. It was argued by the government that for some time too great a share of the country's resources had been devoted to consumption, including public services, and too little to manufacturing investment and exports. The growth in public expenditure in relation to that of other sectors had required increased taxation and borrowing which had created problems of economic and financial management. Those who opposed the cuts in principle, and this did not include the Institution, argued that there was no evidence that the lack of investment in British industry resulted from lack of funds for investment. The cuts, said the critics, would simply add to the level of unemployment, already high, and would not produce a shift of labour into manufacturing industry.

In its White Paper *Attack on Inflation*, published in July 1975, the government said that it intended to reinforce its control of public expenditure by the introduction of cash limits. In April 1976, in its White Paper *Cash Limits on Public Expenditure*, the government dealt with central and local government expenditure and the finances of the nationalised industries and explained that the cash limits for central government expenditure would represent 'a planned limit on the amount of cash that the government propose to spend on certain services or blocks of services, during the coming financial year'. The limits would cover some three-quarters of central government expenditure other than social security benefits.

The cash limits were intended as a long-term method of keeping public expenditure under control but the White Paper set overall cash limits for 1978/9 which entailed savings of £190m. in defence, £620m. in education, £300m. on roads and transport, £220m. on other environmental services and £150m. on health and social services. In addition to such programme reductions the White Paper stated that it was the government's intention to save an additional £140m. in 1978/9 by reductions in planned expenditure on staff and related administrative costs.

Although no immediate details of where the cuts would fall had been released the Institution was fearful that, as usual, specialists would be hard hit. The NEC therefore sponsored a motion at the 1976 conference seeking a mandate to ensure that, in any cuts in public expenditure, full consideration was given to the long-term value of particular projects, especially in the research and development field; that such cuts did not bear unduly on the specialist areas; that reductions in manpower were accompanied by corresponding reductions in workload; and that any manpower cuts should be implemented in such a way as to avoid compulsory redundancy. The motion was passed, although some delegates argued that the Institution should take a tougher line and resist any manpower cuts.

Although the Staff Side had been given advance warning of the impending manpower cuts, and had been informed that departments were considering options based on cuts of 5, 10 and 15 per cent in expenditure up to 1978/9, it was not until the summer of 1976 that the extent and nature of the proposed cuts became clear and then only in broad outline. In December, following negotiations to secure a further loan from the International Monetary Fund, further massive public expenditure cuts were announced and it became clear that the DoE would be particularly hard hit. Throughout this period the Institution's NEC attached top priority to seeking to obtain detailed information about the precise staffing implications of the cuts so that problem areas could be identified early and appropriate steps taken to avoid or minimise redundancy.

The Staff Side took the view that before any forced redundancy occurred the position should first be eased by the provision of facilities for voluntary premature retirement, as provided for in the previously negotiated premature retirement agreement. The Official Side, however, anxious to avoid the massive expenditure which the operation of that agreement would imply, proposed the early retirement of staff over 65 and a review of the retirement policy for those between 60 and 65, and sought to apply the job release scheme in the civil service without consultation. The Staff Side resisted these proposals and suggested that there should be a comprehensive review of manpower policies. In the meantime pressure was being maintained within departments to obtain details of proposed future manpower cuts.

As feared, the projected cuts fell very heavily on specialists, particularly those in research and development. This was despite the fact that the White Paper published in August 1977 giving the provisional outturn for expenditure for 1976/7 showed that there had been a major underspend below the agreed cash limits. Immediately representations were made to the CSD suggesting that this major underspend had already met the targets set out in the Chancellor's earlier programme for reductions in expenditure up to 1978/9.

At the 1977 conference Cyril Cooper moved the NEC motion which recognised the need to give priority to the regeneration of manufacturing industry but expressed concern about some aspects of the public expenditure cuts. It proposed a full debate of the cuts before decisions were taken, no short-term cuts in R&D which could have long-term disadvantages, a review of the manpower implications of the cuts, a comprehensive manpower policy and the avoidance of compulsory redundancy. In his speech he said that the cuts proposed in the MAFF, the DoE, DTI, COI and DHSS would result in a widespread reduction in the quality of service to the public. In the DoE and DTI not only were manpower cuts proposed but the Official Side were also proposing restrictions on promotions in the science area.

The delegate from the DTI Industrial Research branch pointed out that 80 per cent of the cuts in manpower were being made on 30 per cent of the department, namely, in the research establishments. She described as immoral and underhand the behaviour of the CSD, which was interfering with departmental model redundancy agreements, and imposing restrictions and package deals which affected promotion structures and retirement. Naively it had been thought that the motivation behind its attitude was to save money but it was now apparent that the Institution was witnessing a serious attack on the structure and careers of its members.

In the event compulsory redundancies were avoided and a number of volunteers were offered voluntary premature retirement terms. However, in the case of the DoE Directorate General of Research the difficulties were more prolonged and more serious. In the middle of July 1977 the Official Side had offered a package of proposals to cut the normal promotion rates for 1977 and 1978 to one-third of the historic rates, to reduce the retirement age to 60 for all staff with a minimum of thirty years' reckonable service and to conduct a survey of all scientific staff in the grades HSO to SPSO inclusive to discover the number of staff who would be likely to accept an offer of voluntary premature retirement. The Institution informed the Official Side that the first two proposals were totally unacceptable and offered an alternative proposal based on natural wastage and the use of voluntary premature retirement. The Official Side replied that they could agree to a small number (just over twenty) of voluntary premature retirements on the agreed terms but only if the retirement age was reduced to 60 as suggested and if promotion rates were cut by no less than 60 per cent. This was implemented administratively for 1977.

The Institution made representations to the Lord Privy Seal to ensure that the same attitude did not prevail in 1978, especially since the manpower targets had been met. The response was unsatisfactory and the NEC accordingly authorised a half-day strike by the scientists concerned on 10 May 1978. The strike was well supported and the protest demonstration outside DoE headquarters attracted favourable publicity from the media. In addition questions were raised by a number of MPs, articles were written in the trade and national press, and letters sent to universities warning graduating students that careers in the civil service did not provide the glowing conditions and prospects painted in the recruitment literature.

Shortly after the strike, the Lord Privy Seal addressed the 1978 conference and the DoE, DGR branch delegates took the opportunity to carry on informal discussions with him in the bar and over the snooker table. Negotiations were resumed after conference in an obviously improved atmosphere and agreement was eventually reached in late August. Staff retired at 60, including those already retired, were to be allowed to revert to the SO grade, promotions were to be in the normal range in 1978 and a full manpower planning exercise was to be conducted with a view to establishing in due course a new agreement on retirement and recruitment policies.

THE CAMPAIGN AGAINST DISPERSAL

One area where the government was not prepared to envisage public expenditure savings in the short term was the costs involved in the large programme of dispersal to the regions to which it was politically committed.

Further dispersal of some civil servants from London had first been suggested in the White Paper *The Reorganisation of Central Government* and had been referred to Sir Henry Hardman, a former permanent secretary in the Ministry of Defence, to conduct a review and make recommendations.

The Hardman Report on dispersal was published on 13 June 1973 and recommended that over 31,000 posts should be dispersed from London. In a covering statement the government said that it wished to consider Sir Henry's recommendations further before making final decisions and was arranging for consultations through the national and departmental Whitley Council machinery. At a meeting with the Lord Privy Seal in December 1973 the National Staff Side representatives stressed the importance of accepting, as far as possible, the principle that movement should be on a voluntary basis, that dispersal should be to a relatively small number of acceptable locations and that there should be arrangements for facilitating career development without unnecessary transfers. It was made clear that the Staff Side was not committed to dispersal in principle and that it must reserve its position until the specific proposals emerged.

The election of the Labour government in 1974 added a new dimension to the dispersal proposals. The Hardman recommendations had struck a balance between the costs and benefits to operational efficiency and the need to take account of regional policy. The new government laid much more emphasis on regional policy. In July 1974 the Lord President of the Council announced in the House of Commons that some 7,000 posts from the MoD would be dispersed to Glasgow, a similar number from the MoD and other departments would go to Cardiff and Newport and some 4,500 posts would go to the North-West region, including some sections of the Ministry of Agriculture and the Home Office. About 3,000 posts at the headquarters of the PSA would go to Teesside and the Laboratory of the Government Chemist would move to West Cumberland, with 500 posts from the DHSS joining its units already in Newcastle. Whereas the Hardman recommendations would have transferred about 12,000 posts from the London area to other parts of the South-East region the number now moving there would be only 850.

The National Staff Side protested at the lack of consultation and the abandonment of all the work already undertaken jointly in departments on the Hardman proposals. A joint committee was established to review all aspects of dispersal and to challenge in detail schemes which appeared not to be viable.

At the 1974 conference the Institution had decided to accept dispersal in principle but with the insistence that full consultation should take place and that the interests of the staff concerned should be fully protected. The government's assurance that moves would be made on a voluntary basis was welcome but it was clear that for Institution members there were less likely to be alternative posts available in London than in the case of other civil servants.

Some of the proposed dispersal moves progressed smoothly, but real difficulties arose with several of the projected moves. There was evidence, said the general secretary in his address to the 1975 conference, that as far as the government was concerned 'regional and political considerations [had] ridden roughshod' over considerations of efficiency, and of staff opposition to certain dispersal moves. This was well illustrated by four examples in which Institution members were involved – the Department of Overseas Surveys' dispersal to Glasgow, the dispersal of sections of the MoD staff, the move of the Laboratory of the Government Chemist to Cumbria and the dispersal of the Office of Population Censuses and Surveys.

During 1976 the attitudes of Institution members hardened towards dispersal moves which they felt would damage efficiency and were unattractive to the staff concerned. At the 1976 conference a motion was carried calling on the government to reconsider those dispersal proposals which would involve vast sums of public money, reduce efficiency, fail to fulfil the objective of creating extra jobs in development areas and which were strongly opposed by the staff involved. In moving the motion the NEC speaker said that the dispersal moves made no sense to members. At a time when the civil service was under attack for squandering money, when it was faced with severe expenditure cuts and possible redundancies, and at a time when the government was urging everyone to tighten their belts, the government was proposing to spend a vast amount on dispersal. Many Institution members would be compulsorily dispersed which would produce a massive deterioration in morale.

Despite a series of representations in which the Institution played a leading part, the government refused to review the dispersal programme. In November, therefore, the National Staff Side, with the Society of Civil and Public Servants, who favoured dispersal, dissenting, took a new initiative and adopted a revised policy. The main features were:

(*a*) To draw up a list of the disputed areas of dispersal and to express the strongest opposition to any moves for dispersal in these areas;

(*b*) To renew the demand for a comprehensive review of the dispersal programme against the background of current reductions in public expenditure and in civil service manpower costs;

(*c*) if no progress were made, to undertake a vigorous campaign for an independent inquiry into dispersal arrangements with the broadest terms of reference.

The Institution NEC fully supported this policy.

At about the same time members at the Laboratory of the Government Chemist were engaging in their own campaign to publicise what they regarded as the folly of their projected move to West Cumbria. They organised a half-day strike on 9 November and amid considerable publicity lobbied MPs. Similar action was taken by the Directorate of Overseas Surveys staff at Tolworth on 16 November. Early in 1977 the PSA members initiated a campaign against the dispersal to Teesside.

In January 1977 the Institution convened a meeting of representatives from those areas where the dispersal move was disputed in order to review developments and to consider how best the disputed moves could be contested. A dispersal co-ordinating committee was established. A meeting of a similar nature between National Staff Side and Departmental Staff Side representatives took place in February. As a result of that meeting the National Staff Side decided to proceed with the campaign for an independent inquiry into the disputed moves. The issue was brought to the attention of MPs and publicity was secured for the Staff Side case. The Staff Side also decided to discuss the purported economic benefits with receiving local authorities and to continue to co-ordinate research on this and other aspects of the problem. The 1977 conference of the Institution endorsed these policies.

In July 1977 the government announced that it intended to go ahead with the disputed dispersal moves although most of the specific proposals would be deferred by one year. The Institution continued to press for a review of the dispersal programme and made representations to MPs both on the general issue and in relation to specific dispersal moves. It also raised the matter with leaders of the Greater London Council and with ministers in departments affected by dispersal. Institution representatives also took part in television and radio programmes on the subject.

In the summer of 1978, the National Staff Side, having failed to persuade the government of the need for an independent inquiry, commissioned the University of Strathclyde to carry out independent academic research into the economic and social benefits of the dispersal programme. Before the research report was received, however, there was a change of government (May 1979) and the new Conservative government, having reviewed the dispersal proposals, cut dramatically the number of dispersal proposals including the majority of those to which the Institution had objected.

DEVOLUTION

Another aspect of regional policy to which the Labour government was heavily committed was the devolution of certain functions of central government to Scotland and Wales. The implications of this policy for civil servants, although less controversial than dispersal, were substantial. The main concern of the Institution and other unions within the Staff Side was to ensure that there were the fullest safeguards for existing civil servants written into any scheme which might be worked out. A motion passed at the 1975 Institution conference instructed the NEC to ensure that civil servants working for the projected Scottish and Welsh assemblies should receive the same pay and conditions of service as those serving in the UK central government.

Staff Side fears that the UK civil service might be split to produce separate services for Scotland and Wales were allayed by the White Paper *Our Changing Democracy, Devolution to Scotland and Wales,* published in November 1975, which stated that 'in the view of the government it would be in the best interests of all to keep a unified United Kingdom civil service'. This preference was endorsed by the 1976 Institution conference, and the Institution, together with other civil service unions, made strong representations to the Scottish and Welsh TUC along those lines.

Following the 1976 conference the Institution established two committees, one for Scotland and one for Wales, consisting of representatives from branches who had an interest in the devolution proposals. Both were to hold a watching brief on devolution developments and to advise the NEC on ways in which groups of members could be affected by the devolution proposals. In the event, in the referenda conducted in Scotland and Wales early in 1979 the proposals for devolution failed to achieve the support which Parliament had stipulated as necessary. The devolution issue was effectively shelved for the time being.

HEALTH AND SAFETY AT WORK

In 1974 the Health and Safety at Work Act was passed. It provided for the establishment of a Health and Safety Commission to develop policy for health and safety at work, a Health and Safety Executive to be the executive arm of the Commission and responsible for the day-to-day operation of the new health and safety organisation and for enforcing statutory requirements on safety and health, and for a network of safety representatives to be elected by the workforce in each employing organisation.

The legislation arose out of the recommendations of the Committee on Safety and Health at Work, chaired by Lord Robens, which reported in July 1972. The Institution, representing the majority of HM inspectorates concerned with health and safety, had given evidence to the Robens Committee covering the whole field of health and safety, largely from the inspectorate's point of view.

The Robens Report was strongly in favour of a system which relied heavily on the involvement of employers and employees in a self-regulating system rather than a substantial expansion of the professional inspectorates for which the Institution had pressed. The Institution continued to press its own views during the consultative process on the document *Proposals for a Safety and Health at Work Bill* published by the government in 1973. It failed, however, to change the major features of the proposals which closely followed the Robens recommendations. In particular the Institution held strongly to the view that the staff of the Health and Safety Commission should remain civil servants, and that the position of the inspectorates as enforcement agencies could be jeopardised if they were employed by a Commission composed of representatives of organisations, i.e. the CBI and the TUC, against whose members enforcement action might have to be taken.

Once the Health and Safety at Work Act was passed the Health and Safety Commission, chaired by Mr William Simpson, formerly general secretary of the Amalgamated Union of Engineering Workers (Foundry Section), and with nine Commissioners, three each from the CBI and the TUC and three others, was established. Throughout 1974 the Institution pressed for the appointment of a director of the Health and Safety Executive at permanent secretary level to be chosen from among the chief inspectors of the four inspectorates. In the event the appointment went to a deputy secretary from the Department of Employment at deputy secretary level, with an allowance. The Chief Inspector of Factories was appointed deputy director, and the Chief Nuclear Installations Inspector was appointed the third member of the executive. Both of these appointments were at deputy secretary level. The original intention to hive off the Executive and its staff from the civil service was not proceeded with because of strong pressure from the National Staff Side. The Institution also managed to ensure that the 'top structure' of the Executive was composed of specialist staff.

The functions and staffing of the Health and Safety Executive and Commission having been resolved, some of it along the lines advocated by the Institution, attention turned to the implications for members at large in relation both to their management responsibilities under the Act and to their rights and duties as safety representatives. In the debate on health and safety at the 1976 Institution conference it became clear that members were uncertain and confused about the implications of the Health and Safety at Work Act. Delegates were fearful that the legal liabilities arising from their role as managers and supervisors, and thus agents of the employer, might lead to the prosecution of individuals. They also sought guidance from the NEC and the Institution on the role and training of safety representatives provided for in the new Act.

After pressure from the Staff Side the CSD confirmed the assurances given by the Health and Safety Executive that an individual civil servant would be prosecuted only in the same circumstances as an individual employee outside the civil service, for example, where there was a wilful or reckless disregard of health and safety requirements. There was no question, as members had feared, of individuals being prosecuted in lieu of the Crown, because of the difficulties arising from the concept of Crown immunity. Satisfactory arrangements were also agreed for legal advice and representation in the event of prosecution.

On the question of training of safety representatives, members of the NEC and headquarters officers attended courses run by the TUC for tutors in health and safety and the Institution embarked on an extensive programme devised by the TUC for the initial training of safety representatives. Institution members from the health and safety inspectorates were involved as advisers and tutors.

Two other issues concerning the application of the health and safety legislation to the civil service exercised the Institution and other civil service unions. The first was the failure of the government in its role as an employer to make available additional resources to introduce measures in the civil service which resulted from the implementation of the Act. The unions objected to what they regarded as the consistently obstructive attitude of the CSD in discussions at national level on the implementation of the Act and, in particular, on the implementation of the regulations on safety representatives and safety committees. The TUC also brought pressure to bear but to little effect.

The second was the issue of Crown immunity in the whole range of protective employment legislation including the Health and Safety at Work Act. Under the terms of the Act the Health and Safety Executive could not prosecute the Crown for infringement of health and safety legislation and regulations; nor could it issue a legally binding improvement or prohibition notice to any government establishment. The Institution successfully moved a motion at the TUC in 1978 in the following terms:

Congress notes with concern that, in general, legislation designed to protect the interests of workers does not apply to Crown employees. It urges the General Council to seek the extension of all labour laws to cover this group of workers, and to ensure that there are no such exclusions in future legislation.

INDUSTRIAL DEMOCRACY

In December 1975 the government established a committee of inquiry, chaired by Lord Bullock, 'to advise on questions relating to representation at board level in the private sector', with the following terms of reference:

Accepting the need for a radical extension of democracy in the control of companies by means of representation on boards of directors, and accepting the essential role of trade union organisations in this process, to consider how such an extension can best be achieved, taking into account in particular the proposals of the Trades Union Congress report on industrial democracy as well as experience in Britain, the EEC and other countries. Having regard to the interests of the national economy, employees, investors and consumers, to analyse the implications of such representation for the efficient management of companies and for company law.

Although the committee of inquiry was specifically concerned with the private sector, parallel discussions were to take place in the public sector with the intention that the government should take them into account when considering its response to the Bullock Report. The government subsequently announced that a number of departmental committees would review the arrangements in the public sector.

The National Staff Side prepared evidence for the committee with particular reference to the civil service. The evidence recognised the limitations deriving from the accountability of ministers to Parliament and of Parliament to the electorate. It therefore made its first priority to improve the existing industrial relations procedures in the civil service. It also included proposals for staff representation on certain management bodies. The main proposals were:

(1) To seek the fullest possible prior consultation regarding the make-up of estimates, including cash limits, imminent new legislation and the proposed location or relocation of work, in so far as they affect the interests of staff.
(2) Where it is impossible for constitutional reasons for staff to be represented on management boards, civil service staff unions should enjoy similar full disclosure of information as would be forthcoming were they represented on the Board.
(3) That in situations of dispute there should be a 'standstill' period applying to both sides, during which the management would have to suspend the disputed action and the staff suspend any direct action against it. In this way a neutralised situation would be created in which it would be possible to consider the dispute in an objective and constructive atmosphere.
(4) That the National Whitley Council and each Departmental Whitley Council should establish joint disputes committees, each of which would be available for the resolution of disputes (normally registered disagreements) arising at the level immediately below.
(5) Conciliation should be available after the procedure has been exhausted and no agreement reached. A 'standstill' would apply pending conciliation.
(6) Arbitration should be extended to include all grades below the under-secretary pay point and further issues brought within its scope e.g. grading, complements and conditions under which allowances are paid.
(7) There should be a series of experiments in representation on management boards to test the various options available. This would be without prejudice to any permanent system of representation which might subsequently be agreed.

There was no response from the Official Side for seventeen months following the submission of the National Staff Side's proposals. The reply, when it did come in March 1978, caused dismay and disappointment on the Staff Side. The Official Side argued that the existing civil service industrial relations system was broadly satisfactory but they were, nevertheless, willing to undertake a joint review of the procedures. They also argued that the special position of the civil service as the servant of ministers placed severe constraints on the scope for shared decision-making. By the end of 1978 little progress had been made in discussions with the Official Side.

It would have been easier to attack the stance of the CSD and the evident lack of enthusiasm among senior officials had the climate outside the civil service been more favourable. With the exception of the Post Office, which rapidly implemented a Bullock-type system of worker representatives on the Board, even though it was a public sector organisation, progress elsewhere was slow. In nearly all parts of private industry employers were opposed to the Bullock proposals and the unions were divided.

The prospect of early legislation quickly faded. Moreover, the Bullock Committee itself had been divided and unable to agree on a unanimous report. The majority report, published in January 1977, was signed by the chairman and six members of the committee, of whom one submitted a note of reservation, while the three members nominated by the CBI submitted a minority report disagreeing in certain fundamental respects with the majority one. The two crucial recommendations of the Bullock Report, both of which were opposed by the three employer members of the committee and by employers in general, concerned the composition of company boards and the method by which employee representatives were to be elected. The report recommended that in any company employing 2,000 people or more an equal number of employee and shareholder representatives should be elected with a smaller group of independent members jointly agreed by the other two groups holding the balance (the $2x+y$ formula). The employee representatives were to be selected through the existing trade union machinery (the 'single-channel' approach).

WOMEN'S RIGHTS

Although no legislation was forthcoming from the Labour government on the issue of industrial democracy, it did, early in its term of office, give much attention to the promotion of women's rights. At the end of 1975 both the Equal Pay Act and the Sex Discrimination Act came into full operation. The Sex Discrimination Act had been preceded by a White Paper, *Equality for Women*, published in September 1974, on which interested parties were asked to submit comments. The Institution, after consulting branches, submitted its comments in October. The Institution also submitted further comments during the passage of the Bill through Parliament. Under the Act discrimination on the grounds of sex became unlawful in employment, education, housing and the provision of goods and services.

During 1975 the TUC published a revised *Charter for Working Women* listing twelve objectives. Many of those objectives had already been achieved within the civil service, and those which had not were largely covered by the Committee on the Employment of Women in the Civil Service which reported in 1971. As an article in the September 1975 issue of *State Service* pointed out, however, there was no room for complacency. Despite the fact that all the recommendations of the 1971 Report were accepted in principle, progress on many of the recommendations had been painfully slow. The Sex Discrimination Act, the article said, was likely to add some urgency and impetus to developments within the civil service.

The legislation of 1975 laid the groundwork for equal rights for women. Once formal equality seemed to be largely achieved, the emphasis shifted to policies required to make the formal equality a reality, by providing the facilities and opportunities without which the majority of women would be unable to take advantage of the equality to which they were now legally entitled.

Nursery provision was one such facility. On this issue women in the civil service suffered a major setback in 1976 when to the shock and dismay of the Staff Side the CSD announced that it was considering closing its experimental nursery in Llanishen and in 1977 decided against any further nursery provision on grounds of economies in public expenditure. The Institution passed a resolution at its 1977 conference deploring the decision, as did many other civil service unions.

The campaign for nursery provision, however, received a fillip with the publication in 1978 of a TUC working party report, *The Under-Fives*, which recommended as its major long-term objective the comprehensive and universal provision of free nursery services for the under-5s. The report was endorsed by the Institution conference in 1978 in a resolution which pledged the Institution to implement the proposals where possible in the civil service and to support a TUC campaign. Following its endorsement at the TUC in September 1978 the recommendations of the report became TUC policy. The possibility of making rapid progress was undermined, as in the civil service, by the climate of public expenditure cuts.

THE ARMITAGE REPORT

An issue which was causing increasing concern to civil service unions during the second half of the 1970s was that of the political rights of civil servants. At the 1975 Institution conference a resolution, moved by the MoD Atomic Weapons Research Establishment branch, was passed instructing the NEC to seek a review of the restrictions placed on the political activities of civil servants with the aim of ensuring that these were minimised. Similar resolutions emerged from other civil service union conferences. The National Staff Side urged the government to appoint an independent committee to undertake a review. The last such review had been undertaken by the Masterman Committee in 1949, resulting in agreed proposals in 1952 which severely limited the political rights of civil servants.

In August 1976 the government appointed a committee of inquiry under the chairmanship of Sir Arthur Armitage, vice-chancellor of the University of Manchester, with the following terms of reference: 'to review the rules governing the active participation by civil servants in national and local political activities and to make recommendations'.

Stanley Mayne, former general secretary of the Institution, and a fierce opponent of the Masterman proposals and campaigner for civil rights, was appointed a member of the committee, along with Lord Amulree, Liberal Whip in the House of Lords; Lord Brimelow, former head of the diplomatic service; Lord Carrington, leader of the opposition in the House of Lords; Mrs Judith Hart, former Minister for Overseas Development; Sir Frederick Hayday, former chairman of the International Committee of the TUC; Sir Peter Matthews, managing director of Vickers; and Sir William Nield, former permanent secretary at the Cabinet Office. Judith Hart was later appointed to a ministerial post and was replaced by Mrs Barbara Castle.

The National Staff Side gave evidence to the committee in which it recommended a radical change in the rules governing the political activities of civil servants. They proposed that the existing rules should be replaced by a simple proviso that, before a civil servant took an active role in political affairs at either local or national level, he should be required to notify his intention to his department and that a period of one month should be given within which it would be possible for the department to argue that, because of the nature of the individual's position within the civil service, the proposed course of action ran counter to the public interest. There would need to be provision for reference to adjudication on the grounds for refusal. The committee asked the National Staff Side to elaborate in detail on several aspects of its evidence, particularly the procedures for adjudication. This the Staff Side did.

The committee reported on 11 January 1978. It did not grant what the National Staff Side had asked for but did recommend substantial improvements in the existing position. Stanley Mayne and Barbara Castle signed the report but also added four footnotes showing where they thought the committee might reasonably have gone further than it did. These footnotes proved to be valuable in the negotiations which followed the Armitage Report. The effect of the recommendations was to reduce substantially the number of the civil servants in the 'politically restricted' category from 196,000 (26 per cent) to 23,000 (3·1 per cent) and correspondingly to enlarge the 'intermediate' category, in which permission to participate in political activities had to be given, from 333,000 (45 per cent) to 506,000 (67·9 per cent). The category of those 'free' from political restrictions remained unchanged. The report laid down criteria by which decisions concerning the 'intermediate' category should be made. It also suggested that certain groups of staff in the 'intermediate' category could be granted permission *en bloc*. The committee also took up the National Staff Side suggestion of an appeals procedure to be devised by the two sides of the National Whitley Council. At the end of 1978 discussions on the Armitage Report were still proceeding.

27 Science and Technology

Despite the changes of government in Britain in the 1960s and the early 1970s the relative decline in Britain's industrial strength continued. Neither Labour nor Conservative governments had found a solution to the related problems of a low rate of economic growth, continuing inflation, periodic deficits in the balance of payments, a rising trend of unemployment and increased import penetration. A falling proportion of the working population was engaged in manufacturing industry. These problems confronted the newly elected Labour government in 1974.

In accordance with its traditional policy of neutrality between political parties the Institution did not make any pronouncement·on the wider economic and political tasks facing the new government. It recognised, nevertheless, that its own concern about the role of science and technology in society and the status of scientists and technologists, whether in the private or public sector, could not be isolated from Britain's relatively poor industrial performance. Hence the Institution felt strongly that in calling consistently for the development of science and technology in areas of government responsibility it was not only protecting the interest of its own members but was also serving the national interest.

SCIENCE AND TECHNOLOGY ISSUES

The period from 1974 to 1978 provided a welcome respite from the decade of reorganisation of the government research and development effort. The reorganisation following the Rothschild Report was still causing repercussions but by August 1975, when the Institution submitted a memorandum to the Official Side on the experience so far, the situation was beginning to stabilise. Although there were still some problems, the Institution accepted that the customer/contractor relationship was 'here to stay', and that the approach should be to try and smooth the rough edges rather than demolish and rebuild.

The Institution, however, made it clear in talks with the Lord Privy Seal that it was fundamentally opposed to the new arrangements introduced by the government for the co-ordination of research and development policy. In particular, it strongly criticised the decision not to appoint a chief scientific adviser to the government who could provide an independent scientific voice in the formulation of policies at the highest level.

Rothschild apart, however, the Institution was able to focus its attention on certain important and in some cases highly controversial science and technology issues such as the role of nuclear power and the growing science of genetic manipulation. In both these areas the Institution was in a unique position to contribute to the debate within the Institution, in the TUC and within the community at large.

On the issue of genetic manipulation the Institution was asked in February 1976 to submit comments on an interim report of the Williams Working Party on the experimental manipulation of the genetic composition of micro-organisms. Written evidence was submitted and supplemented by oral evidence. By the time the final report of the working party was published, however, the Institution had affiliated to the TUC, and further comments on the report were forwarded through that channel. One of the recommendations of the working party was that a central advisory body – the Genetic Manipulation Advisory Group – should be established. The TUC pressed for trade union representation and received three seats on the group of which, as mentioned earlier, one went to Dr Ellwood, an Institution member.

The Institution also submitted evidence to the Select Committee on Science and Technology in 1976 in connection with its review of scientific research in British universities. The evidence referred to the Institution's fears that the impact of public expenditure cuts would be allowed to fall disproportionately and indiscriminately on the government's science and R&D budgets and asked the select committee to impress on the government the special needs of the research base, not just in the universities but in the public sector as a whole.

The Institution found the report of the Select Committee, *University–Industry Relations*, disappointing in that it did not get to the heart of the role of R&D in the regeneration of British industry, and alarming in its references to the salaries and conditions of scientists and technologists in the public service. The committee received evidence from the CBI with the now-familiar complaint that 'the civil service offers higher salaries and more attractive conditions and that makes it very difficult for industry to recruit in competition with the civil service'. Without receiving evidence from any public sector organisation the select committee proposed an examination of changes in incomes over recent years between scientists and technologists in industry and similarly qualified employees in the civil and other public services.

The Institution quickly made it clear that it would oppose any such limited inquiry and in its comments on the report, submitted to the government, made it clear that the real question was why scientists and technologists in industry tended to get paid so much less than other employees with similar levels of qualification. In the government's White Paper replying to the select committee the Institution's views were endorsed. It declared that the more industry could do to establish good career prospects for scientists and technologists, the more it would make industry attractive to able and ambitious men and women. Similarly, on pay the remedy lay with private industry itself.

THE NUCLEAR DEBATE

The Institution entered fully into the debate on energy policy and the choice of nuclear reactors. Early in 1974 the NEC submitted a paper to the government on energy resources and their use. The paper dealt with the whole range of energy problems and material resources including conservation, additional sources of supply and the recovery of waste materials. Central to the Institution's proposals was the need for a programme of action, phased and co-ordinated within central government with overall responsibility vested in Energy. The Secretary of State for Energy welcomed the paper and announced the appointment of Dr Walter Marshall as his chief scientific adviser on a part-time basis. The Institution also prepared comments on the government's Green Paper *War on Waste*.

At the same time the Institution pressed the government to continue to support the advanced gas cooled reactor (AGR) programme and to include at least one steam-generating heavy water reactor (SGHWR) in its programme. It opposed the adoption of the American pressurised water reactors (PWR) because, in the view of the Institution, it did not meet the requirements of being a safe and proven system capable of construction within a known time-scale. With the change of government the Institution continued to press these points to the new Secretary of State for Energy. Additionally it made its views known to the Energy Resources Sub-Committee of the Select Committee on Science and Technology and to the public at large. The select committee supported the Institution's view on the PWRs and in July the Institution had the satisfaction of welcoming a government decision to base its modest nuclear power programme on the SGHWR.

In 1976 the UKAEA advised the government not to proceed with an SGHWR programme on the grounds of escalating costs. Instead, it advised the adoption of either the AGR or the PWR, commenting at the same time that in its view the safety doubts surrounding the American PWRs could now be disposed of. Thus the issue of reactor choice was thrown back into the melting pot, while the need to choose a reactor system and to decide whether to build fast breeder reactors became increasingly urgent if energy requirements at the turn of the century were to be fulfilled.

In July 1976 the new Secretary of State for Energy, Tony Benn, with his declared preference for open government, held his much-heralded national energy conference to cover the whole range of energy issues. The one-day conference of 470 representatives, including some from the Institution, faced an agenda and thirty written papers covering every conceivable aspect of energy policy. Nevertheless, according to the Institution representatives, it was a useful conference. The unions present mounted a strong case for continuing and expanding the SGHWR programme, and were disappointed that the secretary of state made no response in his summing-up to their challenge that he should say where the government stood on the issue.

In late 1976 the Royal Commission on Environmental Pollution issued its sixth report, *Nuclear Power and the Environment*. The Royal Commission, which had been chaired by Sir Brian Flowers, FRS, since 1973, had been established as a standing commission in 1970 with the following terms of reference: 'To advise on matters, both national and international, concerning the pollution of the environment; on the adequacy of research in this field, and the future possibilities of dangers to the environment.'

The report raised major questions on the environmental impact of various levels of nuclear power capability and the Institution, aware that the issues were already being hotly debated in the community at large and in the scientific community, took steps to sound out the views of a whole spectrum of Institution expertise in preparing its response. A committee was established to advise the Public Research and Development Committee and hence the NEC. The committee consisted of representatives from Institution branches in the UKAEA, BNFL, the Nuclear Power Company, the National Radiological Protection Board, the Natural Environment Research Council, the Freshwater Biological Association, the MAFF and the DoE. As a result in April 1977 the NEC issued an internal discussion document 'Nuclear power and the environment' which set out the NEC's preliminary comments on the Royal Commission's report. The replies from branches were considered, together with the government's own response. A further discussion document on the wider issues of energy policy was then prepared and circulated to the membership in December.

There was a full-scale debate on the issue at the 1977 conference. The general secretary in his presentation of the annual report, which took place before the debate, said that the Royal Commission's report *Nuclear Power and the Environment* had provided a thorough and comprehensive basis for the debate which was now taking place in the community

and to which the Institution is uniquely well equipped to make an informed contribution with a membership which contains so many leading nuclear scientists and engineers and so many distinguished environmental scientists.

We therefore have a special responsibility. Our decisions must not be taken by emotional spasms on one side or the other, but by thorough debate and discussion and by the process of exhaustive consultation which the National Executive Committee is following.

The conference debate on nuclear policy lived up to these expectations. Assistant general secretary Margaret Platt prefaced the discussion of the motions by making a statement on behalf of the NEC. She pointed out that the NEC was only part of the way through its detailed consultation with the membership but that decisions would need to be taken soon to safeguard the energy position in the 1990s. The NEC believed that there should be a balanced programme of research keeping all the options open – including a nuclear option. There were grave concerns about the safety of nuclear power which it would be wrong to underestimate. The community needed to be sure that if nuclear power were needed to supplement other sources it could be produced economically and safely. The NEC was recommending cautious development on a step-by-step basis for both fuel re-processing and the development of reactors.

Following the NEC statement the delegates proceeded to debate a motion, moved by a representative from the ARC, that the conference should reconsider its attitude to the construction of nuclear power stations in the light of the uncertainties regarding long-term safety expressed in the Flowers Report. The motions called for the establishment of a multi-discipline working party to review the evidence, in terms of both energy and ecology, and to report in April 1978. The Institution was not to support an expanding role for nuclear energy before that date. A full and lengthy debate followed, ending with a spokesman for the NEC who said that consultation on a multi-disciplinary basis was already taking place. It would take into account the evidence from the public inquiry into the re-processing of residual waste at Windscale which was shortly to begin under Lord Justice Parker. Nevertheless, decisions to order the next generation of reactors could not be deferred indefinitely and it would therefore be wrong to pass the motion. The motion was remitted. Two motions supporting the need for further research into the environmental consequences of nuclear power, as indicated by the Flowers Report, were then carried by the conference.

In the light of the decisions of the conference the Institution submitted a motion on energy policy to the TUC. It said:

This congress, noting the expanding world demand for energy and the limited supply of fossil fuels, instructs the General Council to press the government to formulate a plan for energy with the following objectives:

(1) To promote an effective energy conservation programme.
(2) To expand research and development on renewable energy sources.
(3) To secure the prudent use of this country's vitally important and substantial stocks of coal.
(4) To maximise the contribution of nuclear power consistent with the maintenance of a safe environment.
(5) To provide full opportunities for British industry in both the domestic and overseas markets.
(6) To ensure that decisions are taken in good time to avoid any threat to our economic expansion and standards of living.

The motion became part of a composite motion which was moved at the TUC by the chairman of the Institution, Don Downton, and carried by the congress.

A final version of the paper on 'Nuclear power and the environment' was prepared after extensive consultation with branches. This was presented to the 1978 conference together with an NEC motion welcoming the conclusions on conservation and the development of energy resources. The motion instructed the NEC to pursue the policies set out in the paper. After debate the motion was carried.

THE FINNISTON INQUIRY

Another important issue raised at the 1977 Institution's conference was the call by the general secretary for a full inquiry into all aspects of the recruitment, education, training, standards and qualifications of engineers, including the question of registration. He asked the government to appoint a Royal Commission without further delay. Following conference, approaches were made to the Secretary of State for Industry, to other ministers and to the TUC. In July 1977 the government appointed a committee of inquiry, to be chaired by Sir Montague Finniston, FRS, previously chairman of the British Steel Corporation and at the time of his appointment chairman of Sears Engineering. Bill McCall, general secretary of the Institution, was also invited to serve on the committee, together with sixteen others.

The terms of reference of the inquiry were:

To review for manufacturing industry, and in the light of national economic needs:

(i) the requirements of British industry for professional and technical engineers, the extent to which these needs are being met and the use made of engineers by industry;
(ii) the role of the engineering institutions in relation to the education and qualification of engineers at professional and technician level;
(iii) the advantages and disadvantages of statutory registration and training of engineers in the United Kingdom;
(iv) the arrangements in other major industrial countries, particularly in the

EEC, for handling these problems, having regard to relevant comparative studies;
and to make recommendations.

Institution branches were invited to submit nominations to a working party set up to produce the Institution's evidence for submission to the committee. The working party got under way at the end of the year. By the end of 1978 the evidence was receiving consideration by the NEC ready for submission in early 1979.

FULTON REVISITED

Two opportunities for surveying progress since Fulton were offered during the second half of the 1970s. The training effort of the civil service and in particular the effectiveness of the Civil Service College, established on the recommendation of the Fulton Committee, were put under the microscope in a review conducted by Sir Leslie Williams and Mr R. N. Heaton. Their *Review of Civil Service Training* was published in September 1974 and its major themes were the need for greater involvement of line management in the training process, the raising of the status of training and training personnel within the civil service, the need for a training strategy for the service as a whole and the need for a more professional approach to training. The report was also critical of the performance of the Civil Service College, a view which was shared by the Institution. Following the Heaton–Williams Report a joint review committee under the National Whitley Council Joint Committee on Training was established to discuss the issues arising from the report.

More far-reaching, however, was the decision by the General Sub-Committee of the Parliamentary Expenditure Committee in late 1975 to carry out an investigation into the implementation of the Fulton Report. This gave the Institution an opportunity to air the dissatisfaction and disappointment expressed at successive Institution conferences over the lack of progress on Fulton recommendations and opened up the possibility of a new impetus being given to a whole range of issues.

The Institution's evidence to the Sub-Committee was presented in two parts and identified four major areas of concern. These were the application of the principles of accountable management; structure and grading; career management and development; and the relationship of the civil service to the community. The Institution pointed out that the Fulton Committee had regarded these issues as crucial to the reform of the civil service. In the Institution's view the Fulton recommendations had either not been implemented or had been only partially implemented.

The Fulton Committee had identified two major obstacles to accountable management; the civil service's traditional accounting methods, and the form of organisation in departments. Some progress had been made in the former but the Institution expressed the view that the time was overdue for a complete re-appraisal of the questions of financial accountability and a much greater role for professional accountants within the civil service. On the latter, little progress had been made on the substitution of integrated administrative and specialist hierarchies which the Fulton Committee had recommended should replace the existing structure of parallel hierarchies.

On grading and structure, the Fulton recommendation for unified grading throughout the civil service had only been implemented down to under-secretary level, despite investigations which had shown that it could be extended at least down to principal level. The Institution urged the rapid extension of unified grading to principal level and the much more rapid absorption of the remaining classes into the major categories at principal level and below.

The Institution also argued that although much had been done in the field of career management and development the specialist classes still found themselves at a disadvantage in competing for posts in the open structure. The dominance of staff with administrative backgrounds at under-secretary and above had scarcely changed since Fulton reported.

Finally, the Institution's evidence made a plea for much more 'open' government. There was no dramatic innovation which could transform the position, the Institution said, but it believed that there should be a cautious and deliberate policy supported at all levels, and particularly by the Cabinet, to make a greater reality of the democratic process.

The Institution appeared twice before the committee to give oral evidence. Other civil service unions submitted written evidence and the SCPS and CPSA appeared once before the committee.

The Eleventh Report of the Select Committee on Expenditure, *Reforming the Civil Service*, was published in September 1977. Despite the prolonged campaign against the civil service conducted by the press, which formed a backcloth to the committee's deliberations, the report was one to which in part the Institution could offer a warm welcome.

In its report the committee endorsed much of the evidence given by the Institution and reaffirmed many of the objectives laid down by Fulton. It made several additional proposals designed to increase the efficiency and effectiveness of the civil service, some of which were opposed by the Institution and other members of the Staff Side. In particular the Staff Side objected to the suggestion that cash limits should be fixed before pay negotiations took place. Such a procedure, the Institution argued, could impose highly discriminatory treatment on civil servants and was totally at odds with the committee's endorsement of the principle of fair comparisons. The committee suggested that the Pay Research Unit should be made responsible to a board which should include outside appointees. It made other suggestions for making the pay research procedures more open to public scrutiny. The Institution did not object to these proposals in principal but felt that care would need to be exercised in their implementation.

A recommendation of the Committee which caused consternation on the Staff Side was the suggestion that the functions of the CSD should be split and that those parts of the CSD concerned with control of manpower and efficiency should go to the Treasury, leaving the CSD with responsibility for personnel, appointments, recruitment, training, pay and pensions. Although it regarded the existing CSD arrangements as unsatisfactory, the Institution felt that the committee's proposal would make the CSD even weaker in its relations with the other departments and with the Treasury. The need was to build up the authority of the CSD, not to reduce it still further.

The NEC and the National Staff Side gave detailed consideration to the committee's report. Substantial agreement was achieved between the Institution and other unions on the Staff Side in formulating their response to the report. This was particularly the case with the FDA, whose support for Institution objectives was vital and with whom the Institution conducted close and detailed consultations on the response. By this means, the Institution hoped to remove the danger of disunity in the Staff Side which in 1968 effectively prevented the implementation of many of the Fulton recommendations. Particularly significant was the joint IPCS/FDA support for a common pay and grading structure down to principal level, with career development based on existing occupational groups and with the opportunity of movement between them.

In March 1978 the government produced its White Paper *The Civil Service: Government Observations on the Eleventh Report from the Expenditure Committee,* giving its considered response to the report. Its general attitude was a cautious one but, to the Staff Side's relief, the government rejected the committee's suggestion that cash limits should be fixed before pay negotiations took place. On the suggested split in the CSD's functions the government adopted a cautious 'continuing to study the issues' approach. In many areas of particular concern to the Institution the reaction of the government to the committee's proposals, while not enthusiastic, was broadly sympathetic.

In his address to the 1978 Institution conference the general secretary pointed out that there were already attempts within the civil service to play down the significance of the Select Committee's report, just as had happened with the Fulton Report a decade earlier. He added, however, that this time it would be more difficult for those opposed to change to bury the issue. The Select Committee had said in its report that it would continue to keep a watchful eye on the implementation of the recommendations and would call the government to account for the organisation and efficiency of the civil service.

TRADE UNION STRUCTURE

The close co-operation between the Institution and the FDA on the response to the Select Committee's report was indicative of the closer working relationships developing between the two organisations. At the end of 1973 the FDA and the SCS broke off the agreement of the previous two years whereby the two organisations had close working relationships. Indeed, for a time, the secretary of the FDA was a seconded full-time official of the Society. The Joint National Committee comprising the Society, the FDA and the Institution, however, continued as a useful forum for co-ordinating views among the three organisations representing most of the higher grades in the civil service. In 1976 the JNC ceased to exist because of continued disagreements between the Society and the FDA on a variety of issues.

Close contact was maintained between the Institution and the FDA which had by now clearly re-established its independence with the appointment of a new general secretary. In early 1977 on the initiative of the Institution the two organisations agreed to establish a joint committee of senior officers from both unions to consider the possibility of bringing the Institution and the FDA more closely together, ideally by amalgamation. By this time the FDA had expanded in size to about 10,000 members, and by amalgamation had embraced a large number of specialist grades, including tax inspectors, education inspectors and civil service lawyers. In addition its membership included the specialist grades of economists and statisticians which it had embraced since their inception in the civil service. The first objective which the joint committee set itself was to sort out any major policy differences and then to move on to organisational matters. Observers from each union attended the other's executive committee meetings.

The joint discussions established that there were no major issues on which there was a material difference of policy. They then turned to organisational matters. In 1978 the Institution's NEC invited conference to recognise the desirability of a more rational trade union structure, to welcome discussions with the FDA and to call for a report on a possible merger which would be considered at the 1979 conference. Although there was some opposition to the proposed merger talks in the debate, the NEC motion was overwhelmingly carried. A similar motion was carried at the FDA conference.

A draft memorandum of understanding was drawn up and approved by the executive committees of the two unions and circulated to the membership. The intention was that the memorandum should be considered at the 1979 conferences. In the spring of 1979, however, the FDA executive felt it could not be sure of carrying support for the memorandum at the annual conference and therefore suggested that the issue should be postponed.

The developments between the FDA and the Institution took place against a background of discussions and developments within the rest of the National Staff Side on the rationalisation of union representation and on the democratisation of the National Staff Side structure. The impending departure of Leslie Williams as secretary general of the National Staff Side in the summer of 1973 and the appointment of John Dryden, general secretary of the SCPS, with only four years to go to retirement (he was succeeded by Bill Kendall, general secretary of the CPSA, in 1976), provided an opportunity for a further examination of the future organisation of the Staff Side and the civil service trade union movement as a whole.

In April 1974, Committee A of the National Staff Side produced a report, *The Future Organisation of the Civil Service Trade Union Movement*. It summarised the objectives to be pursued in any reorganisation. These were the achievement of closer co-ordination in dealing with all aspects of pay policy, the development of democracy and accountability, the creation of machinery which would avoid overlapping representation, the establishment of a powerful, united pressure group which could more effectively influence Official Side thinking, the encouragement of greater efficiency in union representation through the avoidance of unnecessary duplication, the possible development of regional organisation and the necessity of ensuring that the rights of minorities were safeguarded. As to how these objectives might be achieved, the report suggested two alternatives, a single civil service union or a more closely knit federation.

The report was discussed at the 1974 conference under a motion from the NEC asking conference to note the report. After a brief debate the motion was carried. The report was sent out to branches in the autumn for consultation and a similar exercise took place in other unions in the Staff Side. The Staff Side then produced a new paper reflecting the consensus of opinion. The paper recognised that neither a single union nor a federation was a realistic possibility for the immediate future but there was a general wish expressed for all constituents to move towards a closer working relationship. Attention, it said, should therefore be concentrated on reaching that more limited objective and it made proposals by which that could be achieved.

The debate on the revised National Staff Side document at the 1975 conference indicated little enthusiasm for major reforms or for amalgamation with other unions. In particular delegates expressed concern that the Institution should remain as autonomous as possible on the grounds that the interests of the specialist grades were not always the same as those of the 'generalists'. Moreover, the Institution was still seeking to achieve the full implementation of Fulton against the wishes of some organisations on the Staff Side. The general secretary, in a reply successfully defending the NEC's motion in support of the National Staff Side document, pointed out that most of the fears expressed referred to possible amalgamation or federation which had already been ruled out by the document. Other unions, he added, were just as suspicious of the Institution as delegates were of them. There was no threat to the sovereignty of any union in the report. The real issue before the unions was the need to develop confidence and trust between themselves, and this was what the National Staff Side were suggesting by proposing a series of very modest changes designed to improve organisational co-operation.

After 1975, which marked the highwater mark of co-operation and co-ordination in pay policy (see Chapter 25), the possibility of achieving overall unification within the civil service trade union movement receded. Differences over policy and tactics on a variety of issues developed between the SCPS and CPSA on the one hand and the rest of the Staff Side on the other. Nevertheless there were further developments on a bilateral basis, of which the IPCS/FDA initiative was one. By the end of 1974 the Customs and Excise Group and the Association of Officers of the Ministry of Labour had decided to amalgamate with the SCPS, and the Civil Service Legal Society with the FDA. The number of civil service unions was thereby reduced to nine, later to be reduced to eight by the merger between the FDA and the Association of HM Inspectors of Taxes.

The Institution's relations with the AGSRO continued to fluctuate. Having gradually improved during the 1970s there was a setback in 1977 when the IPCS–AGSRO consortium was wound up following a decision to that effect by the AGSRO conference. It was, however, immediately replaced by an AGSRO–IPCS joint committee which met to consider matters of common interest. Thus at national level and in some departments good relationships between the two organisations continued, and the two organisations found it possible to put forward a common view on almost all the issues dealt with by the National Staff Side.

INTERNAL CHANGES

In 1974 the Institution achieved, for the first time, a total membership of 100,000. The membership was to fluctuate during the next four years, partly reflecting manpower cuts, but by the end of 1978 it was back around the 100,000 mark. The large size of the organisation and the growing complexity of the issues with which it had to deal entailed other internal organisational developments.

First, the Institution headquarters building occupied since 1961 when the membership stood at 56,297 was no longer sufficiently large to accommodate the staff and other facilities required. Already groups of staff were in rented office space outside the headquarters building. By 1977 the staff were in two separate sets of offices in addition to the main headquarters building. Finding a new building was therefore becoming urgent. Consideration of the possibility of a new building had begun in 1973. Plans were drawn up by the Institution's architect and an application was submitted for an office development permit for the whole Strand Corner House and Institution headquarters site. The application was submitted jointly by the Institution and J. Lyons & Co. Ltd, the owner of the adjacent Corner House site. It was granted on appeal. Discussions on the details of the financing of the development were then started but in 1977 they were abruptly broken off by the decision of J. Lyons & Co. Ltd to sell their building at a price well beyond that which the Institution could afford. The new selling price was higher than the amount which professional advisers thought the building was worth. The Institution had to begin the search for another suitable building or site.

The Institution continued to review its internal procedures for communications, consultation and training. Great strides were made in the 1970s in extending democracy within the Institution, and the chairman of the Institution, Nick Vint, made greater democracy within the Institution his theme for the chairman's address at the 1975 conference. He said that not so long ago general secretaries of the civil service unions, acting upon the instructions of their executive committees, would take action on subjects which the membership at large would accept without serious question and only a modicum of participation was entered into. Just as society at large was demanding more consultation before decisions were taken, hence the demand for 'open' government, and trade unions were demanding more participation in decision-making with the employer, so the membership of the Institution wanted to be similarly consulted. The NEC had recently begun, and would continue, to seek deliberately to involve members more directly in the formulation and development of all policies on important issues. The chairman returned to the theme at the 1976 conference, recalling the major exercise in consultation on incomes policy and affiliation to the TUC which had just been concluded. He said: 'The NEC is conscious of the new spirit in branches and the desire of members to be consulted and involved before final policies are decided. This is most welcome to the NEC . . .'

Several other aspects of internal organisation were under review. The education programme continued to expand. Superannuation weekend schools had been introduced in 1977 and further ideas for specialist schools were being considered. Following affiliation to the TUC in 1976 Institution members could also take advantage of the wide range of TUC education facilities. Courses for safety representatives were developed in 1977, helped by the TUC teaching aids. A new edition of the Institution handbook was produced in 1977.

The 1977 conference was presented with two reviews on which decisions had to be taken. One concerned the status and structure of the professional groups. A consultation paper suggested various reforms to professional group constitutions, to enable groups to assume executive powers on matters affecting the group alone. This was circulated to branches and subsequently approved by the conference. As a consequence the professional and technology group was launched at an inaugural conference at the end of 1978 as a fully fledged group with executive power and its own annual delegate conference.

The other major internal review debated at conference was on communications. A consultative document presented to conference by the NEC was approved and as a consequence in 1978 the *IPCS Bulletin* became a twice-monthly instead of monthly publication. A new design for heading circulars was also approved.

At the 1978 conference a topic which attracted nine motions and generated some heat was the question of how members could obtain more information about candidates for the NEC and for the TUC delegation. A motion moved by a delegate from the Trustee Museums and Galleries branch was taken as a composite for the others. It sought to instruct the NEC to provide more facilities for information on the candidates so that branches could make an informed choice. A light-hearted note was added to the proceedings by a female delegate from the DES Museums branch who said that it was nice to be able to put a name to a face but the only way to do that at present was to look at lapel badges. It was a debilitating, not to say disturbing experience, spending four days looking 400 delegates in the chest. Delegates were clear, despite the fears of the NEC that the motion might lead to political manifestos and possibly the beginnings of factionalism in the Institution, that they wanted more information. The motion was carried. The NEC promised to produce a consultative paper on the issue before the next conference.

OLD AND NEW FACES

In the early part of 1974 the Institution appointed three women to fill vacancies for negotiations officers. Two of them, Cecile Damon and Margaret Taylor, were promoted from posts as assistant negotiations officers. The third appointment went to Linda Cohen, who joined the Institution from the British Medical Association. She was employed as research officer at the BMA and had previously obtained a degree at Leeds University and a postgraduate qualification in industrial relations at Warwick University. She had also worked for a period for the National Union of Bank Employees. Cecile Damon first joined the Institution in 1952 and worked for John Lyons when he was an assistant secretary and later when he was deputy general secretary. Margaret Taylor joined the Institution as a secretary and was then promoted in 1972 to assistant negotiations officer.

On 31 May 1974 Kay Taylor, who had served the Institution for forty-five years, retired from the headquarters' staff. She joined the staff in May 1929 as an office junior and at the time of her retirement was administration officer. It was said of her at her retirement that she was the most knowledgeable person about the organisation of the Institution. She retained her vitality and good humour throughout her very long service. Upon the retirement of Kay Taylor the post of administrative officer went to Mavis Darley who had joined the Institution during the Second World War when she was employed in the Aeronautical Inspection Department of the Ministry of Aircraft Production.

In 1975 the Institution appointed a part-time public relations officer. He was Mr Jimmy O'Dea, who a short time earlier had retired as editor and public relations officer of the CPSA. Mr O'Dea served for twenty years as editor of *Red*

Tape, the journal of the CPSA. In the same year the Institution promoted two of its negotiations officers, Elizabeth Jenkins and Ron McDowell, to assistant secretary level.

Following a review of the headquarters complement it was decided to fill the two negotiations officer posts, and John Findlay, an executive officer in HM Treasury and an active member of the SCPS, and Wendi Harrison, a graduate of Leeds University who subsequently worked in administration with the Electricity Council and at Lanchester Polytechnic, were appointed. Later in the year George Giles, a negotiations officer, left the Institution to take up a personnel position with the BAA. He was replaced by Tony Cooper, an active Institution member from the Forestry Commission and a graduate of Edinburgh University. A further negotiations officer, John Allison, was appointed early in 1978. He was a PTO III serving in Portsmouth Dockyard and had been an active Institution member for many years.

Bill Palmer, having served the Institution well as an assistant secretary since 1946, formally retired at the end of 1977, but stayed on for a further twelve months as a negotiations officer. Elizabeth Stallibrass was promoted from negotiations officer to assistant secretary in his place. In September 1978 three negotiations officers, Jenny Thurston, Linda Cohen and Wendi Harrison, were promoted to assistant secretary.

Several new honorary members were elected during the second half of the 1970s. At the 1974 conference Phillip Middleton and Jimmy Fry, both past chairmen of the Institution, were elected honorary members. Unfortunately Jimmy Fry died suddenly the following year. He had joined the Institution in 1931 soon after he started work for the DSIR and held many posts. He was a member of the NEC from 1947 to 1959, serving as its chairman from 1953 to 1956, a most important and demanding period. After retiring from the NEC he continued to serve on his branch as an executive committee member where he made an important contribution in his main field of interest, the development of government policy on science. He retired from the branch executive in 1971.

The Institution suffered another loss of one of its outstanding members in 1975 with the sudden death of Dan Dorey. He had been a member of the NEC for fifteen years and its chairman from 1966 to 1968. He had also served as chairman of the staff side of the UKAEA Whitley Council. His death was followed soon after in 1976 by that of his close colleague Bill Bowles, who had combined a highly successful official career with a lifetime's service to the trade union movement. After completing his apprenticeship in 1933 he joined the drawing office and continued a steady climb until he reached the position of director of the Inspectorate of Fighting Vehicles. He was a member of the Institution for forty years and a member of the NEC for twenty-two. He was chairman of the Institution between 1962 and 1964 during the difficult period when the Institution could have been torn apart by the issues posed by the Radcliffe Report. That the Institution emerged united and stronger was a fitting tribute to Bill Bowles' leadership and judgement.

At the 1976 conference Helen Lindley was elected an honorary member. She had been an active member of the Institution since 1942, was elected to the NEC in 1962 and shortly afterwards became assistant editor and later editor of *State Service*, both honorary positions. She was followed in 1977 by J. C. McLauchlan. He had been an outspoken member of the NEC for years and was chairman of the

Institution from 1970 to 1972. In addition he was an enthusiastic contributor to the Institution's education programme, having been heavily involved in the writing of tutor's papers, a short pamphlet on the history of the Institution and the production of case studies.

In 1977 another stalwart of the Institution, Verney Stott, died. He was one of the small band of far-sighted members who, by their efforts during and immediately after the Second World War, laid the foundations on which the modern Institution and its policies were built. He was a physicist at the National Physical Laboratory and towards the end of his career became the training officer for the DSIR. In his youth he was a member of the AScW. He later joined the Institution when it became the appropriate body for government scientists. Verney Stott was elected to the new Emergency Executive Committee in 1942 and became chairman of the Institution. It was his idea to set up the Scientific Staffs Committee (later the Scientific Staffs Group) and he was its chairman, closely associated with Leslie Herbert, throughout the important period of postwar reconstruction for scientists. In 1948 he was elected vice-president and was president from 1961 to 1963.

Another scientist from the DSIR stable was Dr Harold Turner who was elected an honorary member in 1978. He had taken voluntary premature retirement at the end of 1977 and therefore resigned as chairman of the SSG, an office to which he had made a distinguished contribution for two periods, from 1960 to 1962 and from 1969 to 1977. In paying tribute to him on his retirement from the Group, Don Downton said that few members could claim to have put more effort to more effect into Institution activity. Better than anyone else could have done, he had represented the interests of scientists at all levels within the Institution. Over the years his name had become synonymous with that of the Group. Harold Turner was also a member of the NEC from 1957 to 1963 and deputy vice-chairman of the Institution from 1959 to 1962.

28 Some Concluding Observations

The history of the Institution is not just a narrative of the development of a representative professional association. It is the story of the evolution of a trade union. It would be wrong, however, to think that the Institution transformed itself from some kind of professional body into a trade union. It had a trade union role from the very first day of its existence. What was at issue was not what it was but what it perceived itself to be. Only with the passage of time and with experience did many thousands of its members become conscious that it was a trade union.

A TRADE UNION

At the outset the majority of those who came together to form the Institution emphatically denied that it was a trade union. Even then, there was a significant minority, particularly among those who had taken the initiative for the formation of the organisation, who wanted the Institution to acknowledge itself as a trade union and to change its title accordingly. At the time they were outvoted, but they had the good sense to understand that it was not so much the title of the organisation that mattered as the nature of its activity. They accepted the wishes of the majority, confident in the anticipation that experience would show that the Institution had to act as a trade union and would in fact become a trade union.

It is of interest to note that prominent among the founders of the Institution were men who came from the Admiralty. Their views had no doubt been influenced by the industrial associations of the Admiralty, particularly in the shipbuilding and ship-repairing naval dockyards. The shipyard and engineering workers of the Clyde had played a leading role in the upsurge of militant trade unionism in the later part of the First World War and in the immediate postwar period. This influence was felt in the naval dockyards. This, incidentally, was not the last occasion on which events outside the civil service were to influence the mood of active members of the Institution.

Today in its range of functions the Institution acts not only as a trade union but as an effective trade union. The hallmark of trade unionism is participation in collective bargaining and in the joint regulation of employment conditions. The Institution engages in collective bargaining and in joint regulation over a wide range of issues and has done so for many years.

In common with other unions in the civil service the Institution has sought to widen the range of issues regulated by collective bargaining. It has dealt not only with salaries, hours of work and leave but also with the status of professional, scientific and technical staff in the civil service. It has made representations about and joined in the regulation of superannuation arrangements for civil servants. It has also participated in the determination of recruitment and retirement conditions for its members. In the range of its negotiations the Institution, together with the other civil service unions, can be counted as being in the foremost rank of trade unionism. There are many issues on which negotiations take place in the civil service which in some sections of private industry and commerce are still determined unilaterally by managerial prerogative.

It is a reasonable question to ask why the Institution continues to call itself by a name which is clearly misleading. It is not a professional institution in the sense in which that term is normally understood. A professional institution is concerned primarily with the maintenance of professional standards and with the preservation of professional titles by reason of qualification and experience. In more recent times one or two professional institutions have made excursions or attempted to make excursions into the area of collective bargaining, but for the main professional institutions negotiations with employers have always been – if they have existed at all – a very subsidiary activity. It is totally different with the Institution. Collective bargaining is its main activity and the principal reason for its existence.

Of course, the Institution is concerned to uphold the status of its members and to maintain professional standards. It has also played a significant part in the development of public policy on research and development and has always taken a close interest in the role of scientists and technologists in society at large. Nevertheless, the Institution maintains the professional standing of its members primarily through the mechanism of collective bargaining with the employer. The services it provides for its members are neither identical to nor in conflict with those provided by the professional institutions. They are complementary to them.

RECOGNITION

Unlike many other white-collar unions, particularly in the private sector, the Institution almost from birth has been recognised by the employer. To this extent it skipped what is often a vital experience in the development of a trade union. It secured recognition thanks largely to the establishment of the Whitley machinery in the period immediately following the First World War. Recognition provided the Institution with a powerful argument for recruitment among eligible staff and thus gave impetus to the new organisation.

Whitleyism was not applied to the civil service without a struggle. In the first instance the government had no intention of applying to the civil service the Whitley recommendations, which had been intended primarily as an answer to the industrial unrest immediately preceding and during the First World War. Moreover, before Whitleyism was established the early civil service unions, particularly in the Post Office, waged a long struggle for the basic rights of organisation and recognition.

If it was with relative ease that the Institution secured recognition through the Whitley machinery it has, nevertheless, always availed itself of the opportunities for bargaining rights which the civil service has provided. At one time in the 1920s, when little progress was being made through the Whitley machinery and when the pay of civil servants was being cut with the fall in cost of living, the question was asked in civil service trade union circles whether the Whitley system was worthwhile. Though doubts were expressed the civil service unions, including the Institution, continued to support the Whitley machinery. In doing this they were influenced not only by the futility of any alternative course of action but also by the argument, advanced particularly by W. J. Brown of the CSCA, that it was not so much the machinery which was to blame for lack of progress but the social circumstances of industrial depression and mass unemployment in which Whitley negotiations were being conducted.

REGISTRATION

The reluctance of the Institution to regard itself as a trade union during the early period of its existence was reflected in its refusal to register itself as a trade union under the 1871 Trade Union Act. Its existence as a non-registered body made little practical difference to its affairs, though it was symbolic of its 'ideological' stand. Ironically it was not until the controversy about the 1971 Industrial Relations Act that the Institution changed course on registration. When the majority of the trade union movement decided not to register under the 1971 Act because, as it saw it, registration carried with it certain requirements inimical to trade union independence, the Institution decided, in contrast, to register. The Institution expressed concern that if it were not registered under the 1971 Act it might be subject to 'raids' from other organisations.

The rule amendments required for full registration were many and, as the general secretary pointed out at the time, alien to the traditions of the Institution. The Institution, like other trade unions, sought the support of its lay representatives and lay membership by persuasion and voluntary discipline. The branch and departmental representatives of the Institution were not the legally responsible representatives of the Institution. They were people who were doing a job to the best of their ability, based upon their voluntary conviction and readiness to act on behalf of their fellow members. If they were to be held legally responsible then the structure of the Institution would need to be very different. In the light of this experience and the fact that the threat of 'poaching' by other registered bodies receded, the Institution de-registered and to this extent took its place side by side with the rest of the trade union movement.

With the repeal of the Industrial Relations Act, 1971, and its replacement by the Trade Union and Labour Relations Act, 1974, the Institution continued to act in much the same way as the rest of the trade union movement. It is now registered as a trade union.

AN EFFECTIVE UNION

The Institution is an effective union on behalf of its membership. From its earliest years its active membership understood that it would have to depend on skill in negotiations and the careful preparation and documentation of claims to supplement the strength and influence it could bring to bear as a well-organised representative body. Partly this was a reflection of the nature of the membership. Their occupational role, their social backgrounds and the security and superannuation rights which went with civil service employment meant that the majority of members did not turn easily towards militant action.

The style of negotiations, however, is also a reflection of the civil service industrial relations system, which in turn reflects the fact that the government is the employer. The system relies heavily on certain defined pay principles and the use of independent commissions and committees of inquiry. This severely circumscribes the freedom of civil service unions to choose the grounds on which they will negotiate and the weapons they will use. Special emphasis has to be placed therefore upon negotiating skill and the careful preparation of claims. The annual reports of the National Executive Committee provide a yearly testimony to the skill and effort that goes into defending and advancing members' interests in the most diverse occupations and professions.

A crucial facet of the civil service industrial relations system is the provision for arbitration in the event of disagreement. The Institution has on many occasions used arbitration to advantage. The Institution can probably claim to have taken more cases to the Civil Service Arbitration Tribunal than any other civil service union. Usually, because of the care with which cases have been presented to the Tribunal, the Institution has secured some improvement on the final offer of the employer.

This does not mean that the Institution has succumbed to the temptation to refer cases unnecessarily to arbitration as an alternative to negotiation. British trade unions have usually been reluctant to accept obligatory arbitration arrangements because of their feeling that arbitration when used too frequently can undermine the responsibility of negotiators on both sides to strive for and to reach a voluntary settlement. It is a healthy attitude. No one looking back on the history of the Institution could say that it has undermined negotiations by too frequent recourse to arbitration.

The Institution has on a number of occasions joined with other civil service unions through the National Staff Side to defend the right of civil service organisations to go to independent arbitration. For a period in the 1920s the arbitration arrangements were suspended by decision of the government. The civil service unions protested vigorously and eventually the arbitration arrangements were restored.

In periods of incomes policy in postwar years, governments have been inclined to tamper with the independence of arbitration. The methods have ranged from asking civil service arbitrators to confine their awards to issues which the government itself regards as arbitrable within the framework of the prevailing incomes policy to asking that awards should not contravene such policies. On occasions they have declined to reappoint arbitrators who are unlikely to pay heed to their view.

The dangers for civil servants arising from the fact that the government's role as employer can be used as a major weapon in its other role of managing the economy were recognised by the Priestley Commission in 1956. Its recommendation that fair comparisons should be used for determining civil service pay was intended to produce a formula which was fair to the taxpayer and fair to the civil servant. Taking a long view, the system of fair comparisons has probably protected civil servants and has helped to ensure that their pay and conditions have been determined on their merits and not as an instrument of other policies.

Nevertheless, there have been attempts to lean more heavily on public service employees during periods of incomes policy. Increases emerging from the fair comparisons exercise have been staged and phased and in the 1970s the civil service pay agreement was suspended for a period. The civil service unions have always argued that to tamper with independent arbitration and the fair comparisons principle is to impose a double dose of incomes policy on civil servants. For fair comparisons reflect what has been happening to earnings outside the civil service. If those outside are adhering to incomes policy then this will be reflected in the pay research evidence. If they are not, then it is unfair to civil servants to insist that they should strictly adhere to a policy which is being evaded elsewhere.

In recent years the Institution has on a number of occasions found it necessary to exert some kind of pressure in support of particular claims. The initiative has come from the members themselves. The National Executive Committee has not been found wanting in the support it has given to the membership when it has been satisfied that prolonged negotiations have not produced a satisfactory outcome. The dispute affecting the pay of scientists in the civil service in the early 1970s was an example of the use of sanctions to strengthen a claim of the Institution. Thousands of members took part in strike action and participated in meetings and demonstrations. The use of militant action and the membership's willingness to take it has grown steadily during the 1970s, a trend which has also been evident in several other civil service unions and among hitherto quiescent white-collar and public service unions outside.

ACHIEVEMENTS

The Institution began, and has remained, an organisation representing specialists. One of the major preoccupations of the Institution throughout its history has been to raise the pay and status of specialists both within and outside the civil service to a position commensurate with their vital role in a modern technologically based society. This has been its central aim in the mass of detailed negotiations, inquiries and Royal Commissions with which it has been involved. There have been many achievements and some setbacks.

As early as 1929 an article appeared in *State Service* which said: 'Who can expect the classical scholars who control the civil service to have a change of outlook and recognise the strengths of scientists and those with professional and technical training?' The Institution's evidence to the Tomlin Commission argued forcibly that those people whom the Institution represented should have an equal share of the top jobs and that they had an ability to manage and to administer. Disappointingly the Tomlin Report failed to address itself to the problem.

To the Priestley Commission the Institution put the point that the civil service should be able to give a lead on the pay of scientists and technologists and thus boost the contribution of, and the value attributed to, science and technology in Britain. This view was rejected in favour of the principle of fair comparisons.

The next opportunity to put the case for raising the status of scientists and technologists within the civil service came with the evidence to the Fulton Committee. On that occasion the committee endorsed in every important respect the Institution's case for equal status for specialists in the civil service. The euphoria among Institution members which greeted that report gradually evaporated with the realisation that a partially successful rearguard action was being conducted by others who took a less favourable view of the report. Some important gains were made, nevertheless, and a further opportunity to improve the situation came with the decision of the Select Committee on Expenditure to examine progress since Fulton. Once again the aim of providing equal status for specialists was endorsed and at the time of writing the full outcome of that report is still to be determined.

Despite the fact that the Institution's objective of raising the status of specialists has not yet been fully achieved there have been major advances since the Institution was formed. The multiplicity of individual disciplines and classes characteristic of the early years of the Institution have been gradually replaced by coherent professional groupings. For scientists the Carpenter reforms in the early 1930s were the first major step towards an integrated structure. These were followed in 1946 by the crucial Barlow recommendations which proposed that good-quality scientists in the civil service should have similar career expectations and career earnings to the administrative class. Barlow distilled the essence of the specialists' claim to equal treatment and provided the basis for an administration pay link for the scientists which remained, *de facto*, unbroken until 1970.

The intention was that the type of exercise which Barlow performed for scientists would be repeated for the other major specialist groupings in the Institution. The most important of these was the Gardiner Committee which laid the foundations for the works group, bringing together the engineering, building, architectural and other similar professions into a single structure. But although such reviews marked significant improvements in pay and status for most groups, they were not as satisfactory as the Barlow Report was for scientists.

The next major rationalisation of grading structures came with Fulton. As a result of Fulton the science category and the professional and technology category were established alongside the general category (comprising the old administrative, executive and clerical grades). Other occupational groups, for example, for librarians, psychologists and accountants, were formed and linked with one or other of the major categories for pay purposes. By the end of 1978, however, the process of restructuring arising out of Fulton was still not complete.

On pay the watershed for the civil service was the Priestley Commission, from which derived the principle of fair comparisons on which the pay of the civil service is still based. The Institution opposed the principle of fair comparisons at the time for reasons already outlined. Nevertheless, it was able to use the pay research system to advantage in the case of professional and technology grades, who since Priestley have steadily improved their position in relation to the 'generalists'.

This was not the case for scientists, for whom the Institution has never accepted that the fair comparisons method is appropriate. The first pay research exercise for scientists was as unsatisfactory as the Institution had predicted it would be. But the exercise took so long that interim increases had already been awarded and the results of the pay research report were never implemented. In 1970, however, the scientists were forced into pay research again with the result that the issue of the criteria by which scientists' pay should be determined was in dispute throughout the period from 1970.

Another area in which the Institution has made a significant contribution, although more difficult to measure, is on issues which impinge upon the professional interests of the membership, particularly in the field of public research and development. These contributions have ranged in their concern beyond the preservation and improvement of the professional and scientific public service. Thus in the 1930s many prominent Institution members were closely involved in the debate about the role of science in society. The Institution has co-operated with other bodies, particularly the AScW, and latterly, through the Parliamentary and Scientific Committee, has joined in exerting pressure to bring science and technology to the forefront of public debate. Such pressure resulted in the establishment of the Select Committee on Science and Technology to which the Institution has on many occasions given evidence.

There are two other special areas where the Institution can claim particular credit. The first is in relation to the political rights of civil servants and the second is in relation to women's rights. The Institution has sought to extend the right of civil servants to take their place in the democratic life of the community, subject, of course, to the exercise of discretion by staff on issues connected with their employment.

The Institution also has a consistent record of opposition to political discrimination. This was a special problem during the years of the 'cold war'. From the outset the Institution took the view that civil servants should not be penalised solely because of their membership or association with any legal political party. Though it would be absurd to argue that espionage does not take place in the modern world there is no evidence in postwar Britain that active trade unionists, including active trade unionists with pronounced left-wing opinions and affiliations, have been engaged in espionage. As Stanley Mayne so frequently pointed out, it is much more likely that a would-be agent of a foreign power would pose not as a left-wing active trade unionist but as a 'pillar of the establishment' in both his opinions and in his private activities.

Even though the Institution did not succeed in securing the implementation of all the proposals it put forward to safeguard its members against discrimination, there can be no doubt that the safeguards that were ultimately introduced and the eventual decline of the 'purge' was attributable in no small measure to the campaign conducted by the Institution and, in particular, by a number of its prominent members. Stanley Mayne played an outstanding part in this campaign.

The Institution also has one of the best records of all civil service unions on the issue of women's rights. Not only has it consistently supported the principle of equal pay for equal work but it also campaigned for equal opportunities for women. Unlike other civil service unions, it consistently opposed the marriage bar which for many years required a woman civil servant to retire from employment on her marriage.

Many women civil servants with professional experience and qualifications have made a significant contribution to the development of the Institution. Today the Institution is, perhaps, unique among trade unions in that women form as high, if not a higher, proportion of the National Executive Committee and of full-time officials than they do of the membership as a whole.

LOYAL MEMBER OF THE STAFF SIDE

Some of the achievements listed above have been secured primarily by the Institution's own efforts. All negotiations on conditions of service which apply to non-industrial civil servants as a whole are, however, conducted by the National Staff Side. Co-operation between unions within the Staff Side is therefore essential.

The Institution was one of the founding members of the National Staff Side when the Whitley machinery was established immediately following the First World War and it has remained an active and influential constituent ever since. Of the so-called higher-grade organisations the Institution has a record second to none in its loyalty to the wider staff side movement.

It has played a crucial role in holding together the National Staff Side at critical moments in its history. One such was the aftermath of the General Strike in 1926 when some of the associations representing the higher grades withdrew from the National Staff Side. Pressure was exerted on the Institution to follow them. If the dissident associations had been joined by the Institution their claim for separate recognition by the Official Side would have been extremely strong. Largely under the influence of Freddie Menzler the Institution remained inside the National Staff Side and the danger of permanent disruption was averted.

The National Staff Side has been in similar danger of breaking up in more recent times, again under the pressure of external events, such as incomes policy, discrimination against the public services and cuts in public expenditure. The Institution has been able to play the role of 'honest broker' partly because of the calibre of its leadership but also because of the nature of the Institution itself.

As an organisation representing a wide range of occupations and a spectrum of grades spanning the hierarchy from top to bottom, it has been accustomed to accommodating diverse interests both organisationally and in policy terms. It has, therefore, been well equipped to play the role of mediator and, indeed, because of its diverse membership and their associated pay links with other grades in other unions, has had a vested interest in preserving the unity of the Staff Side.

CHANGES IN STRUCTURE

The Institution has changed considerably since its inception in 1919. One of the most obvious changes is its size. In 1919 there were only 1,534 members, by the end of 1978 there were 100,000. Some of this growth has been due to the amalgamation of smaller groups of specialists within the Institution. Of all the amalgamations none was as important as that with the Society of Technical Civil Servants.

The long controversy surrounding the trade union organisation of draughtsmen within the civil service began with the secession of the ACSDD from the Institution in 1948 and ended with the amalgamation in 1969. It provides an interesting commentary not only on the attitude of scientists and professional staff towards their drawing office colleagues but also of the ability of both sides ultimately to recognise that the things which united them were more important than those which divided them. With the benefit of hindsight it is clear that the problem of the divided representation of drawing office staff in the civil service should never have taken the acute form that it did. After all, drawing office staff were among the most likely recruits to a trade union of professional, scientific and technical staff. Many of them served an apprenticeship in one of the manual crafts and had associations with the engineering and shipbuilding industries. Understandably, therefore, there was to be found among them a level of trade union consciousness rather higher than among other specialist staff in the civil service.

There were two basic reasons for the divided representation. The first was that in its early years the Institution tended to regard draughtsmen as a rather subordinate group of employees, not quite high enough in professional status to enjoy equality with other specialists. Secondly, the existence of a strong trade union for draughtsmen in private industry provided for many drawing office staff, particularly those with an engineering or shipbuilding background, an alternative trade union orientation. Many civil service drawing office recruits were already members of the draughtsmen's union in the private sector of industry from which they had come. Despite these difficulties the good personal relationship which existed between leading figures in the Institution and in the STCS was an important factor contributing to an eventual solution.

The process of amalgamation whereby the STCS was absorbed into the Institution proceeded smoothly and has been successful. Former members of the STCS have played a notable role in the Institution, not least the present deputy general secretary of the Institution, Mr Cyril Cooper.

A major change in the Institution has been its transformation from a federal organisation, embracing a large number of independent professions or departmental organisations, into a national trade union with an annual conference and a National Executive Committee, and with a much expanded role for the full-time officials.

The change from a federal to a unified structure did not take place smoothly. The pressure for it built up strongly during the early period of the Second World War. The moment of change was surrounded by intense controversy. Those who sought to change the Institution were clear as to their objective. They wanted the Institution to become an effective trade union. Many of those who played a leading part in bringing about this change were men of strong trade union and political convictions.

The creation of a unified structure was seen as necessary to strengthen the trade union effectiveness of the Institution. At the same time it was recognised that it would be essential to provide for the identifiable interests of different professional groups. Advisory committees were created for this purpose. This arrangement also made it possible to bring into activity a larger number of rank-and-file members. In this way the structure of the Institution provided both for the common interests and for the identifiably separate interests of particular professions and groups of members.

Throughout its history the Institution has maintained a democratic structure. Control has been in the hands of the lay membership. Indeed, for many years one of the main problems was not that there was bureaucratic control by full-time officials but that many of the lay members were reluctant to accept the need for professional, full-time leading officials. The controversy which led to the creation of a unified structure also led to the introduction of the post of general secretary with a degree of authority similar to that in other trade unions. Throughout the postwar period the Institution has operated with a highly competent full-time staff, but effective control has remained in the hands of the delegate conference and the National Executive Committee.

In its early days the Institution adhered to the view that every member should be entitled to attend the annual general meeting. Democracy was held to be direct and personal. In the founding years this arrangement had more to be said for it than in later years. By the late 1920s and throughout the 1930s it had become a facade, and other means had to be devised to ensure democratic control. Even if only a small proportion of the members had taken advantage of their right to attend the annual general meeting there would not have been a meeting hall suitable for the purpose in central London. In reality, of course, the right of every member to attend the annual general meeting did not provide for effective democratic control. Thousands of members worked and lived many miles from London where the annual meetings were held.

Inevitably, therefore, there were demands for change. Instead of an ineffective and unrealistic system of direct participation it was urged that there should be introduced a system of representative democracy. Those who took up this demand were the same active members who advocated a unified structure, the creation of a National Executive Committee and the appointment of more professional full-time staff including a general secretary. They succeeded in their campaign. A system of representative democracy was introduced.

In recent years the system of representative democracy has been further improved by the introduction of much greater consultation. This has been achieved by the distribution of consultative documents on major issues before decisions have been taken at the National Executive Committee or at the annual delegate conference.

TUC AFFILIATION

There was, however, until 1976 an important inconsistency in the operation of this system of representative democracy. It was regarded as a satisfactory system except for the one issue of TUC affiliation. On all other issues the annual conference was regarded as the supreme policy-making body. Delegates were guided by discussion in their respective branches. In this way decisions were reached not only by the counting of heads but, even more important, after full discussion and debate.

On the issue of TUC affiliation the Institution for a number of years before 1976 cast aside its system of representative democracy and opted instead for a ballot of the membership. Those who favoured this system argued that on such an important and potentially divisive issue as affiliation to the TUC every member should have the opportunity to express his view.

In 1976, however, the delegates to the annual conference of the Institution accepted the responsibility given to them by the system of representative democracy. They decided that the conference itself would determine the issue of TUC affiliation. This it did, deciding by a vote of 54,434 to 38,246 to instruct the National Executive Committee to seek immediate affiliation to the TUC. The debate was the culmination of the most extensive consultative exercise ever mounted in the Institution. Thus ended the Institution's self-imposed isolation from the mainstream of the British trade union movement. It could now seek to influence the wide range of issues which are nowadays the subject of discussion between governments and the TUC.

THE LEADERSHIP OF THE INSTITUTION

The development of the Institution, like that of any trade union, has been shaped by external political and economic events and by the actions and attitudes of governments, the employer and other trade unions. But it has also been shaped by the nature of its membership, by the committed effort of countless honorary officers and committees at every level and by the calibre of those who have been elected and selected to lead it. There are certain individuals and groups of members, however, who have had a crucial impact on events at various stages in the Institution's development.

Among these the first mention must go to the small band of like-minded representatives of professional associations in the civil service who met at 28 The Broadway, Westminster, in January 1919 and agreed to establish The Professional Alliance, His Majesty's Civil Service, which almost immediately changed its name to the Institution of Professional Civil Servants. Few individual names from that first group can be traced but clearly their role was vital.

An outstanding figure in the development of the Institution during the interwar period was Freddie Menzler. Within twelve months of joining the Institution in July 1924 he became the Institution's honorary secretary and devoted his tremendous energy and ability to building the Institution, serving in almost every capacity at one time or another.

The vital changes introduced in the organisation and structure of the Institution in the early 1940s were undoubtedly strongly influenced by a group of active members, the most prominent among whom was Leslie Herbert from the Estate Duty Office who became the first general secretary. Some members of that group had been members of the Institution for many years. Much of the impetus for change, however, came from members who had been temporarily recruited to the civil service during the war and who brought with them knowledge and experience from unions outside the civil service. Many stayed on in the civil service after the end of the war and gave the Institution a broader perspective in its policies.

Following the untimely death of Leslie Herbert, Stanley Mayne, another major figure in the development of the Institution, became the general secretary. He steered the Institution through the Priestley Commission and the far-reaching changes in the pay system which occurred thereafter.

From 1963 the Institution has been led by Bill McCall. His period of office has been marked by the merger in 1969 with the STCS, and the emergence of the Institution into the wider trade union movement with its affiliation to the TUC in 1976.

For the most part the Institution has had a leadership with a clear idea of the way in which it would like the Institution to develop. On the issue of TUC affiliation, for example, the majority of full-time officials and the National Executive Committee were convinced of the necessity of joining the TUC long before the conference took its decision to affiliate. Nevertheless, they have not sought to impose their will on a reluctant membership. The membership have always set the limits of tolerance within which the leadership has worked. The latter, whatever their personal political convictions, have always been conscious of the need to maintain the political impartiality of the Institution. They have never conceded, however, that to be impartial in this way is to accept the role of a political eunuch.

WIDER INFLUENCES

During many stages of its history the Institution has been influenced by the prevailing mood of the trade union movement and by the activity of trade unionists in other occupations and industries. It has also been similarly influenced by political events and movements. In the 1920s, for example, the Institution, together with the other civil service unions, campaigned against cuts in pay and in public expenditure. In this the civil service unions were acting in parallel with many other sections of the trade union movement. Attacks upon the policy of the Institution came from certain Conservative newspapers who were conducting a consistent campaign of opposition to the trade union and labour movement.

The depression of the interwar years also strongly influenced the terms and conditions of employment of Institution members. In the 1920s and early 1930s the pay of specialists in the civil service fell. This was not due primarily to any weakness on the part of the Institution. It was the consequence of the economic depression, mass unemployment, the defeat sustained by the trade union movement in other industries and generally deflationary conditions of the time. After the initial burst of postwar prosperity prices fell consistently for a number of years.

In these conditions it was very difficult indeed for the Institution to secure the improvement in grading structure and status which provided such an important part of the motivation for the formation of the Institution. Progress after the Second World War in conditions of full employment was, for example, much quicker than after the First World War.

The Second World War also had the effect of underlining the importance of science and technology. This was bound in the end to be reflected in the structure of the civil service. Consistently throughout the years after the Second World War the Institution argued in favour of higher status for scientists, technologists and professional specialists of all kinds. Progress was made, but the clearest expression of all of the deficiencies of the civil service and the traditional cult of the 'generalist' and the 'amateur' came in the Fulton Report. Fulton provided what can only be described as an extremely sharp criticism of the domination of the civil service by traditional administrative concepts. Even to this day the sharpness of the attack is likely to come as a surprise to nearly every new reader of the Fulton Report.

Fulton was not just a commentary on the deficiencies of the civil service. It was a commentary on some of the traditional attitudes which contributed to the decline of British economic and industrial power. Fundamental to this decline was the subordinate position given to industrial knowledge, to technology and the skills that go with it. Thus the Fulton Report also reflected the pressure of outside criticism on the civil service and the prevailing attitudes dominant in British society. Fulton was a protest against the expression of an aristocratic tradition within the civil service.

Since 1945 the pay and conditions of employment of Institution members have also been very much affected by collective bargaining in other parts of the British economy. The most obvious example is that of incomes policy. Successive governments, whether Labour or Conservative, have found it necessary to introduce incomes policies and all have materially influenced pay negotiations in the civil service. The terms of the different incomes policies have been discussed from time to time between the government and the TUC.

Because of its self-imposed isolation the Institution was not able to participate, except peripherally, in the debates within the trade union movement about these policies. The Institution played no part in the central discussion on the White Paper *Personal Incomes, Costs and Prices,* issued by the first postwar Labour government; no part in the central discussion about Mr Selwyn Lloyd's guiding light; no part in the central discussion about the policies which led to the establishment of a National Incomes Commission; no part in the negotiations which led to the joint statement of intent signed towards the end of 1964; no part in the many negotiations which took place regarding the criteria for the National Board for Prices and Incomes; no part in the discussion about the pay code under Mr Heath's Conservative government; no part in the negotiations which led to the 'social contract'; and no part in the discussions to determine the content of the incomes policy to follow the £6 limit. Yet throughout this period all these policies had a profound effect on the pay and conditions of civil servants.

Members of the Institution have also been affected by the new legislation on employment conditions introduced in recent years. Much progress has been made in the civil service, for example, towards the final elimination of discrimination against women. The Sex Discrimination Act will help the civil service unions to complete the process. The Contracts of Employment Act, the Redundancy Payments Act, the Industrial Training Act and the Equal Pay Act have all helped to create a framework in which further improvements in civil service conditions of employment can be effectively argued. In some respects the civil service has been well ahead of other areas of employment but civil service standards can never be totally divorced from the standards established elsewhere. A further example of this relationship concerns retirement arrangements. The campaign conducted some years ago by the trade union movement against proposed increases in the age of retirement for state pension purposes helped civil service unions to maintain the more favourable superannuation and retirement arrangements within the civil service.

The Employment Protection Act, 1975, which was introduced as a result of an understanding between the Labour Party and the trade union movement, established a series of new minimum employment rights which also affect civil servants. They include, for example, the right to belong to a trade union, the right to engage in trade union activities, the right to time off with pay for trade union representatives engaged in representative duties at the place of employment, the right of women who leave employment to have a child to return to employment in certain circumstances without loss of seniority, the right of workers to be informed in writing of the reasons for dismissal, strengthened provisions for redress against unfair dismissal, the right of workers to receive itemised pay statements giving details of fixed deductions and the right of unions to be consulted on impending redundancy. Many of these provisions were already established practice within the civil service but the introduction of the new legislation will encourage further improvements.

Similarly in relation to superannuation arrangements the progress made by many unions outside the civil service in securing the right of consultation on pension arrangements and participation in the control of pension funds has helped the civil service unions to strengthen their own efforts for improvements. Support for the principle of consultation on pensions and participation in the control of pension funds has been strongly supported by the trade union and labour movement. All these changes in legislation and public policy affecting employment conditions have been of direct interest to civil servants. They would not have been secured without the support of the trade union movement and without the readiness of many unions to support political action.

A major influence on any trade union's development is the attitude and strategy of the employer. This is implied in the very nature of collective bargaining. It takes two parties to make an agreement. In the case of the civil service the situation is complicated by the fact that the government is the ultimate employer. The dual role of the government both as manager of the economy and as an employer has implications for collective bargaining. The immediate representatives of the employer with whom unions do most of their negotiating, however, are the permanent officials who form the management of departments and the central management of the civil service.

Although the broad parameters within which both unions and management work are set by the government and the economic climate, the quality of the relationships between management and unions in day-to-day negotiations is also of importance.

Negotiations on pay and conditions until Fulton were conducted by the Treasury and since then by the CSD. Before the Second World War negotiations between the unions and the Treasury when they took place at all were on a very formal level conducted through the National Whitley Council; 'starch and dynamite' in Sir Albert Day's phrase. During the war, however, partly as a result of the general pressure to streamline procedures and the premium placed on oral rather than written communication, a greater informality developed.

The Priestley Report marked the next stage in the development. The new pay system resulted in a much greater centralisation in pay negotiations. Unions could gain direct access to the Treasury to discuss the major issues, and the Treasury now had the power to deliver.

After 1958 more flexibility in negotiations occurred with a new generation of pay negotiators in the Treasury who were willing to enter into preliminary discussions and sound out the options. They did not treat each pay negotiation as a set-piece battle. From then until 1970, despite the rigidities of incomes policy, the Institution was able to reach a degree of understanding with Treasury negotiators which enabled real progress to be made on several fronts.

The fact that negotiations were more flexibly conducted, however, did not mean that the battles were not hard fought or that the Institution always won its case. Fulton was a case in point. While the political will was initially there in 1968 to implement the major recommendations to which the Institution attached importance, the Treasury and later CSD negotiators were much less sympathetic. The Institution's efforts were thwarted.

FUTURE PROSPECTS

By the end of 1978 the Institution had many achievements to its credit. But life does not stand still. The skill and strength which the Institution has developed in collective bargaining will be vital for the future. On general claims affecting living standards and conditions of employment, the Institution will need continued close co-operation with other civil service unions. The outcome of its efforts will also be materially influenced by the course of economic policy and industrial relations throughout Britain.

Throughout its history the Institution has sought to win greater recognition and status for specialists in the civil service. Much has been achieved but much still remains to be done. This problem has wider significance. All too often in Britain those with specialist knowledge and skill have been held in subordinate positions. Industry, and the skills that go with it, has not been given the esteem which it enjoys in a number of other countries which have now surpassed Britain economically. In speaking for the specialist, the Institution is speaking for the well-being of Britain.

BIBLIOGRAPHICAL REFERENCES

L. J. Callaghan, MP, *Whitleyism: A Study of Joint Consultation in the Civil Service,* Fabian Research Series No. 159 (London: Fabian Society, 1953)

Ronald W. Clark, *The Rise of the Boffins* (London: Phoenix House, 1962)

Sir Albert Day, *Whitley Bulletin,* vol. XXXIII, 1953

Sir James Dobbie, presidential address to the Institute of Chemistry, in *Proceedings of the Institute of Chemistry,* pt 1 (London: Institute of Chemistry, 1918)

B. V. Humphreys, *Clerical Unions in the Civil Service* (Oxford: Blackwell & Mott, 1958)

McDonnell Report, *Report of the Royal Commission on the Civil Service* (London: HMSO, 1914)

F. A. A. Menzler, 'The expert in the civil service', in *The British Civil Servant,* ed. W. A. Robson (London: Allen & Unwin, 1937)

H. Parris, Constitutional Bureaucracy (London: Allen & Unwin, 1969)

H. Parris, *Staff Relations in the Civil Service* (London: Allen & Unwin, 1973)

HM Treasury, *Introductory Memorandum to the Tomlin Commission* (London: HMSO, 1930)

LIST OF ABBREVIATIONS

ACSDD	Association of Civil Service Designers and Draughtsmen
ADA	Admiralty Draughtsmen's Association
A&E	architectural and engineering
AESD	Association of Engineering and Shipbuilding Draughtsmen
AEU	Amalgamated Engineering Union
AGGAT	Association of Government Geographers and Allied Technicians
AGM	annual general meeting
AGR	advanced gas cooled reactor
AGSRO	Association of Government Supervisors and Radio Officers
AIT	Association of HM Inspectors of Taxes
APOE	Association of Post Office Executives
APST	Association of Professional Scientists and Technologists
ARC	Agricultural Research Council
AScW	Association of Scientific Workers (formerly NUSW)
ASO	assistant scientific officer
ASTMS	Association of Scientific, Technical and Managerial Staff
ATCO	air traffic control officer
AUEW	Amalgamated Union of Engineering Workers
BALPA	British Airline Pilots Association
BMA	British Medical Association
BNFL	British Nuclear Fuels Ltd
CBI	Confederation of British Industry
CIR	Commission on Industrial Relations
COI	Central Office of Information
COPOU	Council of Post Office Unions
COPPSO	Conference of Public and Professional Service Organisations
CPSA	Civil and Public Services Association (previously CSCA)
CS	Civil Service
CSAT	Civil Service Arbitration Tribunal
CSCA	Civil Service Clerical Association
CSD	Civil Service Department
CSU	Civil Service Union
CVL	Central Veterinary Laboratory
DATA	Draughtsmen and Allied Technicians' Association (formerly AESD)
DCSO	deputy chief scientific officer
DES	Department of Education and Science
DHSS	Department of Health and Social Security
DoE	Department of the Environment
DoE, DGR	Department of the Environment Directorate General of Research
DSIR	Department of Scientific and Industrial Research
DTI	Department of Trade and Industry
EDO	Estate Duty Office
EDOA	Estate Duty Office Association
EO	executive officer
FBU	Fire Brigades Union
FDA	Association of First Division Civil Servants
FSSU	Federated Superannuation Scheme for Universities
HMSO	Her Majesty's Stationery Office
HSO	higher scientific officer
IPCS	Institution of Professional Civil Servants
IRSF	Inland Revenue Staff Federation

JCC	Joint Consultative Committee
JNC	Joint National Committee
MAFF	Ministry of Agriculture, Fisheries and Food
MoD	Ministry of Defence
MoD (PE)	Ministry of Defence (Procurement Executive)
MPBW	Ministry of Public Building and Works
MRC	Medical Research Council
NALGO	National and Local Government Officers' Association
NBPI	National Board for Prices and Incomes
NCCL	National Council for Civil Liberties
NCL	National Chemical Laboratory
NEC	National Executive Committee
NEDC	National Economic Development Council
NERC	Natural Environment Research Council
NFPW	National Federation of Professional Workers
NIRC	National Industrial Relations Court
NPL	National Physical Laboratory
NSS	National Staff Side
NUBE	National Union of Bank Employees
NUJ	National Union of Journalists
NUSW	National Union of Scientific Workers
NUT	National Union of Teachers
OPCS	Office of Population Censuses and Surveys
POEU	Post Office Engineering Union
POMSA	Post Office Management Staffs Association
PRU	Pay Research Unit
PSA	Property Services Agency
PSO	principal scientific officer
PTO	professional and technology officer
PWR	pressurised water reactor
R&D	research and development
ROF	Royal Ordnance Factory
RT	radio technician
SCPS	Society of Civil and Public Servants (formerly SCS)
SCS	Society of Civil Servants
SGHW	steam-generating heavy water reactor
SO	scientific officer
SPOE	Society of Post Office Engineers
SPOED	Society of Post Office Engineering Draughtsmen
SPSO	senior principal scientific officer
SRC	Science Research Council
SSG	Scientific Staffs Group
SSO	senior scientific officer
SSRC	Social Science Research Council
STCS	Society of Technical Civil Servants
TSRB	Top Salaries Review Body
TTO	telecommunication technical officer
TUC	Trades Union Congress
UKAEA	United Kingdom Atomic Energy Authority
UKAPE	United Kingdom Association of Professional Engineers
UNESCO	United Nations Educational, Scientific and Cultural Organisation
UPW	Union of Post Office Workers
USA	United States of America
USSR	Union of Soviet Socialist Republics

Appendix 1: THE COMPOSITION OF THE COUNCIL OF THE INSTITUTION IN 1920

Association	No. of Representatives
Board of Admiralty, Association of Cartographers	1
Board of Admiralty, Professional Association, Contract Department	1
Board of Admiralty, Association of Electrical Engineers	1
Board of Admiralty, Royal Corps of Naval Constructors	2
Board of Admiralty, Professional Association, Works Department	2
Air Council, Association of Professional Civil Servants	1
Board of Trade, Association of Ship Surveyors	3
Board of Trade, Patent Office Examining Staff Association	2
Board of Inland Revenue, Association of Valuation Office Valuers	3
Board of Inland Revenue, General Valuation and Boundary Survey Office, Ireland, Professional Association	1
HM Office of Works and Public Buildings Professional Association	1
Ministry of Health, National Insurance Audit Department, Association of Inspectors of Audit	1
Scottish Board of Health, Professional Civil Servants' Association	1
Ministry of Munitions of War, Royal Ordnance Factories Association of Professional Staff	1
Office of Land Registry, Technical Staff Association	1
Royal Mint Professional Association	1
Public Trustee Office Surveyors' Society	1

Appendix 2: HONORARY OFFICERS OF THE INSTITUTION, 1919–78

President
1921–55 Sir Richard Redmayne, KCB, MSc, M.Inst.CE, MIME, FGS
1957–61 Sir Graham Sutton, CBE, DSc, FRS
1961–63 V. Stott, MA, F.Inst.P, FSGT

Chairman
1919–20 H. E. Seccombe, ARIBA
1921–22 F. L. Mayer, MINA, AM.Inst.CE
1922–26 J. C. Bridge, FRCSE, MRCPE, DPH
1927   F. Bryant, OBE, MINA
1928–29 F. A. A. Menzler, BSc, FIA
1930–31 J. C. Bridge, FRCSE, MRCPE, DPH
1932–33 S. Martin, FSI
1934–36 R. A. Watson-Watt, BSc, F.Inst.P, MIEE
1937–41 G. L. Pepler, FSI, PPTPI
1942   H. W. Monroe, BSc
1943–44 L. A. C. Herbert, LLB
1945–47 V. Stott, MA, F.Inst.P, FSGT
1947–49 E. J. Widdowson, MSc, BSc.Tech, A.Met, ARIC
1949–51 J. A. Nicol, ACA
1951–53 E. Lawson, ACA
1953–56 J. F. Fry, BSc, AMICE
1956–59 E. Hewlett
1959–62 W. F. Bailey, MI.Mar.E, M.Inst.F
1962–64 W. J. Bowles, AMI.Mech.E
1964–66 R. G. Fall, OBE, BSc, AFR.Ae.S
1966–68 W. A. T. Dorey
1968–70 R. J. P. Middleton, OBE, C.Eng, MIEE
1970–72 J. C. McLauchlan, MA
1972–74 M. W. Sackett
1974–76 G. B. Vint, Dip.Arch., ARIBA
1976–78 D. W. Downton
1978   J. S. Sim

Vice-Chairman
1947–49 J. A. Nicol, ACA
1949–50 N. E. G. Hill, BSc, Eng.EE, MIEE
1950–51 E. Lawson, ACA
1951–52 E. Hewlett
1952–53 J. F. Fry, BSc, AMICE
1953–56 E. Hewlett
1956–59 W. F. Bailey, MI.Mar.E, M.Inst.F
1959–62 W. J. Bowles, AMI.Mech.E
1962–64 R. G. Fall, OBE, BSc, AFR.Ae.S
1964–66 W. A. T. Dorey
1966–68 R. J. P. Middleton, AMIEE
1968–70 J. C. McLauchlan, MA
1970–72 M. W. Sackett
1972–74 G. B. Vint, Dip.Arch., ARIBA

1974–76   D. W. Downton
1976–78   J. S. Sim
1978   V. C. Moores

Deputy Vice-Chairman
1947–50   E. Lawson, ACA
1950–51   E. W. C. Lewis, LLB
1951–52   A. J. Owston, MA, MRCS, LRCP
1952–53   E. Hewlett
1953–56   W. F. Bailey, MI.Mar.E, M.Inst.F
1956–57   G. H. Robertson, BL
1957–59   W. J. Bowles, AMI.Mech.E
1959–62   H. S. Turner, PhD, BSc, FRIC
1962–63   T. H. Clifton
1963–64   W. A. T. Dorey
1964–66   R. J. P. Middleton, AMIEE
1966–67   T. D. Flavin, LLB
1967–68   J. C. McLauchlan, MA
1968–70   M. W. Sackett
1970–72   G. B. Vint, Dip.Arch., ARIBA
1972–74   D. W. Downton
1974–76   J. S. Sim
1976–78   V. C. Moores
1978   E. T. Manning

Honorary Secretary
1919–20   R. C. Bristow, AM.Inst.CE
1920–25   J. H. Salmon, MBE, FSI
1925–28   F. A. A. Menzler, BSc, FIA
1928–35   H. W. Monroe, BSc·
1928–37   S. H. Bales, MSc, FIC
1929–30   A. O. Gibbon, MIEE
1936–37   H. R. Lintern, MSc, AM.Inst.CE, Barrister-at-Law
1938   I. Bowen, MSc
1938–39   H. Whittaker, MSc
1939–40   O. C. Watson, LLB, BSc(Econ)
1941   L. Lanham, OBE, FSI
1942   J. Fraser
1943–44   G. C. Allfrey, BA, MI.Mech.E
1945–47   J. A. Nicol, ACA

Honorary Treasurer
1919–29   E. Ainsworth
1929–35   H. V. Taylor, OBE, DSc, ARCSc, VMH
1936–40   H. Kidd, MINA
1941   I. Bowen, MSc, AFR.AeS
1942–46   F. M. Dean
1946–47   E. Lawson, ACA

Assistant Honorary Secretary for Women's Questions
1936–40   Mrs S. G. Horner, MB, BSc, MRCS, LRCP, DPH

Honorary Officer for Recruitment
1939–40   H. F. Trewman, MA, MIEE

Appendix 3: HONORARY MEMBERS OF THE INSTITUTION*

1954 V. Stott, MA, F.Inst.P, FSGT
1955 I. Bowen, CMG, MSc, AMIEE, FRAe.S
1956 M. E. Adams, OBE, M.Inst.CE
      G. C. Allfrey, BA, MI.Mech.E
      Sir Edward Appleton, GBE, KCB, DSc, LLD, FRS, M.Inst.CE
      N. Black, CBE, FAI
      Sir Frederick Brundrett, KCB, KBE, MA
      Sir Hamish MacLaren, KBE, CB, DFC, BSc, MIEE
      J. A. Nicol, ACA
      Sir George Pepler, CB, FRICS, PPTPI
      Sir Graham Sutton, CBE, DSc, FRS
      Sir Owen Wansbrough Jones, KBE, CB, MA, PhD
      Sir Robert Watson-Watt, CB, LLD, MIEE, FRS
      E. J. Widdowson, MSc, BSc.Tech, A.Met, ARIC
1965 J. Beaton, BL
      S. Mayne
1969 W. F. Bailey, MI.Mar.E, M.Inst.F
      R. G. Fall, OBE, BSc, AFR.Ae.S
      E. Lawson, FCA
      T. H. Profitt, BA
      J. R. Watson
1973 J. Fraser
1974 R. J. P. Middleton, OBE, C.Eng, MIEE
      J. F. Fry, BSc, AMICE
1976 Helen Lindley, BSc
1977 J. C. McLauchlan, MA
1978 H. S. Turner, PhD, C.Chem, FRIC
1979 G. B. Vint, Dip.Arch., ARIBA
      R. H. Firkins, MBE

*Rules of the Institution approved in 1946 laid down under Rule 13 that the following persons shall be honorary members:
(a) the presidents and vice-presidents of the Institution, unless otherwise honorary members;
(b) such other persons as conference may elect from nominees of the National Executive Committee, or branches the members or some of the members belonging to which are connected officially with the nominees.
At the 1963 conference Rule 13 was amended to include only category (b). At the 1964 conference the criteria were further amended to provide under Rule 12 that: 'conference may elect honorary members from nominees of the National Executive Committee from members of the Institution who have rendered outstanding service to the Institution'.

Appendix 4: RECIPIENTS OF NEC SPECIAL AWARD FOR LONG SERVICE*

1967	R. Burtt	MoT, Technical Staffs Branch
	M. Cole	MoD (N), Executive Technical Branch
	W. C. Jackson	MoD (A), Artists and Photographers Branch
	T. Jenkins	MoD (A), Technical Staffs Branch
	T. W. V. Jones	MoD, Meteorological Branch
	D. W. King, OBE	MoD (A), General Branch
	D. J. Lodge	Post Office, General Branch
	V. F. B. Mason	MoD (A), Technical Staffs Branch
	H. I. Moss	MoD (N), Executive Technical Branch
	D. W. H. Roberts	Home Office Branch
	A. Shaw	Association of Valuation Office Valuer's Branch
	F. Taylor	MoD (A), Technical Staffs Branch
	G. Vincent	DES, Museums Branch
	F. S. Waters	MoD (N), Executive Technical Branch
1968	W. F. Bailey	MPBW, Technical Staffs Branch
	P. G. Chamberlain	MoD (A), Scientific Staffs Branch
	M. Fry	MoD (A), Technical Staffs Branch
	R. D. Hails	Ministry of Technology, Professional Accountants Branch
	Miss H. Hughes	MAFF Branch
	A. Lynn	MoD (A), Technical Staffs Branch
	A. Nilson	MoD (N), Scientific Staffs Branch
	S. G. Owen	MoD (A), Professional Staffs Branch
	J. Randle	Ministry of Technology Branch
	M. W. Sackett	MoD (A), Technical Staffs Branch
	M. G. Sawyers	British Museum Natural History Branch
	E. S. Spencer-Timms	MoD (A), Scientific Staffs Branch
	J. H. Stevenson	MoD (A), General Branch
1969	H. J. Barnes	Ordnance Survey Branch
	B. Barraclough-Fell	War Damage Office Branch
	W. H. Boddy	MoD (A), Scientific Staffs Branch
	J. C. Denbigh	MoD (A), Professional Staffs Branch
	D. W. Downton	MoD (N), Scientific Staffs Branch
	S. Head	Ministry of Technology, Technical Staffs Branch
	B. Kauffman	Post Office, Scientific Staffs Branch
	S. W. J. Kiddle	MoD (N), Scientific Staffs Branch
	L. R. Knight	MoD (N), Scientific Staffs Branch
	F. Lazenby	Post Office, Scientific Staffs Branch
	E. S. Milne	MPBW, Drawing Office Branch
	D. S. Papworth	MAFF Branch
	W. R. Parsons	MPBW, Drawing Office Branch
	B. R. Speer	MPBW, Drawing Office Branch
	R. K. P. Stevens	Ministry of Technology, Professional Staffs Branch
	H. R. Waller	United Kingdom Atomic Energy Authority Branch
	C. A. Wright	MoD (Air), Engineering Branch

* In 1966 the National Executive Committee resolved to introduce a Special Award for Long Service as a mark of appreciation to members of the Institution who render service in one or more capacities over a long period.

1970	J. Allan	MoD (N), Executive Technical Branch
	J. G. Armour	Central Branch
	C. Badcock	Atomic Energy Branch
	J. Bowerman	MoD (A), Scientific Staffs Branch
	W. J. Bowles	MoD (A), Professional Staffs Branch
	R. H. Campin	Metropolitan Police Branch
	L. Cockcroft	MoD (A), Technical Staffs Branch
	D. Cook	MoT, Professional Staffs Branch
	R. H. Cook	Post Office Branch
	E. H. J. Edwards	Ordnance Survey Branch
	Miss O. Emmerson Price	DES Branch
	R. H. Firkins	MPBW, Technical Staffs Branch
	G. H. Heath	Society of Technical Civil Servants Division
	A. Hide	MoD (N), Ships' Officers Branch
	I. C. Hill	MPBW, Technical Staffs Branch
	S. H. J. Jeffery	MoD (A), Scientific Staffs Branch
	Miss H. M. Lindley	MoD (A), Scientific Staffs Branch
1970	A. J. Lovell	MPBW, Technical Staffs Branch
	A. G. Oxford	MPBW, Drawing Office Branch
	A. G. Parsons	MPBW, Drawing Office Branch
	D. A. Perfect	Ministry of Technology, Scientific Staffs Branch
	B. Sutton	MoD (A), Scientific Staffs Branch
	L. J. Taylor	MPBW, Technical Staffs Branch
	A. Tithinus	MoD (N), Executive Technical Branch
	R. J. Truscott	MPBW, Drawing Office Branch
	E. Williams	Metropolitan Police Branch
	J. K. Williams	Ministry of Technology, Technical Staffs Branch
	J. V. Wood	MPBW, Technical Staffs Branch
	Miss B. Woolgar	Central Office of Information Branch
1971	Miss M. L. de Azevedo Amaral	DES Branch
	E. W. Baldwin	Ministry of Aviation Supply Drawing Office Branch
	F. Burrows	DoE (MPBW), Technical Staffs Branch
	V. Church	MoD (A), Technical Staffs Branch
	J. A. Dawson	Overseas Development, Administration Branch
	Miss M. E. Deering	Ministry of Aviation Supply, Technical Staffs Branch
	F. Dimes	Natural Environment Research Council Branch
	C. Dowle	MoD (A), Technical Staffs Branch
	H. A. T. Dyke-Hart	MoD (A), Scientific Staffs Branch
	J. Ellis	MoD (A), Technical Staffs Branch
	G. Giles	MoD (Air), Meteorological Office
	W. G. Griffith	MoD (N), STCS Division
	H. Holden	Atomic Energy Authority Branch
	G. F. Ibison	Atomic Energy Authority Branch
	M. Jones	Home Office Branch
1971	I. McDonald	DoE (MPBW), Technical Staffs Branch
	V. C. Moores	DTI, Air Traffic Control Officers' Branch
	J. E. Pearson	DoE (MPBW), Technical Staffs Branch
	E. W. Pratt	DoE (MPBW), Technical Staffs Branch
	H. P. T. Roberts	MoD (N), STCS Division
	J. C. Roylance	MoD (A), Scientific Staffs Branch
	A. M. Smith	Meat and Livestock Commission Branch

	H. Smith	MoD (A), Technical Staffs Branch
	A. Stockley	Ministry of Aviation Supply Drawing Office Branch
	T. Williams	MoD (A), Professional Staffs Branch
1972	O. Barden	MoD (N), Drawing Office Branch
	J. C. Bowen	MAFF Branch
	R. G. H. Chadwell	Association of Valuation Office Valuers Branch
	D. R. K. Coleman	Atomic Energy Authority Branch
	W. A. T. Dorey	Atomic Energy Authority Branch
	W. G. C. Hall	DoE, (MPBW), Technical Staffs Branch
	F. M. Hicks	MoD (N), Drawing Office Branch
	R. Hodges	DoE (MPBW), Drawing Office Branch
	O. R. Hulton	MoD (A), Technical Staffs Branch
	E. Jones	MoD (A), Professional Staffs Branch
	J. S. Pearson	DoE (MPBW), Technical Staffs Branch
	R. A. G. Powell	Ordnance Survey Branch
	F. Scotton	MoD (A), Drawing Office Branch
	F. A. Sewell	MoD (A), Drawing Office Branch
	P. Simons	MoD (A), Technical Staffs Branch
	S. Wyatt	MAFF Branch
1973	D. Cram	MoD (Air), Engineering Branch
	E. A. Ellerby	MAFF Branch
	Dr R. Fletcher	DHSS Branch
	F. W. Gallimore	MoD (A), Scientific Staffs Branch
	R. J. Holland	MoD (A), Scientific Staffs Branch
	J. Hoskin	MoD (N), Executive Technical Branch
	G. J. Jeacocke	Home Office
	H. A. Kempton	Diplomatic Service Branch
	R. J. P. Middleton	MoD (PE), Professional Staffs Branch
	S. H. Parker	Meat and Livestock Commission Branch
	Dr R. E. Pattle	MoD (A), Scientific Staffs Branch
	L. Pearson	MoD (PE), Professional Staffs Branch
	J. Smothurst	Post Office Professional Accountants Branch
	G. P. Tipler	Meat and Livestock Commission Branch
	W. M. White	MoD (N), Executive Technical Branch
	K. Woodley	MoD (Air), Meteorological Office Branch
1974	W. J. Bradley	British Airways Authority Branch
	H. V. Foord	MoD (Air), Meteorological Office Branch
	J. Garland	MoD (A), Professional Staffs Branch
	R. Good	MoD (A), Scientific Staffs Branch
	L. A. Lauener	Scottish Office Branch
	J. May	British Nuclear Fuels Ltd
	R. Morley	MoD (A), Drawing Office Branch
	J. H. Pitt	MoD (PE), Headquarters Branch
	Miss Joyce Price	MoD (A), Drawing Office Branch
	G. Stephens	Commonwealth War Graves Commission Branch
1975	C. W. Bramhall	Ordnance Survey Branch
	R. J. L. Eldridge	MoD (Land Systems), Headquarters PTO Branch
	C. Fazackerley	Atomic Energy Branch
	C. Hutchinson	MoD, REME Branch
	D. B. James	DHSS Branch
	R. Lumley	MoD (Air), Meteorological Office Branch
	L. S. A. Moores	Ordnance Survey Branch
	D. J. Norman	Government Actuary's Department Branch

	M. S. Ridout	Atomic Energy Branch
	A. Stark	CAA Air Traffic Control Officers Branch
	B. J. V. Wechsler	MoD, Mapping and Charting Branch
	N. White	MoD (Navy), Drawing Office Branch
	R. Willmott	MoD (PE), Headquarters Branch
	L. Wright	MoD (Air), Engineering Branch
1976	W. Amer	MoD, ROF Branch
	L. Brown	MoD (Air), Engineering Branch
	R. Cobill	MoD (A), Scientific Staffs Branch
	K. Irwin	CAA General Branch
	J. C. McLauchlan	MoD (MOAS), Scientific Staffs Branch
	D. Moore	MoD, Air Technical Publications Branch
	L. S. O. Morris	Natural Environment Research Council Branch
	A. Pickford	MoD Photographers
	D. Poole	MoD (Air), Engineering Branch
	D. W. Rayner	MoD, ROF Branch
	J. Rearden	MoD (PE), AQD/EQD Branch
	T. W. Thomas	DoE, PSA Technical Staffs Branch
	E. J. Trobridge	Home Office Branch
	G. B. Vint	Metropolitan Police Branch
	N. Webster	Central Office of Information Branch
	K. A. Weller	HM Stationery Office Branch
1977	G. Ansell	MoD Principal Directorate of Technical Cost Branch
	L. Collins	MoD (PE), DGW (Navy) Branch
	W. Harris	MoD (Air), Engineering Branch
	W. Haslem	MoD, ROF Branch
	L. Hatch	Ordnance Survey Branch
	I. MacKay	DoE, PSA Technical Staffs Branch
	H. G. Millen	MoD, Marine Staffs Branch
	W. Nelson	MoD (Land Systems), Quality Assurance PTO Branch
	J. Parry	MoD (PE), DGW (Navy) Branch
	Joy Penny	Science Research Council Branch
1978	I. Hamley	MoD, Medical Branch
	I. A. Ford	Home Office Branch
	E. Walkley	PE/MoD (Army), Scientific Staffs Branch
	A. Charter	PE/MoD (Army), Scientific Staffs Branch
	B. J. Harness	MoD (Air Systems), R&D PTO Branch
	G. J. West	MoD, ROF Branch
	Dr H. Turner	DTI, Industrial Research Branch
	B. Selton	DTI, Industrial Research Branch
	G. McPherson	Scottish Branch
	J. M. Warnes	PSA/DoE, Directorate of Estate Surveying Service Branch
	I. St G. Light	MAFF Branch
	E. F. Evans	MAFF Branch
	W. A. Smith	PE/MoD (Navy), Scientific Staffs Branch
	J. D. Kinder	PE/MoD (Aviation), Scientific Staffs Branch
	E. R. Williams	PE/MoD (Aviation), Scientific Staffs Branch
	L. Fsadni	Malta Branch
	G. Brindley	DOE/PSA, Technical Staffs Branch

Appendix 5: INSTITUTION MEMBERSHIP, 1919–78

1919	–	1,534	1949	–	33,740
1920	–	2,917	1950	–	34,354
1921	–	3,150	1951	–	40,295
1922	–	2,900	1952	–	43,801
1923	–	2,700	1953	–	43,221
1924	–	2,800	1954	–	47,284
1925	–	3,046	1955	–	49,458
1926	–	3,783	1956	–	51,486
1927	–	4,294	1957	–	52,925
1928	–	5,308	1958	–	52,239
1929	–	6,560	1959	–	51,632
1930	–	8,452	1960	–	53,923
1931	–	8,564	1961	–	56,927
1932	–	8,597	1962	–	57,676
1933	–	8,894	1963	–	57,520
1934	–	9,029	1964	–	55,142
1935	–	10,152	1965	–	56,961
1936	–	11,632	1966	–	62,016
1937	–	13,896	1967	–	70,478
1938	–	14,139	1968	–	75,138
1939	–	16,378	1969	–	85,617
1940	–	18,845	1970	–	92,418
1941	–	20,846	1971	–	94,356
1942	–	23,190	1972	–	96,608
1943	–	27,491	1973	–	97,234
1944	–	31,020	1974	–	101,671
1945	–	30,278	1975	–	103,502
1946	–	29,953	1976	–	100,233
1947	–	29,785	1977	–	99,009
1948	–	31,491	1978	–	99,051

Index